AMERICA'S PASTOR

AMERICA'S PASTOR

Billy Graham and the Shaping of a Nation

GRANT WACKER

The Belknap Press of Harvard University Press
Cambridge, Massachusetts
London, England
2014

Library of Congress Cataloging-in-Publication Data
Wacker, Grant, 1945–
  America's pastor : Billy Graham and the shaping of a nation / Grant Wacker.
    pages cm
  Includes bibliographical references and index.
  ISBN 978-0-674-05218-5 (alk. paper)
 1. Graham, Billy, 1918–. Christianity and culture—United States—
  History—20th century. I. Title.
  BV3785.G69W33 2014
  269'.2092—dc23
  [B]
                                                      2014014155

For
Gretchen, Nicholas, and Charlie Stern
Henry and Silas Beck

Children's children are the crown of old men.
Proverbs 17:6

CONTENTS

AMERICA'S PASTOR

But he had in his Pocket a Map of all ways leading to, or from
the Celestial City;
wherefore he struck a Light (for he never goes also without his
tinder-box).

—John Bunyan, *The Pilgrim's Progress*, 1678/1684

PROLOGUE

Billy and I descended on New York City at the same time, the summer of 1957. He was thirty-eight and about to clinch his reputation as the premier evangelist of twentieth-century America. I was twelve and about to taste freedom. But not that summer. One humid night my parents packed themselves and me—entirely without my permission—into a subway car bound for Madison Square Garden. The Great Man was preaching.

I was a kid from a small town in southwest Missouri, and that was the biggest crowd I had ever seen. I remember that the choir alone seemed larger than my whole church. After a lot of music, including a dirgeful rendering of "The Old Rugged Cross" by "Bev" Shea, Graham finally stepped to the pulpit. The Garden fell silent. The anticipation was electric. He was handsome and charismatic and funny. Focusing on the great number of young folks in the audience, he quipped something about puppy love being utterly real to the puppy. The audience roared. By the end of the sermon, however, he had grown deadly serious. When he invited people to stand up and walk to the front to commit or recommit their lives to Christ, hundreds surged forward. For a while I thought I should go too, but then I remembered that I had already been saved when I was four.

Beyond that, not much stuck. Soon our first family trip to the Big Apple was over and we headed back home. At the time I had no idea what the big whoop was all about. I eventually realized, however, that Graham's core constituents—the millions of mostly white, middle-class, moderately conservative Protestants we might call Heartland Americans—did not share my puzzlement. They knew exactly what it was all about.

America's Pastor: Billy Graham and the Shaping of a Nation explores Graham's place in the great gulf streams of American history in the long second half of the twentieth century. It is not a conventional biography. Numerous studies of Graham's life or aspects of it already grace the shelves of public libraries, and many of them are excellent. My aim is different. I try to step back and ask another question. Why does Graham matter? What does his story say about the construction of charismatic leadership? More important, what does it say about how evangelical religion became so pervasive? Most important, what does it say about the relation between religion and American culture itself? The short answer to all three of these questions is, a great deal. Graham's long life (born 1918) and sixty-year ministry (roughly 1945 to 2005) offer a means for hearing the conversations of the age.

But there is more. Graham's story not only registered other Americans' stories but also shaped them. I do not suppose that he exercised much influence in the formation of public policy. For that matter, with the possible exception of Martin Luther King, Jr., I do not suppose that any clergy person did. But I do think Graham exercised influence in another, subtle, and deep way. He played a large role in the shaping of public consciousness: how Americans perceived the world around them, how they interpreted those perceptions, and then how they acted upon them. He gave them tools to help them see themselves as good Christians, good Americans, and good citizens of the modern world all at the same time. He also called them to accountability on each of those scores. Graham did not speak for everyone. Millions knew or cared nothing about him. But many millions did. In a very real sense those millions—the ones I variously call Heartlanders, ordinary Americans, or simply supporters—constitute along with Graham himself one of the two main players in this narrative.

The days are long gone when historians can credibly pretend to hold a mirror up to the past and simply report what they observe. They see what they are prepared to see. So it is only fair to let readers know ahead of time what I think I see in Graham's career. On one hand, Graham ranks with Martin Luther King, Jr., and Pope John Paul II as one of the most creatively influential Christians of the twentieth century. One could make a case for others, too, such as Professor Reinhold Niebuhr, Bishop Fulton Sheen, and Mother Teresa, but all of them spoke for a more limited constituency and for a briefer stretch of time. On the other hand, Graham was not a marble statue, and he was the first to say so. He made mistakes, and some of them were grievous. "A hero," said the historian Michael Kazin of three-time failed presidential candidate William Jennings Bryan, "is not a man whose life is free of errors and contradictions." Rather, he is (quoting classicist Moses Hadas), "'a man whose career has somehow enlarged the horizons of what is possible for humanity.' . . . A man without flaws, adds Hadas, 'is not apt to possess the determined energy heroism requires.'"[1] Graham's achievements loom all the larger when we recognize that he did not tumble from the sky fully formed and perfectly chiseled like an American Moses.

He grew gradually, and sometimes fitfully, into the imposing figure that millions of Americans carved for him and that he carved for himself.

Since feelings about Graham run strong, I should say a few words about my method and point of view. As for method, I hope simply to be fair. That means that I try to treat him as I hope others would treat me, by giving him the benefit of the doubt when the evidence allows it but also by telling the truth without flinching when it does not. Graham made clear to historians and journalists that he wanted it no other way. I have talked about the project with members of Graham's family and several of his close associates. They caught factual errors and offered perspectives I had not thought about, but the overall interpretation is mine alone. Readers on Graham's left will find my account too positive, and those on his right too negative. Long ago I decided that I would have to proceed as my grandmother proceeded onto freeways: buckle up, close your eyes, and just do it.

As for point of view, I count myself a partisan of the same evangelical tradition Graham represented, especially the irenic, inclusive, pragmatic form of it that he came to symbolize in the later years of his public ministry. That identification comes from my upbringing and from adult choice. To be sure—to steal a line from the historian Ron Wells—I have often thought of resigning from the movement, but I did not know where to send the letter. Besides, who else would have me? Sunday mornings usually find my wife and me in our accustomed pew in a small United Methodist Church in Chapel Hill, North Carolina, seated on the cemetery side of the building. Just outside the window, the weather-beaten tombstones dating back to 1859 remind me of the enduring power of the gospel message, generation after generation. At the same time, I know that the eroded tombstones with no names at all may well mark the graves of Methodist slaves. They remind me of the tradition's failings.

I started this Prologue with a personal recollection because I thought my experience represented many others. I will close the same way and for the same reason. In the summer of 2009, I escorted my four-year-old granddaughter, Gretchen, to the Billy Graham Library in Charlotte, North Carolina. Mostly, we wanted to see the famous talking cow just inside the entrance. After a long time—a *very* long time—admiring the cow, and then walking through several rooms of exhibits celebrating (and celebrating is the right word) the evangelist's life, we ended up, as all visitors do, in a theater with an enormous cinema screen. Across the screen flashed a five-minute clip of Graham, in his prime, preaching to a vast stadium audience. Significantly, the place and date of the event went unnamed, creating a sense of the universal and timeless relevance of his message.

When the sermon—a well-rehearsed story of God's love for broken humanity—drew to a close, the evangelist encouraged potential inquirers, as he called them, to stand up and walk to the front. "Come. You come. We will wait." And wait he did, as hundreds, perhaps thousands, wordlessly streamed toward the counselors standing near the podium. When the lights in the theater came back on, Gretchen demanded in wide-eyed wonderment, "Grandpa, what's this all about?" I doubt that any book will ever fully answer her question, but I hope this one makes a good start.

Billy Graham's long life started inauspiciously enough on a dairy farm near Charlotte, North Carolina, on November 7, 1918. The guns of the Great War in Europe fell silent on November 11. As an adult, Billy Frank—as his family called him—liked to quip that it took the world only four days to hear about his birth. Though the comment was typically tongue-in-cheek, it foreshadowed, with brilliant succinctness, an authentic American nativity story. By the 1950s, Graham would be a national personality, by the 1960s an international celebrity, and by the 1970s an icon everywhere. That status would stay with him until he effectively retired from public ministry in 2005. By then his name had become common currency in millions of American households.[1]

America's Pastor: Billy Graham and the Shaping of a Nation offers an interpretation rather than a strictly chronological account of the evangelist's life. The rise, singularity, and longevity of the career of a lanky farm kid from North Carolina help us understand how Americans constructed and experienced leadership. More important, Graham's story sheds light on the formation of a moral vocabulary that expressed the grievances and aspirations of millions of people. Graham's voice helped guide that process. And most important, his story reveals the influences of religion, especially evangelical religion, on larger trends in the culture. After all, Graham intersected with many of the most compelling public events of the era, including the growth of a celebrity ethos, the geographic expansion of Southern habits, the galvanization of the evangelical movement, the normalization of religious cooperation, the awareness of military threats, and the quest for global justice. His tenure also coincided with the public discussion of many of the most compelling private events of the era—aging, loneliness, broken marriages, wayward children, and, of course, the ever-present fear of death. Though private experiences of this sort had marked American life from the beginning, people described them in the vocabulary of the time.

This book provides a tool for making sense of the complexities of American culture in the six decades following World War II. But it rests on a foundation of basic biographical details. Fortunately the most important details are fairly easy to come by. The archival resources are vast. Moreover, Graham told his story often, as did historians and journalists, and their renderings show little variation. The differences lie mainly in emphasis and point of view.[2]

Perhaps the most remarkable thing about Graham's childhood and early adolescence is how unremarkable they really were. The oldest of four children, Graham grew up in the security of a moderately prosperous farm family. Both parents were, from the time of his birth, members of a nearby Associate Reformed Presbyterian Church. This small but sturdy sect was known for its rigorous Calvinist theology, strict rules about Sabbath observance, and tradition of singing psalms instead of hymns. Graham proved an ordinary student, neither strikingly good nor strikingly bad. He displayed normal teenage interests, especially, he later suggested, girls, baseball, and fast cars.

The story of Graham's adolescent conversion has been rehearsed so often it has acquired the patina of a Damascus Road experience. Still, there is no reason to doubt the basic outline. In the fall of 1934 an itinerant evangelist named Mordecai Ham set up his tent not far from the Graham farm. Ham was a classic Southern barnstormer, later associated with anti-Semitism and right-wing causes, but in 1934 known mostly for excoriating immorality, upbraiding lax clergy, and calling lost souls to Christ. The revival waxed for six weeks. Graham visited several times, apparently more from curiosity than conviction. But Ham's preaching finally struck a spark. On November 1, six days before Graham's sixteenth birthday, the young man made his way down a sawdust-covered aisle in the revival tent.[3] The commitment involved no tears, no epiphany, and little emotion, but it did produce a granite determination to commit his life to Christ. Graham and sympathetic biographers portrayed the Ham revival experience as his conversion to evangelical Christianity. But there was not much to be converted from. He already upheld all the major tenets of evangelical Protestant faith, fortified with a morally upright life. The occasion seems better understood as a moment of self-definition.

The year 1936 marked major transitions in Graham's life. After graduating from Sharon High School in May, he spent the summer selling Fuller Brushes door-to-door in South Carolina. The young man proved exceptionally good at it too, earning more money than any other Fuller Brush salesman in the state. Someday those selling skills would manifest themselves in the great stadiums of the world. In the fall of 1936 Graham matriculated at Bob Jones College in Cleveland, Tennessee, not realizing that the school was unaccredited.[4] Though there was no evidence that he objected to the school's fundamentalist theology, he did find its regimented social rules as oppressive as President Jones's authoritarian control. A damp climate, "a flu bug," and class work in "a shambles" did not help.[5]

Sometime that autumn Graham received a letter from a friend at Florida Bible Institute (FBI, later Trinity College) near Tampa. The note described the sunshine, orange trees, relaxed atmosphere, and evangelistic focus. Graham's mother, Morrow Graham, had read about the school in *Moody Monthly*. It was an independent institution with a Christian and Missionary Alliance flavor. (The CMA, as it was commonly called, flourished as a Northern-based holiness sect emphasizing divine healing, overseas missions, and Christ's second coming.) Morrow Graham liked what she read. Billy transferred in January.

Florida Bible Institute offered Graham a range of opportunities that proved crucial for his career. He honed his preaching skills by emulating the style of fundamentalist warhorses wintering at the school, memorizing passages from famous evangelists' sermons, and practicing in front of mirrors as well as alligators in the nearby Hillsboro River. Soon he graduated to street corners, storefront missions, local jails, youth camps, and mobile-home parks. The aspiring evangelist went on the radio and served as assistant pastor at Tampa Gospel Tabernacle, a start-up congregation affiliated with the CMA. Astute observers might have suspected that even then his greatest gift would lie in his ability to persuade his audience to make a decision for Christ—to "close the deal," as outsiders put it.

Professional opportunities arose too. In the spring of 1939 Graham received ordination from the Southern Baptists, a denominational identification he held ever after. The following year a chance encounter with visitors from Wheaton College near Chicago led to the promise of a scholarship to that institution. Graham accepted Wheaton's offer. Armed with an unaccredited Bachelor of Theology degree awarded in May, the aspiring preacher headed north in the summer of 1940. Wheaton was fundamentalist but serious. It gave him only one semester of credit for three years of Bible institute work.

In many ways Wheaton, not the Ham revival, proved the defining experience of Graham's early career. There he met his future wife, Ruth Bell, the precocious daughter of staunchly Presbyterian China missionaries, Dr. L. Nelson and Virginia McCue Bell. He majored in anthropology, not Bible or missions, a choice with portentous implications. At Wheaton, anthropology did not signal cultural relativism, as it did in secular colleges, but it did signal awareness of a wider world. And once again Graham spent a great

deal of time preaching, both on the road and at a local CMA tabernacle—
"The Tab"—where he served as a pastor for the final two years of college.[6]
And, critically important, Wheaton introduced Graham to a dense network
of friendships with talented and ambitious evangelical divines very much
like himself.

After graduating in May 1943, the young preacher accepted the pulpit
of a tiny nearby Baptist church. Billy and Ruth married in August. (They
would parent five children: Virginia, 1945; Anne, 1948; Ruth, 1950; Franklin, 1952; and Ned, 1958.) A great pastor he was not, and his term of service lasted slightly more than a year. But the incurably restless Graham knew
how to reach a wider audience. First, he changed the congregation's name
from Western Springs Baptist Church to the more expansive Village Church.
He inaugurated a monthly lunch meeting, significantly dubbed the Suburban Professional Men's Club, at a local restaurant. It won the support of
celebrities such as the Pulitzer Prize–winning cartoonist Vaughn Richard
Shoemaker.

In January 1944 Graham shouldered a Chicago radio program called
Songs in the Night, which aired every Sunday night from 10:15 to 11:00
over Chicago's powerful WCFL Radio. Though the broadcast included a
sermonette by Graham, it emphasized organ and vocal music, especially the
dulcet voice of baritone George Beverly Shea. Graham had persuaded Shea,
a Canadian crooner already famous in the Chicago area, to join the program
on a regular basis. As things turned out, the team of Graham and Shea, like
the teams of Dwight L. Moody and Ira Sankey in the late nineteenth century
and then of Billy Sunday and Homer Rodeheaver in the early twentieth century, proved for keeps. Graham and Shea stayed together, colleagues and
fast friends, until the end of Shea's long life in 2013.[7]

The mid-1940s saw Graham twice applying for service as a military
chaplain. Prefiguring his chronic struggles with ill health (despite remarkable physical stamina and athletic ability), the army turned him down both
times: once for being underweight and once for a severe case of mumps. Yet
the lack of military service did not harm his reputation, even in times of
nationalistic fervor. That irony may have found resolution in another way:
Graham's deep involvement in a Protestant movement attuned to the blend
of religious and patriotic zeal that marked the years preceding and following the end of World War II. It went by the name Youth for Christ (YFC).

This fledgling nondenominational organization featured entertainment,
patriotic fervor, and spiritual uplift for young adults and returned servicemen

and women. Riding a wave of interest in (and sometimes fear of) adolescent culture, YFC paralleled other evangelical organizations founded in the early 1940s with youth in mind, such as Young Life (1941), InterVarsity Christian Fellowship (1941), and Word of Life (1940). YFC services showcased, as one admission ticket headlined it, "Sparkling Singspiration" and "Timely Testimonials." They also offered "all the gimmicks that reason would allow: famous athletes, stunts, music."[8] In the fall of 1944 Graham became its first full-time evangelist. Historians debate whether Graham made YFC or YFC made Graham. Either way, the match was made, if not in heaven, at least in the cultural effervescence of postwar America. The initial Chicagoland Youth for Christ Rally, held May 27, 1944, at the city's prestigious Orchestra Hall, marked Graham's first major public meeting. Swallowing his fears, the twenty-three-year-old firebrand thundered to three thousand partisans, for by all accounts the young evangelist mixed volume with light in roughly equal measure. At the end, forty souls streamed forward to give their lives to Christ. By then Graham, too, surely realized that "closing the deal" constituted his greatest gift.

The marriage between Graham and YFC flourished. He relentlessly crisscrossed the northern Midwest preaching under its auspices. In 1945 he spoke to sixty-five thousand at a YFC rally in Soldier Field, Chicago, and logged at least 135,000 miles, more than any other civilian passenger on United Airlines. Between 1946 and 1947 a series of YFC events in Europe enabled Graham to build his repertoire of sermons, polish his preaching style, organize large meetings, engage the press, deal with criticism, nurture support groups, and, again, network with other rising evangelical leaders.[9] Graham continued to speak at YFC meetings in the United States off and on until 1950.

In the late 1940s one of the most important but least analyzed features of Graham's ministry realized its final form: the establishment of the Graham "Team." It consisted of Shea, the musical soloist, and Cliff Barrows, the announcer, choirmaster, and unofficial front man. Shea won distinction for his resonant renderings of favorites such as "Just As I Am" and "How Great Thou Art." Barrows—like Graham a YFC man—made his mark with his seemingly unique ability to organize and lead massive choirs, often numbering in the thousands. Other associates—preeminently Grady Wilson, Graham's childhood friend and Wheaton classmate, and, later, Leighton Ford, Graham's Canadian-born brother-in-law—served as regular alternate preachers. Ford sounded so much like Graham on the radio that listeners often confused them. But in the public eye Shea and Barrows (who, like Shea, remained a colleague and fast friend for some seven decades) formed the irreplaceable wings of the Team.[10]

The years stretching from December 1947 to February 1952 cradled the strangest interlude in the evangelist's life. In 1946 the aging fundamentalist William Bell Riley repeatedly urged Graham to succeed him as president of Northwestern Schools—a Bible-training institute, liberal arts college, and seminary—that he had started in Minneapolis in 1902. Though Graham initially resisted, he eventually succumbed to the patriarch's deathbed entreaties. So it was that at age twenty-nine Graham became the youngest college president in the nation. He held only bachelor's degrees from Florida Bible Institute and from Wheaton College. Though Graham entertained no illusions about his credentials, he felt somehow obliged to accept Riley's importunate requests. Despite his youth, inexperience, and frequent and prolonged absences on the itinerant circuit, he acquitted himself in the president's role surprisingly well. He oversaw, or at least authorized, a major building program, started a radio station, and received credit for dramatically rising enrollments. He learned how to delegate. And he discovered that he was a preacher, not an administrator. Moreover, Graham again forged ties to other rising evangelical leaders. Realizing that he could no longer function as president of Northwestern Schools and remain on the road so much, he resigned in February 1952, slightly more than four years after taking the helm.

In the fall of 1947, following two major endeavors in Europe, Graham held his first urban revival campaign in the United States, independent of YFC auspices, in his hometown of Charlotte, North Carolina. In many ways this set of meetings anticipated the hundreds of urban revivals he would lead in America and elsewhere in the decades ahead. It involved advance planning, systematic organization, prayer chains, extensive publicity, and sponsorship by local churches and business groups. It also involved Graham's trademark instinct for maximizing effectiveness with celebrity testimonies. Three years later one of Graham's associates changed the name of his meetings from *campaigns* to *crusades* in order to emphasize that the work would continue after the Team left town.

Enter Modesto. The site looms large in virtually all accounts (including Graham's own) of his career in the late 1940s. As the story goes, in the fall of 1948 the Team met in a motel in this central California town to discuss revivalists' historic pitfalls. After extended prayer and thoughtful discussion, they settled on four: misuse of money, sexual immorality, exaggeration of results, and criticism of other clergy. They determined that they would not only avoid those snares but also take measures to prevent them in the first place. The precautionary steps eventually acquired a life of their own and set the gold standard for other evangelists. They included conducting regular audits with full disclosure; never traveling or dining alone with a woman other than family; relying on outsiders' enumeration of attendance records; and emphasizing areas of agreement rather than disagreement with other clergy and Christian traditions. Over the years Graham received intense media scrutiny, but hardly anyone accused him of violating any of those four principles. Supporters (though not Graham himself) soon started to call the agreement the Modesto Manifesto. Modesto Covenant would have been more apt, for it relied on the tensile strength of mutual accountability.

Charles (Chuck) Templeton also loomed large in Graham's early career. Templeton was a man of extraordinary gifts. Born into a working-class family in Toronto in 1915, he experienced a powerful religious conversion in a local fundamentalist church in 1936. Though he never finished high school, he became an itinerant evangelist for YFC. In 1945 Graham and Templeton met on the YFC circuit. Acquaintance soon blossomed into friendship, and they started traveling and preaching together in Canada, the United States, and Great Britain. By all accounts, including Graham's own, the handsome Canadian was the better preacher.

In the late 1940s, however, Templeton began to experience doubts about the conservative message that they were preaching. Determined to tighten his theological grip, he successfully petitioned Princeton Theological Seminary to admit him into a special program. The encounter with modern theology and biblical criticism only deepened Templeton's doubts. He challenged Graham, too, to go to seminary and grapple with these troubling problems. After a year, Templeton left Princeton and started working for the National Council of Churches as a Presbyterian evangelist. Later he hosted a weekly CBS television program on religion. In 1957 Templeton announced that he had grown agnostic and honorably resigned from Christian ministry. He returned to Toronto, where he distinguished himself as a novelist, journalist, politician, toy designer, and television news commentator. In 1996 he published a poignant spiritual autobiography, *Farewell to God*, which detailed the reasons for his loss of faith. Both men bravely tried to maintain their friendship into the 1970s. Templeton died in 2001.[11]

The Canadian evangelist's narrative holds significance for its own sake, of course, but also for what it tells us about Graham. First, Templeton challenged Graham to re-examine the theological bases for the views he espoused. In his own way, Graham accepted Templeton's challenge. Late in the summer of 1949 Graham emerged from a short but intense period of theological self-examination. His old views remained pretty much intact but were now fortified with faith-based and pragmatic arguments he found persuasive. Graham's preaching never veered from a forceful—outsiders said dogmatic—assertion that the Bible offered authoritative answers for all of life's truly important problems. Templeton called Graham's approach "intellectual suicide."[12] Second, Templeton appears in most renderings of Graham's life, ranging from hagiographic to debunking, as the foil that defined him. Graham emerges either as an obscurantist who timidly avoided the hard edge of Templeton's challenge, or as a man of deep faith who courageously wrestled it to the ground. Graham's faith-based approach to the Bible proved baffling to many partisans of the mainline Protestant—not to mention the academic—establishment.[13] But Graham's supporters did not care. Sooner or later everyone had to settle on a few axioms that made daily life possible.[14]

In many ways the eight weeks from September 25, 1949, to November 20, 1949, served as the springboard for Graham's entire career. After unsuccessful attempts to evangelize Los Angeles with other preachers, a group of Christian businessmen working with the local YFC chapter invited Graham to try his hand. The campaign was centered in a mammoth circus tent pitched in the heart of the city. The tactics that Graham deployed that fall dictated the template for virtually all the crusade meetings for the next six decades. Most of the components had appeared in Billy Sunday's revivals before and after World War I, and in nascent form in Graham's own Charlotte campaign in 1947. But in Los Angeles the combination proved more than the sum of the parts, not least because of the sheer size and complexity of the endeavor. It included extensive planning, lavish publicity, meticulous organization of ushers and choir members, and concerted prayer chains meeting months in advance. The services featured celebrity testimonies, both old and new music, electrifying preaching, boilerplate evangelical theology, prayer with converts, and lots of Southern charm—all delivered with smashing sincerity and effectiveness.

Graham's early theology represented a tradition of assertions that many Americans found reassuringly familiar. God had revealed his will in the Bible, which taught that all humans had sinned. But Christ offered forgiveness and new life through faith in his atoning death and resurrection. Personal transformation did not come cheap, however. It demanded a life of moral rigor, ethical integrity, and readiness to share this good news—or "gospel"—of salvation. The result was everlasting joy in heaven for the saved or everlasting separation for the lost.

Graham placed this theological message in a context of domestic and international threats, especially lawlessness at home and communism abroad. That context resonated with his audience in Los Angeles and, soon, across the nation. Less than a month before the crusade began the Soviets had exploded an atomic bomb, and six days after it started the Reds, as many Americans called them, took over the Chinese mainland. Graham's ability to set traditional theological claims in a setting of national and world crises would rank as one of the hallmarks of his long career.

Things got off to a slow start—not least because of unseasonably cold weather and scant attention from the media—but the conversions of celebrities, such as the Country Western singer Stuart Hamblen and the Olympic track star and war hero Louis Zamperini, as well as the priceless publicity bestowed by the newspaper magnate William Randolph Hearst, helped generate a cumulative attendance of 350,000 with 3,000 converts. (Soon Graham would call them inquirers, not converts, because no one except God knew the heart well enough to call anyone a convert.) Those numbers likely exceeded Graham's previous endeavors put together. The size and publicity of the Los Angeles project triggered extensive coverage in the national and international media, including in *Time*, *Life*, *Newsweek*, and the *New York Times*. Their stories transformed Graham into a national personality.

If the events of the late 1940s served as the launchpad for Graham's career, those of the 1950s established him as the premier Protestant evangelist of the twentieth century. We can conveniently group the developments of the 1950s into three categories: the crusades, the media enterprises, and the issues of the day.

The crusades steadily grew in size, frequency, and types of venue. Immediately after the Los Angeles meeting Graham opened a crusade in Boston, with less advance planning but greater media attention and penetration into both Roman Catholic and mainline circles. The Boston meeting was followed by highly publicized ventures in Columbia, South Carolina; Portland, Oregon; and Atlanta, Georgia, all in 1950. In 1951 Graham introduced a systematic program of on-site counselors to instruct inquirers in Christian essentials and then guide them to local churches. To the end, Graham considered counselors and follow-up guidance fundamental to the crusades.

The year 1954 saw Graham's massive crusade in London, and then the most famous extended meeting of his career in New York City in 1957.

Held in Madison Square Garden, the highly publicized event ran sixteen weeks, from May 15 to September 1. In the months leading up to the New York crusade, Graham appeared at a flurry of press conferences and in network television interviews. A gathering in sweltering heat in the middle of July in Yankee Stadium broke attendance records at the venue. In a telling portent of things to come, Vice President Richard Nixon visited. At the end of the crusade, counters recorded a staggering 2,400,000 cumulative attendees and 61,000 inquirers.[15]

The New York crusade was significant for another reason. Graham's cooperation with mainline Protestants and Roman Catholics turned a growing rift between him and his fundamentalist friends into a permanent and unbridgeable chasm. From that point forward, Graham, more than anyone else, both galvanized and exemplified a rapidly growing faction in American Protestantism. The new evangelicals, as they sometimes called themselves, affirmed most of the doctrinal cornerstones that fundamentalists affirmed, but with less dogmatism and with little inclination to fall into arcane debates about how the world would end. At the same time, they placed more emphasis on evangelism, social reform, and cooperation with other Christians.

In the 1950s Graham moved decisively into his own media enterprises. The first three years of the decade marked serious expansion into radio, television, movies, and book publishing, followed in the middle years by equally serious expansion into high-profile journalism. The *Hour of Decision* (actually, half-hour) radio show made its national debut over the ABC network in November 1950. It consisted of the choir leader, Cliff Barrows, summarizing crusade activities elsewhere, one or two chestnut hymns from songster Bev Shea (as he was affectionately known to millions), testimonies from celebrities (often entertainers or sports stars), a brief and very low-key appeal for "support" from Barrows, and then a forcefully delivered sermon from Graham. As before, his message invariably began with a litany of national and world crises. He preached, in the words of one biographer, "with a Bible in one hand and a newspaper in the other."[16] The litany soon yielded to a rehearsal of the kinds of personal distress most Americans encountered in their daily lives. Those dire words told the "Wondrous Story," as one of Shea's most beloved hymns called it, of God's redeeming love for wayward humans. In Graham's presentation, the transformation that Christ alone made possible offered peace with God, peace with other people, and peace within.

Though the *Hour of Decision* radio broadcast embodied Graham's best-known media outreach in those early years (if not of his whole career), other endeavors followed in quick succession. First came a foray into television, a half-hour program also called *Hour of Decision*, recorded and edited in a studio, which ran from 1951 to 1954. This short-lived venture yielded to live broadcasts from his crusades, starting on Saturday night, June 1, 1957, at Madison Square Garden and running for fourteen successive Saturdays. After the New York crusade, hoping to avoid overexposure and the staggering cost of a regularly scheduled program, Graham moved from this format to quarterly network television broadcasts, drawn from actual crusade meetings.[17] Graham's film ministry, which eventually reached more than 100 million viewers, began in 1951 with *Mr. Texas*. Over the years, more than thirty additional feature-length films appeared. Though none achieved Hollywood writing or production standards, some, such as *The Hiding Place*, ranked highly in the evangelical market. In those various programs and movies Graham showed once again that he knew how to speak both for and to ordinary Americans with consummate skill.

Along with radio and television, Graham embraced print media, possibly with even more enduring results. In 1952 he moved into the newspaper mass market with a daily syndicated Question and Answer column called "My Answer." More important was Graham's remarkably successful entry into the semi-academic periodical market with the evangelical fortnightly *Christianity Today*. Though he rarely wrote for the magazine himself, he served as its principal founder and theological guiding light. First published in 1956, *Christianity Today* had two purposes: to speak to evangelicals in the mainline and to offer an alternative voice to the mainline's real or perceived domination of American theological discussions. By the ninth issue the fortnightly's circulation had eclipsed that of the *Christian Century*, the mainline's principal literary voice. *Christianity Today* soon became—and in 2014 remained—the most widely read serious Christian periodical in the world. In 1960 Graham discerned a market for a more popular organ, something like *Guideposts* or the Roman Catholic *Our Sunday Visitor*. This interest culminated in *Decision* magazine, a tabloid-sized glossy monthly adorned with large photos, uplifting stories, and a brief devotional rendering of a Graham sermon.

The Billy Graham Evangelistic Association (BGEA) managed these multiple ventures. Established in 1950 as a nonprofit religious corporation to oversee finances, the BGEA won recognition for organizational efficiency and financial accountability in the evangelical world.[18] The BGEA's board of directors consisted of successful business leaders (almost all men) who knew how to swim in the fast-running rivers of government regulation and religious competition. Perhaps the BGEA's most important accomplishment lay in its rigorous oversight of Graham's revenue, a perennial bog for evangelists. As early as 1950 Graham had started to grow uneasy with the real and perceived abuses of the venerable "love offering" tradition. Two years later the BGEA placed him and the other Team members on publicly stated annual salaries—in Graham's case, a wage pegged to that of a successful urban pastor, initially $15,000.

The 1950s also marked Graham's public involvement in matters of compelling political and social concern. Most conspicuously, he preached frequently and often stridently about the peril of communist expansionism abroad and infiltration at home. Like millions of American Christians (and non-Christians), including the most respected public figures of the day, he saw communism as both a military threat and a religious menace. Communism's spiritual character stemmed from its self-understanding as an alternative worldview that lured gullible minds with promises of material prosperity. Graham's fear of communism loomed largest in the early years of the decade. It continued, with diminishing urgency, into the 1970s.

In the same years the rising civil rights movement also captured Graham's attention. Initially he, like most Southern white preachers, had uncritically followed Billy Sunday's practice of abiding by local racial customs. In the South that meant of course that blacks and whites sat separately. By 1951 Graham's conscience had started to stir. That year he chastised his own Southern Baptist Convention for their discriminatory admission policy in Baptist schools. The following year he told a crusade audience in Jackson, Mississippi, that there was no room for segregation at the foot of the cross. In March 1953, at a crusade in Chattanooga, Tennessee, he personally removed the rope separating the races.[19] Graham later waffled, allowing a rope to go back up at the Dallas crusade in May. But after *Brown v. Board of Education* in 1954, he never again permitted ropes at his meetings—despite stinging criticism from many white supporters.

That slow but continually growing awareness of racial injustice persisted. In 1957 the evangelist boldly invited Martin Luther King, Jr., to offer an invocation at his New York crusade, and just as boldly King accepted. Three years later, in a story published in the high-circulation *Reader's Digest,* Graham excoriated America's churches for making eleven o'clock Sunday morning the most segregated hour of the week (King often used the same phrase). To be sure, Graham never felt comfortable with confrontational tactics about race—or about anything else, for that matter. He never marched in the streets, and his relationship with King proved unsteady. Yet Graham's determined refusal to allow segregated seating in his meetings, or to speak in countries that did (such as South Africa), along with his drumbeat naming of racism as one of America's lethal sins (not just mistakes but sins), told millions of Christians that authentic faith offered no room for racial prejudice.

The 1960s and 1970s witnessed an amplification of trends established in the 1950s. Each year Graham averaged six to eight major crusades at home and abroad (the balance gradually tipped toward those abroad). Along the way he maintained a punishing schedule of appearances at colleges, universities, seminaries, civic events, invocations at political conventions, and symbolic occasions such as national prayer breakfasts and presidential inaugurations. His personal friendships with Presidents Eisenhower, Johnson, Nixon, Ford, Reagan, Clinton, and both Bushes landed him on the front page of countless newspapers on countless occasions. Scattered evidence suggests that Graham's golfing with presidents and overnighting at the White House won the admiration of millions of Americans, who saw him as their vicarious representative. At the same time, however, his connection to the White House provoked sharp criticism from other Americans, who saw him more as a chaplain to the powerful than a preacher to the masses.

The 1960s and early 1970s witnessed both bright days of praise and dark days of criticism. The sharpest attacks centered on Graham's involvement in the Vietnam War quagmire and the Watergate fiasco. Like most Americans, he initially supported the Asian conflict as a warranted response to communist aggression. But by the early 1970s he had grown ambivalent about its aims. That pattern of belated reassessment replayed itself with Watergate. A strong admirer of Nixon's knowledge of national and international affairs, as well as of his personal integrity, Graham simply could not bring himself to believe that the president could have obstructed justice.[20] Following the release of the White House tapes in April 1974, however, Graham reluctantly accepted the hard truth. Shocked by Nixon's betrayal, the preacher vowed not to fall into partisan politics ever again. In both sets of controversies, Graham's change of heart came long after most Americans had grown doubtful of Presidents Johnson and Nixon's war policies and of Nixon's truthfulness about Watergate.

To the dismay of foes and the discomfort of friends, the middle career years, and especially the early 1970s, marked the apogee of Graham's elite status. Perennially hobnobbing with the rich and the famous, Graham seemed to represent not only Establishment Evangelicalism but also Establishment America. His strikingly handsome face recurrently graced the covers of the nation's magazines. Accounts of his every move—religious, political, and recreational—turned up in dailies everywhere. Sometimes it proved hard to tell whether Graham was best viewed as a preacher, a pundit, or a celebrity. The one label Americans rarely heard was prophet.

But things changed as Graham more clearly saw the evangelical movement's global reach and responsibilities. In 1974 he delivered the keynote address at the International Congress on World Evangelization in Switzerland. The BGEA had spearheaded and largely funded this meeting of world Christian leaders. Growing from the Berlin World Congress on Evangelism in 1966, which the BGEA had funded, the Lausanne meeting sought to provide an alternative—not adversarial but alternative—voice to the World Council of Churches. Graham had attended the gatherings of the World Council of Churches since its inception in Amsterdam in 1948. Though he believed that the council represented the views of sincere Christians, he also felt it had largely substituted social reform for evangelism. Lausanne would recognize both, but it would give priority to evangelism. It also would enable evangelicals around the world to meet personally—more or less for the first time—and learn what others were doing. Graham knew from his YFC days the importance of developing a sense of a worldwide community of fellow travelers. Massive follow-up meetings in Amsterdam in 1983, 1986, and 2000 carried forward that task, along with much greater representation from women, Pentecostals, and lay people from all parts of the globe, including, most notably, developing nations.

The mid-1970s provided the springboard to another dramatic change in Graham's outlook. From the beginning Graham, by his own admission, loved the sport of partisan politics. He generally supported, implicitly if not explicitly, Republican candidates. Murray Kempton's quip that Graham "prays Republican" bore more than a sliver of truth.[21] But not always. A life-long registered Democrat, he refused to support Barry Goldwater's campaign for president in 1964, maintained a deep comradeship with Lyndon Johnson, and held enduring friendships with figures as politically progressive as Sargent Shriver, Mark Hatfield, Bill and Hillary Clinton, and the rock star Bono. What changed in the mid-1970s was Graham's decision to avoid partisanship of any kind, Republican or Democratic. The Nixon fiasco had damaged his confidence both in Nixon and in his own political judgments. From that point until his retirement three decades later, Graham tried, with mixed success, to avoid explicit partisanship. He declined to sign or explicitly endorse political statements, including those with which he agreed, and distanced himself from the Christian right as well as from his son Franklin Graham's harsh statements about Islam.[22]

In the long arc of history, Graham's move into the "Restricted Access" countries of Eastern Europe, the Soviet Union, the People's Republic of China, and North Korea in the final decades of the century may prove to be his most courageous and far-reaching gesture. His visit to a "peace conference" in Moscow in 1982 provoked a firestorm of criticism back home from the left as well as from the right. To be sure, during and after the trip he made some ill-considered—and misquoted—comments about the amount of religious freedom he had seen in the Soviet Union. Yet his commitment to carry the gospel, along with a growing conviction that humans were plunging toward nuclear destruction, propelled him. In time, all but the most obdurate critics would applaud his determination to take his message to oppressed peoples. Some considered it a contribution to the dismantling of the Berlin Wall and the defusing of the Cold War.

The ministry of the mature Graham of the 1980s and 1990s seemed both continuous and discontinuous with the ministry of the young Graham of the 1940s and 1950s. The 1980s and 1990s saw some of his largest American crusades. Nineteen of them drew an aggregate attendance of more than 200,000 people each.[23] The three-day outdoor meeting in Flushing Meadows, New York, in 2005, located on the site of the 1963 World's Fair, and his final such gathering, also attracted more than 200,000 people. It ranked as one of the most multiethnic events in the city's history. The evangelist's cornerstone insistence on God's redeeming love, effected through faith in Christ's death and resurrection, remained untouched. And so did the conviction that enduring change had to begin in the hearts of men and women. Laws and structural reforms were needed, but they were not enough.

Other things did change, however. The fiery sermons slowed to fireside chats. The fierce anticommunism yielded to heartfelt pleas for mutual disarmament and attention to the worldwide AIDS epidemic, hunger, poverty, and environmental threats. The vigor of a physique that once seemed invincible succumbed to a body weakened by the debilities of old age. And the reins passed to other hands, as Franklin Graham took control of the BGEA in 2000. Ruth died in 2007. By then Graham had retired to a quiet life in his mountaintop home near Asheville, North Carolina. Many believed that the nonagenarian Graham's apparent turn to Culture War politics before and after the 2012 election reflected Franklin Graham's views more than his father's.[24] At the very least, it signaled a departure from the position

Graham had maintained since the mid-1970s that high-profile preachers in general, and he in particular, should stay out of partisan politics.

In 2014, Graham's place on the Mount Rushmore of American religious icons seemed secure. By then, the task was less to take the measure of the image—many hands already had done so—than to ask what it told Americans about themselves.

Influence

World War II officially ended on September 2, 1945, but the changes it unleashed lingered into the following century. Those decades saw the surge of America's strength worldwide, the polarization of the world into free and communist regions, the rise of political Islam, and racial, gender, and cultural upheavals everywhere. Developments within the United States seemed no less momentous. Unprecedented though uneven prosperity invited turmoil, not peace. Relaxed sexual mores and lifestyle options multiplied in ways that seemed as confusing as they were dazzling. The wrenching changes that marked the wider culture replayed themselves in the religious culture. The seeming consensus of the immediate postwar years harbored fissures that would crack open in the 1960s and turn into gaping chasms in the 1970s and later. For many, those developments signaled opportunities for growth and renewal, but for many others, perils both ominous and imminent.[25]

Evangelical Protestants found themselves in the middle of these tectonic shifts. The tradition had emerged on the European continent and in Scotland, England, and most of the American colonies in the early decades of the eighteenth century. Like all Protestants, evangelicals affirmed the authority of Scripture, the sovereignty of God, the brokenness of humans, the promise of redemption through faith in Christ, the necessity of personal and social holiness, and hope for the life to come. Unlike most Protestants, however, they downplayed the role of tradition in general and the historic church and sacraments in particular. They especially emphasized a new life in Christ, appropriated through a personal decision to repent of sin and receive God's grace by believing the good news of Christ's death and resurrection. They stressed the mandate to share this gospel through missions. God's Holy Spirit enabled and vivified the commitment with heartfelt emotion.[26]

This cluster of beliefs and practices had served evangelical Protestants in America well enough through the eighteenth and most of the nineteenth centuries, when they gradually achieved something like dominance (never control, but dominance) over the wider culture.[27] But in the late nineteenth and early twentieth centuries the winds of modernity blew that once wide river into two broad streams. One came to be known as liberal or modernist, and the other as conservative or fundamentalist. The former sought to capture the best of the new while the latter sought to preserve the best of the old.[28] But just when it seemed that everything had settled into this neatly bifurcated pattern, the turmoil of the post–World War II era reconfigured the landscape once again. The older liberal and conservative currents started to rearrange themselves. Billy Graham turned his hand to cutting a third channel for powerful surges of religious and cultural energy.

Graham's achievements took multiple forms. Attendance statistics at his meetings piled up like snowdrifts. By the time he effectively retired in 2005, he had preached to nearly 215 million people in person in ninety-nine countries and perhaps to another two billion through live closed-circuit telecasts.[29] Those numbers may have swelled in the telling, but—with the possible exception of Pope John Paul II—the evangelist likely addressed more people face-to-face than anyone else in history. He set multiple attendance records, including 185,000 people at Wembley Stadium outside London in 1955 (when he was thirty-six years old); 100,000 in Yankee Stadium in 1957—the largest crowd since Joe Louis had fought Max Baer on that site in 1936; 130,000 at the Rose Bowl in 1963; 250,000 at Maracanã Soccer Stadium—the largest stadium in the world—in Rio de Janeiro in 1974; 250,000 in Central Park in 1991, at that time the largest religious gathering and the second largest gathering of any kind on that site; and as noted, 200,000 at Flushing Meadows, New York, in 2005. Yet all of those record-breaking appearances paled before his achievement in Seoul, Korea. A five-day meeting in the spring of 1973 drew three million attendees, with 73,000 decision cards turned in. On the final day, with more than 1,100,000 souls crowded onto a converted airport tarmac, Graham delivered the Good News to what may have been at that time the largest gathering of humans for a religious purpose in history. Taken together, those six decades of evangelism yielded more than three million recorded commitments for Christ.[30]

Before Graham set attendance records in the world's stadiums he cornered other records in electronic and publishing media. The *Hour of Decision* radio program, started in 1950, soon eclipsed Charles E. Fuller's *Old Fashioned Revival Hour* as the most widely heard religious broadcast in the nation, streaming into twenty million homes every Sunday afternoon. *Peace with God*, Graham's third book, appeared in 1953. Repeatedly reissued and never out of print, it eventually sold more than two million copies in fifty languages. In 1997, HarperCollins's first printing of Graham's autobiography, *Just As I Am*, totaled one million copies. Altogether Graham and his editorial assistants would author thirty-two books, translated into fifty languages. The syndicated advice column "My Answer" (1952) appeared in two hundred newspapers with a potential readership of twenty million. Graham's devotional monthly, *Decision* (1960), eventually posted a circulation of six million and saw publication in six languages and a braille edition. Except for two Jehovah's Witnesses publications, *Decision* may have been the most widely distributed religious publication in the English-speaking world.[31]

The evangelist's close relationship with American presidents was probably unique in U.S. history. Graham knew all eleven from Truman to George W. Bush, enjoyed friendships with all except Truman, and very close friendships with Johnson, Nixon, Reagan, and George H. W. Bush. President Barack Obama visited Graham in his home in 2010, the first sitting president to do so. Less noticed but important friendships also flourished with four First Ladies: Lady Bird Johnson, Pat Nixon, Nancy Reagan, and Barbara Bush. Journalists and historians have invested considerable energy exploring the significance of those presidential ties. At the very least, they expressed perennial access to the pinnacle of American power.[32]

Awards and honors cascaded on Graham. Between 1955 and 2013, the evangelist won a spot on the Gallup Organization's roster of "Ten Most Admired Men" anywhere in the world fifty-seven times, easily trumping his closest rival, President Ronald Reagan, who appeared "only" thirty-one times.[33] In a 1978 *Ladies' Home Journal* survey, under the category "achievements in religion," the preacher outstripped everyone except God.[34] The United States government awarded him the two highest commendations a civilian could receive: the Presidential Medal of Freedom in 1983 and, with his wife, Ruth Bell Graham, the Congressional Gold Medal in 1996. He received, among countless other awards, the Torch of Liberty Award from B'nai B'rith (1969) and the Templeton Prize for Progress in Religion (1982).[35] Honors paralleled awards. He served as the featured speaker at the Honor America Day in Washington, DC, on July 4, 1970; the Honor Billy Graham Day in his hometown of Charlotte, North Carolina, on October 15, 1971; and the Grand Marshal of the Tournament of Roses parade in Pasadena, California, on January 1, 1972. He was the only living American to be imaged in the glass of the National Cathedral in Washington.

Rankings and titles followed. In 2001 a jury of distinguished Southern Studies scholars included Graham on a list of "Twenty Most Influential

Southerners." The panel placed him among the top six (which they could not rank).[36] The titles that journalists conferred on him left little doubt that this lofty evaluation was not far off the mark. In 1970, Kenneth L. Woodward, *Newsweek*'s distinguished religion editor, said that Graham's image floated over the American horizon like "a celestial Southern Cross."[37] In 1987 one CNN correspondent went so far as to say that "some would call him the 13th disciple."[38] Two years later the British journalist David Frost said that Graham was the nearest thing that America had to an established church.[39] At the end of the century, *Time* magazine featured him in a 1999 cover story titled "100 Heroes and Icons of the Twentieth Century."[40] Just after the turn of the century, a journalist for Scripps Howard dubbed him "America's Pope."[41] At the dedication of the Billy Graham Library in Charlotte in 2007 the senior President Bush named him "America's pastor."[42]

To be sure, not all titles were flattering. In 1957 Murray Kempton, the Pulitzer Prize–winning *New Republic* editor and pundit, mocked him as "the Pope of lower Protestantism."[43] Marshall Frady, one of his premier biographers, depicted him as "sort of like Christ's American son."[44] The Catholic polymath historian Garry Wills pegged him as a creator of the "golf-course spirituality" of the 1950s.[45] Graham's association with Nixon also got him into trouble with the left-wing journalist I. F. Stone, who dubbed him Mr. Nixon's "smoother Rasputin."[46] Yet ridicule, too, counted as an index of influence.

Perhaps the most telling marks of Graham's influence are simply anecdotal—cultural snapshots, we might call them. A sampling suggests the richness of the menu. Except for elected officials, Graham may have been the only person in the United States who, at the height of his popularity, needed no mailing address beyond his name. Just "Billy Graham" scratched on an envelope would do.[47] Children bore testimony to Graham's status in their own ways. Of the thousands of letters they sent to him, one, posted in 1971, probably from a first- or second-grader, seemed to speak for all. After requesting a free book, the young author signed off, "Tell Mr. Jesus hi."[48] Unheralded ordinary people contributed to the Graham mystique. On hearing that Graham had suffered an arterial spasm that impaired his vision, some people offered their eyes.[49] During his 1957 New York City crusade, a Long Island woman wrote to Vice President Nixon asking if he could arrange for her to meet Graham, adding, "believe me I am not a crank."[50] And then there was the story of a political delegate in the 1980 Republican Convention who told Graham he would vote one way but actually planned to vote another. Hearing about the switch, a different delegate remarked, "It's okay to lie to another politician, but you just don't lie to Billy Graham. That's going too far."[51]

In the face of such acclaim, it is predictable that distinguished analysts of the culture, viewing Graham from different angles, would also acknowledge his mythic status. In the 1972 movie *Sleeper*, the comic Woody Allen quipped that Graham and God "used to go out on double dates together." Allen knew that sophisticated audiences, domiciled well outside evangelical America, would recognize both the name and its emblematic significance. The literary critic Harold Bloom summed up the preacher's impact with memorable succinctness: "You don't run for office among us by proclaiming your skepticism or by deprecating Billy Graham."[52] In 1988, on Graham's seventieth birthday, the historian Martin E. Marty—as famous in the academic realm as Graham was in the religious one—judged that the preacher had come to be, along with the pope, "one of the two best-known figures" in the Christian world.[53]

It is important not to overstate the case. Graham did not rival Lyndon Johnson in terms of influence on public life. Indeed, he did not make *The Atlantic*'s "Top 100 Influential Figures" list.[54] And extensive anecdotal evidence in the press over six decades leaves little doubt that Graham remained unknown, little known, unappreciated, or disliked among great segments of the American population—especially academics, secular thinkers, ethnic minorities, non-Protestants, and a good many Protestants too. Those are the dissenters we know about. Though one poll in the late 1950s showed that 85 percent of American adults recognized Graham's name, and 75 percent of them viewed him favorably, that still left a great slice of the public either oblivious or doubtful about him.[55] Which is to say, Graham spoke for millions of Americans, but not for everyone.

Nonetheless, the register of attendance records, media data, awards, honors, rankings, titles, and cultural snapshots suggests that Graham's influence, like that of his contemporaries Martin Luther King, Jr., and Pope John Paul II, reached beyond passing fame to enduring influence. For millions, Graham functioned very much as a Protestant saint. By the mid-1950s, he had eclipsed all rivals among postwar Protestant evangelists, and—with the possible exceptions of the English hymn writer Charles Wesley and the trans-Atlantic evangelist George Whitefield, both in the eighteenth century, and the American hymn writer Fanny Crosby in the nineteenth century—he had eclipsed all competitors in Anglo-American religious history.

By the mid-1960s Graham had become what we might call "The Great Legitimator." By then his presence conferred status on presidents, acceptability on wars, shame on racial prejudice, desirability on decency, dishonor on indecency, and prestige on civic events, at least if the newspaper coverage of his ministry serves as a reliable index.[56] In 1972 the *Saturday Evening Post* judged that the preacher might "very well be the best-known man in the world today. He is the greatest personal phenomenon of the age."[57] Twenty years later the former CBS News anchor Dan Rather said much the same: "He stands with a handful of American religious leaders from the Great Awakening forward who helped define the country."[58] One prominent historian would summarize it well: "Billy Graham is an epic figure that towers head and shoulders over the American landscape—Olympian in size and handsomeness, unrivaled in outreach to the world and inroads on the rich and powerful—enormously large of spirit."[59] Not surprisingly, when the Billy Graham Library opened, all three living U.S. former presidents graced the platform. By then the preacher seemed to stand above the fray, transcending denominational boundaries, theological disputes, and partisan agendas.

Complications

The reasons for Graham's prominence on the American religious landscape are not obvious. For one thing, the likelihood that any evangelist would become a national celebrity in the 1950s was not self-evident. To be sure, the most conspicuous evangelists of the post–World War I era, Billy Sunday and Aimee Semple McPherson, had attracted eye-popping crowds and garnered wide publicity in the religious and secular media.[60] And many others would win impressive crowds in the 1930s, 1940s, and 1950s. Their ministries provided a springboard that helped propel Graham. But the age of front-page coverage of mass evangelism in the nation's largest and most influential newspapers had largely passed.[61] What *did* win wide recognition in the interwar years was Sinclair Lewis's 1927 novel, *Elmer Gantry*. The image of the skirt-chasing charlatan preacher proved vibrant enough for Broadway to turn it into a play in 1928 and for Hollywood to turn it into a feature-length movie, starring Burt Lancaster and Shirley Jones, in 1960.[62] Little wonder that Willard Sperry, dean of Harvard Divinity School, would say in 1946, "We are tired of religious revivals as we have known them . . . Among all but the most backward churches it is now agreed that education ought to be . . . the best way of interesting our people in religion."[63] In 1957 the historian William McLoughlin would predict: "If history is any guide, Graham's popularity has about two more years to run."[64]

Graham's childhood and adolescence also offered few hints of things to come. Except for short family vacations to the North and South Carolina coasts and brief visits with relatives in Oklahoma, he never traveled far from the dairy farm where he was born and reared. His education at Bob Jones College, Florida Bible Institute, and Wheaton College launched him into a modestly successful career as a local pastor, itinerant evangelist, and YFC speaker. All of this would change, and dramatically, with his crusade in Los Angeles in September 1949. But until then, his family connections, education, and early ministry choices prefigured little more than a respectable but unexceptional career on the revival circuit.

At first glance, Graham's early career in the middle and late 1940s seems as barren of hints about his future as his salad days. He often appeared to personify the proverbial stump orator, firing 240 words a minute, feet pacing, hands chopping, and fingers stabbing.[65] On-stage dramatizations of biblical stories were marked by slang and preposterous renderings of scriptural texts.[66] The public heard enough factual blunders to sink lesser ships. Nor did his theology help much in mainline Protestant circles. The early Graham projected moralism, apocalypticism, and boilerplate literalism without flinching.

The intermediate career years—the mid-1950s to the mid-1970s—featured a more polished figure, yet they too raised questions about the reasons for his ascendency. To be sure, Graham's preaching slowed to a more dignified pace and his theology lost some of its hard edges. And some of his misfires were the expected mistakes of comparative youth, for he experienced a great deal of fame very early, and it took a while for him to figure out who he was. Yet many of the flaws seemed to run deeper and could not be waved away. His fraternizing with the rich, the famous, and the powerful worried his friends and energized his foes. The bill of particulars included his odious remarks about Jews and the media, uttered in private in President Richard Nixon's office in 1972 but secretly recorded and subsequently revealed in 2002. Though Graham repeatedly apologized to Jewish leaders, in print and in person, the episode stained his record. Most disturbing, for all but his most ardent followers, was his political posture from the mid-1960s to the mid-1970s. His early strong support for the Vietnam War, and then waffling on it, and then his rock-ribbed defense of Nixon during Watergate persisted long after most Americans had given up on both causes.

Outsiders, noting Graham's flaws and failures, subjected him to merciless criticism. Besides a steady flow of hate mail and death threats to him and his family each year, the assaults came from all directions: the left, the right, the academy, the media, and the church.[67] After the young evangelist bungled a White House meeting with Harry Truman in 1950, the president soured on him. Two decades later, the older man still remembered the younger one as a "counterfeit." "I just don't go for people like that," he groused. "All he's interested in is getting his name in the paper."[68] College students pummeled Graham too. When he held a crusade at the University of Tennessee in 1970 and invited President Nixon to speak, the student newspaper slammed the event as a "one-man circus" complete with an "elephant."[69] The right showed no mercy either. In 1966, following Graham's interdenominational crusades and ecumenical overtures, Bob Jones, Sr., president of Bob Jones University, judged that Graham was "doing more harm to the cause of Jesus Christ than any other living man."[70] As Graham grew older, the attacks generally softened. But not always. After his visit to a controversial Moscow disarmament conference in 1982, the conservative columnist George Will surmised that Graham was "America's most embarrassing export." Will hoped that the preacher would "stop acting as though pious intentions are substitutes for intelligence, and excuses for irresponsibility."[71] As noted, in 2002 the National Archives released tapes of Graham's conversation in the Oval Office in 1972 with President Richard Nixon about Jews' alleged control of the media. When the news broke, the secular essayist Christopher Hitchens pounced. He called the aging evangelist an "avid bigot as well as a cheap liar," "a gaping and mendacious anti-Jewish peasant."[72]

Graham's multiple public images made his success even more puzzling. That the fiery anticommunist of the 1940s differed from the irenic senior diplomat of the 1980s seemed easy enough to explain. People changed. But that explanation did not solve the problem. The deeper and more difficult issue was that many of Graham's faces continually appeared, disappeared, and reappeared, not sequentially but more or less at the same time. That pattern repeated itself throughout his career. Which was normative, the savvy CEO or the simple preacher? The uptown sophisticate or the downhome country boy? The globetrotting absent father or the attentive family man? The name-dropping partisan of the White House or the humble servant of the church? Above all, the self-promoting entrepreneur or the self-effacing saint?

For serious students of Graham's role in the shaping of modern America a family of related words keeps cropping up, each carrying a slightly different connotation. Are we looking at adroitness or adaptability? Ambiguity or complexity? Slippage or paradox? These words, which suggest multiple public images, must be balanced against an even more powerful and pervasive public conviction that Graham represented a man of uncompromised sincerity and integrity, "a man without shadows," as one biographer put it.[73] Possibly another biographer came closer to the mark: Graham was "perhaps America's most complicated innocent."[74]

Adding to this complexity was the plain fact that Billy Graham was not always Billy Graham—just as Martin Luther King, Jr., and John Paul II were not always Martin Luther King, Jr., and John Paul II. All of them grew in their self-understanding and in the public imagination. At some point very early on Graham the itinerant preacher became Graham the towering phenomenon, something larger than himself. The question was, then, when did Americans stop dealing with an ordinary man and start dealing with a cultural myth?

So it was that along with Olympian fame, Graham brought to the table a long list of liabilities: conventional beginnings, serious mistakes of judgment, mordant criticism from others, shifting public identities, and elusive mythic dimensions. His success does not explain itself. It requires analysis and interpretation.

Explaining Graham's Success

Three closely related but distinct questions propel this book. The first one is about Graham himself. How did he become, in the words of one historian of celebrity pulpiteers, "the least colorful and most powerful preacher in America"?[75] The second and more important question is about Graham and American religion. How did he help expand traditional evangelical rhetoric into the moral vocabulary that millions of Americans used to make sense of both their private and their public experiences? The third and most important question is about Graham and the great gulf streams of post–World War II American history. How did he help mold the culture that created him and that he created? More precisely, how did he speak both *for* and *to* modern America?

I propose one answer for all three questions. It applies mainly to the United States but with important qualifications illumines Graham's career in other countries too. *From first to last, Graham displayed an uncanny ability to adopt trends in the wider culture and then use them for his evangelistic and moral reform purposes.* To be sure, successful evangelists from George Whitefield in the 1730s to Billy Sunday in the 1930s had followed pretty much the same strategy. The difference was that Graham did it with greater skill for six decades and, despite innumerable opportunities for slipping, comparatively few missteps. Sometimes he seemed to move by instinct, sometimes by design, and sometimes by both at once—all on the "back stroke," as one associate put it.[76] In most cases it is hard to tell which was which, and probably it does not matter very much if we could. The key point is that Graham, like a finely calibrated barometer, proved acutely responsive to changes in the world around him. The enduring meaning of his career lies precisely there, in the intersection between his extraordinary agency and the forces shaping modern America.

In the following pages, I look at Graham through different interpretative lenses. Though the book follows a roughly chronological order, taking up features of Graham's ministry in the sequence in which they began to loom large on the horizon, the treatment is largely thematic, like pages in a scrapbook of American life. The chapters highlight the varying roles that Graham played on the nation's stage. As "Preacher," he articulated a traditional evangelical theology but presented it in increasingly appealing ways. Amid the complexity of the crusades and the Graham media machine, his preaching remained the centerpiece of his ministry. As "Icon," Graham capitalized on both inherited and acquired qualities. A Hollywood face and other winsome traits came naturally, but he tended them—along with honesty, modesty, marital fidelity, and financial integrity—very carefully. The press knew good copy when they saw it. As "Southerner," Graham reinforced his personal gifts through his identification with the New South. He deployed a genteel yet downhome style that other Americans found increasingly attractive, along with a measured but steady embrace of racial civil rights. As "Entrepreneur," he built from the ground up a crusade structure and organization of remarkable durability and streamlined efficiency. As "Architect," Graham pioneered evangelical ecumenism, which pivoted on his willingness to work with almost anyone who would work with him as long as they did not ask him to change his message. As "Pilgrim," he displayed a circuitous yet inexorable march toward a progressive position on most of the key social issues of the era, including disarmament, nonpartisanship, and global poverty (though not feminism). As "Pastor," he and his writers fashioned standardized yet remarkably relevant responses to the thousands of letters that cascaded into his mailbox every week. And finally, as "Patriarch," he fathered a legacy that manifested itself in figures as different as Franklin Graham, Rick Warren, and Bono. He also exemplified a personality profile that millions of Americans found both complicated and enormously appealing.

Five boundaries define the scope of this work. The first and most important is that I focus on Graham's *public* career—the things he said and did

on the nation's stage for all to hear and see—and not on the things he said
and did in private, behind the scenes. For this reason I have drawn primarily on published sources, documents that represent his public voice, rather
than on his extensive private correspondence or on interviews with family,
friends, or associates. Those details would be crucial for a conventional
biography, but that is not my aim. So, too, I usually do not try to distinguish between Graham's own words and the words of people who spoke
and wrote on his behalf—the Graham Voice. One important exception
modifies this pattern: Graham's extensive correspondence with presidents
of the United States, which I regard as automatically public documents.

Looking at the public Graham comes with costs. It bypasses some of the
most interesting features of his daily life, including chronic insomnia, habitual nail biting, fondness for sunny beaches, taste for Carolina barbecue,
and constant efforts to gain weight, to name a few.[77] But interesting is not
the same as important. A bigger cost is that it largely elides his family relationships. By all accounts, Graham's wife of sixty-three years, Ruth Bell
Graham, played a quiet but powerful role in just about everything he said
and did, on stage and off. Indeed, after her death in 2007, when the stories
about her influence began to grow, it became increasingly clear that a major part of any conventional biography of Billy would also have to be about
Ruth.[78] Graham's grandfathers, parents, three siblings, five children, and
brother-in-law, Leighton Ford, shaped him too. I touch on those relationships when they became artifacts of public attention, as when reporters
used Ruth to score points about strong women staying at home, but in
general I leave the job of exploring Graham's personal and family relationships to historians with a more strictly biographical agenda.

The second boundary is methodological. I conceive this study to be sug-
gestive, not exhaustive. Many aspects of Graham's public career, such as his
frequent pronouncements on sex and youth, receive little attention. Other
important topics, such as the internal machinery of the BGEA, also receive
little attention. I justify such omissions with the journalists' adage that less
is more. A handful of well-chosen examples speak for most of the others.
Admittedly, fair selection is no small challenge. Graham talked, wrote,
traveled, and changed a great deal, and all of it received exhaustive coverage in the media. In the end I can only invite the reader's trust that I have
tagged the dominant pronouncements and not stray counterpoints.

The third boundary is geographic. I examine Graham's ministry primarily in the United States. His international career merits a book in itself, for
eventually it may prove more significant than anything he did at home.

Except for New York in 1957, all of his largest crusades took place overseas. His rise as a global religious presence paralleled America's rise as a global political presence in the same postwar decades. But figuring out how Graham's story illumines America's story is my focus.

The fourth boundary is procedural. When I speak of what Graham "knew" or "believed" or "felt," I should stress that I do not presume *really* to know his states of mind. My statements are informed guesses, based on long acquaintance with the primary and secondary data. Yet it is important to remember that they remain no more than that: informed guesses.

The fifth and final boundary pertains to audience. This book does not presuppose close knowledge of American history and certainly not of American religious history. Rather, I have written for the person more interested in Graham's significance than in the details of his life or in professional historians' debates about him.

In 2007, poll data showed that nearly a third of Americans under the age of thirty did not recognize Graham's name.[79] When I find that I need to explain to my students who he was, I know that a new day has dawned. The closing of Graham's era offers a fresh opportunity to think about how he contributed to the shaping of modern America. It invites us to think about why Billy Graham matters.

CHAPTER ONE

Preacher

Blessed with an uncanny sense of the opportunities afforded by the media revolution, Graham adapted his old-fashioned message to new venues. Sensing the possibilities of an age increasingly given to sound bites, hurried interviews, and arresting visual images, he delivered his ideas in crisp and compelling forms. Journalists, academics, and ministers endlessly analyzed his public-speaking practices, especially in the crusade meetings in which the most memorable deliveries took place. Sympathetic observers touted them and critics lamented them, but no one doubted their power.[1] Admittedly, besides speaking, Graham and his editorial assistants wrote copiously. Though the prose proved clear and accessible, little of it was memorable, and much of it soporific. Sometimes he seemed to turn wine back into water. So it is that we probably would not care all that much about Graham today if millions of Americans had not first encountered him as a preacher, either face-to-face in the great stadium crusades or broadcast over radio and television. His publications elaborated themes that in most cases had been more forcefully articulated in the sermons. Faith, after all, came by hearing.

What was the substantive theological content of his sermons? What concepts did his words convey? The secondary literature about Graham is vast. Yet it seems fair to say that the great bulk of it discusses features of his ministry that he would have regarded as secondary or tertiary or less: his looks, style, relation to presidents, views of social and political issues, international travels, ability to evoke both adulation and contempt, friendships with the high and the mighty, reportedly storybook family life, and (indubitably) impeccable personal integrity, among others. Though he was a willing participant in all of those interests, he made clear—repeatedly—that he saw himself as an evangelist with one purpose: to win people to Christ. And that required him to think through and then communicate a bundle of theological concepts. He was not a theologian and never pretended to be. But he did know that he was a craftsman who worked with theological materials. And that is where students of Graham's role in the shaping of a nation's consciousness should begin: with the theology.

Theological Core

Logically, if not always in practice, Graham's thinking about this subject started with the problem of authority. Who or what established the final rule of measurement for everything Christians should believe and practice? The answer, of course, resided in a single source, the Bible. That sacred text talked about many things but above all God, humans, and God's relationship with humans. The Bible's narrative arc was clear. It taught that the first human, Adam, had sinned by willfully rebelling against God's rules. So did every person who came after. Human pride formed the toxic well that polluted the entire created order. Yet God, in his infinite love, chose to save people by revealing himself in his son, Jesus Christ, who was simultaneously fully God and fully man. Because Jesus lived a sinless life, his death paid the penalty for sin and his resurrection defeated the grave. If people repented of their sin and embraced Christ as Lord and Savior, the Holy Spirit would enable them to live lives of inward holiness and outward integrity. Christians could be confident that Christ would return at the end of human history. After death, believers would enter into the everlasting joys of heaven and nonbelievers the everlasting sorrows of hell. Believers were obliged to share this good news—or gospel—of salvation with others. The whole of it was this. Things were broken, but God offered a solution. Humans needed only reach out and take it.[2]

Graham repeated this core message, with little variation, on countless occasions. It formed the substance of the first formal compilation of his thought, his best-selling and eventually signature book, *Peace with God* (1953).[3] The message could be summarized in—or reduced to, according to one's point of view—something like a dozen words: Bible, God, sin, Jesus Christ, new birth, growth in grace, second coming, reward (or punishment), and mission. Of course, Graham knew that theologians used formal labels for each of those constants—authority, Trinity, depravity, Christology, soteriology, justification, redemption, sanctification, eschatology, and evangelization, among others—but he preferred the language of everyday experience. For that reason, he endorsed and sometimes preached from newer translations of the Bible, especially the vernacular *Living Bible*.[4] He aimed to show that however phrased, the New Testament's central message—the gospel—represented *truly* good news.

In Graham's preaching the new birth constituted the centerpiece of the gospel. He knew perfectly well, of course, that Christian theology entailed many other claims. But since he saw himself as an evangelist called by God to invite people to faith, the new birth stood at the center of his own work. Many evangelicals used the term *born again*, and sometimes he did too, but he preferred *new birth*. He described the experience in various ways. In a theological mood he depicted it as a "saving knowledge of Jesus Christ." It was not reformation but regeneration—literally, *re*-generation, *re*-creation, *re*-birth—of the person from the ground up. In February 1951, in one of his earliest nationally broadcast sermons, Graham articulated the position he would repeat thousands of times, nearly word for word, for the next six decades: "God gives a new nature to those that receive by faith His Son, Jesus Christ. . . . Reformation cannot be substituted for regeneration. . . . God's standard . . . demands regeneration."[5]

Authentic regeneration produced peace. It is significant that Graham's foundational theological work would bear the title *Peace with God*. In 1986 he told his hometown paper, "I am for peace . . . first in our relationship with God through Christ; secondly that he can give us peace here and now in our daily life. . . . And thirdly, peace among people and nations. Peace in families. Peace in community. Peace between the races."[6] He captured the sum of the problem and the sum of its solution in two often-quoted sentences: "We need a new heart that will not have lust and greed and hate in it. We need a heart filled with love and peace and joy, and that is why Jesus came into the world . . . to make peace between us and God."[7] Reflecting on the whole of Graham's publically presented theology after the preacher retired, the historian David Steinmetz captured the central point more succinctly than Graham himself usually did: The new birth offered not a problem-free life but "a relationship to God that transforms all other relationships."[8] Graham did not worry very much about rhetorical precision. Getting the point across *was* the point. Grace-filled hearts should result in grace-filled lives.

Throughout his ministry Graham emphasized the practical results of the new birth. Since the evangelical movement's beginning in the early eighteenth century, partisans had viewed it as a means for imposing discipline on one's life. Fully realized, it meant a heart freed from greed, revenge, violence, selfishness, and racial prejudice. Graham never budged from the insistence that the origin of humans' problems, both personal and social, resided in the corrupt heart. Enduring solutions to the world's problems—as opposed to temporary ones—required people to deal with the issue at its root, where it started. Later we will see that the middle-aged and mature Graham said more than the younger Graham did about the social effects of the new birth—more just, more equitable relationships among groups, races, and classes—but he never reconsidered his analysis of where the problem originated.

Contrary to the impression commonly conveyed by many academic studies of Graham, the priority he gave to the personal was shared by many thoughtful Americans outside the evangelical subculture. In 2008, to take one of countless possibilities, Duke University president Richard H. Brodhead remarked—in the wake of a university sports scandal—that "the integrity of the judicial system is no greater than the integrity of the individuals that constitute it."[9] Brodhead's comment had nothing to do with religion, let alone Graham. And the analogy should not be pressed too hard. Nonetheless, the larger point held. Sturdy bridges required sturdy foundations.

PROVIDENCE AND MORAL THEISM

Besides the theological tenets sketched above, two additional principles marked Graham's preached message: the concepts of providence and of "moral theism." They did not show up, at least not explicitly, in *Peace with God*, but they functioned prominently in uncounted sermons, press conferences, and civic occasions.

Providence embodied the evangelist's view of how God superintended the world in both the natural and the historical realms. That arrangement applied both to natural and human history. Nature's laws normally prevailed, but occasionally God intervened in the form of miracles, which shattered nature's continuity. As for human history, Graham, like most evangelicals, believed that it was neither determined nor random but something in between: contingent.[10] That meant that God maintained a plan for the final hour of the final day, but he had given humans the ability to speed up or slow down the process. More precisely, God ultimately oversaw everything but left many of the details open-ended. Humans operated more or less freely within a framework of divine oversight. Well into his later years, Graham quoted the nineteenth-century Africa missionary David Livingstone in these terms: "We work for a glorious future which we are not destined to see."[11] If Graham was vague about just how God's superintending providence intersected with the natural and the historical realms, so was the Bible.

"Moral theism" was not a term Graham used—I adapt it from a similar term from the sociologist of religion Christian Smith—but it captures a second pervasive theme in his outlook.[12] Simply defined, it meant something like fundamental morality, based on the premise of a benign personal

God. For Graham himself morality rested on Christian assumptions, but people did not have to be Christian to appreciate its relevance to their daily lives. Moral theism resulted in common-sense guidance for normal living. Its vagueness lent itself to capacious and flexible application. It allowed Graham to address dilemmas of daily life in a way that crossed theological and sectarian boundaries. And it won wide audiences while alienating few. So it was that on June 25, 2005, in Flushing Meadows, New York—the second evening of the final major crusade meeting of Graham's life—the platform guests included former president Bill Clinton, New York City Mayor Michael Bloomberg, and New York Senators Hillary Rodham Clinton and Charles Schumer. "New Yorkers share an appreciation for faith," said Bloomberg, "after all, our city was built by people who came here to worship God freely."[13] Graham's moral theism drew on deep-running streams in American life that esteemed (albeit with mixed outcomes) ideals of decency, pluralism, and fair play.

The cluster of convictions set forth in *Peace with God*, along with providence and moral theism, constituted American evangelical boilerplate. It also marked Graham's preaching from the beginning to the end of his career. He helped make it boilerplate. Looking inward, it formed the intellectual benchmark that enabled evangelicals to define the boundaries of orthodoxy. Looking outward, it enabled them to gain their bearings on the religious landscape.

Changes

Over the years Graham's preached theology evolved in some ways. It is important to stress "some." The core conviction of biblical authority, human sinfulness, divine grace, and Christ's return remained impregnable throughout. And most of the changes were gradual shifts of tonality or emphasis or new ways of phrasing old positions. Sometimes the changes were mainly a matter of bringing to the surface themes that had been there all along. Nonetheless, tonality, emphasis, phrasing, and position counted, precisely because Graham's audience also changed when it came to the ideas they were prepared to hear and support. The main developments applied to his understanding of the Bible, the new birth, and providence.

BIBLE

The final and sole authority of the Bible in matters of salvation remained unchanged, but how Graham conceived and articulated that concept evolved.

His college training and early sermons left little doubt that he started out with a fundamentalist view that Scripture, reasonably read, did not make mistakes of any kind in matters of faith, science, or history.

The story of the Bible, fundamentalism, and fundamentalism's stepchild, evangelicalism (or the new evangelicalism) is long and complex. Historians have given it sustained attention.[14] The details need not detain us at this point—we will return to some of the more pertinent ones later—but here a word about words may be helpful.

Before the World War II years, fundamentalists, especially in popular writing and preaching, used the words *authoritative, infallible*, and *trustworthy* more or less interchangeably. They denoted the conviction that the Bible, fairly interpreted, told the truth about everything that mattered. After the war years, in the face of controversy, the words began to take on separate meanings. *Authoritative* emphasized the Bible as the final authority in the face of competing authorities. *Infallible* stressed the Bible as a reliable guide to salvation, something people could count on. *Trustworthy* underscored the Bible's ability to speak truth to the heart, a source of spiritual enrichment. All of these terms—*authoritative, infallible,* and *trustworthy*—implied that the Bible mainly aimed to address ultimate questions of faith and salvation. They implicitly set aside the assumption of the Bible's literal accuracy in matters of science and history as less important, and perhaps less clear, for it fell outside the Bible's primary goal of providing life-giving good news.

The words *inerrancy* and *inspiration* dropped into the mix as well. Though theologians had argued about the precise meanings of these words for decades, in the postwar years they, too, acquired more differentiated connotations in popular usage. Inerrancy emphasized the Bible's accuracy in science and history in order to underscore its accuracy in matters of faith and salvation. If the Bible made mistakes in one area, how could it be relied on in other areas? The meaning of inspiration (and plenary inspiration) proved particularly elastic, depending on who used it and in what context, but the larger point remained clear enough: God, not human ingenuity, ultimately stood behind the writing, transmission, and proper interpretation of all of Scripture.[15]

In *Peace with God*, Graham used *authoritative* but not *infallible* or *inerrant*. He did not explain why. There is no reason to think that he doubted the Bible's accuracy in all respects, but he seemed to want to emphasize its truth in matters of faith, as a guide to Christian salvation and Christian living. In the 1940s through the mid-1950s he signed statements of faith that used the word *inerrancy,* but he himself did not use it.[16] He thought it was "too brittle."[17] The word *infallible*—carrying the connotation of accuracy in science and history but with an emphasis on salvation—did figure in his writing and preaching. Though it would be difficult to prove quantitatively, my reading of Graham's sermons and writings over the years suggests that the concept of accuracy in science and history, though never absent, yielded more often to the concept of the Bible's final authority, infallibility, and trustworthiness.

"We must read the Bible, not primarily as historians seeking information, but as men and women seeking God," Graham urged in 1999.[18] Biblical authority figured prominently in the editorial focus of the evangelical flagship periodical, *Christianity Today*. He wrote the blueprint for the point of view it would project. The premier issue declared that the magazine would "unreservedly" teach the "complete reliability and authority of the Word of God," as well as "the doctrine of plenary inspiration."[19] In his memoir, published in 1997, Graham remembered that the "hallmark distinguishing *Christianity Today* was a commitment to the trustworthiness of Scripture as the Word of God, with all of the ramifications of that commitment."[20] In the evangelical subculture, the shift from explicit insistence on inerrancy to infallibility, and then to authority, and even more to trustworthiness, was not minor. It provoked fierce debates and left wounded relationships.[21]

Fuller Theological Seminary's connection to these questions offers a case study of a debate that seemed arcane to mainline Protestants (not to mention secular writers) but proved the breath of life for evangelical insiders. Fuller Seminary began in 1947 with the notion of biblical inerrancy in its Statement of Faith.[22] By 1972, however, the seminary had moved from inerrancy to "the inspiration and authority of the Scriptures." The president, David Allan Hubbard, defined that principle to mean "loyalty to the trustworthiness, the inspiration, the authority and the power of Scripture."[23] Graham served on Fuller's Board of Trustees. Privately he opposed the change. He might have been worried that an institution charged with training the next generation of clergy should err on the side of caution. Or he may have been of two minds about the matter. Whatever the reason, he said to Hubbard in private that the disagreement about terms and the fine points of meaning that they conveyed was one of the "peripheral matters" that unfortunately divided the evangelical community. Publically he supported Fuller's shift.[24] In one of the most important talks Graham ever gave, the opening address to the International Congress on World Evangelization at Lausanne, Switzerland, in 1974, he used both *authority* and *infallibility,* apparently interchangeably. He declared that evangelicals worldwide were "committed to the authority of Scripture. We hold that the entire Bible is the infallible Word of God."[25]

If Graham's views about the Bible's truthfulness rested (at least most of the time) on a capacious sense of it as authoritative, infallible, and trustworthy—but with no mention of inerrancy—his views on how the Bible should be interpreted rested on a capacious foundation too. His preaching in the 1940s and early 1950s suggested that the Bible should be interpreted as literally as reasonably possible.[26] But over time that position grew more flexible. In 1964 the BBC correspondent David Frost asked Graham, "Are you a biblical literalist?" Graham answered—we can almost see the smile—"I don't think anyone is really a literalist." He immediately explained that metaphors—such as the parable of the rich man who died and went to hell—should be understood as exactly that: metaphors. Here Graham was not unusual, even among fundamentalists, and certainly not among evangelicals, who similarly felt that something like a rule of reason had to be applied to Scripture. But when Frost pressed about the creation story, Graham allowed that the Bible was not a "scientific book." It was a "book of redemption." The key point, he said, was to affirm that God had created humans, whether by evolution or by blowing on "some dust."[27]

Following a wide-ranging conversation with Graham in 2006, *Newsweek*'s Jon Meacham would say, "While he believes Scripture is the inspired, authoritative word of God, he does not read the Bible as though it were a collection of Associated Press bulletins straightforwardly reporting on events in the ancient Middle East." "I'm not a literalist in the sense that every single jot and tittle is from the Lord," Graham told the journalist. "This is a little difference in my thinking through the years."[28] Graham's comments to Frost and Meacham surely seemed tame enough in mainline Protestant circles, but they both registered and portended an important shift of emphasis in the evangelical subculture.[29]

There is little evidence that Graham clearly understood, let alone supported, the principles of biblical higher criticism or related critical methods taught in mainline Protestant seminaries and in secular colleges and universities. Yet his legendary encounter with his critic-friend Charles Templeton in the summer of 1949 ironically freed him from the shackles of inerrancy and literalism. He embraced a faith-based foundation that trumped any sort of empirical or logical demonstration of the Bible's factual accuracy—or inaccuracy, for that matter. In the pivotal talk he gave in Lausanne, Switzerland, in 1974, just after speaking of the Bible's infallibility, he went on: "Many years ago I had to accept this position by faith. Even though I myself cannot understand it all, it is taken by the Holy Spirit and made inerrant *to my spirit*" (my emphasis).[30] That outlook had been developing for at least the better part of two decades. As far back as 1956 he had noted, "One can be a Christian without reading the Bible . . . because it is faith in Christ which makes one a Christian and not reading the Bible." To be sure, Graham added, a person could not be an "intelligent and instructed Christian," or likely remain one for very long, without reading the Bible.[31] Still, the foundation was Christ, not the Bible. He reminded David Frost in 1964 that early Christians had no Bibles or theological colleges. Yet they "turned their world upside down. What did they have? An experience with the living Christ." Graham said that he would be a Christian even if the Bible proved untrue: "My faith is grounded in a personal encounter with Christ."[32]

Graham returned to the subject with Frost three decades later. The Bible was "inspired of God to help us in direction of our lives, in our salvation, and in doing what God wants us to do. . . . A mistake many make is that they worship the Bible, they make it into a fetish. But they never look at it." They make it into "sort of an icon."[33] Graham's position was a classically pragmatic one. Some things just have to be settled. People like Templeton might be able to live a life of questions, but Graham had to take his bearings by the stars he saw in Scripture and go from there. The Bible brimmed with assertions he did not understand, he admitted. But it also contained enough that he did understand that he could proceed with confidence.

This faith-based approach to the Bible proved effective for all the moral questions of daily life. In *My Answer*, a compilation of some of the responses that had appeared in his daily syndicated newspaper column "My Answer," Graham addressed a wide array of problems, mostly dilemmas of daily life—aging, loneliness, empty nest syndrome, bad habits, bad health, conflicts with co-workers, even what to believe about outer space. Significantly, none of the questions or answers bore dates. The reason was simple: Graham based his answers on the Bible, and the Bible was timeless and universal. The book was called *My Answer*, but he hoped it relayed God's answer, for "the Bible has the answer to every moral situation known to man."[34] The volume was reissued in 1988—tellingly retitled *Answers to Life's Problems*—with minor changes, but the introductory guarantee of timeless and universal relevance remained untouched: "The Word of our God stands forever as an unchanging source of answers to all of life's problems."[35] Graham nowhere claimed that the Bible answered questions of history and science, but it did answer everything that truly counted.

The faith-based approach to the Bible proved effective for mass evangelism too. For one thing, the "Bible wars" among fundamentalists over the inerrancy of Scripture versus the authority of Scripture were more important for intellectuals within the movement than for rank-and-file believers. Intellectuals had positions to defend.[36] Graham, in contrast, did not engage in debates, let alone polemics, about the Bible's reliability. Rather, he focused on real-life answers to real-life questions. Graham knew his audiences. He knew that they esteemed the Bible less as a storehouse of inerrant facts and doctrines than as a living, breathing authority that addressed the dilemmas people faced day in, day out. Steeped in Bible stories, millions of them knew its content from cover to cover. Its stories were their stories. Graham's drumbeat quoting of the *King James Version* (and later, the *Revised Standard Version* and colloquial translations), amplified by his prodigious memory of the text and ability to cite it on cue, underscored his connection with his constituency. In 2003, looking back on a lifetime of preaching, he knew where his success had lain: "I have found that if I say, 'The Bible says' and 'God says,' I get results."[37] Graham and his supporters, millions strong, were slices from the same pie.

New Birth

These considerations bring us to the second shift of emphasis: Graham's preaching about sin and the new birth. In his early sermons he often fell into moralism, framing sin as an infraction of rules. Those transgressions were not trivial. Gambling, alcohol, tobacco, the misuse of sex, and other forms of illicit behavior betokened a tear in the social fabric. He also underscored the pernicious dispositions that gave rise to such lapses in the first place: lust, greed, selfishness, materialism, and racism. But he also knew that the problems ran deeper than breaking rules or giving vent to carnal dispositions. More and more he focused on original sin and its corruption of human nature, both personal and social. "There is a difference between sin and sins," Graham said in 1981. "There is sin (singular), which is the heart of our spiritual disease, and there are sins (plural), which are the fruit or signs of the disease. If I spent all of my time on sins (plural) I might never be able to get at the root cause which is sin (singular)."[38] That fatal flaw marked the intractable fracture in the human condition: "We all have a terminal disease far worse than cancer, that will kill us morally and spiritually. It's called sin."[39]

With those strokes Graham embedded evangelicals in larger currents of postwar anxiety, offering tools for a more realistic reading of their daily newspapers. The historian Andrew Finstuen captured the point precisely.

Graham's message about sin was a message about human finitude, the limits of humans' ability to change themselves and the natural and social world around them. Observers—even sympathetic ones—sometimes took Graham's words as counsel to accept, or at least acquiesce in, unjust social structures because not all that much could be done until Christ came back.[40] Yet a more accurate reading, and one that better fit the temper of the times, would see Graham's words as an honest appraisal, the kind of realism that stood as a necessary precursor to responsible reform, personal no less than social. He preached a democracy of sin.[41]

But Graham also preached a democracy of grace, and there too the emphasis evolved. In the early years he stressed the need for a decision for Christ that led to a new birth. He did not exactly say that new birth would occur at a definable time and place, but the testimonies, including his own, strongly implied it. In time, however, he gave more room to the great variety of ways that new birth could come about, gradually as well as instantly, through the instrumentalities of the church (including sacraments) as well as through the personal decision of the individual seeker: "Now different churches interpret that slightly different . . . Some people think that that happens at baptism . . . some think it happens in the communion service. Some think it happens on other occasions. Whenever it happens that's not the important thing. The important thing is[,] are we being a Christian every single day? Jesus said 'by their fruits you shall know them.' "[42] And he showed more appreciation for the significance of recommitment, a determination by lax or nominal believers to stop drifting and self-consciously shoulder the responsibilities of being a Christian. Little wonder. On his own conversion card in the Ham revival back in 1934 he had checked "recommitment."[43]

Though the younger Graham emphasized the practical results of the new birth, both personally and socially, the middle-aged and mature Graham thought and preached about it more often and with more force. Having been "reared on a small farm in southern America," he admitted to a crowd at Harvard in 1982, it had "rarely occurred" to him to think about "the difficulties, problems, and oppressions of black people." In high school he did start to think about such injustice. With his commitment to Christ, he "began to realize" that he would have to take a stand.[44]

The practical results took time to come to fruition: "I never thought of it in terms of corporate responsibility. I had no real idea that millions of people throughout the world lived on the knife-edge of starvation and that . . . I [had] a responsibility toward them. Later, as I traveled and studied the

Bible more, I changed."[45] To be sure, Graham rarely if ever used the terms *social gospel* or *social Christianity,* which he associated with liberal programs that started at the wrong end, with abstract structures rather than with the persons constituting the structures. And he never believed that legislation was sufficient. People could and would subvert any regime they did not embrace from the inside.[46] He offered the failure of Prohibition as Exhibit A.[47] But he understood that social holiness was not an automatic result of personal holiness. It needed to be secured through legislation. Graham started publically calling for the passage of civil rights legislation as early as 1957 in a massive outdoor meeting in Brooklyn, New York.[48] Laws such as the federal civil rights laws enacted in 1964 and 1965 served the vital purpose of *helping* to solidify the moral reform that personal transformation initiated.

Finding the right balance between personal and social holiness remained a challenge for Graham, as for many thoughtful evangelicals. He worried that clergy would fall into misplaced priorities and see moral reform as their primary task. It was not. Their primary task was to preach the gospel of personal transformation. But if personal transformation was rightly proclaimed in all of its dimensions, and then appropriated and put into practice, it would *result* in social and personal holiness. In 1974 Graham told a Dayton, Ohio, journalist that he agreed with 90 percent of what politically radical young evangelicals were saying: "We need to read the Book of Acts again."[49] A full-orbed evangelical theology offered a shining vision of what the kingdom of God on earth really would look like.

PROVIDENCE

Graham's views of providence, like his views of the Bible and of new birth, also underwent a subtle but important evolution of emphasis. Though he preached more—far more—about other topics, this one captured a disproportionate share of journalists' and historians' attention. So it calls for careful consideration here.

First came the providential ordering of nature. Graham's preaching distinguished between divine superintendence in general and miraculous interventions in particular. With the exception of the New Testament message of Christ's physical resurrection and return at the end of history, he increasingly spoke of the divine superintendence of all of nature and history rather than emphasizing miracles as definable interventions in nature or history.[50] Joe Barnhart, an unsympathetic biographer, judged that Graham believed in miracles, but "not the kind [of miracle] that raises people from the dead and makes the sun to stand still." For him, Barnhart thought, "modern miracles are more subjective and psychological in nature."[51] "Could it be that signs and wonders were gifts particularly appropriate to the special circumstances of the early Church? I think so," Graham wrote in 1978. The evangelist allowed that when the gospel was proclaimed on "the frontiers of the Christian faith," and at the end of history, "we may expect miracles to increase." But that outcome lay elsewhere or in the future.[52]

What about today? "What is the nearest to proof of the existence of God?" asked David Frost. "The birth of a baby," was the evangelist's answer. Quoting the doctor who delivered his son Ned, Graham wondered, "How can anyone watch this birth and deny a God?"[53] In 1972 the entertainer Dinah Shore asked Graham, on national television, if he believed in miracles. He responded without hesitation: "Yes, Jesus Christ performed miracles. [There are many] miracles around us today, including television and airplanes. But the greatest miracle of all is to take a person and give them a new nature." The greatest miracle, then, was Christ's transformation of the heart.[54]

Graham never denied the possibility of the kind of overt miracles that Pentecostals, Mormons, and Catholics, among others, emphasized, but with the important exception of his hugely successful book, *Angels: God's Secret Agents* (1975), he rarely talked about them. In this respect his views ran closer to both the dispensationalist fundamentalist (a group we will take up shortly) and the mainline Protestant outlooks. The two groups avoided miracles for very different reasons—the former because they believed that God had suspended them at the end of the apostolic era, the latter because of a strong sense of the unbroken continuity of all of history—but the outcome was the same. For Graham, too, the outcome was the same. He rarely elaborated how he got there. He did not need to wander down those dimly lit hallways of theological argumentation because the goal was converts, not disciples.

END OF HISTORY

The evangelist's preaching about the study of history's final scenario—what theologians called eschatology—proved more complicated than his preaching about nature. Throughout the nineteenth century American evangelicals had shown intense interest in the question of endings. Before the Civil War the great majority were postmillennialists, which meant that they expected Christ to return as the crowning culmination of a millennium (usually conceived metaphorically as a very long period) of steady improvement in humans' material and spiritual lives. After the Civil War most became premillennialists, meaning they expected Christ to return and inaugurate, not crown, a millennial age.

Of those evangelicals a great many, probably a majority, also embraced a subset of premillennialism commonly called dispensationalism. Influenced by fundamentalist Bible teachers in Ireland and England in the late nineteenth century, dispensationalists held that God had divided history into distinct eras, or dispensations. The church dispensation—running from Christ's birth through the end of the period covered by Acts—included miracles. Those events attested to the Holy Spirit's power in the founding of the church. When that dispensation ended, God suspended miracles until the end of history. The present dispensation would end when Jesus "raptured" his saints from earth. That meant, among other things, that they would escape the Great Tribulation, or the time of terrible suffering that the Bible foretold would take place just before the Battle of Armageddon. At the height of the battle, dispensationalists argued, the Lord would return to earth with his saints, bind the forces of evil, and then rule throughout the millennial age. It would be an age of healing, peace, and justice. The lion would lie down with the lamb. At the close of the millennium the Lord would judge all people, sending some to their final reward and the others to their final punishment.[55]

Graham inherited this scheme of dispensationalist premillennialism. To outsiders it seemed arcane if not preposterous. To evangelical insiders, however, it felt as familiar as an old flannel shirt.[56] Within that context, three continuities marked his thinking and preaching from the beginning to the end of his public career. First, the premillennialist part of the scheme loomed much larger than the dispensationalist part. He always made clear that he expected the physical return of Christ to earth. Christ and Christ alone would inaugurate the final chapter of history when the lion would lie down with the lamb. To be sure, humans must do all they could in the meantime to bring about peace and justice, but their efforts would never prove sufficient or permanent. Graham avoided giving dates for Christ's return, though in the early years he did succumb to the temptation to set an outer limit, once saying before 2000.[57] Later, he scrupulously avoided setting any sort of date, stressing instead the importance of working and waiting.[58]

Second, Graham, like Dwight L. Moody (whom he effectively took to be his role model), held dispensationalist views too, but he downplayed them. They remained artfully vague in his preaching, as they did in Moody's.

More to the point, by the middle years of Graham's ministry, dispensation-alism had receded to something like wallpaper: always present, but hardly more than a backdrop. Indeed, in his architectonic vision for *Christianity Today*, he urged the editors to avoid the topic altogether. Always alert to the evangelical (not to mention the wider) reading market, he warned that the magazine would lose the support of "thousands of ministers" if they waded into the subject.[59]

Third, Graham invested a great deal of energy in "prophecy watching." Throughout his life he continually scanned the newspapers for particulars about developments that might serve as indicators of where humans stood in the unfolding of history. He paid attention to both negative and positive developments, and, like most fundamentalists, gave special attention to events in Israel. But here things grew tricky. On one hand, into the 1980s, Graham took no vacation from prophecy watching, continually looking for signs of the times that portended the end of the world. (The garish doomsday cover of Graham's book *Approaching Hoofbeats: The Four Horsemen of the Apocalypse* [1983] left no doubt that Graham's publisher knew a good marketing tool when they saw one.)[60] On the other hand, he said comparatively little about how *specific* times, places, events, or people would figure in the last-days scenario. He focused instead on broad trends such as wars and famines or medical and spiritual advances. Unlike many fundamentalists, who seemed determined to pin down the exact identity of the Anti-Christ or the exact timing and site of Christ's advent, Graham left all that indefinite. What he did not leave indefinite was the promise that Christ would return to right every wrong and dry every tear.[61]

The relationship between threat and hope merits closer analysis. Critics charged that Graham preached opposite messages about the future. On one hand he railed about imminent doom, triggered by humans' sinful and reckless behavior, both personal and social. Unless men and women mended their ways, the world was headed for calamity. Without question, his preaching about how the world would end produced some of his most apocalyptic rhetoric. A typical case in point was a February 1953 *Hour of Decision* sermon that bore the alarming title "Three Minutes to Twelve." Pivoting on the urgency of President Eisenhower's Inaugural Prayer the previous month, as well as on the cover of the *Journal of Science*, which pictured a clock set at 11:57 PM, Graham thundered: "How can I make you realize the tenseness . . . of the present world situation? We have allowed ourselves to be lulled into a stupor, somehow thinking that the whole matter is not urgent after all."[62] On the other hand he also exulted about imminent revival and the salvific results that would come from it, both personal and social. This second clock was perennially set at 12:03 AM. So it was that in 1985 he told an audience, as he had told countless other audiences on countless other occasions, that in the United States, "despite many human problems, 'we are in the midst of probably the greatest spiritual revival in American history.' "[63]

Which was it? Was history's clock set at the ominous hour of 11:57 PM or at the glorious hour of 12:03 AM? The answer, of course, was both. Church-going evangelicals were accustomed to the paradox of history's clock being simultaneously set at 11:57 PM. and at 12:03 AM. That paradox had served as a staple of Puritan preaching, and as a young man growing up in a Puritan-rooted Associate Reformed Presbyterian congregation Graham undoubtedly heard it so often that he thought nothing of the tension.[64] The reason was simple: the tension was more apparent than real. In Graham's rhetoric some aspects of history portended evil and some portended good. The key point was that people had the power to make the bad worse and the good better. That did not mean they could change the overall scheme. No matter what they did, the Lord would return when he wished, judge the wicked, reward the righteous, and inaugurate the New Heavens and New Earth. But humans could do a great deal in the meantime to make the world a less or a more humane place.

The question then is whether the balance shifted. Did the mature Graham see more reasons for despair or for hope? Graham publicly spoke so many words—easily, millions—on so many topics on so many occasions that it is hard to know how to answer this question. It is also hard to know what people heard. Yet one possible yardstick is to compare his first major book on the topic of end-times, *World Aflame*, published in 1965, with his third, *Storm Warning*, published in 1992. In *World Aflame*, images of conflagration, imminent doom, and social crisis prevailed. Chapter titles conveyed the urgency of the world's situation: "Flames Out of Control," "Our Psychological Jitters," "National Idolatry," "Man's Fatal Disease," "Signs of the End," "Coming Judgment," "World on Fire," and "World of Tomorrow." Elements of classic dispensationalism appeared without apology: Christ's unexpected, sudden, dramatic return, the rapture of Christians to meet him in the air, the resurrection of all believers of all ages gathered together with all living believers, the time of great suffering (Tribulation), the rise of the Anti-Christ, and the Battle of Armageddon.[65]

Storm Warning, published nearly three decades later, offered a similar picture but with different shadings. Focused on the symbolism of the four horsemen of the apocalypse detailed in Revelation 6—false religion, war and peace, famine and pestilence, and suffering and hell—it, too, projected apocalyptic warnings. But the overall coloration was different. Graham explicitly avoided discussion of rapture, tribulation, and millennium.[66] The titles of the first four parts were still alarming—"Storm Clouds," "Lightning," "Tempest," and "Hurricane," but the title of the fifth and final part, "Toward the Coming Sunrise," and the titles of the final two chapters, "A Voice in the Storm" and "The Promise of Peace," conveyed hope. The back cover featured a photo of Graham sitting at a desk, impeccably dressed, smiling warmly, ever so much the comforting family doctor-pastor. To be sure, the toxins of personal sin would persist: deceit, promiscuity, child abuse, self-absorption, and "erotic, violent" music lyrics, among others.[67] And so would the toxins of social sin: racism, crime, environmental degradation, and uncontrolled militarism. And that kind of destructive behavior would not be eradicated until Christ returned. Yet a spiritually renewed church and morally reformed nation offered resounding reasons for hope. The global expansion of Christianity and revival fires among the nation's youth inspired confidence that history was moving in the right direction.

These considerations bring us finally to the effort to explain why an always-good God allowed terrible things to happen to generally good people. Graham did not address the problem often, or at length, but he did confront it at times of national mourning when millions of people found themselves in anguish. Graham, unlike Puritans of old, and not a few evangelicals, too, had rarely portrayed natural disasters and human atrocities as inexplicable. Rather, they represented God's just retribution for the nation's errant ways. Disarray and suffering lay all around and doom just ahead, but those sorry states were the inevitable results of human transgressions.[68] The topic that did arise with increasing frequency was simpler but more terrible: How do we explain situations that seemed to lie outside human complicity?

In most cases, said the mature Graham, God's ways remained mysterious, simply beyond human reckoning. Inexplicably tragic events (versus those that resulted from defiance of natural and moral laws) built character. They called Christians to trust God's wisdom, and they called believers to arms to alleviate the suffering. Yet Graham did not flinch about ultimate causation. He did not duck behind the venerable evangelical subterfuge that God allowed but did not cause such events. If they happened, God bore responsibility. Though it would be hard to prove, one suspects that in the wake of Auschwitz and Hiroshima millions of Americans found Graham's rigorous honesty somehow comforting.[69]

Graham's thinking about providence—God's grand superintendence of the unfolding of history—seemed, then, to grow more generous in tonality and emphasis, if not always in all of its technical details, as he grew older. In the well-worn words of a popular revival hymn Shea and audiences often sung in his crusades, providence formed a sobering yet invigorating vision of the "great things God has done"—and will do—in the unfolding of time.

END OF LIFE

But what about the individual believer? What did Graham have to say about death and the state to follow? His preaching about death underwent little change, except perhaps that he seemed to address the topic more often as the years slipped by. For the individual, death was of course unavoidable and, viewed from afar, always imminent. Critics who charged him with sentimentality were not paying attention. Sermon after sermon reminded listeners of death's absolute inescapability. Once, when he was in his mid-sixties, a teenager asked him what surprised him most in his "old age." He answered without hesitation, "the brevity of time."[70] Listeners heard no loopholes.

Though his preaching about death remained largely the same, if not more importunate, heaven and hell gradually took different forms. In the early preaching, both destinations emerged in starkly literal terms. Drawing on the Book of Revelation, which he read as literally as the most fact-minded fundamentalist, Graham described heaven's exact dimensions and streets of glistening gold. Within a few years, however, heaven became a place of glorious fellowship with God, saints, loved ones, and invigorating work to do. Perhaps even planets to rule: "Think of a place where there will be no sorrow and no parting, no pain, no sickness, no death, no quarrels, no misunderstandings, no sin and no cares."[71] Graham even speculated about golf courses and beloved pets—whatever it took to make folks happy.[72]

Hell underwent discernible changes too, both in what he affirmed and in what he refused to affirm. In a 1966 *Hour of Decision* sermon, "Hell," he argued that he could not say whether it was a state or a place or even a literal fire. Mystery surrounded it. But he knew this much: Hell was "separation from God . . . 'the second death.'" It was "banishment from the presence of all that [was] joyous, good, righteous and happy." Moreover, hell might well begin in the midst of earthly life. And what could be worse than separation from the source of all light and goodness? More important, the mature Graham steered away from hell in general, and when he did talk about it, all that he would affirm with certainty was that it meant separation from God. Beyond that, he fell back on the Graham trademark of principled refusal to speak about mysteries reserved for God's knowledge alone. In 1997 David Frost asked if he believed in something like purgatory or a "holding pattern" for the person "who never had a chance to know God." Graham said no, he would not go that far. But he would say that no one would be in heaven or in hell who was not supposed to be there. "I'll leave it at that," he stated. "And then there are people that say that hell is not eternal. . . . I leave all that in God's hands."[73] Two years later he told *Time*: "The only thing I could say for sure is that hell means separation from God. We are separated from his light, from his fellowship. That is going to be hell. When it comes to a literal fire, I don't preach it because I'm not sure about it."[74]

Graham's mainline Protestant listeners probably did not hear much of a concession to the winds of change, but for evangelical followers, accustomed to hearing conservative preachers' insistence on everlasting torment for the lost, Graham's diffidence sounded a new key. As far back as 1963 a *Saturday Evening Post* interview headline had read: "To some, he seems too soft on hell."[75] Even in the 1966 sermon he had described hell as the destiny for "men who have deliberately ignored God during their lifetime." Deliberately. If pressed, is it possible that the later Graham might have endorsed C. S. Lewis's view that the gates of hell were locked from the inside?[76] Probably not. He did not think in metaphors.[77] And in the final major crusade sermon of his life, he reminded the audience that "some will be eternally lost and some will be eternally saved."[78] If God's love had come decisively to dominate the rhetoric, the old notes of judgment still echoed in the background.

None of this minimized the grim certainty of death. During his Las Vegas crusade in 1980 the MGM Grand Hotel burned. "Some day, for all of you, if you don't know God, the music will stop. It will all be over," he warned.[79] First, "accept the fact that you will die." Second, "make arrangements." Third, "make provision for those you are leaving behind." And finally, "make an appointment with God."[80] Graham was not a profound thinker or preacher, but he dealt with serious things in serious ways. Millions listened. And what they heard, their letters to him suggested, was a message about dark clouds overhead but always limned with blue skies beyond.

Taking a Second Look

Several features of Graham's preached theology now call for closer attention. The first is that it rested on assumptions going all the way back to eighteenth-century rationalism. The evangelist simply assumed the transparency of Scripture. Differently stated, he simply assumed that the Bible said what it meant and meant what it said. He gave lip service to the illumination of the Holy Spirit, but there was little practical evidence of it in how he actually read the Bible's pages and applied them to daily life. Mystery, paradox, and the contingencies of interpretation remained foreign to his thinking. Here as elsewhere he followed one of the deepest and most pervasive streams in American culture.

A second feature is that the rhetoric appeared simple but actually served as specialized language functionally similar to the technical vocabulary of a social science. Terms like "born again" or "new birth" carried layers of meanings, comprehensible mainly within the community. As a result, Graham's lexicon also functioned as a code language, like a set of secret passwords, separating insiders from outsiders, experts from dabblers, true believers from fellow travelers. It also provided the comfort of a deeply ingrained ritual, which was exactly what it was: an orally delivered, aurally received ritual of reassurance. Though in principle Graham spoke to all Americans, in practice he spoke mainly to an audience that already agreed with most of what he said. The language was familiar. Everyone knew what to expect, and few went away disappointed.[81]

This point brings us to third and fourth characteristics of Graham's preached theology. It was communal, and not always consistent. Though it aimed to encourage the conversion of individuals, it also sought to define and invigorate local congregations, families of believers, and ultimately the nation. Conversion might have started as a private transaction between the person and God, but if it remained that way, it was a stunted experience that did not fulfill its intended purpose.[82] Inconsistencies intruded too. Rarely a man of measured, let alone few, words, he proved a speaking and writing machine. He and his editorial assistants churned out thousands if not hundreds of thousands of words on topic after topic year after year. Like John Wesley and Jonathan Edwards before him, he addressed disparate subjects in disparate settings as they arose. Also like them, he just did not possess the time or inclination to draw them into a systematic statement.[83] Beyond that, by any reasonable measure of such things, he simply talked too much, expatiating on subjects about which he knew little, and that habit created inconsistencies too.[84]

A fifth notable aspect of Graham's preached theology lay in the streamlining—or, according to one's point of view, the elisions and omissions. He left out many things in order to focus on perceived essentials. So we find virtually nothing on the liturgy, or on the historic rituals of the church (whether conceived of as sacraments or ordinances), or on ecclesiology—the nature of the church itself. His inability to understand let alone appreciate the historic Christian notion of the corporate Body of Christ as a means of conversion and ethical living severely compromised his appeal to High Church traditions of Lutherans, German Reformed, and Roman Catholics.[85] On the other hand, that streamlining served his larger purpose of appealing to the widest possible base of broadly evangelical or evangelically minded people.

Streamlining also prompted Graham to elide alleged subtleties or "fine points" of sectarian distinction like the proper mode of baptism or the proper understanding of speaking in tongues. Of course, the definition of what was or was not a sectarian specific distinction—versus a fundamental belief or practice—lay in the eye of the beholder. Graham knew this but remained undeterred. He sought to preach a message with maximum appeal to a maximum number of people. The media he chose—crusade sermons, radio, television, popular magazine articles, and a slickly produced popular magazine—reduced the chance for theological depth in order to achieve a broadly defined evangelistic purpose.

Graham's preached theology also reflected a clear sense of priorities, and that was a sixth defining feature. Some affirmations were more important than others, both absolutely and for his purposes of evangelism and moral reform. Simply put, priorities mattered, and in all cases, charity should prevail. Homosexual practice served as an example. Graham never questioned that the Bible taught that it was sinful—and a sin for which Christians must repent and change if they wished to be welcomed into the church.[86] Yet he also insisted that the church should see it as one sin among others.[87] He affirmed God's love for gay persons.[88] He greeted a crowd of ten thousand at San Francisco's Cow Palace in 1997: "Whatever your background, whatever your sexual orientation, we welcome you tonight."[89] When 20/20 anchorman Hugh Downs asked Graham point blank on network television if he would love a gay child, Graham answered without hesitation: "Why, I would love that one even more."[90] And he once told reporters that AIDS could be a judgment from God—then almost immediately retracted his statement: "To say God has judged people with AIDS would be very wrong and very cruel. . . . I am very sorry for what I said."[91] Christian wisdom was the art of knowing what to worry about first.

Latitude of interpretation followed from a sense of priorities. Precisely because he proved so firmly tethered at the center when it came to a handful of non-negotiable convictions about human sin and divine forgiveness, Graham proved able not only to grow and change but also to be humble about the things he was not so sure about. It enabled him to say, too, that Christians and denominations outside his own Southern Baptist fold might hold differing views about many contentious issues—including justifiable reasons for abortion, capital punishment, women's ordination, and even the Virgin Birth (which he personally strongly affirmed)—without running the risk of tumbling over the cliff. Scale mattered.[92] The periphery really did differ from the center.

This sense of rightly ordered priorities coupled with latitude of interpretation fostered an awareness of timeliness, and that awareness constituted an eighth characteristic of his thinking. The gospel remained the same but each generation had to hear it anew in their own language. For that reason, he liked to say, every generation was strategic.[93] Although the famously mixed metaphor of the Youth for Christ movement, "geared to the times, anchored to the rock," preceded Graham, it well conveyed the conviction that a timeless message required timely application.

Graham's preached theology reflected a perennial balance—or tension—between judgment and love. That balance constituted another distinctive feature. Judgment rose from the theologian's head while love flowed from the pastor's heart. By his own reckoning, in the beginning of his ministry judgment often outweighed love, but as he matured the balance shifted. At the same time—and this is crucial—neither judgment nor love ever totally eclipsed the other. The most judgmental early sermons invariably moved toward hope born of love, while the most loving of the later sermons invariably carried a shadow of judgment. Death and resurrection marched together. Graham's theological genius lay in the tension that insisted on linking them, indissolubly.

A comparison of the first sermon he preached in his highly publicized crusade in Los Angeles in 1949 with the three sermons he preached in his final crusade makes the point with power. The inner theological scaffolding was the same: God, humans, sin, Christ, salvation, judgment, heaven, and hell. Yet the tonalities were dramatically different. Tellingly, in the 1949 sermon the text was Amos 4:12: "Prepare to meet thy God O Israel." Then came the drumbeat litany of sin—divorce, crime, addiction, materialism, sex, fear, and the "lashing of conscience." Heed the peril of sudden death by cancer, heart attack, or motorcar. Christ alone was the answer: "Without old fashioned revival we are done for."[94]

In the New York sermons, in contrast, the texts came from John 3:16: "For God so loved the world . . ."; Mark 10:17: "Good teacher . . . What must I do to inherit eternal life?"; and to be sure, Matthew 24:36: "No one knows about that day . . . but only the Father." Love outweighed judgment but did not obliterate it. Yet Graham's written postscript to the published version of the three sermons, nearly six decades after the first one in Los Angeles, spoke worlds within worlds about how he had changed: "I . . . want to tell you one great truth: God loves you, and He can make a difference in your life if you will let him. . . . He gives us strength for the present and hope for the future. . . . He alone can bring—peace with God, peace in your heart, and peace with those around you."[95]

Graham's preaching about the future said important things about the present. Most obviously it served as a warning that time counted. It paid to pay attention. Life was short and unpredictable, and the inevitability of its shortness was heightened by the drama of its unpredictability. Graham's preaching also showed people that their lives were not trivial, let alone meaningless, but enmeshed in a larger plan. Outside the plan darkness prevailed, and nothing ultimately made sense. Inside the plan light prevailed, and everything ultimately made sense. Only the biblical vision of providence offered believers the possibility of playing life's role on the world's stage in a truly meaningful way.

Most important, Graham's preaching about the future offered hope. For every dire statement about the certainty of apocalypse one finds many more about the certainty of redemption. One journalist observed that in Graham's hands "the message of God's imminent judgment somehow has a soothing effect."[96] Everything rested in God's hands. Tellingly, his 1981 title, *Till Armageddon*, was not about future things at all but about the little Armageddons everyday people suffered in their everyday lives.[97] If the tens of thousands of letters posted to Graham served as an index, the evangelist emerged not as a doomsayer but as a friendly neighbor here to help them move safely from today to the end of days.

Finally, we need to ask not only what Graham said but also what America heard. First of all, what appeared to be boilerplate to the outsider, or even the church-weary insider, was not boilerplate for the believer. It was sacred doctrine, and sacred doctrine housed vibrant inner convictions. It clarified the life of God in the life of the believer. Analyzing popular reception of Graham's preaching about original sin, to take one example, Andrew Finstuen argued that it is a grave mistake to presume that "the religion of ordinary people is mostly, if not completely, a-theological." Countless ordinary people—Finstuen called them "lay theologians"—seriously pondered "the nature of sin and its meaning for their lives."[98]

Without question, Graham's sermons, books, articles, and press conferences often echoed one another. Was that similarity mind-numbing repetition? Or mind-comforting consistency? If repetition proved soporific for some, it proved gratifying for others, helping them store winsome formulations in the memory vault. It intimated steadiness at the helm, the security of settled beliefs, and the rewards of predictability. In matters of culture as well as religion, he seemed to say, kissing might kindle a marriage but it was cooking that kept it going. And for many, consistency counted more than originality

Or again, did Graham's words suggest simplemindedness—or clarity? Which is to ask, did they come across as banal—or as time-tested? Did he avoid important subtleties of the historic Protestant theological tradition, or did he cut through the clutter? Those inclined toward the former verdict felt that he reduced complex matters to glib formulas. Those inclined toward the latter agreed that he reduced complex matters into a different language, but it was the language of common sense, one that turned complex matters into useful tools for navigating the dilemmas of everyday life. Partisans appreciated Graham's spotlight on the evangelical essentials of human sin and divine forgiveness. In the approaching darkness (or glorious light) at the end of history, there was, Graham insisted, no time to trifle with subtleties or fuss about matters in dispute.

In sum, if outsiders heard a boring and platitudinous preacher, insiders heard an exciting and prophetic one. For them, Graham's theology cohered. It explained their experiences and enabled them to paint their lives onto a grand canvas. It cemented the conviction that he told the truth, not just about this or that particular thing, but also about reality itself.[99]

Delivering the Message

Recurrent patterns marked the thousands of sermons Graham preached to crusade audiences over the years.[100] To be sure, he spoke in different ways in different contexts. For example, he adjusted the usual "altar call" at the end of the sermon as the situation dictated. He found substitutes for it in secular university settings, where it might have caused discomfort, or avoided it altogether in civic or nonreligious occasions, where it clearly would have been inappropriate.[101] But the crusade sermon, Graham's signature form of public expression, reflected a signature structure.

Heard or viewed in the aggregate, Graham's messages seemed to unfold like a script sent over from central casting. Flashing a million-dollar smile, he invariably started with icebreaker lines and warm-up jokes. He subscribed to local newspapers six months ahead of meetings to catch up on local news and sports.[102] His opening lines typically referred to the natural beauty of the setting or the historic charm of the city. The jokes flowed easily, chestnuts that he repeated uncounted times, constantly improving his timing and choice of words. On his first trip to England in 1946, he later quipped, he "endured the darkest days of post-war British cooking."[103] Frequently he poked fun at himself and his fame. He liked to tell about the man in an elevator who looked him up and down for about thirty seconds and then said, "My, what an anticlimax."[104] Or of the woman who strolled over to his restaurant table and declared, "You look just like Billy Graham." To which he drolly responded, "Yes, people often say that."[105] Or of the woman who accosted him in an airport, insisting that she knew exactly who he was: James Arness, the star of *Gunsmoke*.[106] Graham's preaching foibles often came up too. "I will talk for only a few hours tonight," he deadpanned at the outset of a sermon.[107] Graham avoided jokes about particular persons, including particular critics. When he directed his humor outward, away from himself, he usually targeted entire occupations like farmers, lawyers, and especially preachers, but in an obviously benign way. Marriages, he joked, prove that "preachers can still out talk lawyers."[108] Humor reminded audiences that Graham did not take himself all that seriously and by implication, other Christians should not do so either.

Graham's fans knew that the jokes and quips were recycled but laughed harder every time. Humor was not the icing on the cake but an intrinsic part of the performance. Laughter brought Graham and his listeners into the same emotional range. It signaled acceptance of him and openness to his message. And it enabled Graham to intuit their receptivity when the subject turned serious. By all accounts Graham's personal humility was the real deal. Yet humility did not compromise his confidence in himself or in the message he came to deliver. His humor worked precisely because it led to something else.

The serious part began with a pair of disclaimers. First, Graham made clear that he did not come to entertain, and second, he served only as a mouthpiece for the Holy Spirit. Both disclaimers were of course only partly true. Whatever Graham's intentions, crusade visitors knew that the meeting offered a fine night out. It introduced them to toe-tapping music, testimonies from notable people, and a face-to-face view of the world's most famous preacher. The second disclaimer ran deeper: "I sat on the platform many nights with nothing to say, nothing. Just sat there. And I knew that in a few minutes I'd have to get up and preach, and I'd just say, 'Oh, God, I can't do it. . . . Yet, I would stand up and all of a sudden it would begin to come—just God giving it."[109] Though Graham undoubtedly believed that he served as only a mouthpiece for the Holy Spirit, he took great care to make sure that the mouthpiece was well prepared.

And then came the sermon itself. Sermons typically addressed a single topic but not in a tightly focused way. They contained many points, once, he admitted, as many as seventeen.[110] The messages were more of a pastiche, conveying impressions rather than a closely reasoned or systematic presentation of a topic. One associate aptly said that Graham leapt from "one lily pad to the next."[111] The sermons usually ran forty minutes, later edited and adjusted for television, so most Americans heard a more streamlined version. They contained many stories but rarely sentimental ones or tear-jerking deathbed tales. The countless photographs of Graham preaching invariably show him looking straight ahead, eyes open, or head bowed, eyes closed. They do not show moist eyes or a handkerchief dabbing the eyes. A man of tears he was not.

Mistakes abounded, yet no one cared since meticulous accuracy was not the point anyway.[112] Besides, factual gaffes contrasted with impressive evidence of Graham's command of biblical passages, which he accessed rapidly and accurately. For his audiences there was no such thing as objective disconfirmation. Graham's partisans not only caught the larger point but also heard what they came to hear.

Name-dropping popped up throughout. Examples included famous people he had personally known and authorities he had encountered in his global travels. Mention of the numerous overseas places he had preached in or simply visited added the gravitas of the seasoned traveler to his remarks. But for homiletic purposes the most important names were the ones he had encountered in his reading. Some of the favorites included (in alphabetical order): John Adams, Konrad Adenauer, Karl Barth, Winston Churchill, Noel Coward, John Dewey, Sigmund Freud, Robert Ingersoll, Thomas Jefferson, Samuel Johnson, John Lennon, C. S. Lewis, Abraham Lincoln, Walter Lippmann, Douglas MacArthur, Karl Marx, Somerset Maugham, Thomas More, G. Campbell Morgan, John Newton, Friedrich Nietzsche, Plato, Franklin Roosevelt, Fulton Sheen, Pitirim Sorokin, and H. G. Wells.[113] Exactly how deep those encounters ran remained open to question. One suspects that Graham invoked names he had run across in his manifestly avid reading of newspapers and newsmagazines—and perhaps a few that his researchers brought to his attention—but that he possessed little deep or firsthand acquaintance with their actual texts. Associates attested that he did read biographies. Yet clearly none of that mattered to Graham's listeners. They did not come for learned exegesis. They came to see and hear God's messenger for the hour.

Yet there was more to it than that. Graham took a course in homiletics (the discipline of preaching) at Florida Bible Institute. Wheaton College offered a course in speech/homiletics when he was a student there, but the records are closed, and (to the best of my knowledge) he never mentioned pursuing the practice systematically, as ministerial students normally would do in an established seminary.[114] Even so, he carefully studied—and copied—the style of fundamentalist paladins of the age.[115] He instinctively understood that good preaching embodied both art and craft. It was not a trade and certainly not a job. Contrary to stereotype, Graham took seriously the relevant reading for his line of work. He committed to memory great stretches of the text of the Bible. Graham also read voraciously about current affairs in newspapers and magazines, and that information spilled into his sermons.[116] Equally important, he knew what he did not know.[117] Graham freely admitted his lack of seminary education and never pretended to possess deep scholarly knowledge of the tradition. In short, Graham's reading took a form not taught in seminaries but well suited for the work of a mass evangelist.

The expository heart of the sermon almost always stemmed from a biblical passage. Graham paid no attention to any Christian lectionary. Rather he preached from any text that served his evangelistic purposes. That being said, it would be no great exaggeration to say that John 3:16—"God so loved the world he gave his only begotten son so that whoever believes in him shall not perish but have eternal life"—served as the implicit text of *every* sermon. "If you have heard Billy ten times," a close friend remarked, "you probably have heard all of his sermons."[118] One could go further. Graham likely would have felt complimented if the friend had said that if you have heard *one* of Billy's sermons, you have heard them all.

Graham rarely took time to elaborate the historical and theological implications of the text *du jour*. Instead he hurried on to a laundry list of national and world crises—economic, political, social, and cultural—often collapsed into a single overpowering message of impending doom: "Probably not in modern times has there ever been such a week—the whole world confused and taking sides on an issue so far reaching that it could well decide the future of world history." Thus began his first published sermon, preached on the nationally broadcast *Hour of Decision*. Though purporting to be apolitical, he moved immediately to President Truman's dismissal of General

Douglas MacArthur, thundering, "Ever since Tuesday morning at one o'clock the Nation has been in an uproar that is threatening our unity in an hour of our greatest peril." From there he moved to the worldwide persecution and killing of Christians, then to hatreds tearing apart the fabric of American life, and then to disarray in the home, and then to the poison of sin in the individual heart. But "Jesus Christ answers the problem. . . . Right now you can settle it—you can say 'Yes' to Christ! You can make this your 'Hour of Decision' for Him."[119] Unlike many fundamentalist preachers, who made arcane connections with the prophetic books Ezekiel and Revelation, Graham normally took his examples from everyday voices such as *Time*, *Newsweek*, the *Washington Post*, and the *New York Times*. If he enjoyed credibility in Heartland America it was partly because he drew on sources ordinary folks drew on too.

If listeners agreed with Graham's theological reasoning about the causes and implications of those crises—and millions did—the effects proved multiple. Most obviously, he ratcheted up the stakes. He pinpointed issues of momentous public concern. He prompted people to see that seemingly routine events were not routine at all but carried lofty theological meaning. The strategy showed that Graham was in touch with the age. He could be trusted because he knew what was going on. And he brought his audience into conversation with those events—events that touched their very own lives. The preacher's next move was to identify an array of personal crises that sooner or later virtually everyone would know all too well: illness, addiction, divorce, unemployment, cheating spouses, rebellious children, parents slipping into dementia. Here too he ratcheted-up the stakes by highlighting issues of momentous personal concern. He could be trusted because he was in touch with trials others experienced too.

So it was that the great public crises of the age mirrored and portended the great personal crises and vice versa. That meant that the threat was imminent, here and *now*—not removed to some hazy point in the distant future. If listeners were concerned about one, they could hardly shrug their shoulders and remain unconcerned about the other. But the good news—the *truly* good news—was that both crises were fixable. In Graham's preaching Christ offered the solution for one as much as for the other.

Preaching Style

Graham instinctively appreciated the evangelist Aimee Semple McPherson's recipe for rabbit stew: first, "you have to catch the rabbit."[120] The

practical result of that conviction was that he took great care to bring inquirers into the range of his powerfully persuasive preaching.

Graham prepared carefully. The preacher said he matriculated at Bob
Jones College because Jones had spoken at his high school and he had found
the patriarch's commanding style impressive. As a student at Florida Bible
Institute he carefully observed the style of fundamentalist celebrities like William Bell Riley, Homer Rodeheaver, Gipsy Smith, and Mel Trotter who came
south for the winter. He knew that effective preaching was a trade, a skill
that had to be learned and polished like any other. At Florida Bible Institute he worked very hard to refine his technique, preaching in front of
mirrors, memorizing paragraphs from published sermons, and mixing
them with extemporaneous remarks until he got it just right.[121] "You learn
to preach by preaching," Graham remembered his Florida Bible Institute
dean instructing him.[122] He said that before preaching to great stadium
audiences he rested and prayed for hours in the quiet of his hotel room,
husbanding his energy, sometimes napping with a baseball cap on (to protect his unruly hair from getting mashed up). One associate remembered
him sitting up in bed in the afternoon before he preached, scribbling updates into his sermon notes.[123] (Those notes—recently placed online—
reveal a profusion of personal stories, current events, and biblical passages
he wanted to include.) He took every preaching occasion seriously. Momentous things were at stake.

Graham rarely read his sermons, which would have transgressed the
Southern style of evangelistic preaching.[124] Given mainline clerics' tradition
of reading or preaching from a memorized text, it also would have suggested
a denominational and class standing different from the one he possessed or
wanted to project. But he did preach from comparatively fulsome outlines
(typed triple-spaced), often amended in his own hand just before the service
and packed with Bible passages.[125] That pattern helps explain how he conveyed an image of artlessness without stumbling for words or veering off
course. It also helps explain his no doubt genuine sense of preaching by divine inspiration.[126] Clearly, when he stepped behind the pulpit he already
knew pretty much what he was going to say, but working from notes allowed a kind of flexibility that old-time Methodist camp meeting speakers
had called "liberty in the Spirit." That sense also proved enormously empowering, for it freed Graham from responsibility for the final outcome. This was
God's charge to keep, not his.

Graham's preaching style bore many distinctive characteristics. Audiences probably first noticed the voice. Two *Time* journalists called his resonant baritone an instrument of "vast range and power."[127] A writer for the

New Yorker spoke of the "deep Carolina timbre."[128] It compared well with Graham's exact contemporary, Walter Cronkite. Another said that he "could make the simplest sentences sound like sacred scripture."[129] The preacher knew his voice was special. Like an opera singer, he took care to rest it on working days and practice it on nonworking days.[130] It buttressed the authority of the words he uttered. The BGEA knew it too. Crusade organizers transported their own sound system wherever Graham traveled in the world. They wanted to make certain that his voice was transmitted flawlessly.[131]

After the voice, listeners likely noticed the speed of the delivery. When Graham preached, said one editor, he "announced his presence with a fast ball."[132] Many dubbed him "God's machine-gun."[133] Looking back, Graham remembered that he self-consciously adopted the rapid-fire style of newscasters like Drew Pearson, Walter Winchell, and H. G. Kaltenborn. Verbal athletes, they had mastered the art of delivering words as fast as the tongue could speak and the ear could discern.[134] In the middle years, the speed slowed to a brisk pace, and later to that of an avuncular fireside chat. But even in the later decades Graham's fans remembered—and still talked about—the youthful preacher's blazing speed.[135] He did too. "Back then," he recalled with a touch of embarrassment in 1994, "I preached with much more fire and vigor. Part of that was youthfulness, part of it was intensity, part of it was conviction. And . . . part of it was ignorance."[136] Even so, the younger Graham knew his audiences. He knew what worked.

And then there was the volume, the accent, and the clarity. Though the stentorian volume gradually diminished to that of normal public address (aided by a microphone), in the beginning *Time* magazine called Graham "trumpet lunged."[137] His hometown newspaper remembered him "shouting the Word and threatening the wayward with God's wrath."[138] The accent was recognizable but hard to peg. It did not resemble the drawl of the South Carolina lowlands or the lilt of the North Carolina uplands. A journalist in Ohio said he preached in the "curled, buttery rhythms of the South."[139] A writer for the *New Yorker* described it somewhat cryptically as "Carolina stage English." Whatever that meant, Americans twirling the radio dial knew Graham's reassuring voice and accent the instant they heard it. The preacher's enunciation merited notice too. He rarely if ever muffled a sound or paused to find the right word. No matter the context— crusade stadiums or press conferences or talk shows—the words flowed effortlessly.

Graham chose a vocabulary range designed to communicate with mass audiences. Critics complained about many things but rarely about obscurity at one end or pandering at the other. They knew he was master of the art. Believing that the average person possessed a working store of six hundred words, he sought common one- or two-syllable terms, arranged in paragraphs stacked high with action verbs and short vivid sentences.[140] He did not talk down, as if he were explaining difficult theological concepts to students, or talk up as if he were trying to impress himself. "The average American has the intelligence of a twelve-year-old: religiously," he told correspondent David Frost.[141] The point was to connect.

Graham aimed to be simple but not simplistic. The sermons revealed no equivocation or qualification. Listeners rarely heard limiting phrases such as "it seems to me," "on the whole," or "more often than not." (Press conferences, in contrast, were inexplicably littered with the distracting locution, "I think.") He also spoke directly, rarely allusively or metaphorically, and hardly ever obliquely. Graham's diction bore trademark lines. Just as Americans expected the nation's newscaster, Cronkite, to conclude each broadcast with the magisterial statement "and that's the way it is," they also came to expect Graham to introduce sentence after sentence with the equally magisterial words "the *Bible* says," and to conclude sermon after sermon with the directive, "Come. You come. We will wait."

As noted, Graham repeated phrases and paragraph chunks in sermons and in press conferences, sometimes almost word for word. Though some listeners undoubtedly found that pattern repetitious, it enabled him to hone his words and sharpen their impact. He proved a master of angular, arresting phrases. He described the arms race as a "push button war," global conflicts leaving "rivers clogged with bodies," and Americans suffering from "moral laryngitis."[142] "While the world totters on the brink of destruction," he warned, "millions . . . snore in comfortable complacency."[143] We live in days of "tangled thinking."[144]

The physicality of Graham's preaching, especially in the early years, riveted visitors' attention. Feet paced, hands chopped, fingers stabbed like cocked pistols. He said he routinely lost twenty to thirty pounds during crusades. Videos of those performances—and performances is the right word, too—leave no doubt why. One journalist called him a "preaching windmill," another said his style suggested "the coiled tension of a panther."[145] Yet the explosive animation was punctuated with precisely timed dramatic pauses and changes of pace. Staccato bursts and short pauses combined to form Graham's signature cadence. There were no tears or (after the earliest outings) histrionics. Even when he was preaching to thousands in the great stadiums he said he paid attention to the audiences' response, from the front row to the back. And never to be forgotten was the ever-present Bible. Clutched in the left hand, thrust aloft, it served as a material emblem of his jurisdiction, rather like a bishop's staff and mitre, reminding visitors that Graham represented an authority greater than his own.

The cumulative effect left its mark. Visitors of all stripes, including those who self-consciously rejected Graham's message, commented on his manifest sincerity. No one doubted that he believed everything he said, absolutely, without mental reservations. That trait recurred in uncounted reports. And so did the appearance of utter effortlessness, like a professional athlete executing a play. Of course it was not effortless, but he made it look that way. Visitors did not feel that he was unprepared or did not know what to say or did not want to be there. In truth, before crusades began he prepared with days or weeks of physical exercise, study, and prayer. Graham acknowledged the tension of speaking to thousands of people, a tautness undoubtedly intensified by radio microphones and rolling television cameras transmitting every word and gesture to millions more. One crusade chairman said that before Graham went on, he carried "an inner and very finely controlled tension . . . a man under immense strain."[146] Yet when he entered the pulpit, his biographer William Martin aptly said, "fear departed and fire roared."[147] One more ingredient, rarely noted but crucial, was simple, old-fashioned enjoyment. Clearly the evangelist loved his work. He was comfortable in his own skin. How could he not be?

Preaching Goals

The theological content, rhetorical structure, and style of Graham's sermons flowed together to secure a single aim: to draw men and women to make a decision for Christ. Whatever the specific topic, the overarching pattern invariably took the same form. First acknowledge sin's destructive power. Second embrace God's redeeming power. Graham effectively inserted two adverbs into the genre: *nearly* and *only*. Everything was *nearly* lost, but not quite, if people would *only* accept Christ's forgiveness and gift of salvation. Why not? Sinners' only task was to reach out and take it.

The concluding segment of the sermon—the invitation—displayed remarkable consistency, year after year, at home and abroad. "How many of you here tonight are broken? God is not waiting to judge . . . or condemn you. He's waiting to receive you with open arms. You may not have another chance. [You] say by coming, I open my heart to Christ. Whatever

your race, whatever your religion, you need Jesus Christ as your savior.
You will have supernatural help in breaking those chains that bind."[148]
Graham repeated those words, or words to that effect, countless times in
countless places. They constituted the dramatic center of the entire meeting
and of Graham's entire career. The invitation was deeply ritualized.[149]
Evangelicals, revealing their populist roots, typically resisted the idea that
an event that felt so sacred might have been ritualized. The concept seemed
to minimize the Holy Spirit's role and smack of human contrivance.
Graham knew that, of course. In his more pragmatic moments he readily
acknowledged the interplay of divine and human agency. He often said that
he had the best product in the world, so why not present it in the best way
possible?: "If God expects me to give thought to what's in my sermons, as I
know He does, isn't it likely He expects me to give some thought as to how
to deliver them?"[150] That notion applied to the invitation with particular
force. The stakes were high.

Graham signaled the transition from exposition to invitation by slowing
the tempo, carefully choosing each word, and requesting silence. He asked
that no one move around. Even in a vast stadium, the slightest distraction
could eclipse the momentousness of the decisions at hand. Great battles
were taking place. Supernatural? Psychological? Ordinary time melted into
extraordinary time. The silence added dramatic power to the moment. The
preacher quickly switched into the second-person imperative: "There is no
decision in your whole life that compares to this. You come."[151] His physical posture sharply etched the scene. Tearless, standing tall and arrow
straight, with left elbow resting in right palm, Graham's entire body signaled the weight of the decision at hand: "No matter what they do for the
rest of their lives, for one moment they've stood before God."[152]

The invitation ritual rested on a cluster of assumptions. The most obvious was the underlying theory behind the transformation experience. At
first blush it called for a straight-up conscious act of the will: make a *decision* for Christ: "Loving Christ was a choice." It was no accident that
Graham called both his radio and his television programs *Hour of Decision* and that his mass-circulation periodical bore the arresting one-word
title *Decision*. He detailed his own conversion experience with virtually no
variation numberless times. It involved a clear-eyed choice to stand up and
walk to the front to commit his life to Christ. That night, kneeling beside
his bed, he decisively, self-consciously reaffirmed that commitment. He
later said that the world looked different the following day, but he rarely
intimated that special emotions played a role.[153]

Yet in Michael Hamilton's words, Graham's preaching also sought to awaken desire—the *desire* to decide for Christ.[154] "Listen with your soul, tonight," he urged in the opening of his first sermon in New York City in 1957, for "your heart also has ears."[155] Here, perhaps without realizing it, Graham drew on a deep-running tradition in American evangelicalism. He reached back to both Puritan/Presbyterian and Wesleyan/Methodist impulses in the Great Awakenings of the early eighteenth century. Jonathan Edwards taught that rightly ordered lives flowed from a fount of "true affections." The best known of Charles Wesley's nearly nine thousand hymns called for "a thousand tongues to sing / My dear Redeemer's praise." Graham instinctively discerned the mutually re-enforcing bond of desire and decision.

Several additional assumptions undergirded the invitation segment. Standing front and center was an unarticulated but powerful conviction that the future remained open-ended. Nothing had to stay the same. Everything could be changed. As noted, Graham's message, like that of countless evangelical preachers before him, pivoted on "re-" words: reform, rebirth, renewal, and regeneration, among others. A second assumption intimated the democracy of the problem. People's experiences of brokenness were neither unique nor irreparable. Like an astute therapist, Graham made clear that other people had suffered those burdens too, they had made it through, and so could you. And yet—this was a third assumption—Graham's gospel offered no hint of escape from life's trials as deliverance healers and prosperity marketers did. "The Christian life is not a way 'out' but a way 'through.' "[156] God had promised to walk *with* believers—to provide strength for the journey—but not to fix things like a cosmic repairman.

The fourth and fifth assumptions were closely related: Come as you are. "You don't have to straighten out your lives first," he told his audience in the Columbus, Ohio, crusade in 1993. "You don't have to make yourself well before going to a doctor."[157] The altar served as a clinic for sinners, not a resort for saints. And finally the fifth: problems would persist. There were no silver bullets. Graham's theology taught Americans that becoming a Christian was easy but living as one was not. Creation was broken. The dolorous legacy of original sin would endure and daily sins would intrude. That tension did not bother Graham or the millions who followed him. They experienced those strains as simultaneously true in their daily lives.

By all accounts, including that of Graham's friendly foil Charles Templeton, the preacher excelled at winning decisions. Time after time reporters spoke of his uncanny ability to connect, to speak to people at some deep level where their fears and aspirations coalesced. One of his associates captured the point perfectly: "Billy could get up and quote a telephone book and . . . people would come."[158] The power that he alone held at that point weighed heavily. The intensity of the moment proved palpable. "They've come to make life's most important commitment," he judged. He sometimes talked about the energy that drained from him when he gave the invitation. Another associate remembered that sometimes when the service was all over the exhaustion was so great he had to be helped from the platform into a waiting car.[159]

The number of inquirers who responded to the invitation constituted the acid test of the evangelist's effectiveness. To be sure, that is not how Graham saw it. "If I talk to one person and get him to say yes to Jesus Christ," he stated, "I consider that to be a successful meeting."[160] Still, what if no one came? Since he preached for a "verdict," up or down, that aim made the results clear.[161] Viewed theologically, the invitation collapsed the worth of his calling into a single instant. The work of an ordinary parish pastor could take a lifetime to show its worth. Not the evangelist's. The BGEA claimed more than three million inquirers in face-to-face meetings over the course of the preacher's career.[162] That figure may have been too high, or it may have been too low. Or there may have been other ways to measure success. However interpreted, the visual evidence of hundreds and often thousands of men and women streaming forward wordlessly attested to the power of Graham's uncommon presence in American life. Insiders called it anointing. Outsiders called it magnetism. Almost everyone called it charisma.

At first glance Graham did not rank very high in the art of preaching. He was not flamboyant as Billy Sunday, or dramatic as Aimee Semple McPherson, or soaring as Martin Luther King, Jr., or memorable as Harry Emerson Fosdick. Granted, preaching textbooks usually mentioned Graham, and anthologies generally included a chunk or two of his sermons, but seemingly from a sense of duty rather than from conviction of any special mastery on display. "Homiletically," said W. E. Sangster, a friend and leading cleric in England, "his sermons leave almost everything to be desired."[163] Even Graham's wife, Ruth, admitted that he was not eloquent, "as men count such," but she added, with telling insight, that perhaps "he'd not have spent his life this way if he were eloquent."[164] Graham himself bore no illusions about greatness behind the pulpit. He often said that he knew he was not a learned or polished or even well-organized speaker.[165]

Yet the convention that Graham's preaching left "almost everything to be desired" should be taken with several grains of salt. Not being a parish pastor, burdened with ceaseless rounds of baptisms, marriages, funerals, counseling sessions, and hospital visits, he enjoyed the luxury of perfecting his craft. In 2010, *Preaching* magazine, a journal of record in the field, ranked him the most influential preacher in America in the previous half-century. It said he stood "in a category unto himself."[166] The magazine spoke for many people. A 2005 Barna poll of "Protestant senior pastors" judged Graham "the most influential Christian figure and most trusted spokesman for the faith." That was not quite the same as most influential preacher, but it was not far off.[167] They saw that Graham possessed the gift—The Gift—that elusive combination of content, form, style, diction, voice, gesture, conviction, and sincerity that proved inimitable. And for millions, the result was electrifying.

The evangelical tradition had rarely prized eloquence as highly as effectiveness. By most accounts, Dwight L. Moody, one of the greatest of Graham's predecessors on the evangelist circuit, was not eloquent either. But he was effective. If the number of inquirers who walked forward to commit their lives to Christ measured effectiveness, Graham was the best in the world at what he did. For that matter, he may have been the best ever.

CHAPTER TWO

Icon

After World War II the United States experienced a surge in celebrity culture. Celebrities were nothing new, of course, but the postwar era saw a qualitative jump in their visibility and influence. The reasons were diverse. One was the ending of the war, which brought home millions of veterans, many of whom held the status of heroes in the eyes of family and friends. Another was the rise of electronic media, first radio and then movies and television, which facilitated the transmission and dissemination of information about stars. With enhanced sound technology and color television, personal traits not readily accessible before—such as the timbre of the voice or the color of the eyes—became common currency. A third reason involved the solidification of mass consumer culture. Just as material goods could be mass produced, so too celebrities could be marketed as generic commodities.

Celebrities were not all alike, however. Some male figures, such as James Dean and Jimmy Stewart, functioned as entertainment idols. Others, such as Douglas MacArthur and George S. Patton, were military heroes. Still others, such as John F. Kennedy and Albert Einstein, were figures of singular achievement. And some—think Mother Teresa, Bishop Fulton Sheen, the Reverend Norman Vincent Peale, or the Reverend Professor Reinhold Niebuhr—were religious icons. Being religious icons distinguished them from other celebrities in two ways: first, they stood somehow above and apart from mundane affairs; and second, an aura of veneration entered the mix. For millions of Americans, Billy Graham, too, occupied that special kind of gravitational field.

Creators of the Icon

The story of Graham's rise, singularity, and longevity as a religious icon is a constructed story. To be sure, everyone's story is constructed. But the layers that marked Graham's presentation were more complex than most people's. That did not mean that his story was fabricated out of whole cloth. Most of it grew from objectively confirmable information. But different groups arranged that information in different ways according to what they were able—and wanted—to see. Few if any aimed to create a false image of the preacher. Rather, they saw the world, as all people do, through glasses colored by their time and place and personal and group interests. And Graham's story, like the stories of most prominent people, reflected the work of multiple hands. Graham himself, the BGEA, the media (evangelical and otherwise), and the consuming public all contributed to the creation of the icon.

First Layer: Graham (Himself) and the BGEA

The story began with Graham's own contribution to his public image. First of all, he portrayed himself growing up as an altogether ordinary farm kid. Speaking through the medium of an authorized (effectively first-person) biography/autobiography, he said that "he was born to a typical American family on a farm outside a small southern town." His grades were "average." "Nothing special." He got up at 2:30 in the morning to milk the cows. "He dated girls, played baseball, did his chores, and grew up."[1] Few autobiographical details went unused. They all went into the sausage of making his biography one with common folk everywhere.

The second and more conspicuous image emerged from Graham's self-understanding as a man whom God had called to be an evangelist—and only an evangelist. He never imagined that he chose the vocation of evangelist on his own. God had called him. He had no choice in the matter. He said it repeatedly and in multiple contexts. Significantly Graham emphasized this fact in the concluding paragraphs of the preface of his autobiography, *Just As I Am*, published in 1997. After explaining the Greek etymology of the term *evangelist* as "one who announces Good News," he moved on to outline the task of the evangelist. As with a newscaster or journalist, the evangelist's job was to proclaim the truth, in Graham's case, that "Christ came to forgive us and give us new life." The evangelist was not summoned to do everything that needed to be done: "On the contrary, the calling of the evangelist is very specific." The evangelist has been "called and especially equipped by God to declare the Good News to those who have not yet accepted it."[2] Elsewhere the preacher made clear that God had not called him to be a pastor or a theologian or a social reformer. Rather, God had summoned him to do one thing: invite people to repent, accept God's forgiveness, and enter into a new (or renewed) life of faith.

Graham did not make this up. Looking back, he saw numerous signs sprinkled throughout his life that confirmed that God had called him to be an evangelist. As far back as the summer of 1934, before his conversion, at a revival held on his father's land, one stalwart had prayed that God would "raise up" a prophet to bring revival to the land. At Florida Bible Institute, on a moonlit night on a golf course after a romantic disappointment, Graham had fallen to his knees and experienced a profound sense of calling.[3] As he practiced his craft at the institute, standing on a cypress stump, calling sinners to come forward, he "seemed to hear a voice within . . . saying, 'One day there will be many.' "[4] In 1947 the fundamentalist veteran William Bell Riley persuaded Graham to take the presidency of Northwestern Schools so that Riley could pass along the "mantle" of his own calling.[5] Three years later the noted Lutheran radio Bible teacher Walter Maier died. When Graham heard about it, he knelt "and prayed that someone might raise up someone to take his place on the radio." Yet Graham did not launch the *Hour of Decision* national radio broadcast until financial support in the exact amount needed—$25,000—arrived at his hotel room in answer to a "fleece" (a test for God's approval).[6]

Providential calling took less explicit but no less persuasive forms too. Before heading to the most challenging and, as it turned out, most grueling crusade of his life—the sixteen-week enterprise in Manhattan in the summer of 1957—he confided to his diary that he "wept" in prayer for New York City, and then rested in the conviction that "now it is in God's hands." Graham's account paralleled the story of Jonah preparing to go to Nineveh as well as the story of Jesus in the Garden of Gethsemane preparing for his terrible ordeal. He acknowledged that both biblical precedents influenced his thinking.[7]

There is no reason to think that any of those experiences were contrived in order to bolster his self-presentation as a divinely called evangelist. Yet providential calling equaled providential legitimation. And legitimation bore several results. One was empowerment. It enabled him to frame his life in terms of a divinely ordained plan. Often he said that he had no idea why God had chosen him: "The first thing I am going to do when I get to heaven is to ask, 'Why me, Lord?' "[8] Yet he remained absolutely certain that God *had* chosen him. Divine legitimation yielded a sense of time out of time too. Graham saw and often presented himself as just a spectator. One thinks of the words of Ronald Reagan's biographer Lou Cannon, describing the president's final departure from the White House: "Then he closed the door and left the judgments to history."[9] Graham, too, was convinced that he could leave the judgments to history because the final outcome lay in God's hands.

Providential legitimation also afforded absolute single-mindedness about his vocation as an evangelist. The calling remained unchangeable and non-negotiable, despite lucrative offers for movie, television, and talk show roles, not to mention an offer from Lyndon Johnson of an ambassadorship.[10] It steeled him against discouragement in the face of relentless and often vitriolic criticism. It afforded a sense of great adventure, a personal challenge to take the gospel to exciting places—behind the Iron Curtain and into North Korea, to name but two. Graham did not exactly say so, but the buoyancy of adventure peeks out from between the lines. Finally, and important for understanding Graham's place in contemporary culture, providential legitimation helped cement Americans' commitment to him. Who would contest *God's* choice for the hour?

Graham's organization, the BGEA, played an important and often over-looked role in the construction and projection of the Graham icon. Though the evangelist himself proved remarkably free of defensiveness, the BGEA was not. Its habit of either ignoring or spinning Graham's missteps in a favorable light was unremitting.[11] The pattern should surprise no one. The organization existed, after all, to further his cause, not critique it. And abundant evidence shows that many staffers not only loved Graham personally but also remained absolutely convinced that through him they too served a higher cause.[12] The challenge, then, is not to puncture the BGEA's solid front but rather to analyze how it framed his public presentation.

Several features stand out. The first was historical legitimation. In 2014 the Billy Graham Museum (closely associated with the BGEA) at Graham's alma mater, Wheaton College, welcomed the visitor with a long hallway maze celebrating his life and achievements.[13] Notably, the walk began with visuals of Justin Martyr, Gregory the Great, St. Francis of Assisi, John Wycliffe, Martin Luther, Blaise Pascal, John Eliot, George Whitefield, Jonathan Edwards, Francis Asbury, Richard Allen, Pandita Ramabai, Evangeline Booth, Oswald Chambers, Charles Finney, Dwight L. Moody, and Billy Sunday. The sequence ended with Billy Graham's birth and life story. That arrangement symbolically placed Graham squarely among the giants of the historic Christian and especially the historic evangelical Protestant tradition, with special emphasis on the most famous revivalists.

The second feature showcased a theme that might be called the "How Could It Be?" motif. In a variety of ways, museum presentations, motion pictures, and published accounts set up a dramatic contrast between the ordinariness of Graham's roots and the extraordinariness of his success later on. To take but one example, *The Canvas Cathedral*, Graham's first film, was released in early 1950 (a few months before the formation of the BGEA). The crackling black-and-white talkie told the story of the Graham revival in Los Angeles in the fall of 1949. It showcased the failure of previous evangelists to awaken the spiritually dormant city, the cold weather, and the ordinariness of the people who streamed from all parts of the sprawling metropolitan area to hear the preaching of a relatively unknown and untested young man from far away. The announcer then turned to the unexpected publicity given by newspaper magnate William Randolph Hearst and the unexpected conversions of radio star Stuart Hamblen and war hero Louis Zamperini. It all seemed to be a great drama in which Graham, God's specially called servant, played the leading role. How could it be?

The third feature is how tightly the BGEA controlled the production and dissemination of Graham's image. All *Hour of Decision* radio broadcasts and the first round of *Hour of Decision* television programs—1951 to 1954—were edited in studios. In June 1957 the BGEA decided to air Graham's Saturday night meetings at Madison Square Garden live, but after that, organizers moved to quarterly telecasts of streamlined versions of actual services. Moreover, no one in the Graham organization was more important than Russ Busby, his ever-present and extremely skillful photographer. Busby's oversized, beautifully produced coffee-table book of pictures, *Billy Graham: God's Ambassador; A Lifelong Mission of Giving Hope to the World*—which soon became something of an icon itself in evangelical circles—portrayed the preacher in a great array of settings, with a great array of people, but not in a great array of ways.[14] On every page Graham emerged as the Cary Grant of the evangelical world. To be sure, Busby had splendid material to work with. The evangelist was nothing if not photogenic. Nonetheless, the absence of a bad day suggests that the BGEA knew perfectly well that first—and for that matter subsequent—photographic impressions formed an important part of the calculus of effectiveness.

It is important not to overstate the case. In 2012, the BGEA placed more than 1,600 of Graham's live audio sermons online, apparently without editing.[15] In October 2013 the BGEA also made available to researchers 66,000 pages of fulsome sermon outlines, with Graham's handwritten emendations, and all of it went online in February 2014.[16] By any reasonable measure, that gesture represented a vast transfer of data directly to the public, without visible filtering or editing. At the very least the development represented an implicit acknowledgment by the organization and perhaps by the nonagenarian evangelist himself that the icon did not need all that much burnishing after all.

Second Layer: Journalists

Though academics working in a variety of disciplines—history, theology, sociology, and homiletics—contributed their voices to the construction (and deconstruction) of the icon, journalists proved by far the most influential. It would be difficult to exaggerate the extent of their attention. It started slowly in the mid-1940s. *Youth for Christ* magazine gave laudatory but passing attention to the meetings Graham held under YFC auspices. Coverage picked up in the late 1940s as Graham (accompanied by his associates) crisscrossed the United States, twice toured Britain and the Continent, and then launched out on his own in Charlotte, North Carolina, in November 1947. But the Los Angeles crusade in the fall of 1949 marked the springboard event. From that point forward, he served as the topic of—a good faith estimate would be—thousands of newspaper articles, magazine stories, press conferences, television appearances, and cartoons and photographs. If we throw in letters to editors, the number easily would soar into the tens of thousands. Newspapers in the cities where he held crusades published recaps of his sermons and sometimes full verbatim transcripts as well.[17] Many of these documents—laboriously clipped out of newspapers from around the globe by faithful assistants for six decades—snooze in great bulging scrapbooks housed at the Billy Graham Center Archives at Wheaton College. Thousands more respond to word searches for "Billy Graham" on Internet search engines. And this tabulation refers only to coverage in the United States in English. Measuring the amount of journalistic attention worldwide in the fifty or more languages in which Graham's work appeared daunts the imagination.

The reasons for the breadth and depth of journalistic interest in Graham reached beyond Graham himself. One of course was the surge of radio and television in general, and of radio and television religious programming in particular.[18] Graham profited from changes in Federal Communication Commission regulations after World War II that helped evangelical broadcasters by enabling them to buy airtime rather than wait in line for free public-service airtime (which usually went to mainline Protestant groups).[19] He also profited from the comparative scarcity of radio and television networks, which focused attention on the few broadcasters who enjoyed such access. The radio dial tuned to a dozen AM stations, and the television dial to three or at most four. By the time the radio dial reached scores of AM and FM stations, and the television dial some five hundred channels, Graham's voice and presence already had established themselves as known commodities.[20]

Another independent factor stemmed from the expansionist consumer ethos that both print and electronic media projected in the postwar years. Just as the *Dinah Shore Show* presented its trademark jingo for Chevrolet— "See the USA in your Chevrolet, America's the greatest land of all"—so too the media presented Graham as a commodity in the big box store of American religion. His organization marketed him in Seattle pretty much the same way they marketed him in Miami. Like Chevrolets, he too was good for America. And finally, Graham likely profited from growing pluralism in American life, both demographic and cultural. That pluralism prodded the secular media to begin to imagine the marketability of religious traditions outside the center stream. Even if the technology had been available, it is difficult to imagine Bishop Fulton Sheen's immensely popular weekly telecast, *Life Is Worth Living,* flourishing as it did much before the 1940s.[21]

Graham's serious relationship with the press began with William Randolph Hearst's involvement in the 1949 Los Angeles revival. The story has been told so many times that it has acquired the sanctity of a creation story, replete with its founding myth. Graham's Los Angeles crusade started September 25 in an oversized circus tent pitched in the center of the city. The Los Angeles Christian Businessmen's Association, which sponsored the crusade, as well as Graham himself, initially planned three weeks. The coverage in local papers came mostly from Graham's own advertisements. Attendance sputtered. Yet near the end of the three weeks attendance boomed, and one morning reporters and photographers swooped down on the tent. Puzzled, Graham learned that he had "just been kissed by William Randolph Hearst."[22]

The newspaper tycoon owned an imposing chain of papers and magazines, including the Los Angeles *Examiner*. Exactly how he heard about the little-known preacher remains fuzzy. It might have been through one of his housekeepers attending the meeting. A more credible narrative is that the organizing committee had worked hard behind the scenes, through intermediaries, to win Hearst's attention.[23] However it came about, Hearst purportedly told his staff to "puff Graham." The story probably was an urban legend. Hearst himself was not notably religious, but he approved the traditional morality that Graham represented, and he certainly echoed Graham's fierce anticommunism. That being said, Hearst likely said *something*, as the *Examiner* and other Hearst papers began to cover the revival.[24] By the end of the year the Associated Press, United Press, International News Service, and *Time*, *Life*, and *Quick* had followed.[25]

Graham's connection with Henry R. Luce received less attention but was more important. Luce owned or would own *Time*, *Life*, *Fortune*, *Sports Illustrated*, and other enterprises. His influence rivaled Hearst's. He was the son of missionaries to China and a life-long member of the Presbyterian Church. Luce and Graham met in Columbia, South Carolina, in the spring of 1950. The financial tycoon Bernard Baruch had read about Graham and urged his friend Luce to look him up.[26] They immediately struck up a friendship that lasted till Luce's death in 1967. The alliance proved portentous in several ways. The key point just now is that Luce directed the editors of *Time* and *Life* to devote attention to Graham's meetings. The preacher was airborne.

A cluster of elements came into play. First, of course, was Graham himself, who possessed an exceptional aptitude for working with the press. Second, a message that proved timely, accessible, and exportable. Third, new media technology that spread Graham's message, with speed, breadth, and depth that would have been unimaginable much before the 1950s. Fourth, a mass audience receptive to a mass message: one that sounded and functioned very much the same wherever he went. Fifth, a journalistic empire possessed of the financial means and power to project it. And sixth, the attention of Hearst, Luce, and savvy figures like them who saw that the other five elements were in place. They had the moxie and determination to make it all happen.

Graham's personal contribution to the press's fascination with him merits a closer look. For one thing, he was never shy about enlisting journalists in his cause. He invited them up to the house.[27] On the road, he actively sought their coverage.[28] Knowing their power, he took them seriously, once telling the *New York Times*'s Edward Fiske that he was "more nervous in front of some of those newspaper people and television people than the president."[29] Even so, the preacher knew how to talk with the press. He was polite and answered their questions directly and (with occasional exceptions) succinctly. He came across with a downhome attitude buttressed with the confidence of a man who knew what he was talking about.[30] Aware that he was not conversing with a platoon of Baptist Sunday school teachers, he even took time to prepare a glossary of religious terms for them, offering clear one-line definitions of *Grace*, *Heart*, *Faith*, and *Born Again*.[31]

The transcripts of the press conferences and talk shows reveal a remark-able amount of bantering—often with the bracketed word *Laughter* tucked between sentences.[32]

On talk shows Graham appeared relaxed, grinned readily, and quipped with the best of them. His body language signaled relaxed self-assurance as he sat with his legs crossed jauntily and his jacket flung open.[33] In a classic 1969 exchange with Woody Allen, which eventually "went viral" on You-Tube, Allen asked Graham what his favorite Commandment was. Without missing a beat, Graham shot back: "Right now, with a lot of teenagers, it is to honor thy father and thy mother."[34] The studio audience, presumably largely nonevangelical, roared. Yet on such occasions Graham invariably brought the conversation back around to the reason for his visit in the first place: to share the gospel. With such tactics, which seemed more instinctive than deliberate, he managed to win the friendship of outsiders, insiders, and millions in between.

Graham manifestly enjoyed the press corps. He said that they almost always treated him fairly and quoted him accurately.[35] He quipped that sometimes they quoted him accurately when he wished they had not.[36] In the words of a *Saturday Evening Post* writer: "One gets the impression that an interview is a game with him, but one played seriously, and which he proposes to win. He faces the music with relish."[37] Another journalist, Andrew Walsh of the *Hartford Courant*, described Graham's approach as gracious and professional. Walsh said Graham was able to take tough ques-tions in stride without growing defensive.[38] Graham made it all look easy, when of course it was not.

The press, in turn, liked Graham. Before exploring the reasons for that affinity, however, we should note that journalists sometimes had a hard time figuring him out. Any reasonably objective observer recognized that his faces shifted according to context. How much Graham himself was aware of those shifts is debatable. On one hand he was naïve about the legitimat-ing power of his presence. On the other hand he was not, as the saying goes, born yesterday. If challenged he undoubtedly would have said that it was altogether appropriate to present one side of himself in one context and another side of himself in another context, as long as there was no contradiction between them. He was just doing his job—or perhaps just being his agreeable self. The problem was that journalists did not always know which was which. They needed a story line. When he did not fit their predefined frame of reference, even sympathetic writers found him baffling.

That being said, Graham made good copy. The crusades offered attrac-tive stories because they were spectacles, and spectacles sold papers. For the press, Graham functioned as a "contrast gainer." Compared with Graham, previous and contemporary evangelists seemed like a "field of stutterers." Graham, in contrast, filled the air with words that counted. The preacher related to the press in their language and in their way. He claimed—and most who knew him personally attested—that he was an avid daily reader of newspapers and news magazines, especially the *New York Times*. At one point he even had a UPI Teletype machine installed in his home.[39] He knew what the press was interested in. More important for measuring Graham's influence on modern America, they treated him as an authority on numerous subjects, whether or not he possessed adequate credentials for talking about them. "When he first began making headlines," said one early journalist/biographer, "reporters could get an opinion from him on almost anything."[40] In later years Graham admitted that sometimes he spoke beyond his knowledge.[41]

What did Graham and journalists gain from each other? At the most basic level, Graham won exposure and the press won revenue. But the mutual benefits ran deeper. By 1950, when Graham was just thirty-one, the media was depicting him as America's leading evangelist.[42] By 1957—the date of his New York City crusade—they were treating him as unique, as if he occupied a stratum qualitatively different from all competitors.[43] What the press gained from Graham, in turn, was a narrative. Sprawling and amorphous, the American evangelical movement enjoyed no headquarters, no encompassing doctrinal statement, and no periodical that spoke for everyone. But Graham offered the press a fixed point of reference. For sure, from time to time the press proved entirely capable of savaging him.[44] (More on that shortly.) Yet on the whole they treated him fairly during his early years, respectfully during his middle years, and with admiration bordering on veneration in his later years. By then he was effectively bulletproof.

Much that we know or think we know about Graham, outside his own and his organization's projection, resulted from the press's construction of him. Three bodies of data seem especially relevant. They were Graham as Myth, Graham as All-American Male, and Graham as Ideal Family Man. In each case, the veils of construction were so thickly layered that it is often difficult to know how to separate them.

MYTH

For the better part of six decades, stories about Graham's evangelistic feats, like those of a spiritual Paul Bunyan, loomed over the press. His every move, religious and otherwise, received coverage in excruciating detail. Narratives about his family, even his dogs, abounded. Pictures, caricatures, and cartoons ran close behind.[45] (Cartoons captured some of the most perceptive—and often biting critiques—of Graham.)[46] For two years in the mid-1950s—long before Graham's star had risen to its full altitude—he won more press coverage than any other person in the United States, including President Dwight Eisenhower.[47]

A sample of the many periodicals that carried articles about Graham in English includes major city dailies (such as the *New York Times*), local dailies (such as the *Springfield Republican*), ethnic dailies (such as the *Chicago Defender*), college and university dailies (such as the *Yale Daily News*), periodicals of business and civic groups (such as *Holiday Inn Magazine*), periodicals of denominations (such as *Commonweal*), periodicals of parachurch groups (such as *World Vision*), geographically focused periodicals (such as *Arkansas Baptist News)*, general-reader periodicals (such as the *Nation*), and stand-alone religious periodicals (such as *Christianity Today*). Some of these publications—such as the *Washington Post*, the *New York Times*, *Christianity Today*, and *Christian Century*—carried dozens of articles about him.

Headlines in secular dailies offer additional insight into how the press turned Graham into a figure of larger-than-life proportions. Leafing through the pages of the newspapers in the 1950s alone, one gains an impression, first of all, that the headlines about Graham received prominent placement: boldly rendered, in full caps, and often placed on the front page. Publishers knew that the two words *Billy Graham* sold papers. In terms of content, the most conspicuous feature of the headlines was the drumbeat references to the size of the audiences. Nouns such as *throngs*, *crowds*, and *masses* recurred year after year. After that, papers focused on the number of converts, along with references to the forcefulness of Graham's injunctions to make a decision for Christ. And after that, the dominant themes were Graham's warnings about imminent doom if the nation (or world) did not change its ways—along with portents of imminent revival if it did. Closely related were depictions of contemporary cultural crises, especially crime, communism, war, racial tension, and economic collapse. Many headlines referenced famous people involved in the crusades (especially high-ranking politicians). Some highlighted Graham's travels, which undoubtedly seemed both glamorous and unreachable for the vast majority of readers. Others spoke frankly about opponents and opposition, especially from other religious groups. Most headlines featured action-packed verbs: *challenged*, *warned*, and *pleaded*.

And then there was the visual presentation. Most stories appeared with a photograph or caricature of a young or middle-aged preacher blessed with a handsome face, trim physique, spiffy wardrobe, and forceful gestures, all suggesting he was not a man to be toyed with. Images of packed auditoriums and stadiums and of long lines of seekers hoping to get in proliferated too. Many interior pages featured photos of Graham's attractive wife and attractive children and attractive dogs and attractive mountain home. Some gave the word *sappy* new dimensions of meaning. Yet many were powerfully evocative too, especially those of Graham in un-posed settings in the developing world.[48] Russ Busby's photograph—shot from behind—of Graham standing on a platform speaking to 1.1 million people in Seoul in June 1973 became iconic in evangelical circles.[49] What was missing was important too. Readers saw few representations of Graham engaged in mundane activities such as yard work or washing dishes or just relaxing in front of a television (which, remarkably, he once wished that he had "watched less").[50] Photographers rarely if ever captured healing lines, ecstatic trances, or any sign of raucous behavior. The gallery showed crusade audiences uniformly well dressed and well behaved.

Graham's face graced the covers of major national magazines at least twenty-eight times. He appeared on the cover of *Time* at least six times, *Newsweek* five times, *US News and World Report* four times, *Look* and *Parade* three times each, *Life* and *Saturday Evening Post* two times each, and *New Man*, *Texas Monthly*, *American Mercury*, and *People Weekly* once apiece. The cover banners bore many of the same features as newspaper headlines. In most cases they showcased action-packed verbs and strong nouns: *Surging, Invasion, In Action, World to Win, Most Influential, Most Extraordinary, Hard-Hitting, Billy Pulpit, Millions Heed His Call, The World Is His Pulpit*. Several of the covers promised an interview, sometimes an exclusive one, with Graham, clearly an invitation for readers who wanted to get the word straight from the source. Cover stories published in Graham's later years presented a magisterial if not elegiac tone. *Pilgrim's Progress* ran the cover of *Newsweek* the year after Graham's final crusade.[51]

And then the press constructed the Graham Myth as a benchmark for events or people related to him indirectly or not at all. Examples turned up everywhere. A few illustrate the different genres. Most predictably, perhaps, the press framed other religious leaders in terms of their theological proximity to Graham. For example, journalists depicted the Argentine-born Luis Palau (who was in fact a celebrated revival figure in Latin America) as the "Hispanic Billy Graham."[52] That rendering was positive, but some were not. When John Paul II announced his seventeenth overseas trip in just four years, some Catholic leaders scored him as the "Billy Graham of the Catholic Church."[53] The reference applied to Graham's peripatetic ways, not to his evangelistic successes.

Representatives of other religions scored a spot on the roster too. One reporter judged that the Libyan dictator Muammar Qaddafi was "sounding at times like a Moslem Billy Graham" as he assailed both the capitalist and the communist worlds for "destroying man's spiritual and family values."[54] Fighting "spiritual genocide" among the nation's secularizing Jews, the Jewish activist Esther Jungreis did not mind being called "a Jewish Billy Graham." That being said, Jungreis added, with telling precision, that she was a revivalist, not an evangelist, for she wanted to recall Jews to their heritage, not convert outsiders.[55] At the same time, some religious figures went out of their way to sever any connection between what they and Graham did. The witch Sybil Leek disavowed any desire to convert anyone else to witchcraft, saying, "I'm not the Billy Graham of the witchcraft world."[56]

Persons of other races or ethnicities claimed Graham as a comparative point of reference, up or down, or others did it for them. South African evangelist Nicholas B. H. Bhengu, also known as the Zulu evangelist, was dubbed "South Africa's so-called 'Black Billy Graham.'"[57] So too Malcolm X said he would "preach the gospel of Black Nationalism in the same manner that the evangelist Billy Graham spreads the gospel of Christ."[58] A *Time* cover asked if prosperity megachurch pastor T. D. Jakes would fill Graham's role: "Is This Man The Next Billy Graham?"[59] On the other hand, Jesse Jackson, an ordained Baptist preacher and civil rights activist, did not want to be mistaken for a "'Black Billy Graham.'" Jackson's gospel would offer a balance of spiritual and moral values, not just "Jesus is the answer."[60]

Then too Graham served as the benchmark of comparison for achievement in other lines of work. A 2008 PBS *American Experience* special whimsically described the Transcendentalist Ralph Waldo Emerson as something like a combination of Oprah Winfrey and Billy Graham.[61] An "economic Billy Graham" was how the famed New York *Herald Tribune* journalist Joseph Alsop depicted Lyndon Johnson's efforts to make business and government work together.[62] The comparisons ran far off into the horizon. According to one account, fitness guru Dr. Kenneth Cooper found himself portrayed as a "sort of Billy Graham of physical fitness" as he preached to United States congresspersons about the "evils"—a telling term—of "inactivity, smoking, and obesity."[63] Most arresting, perhaps, was the depiction of Amsterdam Dadaist painter Robert Jasper Grootveld. A "sort of Dadaist Billy Graham," Grootveld emerged as a "mob orator of great Power" and "initiator of weekly madcap happenings."[64]

Billy Graham may not have been a man for all seasons, but for America's journalist corps, he came close.

ALL-AMERICAN MALE

In Graham's career the All-American Male image expressed itself in multiple ways. Appearance constituted the most visible one, especially in an age of color television. Scottish genes and Nordic looks gave him a head start. When the preacher looked in a mirror, he saw advertisers' male ideal: craggy face, blue eyes, square jaw, and wavy flaxen hair. A memorable physique matched a memorable face: six feet two inches tall, 180 pounds, broad shoulders, and narrow waist. Lean but not skinny, and never remotely close to heavy. A régime of jogging, swimming, weight lifting, mountain climbing, and, of course, golf kept him in shape.[65] Even when he was on the road, which was eight months a year, he maintained a schedule of rigorous daily exercise.[66] One worker said he was "hard as a rock."[67] In 1972 he proudly told the *Saturday Evening Post* that he ran a mile in six minutes and tried to run 1.5 miles every day.[68] Before crusades, Graham claimed, he trained like a prizefighter.[69]

For the better part of sixty years, virtually every newspaper article about Graham commented on his appearance. During his 1949 Los Angeles revival, right at the very beginning of his career, the Hollywood, California, *Citizen-News* described him (slightly inaccurately) on page 1 as "six-feet-four, with broad shoulders, blue eyes, wavy blonde hair and a beguiling southern drawl. They come see him pitch woo to some luscious movie siren."[70] During his first outing in England, the London *Evening News* called him, "Charles Atlas with a Halo."[71] An appreciative retrospective written by the veteran *Newsweek* columnist Kenneth Woodward started with the obvious: "His face was Hollywood handsome."[72] Popular magazines juxtaposed photos of him on one side of the page with shots of glamorous women on the other. A 1951 *Look* cover, for example, sandwiched the preacher, Bible in hand, between a scantily clad Marlene Dietrich and a caricature of a bathing beauty lounging on a beach.[73] The image of a buff preacher grabbed headlines. "Grueling Life Led by Preacher: Eats 4 Meals a Day, Keeps in Trim Like a Prize Fighter," boomed one; "Billy Graham's Physical-Fitness Program Can Help YOU," boomed another.[74] An early biographer said he possessed a "laminated, heroic, commanding, Viking-like" visage.[75] In the eyes of the press, Graham grew even better looking as he matured. In 1993 one journalist said: "He looks like the aging athlete."[76] Some compared him to Burt Lancaster or to Gregory Peck. Graham bore the image of the seasoned yet virile male.

The BGEA appreciated the power of rugged good looks in a media age. Graham's rising visibility paralleled the rising visibility of Warner Sallman's paintings (which sold in the millions) of a tanned, angular, hirsute Jesus.[77] Graham described his associate George Beverly Shea as a "handsome bass baritone" and his friend Prince Philip as "every inch a man's man."[78] When the historian Marshall Frady asked another aide what would have happened if the evangelist had been podgy and scrappy of hair, the aide smiled, "Well, but he wasn't, was he? The Lord worked it out so that he wouldn't be."[79] Of course, Graham did not say anything like that about himself, but clearly he appreciated the cultural power of a manly presence. A skillful dentist guaranteed the Hollywood smile.[80] When a *Harper's Magazine* profile depicted Graham's smile as "pleasant and manly," one suspects that the preacher took the compliment to heart.[81] Appearance did not make a man better, one aide allowed, but it did reduce "the limitations a man faces if he is to present himself well."[82]

Manly looks found their complement in manly threads, and the press noticed that too. Graham presented himself to his audiences and to photographers as stylish but not foppish. In his adolescent days, a friend remembered, his navy jacket, white slacks, and white shoes made him stand out from the crowd.[83] In 1940 he moved from the rural South to the suburban North. His destination was Wheaton College, located in Wheaton, Illinois, a decidedly uptown community twenty miles west of Chicago. The college enjoyed a reputation as the Harvard of the fundamentalist world, and that reputation applied to the social class of its students and faculty as well.[84] Yearbook photos suggest a corresponding primness of attire. Initially Graham felt out of place, discomfited by his "Lil Abner" wardrobe. But Graham's attire changed with the setting. Photographs of him as a well-dressed upperclassman show that he adapted quickly.[85]

On the itinerant evangelist circuit, the young preacher responded to sartorial cues appropriate for a man in his line of work. As a traveling speaker for the YFC in the middle and late 1940s, he sported hand-painted ties— when he was not wearing a flashing (yes, flashing) bow tie—and showy suits.[86] One writer called him "Gabriel in Gabardine."[87] Yet Graham's

1949 Los Angeles crusade showcased an evangelist changing with the set-ting. Photographs revealed a handkerchief billowing from a double-breasted suit coat pocket.[88] When he got to Boston the following year, a *National Review* writer would say that he looked like a "knowing Esquire gent." There he was "the Arrow Collar man!"[89]

Misreading the protocol for the situation, Graham and three associates showed up at a 1950 White House meeting with President Harry S. Truman gloriously arrayed in cream-colored suits, hand-painted ties, rust-colored socks, and white buck shoes. Graham said that he had seen pictures of Tru-man in white buck shoes and felt that he should wear the same.[90] Nearly fifty years later, Graham still cringed, remembering that Truman proba-bly viewed them as if they were a "traveling vaudeville team."[91] As things turned out, overdressing proved the least of Graham's mistakes that day. Yet the scene symbolized Graham's awareness of the importance of self-presentation.

As the setting changed, so did the wardrobe. By the time of Graham's first major international crusade in London in 1954, his customary dress had evolved into smart business attire. In time the press would speak of his impec-cably tailored "trademark" dark suits, starched white shirts, and ever-present accessory handkerchief. He took care not to dress too well, however. No one thought of him as a dandy, which would have derailed him in middle Amer-ica. When photographers caught him at his mountaintop home in North Carolina, often outdoors in a rocking chair looking out over his beloved Smokies, loafers, blue jeans, polo pullovers, and turtleneck sweaters pre-vailed. At work or play, the preacher was a haberdasher's dream.[92]

The glamor of youthfulness marked story after story too. Several factors played a role here. Part of it, of course, was that Graham fit the idealization, if not idolization, of the post–World War II youth culture.[93] Not accidentally, Aimee Semple McPherson had walked into the national religious limelight in the prime of her own youth in the 1910s and 1920s. When Graham first hit the itinerant circuit in the small towns of central Florida in the late 1930s, the advance publicity recurrently underscored his youth, turning inexperi-ence into a virtue. Said one poster: "Hear Billy Graham / 21 Year Old Evan-gelist of Tampa, Florida / A Young Man With a Burning Message."[94] Good looks and youthfulness, now coupled with athleticism, played well in the North too. In the late 1940s a *Grand Rapids Press* ad promised a winning combination of aptitude, appeal, pre-eminence, and athleticism: "Here's a Talent Line-up to Delight You!' " Under Graham's photo, the caption blazed:

"America's foremost youth leader and speaker. A young athlete with a 20th Century Gospel Message."[95] Elsewhere advertising posters show-cased Graham slightly crouched, with clenched fist thrust forward. Underneath his image ran the by-now familiar caption: "Billy Graham / America's Dynamic Young Leader and Evangelist."[96] Visual intimations of Graham as a man in the prime of life continued in newspapers and news magazines, including, especially, cover stories, until he was well into his sixties.

Images of inexhaustible vitality energized the published narratives of Graham's career. His ministry grew from roots in YFC, an organization that featured splashy dress, lively music, evangelistic fervor, and patriotic enthusiasm, and in its stunningly successful Saturday night "rallies" across the United States and postwar Europe.[97] The preferred venue (Saturday nights) and nomenclature ("rallies") perhaps enlivened the stories about the meetings as much as the meetings themselves.

Journalists fixed on Graham's stamina too. He gave them plenty to work with. His crusade in Los Angeles in 1949 equaled a great public marathon. In the eight weeks stretching from late September to late November, he held seventy-two meetings, preached sixty-five full sermons, and gave hundreds of additional talks to small groups and on the radio.[98] Yet that marathon paled before the Madison Square Garden meeting in 1957, which saw Graham preach exactly one hundred times in person to more than two million people. He also spoke on live network telecasts almost every Saturday evening and made uncounted additional appearances to civic and church groups along the way.[99] Newspaper and magazine articles, replete with photographs, conveyed an image of a man relentlessly on the go, flying from city to city around the world. Though he took regular breathers—down time at home and on Florida beaches—those moments of repose largely escaped the press's attention. What they saw and what they reported was a man always in a hurry.

Finally, the press projected moral backbone—alongside appearance, dress, and youthfulness—as one more feature of the All-American Male image. Here we must be careful. Over the years, and especially in the middle decades of his career, some journalists (and others) assailed Graham for failing to exhibit moral backbone when it came to the issues they themselves considered especially important.[100] Yet for other writers he stood tall for the principles he believed in, regardless of personal consequences. Courage was a key part of the icon. They observed that he readily engaged real or perceived opponents in public discussion. They included audiences as diverse as Students for a Democratic Society at Columbia University, a debating club at Oxford University, theology professors at Harvard Divinity School, law professors at Harvard Law School, students and faculty in at least twenty mainline Protestant seminaries, including Princeton, Colgate Rochester, and the effective command center of the mainline Protestant Establishment, Union Theological Seminary in New York City. The extant evidence (strangely scant in this respect) suggests that audiences in those institutions occasionally responded derisively, but usually respectfully and sometimes with surprising warmth. Like a skilled barrister, he deflected barbs and elicited both laughter and applause with a quick wit and a light touch.[101]

Little or no evidence suggests that Graham ever backed down or declined an invitation because of the potential hostility of an academic audience. Needless to say, learned elites held credentials that Graham, who never went to seminary, could only dream about. Yet time after time he accepted invitations from intellectual heavyweights and then shifted the discussion onto moral or spiritual grounds, where he felt comfortable. Besides events of that sort, Graham recurrently took the initiative to meet or try to meet formidable foes in private to talk things over. One of his most vocal critics, Reinhold Niebuhr, refused, but others, especially journalists, accepted his offer.[102] The theological and especially political content of those exchanges was not especially important. But for students of Graham's place in American life, his willingness to step into the ring in the first place *was* important.

Perhaps the best example of moral backbone resides in one of the most publicized—and demonized—events of Graham's career: his decision to participate in a transparently anti-American "peace" conference in Moscow in 1982. We will examine the background and details of this story later. Here it suffices to say that the trip aroused resistance from his wife, the BGEA, and the U.S. State Department. Graham went anyway. Some of the statements he made about freedom of religion in the Soviet Union during and after the trip provoked stinging responses from the political left as well as from the political right. He never backed down.[103]

FAMILY MAN

For many Americans, including journalists, Graham the Myth and Graham the All-American Male blended into another iconic image: Graham the

Family Man. That image took two forms, and both emerged in Graham's preaching and in popular magazines' depiction of his long marriage to Ruth Bell Graham. In his early ministry he endorsed hierarchical, or what evangelical biblical scholars called complementary, gender roles in the family. In the 1950s, Graham's views about the distinctive roles of husband, wife, and children paralleled those found in popular magazines, such as *Ladies' Home Journal* and *Saturday Evening Post*. Though he made clear that the New Testament called husbands and wives to love and mutually to submit to each other, he left no doubt that they should uphold definably different roles. Seemingly without a second thought, Graham judged that the husband normally should be the breadwinner and the wife normally the keeper of the hearth. The early Graham said little or nothing about duties specific to the husband, aside from earning a living and maintaining absolute sexual fidelity. Wives' duties were different. He urged women to keep themselves and their homes attractive for their husbands. Striving to be a good cook for the family was important too.[104] A 1957 photograph by the redoubtable Cornell Capa captured Ruth Graham ironing one of her husband's shirts after "retreating from a round of newspaper interviews" in New York.[105] The photograph spoke volumes.

As the decades passed, however, Graham's views about gender followed the arc of changing conceptions in the wider culture. In a move rare among evangelical men in the 1940s, in the summer before his 1949 Los Angeles crusade, Graham placed himself under the spiritual instruction of a woman, Henrietta Mears, director of religious education at Hollywood First Presbyterian Church.[106] He stopped talking about defined roles in the home, and, with second-wave feminists, insisted that women should enjoy equal pay and equal privileges in the workplace.[107] He pointed to women's record of exceptional accomplishment on the mission field, frequently highlighting instances in which women, including his own wife and daughters, excelled as preachers and Bible teachers.[108] At the 1986 Amsterdam Congress for Itinerant Evangelists, sponsored by the BGEA, drawing itinerant evangelists from around the world, approximately 500 of the participants were women.[109]

Equally important, Graham increasingly espoused a companionate or equalitarian ideal within marriage.[110] More and more he stressed what some evangelical Protestants had always stressed and what television sitcoms like *Father Knows Best* were beginning to convey to many Americans: that honesty, sobriety, gentleness, and, above all, sexual fidelity served as *both* Christian and manly virtues.[111] The macho imagery that had pervaded cinema in the 1950s—hard-living men exemplified by figures such as Marlon Brando and James Dean—shared the screen with the imagery of disciplined men, exemplified by figures such as Charlton Heston and Jimmy Stewart, strong enough not to fall into male vices in the first place.[112] Increasingly Graham spoke specifically of a father's responsibilities. He urged fathers not only to love their children but also to take time to play with them and share responsibility for their spiritual nurture. With no apparent sense of irony, he added that fathers could not be away from home all the time and expect things to go well.[113]

Graham's evolving views about gender probably ran closer to those of many average Americans than to those of the secular and feminist elite.[114] In the 1970s, he quietly avoided controversies about the Equal Rights Amendment, as well as about women's ordination, which he held was a matter for each denomination to decide for itself.[115] Though insisting that he supported the larger goals of the women's movement, he cautioned that some partisans had gone too far with "ridiculous demands" such as taking down the signs from the restrooms.[116] One of the most influential articles he ever wrote—"Jesus and the Liberated Woman," published in 1970 in the popular magazine *Ladies' Home Journal*—was a masterpiece of equivocation.[117] At the same time, a typical 1980 sermon urged both husbands and wives to expect disappointments in their marriage: "some dips and some highs." But counter them, he urged, with commitment, tenderness, and understanding. The same guidelines held for children: "If they are breaking your heart right now, don't give up—have patience and perseverance."[118] Whether Graham reified the older gender ideals by not explicitly endorsing the newer ones, or the reverse, is hard to say.

Ruth Bell Graham was less complicated. By all accounts she was extraordinary.[119] As noted, the daughter of Presbyterian missionaries in prerevolutionary China, she had witnessed as a child and young adult a world of violence, poverty, and suffering that most Americans could scarcely imagine. Ruth and Billy met at Wheaton College in the fall of 1940, shortly after he entered. Ruth was a junior. Smitten on first sight, Billy later remembered her as "a slender, hazel-eyed movie starlet!"[120] Ruth dropped out of school for a time to help care for an ill sister, but they married in August 1943, the summer after they both graduated. Blessed with the kind of wit that bespoke razor-sharp intelligence, Ruth proved a ready conversationalist, gracious companion at Billy's countless honorific events, and prolific author of best-selling books of poetry, devotions, and autobiography.[121] Those daunting tasks she somehow managed while taking principal responsibility for rearing the Grahams' five children. Besides all that, her appearance—like Billy's—arrested journalists' attention.[122] They repeatedly described her as "attractive," "pretty," "lovely," "radiant," and "beautiful." With Billy, she received the Congressional Gold Medal in the U.S. Capitol Rotunda in 1996. The press portrayed her—a life-long Presbyterian—as more politically and culturally conservative than Billy.[123] When Ruth expressed satisfaction with more or less traditional gender roles, which put the husband in charge of what took place outside the home and the wife in charge of what took place inside it, Billy amiably agreed.[124]

Billy and Ruth's family life was a subject of endless fascination for journalists, especially magazines targeted at a mass-circulation audience. The press told and retold the story of the Grahams' rocky, three-year courtship while they were students at Wheaton. Ruth had planned to serve as a missionary in Tibet. Marrying an itinerant evangelist was not in the cards. At one point, she even returned Billy's engagement ring. Yet love won out. Their six decades together proved a storybook marriage. Billy at home was a "gentle patriarch" who left the hard work of serious discipline and child rearing to Ruth.[125] Popular magazines showcased saccharine photographs of Billy and Ruth happily posed in their rustic mountain redoubt, often in front of the great stone fireplace or at the kitchen table, surrounded by their ever-growing brood of children. Not rarely everyone was dressed as if they were just about to head out for church. Large dogs—perhaps symbols of a more carefree time in the American imagination—figured prominently.[126] Billy and Ruth's appearance on the *Person to Person with Edward R. Murrow* television show in 1956 rounded out the picture of a Norman Rockwell family.[127] In later years, readers were more likely to see the pair relaxing in rocking chairs on their porch, gazing over the surrounding mountains.[128]

Though Billy and Ruth were, obviously, willing participants in this idyllic presentation, they also poked fun at it. They freely acknowledged that profound and lasting love had not shielded their marriage from its fair share of ups and downs.[129] "If two people agree on everything," Ruth quipped, "one of them is unnecessary."[130] The story contained just enough romance and just enough grit to be both credible and appealing for millions.

Gender was one thing, sex another. In a culture scarred by divorce and infidelity, Graham repeatedly targeted the unhappy personal and social consequences of sex outside of marriage. Though rarely the sole topic of a sermon or of a "My Answer" column, sexual misconduct appeared often in Graham's lists of behaviors that harmed individuals, wrecked marriages, and damaged a person's relationship with God. "Moral Degeneration and Its Cure," a sermon preached on *The Hour of Decision* in 1959, spoke for countless others.[131] The early Graham allowed that sex between spouses could be a vehicle for love as well as for procreation, but sex simply for pleasure appeared rarely in his rhetoric. Indeed, married couples who failed to use "self-restraint and temperance in their relations with each other" committed gluttony, one of the seven "deadly sins."[132] In 1953 Graham denounced "Dr. Alfred Kinsey's newest book" as "an indictment against American womanhood." He was certain that Kinsey had failed to interview the millions of Christian women "who put the highest price on virtue."[133]

Graham insisted without qualification that he had remained entirely celibate before his marriage and faithful to the bride of his youth after their marriage.[134] Marital fidelity was so much a part of Graham's public image that it is hard to imagine what proof of an extramarital lapse might have done to his career. Part of his aura grew from the real and supposed contrast between him and other evangelists in this respect. Yielding to desire was easy; resisting was hard. The sum of it was simple: sex outside of marriage, forbidden; within marriage; a gift from God.[135]

Yet the public Graham was never simple. The pastor's heart had its own voice. He said sexual sins were no greater (or smaller) in God's eyes than other sins. He urged repentance and forgiveness for mistakes.[136] And he did not pretend to stand above everyday male attractions. When he was a teenager, he told *The Door*, his "hormones were as active as any other healthy young male's," but God gave him strength to resist.[137] Graham admitted that in his early years, on the road after he had been married, "the temptation was great."[138] And Billy never pretended that his attraction to Ruth was purely spiritual. But the point, said Graham, was that "Agape" love— "chaste, transcendent love"—was "a deeper love than Eros love."[139] The later Graham would affirm sex "for enjoyment within the confines of marriage." Here, he said, he disagreed with the pope. Sex was not simply for propagation but also "for the fulfillment of the couple."[140]

The later Graham's frankness about the marriage bed might have helped open—though inadvertently—the public space that popular writers such as Marabel Morgan, Beverly LaHaye, and highly trained therapists such as Joyce and Cliff Penner, as well as other evangelical sex, sexuality, and marriage counselors, eventually occupied.[141] Here as elsewhere

Graham probably marched somewhat ahead of his evangelical constituents but not so far ahead as to alienate them with a move that appeared to compromise with an emerging culture of sexual freedom.

Dismantlers of the Icon

If Graham received roses from the media, he also received plenty of thorns. Though there is no way to know for sure, the positive outweighed the negative, probably by a factor of ten to one. Perhaps one hundred to one. Nonetheless, it is important to take account of the criticism, for that too tells us something important about Graham's role in the shaping of the nation's consciousness. Sometimes the critics were more perceptive than the admirers.

Disgruntlement about Graham came from a great many quarters and took a great variety of forms. The breadth and depth of the dissent were in themselves a telling mark of his influence. At one extreme stood thugs, people who threatened Graham's life or the lives of his family. Details are murky, but Graham talked about such threats many times, and close associates spoke of seeing a "fat folder" full of menacing letters.[142] In 1968 FBI Director J. Edgar Hoover found the intimidation serious enough that he persuaded the family to erect a tall iron fence around their home and buy guard dogs.[143] The threats also emerged as a recurrent detail in biographical accounts. They sharpened the profile of a man under siege, which helped chisel the icon in the public imagination.

Without question fundamentalists constituted the largest number of serious critics. The story contained surprising turns. As noted, in the beginning of his public ministry Graham himself certainly qualified as a fundamentalist, at least if measured by the conventional ideational and behavioral criteria. To be sure, from the outset he proved more irenic and less doctrinally defined than classic figures in that tradition. Nonetheless, his outlook fit the pattern. His early institutional support came from stars of the fundamentalist movement, such as John R. Rice, Jack Wrytzen, Torrey Johnson, and especially his one-time patron William Bell Riley. George Marsden, the premier historian of the tradition, stated the point with lapidary precision: the young Graham was a "purebred fundamentalist."[144] By the early 1950s, however, Graham had started to reassess his relationship to the fundamentalist community. In Scotland in 1954 he disassociated himself from the label because of its combative connotations. He preferred the label "evangelical" or simply "Christian," making clear that charity was important too.[145] For about five years, 1952 to 1957, he lingered in the theological borderlands between fundamentalism and the emerging, more irenic, more politically centrist, and more culturally outward-looking evangelical movement.[146]

Graham's crusade in New York City in 1957 proved the pivot point. He was initially invited by a conservative evangelical consortium of churches in 1954 but refused the invitation because it did not represent a broad enough base of support. That broad base came in a 1955 invitation from the New York Council of Churches, representing the majority of Protestant churches in the city. As we have seen, Graham said that he would work with anyone, without a doctrinal litmus test, if they would work with him and not ask him to adjust his message. "I intend to go anywhere, sponsored by anybody, to preach the Gospel of Christ, if there are no strings attached to my message," Graham told the annual convention of the National Association of Evangelicals six weeks before the crusade opened. "*I intend to continue*." (Emphasis in original.)[147] He invited putative liberals such as John Sutherland Bonnell, pastor of Madison Avenue Presbyterian Church, to sit on the platform. Martin Luther King, Jr., offered one invocation. Graham's fundamentalist supporters were outraged, less by changes in Graham's own theology than by his willingness to work with alleged liberals. By doing so he seemed to be saying that doctrine was less important than success.[148]

The narrative of Graham and fundamentalists contains at least four subplots. The first is that most professional historians have a hard time sympathizing with Graham's fundamentalist foes. Their theology often emerges in academic accounts as dogmatic rather than rigorous and their behavior as angry rather than principled. Aside from the question of fairness, the point here is that fundamentalists' response expressed "the anger of disillusioned love."[149] In the eyes of fundamentalists, Graham betrayed their trust. He started out as one of them, they supported him, and then he sold them out. There was a line between cooperation and compromise, and Graham crossed it.

The second and third subplots were two sides of the same coin. By working with the mainline in New York (and elsewhere) Graham helped solidify the identity of the sprawling postwar mainstream evangelical movement. That development carved the American religious landscape into three large streams: mainline Protestant, mainstream evangelical, and fundamentalist.[150] Graham also helped create the postwar fundamentalist movement itself, and that is a third subplot. From 1957 forward fundamentalism took its identity from the fact that it was not cooperative in general and most definitely not a friend of Billy Graham in particular. Graham and Friends now dominated the middle of the playing field. To split with him was to position oneself outside the boundaries of the credible, respectable, Protestant religious landscape, whether mainline Protestant or mainstream evangelical.

And finally, it is important to remember that some fundamentalists stuck with Graham even though they did not like all that he was doing. A. W. Tozer, pastor of a large Christian and Missionary Alliance Church in Chicago, offered a case in point. A prolific author and powerful preacher known for his wit, Tozer himself was something of a legend in fundamentalist circles. When Graham accepted an invitation from "more liberal churches" to hold a crusade in the city, a group of fundamentalist pastors called a meeting to decide "their stance." After defending Graham, Tozer concluded: "Brethren . . . let's let our hair down. You could stand all the fundamentalists in the United States in one line and start them preaching and they would have less effect on the United States than Billy Graham would have just clearing his throat."[151]

Even so, many, perhaps most, fundamentalists never forgave Graham. When Bob Jones—once Graham's hero—died in 1968, his son, Bob Jones, Jr., telegrammed one of Graham's top associates that the associate (and by implication Graham himself) would not be welcome at the funeral.[152] In 2014, a quick look at the Internet revealed that the great majority of attacks on Graham still came from fundamentalists.[153] The stakes were not just high but ultimate. If souls were perishing into an eternal hell one reason was their dalliance with the compromising preacher from North Carolina.

Fundamentalists were not the only Christians who spotted grievous faults in Graham. In the early years, many Roman Catholics joined the charge. Their reasons, of course, proved quite different. Mostly they scored him for his obliviousness to the cardinal doctrinal truths and practices of historic Christianity. Among those were the centrality of the papacy, the sacraments, the church, and the normative authority of tradition. To the Reformation heritage of the Bible alone, Christ alone, and faith alone, Graham's (perceived) focus on the decision-making power of the solitary individual seemed to add one more: me alone.[154] In time, however, many, perhaps most, American Catholics would follow Pope John Paul II in embracing Graham as a fellow brother in Christ.

Though the chorus of critics on Graham's left represented diverse voices— serious theologians, denominational leaders, academic elites, and practiced journalists, among others—they sounded many notes of concern, ranging from raised eyebrows to clenched fists. As far back as 1952 the British Council of Churches, which spoke for the majority of British Christians, refused to join the British Evangelical Alliance's invitation to Graham to speak in London.[155] When he actually arrived on the scene two years later, Graham still remembered, nearly a half-century after the fact, that one newspaper claimed he displayed "all the tricks of the modern demagogue."[156] Canon Stanley Evans of Southwark (England) Cathedral asserted that Graham's theology was "the Gospel degutted," not speaking "of anything but a sentimental relationship between the individual and God."[157] Back home on college campuses Graham often did not fare well either. When he visited Yale in February 1957, the Yale Daily News found him "clearly underintellectual" and "embarrassingly overdramatic." His insights were "banal" and his message irrelevant.[158] Ten years later, when Graham spoke at the University of California, Berkeley, he was greeted with posters that called for "investigating" him.[159] By the mid-1950s Graham was under steady and heavy bombardment from the mainline. In the course of a 1956 trip to India, he surmised that if the U.S. government gave Mr. Nehru a "white air conditioned Cadillac," it might serve as a powerful symbolic gesture of good will. That recommendation prompted the Christian Century to conclude that Graham "hasn't a glimmer of a notion about what is really going on in the world."[160] When Graham's crusade opened in Madison Square Garden in May 1957, the Century did not pull its punches, editorializing: "the Billy Graham campaign will spin along to its own kind of triumph because canny, experienced engineers of human decision have laid the tracks, contracted for the passengers, and will now direct the traffic which arrives on schedule."[161]

Other New Yorkers seemed to feel pretty much the same. Walter Donaid Kring, pastor of the city's prestigious (Unitarian) Church of All Souls on Lexington Ave., declared (or perhaps quipped): "I predict that not only will there be more Unitarians after this revival campaign, there will also be many more 'unchurched.'"[162] Across town, Reinhold Niebuhr, a professor of Christian ethics at New York's Union Theological Seminary, may well have been the most influential theologian in the nation.[163] Niebuhr's biographer tells us that he was "angry" when the New York City Protestant Council of Churches invited Graham to hold meetings. Writing in March of that year, Niebuhr acknowledged that Graham was a "personable, modest and appealing young man," but he dreaded Graham's "rather obscurantist version of the Christian faith." Graham's crusade opened on schedule.

Niebuhr remained unconvinced, even after watching the preacher on the job for a month. Mass evangelism's success, he judged in the July 1 issue of *Life*, "depends upon oversimplifying every issue." Graham's version "offers . . . even less complicated answers than it has ever before provided." Niebuhr concluded that Graham's bland message "promises a new life, not through painful religious experience but merely by signing a decision card. . . . A miracle of regeneration is promised at a painless price by an obviously sincere evangelist. It is a bargain."[164] Niebuhr also thought Graham publicly (though not personally) dragged his feet on civil rights and seemed oblivious to the excesses of consumer capitalism. "Graham Ballyhoo Cheapens Ministry, Niebuhr Says," was how a *New York Post* headline summed up the professor's view of the preacher.[165]

Others followed these astringent paths. Two years after the New York crusade, William G. McLoughlin, a highly regarded historian at Brown University, weighed in. McLoughlin—Graham's first scholarly biographer—did not pretend to be sympathetic, but he did try to be fair. He found that as a "rallying center for many persons in a state of confusion, he was a typical revival figure." McLoughlin allowed that "Graham's decline might be gradual . . . or it might be precipitous." Either way, professional evangelists like Finney, Moody, Jones, Sunday, and Graham were "not likely to provide the key to [America's fourth great awakening] or to stand long as a symbol of it."[166] Shortly afterward, Paul H. Lehman, a prominent systematic theologian at Union Theological Seminary, acknowledged that "at times the power of the Holy Spirit seem[ed] to be manifest in Mr. Graham's meetings." Yet Graham's evangelism was "evangelism with a backward look," presenting Christianity "in terms of ideas, values, and individual decisions which have steadily lost significance."[167]

Graham failed to slip out the back door as predicted, but doubts about his theological sturdiness persisted. After preaching to more than one million people in one service in Seoul, Korea, some pastors criticized him because, as Graham himself put it, "I did not have enough theological content to my messages."[168] The Korean pastors were not alone. In Graham's memorial talk at the National Cathedral on September 14, 2001, he sought to comfort the grieving by saying that many of the victims of the September 11 terrorist attacks were now in heaven and would not want to come back. "It's so glorious and so wonderful," he urged. Leon Wieseltier, literary editor of the *New Republic*, recoiled. Likening Graham's words to "Mohamed Atta's eschatology," Wieseltier judged that "mourners can be imbeciles, too." He offered Graham's remark as evidence. "It is not consoling, it is insulting. We are not a country of children. Nothing that transpired on September 11 was wonderful, nothing." There was a vocabulary in which people disagreed about belief and unbelief but not "about what is significant." Graham had degraded that vocabulary. His words "should have sent all intelligent souls in perplexity running from the church."[169]

The evangelist's perennially cozy relationship with the rich and the powerful only aggravated the criticism. In the 1970s his dogged friendship with President Richard Nixon—insiders considered it loyalty, outsiders considered it blindness—coupled with his ill-disguised support for Nixon's political ambitions, probably marked the nadir of his reputation in secular universities, mainline Protestant seminaries, the establishment press, and not a few politically progressive evangelicals too. In 1990 Garry Wills charged that politicians had "somewhat cynically" manipulated Graham. That Graham was the kind of lightweight who allowed himself to be manipulated apparently seemed self-evident to Wills.[170] Near the end of the decade, the *Nation* quoted Graham's fellow Baptist clergyman Bill Moyers along the same lines. Graham represented, said Moyers, "an unquestioning, obeying patriotism, a loyalty to the authority of the president. Billy was always uncritical, unchallenging, unquestioning."[171]

The op-ed and letters-to-the editor columns of American newspapers and magazines bore testimony to the breadth of the distaste for Graham. This is not to say that grassroots criticism of Graham ever eclipsed praise for him in these columns, or even came close to it, but it is to say that casual readers did not have to spend a lot of time looking for it either. Some writers objected to one or another aspect of his theology, some to his lifestyle or personal bearing, some to his politics, which they thought too liberal or too conservative, but the greatest number objected to his alliance with the power Establishment.[172]

Other thoughtful observers, who might be called supportive critics, found much to approve about Graham himself or his goals or both, yet distanced themselves for one reason or another. The towering European theologian Karl Barth, for example, approved of Graham's commitments but felt that Graham elided important Christian notions such as the Holy Spirit's role in bringing about the Kingdom of God.[173] Daniel Aleshire, the long-term executive director of the American Theological Society, judged that Graham did not appear to see how severely his seeming fixation on moral peccadillos such as the shortness of skirts compromised his laudable overall aims.[174] Donald G. Bloesch, an influential "progressive evangelical" theologian, felt that Graham's theology fell into romantic optimism, tended to link conversion with momentary experience, and failed to attack social sins with sufficient specificity.[175] Joel Carpenter, a leading American historian of the movement and an expert on Graham, supported the preacher's larger purpose yet worried about the danger of allowing one person to speak for an entire movement.[176] In 2013 the television talk show host Larry King—a self-described nonbelieving Jew—affirmed his personal affection for Graham. Yet King acknowledged his disappointment with Graham for failing to challenge President Nixon's anti-Semitism.[177]

A final category of critics consisted of former doubters: people who had once opposed Graham but changed their mind. They came to see him more favorably because he changed, they changed, and the culture changed. One example suffices. In 1988, on the occasion of Graham's seventieth birthday, Martin Marty, one of the most distinguished historians of the twentieth century, admitted that in former years he had grumbled about Graham's style of Christianity. "Reflections on Graham by a Former Grump," Marty called it. To be sure, about the worst Marty ever had to say about Graham back in the 1950s was that "in the olden days they stoned the prophets; now they invite them to dinner."[178] Even so, Marty now mused, when Graham first appeared on the religious landscape, he was "still part cornball, part jejune analyst of 'the signs of the times,' part misusable young comer." He gave others "good reasons" to criticize him. But in 1988 Marty judged that "Left and Right, liberal or conservative mean less than mean and non-mean and Graham—to our great fortune—has been 'non-mean.'" And in that spirit he was "first of all and always, a witness to Jesus Christ."[179] Marty kept moving. In an academic conference in 2013 devoted to analyzing the preacher's legacy in American history, Marty said that the Mt. Rushmore of American religious history included Jonathan Edwards, Martin Luther King, Jr., and Billy Graham. (Marty added, with a characteristic twinkle, that he had not yet decided on the fourth.)[180]

There is no reason to think that Graham intentionally courted censure, let alone hate mail or threats on his life. But he did not try to avoid it either. He knew that it came with the territory. He also knew its value. Graham was astute enough to recognize that criticism was, as historian Harry Stout said of George Whitefield, a public relations dream come true.[181] Within broad limits there was no such thing as bad publicity. Even his blunder with Truman in 1950 proved an image-management bonanza, for it humanized him, showing that even the most skillful figures had to learn their craft the hard way.

How did Graham respond to criticism? The short answer is that he either did not respond at all or did not respond in kind. He said that if he tried to respond to each attack he would not get anything else done.[182] To be sure, he countered whole classes or categories of people who challenged his approach—secularists and fundamentalists—but not by individual name. "If this extreme type of fundamentalism was of God," he said, a bit testily, in 1955, "it would have brought revival long ago. Instead, it has brought dissension, division, strife, and . . . produced dead and lifeless churches."[183] Sometimes he tried to meet with critics in person to talk things over, with mixed results. Sometimes he sent personal letters, thanking the person for taking time to write or speak. He said that he would carefully consider their criticism, or ask them to correct factual mistakes, but rarely if ever more than that.[184] He rightly viewed criticism as opposition in varying degrees but did not portray it as persecution. Close associates acknowledged that some of the criticism smarted, especially the rocks hurled by his former fundamentalist friends. Graham admitted that early on the criticism had caused insomnia.[185] But he did not retreat from the strategy of responding, if at all, with a soft touch.

The public ramification of Graham's refusal to respond to his critics in kind merits brief comment. To some extent his approach grew from his personal disposition. By all accounts he was irenic and just did not like to fight with anyone about anything. To some extent it grew from principle. Christians were not supposed to fight. But it also grew from a pragmatic recognition that if he held his fire he would gain more than he would lose. Refusing to respond made him look both manly (he could take it) and self-confident (he knew his message was true). In the meantime, the criticisms themselves—except perhaps for Niebuhr's sharply worded reservations—largely faded from view as the preacher's hair grayed and his positions grew more inclusive. The challenge for students of Graham's place in American history is to discern how the discussion helped carve the face of the icon.

Results

How did Graham's rise, singularity, and longevity on the American religious landscape contribute to his iconic status? Of course this question could be turned around. But for analytic purposes it seems more useful to imagine rise, singularity, and longevity as the independent variables and ask how they helped fashion the icon.

First, rise. To start with the obvious, Graham did not carry the baggage that limited the appeal of some of his predecessors. He was not burdened with arcane theological views like William Bell Riley, or a controversial lifestyle like Aimee Semple McPherson, or a Prohibitionist agenda and confrontational style like Billy Sunday, or divisive healing and money-raising practices like Oral Roberts. It might be an exaggeration to say that he hit the ground running in the late 1940s, but he came as close as anyone.

What Graham did possess was a wealth of native gifts and graces. Though classic good looks gave him a head start in a Hollywood-saturated culture, he carefully cultivated them. The same proved true for his personality. He cultivated graces he acquired on his mother's knee. Three examples suffice. An interviewer from the *Saturday Evening Post* would say that his "emotional power, even held to a calmly conversational level, is hypnotic."[186] The country music star Barbara Mandrell said she had known two people whose presence you could sense "when they were in the building": Johnny Cash and Billy Graham. "The air would just get exciting and stimulating and electric even if you couldn't see them."[187] And then there was the experience of *Time* journalists Nancy Gibbs and Michael Duffy, who visited Graham when he was well advanced in years. "Unless you've been in his presence," they recalled, "it's hard to capture its effect. Many people said he was the most charismatic man they ever met."[188] Mandrell, Gibbs, and Duffy spoke for many. We also should note a factor that many historians have missed but that the evidence well attests: sheer hard work. The press saw and commented on the vacations on sun-drenched beaches in Florida and Hawaii. What they overlooked were the long days, the punishing travel schedule, and the continual oversight of a mammoth business and media empire.[189]

More broadly, Graham's rise was fueled by his ability to adopt and adapt the trends of the age, and the age provided unprecedented tools and opportunities. One conspicuous example of that interaction between opportunity and creativity lay in Graham's friendships with (after Truman) ten successive U.S. presidents, very close friendships with at least four of them, and (insufficiently appreciated) close friendships with four First Ladies.[190] Probably no other person, and certainly no other evangelical, ever enjoyed that kind of sustained access to the pinnacle of American power. In short, gifts, graces, work habits, and what might be called affability helped explain Graham's rise, and the rise helped explain the icon.

Singularity played a role too. Sometimes the postwar era seemed to be one of "onlys." With some exaggeration one might say there was only one Elvis, only one King, only one Bernstein, and only one Cronkite.[191] First names were not needed. That pattern applied to Graham, too. In the first issue of 1951, the popular magazine *Look* predicted: "Before his candle burns out, Graham will be recognized, on the basis of numbers alone, as the most potent evangelist in American history."[192] If secular newspapers and magazines can be taken as a reliable index, by 1951 no other person came close; by 1957 no one else seemed even to aspire (at least publically) to come close. Potential rivals such as Merv Rosell of Youth for Christ, Harold John Ockenga of Park Street Church, Charles E. Fuller of the *Old Fashioned Revival Hour*, faith healers Oral Roberts and Kathryn Kuhlman, and of course Charles Templeton won substantial crowds but did not approach Graham's visibility in the national secular press. We are left to ask, to what extent was Graham's singularity the result of reporters' decision to report on him and not others? More precisely, what ingredients in his career drew such close, sustained, and, in many ways, singular attention from the press?

Graham's presence constituted the electromagnetic center of the postwar evangelical movement. His voice settled discussions—a feat especially remarkable given the tradition's proudly cacophonous and profoundly fissiparous character. Proximity to him became proximity to normative authority. He represented the right way to do things. Others were forced to justify themselves in terms of the standards he set, not the other way around. Graham's singularity may have gained force, too, from what might be called the finality factor. As the years slipped by, many supporters increasingly saw him as the last man standing. He enjoyed the iconic status that accompanied a sense that he represented the final burst of the revival tradition.

If the first task is to reflect on Graham's rise, and the second his singularity, the third is to examine his longevity on the public stage. By one measure his significant public influence started with his first YFC outing in Chicago in May 1944 and lasted to the end of his public ministry in the Flushing Meadows crusade in 2005—the better part of six decades. Insiders explained that longevity as providential, God's man for the hour. Outsiders explained it as an artifact of good genes, consistent exercise, moderate diet, medical interventions, ability to avoid the traps that had swallowed up other evangelists, and the salubrious effects of a fundamentally happy family life. And of course many explained it both ways at once. However parsed, the result was the same. Graham not only lived longer than most other evangelical leaders of note in American history but also managed to stay actively in the limelight the entire time. More remarkable, until the 1990s, he suffered little loss of physical and mental energy. His record of interacting with so many people and so many issues stemmed in part from the simple biological fact of longevity.

A couple of implications of Graham's longevity in the spotlight merit notice. The first one is that though very early Graham showed little interest in gaining a seat at the table of public influence, by the mid-1950s he clearly did. That he ever gained a seat at the very head of the table may be doubted, but that he gained a seat somewhere near the head seems beyond debate.[193] More important, he knew how to behave at the table—when and how to speak. There were gaffes, but given the number of opportunities for mistakes, remarkably few. And he showed other evangelicals how to do it too. Not all of them did, of course. With the rise of the Christian right in the 1970s many elected to walk away, and some tried to hijack the table and take it with them. But on the whole evangelicals followed Graham's lead. For many, just sitting next to Graham, both literally and figuratively, was all they needed.

A second implication of Graham's longevity on the stage is that it legitimated, even sacralized, events and persons. One example makes the point. In the 1960 election Graham supported Nixon.[194] Later we will see that he worried about Kennedy's possible ties to the Vatican. Yet Graham made plain to JFK and the press that if Kennedy won, Graham would support him. On January 17, 1961, after the election but before the inauguration, a *New York Times* headline declared the news: "Dr. Graham Hails Kennedy Victory: Says It Aids Understanding Among Major Churches—They Dine and Golf."[195] Joseph Kennedy had arranged for Graham to go golfing with the new president the day before. He also had arranged for photographers to catch the two riding together in a Lincoln convertible. That evening Kennedy took Graham to a gathering of 300 members of the press.[196]

White evangelicals, at that point roughly split between parties, and heirs of centuries of bitter hostility between Catholics and Protestants, now saw that they could support the new Democratic Roman Catholic president, at least in his office as president, if not in his policies.[197] Democrats gained something. At the same time, evangelicals saw that one of their own could schmooze with one of the richest and most powerful men in the world. So evangelicals gained something too.

It would be an exaggeration to say that Graham's mere presence—a wave, a grin, or a golf swing—made it all happen. But not totally false, either. He packed muscle with the press. As *Newsweek* later saw it, Graham represented American Christianity at its best: "faithful to the gospel but tolerant of others, dedicated to Jesus but committed to openness and freedom of conscience."[198] That was what icons were supposed to do.

CHAPTER THREE

Southerner

The middle third of the twentieth century witnessed a vast social and cultural transformation that historians have called the "Southernizing" of the United States. Between 1930 and 1970 mass migration from the South to the North and West, involving eight million whites and three million blacks, allowed Southern attitudes and practices to move outward. Dixie traveled with them. Elvis, NASCAR, and the Gunbelt (the California munitions industry, populated by ex-Southerners) symbolized the force of the impulse.[1]

The literature on the process is extensive. Fundamental structural changes following World War II, such as mass advertising and the Interstate Highway System, paved the way for a host of Southern attitudes and practices to swell. (The reverse process took place too, but that is another story.) If we conflate California Sunbelters with traditional Southerners, the outcome of all but one of the presidential elections, regardless of party, from Nixon to Bush II, told a tale of Southern expansion.[2] Perhaps more symptomatic was the Northern provenance of most of the losers.[3] The story grows still more dramatic when we add the extraordinary national visibility of Southern-based sports celebrities such as Bear Bryant, Willie Mays, and Arnold Palmer; musicians such as Johnny Cash, Willie Nelson, and Dolly Parton; writers such as Truman Capote, William Faulkner, and Flannery O'Connor; and performers such as Joan Crawford, Ava Gardner, and Andy Griffith. In the realm of religion, add television evangelists Pat Robertson and Charles Stanley; healers William O. Branham and Oral Roberts; and of course, the sprawling religious empire of the Southern Baptist Convention, sixteen million strong. At its height, the *Old Fashioned Revival Hour*, aired from the Sunbelt city of Long Beach, California, with a dose of Southern gospel music, and Grace "Honey" Fuller reading appreciative letters from listeners, proved one of the most widely aired radio programs in the nation.[4]

The ballooning national and international visibility of Charlotte's hometown boy rounds out the picture. From start to finish outsiders readily identified Graham as a Southerner. In one of his earliest outings, barely six months after he enrolled at Wheaton College, the *Park Ridge Gospel Herald* at the Park Ridge Gospel Church in Park Ridge, Illinois, promised: "Evangelist from the South to Speak Sunday." Lest anyone overlook the opportunity, the *Herald* added that Graham ranked as "one of the most dynamic, appealing young speakers of the South."[5] Sixteen years later, when Graham launched his crusade in Madison Square Garden, a *Newsweek* cover dubbed it, perhaps a bit melodramatically: "The Billy Graham 'Invasion' / Finally the Big One—'Save New York.'" Near the end of the century, a special issue of *Life* titled "The 100 Most Important Americans of the 20th Century" would open its biographical piece on Graham with a nod to his roots: "He came out of Florida in the 1930s. A farm boy born again at 15, a preacher by 20, a legend by 40, William Franklin Graham Jr. was the most sincere—and most incorruptible—evangelist ever to raise a tent or a dollar."[6] There it was in one paragraph: "Florida," "farm," and "tent." With good reason George Marsden described Graham's early ministry as fundamentalism with a "southern accent."[7]

Southerners, too, claimed Graham as one of their own. In a study published in 2001 in *Southern Cultures*, Graham ranked with Louis Armstrong, Jimmy Carter, William Faulkner, Martin Luther King, Jr., and Elvis Presley as one of the six most influential Southerners of the twentieth century.[8] As early as 1955, *Our State: Down Home in North Carolina* magazine—the official unofficial organ of the state's tourism/local color industry—featured Graham on the front cover, emblazoned with the title: "They Like Billy Graham."[9] Two decades later *Dixie Business: The Voice of Southern Progress* bestowed on Graham two awards: "Man of the South" and "A Great American."[10] When Graham returned to Atlanta in the fall of 1994 for one of his largest crusades, the *Atlanta Journal Constitution* headlined the story "Son of the South."[11] In 2012 a writer for *Our State: Down Home in North Carolina* magazine dryly observed that back in the 1970s Graham had been "merely loved" but now he was "revered."[12] If denizens of the South pegged Graham as one of their own, scholars pegged his followers similarly. In 1970, Liston Pope, a Vanderbilt sociologist, judged: "People go to hear Billy Graham speak largely to be reassured that the South of their childhood— what they once knew and thought and counted on—is still to be believed in."[13]

Graham, too, viewed himself as a Southerner. He repeatedly identified himself that way in press conferences and in other public contexts.[14] Sometimes he went out of his way to classify himself specifically as a North Carolinian, especially when he was speaking in his home state.[15] Ironically, in the early years of his ministry he felt, with an obvious touch of regret, that he had not done very well in the South.[16] Though the data belied that self-assessment, it was telling that he wanted very much to prove successful in his home region.

Graham's autobiographical reflections revealed some of his deepest assumptions about himself. He made clear that he not only came from the South but also took a great deal of pride in that heritage. He pointed out, for example, that both grandfathers were Civil War veterans and both had suffered serious wounds fighting for the Confederacy. His father's father, William Crook Graham, took a bullet at Gettysburg, leaving him crippled for life. This depiction cemented personal bravery with loyalty to the region. Crook also emerged in Graham's accounts as something of a hell-raiser. Graham did not tout his grandfather's behavior, stereotypical of the unhitched Southern male, but he made no attempt to hide it either.[17]

When Graham turned to describe his parents, Frank and Morrow Graham, the picture was more prim but still definably Southern. They embodied what the historian Michael Kazin has called the "Jesus and Jefferson" ideal, which pervaded the South in the first half of the twentieth century.[18] In the Jesus and Jefferson frame of mind, white denizens of the region combined religious with secular values. The latter—the Jefferson part—esteemed frugality, rural origins, hard work, self-reliance, local control, tight community ties, a strong sense of honor, doing the right thing, and a paternal relationship with blacks, especially those in their immediate circles. In other times and places, outsiders would call such white people "plain folk" or "salt-of-the-earth types."

Graham's birth family fit the Jeffersonian image. Frank and Morrow emerged in the preacher's memory, in most biographies, and in innumerable magazine sketches as an upwardly mobile farm family.[19] And rural it was. Not more than four or five cars a day passed the Graham holdings.[20] Hard-working, too. Unlike crop farming or cattle-raising, where the rhythms of work offered time off now and then, dairy farming required continual attention. The senior Grahams knew no silver spoon. Though Billy's biographer Marshall Frady portrayed Frank as a hard-driving, hard-dealing businessman, most accounts describe a man with a strong work ethic and rigorous personal discipline.[21] Billy's sister Jean remembered that her father sold part of his land to a developer for a reduced price in order to build affordable housing for returning World War II veterans.[22] There are persuasive reasons to believe that the conventional sketch of the family's middle- or upper-middle-class economic standing was substantially accurate.[23] Though the Grahams suffered a bump when milk prices plummeted during the Depression, they ended up with one of the most prosperous farms and nicest homes in the area, replete with electricity and running water when those amenities were rare.²⁴ They even owned a car. Graham and the media repeatedly reproduced this palimpsest of enterprising Southern rural virtues.

In 2014, visitors to the Billy Graham Library, housed just off the Billy Graham Parkway in Charlotte, immediately encountered a remarkably realistic, Walt-Disney–inspired talking cow, pictures of Billy and other members of the family doing farm chores, milk buckets and cattle stanchions scattered throughout, and an arresting photograph of Billy's younger brother, Melvin, leaning on a wooden fence, with his sleeves rolled up over muscular biceps. The architecture imaged Melvin as a successful rustic in a sturdy Jeffersonian world. Seven years earlier, the library's grand opening ceremony (which featured former presidents George H. W. Bush, Jimmy Carter, and Bill Clinton) took place in a great open-air tent, flanked by an equally great red barn and silo. The cafeteria on the grounds showcased Carolina barbecue, banana pudding, and sweet tea. The scene could have been a page ripped from a rural life sketchbook of the post–World War II South. And most of the speakers and guests on the platform were white males.

By then Graham was eighty-eight. But in autobiographical texts written over the years he invoked pretty much the same rural middle- and upper-middle-class vista of his youth and young adulthood. Time after time he mentioned that he had grown up on a dairy farm, where he had roused himself out of bed long before dawn to milk twenty cows. Though there was nothing distinctively Southern about dairy farming, it fit his evocation of a region commonly identified as predominantly agricultural. He forged close friendships with farm hands, white, black, and Hispanic. One of the hands explained the sexual "facts of life" to him.²⁵ Years later Graham remembered that as a teenager he had considered enrolling at the University of North Carolina at Chapel Hill. Though he did not say so, many considered UNC, like its rival, University of Virginia, a citadel of genteel Southern culture. Graham's first taste of higher education took place at Bob Jones College, in those days located not far away in the southeastern Tennessee berg of Cleveland. He found the school distasteful for the damp cold of a small town wedged into the foothills of the Southern highlands.

So it was that after one semester the young Billy Graham transferred to Florida Bible Institute near Tampa. FBI proved a much happier site, splayed in the sun-splashed greenery of central Florida, rich with palm trees, orange groves, languid rivers, swampy lakes, and a lush golf course nearby. Though we should not make too much of it, well into his later years Graham the inveterate Southerner gravitated toward vacation sites on warm beaches, often in Florida. One of his most frequently recounted moments was a powerful religious experience that took place one evening at FBI as "a soft southern breeze stirred the wispy Spanish moss that draped the trees."[26]

After three years at FBI, Graham matriculated at Wheaton College, in Wheaton, Illinois, thirty miles west of downtown Chicago. He migrated to the Northern school because it had a strong academic reputation among fundamentalist institutions and offered scholarship aid.[27] But the move crystalized his awareness of his Southern roots. Even before he arrived in Wheaton, however, he discovered that his accent posed a problem. Stopping off in York, Pennsylvania, for a revival, he sensed that some people were having trouble understanding him. He tried speaking louder. No success. At first he blamed the communication problem on "their spiritual deafness," but he soon realized that the problem lay in his "heavy accent."[28] When he got to Wheaton things grew worse. Though he was a natty dresser in his own settings in the South, at Wheaton his shoes and clothes—which other students perceived as country—evoked ridicule.[29]

Yet the main thing Graham recalled about his days at Wheaton was the sheer loneliness. Living away from home was not the problem. He had been away from home for three years, working in South Carolina and preaching and studying in Tennessee and Florida. The problem was being a Southerner in the North. "On Wheaton's elm-shaded suburban campus," he remembered a half-century later, "I felt like a hick. Born and bred on a farm in the South, I doubted there was anybody in the entering class as green as I was."[30] For a while, he poignantly remembered, he felt he had made a terrible mistake.

After graduating from Wheaton, Graham served a small Baptist church near Chicago, but after just eighteen months Billy and Ruth headed south. The young couple established their first permanent home, not in Chicago or some other hub of Northern fundamentalism, but in Montreat, North Carolina, a postcard community tucked into the Blue Ridge mountains twenty miles east of Asheville. To be sure, Ruth's parents lived there, which probably meant some free babysitting for a growing family. But given that the young couple had the financial and social resources to live many places, the choice of Montreat symbolized a Southern gravitational pull too. Montreat housed the conference grounds of the (Southern) Presbyterian Church in the United States, Ruth's denomination. Graham's sister Jean once quipped that he returned to Charlotte for the food and to Montreat for the repose.[31] Graham made Montreat his home for the rest of his life. It constituted a bold statement of cultural preference. In 2014 he expected that on his death he would be interred next to Ruth a few hundred yards from the Billy Graham Library in Charlotte.

Graham's identification with the South ran deeper than family, food, and repose, however. Most Americans probably believed—rightly—that his instincts ran moderate Republican. Even so, he told reporters in 1967 that he was reared a Democrat and remained one. This political affiliation was born of regional roots. He said he did not know anyone who was not a Democrat until he was grown.[32] Graham defended the South, too. Where admirable defense of one's birthplace slipped into less-than-admirable defensiveness grew murky. Except for occasional references to poverty in Appalachia, he said little about the South's destitution, humidity, violence, parochialism, or stubborn Lost Cause mythology. And when it came to race, he took pains to say that the South was "making tremendous progress," while the North, with its de facto segregation, still faced "great trouble spots."[33] Many felt that he was only stating the obvious: the South should receive credit for its progress.[34] Others just as surely felt that commendable loyalty to region blurred his vision about the depth and intractability of the injustices that remained.

Talking about being a Southerner was one thing, embodying it was another, and he did both. Graham's accent was unmistakable and for most audiences probably the clearest tip about his origins. Of course, an accent was an accent only to outsiders, but Graham's audience rapidly expanded beyond the states of the Old Confederacy, and Dixie was the language outsiders heard. The earliest recordings of Graham preaching capture a definable Southern inflection.[35] One careful listener later called it "a southern sway in his voice."[36] Contrary to convention, which assumed that Southern pronunciation meant a drawl, the evangelist's earliest deliveries sounded like a machine gun (a very loud one too). Yet the regional markers remained. He toned them down when he preached on the radio or television for a national audience, and they modulated with the passing of the years. But he never lost the accent, especially in private conversation.[37] Graham's accent came across as different enough to be interesting but not so different as to sound aristocratic or backwoods or foreign. The accent also served as a marker of class as well as region.

A second hallmark of Graham's self-presentation as a Southerner took a more elusive yet no less important form that might be called *style*. We might also call it demeanor, or deportment. Some found him courtly.[38] Journalists' accounts consistently projected an image of a mannered man, "unfailingly gracious to others," as one Southern university president put it.[39] Critics nailed him for many things but almost never for being curt or boorish. In old age Graham remembered that as a young man at FBI he had tried to obtain the autograph of Gipsy Smith, a renowned evangelist. Smith declined.[40] Graham said the rebuff steeled his determination never to do the same. By all accounts he kept that promise.

One anecdote speaks for many. In the early 1980s, Andrew Walsh interviewed Graham several times when Graham took his crusades into southern New England. Nearly thirty years later, Walsh, by then a scholar at Hartford's prestigious Trinity University, still remembered two features of those interviews. The first was Graham's personal manner. "He could lay on that Southern graciousness thing with a trowel," said Walsh, with a wink. But the interaction was more complex than that. Walsh recalled that Graham clearly understood the professional character of the interviews. He did not assume a false familiarity or seek to break the ice with chitchat. Rather, he simply went about the business of answering the questions as posed, including hard ones about race, with candor.[41] The subtle protocols of the South, which mixed intimacy with distance in a way that outsiders rarely could figure out, were a hallmark of Graham's style.

And then Graham embodied conventionally Southern traditions in his repeated references to personal character. "Never underestimate a 'small temptation,'" he would say. Or: "When wealth is lost, nothing is lost. When health is lost, something is lost. When character is lost, everything is lost."[42] Reflecting the BGEA ethos, Leighton Ford, Graham's associate evangelist and frequent alternate preacher, similarly remarked: "You won't make a difference by multiplying programs but by investing in people."[43] When Southerners of Graham's generation and social location—middle- and upper-middle-class folk—spoke of character they meant something like treating people fairly, making good on your word, doing not only the correct thing but also the right thing.[44] Racial boundaries and paternalism complicated that formula.

Motives mattered. For Graham, as for many Southerners, the key axis was not the individual versus the structural but the personal versus the impersonal.[45] When Graham delivered Richard Nixon's funeral homily, some people were baffled by the appreciative things he had to say about the former president. Yet on that occasion Graham insisted that the tree could not be reckoned until it fell. When later generations took the measure of the full tree of Nixon's life, he urged, they would see more than the obvious failures. They would see a "personal human side to Nixon that most did not see," an individual who was shy, did countless kind things for unknown people."[46] In Graham's book, Nixon's virtues counted too, along with his flaws.

The Good South

The Southern writer Flannery O'Connor once quipped that a good writer had to be "*frum* somewhere."[47] In her case *frum* meant a set of particularities defined by time and place: a Roman Catholic woman growing up in the Deep South of Milledgeville, Georgia. Graham too was *frum* somewhere: a dairy farm in the South. But which South? There were many. One thinks, for example, of the vast range of cultures evoked in the South's great writers: Flannery O'Connor (eccentric), Margaret Mitchell (paternal), William Faulkner (violent), Erskine Caldwell (impoverished), Pat Conroy (militaristic), Thomas Wolfe (nostalgic), and Wendell Berry (redeemable), among many others.[48] The challenge is to gain a clear sense of the kind of South Graham represented to other Southerners and other Americans at mid-century.

After the late 1940s Graham and his message traveled well for many reasons. One of them resided in his ability to carry with him a bundle of evocations that might be called the Good South.[49] Four of those imaginaries reflected Graham's public style with special clarity: an open, exportable South; an irenic, organic South; a mainstream evangelical South; and a slowly but increasingly racially integrated South.[50]

First, then, Graham staged himself as the herald of an open, exportable South. One biographer reported that Graham accepted the 1949 invitation to hold a crusade in Southern California to see if people in the West would "turn out to hear him."[51] The apparent irony notwithstanding, Graham's South did not appear to outsiders as *too* Southern. He won a national audience precisely because he conveyed a gospel regionally inflected but not regionally limited. His presentation felt Southern but not exclusively so. Its windows opened to the winds of change blowing from other parts of the nation and soon from the entire world.[52] Graham's religion came *frum* somewhere but it was not parochial.

One conspicuous sign of the elasticity of Graham's regional boundaries lay in the BGEA's official business and mailing address: Minneapolis, Minnesota.

When Graham founded the association in 1950, he and his business manager, George M. Wilson, located it in Minneapolis because that is where Wilson lived and because Graham was president of Northwestern Schools, located in that city. The BGEA opened branch offices at various places at various times, including Atlanta, Washington, and London, but until 2002 the primary site remained Minneapolis. In 2002, very close to Graham's effective retirement, the BGEA finally moved to Charlotte to be close to its cousin organization, Samaritan's Purse.[53] But for most of his career, Graham's unmistakably Southern evangelistic presence marched hand in hand with a (very) Northern business presence.

Another sign of regional openness lay in the provenance of the most visible part of Graham's public ministry: the geographic roots of the signature platform Team. By 1947 it consisted of Graham, Cliff Barrows, and George Beverly Shea. By 1951 it had taken its nearly permanent form: Graham, Barrows, and Shea, as well as Tedd Smith, pianist, and Grady Wilson, announcer and occasional substitute preacher. In 1955 Leighton Ford joined the team. Of those figures, only Graham and his high-school friend Wilson were (old South) Southerners. Barrows came from California, Smith from British Columbia, and Ford and Shea from Ontario.

The exportability of Graham's version of the South expressed itself in the mixed regional sites of his meetings. Through the 1950s a majority of the extended crusades took place outside the South, and a great majority of the YFC meetings did too, especially in the Midwest.[54] Most of his early large urban crusades, cumulatively attracting hundreds of thousands of attendees, unfolded not in the South but in Los Angeles, Boston, Portland (Oregon), Pasadena, Washington, DC, and New York City. Even Charlotte, the site of Graham's first independent citywide meeting, merits closer scrutiny for the imagery it conveyed. Along with Atlanta, Charlotte, perhaps more than any other city in the region, represented the New South, the South on the move, both symbolically with its burgeoning financial and insurance concerns, and literally, as a hub of train travel and intersecting highways.[55] Four of Graham's largest urban crusades took place in Atlanta, but it should be noted that the city also housed the nationally oriented Braves, the internationally oriented CNN, one of the busiest air terminals, and, many believed, the most congested traffic corridor in the country.[56]

Finally, the historian Uta Balbier persuasively argued that Graham's message functioned as a consumer item to be marketed, purchased, or declined, everywhere, regardless of region, very much like other items in a consumer-oriented society.[57] Like cash, it flourished in most parts of the nation, shorn of its cultural particularities. Graham's gospel drew people in other regions because he spoke both for and to their concerns, just as he spoke for and to people's concerns in the South. Yet that was precisely the point. Graham was just enough of a Southerner to be appealing, to have a regionally distinctive way of delivering his message, but not so Southern as to seem quaint, an interloper in the North. He knew the danger. In 1954 the British had savaged him: "Yank Says We're Heathens," blasted one headline.[58] In the United States he received every imaginable form of criticism, but rarely that of a latter-day Rebel. Graham began his career in the South and as a Southerner. By the late 1940s, however, he was never "just a Southerner."

This delicate balance between the South as a definable region and the South as an attractive, exportable cultural commodity found instructive parallels in two icons who also came to the front in the later part of the twentieth century: Colonel Sanders and Andy Griffith. Harlan David Sanders lived in Corbin, Kentucky, long enough to persuade the state's governor in 1935 to designate him a "Kentucky Colonel." His habitual garb of white frock coat, black tie, and gray goatee, along with a franchised fried-chicken chain linked with Kentucky, evoked pleasant images of Southern hospitality. In the franchise's international advertising, Southern Everyman Sanders seemed a kindly host, offering good things for families and weary travelers wherever they went, South, North, West, or abroad.[59]

Andy Griffith and the mythical television town of Mayberry (based on Griffith's real-life home town, the village of Mount Airy, North Carolina, one hundred miles north of Charlotte) offered a closer parallel. As sheriff of Mayberry, Griffith carried no gun, embraced everyone, and judged no one, including his oddball assistant, Barney Fife. The sole cell in Mayberry's jail sported an easy chair and a shaded lamp. Most of its citizens were old-stock whites. The real-life Andy Griffith graduated from the state's flagship university in Chapel Hill. He was buried near his home on Roanoke Island, North Carolina.[60] A 2011 poll showed that he was the third most popular person in the state, behind first-place Graham and second-place basketball coaching legend Dean Smith.[61]

Colonel Sanders, Kentucky Fried Chicken, Sheriff Andy, and Mayberry were recognizably Southern. They were also comforting, nonthreatening, transcending time and place. Mayberry in particular symbolized the South's—and America's—self-image as decent, humane, neighborly, and helpful to a sacrificing fault. Obviously that portrait left out the snake of white racism, and much else. Yet the South began to turn a corner on race after the Civil Rights laws of 1964 and 1965. No thoughtful observer believed then or in 2014 that the runners had reached home plate. But increasingly freed from the legacy of Jim Crow, the South found itself an exportable commodity. And so did Billy Graham.

The Southern Evangelical Mainstream

Graham's "curiously angry but also often shrewd" biographer Marshall Frady suggested that the preacher sought "to transform and pasteurize the whole world . . . into a Sunday afternoon in Charlotte."[62] Frady exaggerated, but the deep-running cultural assumptions that Graham exhibited through the first third or even first half of his ministry intimate that Frady was not entirely wrong, either. The form of evangelicalism that Graham projected was not generic but a distinctive version of it—a version found everywhere but most conspicuously and powerfully in the states of the Old South, Upper South, Western South, and large parts of the Sunbelt. The label *mainstream evangelical* seems to work as well as any.[63] To be sure, mainstream evangelicals never owned all of the Southern Christian real estate, let alone all of Southern religion. Catholics, Episcopalians, Lutherans, Pentecostals, Churches of Christ, Jews, and Mormons, among many others, flourished in their own spaces.[64] Yet mainstream evangelicals occupied by far the largest mansion on the block. And it stood squarely in the middle of the block, too. Graham remembered that when he was growing up, Baptists, Methodists, and Presbyterians were normative. Lutherans felt strange. And everyone went to church on Sunday, usually twice.[65]

Respectability marked mainstream evangelicalism. In the South, the most influential voices spoke from the pulpits and occupied the pews of its mostly white churches. Think First Baptist in Dallas, where Graham kept his membership for fifty-five years, or Myers Park United Methodist in Charlotte, or First Presbyterian in Atlanta. In those redoubtable institutions, respectable people ran respectable enterprises during the week and worshiped in respectable ways on Sunday. Politically, they were solidly Democratic, back when *Democrat* connoted a regional identity as much as a political persuasion. Culturally, they were moderately conservative in matters of personal style and moderately progressive (with wide variations) in matters of race.[66] Socially, they were the kind of people who preferred not to see their name in the paper, and saw no need to state their address on wedding invitations since everyone already knew where they lived.[67]

One snapshot revealed worlds within worlds. In 1973 *Dixie Business* touted Graham's upcoming Atlanta crusade. Thomas Graham Cousins, one of the wealthiest and most influential men in the city (also one of the most generous philanthropists) served as chairman of the Executive Committee. Dr. Harry A. Fifield, pastor of Atlanta's First Presbyterian Church, headed the 280-member Council of Ministers. The council supported the crusade with a "vital prayer fellowship." Six area chairs, all Presbyterian, Methodist, and Baptist, assisted Fifield. Three of the chairs' churches bore the word *First* in their names. One of Cousins's two vice-chairmen also served a church with *First* in its name. One of the chairs had been "Man of the South" in 1972. The governor, Jimmy Carter, ranked "among the first to offer his services." The magazine added that it hoped many thousands would "make a public profession of their faith as well as a lasting beneficial effect on the area as a whole." The Council of Women similarly consisted of one head and six area chairs. Each identified herself as "Mrs.," and all but one used her husband's name. The article concluded: "The list of workers includes most of Metropolitan Atlanta's top leaders." No Catholic, Episcopal, Lutheran, Mennonite, Pentecostal, Church of Christ, African Methodist Episcopal, or Christian Methodist Episcopal church, pastor, or leader was named.[68]

The mainstream evangelicals' theology was predictably orthodox, in a vaguely Calvinist/Wesleyan sort of way, and it was also predictably establishmentarian. Theological angularities were sanded down. Congregations heard few if any Pentecostal references to miraculous healings, or Church of Christ references to restorationist purity, or Primitive Baptist references to double predestination, or Plymouth Brethren references to the Mark of the Beast, and no Unitarian references at all to the Resurrection Myth. In a 1973 press conference, Graham told reporters: "I don't like to use the word fundamentalist, because that word carries with it the idea of snake-handling these days and that sort of thing. I believe the Bible and I believe the Apostles' Creed, but I would consider myself a sociological liberal."[69] With "that sort of thing" Graham likely said more—far more—than he realized.

No reporter should have been surprised, at least none who knew how Graham had grown up. Reared in Chalmers Associate Reformed Presbyterian Church near Charlotte, he heard preaching straight out of the Westminster Catechism, which his parents also drilled into him in daily devotions. At church he heard not hymns but versified Psalms and admonitions about strict observance of the Sabbath. That day of the week, his beloved sport of baseball struck out.

When the Christian Businessmen's Association invited the "fire-snorting" (as one journalist described him) evangelist Mordecai Ham to help revive the city's faith, the established clergy proved fearful.[70] Part of the controversy, Graham remembered, ran along denominational lines. "The Baptists in the South generally supported him, but denominations like Methodists and Presbyterians did not care much for either his message or his style," Graham remembered. "It sounded like a religious circus to me."[71] Ham came, but he soon found himself "drummed out" of the Charlotte Ministerial Association for attacking other ministers.[72] After many meetings—the exact number escaped recording—Ham finally won a conversion from the young skeptic. Yet a paradox that lay at the heart of the mainstream evangelicals' tradition—and for that matter Graham's own ministry—was the confluence of expressiveness and restraint. He walked a sawdust trail, but to a decorously tearless decision for Christ.

Not surprisingly, Graham's communication style reflected the dominant aural/oral tradition of the Southern evangelical mainstream too. Words reigned. One journalist perceptively dubbed it "flesh made words."[73] Music, of course, proved important, and so did the powerful implicit liturgy of the closing invitation moments. Yet they remained subordinate to the words at the center. At the same time, if Southerners in general and Graham in particular were talkers, they also were writers. No one accused him of being a great one. He never came close to other Christian writers such as Flannery O'Connor and Wendell Berry. Or close to the literary quality of the publications of his wife, Ruth, for that matter. But he and his editorial assistants proved prolific, thirty-two books in all. Graham esteemed the conversionary power of familiar words and short, clear sentences. The texts offered little hint that he knew broadly mainstream evangelical Southern theologians such as John Albert Broadus, J. Gresham Machen, or E. Y. Mullins. Yet he eagerly embraced their style of lucid declarative prose, effective for its purpose of calling for a decision up or down on the basis of consciously grasped and systematically ordered information.

Mainstream evangelicals projected a definable social ethic too. They enjoined neighborliness, local control, and care for one another, at least within if not between racially and ethnically bounded neighborhoods. This system of implicit protocols favored comfortable whites and disfavored both blacks and uncomfortable whites, but to insiders that flaw in the social structure seemed not a serious one because the lines were, in principle, porous. Anyone blessed with sufficient smarts and determination could cross them. Very few lower-class whites and virtually no blacks ever did.

But the principle encouraged the notion—many outside that circle would say illusion—that engaging, not confronting, people was the most effective way to facilitate enduring change.

Graham's relationship to race and the civil rights movement lies ahead. It almost goes without saying that white mainstream evangelicals did not bear much credit for toppling Jim Crow, especially in its most pernicious *de jure* forms. Nonetheless, as the historian David Chappell has shown, they did not try very hard to stop the toppling either. W. A. Criswell was the pastor of First Baptist Church in Dallas, the largest Baptist church in the nation. In 1968 Criswell effectively apologized for his (and other Baptists') long resistance to government-mandated desegregation. "Never had I been so blind," he lamented.[74] In 1995 the Southern Baptist Convention officially apologized for its role in slavery, legally enforced segregation, and the results of white racism. Graham applauded his denomination's attempt to dismantle a system that he, like most white mainstream evangelicals, had once embraced.

Moral Custodianship

Besides representing the exportable Good South and embodying the Southern evangelical mainstream, Graham reflected his region in a third respect. He perennially assumed that the best way to get things done was to work with, not against, established authorities. To be sure, his genial temperament played a role. By nature, he was a bridge-builder, not a finger-pointer. Moreover, his success in dealing with people had led him to believe that all interpersonal relations could be productive if carried out with the right attitude. But more important, it also reflected a deeply rooted assumption that enduring change grew from persuasion, not coercion. Or to switch the metaphor, he, like his friends Presidents Eisenhower and Johnson, believed that a word in the ear worked better than a hammerlock on the arm. "Over the years," the elderly Graham ruminated, "I had developed a deep conviction that personal relationships sometimes do far more to overcome misunderstandings and tensions than formal diplomatic efforts do."[75] Confrontation might produce immediate results, but as soon as one's foes got back up on their feet, they were certain to come out swinging and undo whatever good had been accomplished.

Collaboration rather than confrontation made sense to Graham at least partly because his class location fit that of the men and women who already ran things. They were cut from the same cloth. Despite—or perhaps because of—a long tradition of subaltern violence, a Christian social system policed by orderly Christians felt eminently sensible.[76] In the "Christ-haunted South," in Flannery O'Connor's famous phrase, white Christians presupposed their right to serve as its moral custodians.[77] Graham instinctively understood the power of social networks among like-minded folk. The church in the South enjoyed solid stature at the time he marched into the public eye. There is little evidence that figures who challenged that snug social order—O'Connor, William Faulkner, Tennessee Williams—found much of a voice in mainstream evangelical pulpits.[78] Graham, like other mainstream evangelicals, presumed his right to speak.

Graham unabashedly networked among the rich and the powerful. Leighton Ford would say that in Charlotte by the 1950s Graham knew everyone of consequence. And everyone of consequence knew him.[79] Clearly he enjoyed those associations throughout his career, as the countless photographs of him on the golf course with highly placed politicians and captains of industry made clear. Golf, stereotypically played on country club courses with hefty greens fees, not only served as a marker of class standing and male camaraderie but also offered an opportunity to talk privately with other men of power.[80] "If you want to judge a man's character," Graham confided to Richard Nixon in 1961, "take him to the golf course."[81]

Graham knew that he needed such people to help him do what he wanted to do. Three examples make the point. James S. Bingay, the executive vice president of the Mutual Life Insurance Company of New York, helped bring Graham to Manhattan for the 1957 crusade. George Champion, the executive vice president (and later chairman of the board) of Chase Manhattan National Bank, the nation's second largest financial institution, chaired the crusade. In the meantime, Graham was working closely with J. Howard Pew, the president of Sun Oil Company (later Sunoco) in Philadelphia, and one of the wealthiest men in America, to maintain funding for the fortnightly *Christianity Today*.[82] The symbolism of those associations spoke volumes.

Graham was part of the club, and so was his cultured and legendarily quick-witted wife, Ruth. Her father (and Billy's father-in-law), L. Nelson Bell, had been a medical missionary in China, and on his return maintained a practice in Asheville, North Carolina. In 1942 Bell founded the *Southern Presbyterian Journal* and in 1956 became the executive editor of the newly formed *Christianity Today*. Ruth knew a measure of privilege. We might even say, with a wink, that Ruth taught her husband which fork to use at the state dinner with the queen.

So it was that Graham—the official unofficial chaplain to the nation's power brokers—carried himself effortlessly in the corridors of power. The sociologist Michael Lindsay has written persuasively about the differences between cosmopolitan and populist evangelicals.[83] Graham not only was both but also knew how to slip back and forth between them as readily as a person growing up in a bilingual culture. When he wanted to speak his cosmopolitan dialect, he knew how. He was not born with a silver spoon in his mouth, but he was born with a nearly inerrant intuition that the path of progress lay in doing the right thing the right way—with the right people.

The preacher's view of church and state provides insight into how the implicit protocols of moral custodianship worked out on the ground. Since the 1830s Northern reformers had challenged the Southern church to confront the evil of the region's "peculiar institution"—the reigning euphemism for slavery. Southerners had retorted with the doctrine of the spirituality of the church. Ministers' job, they said, was to tend to spiritual matters and leave temporal ones to the politicians. As things turned out, however, the Southern myth of the spirituality of the church proved not very sturdy. (For that matter, the Northern myth of the wall of separation between the church and the state proved not very sturdy either.) From the 1890s on, the mainstream evangelicals had waded to the top of their hip boots in politics. Though the exact positions church folk took were more varied than commonly supposed, they threw themselves into segregation disputes in the 1890s, antiliquor fights in the 1910s, evolution debates in the 1920s, civil rights clashes in the 1960s, outsourcing quarrels in the 1990s, and immigration controversies in the 2000s. All of which is to say, they knew how to play "political hardball" when it suited their purposes.[84]

Mainstream evangelicals' willingness to ignore the myth of the spirituality of the church grew from a deep-seated assumption that the private and the public rivers merged. That confluence escaped serious critique because it seemed so natural. After all, both emerged from the same Bible. The idea that the private and the public realms blended was certainly not unique to the South, but it remained especially strong in that region throughout the twentieth and into the twenty-first centuries.[85]

Graham had a personal stake in the outcome. Over the years, he had benefited from countless favors from government officials, who blurred the lines or even bent the rules to accommodate his work. In 1952, for example, Congress passed a law allowing him to hold a service on the steps of the Capitol.[86] In 1968, when he visited Vietnam, the U.S. military ferried him from site to site and took him for a ride off an aircraft carrier.[87] In

1971, the city of Charlotte dismissed public schools so that children could participate in the Honor Billy Graham Day celebrations.[88] In 1991, when Graham held the largest religious meeting in the history of New York's Central Park, the parks commissioner reportedly relaxed the requirement that Graham's group "cover cleanup costs."[89] And so the story ran, decade after decade.

How did Graham view those favors? Clearly he saw nothing wrong with them. If challenged, he probably would have said that he had done many favors for the government, too. More than once he had served, for example, as an unofficial courier for a private message from the president to a foreign head of state or provided a private briefing on his travels for the president.[90] The preacher and the presidents simply helped one another out. But was mutual help of that sort legitimate? Differently asked, in Graham's mind, how did those interactions fit into the First Amendment's limitations on government establishment of religion?

Here Graham's thinking about the Supreme Court is instructive. Early on Graham believed that public schools should permit state-sponsored Bible reading. In 1963 the Court handed down the *Abington v. Schempp* decision, which disallowed it. Graham purportedly called the Court's judgment "a victory for atheism."[91] Soon, however, his Baptist instincts about the separation of church and state kicked in and he offered different reasons for his objection to the ruling. One was the democratic principle: the majority of Americans wanted it.[92] A second reason was the inoffensiveness of the practice if it remained strictly voluntary.[93] Here he betrayed little sensitivity to the coercive power that supposedly voluntary arrangements entailed. Like a true son of a society in which everyone who mattered was of the same mind, he did not grasp that nonincorporation equaled exclusion and effective disenfranchisement. A third reason was historical: the founders had intended to dismantle state-sponsored churches, not denude public life of religious values, including the Jewish-Christian ones that the vast majority of Americans held.[94]

But Graham's main concern—and this would be a fourth reason—pertained less to the present than to what the Court's decisions portended for the future. Did they mean that Congress no longer could begin with prayer? Or that chaplains no longer could serve in the military? The Supreme Court never should have gotten itself into this situation in the first place. There was no telling where it would end.[95]

Displaying the Ten Commandments in classrooms and courthouses rested on a different rationale. Graham did not claim that viewing them should be voluntary or that they should be placed in public places because of popular demand. Rather, he argued that displaying the Ten Commandments was a good idea because they embodied the moral bedrock of Americans' life together. He said they belonged to a "more of a unitarian type of religion." Presidents did not talk about Jesus Christ in public statements, he pointed out. But they did talk about God. "We have on our coins 'In God We Trust.' It's in our Pledge of Allegiance."[96] That kind of rhetoric did not puncture the spirituality of the church or breach the wall of separation. It simply expressed the moral assumptions that undergirded the entire society.[97] On that point, he insisted, Protestants, Catholics, and Jews agreed.[98] The views of secularists and members of other religions did not (yet) enter his mental picture.

When Graham thought about the connected problems of pornography and censorship he came away troubled. Repeatedly he insisted that censorship violated the best of American traditions. No one wanted it. Yet pornography was out of hand. It threatened the nation's moral foundations. On that, thoughtful men and women of all persuasions agreed. So it was that he urged "guidelines" about what was and was not acceptable, but he did not say who should issue the guidelines or how they should be enforced.[99] He may have considered the problem above his pay grade. Or a knot that had to be untangled on a case-by-case basis. Most likely he thought that if upright men and women got together and worked out some clear guidelines, the moral pressure to observe them would be sufficient. Such a solution made perfect sense for a Southerner accustomed to the merging of private and public realms in a society governed by the implicit but powerful rules of moral custodianship.

As the years passed, Graham expressed a more nuanced view of church and state. He rarely explicitly renounced previous positions but started to talk about them in subtler ways. In 1976, for example, he told reporters that churches should pay taxes on income-producing properties.[100] More surprising, when it came to choosing a person for political office, the candidate's competence should take precedence over his or her faith. There are, he said, "many, many great Christians in America that are not qualified for a particular office, such as myself. . . . Morality, character, ability—all of these things must be taken into consideration."[101]

As for pluralism, at some deep level Graham surely *wanted* the nation to become wholly Christian. What evangelist would not? But as a practical matter pluralism was here to stay. He told President Nixon that he should not be the only clergyman to speak at his inauguration. Nixon protested, but Graham insisted, "Dick, you've got to have all faiths represented." The preacher suggested other names, including his "friend and supporter Rabbi Edgar Fogel Magnin."[102]

As Graham matured he consistently affirmed pluralism in the civil sphere. In 1989, for example, the editor of the Salvation Army's *War Cry* asked him about the increasing influence of Islam. "I have some wonderful friends among the Muslim people," Graham replied, "and have great respect and tolerance for them. Because we are a pluralistic society, we are going to have to recognize that we are no longer just a Jewish and Christian society."[103] Four years later, Graham warmly endorsed a new scholarly study of religious pluralism in the United States, tellingly titled *One Nation under God: Religion in Contemporary American Society*. "This study could make a major contribution to reversing this deplorable trend [toward intolerance] and renewing the spirit of genuine tolerance and respect for those of different traditions," he said in a cover blurb.[104]

Graham affirmed pluralism in symbolic ways, too, and those may have proved more forceful. Later we will look at the significance of Graham's participation in the National Day of Prayer and Remembrance, on September 14, 2001, at the National Cathedral in Washington, DC, when he stood shoulder to shoulder with a mainline Protestant clergyman, a Catholic priest, a Jewish rabbi, and a Muslim imam. Here, the key point to notice was his statement, half-way through, that he would now address the Christians in his audience. Unlike many evangelicals, Graham understood that Christians did not own the public forum.

Though Graham did grow more thoughtful about the implications of pluralism, it also should be said that most of the time the complexities of church-state separation remained a nonissue for him. He instinctively sensed that at the level of daily life most Americans and especially most Southerners simply did not care all that much about it. On the big questions, such as explicit government support for a single denomination, especially Catholics, they did, but for the general flow of things, they did not. He intuited that the position later articulated by *Newsweek*'s Jon Meacham was right. The United States was neither a Christian nation nor *not* a Christian nation.[105] Rather, it was a secular nation in which Christians constituted a majority of the inhabitants and held most of the historic oars of power. The results were predictable, especially in the South, where the rivers had blended since time immemorial.

Civil Rights I

Context is important, and nowhere more than with reference to Graham and civil rights. Needless to say, the late 1940s and 1950s saw a growing sense everywhere, including in the South, of the unacceptability of legally mandated and culturally enforced divisions on the basis of race and unearned privilege. Enduring markers of the era included the 1954 Supreme Court's *Brown v. Board of Education* decision, which invalidated the long-standing principle of "separate but equal" in American public education, and the 1964 and 1965 federal civil rights laws, which outlawed discrimination in public facilities and guaranteed voting rights to all citizens.

Crucial developments in the religious culture included the growing refusal of the majority of Southern denominations to support segregation (not quite the same as supporting integration), the firm commitment of the flagship mainline Protestant periodical, the *Christian Century*, to civil rights, the initial foot dragging but ultimately parallel commitment of the flagship evangelical periodical, *Christianity Today*, to the same goal, and the articulation of a powerful agenda for social reform, including racial justice, by leading evangelicals in the landmark 1973 *Chicago Declaration of Evangelical Social Concern*.

No feature of Graham's career has received more scrutiny than his relationship to the civil rights struggles of the era.[106] And no feature has provoked more polarized interpretations, ranging from incredulous to admiring. Unsympathetic observers pointed out that he wavered on the integration of his Southern crusades, in 1958 invited the segregationist governor of Texas to introduce his San Antonio crusade, in 1963 urged Martin Luther King, Jr., to slow things down a bit, and that he never marched in the streets, went to jail, or threw his power and prestige behind fundamental structural reforms. Sympathetic observers, by contrast, countered that he moved to integrate his crusades before *Brown v. Board of Education*, that he forthrightly endorsed the early Martin Luther King, Jr. (until King started attacking the president's Vietnam War policies); that he suffered opposition from White Citizens Councils, multiple threats on his and his family's lives, and, most painful, the loss of friends for his pro–civil rights position, and that he won the support of African American associates, numerous African American pastors, and uncounted African American lay followers. Political figures split, too. In Graham's later years, presidential candidate Jesse Jackson lamented the insufficiency of his efforts for racial justice. Former president Bill Clinton, in contrast, praised his courage in the civil rights struggle.[107]

It is hard to adjudicate among these views. Interpretations said as much about historians and journalists, and the standards they used to evaluate people, as they did about Graham himself and his actual record. How observers evaluated Graham's relation to the civil rights movement depended on the criteria they used. Which was more important: prophetic words and bold actions? Or the steady witness of a half-century of integrated crusades? When it came to race, said William Martin, Graham's premier biographer, the preacher was "typically ahead of his own unit, but never at the head of the parade."[108] Yet figuring out exactly where the front of the parade was, and exactly where the unit was, and exactly where Graham's position was, is not so easy. The task requires examination from several angles.

Besides the major differences of perspective and priorities just noted, two additional problems complicate the analysis. One is the tendency of historians to impose artificial dichotomies on the story, framing Graham as a traditionalist *or* a progressive, a retarder *or* a promoter of racial progress. Those categories prove more ahistorical than not. Close examination reveals a more fluid situation, marked by ambiguity, slippage between motives and the ability to execute them, and significant differences among and within regions where he ministered.[109] The second problem is figuring out which set of years and which geographic location should be regarded as normative. Graham changed, but not always in a linear way. And his efforts toward racial progress bore different results in different places.

It may be most helpful to begin with a bare-bones chronological summary of the key events in the story. With that framework in hand, we can then turn to an analysis of their implications for understanding Graham's relation to civil rights, to the South, and to American life after World War II.

The first task is to place Graham in historical context. His father employed numerous workers on his prosperous 300-acre dairy farm in North Carolina in the 1920s and 1930s. They included African Americans and at least one Hispanic. In 1960 Graham acknowledged that he grew to maturity influenced by the polite paternalism of middle- to upper-middle-class whites of the New South. "Segregation was taken for granted. If there were Negroes who chafed in their status as second-class citizens, I was not aware of them. . . . Even after my conversion, I felt no guilt in thinking of my dark-skinned brothers in the usual patronizing and paternalistic way."[110] (In some ways he never outgrew that outlook. Near the end of his life, in his memoir, he described Reece Brown, a black foreman, as a distinguished war veteran, a man of "great intelligence," and "one of Daddy's best personal friends." He also fondly remembered Brown's wife's "fabulous buttermilk biscuits.")[111] The public schools were of course segregated, and so were the churches. Graham's sister Jean later recalled that when she and their mother went to a church in Charlotte to hear Billy preach, they had to sit in the balcony because the family's black maid had gone with them.[112]

That was about 1937. Not surprisingly, there were no African Americans at either of the Southern colleges Graham attended, Bob Jones College and Florida Bible Institute.[113] Graham remembered that "the first blacks [he] had ever gone to school with" were at Wheaton College, which he entered in 1940 at age twenty-one.[114] One black student came to his room one day and talked "with deep conviction about America's need for racial justice."[115] Graham did not identify the African Americans he met at the college or the one who came to his room. Details about minority students at Wheaton during Graham's tenure remain murky.[116] The key point is that black peers remained either absent or an elusive presence throughout his childhood, adolescence, and young adulthood.

Graham's first serious encounter with the question of race seems to have taken place about 1951. Until then, in his meetings in the South, he had simply reproduced Billy Sunday's pattern of preaching to separate black and white audiences or to audiences with divided seating.[117] Many years later a British evangelist recalled that when he visited Graham in Tampa, Florida, in 1951, he and Graham talked about segregation. Graham saw nothing wrong with it.[118] Separating the races seemed to be the natural order of things.

But about that time he started to reassess. At a meeting of the Southern Baptist Convention in San Francisco that same year he urged his denomination to open its colleges to academically qualified African Americans. The following year, at a crusade in Jackson, Mississippi, blacks and whites sat apart, in segregated sections.[119] During the meeting, Graham told the *Jackson Daily News*, "It touches my heart when I see white stand shoulder in shoulder with black at the cross." The next day, in an interview with a different paper, he waffled, stating: "the Bible . . . has nothing to say about segregation or de-segregation." Yet two months later in a communication to the head of the Detroit Council of Churches he reasserted his critique of segregation.[120] In the words of the historian Steven P. Miller, "The Jackson crusade . . . featured only a premature expression of antisegregationist sentiments that had yet to congeal."[121]

The year 1953 marked a watershed. In March Graham started a four-week crusade in Chattanooga, Tennessee. State laws prohibited miscegenation, with severe penalties for violators, and mandated segregation in schools, transportation, and public accommodations. Graham told the organizing committee that he would not preach if a rope separated the races. Exactly what happened when he arrived is not clear, but either at the outset or sometime during the crusade he personally tore down the ropes. Irate, the head usher stomped out.[122] Later that spring, Graham wavered. In Dallas in May/June the crusade committee designated separate seating for blacks and whites until the services started at 7:30. "Please be courteous in directing our colored friends to their section," read the instructions for the ushers.[123] Graham's authorized biographer, John Pollock, reported in 1966 that Graham "reluctantly accepted their decision."[124] With the likely exception of a meeting in Asheville, North Carolina, in November of that year— the evidence is not definitive—segregated seating never again appeared in a Billy Graham crusade.[125] What *is* clear is that Graham did not go through an epiphany experience about segregation. Rather, he, like many conscience-torn Southern evangelicals—"cautious reformers"—was still feeling his way along the edges of a new social order.[126]

The year 1956 saw significant movement in Graham's approach to non-segregation (as it was called). In that period he published articles in *Life* and in *Ebony* in which he named racism as *sin* and deplored the separation of races in churches.[127] Graham allowed that sometimes the races voluntarily segregated themselves because of cultural preferences, and that was acceptable, but enforced segregation was not. On one hand, the articles were tempered because he did not call for specific legislation or political actions such as school busing. On the other hand, naming racism as *sin* constituted a major step for a Southern white evangelical and for his preponderantly white constituency. He condemned white Christians—the context made clear that he had whites mainly in mind—for allowing "secular influences as the military, sports, and television [to do] more to combat racial prejudice than many churches."[128] People might try to find reasons for defending segregation in the Bible, but they could not. "There are a lot of segregationists," Graham declared, "who are going to be sadly disillusioned when they get to Heaven—if they get there."[129] The best means for dealing with the sin of racism might be debatable but the goal was not. The venues in which he wrote were significant. *Life* enjoyed a readership of twenty-five million.[130] *Ebony*'s readership was smaller, but it reached a mostly black audience. By publishing in those two forums Graham signaled to both whites and blacks where he stood.

Several events of significance took place during Graham's crusade in Madison Square Garden in 1957. Recognizing that the audience in the Garden was overwhelmingly white but the city was not, he invited the Reverend

Howard Jones, an African American pastor in Cleveland, to come to New York to counsel the Team. Jones told him to take the crusade to blacks, not wait for them to come to him. Shortly afterward, Graham conducted meetings in Harlem and in Brooklyn with audiences of 8,000 and of 10,000, respectively. At Graham's invitation Jones stayed, but things were not easy. On the crusade platform, Jones recalled, seats next to him remained empty as white participants moved to the other side. Still, by the end of the crusade, the African American presence may have risen to 20 percent. Graham invited Jones to join the Team as associate evangelist. The following year he came on board.[131]

Detouring for a moment, in 1965, Dr. Ralph S. Bell, an African Canadian-American pastor in Los Angeles, joined Jones on the Team. After King's assassination in 1968, Jones and Bell hoped Graham would commission a film aimed at both whites and blacks that would forthrightly address questions of racial justice.[132] Evidently believing that his record was already clear enough, Graham did not do so.[133] The documents contain intimations that Jones hoped for more visible support for civil rights from Graham in other ways, too.[134] Nonetheless, Jones publically expressed gratitude for what Graham had accomplished rather than targeting what he had not. Reflecting on whites' hostility to Graham's racial overtures, Jones would say in his 2003 autobiography that "no other white evangelical leader of his prominence put himself on the line for civil rights as much as Billy, even if he did not pass each and every litmus test of the black establishment."[135] Jones and Bell remained with the Team until they retired in 1993 and in 2004, respectively.[136]

Returning to the Madison Square Garden crusade, on Graham's invitation, Martin Luther King, Jr., offered the invocation on July 18, 1957. Introducing King, Graham thanked him for taking time from his busy schedule and praised him for leading a "great social revolution." In the prayer, King in turn thanked Graham and asked God's blessing on the meetings.[137] Four days later Graham told a mostly black audience of 8,000 in Brooklyn: "some people are not going to get to heaven because they will not feel at home . . . color is meaningless in the sight of God." A *Baltimore Afro-American* headline declared: "Graham says country needs 'anti-segregation legislation.'"[138] The following month King sent a note to Graham expressing gratitude for "the stand [that] you have taken in the area of race relations. You have courageously brought the Christian gospel to bear on the question of race in all of its urgent dimensions."[139] Neither man explicitly allied himself with the other one's work, but the implication seemed clear.

Beyond the mutual overtures between Graham and King, the Garden saw an additional development of great but underappreciated historical significance. Graham and Barrows enlisted Ethel Waters and Mahalia Jackson, two celebrated black recording artists, to sing there and at other meetings. They launched a tradition. In later decades the crusades routinely featured many—perhaps dozens—of black (and other ethnic minority) entertainers, including Andrae Crouch and the Montreal Jubilation Gospel Choir.[140]

These various events—Graham taking the crusade to Harlem, bringing Howard Jones on board, forging a public link with King, and launching a tradition of minority guest artists—marked a turning point in Graham's relationship with the African American community. By 1964 two of the nine associate evangelists were African American, and another one (Akbar Abdul-Haqq) was Indian.[141] Understandably, the third event—the involvement with King—has received by far the most attention from historians and journalists. Yet common experience suggests that the fourth—the foregrounding of minority artists—may have exerted more influence in the long run. The *New York Times* and *Washington Post* commended Graham for integrating the crusade choirs early.[142] Artists' visible link with Graham was continual, not episodic, and it revolved around music, where emotions ran deep.

Graham's contributions to the civil rights movement in the late 1950s yielded a mixed picture. In the summer of 1958 Graham's relationship with King suffered a blow. Graham had scheduled a two-day crusade in San Antonio for July 25–26. With his approval, the organizing committee invited Price Daniel, the forthrightly Christian and forthrightly segregationist governor of Texas, to introduce Graham.[143] Catching wind of the invitation, the Baptist Ministers Union of the city asked King to approach Graham about rescinding the invitation. Since July 25 marked the eve of the Democratic primary (then the key election in Texas politics), the ministers felt that Price's presence would be taken as Graham's endorsement of Price's segregationist policy.[144] King agreed. He told Graham that "any implied endorsement by you of segregation can have damaging effect on the struggle of Negro Americans for human dignity and will greatly reduce the importance of your message to them as a Christian minister."[145] Graham declined to withdraw the invitation. Through a spokesman, he insisted that the invitation was not political "on one side or the other," and that he had faced opposition for inviting King to New York.[146] Daniel appeared, won the election by 60 percent, and retained Graham's warm friendship through his term of office. The historian Steven Miller judged that thereafter the relationship between Graham and King "vacillated between mostly private warmth and occasional public frostiness" into the 1960s, when their differences widened.[147]

The year 1960 marked progress. In 1960 Graham and King found themselves together at a Hilton Hotel in Puerto Rico, where they had stopped en route to the Baptist World Alliance meeting in Rio de Janeiro. Graham remembered they did "a lot of swimming and praying together." Graham recalled that King asked him to call him by his nickname, Mike, a name reserved for personal friends. In Rio, Graham hosted a dinner in King's honor.[148] Graham later remembered that "early on" King urged him not to demonstrate in the streets, which might cause him to lose the ear of his preponderantly white constituency. Rather, King hoped that Graham would maintain his clear testimony for civil rights by the stance he was taking in his great stadium crusades.[149] King's papers said nothing about the conversation, so it is hard to verify the accuracy of Graham's memory.

Regardless, the point Graham wished to convey at Madison Square Garden and in his autobiography four decades later was that he supported the civil rights movement. He also undoubtedly hoped people would think King endorsed his own, less confrontational approach. The following month—August 1960—Graham published an article in *Reader's Digest* in which he deplored the churches' segregation. Again, the venue was critical. *Reader's Digest*, with a circulation of twelve million, ranked as one of the most widely read periodicals in the world and appealed powerfully to ordinary Americans. In the essay, as noted, Graham quoted the "byword" that Martin Luther King, Jr., often used in the 1950s and 1960s: "the most segregated hour of the week is still 11 o'clock Sunday morning."[150]

The single year stretching from the spring of 1963 to the spring of 1964 in Birmingham, Alabama, cradled both tragedy and courage. King led a major civil rights demonstration in April, which resulted in his imprisonment and the publication of the eloquent and influential *Letter from Birmingham Jail* on April 16. The *Letter* blasted well-meaning white moderates for the timidity of their support. Though King did not specifically name him, Graham surely saw himself in King's crosshairs. On May 18 several hundred people were arrested. Graham famously urged King to "put the brakes on a little bit." The same day the *New York Times* reported that Graham "declined to call himself a 'thoroughgoing integrationist.' "[151] To be sure, Graham was not the only "cautious reformer." Attorney General Robert Kennedy and the *Washington Post* echoed Graham's concerns about the timing and the utility of the demonstrations.[152] Nonetheless, Graham did not attend the March on Washington that King led on August 23, 1963. He may not have been invited (I have found no evidence either way), but he surely could have attended if he had wanted to do so.

Then things changed. On September 15 the Ku Klux Klan bombed the black Sixteenth Street Baptist Church in Birmingham and four girls perished. King's description of Birmingham as "the most thoroughly segregated city in the United States" with an "ugly record of brutality" gained force.[153] Despite threats from the White Citizens Council, Graham accepted an invitation to hold a crusade in Birmingham. The following Easter Sunday, March 29, Graham journeyed to Birmingham and hosted the largest thoroughly integrated audience in the state's history.[154] According to the *New York Times*, the sponsoring committee "was composed of whites and Negroes, Roman Catholic, Jewish, and Protestant laymen."[155] The gathering numbered 30,000 souls, with "thoroughly mixed seating patterns."[156] The audience was equally white and black. The choir, boasting 3,500 voices from 700 Alabama churches, was also roughly divided between whites and blacks.[157] A black minister offered the benediction.[158] The heavy police presence proved unneeded.

The mid-1960s witnessed more twists and turns. When Congress passed the Civil Rights Act of 1964 and the Voting Rights Act of 1965, Graham endorsed both. The endorsement was coupled with the caution that legislation alone would not bring enduring equality. Only Christ could do that by changing people's hearts and the social order when he returned in glory at the end of history.[159] Graham's statement about the civil rights legislation was not enough for listeners on his left and too much for listeners on his right. But then, in the summer of 1965, Watts, California, erupted in flames. Graham attributed the violence to outsider agitators. He insisted that most people in Watts were law-abiding victims, and lawful protest was the only effective way to get things done.[160] Looking back, he appeared to be dragging his feet, and perhaps he was, but he was not alone in his hesitation. The year before Watts, 35 percent of Americans believed that black leaders were moving too fast. The year after, that number had swelled to 85 percent.[161]

Graham had toured the devastated area by helicopter with his close friend, the influential moderate black evangelical pastor E. V. Hill. His friendship with Hill symbolized a large (and underanalyzed) pattern. Hill was the charismatic pastor of Mt. Zion Missionary Baptist Church in Los Angeles for forty-two years. Thoroughly evangelical in theology, he later served on the BGEA's Board of Directors. He represented moderately progressive middle-class blacks uncomfortable with the confrontational tactics of the Southern Christian Leadership Conference. Like Graham, he thought there were more effective ways to accomplish the same goals.[162]

This is the context in which we need to understand the substantial civil rights–related correspondence between Graham and Presidents Eisenhower and Nixon. Typical was a letter from Eisenhower to Graham in 1956, in which the president explained that he would always be "a champion of real, as opposed to spurious, progress, [and] remain a moderate in this regard." Typical, too, was a letter Graham returned to Eisenhower two months later. "I had several private meetings with outstanding religious leaders of both races," Graham recounted. He said he encouraged the leaders to take "a stronger stand in calling for desegregation and yet demonstrating charity and, above all, patience." Then for Eisenhower's own benefit he wrote: "If the Supreme Court will go slowly and the extremists on both sides will quiet down, we can have a peaceful social readjustment. I am more hopeful now than I was . . . in March."[163]

Nixon sought Graham's help in forging positive relationships with middle-class, moderately progressive black pastors.[164] Graham obliged, once organizing a meeting between seven such men and President Nixon—a gathering that ran three and one-half hours. Graham later told the *New York Times* that he was trying to serve "the black community," not Nixon. Presidential advisor H. R. Haldeman told another advisor that the president was "extremely interested" in the work Graham was doing with Negro ministers, especially E. V. Hill. It "may be our best chance to make inroads with the Negro community," Nixon felt.[165]

As the tumult of the mid-1960s grew, the relationship between Graham and King deteriorated. King widened his protests to target the Vietnam War. At that time Graham publically supported the war and sharply criticized King. He condemned King for involving himself simultaneously in the civil rights movement and in war protests—implying that the latter diluted the force of the former. And since blacks, too, surely were divided about the war, King's actions constituted "an affront to thousands of loyal Negro troops."[166] Though Graham did not say so, it is possible that his friend J. Edgar Hoover influenced him about King too.[167]

When King was assassinated in April 1968, Graham was holding a crusade in Australia. He said that the killing left him "almost in a state of shock."[168] He sent telegrams and flowers. "Many people who have not agreed with Dr. King can admire him for his non-violent policies," he stated, "and in the eyes of the world he has become one of the greatest Americans."[169] William Martin, Graham's sympathetic biographer, judged the tribute "muted."[170] Five weeks later Graham told reporters in Los Angeles that the murder was "one of the greatest tragedies in American history."[171]

Regardless, King was the absent presence throughout Graham's life, both before and after King's death. For many Americans, King and Graham were each the standard against which the other was measured. If King called for dramatic change in the structures of public life, Graham called for dramatic change in the structures of personal life. Each had something to learn from the other. Not a few dreamed about what might have been accomplished if they had worked together more closely in the later years of King's life.[172]

If the 1950s represented two steps forward and the 1960s one step back in Graham's relationship to the civil right movement, the 1970s and 1980s represented another two steps forward. In 1973 Graham preached in Durban, South Africa, to a mixed-race crowd of 100,000 in the first major mixed-race meeting in the nation's history. Though some criticized him for avoiding the explosive word *apartheid*, he declared with great vigor that Christ was neither black nor white but the Savior for all people. The Durban Sunday paper headline thundered: "Apartheid Doomed." Graham's next stop was Johannesburg. In 1960 he had declined to speak in that city because his hosts insisted on a segregated audience. This time, 1973, he prevailed. And again, his meeting formed the first major mixed-race meeting in the city's history.[173]

The culmination of Graham's pilgrimage toward a strong racial witness—and one from which he never retreated—took place at the Patriarchal Cathedral in Moscow in 1982. There he stated that he had undergone three conversions in his life: to Christ, to racial justice, and to nuclear disarmament.[174] If pressed, Graham undoubtedly would have given priority to his conversion to Christ. Nonetheless, even with that qualification, the statement stood a universe away from the preacher of the late 1940s and early 1950s who had unselfconsciously reproduced Billy Sunday's system of segregated meetings or seating.

In the remaining years of his public ministry Graham said relatively little about civil rights, as his attention increasingly turned toward the perils of nuclear war. But he routinely included racism in the list of sins—not mistakes, but *sins*—that tore apart the nation's and the world's social fabric.

He spoke of the need for legislative corrections for a problem that started in the heart and would persist in one form or another until Christ intervened.[175] In 1994 he told a *Life* magazine journalist that marriage between blacks and whites was "part of the answer" to America's racial problem: "We've got to be totally integrated—in our homes, in our worship services, even in marriage." In a separate interview he allowed that society would resist miscegenation, but people could find no warrant for resisting it in the Bible.[176] In a related move, Graham would change his mind about capital punishment. By 1976 he was not sure what the Bible had to say about it one way or another, but he was sure that in America it had proved unjust. "White people had somehow been able to get out of it," he declared. The punishment fell disproportionately on blacks. Absent an "ironclad system of absolute justice," he would oppose it.[177]

Civil Rights II

This bare-bones chronology of some of the key events related to civil rights in Graham's career now calls for examination. The story is so charged with political and ethical implications that it is difficult to approach it without assigning blame or praise at every step. The challenge, then, is not to sermonize but to contextualize and then to analyze.

In several respects, Graham's ministry merits critique by both the standards of his time and his own best lights. Working up the ladder of importance, we might begin with the undeniable fact that *Christianity Today*, which he helped establish in 1956 (in 2014 he remained on the editors' page as "Founder" and "Honorary Chairman"), dragged its feet on civil rights until the 1970s and did not get fully on board until the 1980s. On the whole the periodical, like most white evangelicals, especially outside the South, supported the goal but resisted the tactics.[178] Yet two caveats are needed. One is that *Christianity Today* deserved more credit than it usually received. Throughout that period a steady stream of surprisingly progressive editorial and news pieces appeared. They were episodic and constituted a minority view, but they were never absent.[179] The second caveat is that the one who exercised final control over the content of each issue was not Graham but his father-in-law, L. Nelson Bell, who served as executive editor from the magazine's founding in 1956 until his death in 1973.[180] By all accounts, Bell was more conservative on social issues than Graham.[181] Still, Graham's voice was not mute, and common sense tells us he could have intervened more if he had chosen to do so.

A second problem was that Graham recurrently went out of his way to point out that racism was not a uniquely Southern flaw. It existed in the North and for that matter worldwide.[182] Factually, of course, Graham was right. But by universalizing the problem, Graham's words seemed to minimize the South's culpability. Graham was an extraordinarily articulate man. He was capable of making plain that the South's history of legal enslavement of African Americans placed it in a position of peculiar liability, and that the malign effects of Jim Crow persisted in the South more stubbornly than in most parts of the United States. This, Graham failed to do.

A third difficulty was that Graham backed away from confrontations with racial injustice at crucial points. Reasonable critics did not expect him to undergo a personality transplant and trade in his irenic disposition for a confrontational one. But sometimes his pacific instincts seemed to slip into faintheartedness. Graham's unwillingness to withdraw the invitation to the segregationist governor Price Daniel, on the eve of a major election, in the face of impassioned resistance from local black ministers and from Graham's friend Martin Luther King, Jr., constituted one example. In 2014 one outside scholar, otherwise favorably disposed toward Graham, was still scratching his head on the San Antonio debacle.[183]

Often Graham seemed reluctant to take a firm a stand and not hedge it. So it was that in the 1960s and early 1970s, especially, he usually coupled calls for civil rights legislation with warnings that peaceful law-abiding protest was the only practical way to make progress. Gerald Durley, a dean at Clark Atlanta University and pastor of Providence Missionary Baptist Church in Atlanta, became a strong supporter of Graham when Graham brought his crusade to Atlanta in 1994. But back in the mid-1960s, Durley wrote, the message of "the Billy Graham Crusades" had proved "conspicuously silent on the atrocities against God's people."[184]

And finally, throughout his career Graham talked about racial "tension" or "extremists" or the racial "problem" as if it were a matter of mutual intransigence.[185] In some situations, that surely was true, but in the long perspective of American history, no one could reasonably argue for the moral equivalence of the fears held by blacks and by whites. Moreover, talk about tension and extremists and problems between the races trivialized the crisis by suggesting that people could fix it without great effort or sustained sacrifice. Sometimes Graham came across as saying, give your life to Christ, bury your prejudices, and just go out and do the right thing. In his better moments, he knew better. He knew that the corrupt heart, which traded in greed, cruelty, violence, and bigotry, required not only radical regeneration but also radical schooling in how to dismantle asymmetric structures of power. But often that was not how he presented himself.

In the 1950s and 1960s he also explicitly and implicitly urged the gradual dismantling of structures of segregation. In different ways he seemed to say: give everyone time to get accustomed to the new order of things. The most generous interpretation of Graham's view here is that he saw gradualism as the only realistic way to move forward at all. Yet Graham's rhetoric did not show that he understood black desperation in any deep way. His upbringing and his own comfortable social location limited his vision.

The story of Graham and civil rights holds another side, however. First, it is important to avoid the sin of historical anachronism: imposing expectations on Graham drawn from a later era. As noted, he freely admitted that as a child of the South, he simply did not think about the immorality of segregation until he moved north in his early twenties. Context was crucial. In 1970, nearly twenty years after Graham admonished his own Southern Baptist Convention about their racism, only 510 of the its 35,000 congregations claimed one or more blacks among their members, and three-fourths of those were situated outside the South.[186] It is hard to think of another white evangelical of Graham's generation, social location, and breadth of constituency who posted a stronger record. A few outliers come to mind, such as Southern Baptist liberals Will Campbell and Carlyle Marney, but they enjoyed a tiny fraction of Graham's following.[187]

The second and third points bear on Graham's self-understanding. One was the depth of Graham's distaste for confrontation, coupled with his preference for orderly means of redress. In multiple contexts—including, for example, his behind-the-scenes efforts on behalf of Jews in the Soviet Union—Graham endeavored to work with rather than against established authority.[188] And then there was his absolute conviction that enduring change had to begin where the problem started, in the corrupt heart, which would subvert any set of laws it disliked. He often said that laws like the civil rights acts of the mid-1960s were necessary—they should be passed and rigorously enforced—but Americans were fooling themselves if they thought that laws of that sort would remove the poison of hatred and self-interest in the soul. "Now, we have the greatest Civil Rights laws in the history of the World," Graham insisted to reporters in Detroit in 1976, "yet we haven't seen them totally implemented simply because hearts haven't been changed."[189] Only Christ could address the real root of the problem.

The fourth point bears on the criticism frequently leveled by journalists and historians that Graham only dimly understood that reaching out to

black churches was not the same as addressing Jim Crow as a social/struc-
tural problem. Nor did he understand that the goal of "color blindness"
was insufficient. Differently stated, he did not see that color blindness as a
strategy for racial justice worked only if the playing field was level to start
with. The criticism held merit. Graham did not understand that unequal
access yielded unequal results.

Yet Graham was hardly alone. In those mid-century years many white
and some black evangelicals firmly believed that color blindness really was
the goal. "Playing by the rules," so that exactly the same criteria were applied to everyone, regardless of color, when they applied to schools or
sought jobs, formed the heart of the democratic process. When Martin Luther King, Jr., famously proclaimed that he looked for the day when his
children would be judged by the content of their character rather than the
color of their skin, Graham effectively took him at his word.[190] If Graham
had enjoyed the benefit of advanced education he might have seen the flaws
in the color-blind position. Or if racial injustice had formed the center of
his concerns, drawing him into focused, sustained engagement with the issue, he might have seen things differently. But it was not. Racism was rarely
if ever absent from his range of concerns, but it always marched alongside
others.

The most important point is that Graham not only changed but also
changed dramatically. To be sure, it is easy to find instances throughout the
years in which Graham seemed to talk out of both sides of his mouth. In
sermons and press conferences he issued eloquent calls for racial justice, yet
sometimes he also seemed to take it back by suggesting that not much really could be done until Christ returned. Was he soft-pedaling? Or was he
stating that the snake of racism would persist in one form or another till
the end of time? More important, what did Americans hear? Did they hear
an excuse to do nothing? Or did they hear a command to shoulder the task,
knowing that it would never be complete? For supporters, at least, the integration of the crusade audiences, references to racism as sin, diversification
of the platform guests and artists, and incorporation of African Americans
in the planning and counseling phases of the crusades betokened a man
with both a changed heart and clarified vision.

How do these considerations help us understand Graham and race in
modern America? All but the most ardent fans likely would acknowledge
that he could have done more. But he did accomplish something vitally
important: he both legitimated justice and removed injustice from the list.
Though he was not always as forthright as he might have been, even by the

standards of his time and place, he made it difficult for millions of people publically to resist racial justice and still call themselves Christian. Graham took that option off the table.

This argument is impossible to prove in any hard and fast way, but intimations abound. Three examples taken from Southern contexts suffice. In September 1957 both President Eisenhower and Vice President Nixon phoned Graham before sending National Guard troops into Little Rock, Arkansas, to enforce federal law mandating the integration of Central High School. They claimed they wanted his advice. Graham told the president he had no choice.[191] Eisenhower undoubtedly knew perfectly well what he intended to do. Presidents did not take marching orders from preachers. What Eisenhower wanted was not Graham's advice but his support. Within hours Graham's words had been leaked to the press. The president got what he wanted.

The second example also comes from Little Rock, this one two years later. On that occasion Graham traveled to the racially explosive city to hold a crusade. He went despite strident objections from local business groups, the Ku Klux Klan, and the White Citizens Council, which distributed forty thousand flyers opposing his integrationist "agenda."[192] Graham's terms included insistence that the crusade be fully integrated, which it was. Characteristically, he promised that he would avoid "inflammatory statements or preach on the subject of race," but just as characteristically he engaged the issue in a symbolically powerful way: integrated seating.[193] As it happened, a thirteen-year-old boy from Hope, Arkansas, visited the crusade that opening night. Forty-seven years later Bill Clinton vividly recalled how the evening had transformed his life. He saw that Graham chose to confront racial segregation even though his career was already secure and he had nothing to gain from it—except a clear conscience. "He is about the only person I know who I've never seen fail to live his faith," the former president told a sweltering outdoor audience of eighty thousand at Graham's last crusade in June 2005.[194]

A final story illustrates the constructive—if measured—results of Graham's approach to racial justice, especially in the South. Following the three historic marches from Selma to Montgomery in March 1965—including the ill-famed Bloody Sunday trek over the Edmund Pettus Bridge—the (white) Dothan Ministerial Association and the (black) Dothan Ministerial Alliance issued a joint invitation to Graham to hold a crusade in their city.[195] Graham canceled a European tour and agreed to hold a crusade on April 23–24. A white pastor and a black pastor chaired the sponsoring committee. On the eve of the first service, Graham would offer a classic Graham judgment: "the very fact the meeting will be integrated—I believe for the first time in that stadium—conveys enough on the subject of race."[196] On April 23 an estimated 5,500 (some said 7,000) souls filed into the 10,000-seat stadium. About 10 percent were black. The 450-voice choir and the 239 people who responded to Graham's invitation for the two meetings were divided equally between white and black.

The event marked the first integrated public meeting in Dothan's history. Historians' understandable focus on leaders and dramatic scenes has obscured the burden shouldered by ordinary citizens in their ordinary lives in Dothan and elsewhere. "Graham's white supporters experienced the sting of criticism and black ministers felt the humiliation of scandal sheets," said one local student of the event.[197] Nearly a half-century later Harper Shannon, a white Baptist pastor, later president of the Alabama State Baptist Convention, would reflect that with the crusade, "the barriers began to come down. . . . People began to see each other in a different light."[198] The evidence intimated no epiphanies, but it did intimate a start.

Graham regarded himself as a progressive on racial matters. With manifest pride he said he held "demonstrations in big stadiums . . . throughout the country. And that in itself [was] a witness."[199] Near the end of his career, he still averred—on the *The MacNeil/Lehrer NewsHour*—that if he had marched in the streets, he might have lost "the following" and "some . . . of the influence" that he had won in the South. He then added, with telling candor, "I'm not sure."[200] Graham received acidic criticism for letting segregationists sit on his platform. He also received criticism for letting integrationists sit on his platform. Graham did not use a political or even theological litmus test for choosing his supporters, let alone his friends. Yet when it came to civil rights and, we shall see, other crucial social challenges he confronted his friends more often than his enemies. That stance took a special kind of courage too. We do not have to rank forms of courage in order to acknowledge the price paid and the good accomplished.

1. William "Billy" Graham, age 17, at his graduation from Sharon High School in June 1936. (AP Photo)

8 Great Days Of REVIEL

REVIVAL

with Students of Wheaton College

Choruses!

Instrumental Numbers!

Dynamic Preaching!

Solos!

BILLY GRAHAM

Billy Graham, A Young Southern Evangelist With A Burning Message You Will Never Forget!

Al Smith, Nationally-known Composer, Song Leader, Radio Artist!

Lloyd Fesmire, Pianist, Trombonist, Formerly With Percy Crawford's Famous Brass Quartet!

APRIL 13 = 20

The Church With The Sign "JESUS SAVES"

MOLINE, MICH.

Tune in Mel Trotter's Morning Mission Broadcast, Tuesday - Thursday, 7 - 7:30 A.M.

Great YOUTH RALLY, Sunday, April 20, at 3 P. M.

2. A handbill for a Billy Graham revival in Moline, MI, 1941. (Wheaton College/ courtesy of Billy Graham)

3. Graham preaching at a Youth for Christ rally in Grand Rapids, MI, September 1947. (*Charlotte Observer*)

4. Graham's Los Angeles tent revival in 1949, recreated in the Billy Graham Library in Charlotte, NC, 2007. (AP Photo/Chuck Burton)

5. Graham with his four children and wife, Ruth, at a family supper in Montreat, NC, September 1955. (Photograph by Ed Clark/The LIFE Picture Collection/Getty Images)

6. Graham preaching to more than 30,000 people jammed on Wall Street on July 10, 1957 as part of his New York Crusade. (© Bettmann/Corbis/AP Images)

7. Graham enjoys an ice cream soda with a group of teenagers after discussing the problem of juvenile crime at a news conference in New York City, August 8, 1957. (AP Photo/Anthony Camerano)

8. John F. Kennedy and Billy Graham at the White House, December 12, 1961. (AP Photo)

9. Graham delivers the sermon at the 38th annual "Singing on the Mountain" event, at the base of Grandfather Mountain, Linville, NC, August 5, 1962. (Hulton Archive/Getty Images)

10. Billy Graham's Easter Sunday service in Birmingham, AL, March 29, 1964. (Billy Graham Evangelistic Association)

11. American GIs greet Graham, after his speech to 5,000 combat soldiers north of Saigon in South Vietnam, December 22, 1966. (AP Photo)

12. Graham visits former president Dwight Eisenhower in Gettysburg, PA, September 29, 1967. (*Charlotte Observer*)

13. Graham talks with the host on "The Woody Allen Special," July 28, 1969. (CBS via Getty Images)

14. Richard Nixon with Billy Graham at Graham's East Tennessee Crusade at
Neyland Stadium at the University of Tennessee, Knoxville, May 28, 1970. (©
Bettmann/Corbis/AP Images)

15. Graham appears on "The Johnny Cash Show," February 24, 1971. (ABC Photo
Archives/Getty Images)

16. Billy Graham preaches to more than one million people in Yoido Plaza in Seoul, South Korea, June 3, 1973. (Billy Graham Evangelistic Association)

17. Graham visits San Martin Jilotepeque, Guatemala, which had recently lost 3,800 of its 18,000 residents in an earthquake, February 14, 1976. (AP Photo/files)

18. Patriarch Pimen, leader of the Russian Orthodox Church, listens as Billy Graham speaks at the Patriarchal Cathedral of the Epiphany in Moscow, September 21, 1984. (AP Photo)

19. Holding Ruth's hand, Graham poses next to his star on the Walk of Fame, Hollywood, CA, October 15, 1989. (Photograph by Jim Smeal/WireImage/ Getty Images)

20. Graham presents Pope John Paul II a handmade quilt from the North Carolina mountains on a visit to the Vatican, January 11, 1990. (*Charlotte Observer*)

21. Billy and Ruth Graham on the front porch of their home in Montreat, NC in the month of their 50th wedding anniversary, August 1993. (Billy Graham Evangelistic Association)

22. Graham prays during the 55th Presidential Inaugural Prayer Service at the National Cathedral in Washington, January 21, 2005. (*Charlotte Observer*)

23. Billy Graham speaks at Flushing Meadows Corona Park in New York City, June 25, 2005. (*Charlotte Observer*)

24. Graham at home in Montreat, in the mountains near Asheville, NC, July 25, 2006. (Photograph by Charles Ommanney/Getty Images)

25. George H. W. Bush, Bill Clinton, Billy and Franklin Graham, and Jimmy Carter pose in front of the Billy Graham Library in Charlotte, NC, May 31, 2007. (AP Photo/Chuck Burton)

26. President Barack Obama meets with Graham at his home in Montreat, NC, April 25, 2010. (*Charlotte Observer*)

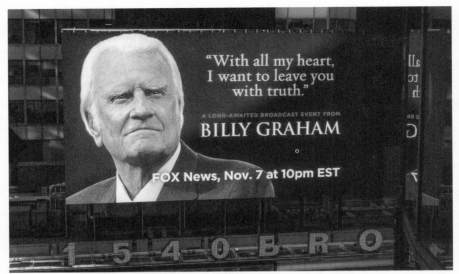

27. A Times Square billboard promoting the television broadcast of "My Hope with Billy Graham." October 21, 2013. (Photograph by George Rose/Getty Images)

28. Billy Graham waving goodbye to the crowd at the closing service at Ericsson Stadium in Charlotte, NC, September 29, 1996. (*Charlotte Observer*)

CHAPTER FOUR

Entrepreneur

Billy Graham would not like to be called entrepreneurial, but he was. In his more otherworldly moments he thought that he served simply as the Holy Spirit's hands and mouthpiece on earth. In his less otherworldly moments, however, he knew perfectly well that revivals had to be worked up as well as prayed down.[1] And why not? He was selling the best product on earth, and that project took the skills of an entrepreneur. There he walked a path staked out more than two hundred years earlier by self-made evangelical leaders. They earned their stripes the hard way, by starting out as itinerant preachers or going out and planting churches on their own. They did not prudently step their way up the ladder by serving as associate pastors under the direction of seasoned seminary-trained pastors. They built their own ladders.

This chapter will look at how Graham constructed the infrastructure of his empire. The next one will examine how he oriented the empire outward to help build the modern evangelical movement. Of course the enterprise represented the work of thousands of entrepreneurial self-made leaders. But somewhere in the early 1950s one leader surged ahead of the others and remained in the vanguard until his effective retirement in 2005—and in symbolic ways afterward.

We have already noted some of the basics of the evangelical tradition that nourished Graham's work, but a closer look now may be helpful. The evangelical story began in the first several decades of the eighteenth century. The tributaries lay in revivals that took place more or less simultaneously among Pietists in southern Germany, Calvinists in Scotland, Wesleyans in England, Puritans in New England, Presbyterians in the Middle Colonies, and Anglicans in the Southern Colonies. Flowing together they produced a recognizable movement. Evangelicals inherited and furthered historic Protestant assumptions about a personal Triune God, mysteriously yet fully expressed in Jesus Christ, and working through the power of the Holy Spirit. They upheld the final authority of the Bible, the bitter reality of human sin, and the glorious truth of redemption through Christ's death and resurrection. Those spiritual verities were mediated through the liturgies (especially baptism and the Lord's Supper) of the church. Beyond those beliefs, evangelicals called for moral probity, ethical uprightness, and commitment to a worshipping community. A solitary believer was a contradiction of terms.

American evangelicals added two features to this mix. The additions were not entirely new; rather, they were strong new emphases in basics already present in the historic Protestant tradition. First and more important, evangelicals called for a heartfelt conversion experience resulting in a change of life. Though evangelicals differed on exactly what heartfelt conversion meant, and exactly how it would take place, they agreed that it involved an affective or emotional feeling of union with Christ. And second, they called for a practice of sharing this *evangel*—or gospel—or good news of salvation—with others. The best way to share it provoked endless discussion, but everyone believed that the experience was too joyous to keep to oneself. Evangelicals who came from a Calvinist (or Reformed) background emphasized God's sovereignty, while those who came from a Wesleyan (or Methodist) background emphasized God's grace. In practice, on the ground, the traditions blended in countless ways.

The evangelical movement boasted many notable leaders. Before Graham, the most remembered names included Jonathan Edwards and George Whitefield in the eighteenth century; Charles Finney, Phoebe Palmer, Dwight L. Moody, and (the African American) Amanda Berry Smith in the nineteenth century; and Aimee Semple McPherson, J. Wilbur Chapman, Reuben Archer Torrey, and Billy Sunday in the twentieth century. As noted, the inspiring hymns of the Englishman Charles Wesley in the early eighteenth century and the American Fanny Crosby in the late nineteenth century rivaled the influence of any—some might say all—of the preachers combined.[2]

Graham did not possess a strong historical consciousness, but when he looked at forebears he most often named Moody, occasionally Sunday. A former shoe salesman, Moody was most visible in the 1880s and 1890s. His ministry proved national and international in scope but was most evident in Boston, New York, and Chicago. This rotund layman's preaching embraced both of the theological emphases noted above—conversion and mission—along with a remarkable ability to draw masses of ordinary men and women to commit their lives to Christ. He pioneered advance planning and systematic advertising. And he featured a staple songster, Ira Sankey, who became nearly as famous as his boss.[3]

Sunday was a former professional baseball player. Like Moody, he deployed advance planning, advertising, and a staple songster, Homer Rodeheaver.

And like Sankey, Rodeheaver became almost as famous as his boss. But Sunday distinguished himself from Moody by adding a paid staff and concerted prayer chains before and during his meetings. He also distinguished himself by his flamboyant preaching style, slang-filled rhetoric, and strident political opinions. He strongly favored America's entry into World War I and just as strongly opposed alcohol. Some credited him for galvanizing the popular support that led to Prohibition. Though no one charged Sunday with personal dishonesty, free will "love offerings" made him very rich. By some accounts he preached face-to-face to millions of people and persuaded more than a million to come to Christ.[4]

Moody and Sunday prepared and in many ways dominated the evangelical revival field, but they never owned it. In the first three decades of the twentieth century they jostled for prominence with J. Wilbur Chapman, Sam P. Jones, Reuben Torrey, and Aimee Semple McPherson.[5] In the 1930s to 1950s other contenders gained prominence. They included Percy Crawford, Torrey Johnson, and Jack Wyrtzen, all radio personalities of Youth for Christ fame. Bob Jones, John R. Rice, Jack Shuler, the Englishman J. Edwin Orr, and, especially, Graham's close friend Merv Rosell drew tens of thousands to their meetings.[6] By one account in the late 1940s Rosell attracted 150,000 people (in aggregate attendance) in a single revival in Long Beach, California.[7] The Los Angeles Bible teacher Henrietta Mears and Boston pastor-scholar Harold John Ockenga reached thousands more through their classes and books.[8]

Historian Garth Rosell aptly called the entire group (with Mears) a "Band of Brothers."[9] Their work found support in a rapidly expanding network of Bible institutes and colleges (including the three Graham attended), missionary sending enterprises, and, perhaps most relevant for appreciating Graham, radio programs.[10] Of the last, the most important was the *Old Fashioned Revival Hour*, pioneered by the California evangelist Charles E. Fuller. Aired on the Mutual and later ABC networks on Sunday afternoons for more than three decades (1937 to 1968), the *Old Fashioned Revival Hour* may have reached twenty million listeners each week. Though the data are elusive, for a time it may have rivaled the top radio broadcasts in the United States.[11]

This rich heritage of evangelical expansion gave Graham a running start. To be sure, when he stepped onto the stage in the late 1940s, mass urban revivalism had lost the steam of the peak Moody-Sunday-McPherson years, and it faced growing disapproval in secular and in Protestant mainline culture.[12] Yet millions of evangelical or evangelically minded Americans were prepared for the kind of messenger and message he had to offer. Graham drew on those swelling resources, and by the mid-1950s he faced no serious rivals.

Crusades

Graham's organizational genius started with the crusades. Just as the preaching formed the cornerstone of his personal ministry, the crusades formed the cornerstone of his institutional empire. It is easy to imagine Graham without one or another of his publications, fairly easy to imagine him without his radio and television broadcasts, difficult but theoretically possible to imagine him without access to the highest echelons of political and social power, but absolutely impossible to imagine him without the crusades.

The crusade structure was not accidental. Partisans would have resisted the word *theatrical*, but they were theatrical, if by that we mean carefully staged in order to produce a desired result. At the very least they were consummately professional, planned and executed with meticulous attention to detail. Graham hired Willis Haymaker, who had organized Billy Sunday's crusades, to make sure that he had an experienced hand at the helm. Graham had studied his predecessors and knew what worked. Drawing especially on Sunday (though giving more credit to Moody), he implemented meticulous planning, advance workers, massive advertising, a paid staff, concerted prayer chains before and during the crusade, and heavy reliance on two associates: choir director Cliff Barrows and soloist George Beverly Shea. More than Moody and Sunday, however, Graham emphasized sustained training and use of counselors before and during the meetings, as well as systematic follow-up measures afterward. New technology—sound amplification, landlines, television, and satellite, among others—created differences too. But most of all, Graham's operation distinguished itself by its sheer magnitude.

The crusade details paralleled mass-market capitalism. Having figured out the most efficient and effective pattern, Graham embellished it in minor ways according to time and place but kept the basic format decade after decade. Everything was predictable. People got what they expected and paid for with their money and their time. And a big part of that bargain was excellence. Nothing unplanned or amateur marred the crusades. In that sense they prefigured the megachurches of the late 2000s. Graham opened public spaces for structures that followed him.

Perhaps the most conspicuous feature of the crusades occurred not in the physical space of the events themselves but in the abstract space of the statistical reports about them. We might call this the rhetoric of crusade drama. Both Graham and the BGEA invested considerable effort in reciting figures about attendance. Russ Busby's pictorial history of Graham's life, *Billy Graham: God's Ambassador*, offered many examples. The volume showcased richly colored one- and two-page photographs of vast crusade audiences. Captions told the eye-popping story: Seoul 1973: "1.1 million people . . . Billy's largest meeting ever held anywhere in the world." Los Angeles Memorial Coliseum 1963: "134,254 inside and 20,000 more outside." Rio de Janeiro's Maracanã Stadium: "In October 1974 the largest crowd to attend an evangelistic service in the western hemisphere—225,000 people." "In March 1973, Johannesburg's Wanderers Stadium held 60,000 people, making it the largest multiracial gathering ever held in South Africa to that time."[13]

And so it ran, page after page. Granted, Graham often said that statistics were not all that important. "The real story of the crusades is not in the great choirs, the thousands in attendance, nor the hundreds of inquirers who are counseled," he explained. "The real story is in the changes that have taken place in the hearts and lives of the people."[14] Graham believed that. And he candidly reported instances when a crusade flopped.[15] Or when smaller-than-expected crowds showed up.[16] Or when he set a stadium record only because people seated themselves on the playing field.[17] Yet the plain truth was that Graham, the BGEA, and the press trumpeted record-breaking statistics constantly and everywhere. So what was going on?

Two preliminary points merit comment. First, it should be stressed that the BGEA made exceptional efforts to guarantee reasonable accuracy. Refusal to exaggerate even in a good cause had formed one of the four tenets of the so-called Modesto Manifesto issued back in 1948, two years before the founding of the BGEA. Besides his personal sense of integrity, there was a contextual reason. Graham competed with contemporary Pentecostal healing evangelists. Many outsiders and not a few insiders suspected healing evangelists of cooking the books.[18] So it was that the BGEA declined to make its own estimates but instead relied on turnstile counts, police estimates, and aerial headcounts.[19] But the determination to gather statistics accurately did not dampen the desire to herald them. Second, statistics rhetoric fit a long tradition. Evangelicals had always "counted the house."[20] As for most expansionist movements, numbers mattered. They formed part of their DNA. They formed part of the press's DNA too. Spectacular numbers made for spectacular headlines, and spectacular headlines sold papers. Moreover, the reporting of impressive statistics, whether by Graham or the BGEA or the press, helped guarantee the success of future crusades. People wanted to be part of the action.

Statistics rhetoric calls for internal parsing. To begin with, in a culture that venerated quantification, numbers felt reliable: hard facts were difficult to dispute. They offered a sharp contrast with mushy narrative accounts about signs of God's blessing.[21] They reflected, too, what might be called the American truck-stop mentality: if a lot of people consistently showed up, the crusades evidently offered something good. The BGEA shrewdly sensed too that numbers portended more than they documented. One hundred thousand souls gathered in one place signaled more than ten thousand souls gathered in ten places.[22] Massiveness impressed. One might even speak of the charismatic power of vast crowds. Beyond that, throngs validated the authenticity of the revivals and of Graham as God's chosen instrument.

Conventional numbers marched with another genre that might be called virtual statistics. They came in a variety of forms but almost always traded on size. They featured adjectives such as *huge, tremendous, dazzling, great, mammoth, dynamic, glorious, heaven-sent, foremost, unprecedented,* and *sin-smashing,* or nouns such as *throngs, crowds,* and *masses.*[23] Another form invoked adversity, especially bad weather and bad health. Again and again we read of sweltering heat, driving rain, and bone-chilling cold.[24] Adverse weather gave the crusade narratives dramatic tension.

Reports on Graham's personal health varied the genre in another way. They exhibited complementary patterns, which were superficially contradictory but actually compatible. On one hand, many accounts stressed his physical stamina. They emphasized his ability to travel constantly, live out of a suitcase, and preach to tens of thousands night after night with undiminished power.[25] On the other hand, many accounts stressed how often he suffered from colds, laryngitis, broken bones, and other ailments. Sometimes he appeared to be Mayo Clinic's most valued customer.[26] The stamina narrative implied God's blessing, the infirmities narrative implied God's testing. Either way, the health rhetoric riveted followers' attention and commitment. In sum, accounts of conspicuous size or adversity or physical status placed the crusades in a new key. Like the tales of George Whitefield's revivals in the early eighteenth century, or Pentecostal revivals in the early twentieth century, the stories of Graham's revivals formed a fresh history of divine blessing.

A third form of virtual statistics invoked a trait that the religion scholar C. Eric Lincoln called *cosmocentrism*.[27] This notion suggested a cluster of related concepts such as center, pivot, springboard, or landmark. So Graham located his meetings in Times Square, or on the steps of the United States Capitol, or at the pavilion of the World's Fair. The crusades started or ended on calendar markers such as New Year's Eve or Labor Day or the Fourth of July. Or they signaled events of global scope or interest. In 1951, hoping (without success) to persuade President Truman to attend his upcoming Washington, DC, crusade, Graham wrote to the president, assuring him that the campaign had captured the interest of "the entire Christian world."[28]

It is possible to overanalyze the language of statistics—to intimate that it offered false reports of what actually took place or that partisans massaged things for purely pragmatic purposes. That would be both unfair and inaccurate. The point, rather, is that Graham and his workers chose to report some things and not others. He and they instinctively understood that Americans desired palpable signs of the wonders that God was working here and now for all to see and hear.

Graham received vastly more invitations than he could accept—more than 8,500 in one twelve-month stretch.[29] Each year he normally accepted three or four in the United States and another three or four abroad. He and his staff chose them carefully. In the beginning they selected sites with an eye to population size or symbolic value, such as capital cities or commercial centers. Later they favored medium-sized cities like Louisville because of lower labor costs and because telecommunications rendered size less relevant.[30] Graham insisted that a majority of all Protestant churches—not just evangelical ones—in the city must support the invitation.

Once a site was chosen, the preparations commenced in earnest. He approached every crusade with the utmost seriousness. None was regarded as an interim engagement between larger attractions. He said that the planning that preceded and the follow-up that succeeded the actual meeting constituted the beating heart of the endeavor.[31] That conviction explained the switch in 1950 from the word *campaign* to the word *crusade*: the latter intimated that the main work took place not during but before and after.[32] After 2001 *crusade* yielded to *festival* because *crusade* had acquired militarist connotations.

Preparation for the crusades proved mind-boggling. The 1996 crusade in Charlotte was typical of the larger ones. It involved 7,000 counselors, 6,000 adult choir members, 1,500 ushers, nearly 900 North and South Carolina churches, a 4,000-voice children's choir, and 1,000,000 brochures and other materials to be distributed. It also involved the Charlie Daniels Band, Maranatha Praise Band, Gary Chapman, Brooklyn Tabernacle Singers, Psalty the Singing Songbook, Michael W. Smith, DC Talk, Johnny Cash, the Gaither Vocal Band, and the Charlotte Symphony Orchestra.[33]

Preparation of that magnitude required advance workers and their families to move to the target city at least a year ahead of the crusade. They set up local organizing committees that embraced as wide a range as possible of denominations, occupations, age groups, races, ethnicities, and both sexes.[34] The mix represented good strategy as well as good theology. It helped ensure success by spreading a sense of ownership widely. The local committees organized themselves like a military hierarchy, with group captains overseeing unit captains. They arranged for weekly training sessions and daily prayer meetings.[35] Graham repeatedly said that the daily prayer meetings formed the soul of the crusade's success. However one judges that claim, it is clear that they fostered a powerful sense of shared responsibility and providential timing. Partisans knew that brothers and sisters around the country and often enough around the entire world were praying for the same thing at the same time.

Even the best product required marketing. Graham never forgot Henry Luce's advice: advertising space paid for itself many times over.[36] The same principle applied to press coverage. Within broad limits there was no such thing as bad press. So Graham sold himself aggressively. He believed that God expected him to use every means possible to advance his message. That meant saturation coverage. Advance workers arranged for the distribution of thousands—or tens of thousands—of flyers, posters, bumper stickers, and television spots. They aggressively sought and secured media interviews with the preacher when he got to town.[37] The secular press acknowledged—and seemed to admire—the effectiveness of the preacher's marketing endeavors. "Graham Superstar: Heaven's Super Salesman: Man Who Has Turned Selling Religion into an Art Form" ran one of countless headlines.[38]

Graham knew that Americans were accustomed to being consumers of a mass-produced product. His shrewdness emerged in minimalist advertising. Many posters simply said "Billy Graham" with a date, time, and place for the meeting discreetly noted below.[39] Some advertisements traded on wit: "Billy Graham Advance Warning."[40] Or sometimes they featured only his face and the meeting information. One associate likened Graham's image to that of a Cadillac: "We don't have to explain."[41] Viewers needed only a glimpse: less was more.

Then, too, Graham's publicity department knew a good idea when they spotted it. One of the more famous instances involved their adaptation of a Microsoft advertisement in Silicon Valley, California. The Microsoft ad showed a hand pointing to the sky, and the question, "Where do you want to go today?" Graham's knock-off ad showed the same image but asked, "Where do you want to go tomorrow?"[42] Just as Graham tightly controlled the production of photographs of himself, he tightly controlled the production of promotional materials about his crusades. Keep them lean—and memorable.

Timing mattered. Graham did not schedule crusade meetings on Sunday morning in order to avoid competing with local church services. Sunday evening services at the 1949 Los Angeles meetings began at 8:45 PM, "for the convenience of church-goers," one poster promised.[43] No one would mistake a crusade event for church as usual, but it was not entirely different from church as usual either. Clearly he did not want partisans to swap one gathering for the other. And though he did not say so, he was astute enough to know that local pastors would resist his work if they saw it as a direct threat.

Site mattered too. In the beginning Graham favored tents, municipal auditoriums, wooden tabernacles built for the purpose, and outdoor venues such as large parks and capitol steps. Soon, however, he moved toward indoor coliseums such as Madison Square Garden in New York, the Cow Palace in San Francisco, and Harringay Arena in London. He also moved toward outdoor stadiums, including some of the largest ones in the nation and world, such as Yankee Stadium in New York, Soldier Field in Chicago, the Rose Bowl in Pasadena, and Wembley Stadium in London. Meetings took place in outdoor venues rich with historic symbolism, such as Times Square and Central Park in New York, the World's Fair grounds in Flushing Meadows, and Trafalgar Square in London. Graham preached on cricket grounds, aircraft carriers, dog-racing tracks, and in bullfighting rings. Crusades rarely met in local churches. He did not explicitly say why, but the reasons are easy to infer. Besides the obvious fact that most churches were not large enough, he wished to show that crusades were nondenominational and posed no competition. More important, he instinctively sought liminal sites for liminal occurrences, extraordinary places for extraordinary experiences. The decision for Christ started as soon as the inquirer stood to start the trek to the front. The entire stadium became a mourner's bench.[44]

Worship Service

Graham's personal role in the crusade worship services formed only half the story, however. The other half was the succession of events that visitors and the press experienced. For most, the meetings proved orderly—but not too orderly. They felt solemn in ultimate intent yet packed with light moments, nostalgic associations, and pleasant informalities.[45] Paralleling the tightly scripted patterns of Graham's preaching and closing invitation, they offered visitors the rewards of predictability. Like satisfied customers, worshipers went away feeling that they got what they came for. That was important, for it involved time (for many the gathering was probably their second or third worship service of the week), money (buses, subways, parking garages), and the hassle of traffic snarls and parking snafus.[46]

Next to Graham's preaching, music ranked as the star attraction.[47] From the earliest days of his ministry he grasped its importance. His first evangelistic outing on the radio as a young man in Florida featured music with a dollop of preaching. Posters advertising his earliest revival meetings in Florida showcased "Song Leader . . . Ponzi Pennington."[48] As noted, in January 1944, just six months after becoming pastor of the tiny Western Springs Baptist Church near Chicago, he agreed to take over a local radio program called—significantly—*Songs in the Night*. The preacher's first move was to enlist the services of the well-known Chicago gospel soloist George Beverly Shea. Like the Florida program, *Songs in the Night* showcased music—heralded by Shea's "deep molasses-barrel baritone"—along with a spoonful of preaching from Graham.[49] On his first YFC venture to England in the spring of 1946, one of the three men who accompanied him was another well-known gospel songster, J. Stratton Shufelt. Graham's second trip to England, in the fall and winter of 1946–47, highlighted another musician, Cliff Barrows. By 1947 the permanent platform Team had gelled, with Graham as the preacher, Shea as the vocalist, and Barrows as, among other things, choir leader and back-up singer.[50]

Though Barrows updated the hymn menu to keep step with the times, in the crusade meetings the congregational singing generally emphasized tried-and-true songs with more than a hint of nostalgia. The same principle applied to the choirs. Often they were massive affairs, sometimes numbering as many as eight thousand volunteer voices. One member of Graham's 1996 Charlotte crusade choir remembered the "angelic wall of sound" of the choir in the 1958 meeting nearly four decades past. "Wow, I'd never heard anything like that," she recalled. "For a while I couldn't sing for listening."[51] "Music is a way we can unite and blend together," Barrows observed. "Melody communicates at a deeper level than the spoken word."[52]

The musical repertoire of crusade meetings gradually widened. Through the 1950s Graham scorned rock 'n' roll. "Anything that whips young people into a frenzy is bad," he scowled. "If I were 17 today I'd stay as far away from it as I could."[53] In time, though, he opened up. By 1972 he would say that "each generation has to hear [the gospel] anew, hear it in their own language and sing it in their own language."[54] Elsewhere speaking of the "younger generation's musical tastes," Graham remarked, "I don't like the music. But I like them. They like it."[55]

In time the crusades would showcase a remarkable variety of styles, ranging from Gaither Family toe-tappers, to Johnny Cash and Ricky Skaggs country, Ethel Waters and Mahalia Jackson spiritual, Robert Goulet and Cliff Richard pop, Jerome Hines and Kathleen Battle classical, DC talk rap, Take 6 jazz, Paul Stookey folk, Marine Corps Band patriotic, Norma Zimmer easy listening, Michael W. Smith and Jars of Clay contemporary Christian, Blackwood Brothers and Statler Brothers Southern gospel, and Brooklyn Tabernacle Choir black gospel. Artists representing one or another so-called ethnic group—Chicano, Latino, Korean, Hungarian, Hawaiian, and Native American—regularly appeared. College choirs and city symphony orchestras performed too. Most guest artists came with well-established reputations in the gospel or secular entertainment worlds.[56]

Graham recognized that he possessed no musical ability himself—Shea quipped that he suffered from the "malady of no melody"—so he soon came to rely on the skills of his associates Barrows and Shea.[57] For a brief time, the three seemed equal, or at least almost equal. A cardboard photograph, possibly advertising Graham's 1949 Los Angeles crusade, presented same-size shots of each man, with their same-size signatures imprinted on their coats.[58] A poster/banner, clearly used for advertising, headlined Graham's name across the top but featured same-size photographs of Graham, Barrows, and Shea just below. The poster described them, respectively, as "America's Outstanding Evangelist," "World-Renowned Song Leader," and "Star Gospel Singer of Radio."[59] Eventually things changed, of course, but Graham never lost sight of the crucial importance of his musician colleagues. He was the first major evangelist to make two music associates part of the platform Team.[60]

Barrows's signal contribution to Graham's story has not gained sufficient attention from historians.[61] Born in Ceres, California, in 1923, Barrows graduated from Bob Jones College in 1944 and received ordination as a

Baptist minister the same year. In 1945 he joined Graham quite by accident at a Youth for Christ meeting near Asheville, North Carolina. When Graham's planned musician for the night became ill, he asked for a recruit from the audience, promising, "We won't be choosy!"[62] Barrows volunteered—and stayed for seven decades. Barrows was very much like Graham himself: tall, handsome, safely married, inexhaustibly vigorous, and blessed with a smooth baritone speaking voice. (Unlike Graham, he also possessed a smooth baritone singing voice.) An advertisement for the 1949 Los Angeles crusade described him: "He is enthusiastic—vital—dramatic! He combines the high spirit of a college cheer leader with the quiet dignity of an expert choral director as he leads thousands in singing praises to God in heavenly harmony!"[63]

Barrows chose all of the songs for the crusade services, determining what the congregation, the choir, and the guest artists would sing (or perform).[64] Graham trusted him to know the chemistry. Besides managing the choir and the lineup of guest artists, Barrows served as the lead announcer and platform manager. Significantly, Barrows, not Graham, gave the brief low-key appeal for money on the *Hour of Decision* radio and television broadcasts. He functioned as the perfect complement. Though the announcer rarely if ever upstaged the preacher, everyone knew that he could have enjoyed a lucrative career on his own.

Shea's contribution paralleled Barrows's. As with Barrows, historians have paid insufficient attention to Shea's crucial role in Graham's story. He was born in Winchester, Ontario, in 1908. His path to Graham wound through schooling at (the Wesleyan Methodist) Houghton College in upstate New York, a decade working for a New York City insurance firm, and a half-dozen years as a featured singer for a variety of Chicago-based gospel radio programs. The most notable was *Club Time*, aired nationally over the ABC network. By the time Graham persuaded Shea to join him as a regular on *Songs in the Night*, Shea had already won wide recognition throughout the Midwest. Graham said he needed a "marquee name."[65]

Shea, like Barrows and Graham, was tall, handsome, safely married, and inexhaustibly vigorous. His voice was deeper than Barrows's, closer to bass. Unlike the highly animated Barrows, Shea worked without gestures. He tried to convey emphasis through the modulation of the words of the lyrics.[66] His dignified singing added reverence bordering on solemnity to the meetings. A handful of songs, such as "Just As I Am," "How Great Thou Art," and "I Will Sing the Wondrous Story," served as his signature hymns. Audiences seemed never to tire of hearing them. Also like Barrows, Shea rarely if ever upstaged Graham, yet his recordings, which sold in the millions, documented that he too could have enjoyed a lucrative career on his own. He stayed with Graham nearly seven decades. Settling in Montreat, North Carolina, in 1985, Shea lived nearly thirty years just a few miles down the road from Graham. He died in 2013 at age 104.

Historian Edith Blumhofer has shown how Barrows's and Shea's careers shed light on Graham's career. First, the three remained close friends to the end. Quoting Ecclesiastes 4:12, they liked to say that "a threefold cord is not easily broken."[67] The image of an irenic, smoothly functioning team countered the frequent picture of evangelical friction and worship wars. At his ninety-fifth birthday celebration in 2013, Graham made just one public remark: to thank the ninety-year-old Barrows, sitting in a wheelchair nearby, "for everything."[68] Second, Barrows and Shea projected a recognizable sound. Guest artists added multiple musical genres but hardly ever dominated the typically decorous aural world of a Graham crusade. Third, Barrows and Shea carefully studied the work of Sankey, Rodeheaver, and other musician associates in the revival tradition.[69] Though they, like Graham, took care to give the Holy Spirit credit, they also took care to prepare. They knew what worked. And once again, audiences received what they expected to receive. No one on Graham's Team believed in accidental excellence.

Testifiers formed another crucial component of the crusade meeting. Over the years they numbered in the thousands. The BGEA did not keep ready records, but we can piece together the broad picture. The cast was divided roughly equally between men and women, likely represented African Americans and other minorities in proportion to the general population, and displayed a range of age groups from young adults to seniors. The occupations they represented included politicians, actors, musicians, athletes, business moguls, military leaders, reformed lawbreakers, and beauty-contest winners.[70] Academics, theologians, and folks off the street rarely appeared. Graham did not lack for supporters in those (and other) occupational groups, but he intuited which ones did—and did not—exercise influence.

Testifiers without exception spoke of the rewards of the Christian life. For virtually everyone, that meant spiritual, not material, rewards. Some articulated the simple contentment that came from knowing Christ. For many that meant purpose: awareness that God had a plan for them, individually. Others spoke of spectacular professional success, yet coupled with a crushing feeling that they had squandered a chunk of their lives in aimless pursuits. Many projected a definable pattern of before-and-after experiences.[71]

Some had lived on the edges of society or well beyond the edges of the justice system. They had fallen into some form of addiction, or run afoul of the law, or suffered financial reverse, or endured social ostracism.[72] Two examples suffice. The testimony of country music star Stuart Hamblen, one of Graham's most famous converts, at the 1949 crusade was typical: "I've done practically everything everybody else has done. I've been a sinner."[73] By his account Jesus brought new meaning to his life. Johnny Cash, one of the more frequent guests, had his ups and downs with drugs and the law and with Jesus. He did not pretend to be a saint, and Graham did not pretend that he was one either. Yet Cash embodied the complexities of many lives. There was a place for him, too.[74]

Several implications of the testimony literature are worth noticing. First of all, Graham intuited that stories proved more powerful than arguments. The star Fuller Brush salesman still remembered that the word of the satisfied customer trumped the word of the smartest theologian. Then too, testimonies served as powerful rituals, public acts that helped solidify the commitment of the speaker. That pattern applied not only to the speakers but also to the audiences hearing them, for the testimonials proved powerfully normative. In effect: "What God has done for me he will do for you. Let my testimony be yours too." In classic evangelical fashion, everything depended on choice. *Your* choice. And finally, once again, it is possible to overanalyze these narratives by suggesting that they were shaped to fit expectations or dreamed up for the status they earned. Undoubtedly some were. Yet when they are considered whole, only the most acidic observer could avoid the overwhelming sense of fulfillment they conveyed.[75]

The final component of the crusade service that calls for attention is the counselors. Historians have paid strangely little attention to the role that the counselors played, but in Graham's view they proved crucial to the crusades' success. Typically drawn from the supporting churches, counselors exemplified the churches' geographic and denominational range. Though the age limits ran from seventeen to seventy, most were twenty-five to forty. Counselors underwent extensive training, including, for some, learning to work with the deaf, with children, or in different languages.[76] The training started nine weeks ahead of the crusade, involved a full morning or evening each week, and called for the memorization of scriptural passages relevant to a variety of spiritual needs. Senior counselors screened applicants for ability and aptitude.[77] With so much time and effort invested, counselors, too, had a stake in the crusade's success.

At the crusade, as inquirers stood to walk forward, a captain signaled a counselor of the same gender and similar age (and if known sometimes similar occupation) to join the inquirer. They walked together to the front, or counselors met them there. After a short exhortation from Graham, counselors escorted inquirers to a separate space or a back room where they briefly prayed with the inquirer and urged a commitment of repentance and faith in Christ. They filled out a decision card listing name, address, occupation, church preference, pastor's name, and a notation about any special status such as service members.

In their training, counselors learned to be courteous and thoughtful, avoid arguments, sidestep "doctrinal" discussions, not press for a decision, and be "clean and neat" and careful about "personal body offenses," as one training manual put it. Inquirers received a Gospel of John and a Bible study lesson book. Local pastors received a copy of the decision card for follow up.[78] Counselors sought to funnel inquirers into local churches, preferably evangelical ones, but if that did not work out, a congregation of their choice.[79]

Sometimes the best pastors were the lay counselors. Though patterns varied, counselors commonly took responsibility for staying in touch with inquirers after the crusade to see if they had associated themselves with a local church. Systematic follow-up measures helped cement conversions or recommitments, win the support of local clergy, and solidify the success of the endeavor. Graham's careful attention to local churches helped allay the historic resentment about evangelists hitting town, capturing glory, then moving on to lusher meadows.

Nothing was left to chance. The crusade procedure books bulged with details about how things should be done before, during, and after the crusade. The BGEA maintained elaborate statistical records about everything. The crusades made good headlines not only because they worked but also because they embodied the entrepreneurial spirit of American evangelicalism at its most efficient best.

The Billy Graham Evangelistic Association (BGEA)

Graham well understood that even if God had called him to his line of work he still had to organize it in order to keep it running. Graham originally conceived the BGEA as a tool for regularizing his finances. But from the outset it was more than that. The organization enjoyed providential legitimation, for it handled the disposition of money that had been received providentially. In the fall of 1950 Graham felt that God was calling him to launch a national radio program. He worried about how to tell the difference between his own ambitions and God's calling. So he set up an unlikely condition. He would need exactly $25,000 to cover the part of the start-up costs not yet funded. As noted, that exact sum arrived that night, right in the nick of time.[80] Stories of that sort were common currency in evangelical literature. What seemed a coincidence for outsiders seemed divinely ordained for insiders.[81]

Graham and George M. Wilson, the business manager of Northwestern Schools in Minneapolis (where Graham was president) set up the BGEA as a nonprofit enterprise. But being providentially sanctioned meant that the BGEA was also a missionary enterprise, which evoked workers' loyalty, commitment, and self-sacrifice. Those virtues fostered others. BGEA soon won a well-earned reputation for integrity and efficiency. Wilson appropriated the latest postal, printing, accounting, and communications technologies. Outsiders traveled to Minneapolis to study its operations.[82] Even William McLoughlin, generally an unfriendly biographer of Graham, acknowledged that the BGEA earned its stripes as a model among such organizations.[83]

Graham himself played a large role in the BGEA's success. For one thing, he always knew what he was and was not good at doing, and so he hired men and women who could do what he could not. To say that he delegated responsibility is not, however, to say that he delegated all of it. Typically he phoned in once a day no matter where he was in the world to check on things. Insiders reported that he gave his associates a long rope but they knew that at the end of the day he kept one end of that rope firmly in his hand.[84] At the same time, he lived in Montreat, North Carolina, nearly eleven hundred miles from Minneapolis. That geographical distance provided just enough separation to maintain both the reality and the appearance of administrative freedom and financial integrity. The image of Graham as a charismatic but naïve country boy, working for others more worldly wise than he, collapses here. Others ran the organization, but he put it together and made certain that it hummed along according to his—and, he would say—God's plan. Graham fit the venerable American ideal of the savvy simpleton—men like his contemporaries Harry Truman and Ronald Reagan—who knew a good deal more than they let on.

The BGEA kept an eye on the ledger book. There, too, it soon won a solid reputation for integrity and efficiency. That image did not drop from the sky. In the revival tradition, local committees had handled local expenses while the preacher passed the hat at the end of the meetings for himself and his associates. In the beginning Graham adopted that pattern.

At the end of the Atlanta crusade in December 1950, however, unplanned events prompted Graham to reconsider. After the final meeting, the *Atlanta Constitution* splashed a pair of photos on the front page. One of them showed ushers scooping up gunnysacks bulging with money—a "love offering" of $16,000.[85] The other showed a grinning Graham hopping into a taxi headed for the airport. The photos were authentic, nothing had been Photoshopped, but the events were unrelated. Yet the juxtaposition implied manipulation at best and subterfuge at worst. Graham resolved to change the practice.[86]

In 1952 the BGEA placed Graham on a published salary. They pegged his compensation to that of a pastor of a typical large urban church. The sum permitted him to live comfortably—he never pretended to lead an abstemious lifestyle—but not lavishly, and nowhere near the opulence he could have enjoyed if he had chosen to do so.[87] In the early 1950s NBC offered Graham one million dollars a year to host a television show to compete with Arthur Godfrey.[88] Cecil B. DeMille dangled a supporting role in a movie about Samson and Delilah.[89] Paramount Studios proposed a role, too.[90] Ruth Graham once said, "Bill literally spends hours, *hours,* trying to figure out how not to make money."[91] Over the years Graham received fierce criticism on many counts but personal financial gain rarely was one of them.

The means for raising money formed another important part of the story. Apt descriptors would be *deft* and *low-key.* Voluntary contributions in the crusade meetings went to the local committee for local expenses. Surpluses were plowed back into the BGEA for operating costs and, later, disaster-relief programs. But the greater part came through the mail in the form of greenbacks mom and pop tucked into the millions of letters they sent over the years. In 1976 Graham told reporters that the average contribution ran about $7.00.[92] The following year BGEA's business manager, George M. Wilson, told *Corporate Report* that 80 to 90 percent of the organization's support came in those letters. He said the average contribution ran between $10 and $12 per letter, adding, "$50 is large for us."[93] The *Hour of Decision* established this understated yet financially productive approach at the outset. At the end of the broadcast, Barrows briefly mentioned that the ministry relied on listeners' prayers and "support."[94] He invited them to drop a line to "Billy Graham, Minneapolis, Minnesota. That's all the address you need, just Billy Graham, Minneapolis, Minnesota." Call it the blue-ribbon approach.

If Graham's ministry did not need to beg, it also did not need to spell out the full address. Listeners already knew how to reach the preacher. Deck hands converted return addresses into a mailing list.[95] Graham was one of the first evangelists to appreciate the utility of a mailing list. Supporters received quarterly newsletters, which resembled Graham's sermons by framing his ministry against a backdrop of dire world, national, and personal crises. Following Willis Haymaker's advice, Graham sent supporters an invitation to write back for a free gift, usually one of his books. He shrewdly recognized that when readers requested a gift, they typically sent a donation larger than the gift cost to produce and mail.[96]

And that point leads to a larger one. Backers supported Graham with their wallets because they trusted him. As in the crusade meetings, they got what they paid for. Americans looked for investments that paid reliable dividends. Graham got something too—beyond the obvious wage to live on. He received an independent financial base that enabled him to follow his entrepreneurial instincts without the interference of a denominational hierarchy.[97]

Graham enjoyed numerous long-standing relationships with men of great wealth and manifest business ability—a story that only recently has started to receive the attention it deserves.[98] For Graham, there was nothing new about that kind of link. As far back as 1944, when he became pastor of a tiny church on the outskirts of Chicago, he immediately launched the Suburban Professional Men's Club, consisting of "business executives of highest rank and tightest schedules."[99] The club's name and constituency intimated things to come. Some magnates—George F. Bennett, treasurer of Harvard University and president of State Street Investment Corporation; Allan C. Emery, Jr., president of the National Wool Trade Association; Bill Pollard, CEO of ServiceMaster; and William Walton, president of Holiday Inn—became members of his board. George Champion, chairman of the Chase Manhattan Bank; Roger Hull, CEO of Mutual Insurance Company of New York; and Tom Cousins, Atlanta philanthropist, sports franchiser, and real estate developer, all chaired major urban crusades. Other moguls such as Earl Hankimer, H. L. Hunt, Maxey Jarman, Tom Landry, R. G. LeTourneau, J. W. Marriott, John D. MacArthur, Clint Murchison, Sid Richardson, and especially J. Howard Pew fell into Graham's network too.

The lives of these very wealthy and very powerful supporters had followed a variety of paths. Marriott was a devout Mormon. Hunt marched as an archconservative. On his demise, he purportedly ranked as one of the half-dozen richest men in the world. MacArthur, who won his fortune in insurance, established the prestigious MacArthur Fellowships. A disproportionate number made their money in oil or in extractive enterprises such as

mining or earthmoving. Hunt's son, Nelson Bunker, dominated silver mining. LeTourneau, a particularly generous philanthropist, founded the largest
heavy earthmoving company in the world. The reclusive Richardson, known
as the Texas Oil Baron, was a strong supporter of Dwight Eisenhower and
Lyndon Johnson. As noted, Pew established Sun Oil (later Sunoco) and
served as principal bankroller behind *Christianity Today* and Gordon Conwell Theological Seminary. Cousins, on the other hand, established and ran
the East Lake Foundation, which poured great financial and business resources into the renewal of impoverished areas of Atlanta and served as a
model for Habitat for Humanity.

Not accidentally, Graham's second and in many ways signature feature-
length movie bore the telling title, *Oil Town U.S.A.* Released in 1953, the
film told the fictional story of Houston native Lance Manning, a ruthless,
hard-driving, emotionally callused oil tycoon. In the movie, Manning remarked: "My God? My two strong hands." A friend of Manning concurred:
"His God is gold, black gold, and he can find it even if is three miles straight
down." Manning eventually found Christ through the ministry of his college-
age daughter. Still, the film left no doubt that Manning was a swashbuckler
at heart.[100] In his own way, so was Graham. And everyone kept an eye on
the store.

Exactly how much money such men contributed to Graham's ministry
remains largely unknown. In the late 1940s Graham, facing financial hard-
ship during an evangelistic tour in Europe, successfully tapped LeTourneau
for $7,000.[101] Controversial right-wing industrialist Russell McGuire gave
him $75,000 to start a film ministry.[102] But beyond that, it was hard to tell,
since the BGEA did not break down those data in their public disclosures.
MacArthur offered to underwrite a Billy Graham University in Florida.
Graham initially embraced the plan, then experienced second thoughts and
withdrew (permanently alienating MacArthur).[103] Graham also declined at
least one major gift for a crusade because "it would look like a rich man
would be paying the bill and we wouldn't want that—a rich man's Crusade."[104] He did seek major donations for specific projects, such as the magazine *Christianity Today* and Gordon Conwell Theological Seminary, yet
not for the BGEA.[105] He accepted favors from mogul friends, such as free
lodging in Marriott hotels anywhere in the world, and vacations in sunny
climes, but nothing substantial for men of their means.[106]

It seems Graham simply enjoyed their company. And they enjoyed his. One
person—presumably a soul of significant wealth—once offered Graham
$100 a minute just to talk with him.[107] In Graham's world, as in the rest of

America, there was no shame in financial success, only in its misuse. In the United States members of the religious and economic establishments, both right and left, often had marched together. Tycoons, both religious and business, saw the world in similar ways. Graham admired people like himself: practical, hard-working, with an affinity for personal responsibility, private philanthropy, and meritocratic capitalism. And some of the friendships were born of deep personal affection.[108] Even so, there were limits. Graham's final golf outing was with President Gerald Ford. One associate explained that he stopped partly because it took too much time but also because he did not like the image.[109] For the same reason he refused a private jet and tried to avoid chauffeured limousines.[110]

Women played a mixed role in the front ranks of Graham's empire. On one hand, about half of the counselors, testifiers, and guest artists were female, and that representation sent an important signal. On the other hand, all members of the platform Team, the full Team, and associate evangelists were male. Of the seventy-six persons who served on the BGEA board from its inception in 1950 to 2014, only six were female, and of those, two were members of Graham's family (wife Ruth and daughter Anne).[111] Women testified but rarely if ever preached (in the formal sense of expositing a biblical text for the instruction of adult men as well as women). That pattern may have reflected Graham's personal views or, more likely, his instinctive sense that his tradition-minded audiences would resist female preachers. The minimal presence of women on the BGEA board also undoubtedly reflected Graham's desire to populate the board with individuals of demonstrated success in the business and financial worlds. The number of evangelical women CEOs was too small to offer many candidates.

Media Empire

The transportation and communications revolution of the mid-twentieth century enabled Graham to do things that Moody, Sunday, and McPherson could not have imagined. Viewed from afar, the most striking feature of Graham's media empire is that it really was an empire. The sheer complexity and vastness of it all arrest the imagination: mailings, advertising, magazines, books, movies, radio, television, and more recently a continually updated webpage and social media presence. He pioneered communications innovations, ranging from the newest forms of sound-amplification technology in the great stadiums, to landline relays of his crusade meetings to remote giant television screens, to simulcast satellite broadcasts around the world.

He knew that the storied tradition of homey preachers prowling the kerosene circuit was forever gone.

Graham's first major venture into mass communications appeared in the half-hour *Hour of Decision* syndicated radio broadcast transmitted nationally over the ABC network on Sunday afternoons. Though he felt that the *Hour of Decision* enjoyed divine blessing, he also knew that the blessing was timely. It fit snugly into a powerful heritage of religious radio broadcasts in the pretelevision age of the 1930s and 1940s (and prospered well into the television age of the 1950s and 1960s). In millions of households, Theodore Epp's *Back to the Bible Broadcast*, Walter Maier's *Lutheran Hour*, Aimee McPherson's *Sunshine Hour*, Fulton Sheen's *The Catholic Hour*, and the granddaddy of all, Charles E. Fuller's *Old Fashioned Revival Hour* were as predictable as the Sunday roast.[112]

Graham's sensitivity to the power of radio traced back to his own beginning years. At age twenty-one, he started broadcasting weekly devotionals from a tiny station beaming its signal from St. Augustine, Florida. As noted, in January 1944, just seven months after graduating from Wheaton College, he grabbed the opportunity to take over the late Sunday night program *Songs in the Night*. In March Graham doubled his airtime with a Sunday morning broadcast too. When he became president of Northwestern College in 1948 one of his first endeavors was to raise money for the construction of a college radio station. KTIS started broadcasting on February 7, 1949—and Graham was the first speaker. (Not surprisingly, the station featured student music groups.)[113] Given his street-smart instincts, Graham naturally turned his talents to the creation of a national radio program. Immediately transmitted to 150 ABC stations, within weeks the *Hour of Decision* ranked as one the most widely heard religious radio broadcasts in the nation.[114]

The programming fit the pace of the times. In the very first broadcast of *Hour of Decision*, November 5, 1950, Barrows led off with the emphatic statement, "*This* is the hour of decision." The forceful vocative "*this*" left listeners no doubt that the time of reckoning had arrived. Barrows immediately swept into a rehearsal of the momentous proportions of the meeting taking place in this "great crusade auditorium," the center of a "city wide" revival, backed by the "one thousand voice Atlanta crusade choir," and promising listeners that within minutes they would hear Billy Graham with "God's message for these days of international crises." After a reverent, almost dirgeful favorite from Shea, Graham opened with an explosive riff on "war jitters" everywhere, growing awareness that a "third world war" lay just around the corner, that "atomic judgments" were casting shadows over civilization, and, unless revival came, "we live on the edge of catastrophe."[115] On *Hour of Decision* broadcasts, the apocalyptic tones seemed harder and darker than they did in his face-to-face crusade preaching. The style proved fast and confrontational. Every sermon concluded, of course, with an invitation to give one's life to Christ. And listeners loved it all. Why?

Answers must be inferred, but several present themselves. One was the desire to hear authoritative solutions in uncertain times. It was, after all, the age of the backyard bomb shelter. A second, closely related reason resided in Graham's ability to convey a sense of community: we face this trial together. The third and most compelling reason lay in the dyad that marked Graham's preaching everywhere: first warning, then hope. The warning rarely if ever appeared alone. It marched arm in arm with words of assurance.

Rarely behind the curve, and usually ahead of it, Graham soon complemented the *Hour of Decision* radio program with a television version. The first incarnation experienced a short life, starting in 1951 as a studio program, but going dark three years later.[116] The second incarnation started in June 1957 as a live broadcast of Graham's Saturday night crusade meetings in Madison Square Garden. Lasting fourteen consecutive weeks, the programs were translated into different languages and transmitted by shortwave too. The first broadcast alone elicited twenty-five thousand responses. Fifty to seventy-five thousand letters per week streamed into the Minneapolis offices.[117] Graham later moved the broadcast to an edited one-hour telecast of an actual crusade meeting. Fearing overexposure and staggering financial commitments, he contracted for broadcasts of (usually) two or three consecutive nights four times a year on ABC network television around the nation. This format afforded the best of all worlds: the excitement of a live program with the control of an edited one.[118]

Graham immediately saw the potential of a televised *Hour of Decision* in this hybrid format. It encouraged timely sermons on fresh topics crafted in easily consumable forms. Though he did not say so, he—or at least his advisors—intuited that his looks were made for television, especially when color television came along and featured his arresting blue eyes. The commanding voice complemented the commanding visage to create a sense of authority that few evangelists—that few practitioners of any public profession, for that matter—could match. Far into the 1950s, evangelicals resisted televisions in their homes. By legitimating television Graham may have borne the lion's share of the credit—or blame—for that shift. Here again he embraced trends, technological and otherwise, that served his purposes.

Graham recognized that the preaching in the crusades and on radio and television formed his ministry's centerpiece, but he also recognized that spoken words were evanescent, like a spirit soaring on the wind. So it was that he and his editorial assistants also invested a remarkable amount of time authoring books and articles and helping launch the fortnightly *Christianity Today*. After the microphones were shut down, written words remained. He desired the immediate impact that preaching afforded, but he also wanted the long-range impact that publications secured. The short of it was that Graham's publishing empire was vast. Ultimately it may have reached more people than the telecast empire, and it certainly proved more permanent. By 1999 his books had sold more than thirty million copies worldwide.[119]

But first we need to address the question of authorship. How many of the words released under his name did he actually write himself? For that matter, how many of his sermons—many of which eventually saw publication—did he actually craft himself? In 1971 he told reporters that except for "a man that helps me with my newspaper column" he had "no writers."[120] In his 1997 memoir Graham acknowledged that one assistant provided "background research for sermons and other messages," and that a secretary typed up sermon notes from dictation for his 1954 London crusade, but he denied that other people helped with his "evangelistic sermons."[121] Those statements obscured the truth. Documents housed in the Billy Graham Center Archives show that an assistant supplied a steady stream of "messages" for Graham during his crusade in Europe in 1954. Another assistant performed "research and writing" tasks for Graham from 1951 through 1974. The precise details are not clear.[122] Yet common sense tells us that no person possibly could have drafted at least 1,600 different sermons, produced innumerable civic addresses, traveled eight months a year, preached in nearly one hundred countries, appeared at scores of press conferences and talk shows, produced a daily syndicated question-and-answer column, *and* written thirty-two books, as well as countless articles on countless topics. Clearly Graham had help.

Four lines of response arise. First of all, in the pulpit, in evangelical circles—as in most of Christianity—the line between creating and borrowing blurred. Differently stated, the genre did not encourage the homiletic equivalent of footnoting. Graham probably would have been surprised if reporters had challenged him about it, and, to the best of my knowledge, none did. Sermons were one thing, books another. There, Graham usually—not always but usually—did acknowledge assistance, and that is the second line of response. For example, he allowed that his wife, Ruth, co-wrote *Peace with*

God (after tossing out materials the publisher had drafted).[123] In the "Preface" of his memoir, *Just As I Am*, he thanked "the many individuals to whom I owe an enormous debt because of their help or their friendship, and yet whose names are not mentioned in these pages," and in the Acknowledgments of the memoir he identified a half-dozen specific researchers/writers by name.[124] The "My Answer" column periodically included a statement that he approved but did not actually write the columns. The question, then, is not whether he acknowledged help but whether he was sufficiently fulsome and specific about the extent of the assistance.

The third line of response is simpler. The evidence suggests that on balance Graham's sermons and writings represented his own *thinking*, though not necessarily his own writing. The texts of the 1,600 sermons, released to researchers in early 2014, consist of typed, relatively spare outlines with numerous comments in his personal hand inserted all along the way. Even if editorial assistants created the outline, Graham clearly came up with most of the actual words that he uttered, along with his deletions and additions.[125] Janet Baird, a writer—ghostwriter, if one prefers—for *Peace with God* revealed the pattern. "With the crowded schedule that Dr. Graham maintains," one journalist wrote about Baird, "he doesn't have time to do the actual writing of his book. Mrs. Baird is doing this from scores of radio scripts, sermons and numerous conferences in which the evangelist has given her his thoughts. . . . 'He is simply putting into book form what he puts into his sermons,' she said."[126]

Dr. John Akers, one of Graham's chief editorial assistants after 1977, described the collaborative process that supported the research and writing of Graham's books, columns, and sermons. The original idea for a book always came from Graham. Articles usually arose because a magazine or newspaper requested one. Typically the writers presented drafts to Graham, he worked through them orally and in writing, routed them back to the writers, they incorporated his ideas, routed them back to him, sometimes for several rounds, until Graham felt satisfied. The pattern with the sermons evidently changed as he matured and, like most preachers, developed a storehouse of homiletic material. By the time of Akers's tenure, Graham generated the sermon ideas himself, but he relied on his writers, his wife, Ruth, and others to supplement examples he gleaned from his own reading, especially of newspapers. The procedure always proved a dynamic one.[127]

Finally, did any of these considerations really matter? There is little reason to believe that Graham's supporters spent much time worrying about it. We will come back to this question in a later chapter that focuses on the letters Americans sent by the millions. If those letters can be taken as an index, it is clear that what most partisans heard and read was the Billy Graham Voice, and for them, that was all they cared about.

In October 2013, one month before Graham's ninety-fifth birthday, he released his thirty-second book, *The Reason for Hope: Salvation*. The first book, *Calling Youth to Christ*, was published in 1947. The others appeared in roughly two-year intervals throughout his career. Four dealt with eschatology (the study of how history will end), three addressed teenagers, one took the form of a memoir (in two editions), and two or three (depending on how one defines things) took up specific theological themes such as the new birth. The rest—the majority—focused on how to find hope in the ups and downs of daily Christian life. The titles of the final seven books are telling: *Hope for Each Day* (2002), *The Key to Personal Peace* (2003), *Living in God's Love* (2005), *The Journey: How to Live by Faith in an Uncertain World* (2006), *Nearing Home: Life, Faith, and Finishing Well* (2011), *The Heaven Answer Book* (2012), and *The Reason for Hope* (2013).

Of those thirty-two works, the most important ones for placing Graham in American culture were *Peace with God* (1953, rev. 1984) and *Just As I Am* (1997, rev. 2007). As noted, *Peace with God* sold more than two million copies. Repeatedly reissued, and never out of print, this trademark volume eventually saw translation into fifty languages, as well as a miniaturized version—which likely meant that some viewed it as a devotional object in itself. Those figures proved remarkable for a theological work pounded out—at least in part—by a thirty-five-year-old preacher with no seminary, let alone advanced, degrees. Intellectual historian Andrew Finstuen aptly said that *Peace with God* was heralded as theology for the "common man."[128] Some of the success may have stemmed from its somewhat misleading association with two other popular books published at roughly the same time: Joshua Liebman's *Peace of Mind* (1947) and Norman Vincent Peale's *The Power of Positive Thinking* (1952).

Graham's *Peace with God* articulated themes that recurred in every other book he wrote. One could make a strong case that it proved his most influential work since it prefigured the basic lines of his theology for six decades. The chapter titles offer a glimpse not only of its contents but also of American evangelical boilerplate in the middle years of the twentieth century: Part I: The Problem, The Quest, The Bible, God, Sin, The Devil, After Death; Part II: The Solution, Why Jesus Came, How and Where to Begin?, Repent, Faith, The New Birth, How to Be Sure; Part III: Results, Enemies of the Christian, Rules of the Christian Life, The Christian and the Church, Social Obligations of the Christian, The Future of the Christian, and Peace at Last. More telling than the chapter titles was the book's threefold structure: Problem, Solution, and Results. It is difficult to imagine an arrangement more suited to the pragmatic no-nonsense American cast of mind.

When the book is read whole, several different features stand out. First, as Finstuen noted, the book did not detail peace with self or with society, and it did not offer a recipe for health or wealth. Rather, the subject was God.[129] Graham's God was not, perhaps, the transcendent North Star of Jonathan Edwards's theological imagination. But Graham's deity did prove transcendent yet personal, judging yet forgiving, and timeless yet timely. This God remained the absolute, unqualified anchor for everything else he preached and wrote about for sixty years. Second, Graham underscored the fundamental flaw in humans that no amount of social engineering could fix. That flaw was sin. If a personal God towered at one end of Graham's cosmos, a serpent still lay coiled in the pit at the other. And third came the promise of another chance. To be sure, in *Peace with God* the God of judgment loomed larger and darker than he would in later books, but the promise of a second chance ran close behind. Critics such as theologian Reinhold Niebuhr charged Graham with offering a religion too much at ease with American culture—"a tailored and domesticated leftover from the wild and wooly frontier evangelistic campaigns," the professor said.[130] And sometimes Graham did. But more often than not he offered—or at least supportive readers believed he offered—a real God and real sin and real hope.

Graham's memoir, *Just As I Am,* remains the most valuable resource for his personal history. Since it was published in 1997, in the later years of a very long life, the question of historical reliability necessarily arises. The Preface indicated that Graham and editorial assistants built the text from contemporaneous records. Other accounts have sometimes presented a quite different interpretation of events, but on the whole the basic factual framework has survived intact.[131] It rehearsed the mundane facts of Graham's life in exhaustive—and exhausting—detail. It also painted those details with a thick veneer of devotional uplift.

Except for ardent partisans, the book did not win a great deal of praise. Not a few critics found it banal at best and self-serving at worst. A reviewer for the *Times Literary Supplement* called it "insipid," "self-serving," and "massively protracted."[132] Another, writing for the *Nation*, said that if it were compared with classics of spiritual autobiography such as those by Thomas Merton and Dorothy Day, Graham had written "a comic book."[133] Columbia University's Andrew Delbanco, a distinguished literary historian, acknowledged that Graham—the "Elvis of the evangelicals"—seemed sincere, "winsome," and "genuinely enlarged by his travels." But Delbanco found the book "monotonous" and short on insight. Its humor was mostly "unwitting" and its writing never rose above "genial banality." It was, in short, "little more than just another celebrity autobiography—the fluff one expects from most politicians, newscasters and movie stars."[134] To be sure, many responses proved even-handed, and some warmly appreciative, but the latter tended to focus more on the man than on the memoir.[135]

However evaluated as literature, *Just As I Am* illumined Graham's larger historical significance in several ways. For one thing, though much of the criticism seemed fair enough, some of it missed the mark by failing to grasp Graham's clear intent. He imagined the book as a memoir, not an autobiography, and so the narrative of his life ran on the rails of a theme. That theme was how God worked not because of him but *through* him. Graham's deep sense of providential calling cradled the enormous paradox throughout his career of personal humility and professional self-promotion.

A second revealing feature of *Just As I Am* was the extraordinary—and extraordinary is the right word—density of Graham's interpersonal connections. The index read like the social register of the *Charlotte Observer* and *Washington Post* combined. To some extent the list of names constituted old-fashioned name-dropping, but it also represented the people Graham really did know and trust. Figures as unlikely as Karl Barth, Bernard Baruch, Frank Sinatra, and Aleksandr Solzhenitsyn made the cut. And that said a great deal about the density of the social-demographic scaffolding of evangelicals' leadership in general and of Graham's generalship in particular. It would be an exaggeration to say that all of those figures knew one another, but they all knew Graham. Closely connected to this point was the rich array of photographs of Graham and the human and material settings in which he worked. If he carefully controlled his personal public image, he just as carefully controlled the public image of the evangelical surge he helped create. Evangelicals accomplished a lot partly because they made certain that the world saw them accomplishing a lot.

A final set of revealing features emerged as a paradoxical pair: contrition and artfulness. The book bore repeated apologies for mistakes made and opportunities missed.[136] We will return to complexities of this trait later. Here it suffices to say that contrition said something important about the man. Critics charged Graham with not being "prophetic," and later we will see that to some extent they had a point. But prophetic figures often proved more adept at exposing society's mistakes than their own. Americans evidently appreciated Graham's awareness of his own shortcomings.

Their devotion to him also said a lot about their willingness to forgive his mistakes.

At the same time, however, the book was artfully selective. *Newsweek*'s Ken Woodward, not uncritical but generally sympathetic to Graham, suggested the book was mistitled. It did not present him "as he was." Rather: "Too much has been left out, too little explained."[137] Students of American culture found few surprises and even fewer insights into the inner character of the hundreds of figures that paraded through its pages. Yet Graham clearly did not intend the book as a "tell all," and readers might be grateful he did not attempt much in the way of character analysis since he was not very good at that sort of thing anyway. Rather, he hoped the memoir would not only show that God had worked through him but also serve as a guide for young evangelists eager to avoid his mistakes.[138]

Beyond *Peace with God* and *Just As I Am* (and perhaps one or two other books, especially *Angels*), Graham's most noted print publications were the fortnightly *Christianity Today*, the monthly *Decision,* and the daily syndicated question-and-answer column "My Answer." We will consider the "My Answer" column in a later chapter. The details of *Decision* can be quickly stated. Launched in 1960, it was meant to be a popular version of *Christianity Today*. *Decision*'s long-term editor, Sherwood Wirt—who held a doctorate in theology from the University of Edinburgh—modeled it after the (Catholic) *Our Sunday Visitor. Decision* typically ran the text of one of Graham's recent sermons, several testimonials, and news of current and upcoming crusades. Circulation figures are hard to pin down. One scholar set them at 2.1 million in 1965, 5 million in 1975, and down to 1.7 million in 1992. By 1980 the BGEA was publishing it in six languages and different editions. In 2014 the BGEA reported 400,000 but still rated *Decision* as "one of the most widely circulated religious periodicals in the world."[139]

One of Graham's shrewdest insights lay in the recognition that his ministry ran the best chance for solidifying during his lifetime and surviving after he was gone if he institutionalized it in a periodical. Other evangelists had embalmed their legacy in schools or in mini-denominations. Graham knew that he was not trained for the former and temperamentally unsuited for the latter. So it was that *Christianity Today* came to life in 1956. To race ahead in the story, within four years its circulation had caught up to its mainline Protestant rival the *Christian Century.* In 2014 it boasted a print circulation of 120,000 and readership of 240,000. *Christianity Today*'s website reached nearly 650,000 people, with 2.19 million webpage views, every month.[140]

By one account it all started about 2 AM. As Graham remembered the story, one night in 1953 he thought about founding a periodical. He rushed to his desk to rough out the blueprint.[141] Other evidence suggests that as early as 1951 Graham and a faculty friend at Fuller Theological Seminary had started tossing around the idea of a periodical.[142] However it came about, the year before the magazine began publication Graham said he hoped it would "plant the theological flag in the middle of the road, taking a conservative theological position but a definite liberal approach to social problems."[143] In Graham's chartering vision for *Christianity Today*, he stated two aims. The first was to give evangelicals in the mainline a voice. The second was to give the nascent evangelical movement respectability in the wider culture. Given those aims, it was not surprising that Graham— invariably sensitive to the symbolism of location—felt the high price of locating the editorial offices in Washington, DC, worth the cost.[144] Years later Graham reflected: "We also wanted our editor to mingle with congressmen, senators, and government leaders so he could speak with first-hand knowledge on the issues of the day."[145] Graham's entrepreneurial reflexes were on full display.

The determination to form a normative theological imagination expressed itself especially in the second aim. The periodical's "Editorial Policy" would call for the magazine to be "pro-church," "thoroughly biblical, evangelical, and evangelistic," "anti-communist," "for social improvement," and "down the middle of the road" when interpreting current events.[146] Four decades later Graham remembered that he aimed for the magazine to be "pro-church and pro-denomination," committed to "the trustworthiness of Scripture," and dedicated to a "more gentle and loving direction."[147]

The founders proved surprisingly forthright, acknowledging that they had the *Christian Century* in their sights. The goal was not to push the *Century* off the playing field. By then the *Century* was nearly sixty years old and served as the primary voice for the mainline—which the *Century* magazine had helped create.[148] The goal, rather, was to provide a second voice in the American theological choir, a voice for people who felt they had none, and one that presented itself in a manner both sophisticated and accessible.[149]

The operating tactics proved simple enough. The organizers sent the first ten issues free to every pastor in the United States, Canada, Great Britain, Australia, New Zealand, and to foreign missionaries. Graham expected that the main readers would be pastors, not theologians. He insisted that it should be credible to theologians but not designed for them. Its articles should be serious but not ponderous. That goal proved easier said than done when the heavyweight systematic theologian Carl F. H. Henry became the first editor. After the first installment hit Graham's mailbox, he told Henry that advisors felt that the opening article was "too verbose" and looked like "obscurity reaching for profundity."[150] Elsewhere Graham urged Henry to avoid controversies and go light on doctrinal technicalities.[151] Graham respected Henry's mind, erudition, and academic credentials, but he also kept a clear eye on the audience he wanted the fortnightly to reach.

Historians have looked at *Christianity Today* with several questions in mind. The most persistent and controversial one is to what extent *Christianity Today*'s views of social and political issues represented Graham's own. The question has gained traction partly because *Christianity Today* did not stick to its originating vision of a liberal position—however loosely defined—on social issues. The civil rights struggle offers one example. On the whole the magazine resisted it, affirming equality in God's eyes but not pro-active governmental measures to achieve it.[152] Yet the organ also allowed a minority strain of decidedly progressive editorials and articles to appear.[153] One reporter assigned to cover the 1965 Selma March actually joined it—though significantly his report never saw publication.[154]

Where did Graham himself stand? Did the unsigned positions on the editorial page represent his? Or did they represent those of L. Nelson Bell, the executive editor for the first eighteen years and, by Graham's own account, an "ultra-conservative if there ever was one"?[155] Or did they represent those of J. Howard Pew, the laissez-faire oilman who provided much of the magazine's start-up money—and purportedly tried to press his views on the editors?[156] As the founder and acknowledged head of the magazine for fifty years, did Graham exercise a say?[157]

The answer needs to be carefully parsed. On one hand, Carl F. H. Henry, the first editor (1956–1968), intimated that Graham played little role in the magazine's day-to-day editorial decisions.[158] His pattern was to get things started and then (except for overseeing the BGEA itself) monitor them from afar. On the other hand, Graham did influence the fortnightly's overall editorial direction. He personally chose all board members. One of them openly called it "Billy's magazine." Though Graham himself would never say so, according to a later executive editor, "he served as the final reference point and power, even into the 2000s."[159]

However Graham's own role is interpreted, there can be little question that as the decades passed, *Christianity Today* inexorably inched toward the social outlook of the *Christian Century*. Though it never quite reached the *Century*'s center/left posture on those issues, and never came close to it on theological matters, it did increasingly distinguish itself by the breadth and depth of its concerns about human suffering globally.[160]

Social orthodoxy was one thing but theological orthodoxy quite another. Graham and *Christianity Today* soon came to serve as the gatekeeper for the doctrinal norms of the evangelical movement. Differently viewed, the magazine's doctrinal norms defined the perimeter of the theological playing field, and evangelical orthodoxy found its measure by staying within that perimeter. Pentecostals, Holiness Wesleyans, Churches of Christ, liturgical Lutherans, and fundamentalist Baptists, among others, might not have liked it, but they did not successfully challenge it or provide a viable alternative. Part of Graham's achievement lodged in his ability to see that the emerging evangelical movement, surging with undisciplined energy, needed both a point of reference at the center and a working fence around the perimeter.

It would be a stretch to say that Graham, still years from his prime, understood the implications of all that he was doing. But then, it is worth remembering that entrepreneurs often did their best work on the backstroke.

CHAPTER FIVE

Architect

The six decades stretching from the end of World War II until Graham's effective retirement in 2005 were a time of paradox. On one hand it seemed an age of exceptional turmoil. Battles about war, race, women, sexual orientation, and unborn life raged. The culture split into adversarial camps and the country into rival states, often loosely tagged red and blue. Those labels denoted entire value systems more than geographic regions. On the other hand, the age also seemed marked by exceptional satisfactions. Though recessions came and went, the standard of living continually rose, at least into the early 1970s. By 2005, the year of Graham's last major crusade, basic expectations about comfort, recreation, travel, health, and longevity soared beyond any benchmark realistically available in 1944, the year of his first major public speaking event. The technological revolution at the end of the twentieth century, which made television almost obsolete in the face of the brave new world of the Internet, represented not just a quantitative but also a qualitative advance in the possibilities of life. So if it was an age of anxiety it also was an age of opportunity.[1]

This paradox evident throughout the long half-century following World War II manifested itself with special clarity in the period from 1945 to 1960—the era in which Graham gained national and international visibility. Those years saw economic ups and downs, with a particularly sharp recession at the end of the 1940s. They also saw the specter of worldwide communist expansion, with global nuclear annihilation no longer a science-fiction fantasy but a palpable possibility. At the same time, the United States had emerged from the most terrible war of the century undisputedly the strongest military and economic power on earth. Significant moves toward justice for minorities and for women began to seem a realistic possibility, even within that generation's lifetime. Religious participation in general and church membership and attendance in particular reached unprecedented levels.[2]

In this setting, strong voices in the entire religious establishment—which is to say not just Protestant but the Protestant/Catholic/Jewish establishment—felt they could in some ways speak for the culture as a whole. The aim was not imperialist, not to usurp and displace, but to transcend with a higher set of values. Figures as diverse as Dorothy Day, Georgia Harkness, Abraham Heschel, Martin Luther King, Jr., Reinhold Niebuhr, and Fulton Sheen sought in words and deeds to embrace everyone in a sweeping vision of a more humane life.[3] The redoubtable Henry R. Luce of *Time/Life* fortune imagined an "American Century" ahead.[4] In 1967 Robert N. Bellah famously called the outlook "civil religion." At that time Bellah deemed it a good thing, for it meant that the unifying power of religion might be harnessed to help form the basis of a truly civil society.[5]

Both mainline and evangelical Protestants participated. Mainline Protestants, for example, helped transform the old Federal Council of Churches into the more comprehensive-sounding National Council of Churches. And they helped transform the old Interchurch World Council into the more comprehensive-sounding World Council of Churches (WCC). Many broadly evangelical Protestants also shared an aspiration to influence the entire culture. In 1942, for example, they formed the National Association of Evangelicals to project a coordinated agenda of political and moral reform, along with a somewhat more progressive theological and social outlook than their fundamentalist parents had held.[6]

So it was that a powerful evangelical center, dominated by evangelical Baptists, Methodists, Presbyterians, and, later, the Assemblies of God, aspired, like mainline Protestants, to represent the whole culture. They sought prescriptive authority—a custodial role—for everyone. In the public mind this centrist evangelicalism, normative in aspiration and expansionist in practice, became the key definer of post–World War II evangelicalism. It embodied the form that came to mind most readily when outsiders in general and the press in particular thought about evangelical identity.[7]

The story bore complexities. Not all broadly evangelical Protestants shared that normative expansionist desire. Lutherans, Mennonites, Adventists, and the Churches of Christ, to take four large and important bodies, focused more on their own affairs. They continued to call themselves by their own names, read their own newspapers, and attend their own conventions.[8] At first glance Southern Baptists might not appear to be normative and expansionist either, since they too continued to focus on their own name, newspapers, and conventions. Yet they did not need to flex their muscles. In the South, they already dominated the landscape.[9] When outside forces challenged that dominance in the 1970s, Baptist expansionism was unleashed with explosive power.[10]

How should we label this normative expansionist centrist evangelicalism? *Subculture* is too restrictive because it does not connote the movement's power to shape the larger culture. *Parallel culture* is too muscular because it connotes too much power in the face of the historic privileges that mainline Protestants and secular elites still enjoyed. *Shadow culture* is too furtive because its ambitions were anything but furtive. Evangelicals often fancied themselves a *counterculture,* at least spiritually, but there were too many station wagons in their church parking lots to make that one credible. And so we come to *mainstream evangelicalism.* This phrase carries some limitations too, but it comes as close as any. It intimates both a measure of socially rooted comfort with the surrounding culture and a measure of theologically rooted discomfort. The balance between comfort and discomfort varied from place to place and time to time. In the South the tradition enjoyed something close to establishment status. Outside the South it experienced greater tension.

Mainstream evangelicalism sheltered two impulses within itself: *denominational* and *independent.* They were not mutually exclusive. Individuals often fell into both camps at once. But viewed from afar the impulses proved distinguishable. Denominational partisans were primarily interested in working within the boundaries of their historic denominations. They were not necessarily opposed to independent ventures, but they focused more on taking care of things at home. They kept the fences in good repair. Independent partisans were primarily interested in working outside denominational boundaries in order to achieve their aims more effectively. They kept the gates in good repair.

Peeking ahead for a minute, the independent impulse itself bore two internal orientations. One was a cooperative inclination to join hands with other independent endeavors in order to foster evangelism. Prime examples were the National Association of Evangelicals (1942), Fuller Theological Seminary (1947), and *Christianity Today* (1956). The other orientation was a rigorist inclination to separate in order to foster purity. Prime examples were the American Council of Christian Churches (1941), Bob Jones College (1927), and the fortnightly *Sword of the Lord* (1934). After World War II, the cooperative inclination would come to form a large share of mainstream evangelicalism, while the rigorist inclination would come to form a big part of fundamentalism.

Return to Graham. Throughout his life he exhibited both denominational and independent/cooperative impulses. We will pay more attention to the independent/cooperative side because it was more conspicuous, more distinctive, and did more to change the American religious landscape. But that does not mean that it dominated Graham's self-understanding or interests.

In the pre–World War II days both impulses—denominational and independent—turned up in Graham's birth family. Chronologically the denominational one came first. The family's church connections were rooted in hamlets some twenty miles southwest of Charlotte. Graham's father, William Frank Graham, grew up in the Dilworth Methodist Episcopal Church, South, while his mother, Morrow Coffey, grew up in the Steele Creek Community Church, a congregation of the (Southern) Presbyterian Church, US. After marrying, Morrow joined William's Methodist congregation. Because of bad roads, however, the couple often worshipped with the Steele Creek Church because it was more convenient. Eventually they moved on to Chalmers Memorial Associate Reformed Presbyterian Church (where they had been married). Graham was baptized as an infant at Chalmers Memorial and entered into formal membership at age twelve.[11] Chalmers Memorial represented Scottish Presbyterianism in its most rigorous, denominationally self-conscious American form. Many decades later, in his final Charlotte crusade, Graham would say of Chalmers Memorial: "Now those are real Presbyterians."[12] After Billy left home, William and Morrow moved on to Tenth Presbyterian Church, US. This denomination positioned itself firmly in the middle of the Southern evangelical mainstream. They remained there the rest of their lives.[13]

But for the Graham family denominationalism had its limits. An independent dynamic also energized Billy's early family experience. As the often-told story goes, the elder Graham had proved a faithful church member, but over the years his heart had grown cold. And then a crisis intervened, awakened his spiritual life, and prompted him to find sustenance outside his local church. In 1930 William suffered a severe facial injury on the farm. For a time he feared he might die. After intense prayer within the family and among friends, he recovered. William soon joined the Christian Businessmen's Association, a group of middling farmers and small business owners who met weekly for Bible study and prayer. One afternoon in the spring of 1934 the association met outdoors on William's farm to seek a spiritual quickening for themselves and for their city. The youthful Billy wanted no part of it and found himself dismayed by the whole thing—its freedom from an established denominational church service and, probably, the unfettered prayer style he heard.[14]

The Christian Businessmen's Association had sponsored Billy Sunday in the 1920s. Hoping for a repeat of Sunday's influence, they invited a dapper itinerant preacher named Mordecai Ham to hold a tent revival nearby in the fall. Though Ham was associated with segregation, anti-Catholicism,

Prohibition, and, in the 1940s, anti-Semitism, there was no indication that the Businessmen's Association knew or cared anything about that in 1934.[15] They wanted an old-fashioned revival. Graham remembered that the pastors of the established churches in the area—apparently including the pastor of Chalmers Memorial—remained aloof.[16]

In the meantime Morrow Coffey Graham, though retaining her membership and active participation in Chalmers Memorial, had been tracing an independent journey of her own. Prompted by her sister, Morrow started meeting for prayer and Bible study with a group of women associated with the Plymouth Brethren.[17] This small but influential sect originated in the Church of England in Ireland in the early years of the nineteenth century. Plymouth Brethren associated themselves with an apocalyptic form of premillennialism called dispensationalism. As we have seen, that tradition held that Christ would physically return in glory before the millennium. Dispensationalism equaled only part of the story, however. Another part lay in the sect's fierce distrust of established churches in Great Britain and denominational churches in the United States. They urged their partisans to meet in cell groups in homes for prayer and Bible study. Still another part focused on private devotional times of prayer and Bible study—often alone in the believer's "prayer closet"—as well as evangelism to the lost.[18]

The band that Morrow attended apparently was an entirely informal gathering in friends' homes, not in any way a rival to Chalmers Memorial. Yet she imbibed its independent spirit, especially the emphasis on communal and private prayer and Bible study, as well as evangelism. In those years she started regularly reading *Moody Monthly*. This periodical came from the Bible Institute of Chicago, founded by the roving independent revivalist Dwight L. Moody.[19] Like Moody himself, the *Monthly* was in principle committed to premillennial teaching, but the more important part of the magazine's influence lay in its commitment to bolstering believers' personal spiritual life and to independent evangelism outside the strictures of the historic denominations.[20]

Graham never said that he discussed independent evangelicalism—or anything like it—with either of his parents. But given his age—early to middle teens—and given that the family maintained tight internal bonds, he hardly could have escaped it. The elder Grahams hosted itinerant evangelists in their home. Graham's very first preaching outing unfolded when one of the visitors took him to speak at a local jail.[21] It was telling that William and Morrow sent their son to Bob Jones College, an unaccredited nondenominational Bible Institute. Given the proximity and comparative affordability of the University of North Carolina in Chapel Hill, Bob Jones College likely proved attractive because it fit their religious worldview. A similar logic applied to Graham's transfer at mid-year to Florida Bible Institute. Purely personal reasons such as a fondness for sunshine and a friend already there had something to do with it. Yet Morrow likely found the school's literature, which stressed its independent posture and evangelistic spirit, compelling. Finally the elder Grahams almost certainly encouraged and perhaps helped finance their son's move north to Wheaton College, another independent school with a strong evangelistic emphasis.

In short, William and especially Morrow Graham bequeathed to Billy two heritages: denominational and independent. Over the next six decades, that dual impulse played out in a variety ways. For Billy, like his parents, the denominational disposition came first chronologically and perhaps intellectually too. In autobiographical accounts he made a point to say that he underwent sprinkling and grew up in Chalmers Memorial.[22] Years later, while preaching in small Southern Baptist churches in Florida, Graham's colleagues told him he really should be immersed Baptist-style if he wished to continue holding forth in Baptist churches. And so he was in 1938. The following year he underwent formal ordination at the hands of Baptist colleagues at a Southern Baptist church in East Palatka, Florida.[23] On graduation from Wheaton in 1943, he served a denominational Baptist congregation for eighteen months. In 1959 he became a member of the largest Baptist church in the country, First Baptist in Dallas. Many people regarded that congregation as the "national" church of the Southern Baptist Convention. In 2009, a half-century later, Graham transferred his membership to another historic Baptist church, First Baptist in Spartanburg, South Carolina. The Spartanburg congregation had a strong regional denominational presence.

After graduating from college, Graham invariably publically identified himself as a member of a historic denomination: the Southern Baptist Convention. He shouldered his share of responsibility for its unhappy racial history. Graham remained loyal enough to the Southern Baptist Convention that he refused to join his strong-willed wife in the Presbyterian fold. All of his associates held historic denominational affiliations all of their lives (notably, Barrows Baptist, Wilson Baptist, Shea Wesleyan Methodist, and Ford Presbyterian). Graham accepted no invitation to hold a crusade in a city unless a majority of churches in the city endorsed it.[24] Most churches that signed on for a Graham crusade were Baptist, Methodist, Presbyterian, and, later, Assemblies of God. To take one of countless examples,

in the 1982 Raleigh, North Carolina, crusade, half of the fourteen counselor applications represented Southern mainstream Baptist and Methodist
churches, a third unaffiliated, and a small minority Catholic or Episcopal.
Of the decision cards, again, half were Baptist and Methodist, one-fifth
Catholic or Episcopal, another fifth other Protestant denominations, a bit
more than one-tenth not specified, and a sprinkling of other groups.[25]

What about the other side of the ledger? What data reveal an independent impulse? From first to last Graham also showed a powerful affinity
for independent groups and endeavors operating outside established denominations. He said that he went to Bob Jones College in order to be mentored
by Bob Jones, one of the most famous freelance evangelists of the age.[26]
Graham moved to FBI for many reasons, but preparing for a career as an
ordained minister in a Southern mainstream or mainline Protestant denomination was not one of them. At FBI he served as assistant pastor of Tampa
Gospel Tabernacle, a Christian and Missionary Alliance (CMA) church.[27]
At FBI he took a range of standard Bible school courses—Bible, doctrine,
history, geography—but there is no evidence that he pursued a course in
the history, theology, or polity of a particular denomination, including the
CMA.[28]

Moving to independent Wheaton, Graham signed the denominational
preference card "Presbyterian," although by then he had been ordained
Southern Baptist.[29] In his second and third years at Wheaton he served as
interim or supply pastor of "The Tab" or the United Gospel Church—
which informally aligned itself with the CMA.[30] Though by then the CMA
had acquired the infrastructure of a conventional denomination, it remained well outside the orbit of mainstream evangelical or mainline Protestant bodies.[31] Graham majored in anthropology, which probably meant
that he took courses in ethnology, cultural anthropology, and biological
and cultural evolution, among others, but he never spoke of courses preparing him specifically for seminary (such as Koine Greek or denominational
polity).[32] In light of those developments it seems reasonable to believe that
his ordination as a Baptist reflected a marriage of convenience. He avoided
preaching about Baptist distinctives such as believers' baptism or the theology
of separation of church and state. From 1944, when he spoke for YFC, to
the end of his career, he worked intimately with independent organizations.

To sum up, we see a man stretched between two poles: denominational
on one end and independent on the other. Yet the tension proved productive, not disabling. It meant that on one side he enjoyed roots in a bona fide
American denomination with origins deep in the Protestant Reformation

of the sixteenth century. That identity yielded credibility in the outside world, among other benefits. Despite continual travel for sixty years, journalists rarely if ever called him an "itinerant," let alone a "freelance," preacher. At the same time, Graham's denominational ties remained sufficiently tenuous that he found himself free to move around, not only geographically but also culturally and to some extent theologically, too. He was answerable to no one except his supporters. He enjoyed the luxury of choosing his own friends.

Graham bequeathed this taut yet productive relationship between the stability of a denominational identity on one side and the freedom of an independent identity on the other to the mainstream evangelical movement. It manifested itself in Youth for Christ's motto: "Geared to the Times but Anchored to the Rock." The creator of the motto likely had something somewhat different in mind—a flexible method to convey a fixed message—but the overall point was the same: stability coupled with freedom. That relationship proved enormously effective. It fueled evangelicals' creative energies but kept those energies within manageable boundaries. Though it would be an exaggeration to call it lightning in a bottle, that was the idea.

How did Graham's dual bequest—the combination of denominational and independent impulses—shape mainstream evangelicalism?

First of all, Graham both prompted and enabled mainstream evangelicals (hereafter simply evangelicals) to come out of the closet and fit themselves in wider social circles. They rarely showed much of a presence among the educational elite, and only a limited presence outside the circle of old-stock whites.[33] But they readily moved into the management side of government, business, and technology-dependent circles.[34] Graham showed them how to make this move with integrity and credibility.[35]

Keeping their souls intact and maintaining respectability all at the same time was no small order, but Graham managed it. Respectability, in turn, required evangelicals to seat themselves at a table in the middle of the public square. Graham modeled both open conversation and open scrutiny. In the process evangelicals won not only a place at that table but also a permanent place on the customary guest list: one mainline, one Catholic, one Jew, and one evangelical. That did not mean they always won the day, but it did mean that they received a fair chance to join the conversation.[36]

Graham also provided a model for how to behave once seated, and that was a second element of his bequest. Granted, it would have happened anyway. Graham was not by any means the only evangelical who knew how to rub shoulders with elites, but he helped the process along. By example he tutored evangelicals in the fine art of being polite participants rather than disruptive onlookers taking pot shots from the sidelines. He offered a model of principled yet civil conversation. In important ways evangelical became less a theological position than a style, a way of behaving, not extreme either by evangelicals' own standards or by the standards of secular culture. Samuel S. Hill, an eminent historian of the South, once quipped that Graham taught them when to wear a necktie.[37] To be sure, the quip was only that, a quip. In the 1950s the halls of Fuller Theological Seminary saw their share of bowties and three-piece suits and even a homburg hat from time to time.[38] But the larger point held. Being an evangelical meant not only liking Graham but also being like Graham: well appointed and well behaved.

Third, though Graham himself was not an intellectual, he respected and sponsored colleagues who were, such as Carl F. H. Henry (Ph.D. Boston University), Harold John Ockenga (Ph.D. University of Pittsburgh), and Edward John Carnell (Harvard Th.D., Boston University Ph.D.). Being linked with Graham connoted that they were not just intellectuals but also had something important to say to the spirit. Men like Henry and Ockenga may not have been as irenic or inclusive as Graham but they were not culture warriors like Jerry Falwell or Franklin Graham either. If Henry and Ockenga gave themselves heft, Graham gave them currency.[39]

Then too, Graham provided vicarious elite status for millions of evangelicals. He served as the representative for everyday believers who otherwise did not enjoy a moment in the sun. He became the "very famous evangelical" who hobnobbed with presidents and queens and billionaires and celebrities. And though he did not hobnob with secular intellectuals, he at least got invited to speak at prestigious secular colleges and center/left mainline Protestant seminaries.[40] Of course fundamentalists thought he sold out to liberals and liberals thought he sold out, not to fundamentalists, but to the conservative power establishment in Washington. But evangelicals and many other Americans did not think so.[41]

And finally, under Graham's leadership evangelicals achieved their identity by doing two things at once: first by engaging their mainline Protestant neighbors on their left and second by distancing themselves from their fundamentalist cousins on their right. In the eyes of his fellow mainstream evangelicals he displayed an appropriate sense of priorities when he decided that it was fitting to downplay doctrinal differences with the mainline in the interests of a wider evangelistic message. But shortly we will see that his fundamentalist cousins wondered what the point of cooperating was if it meant that he ended up preaching a lowest-common-denominator religion? To them, Graham had sold out.

Graham, more than any other person, triangulated—to use the apt word of *New Yorker* columnist Peter Boyer—American Protestantism into three distinct groups: mainline Protestants on the left, unreconstructed fundamentalists on the right, and evangelicals in the middle.[42] We are left to wonder how things might have gone if Graham had remained an itinerant preacher marketing his message in the small towns of the South. The triangulation would have taken place anyway, but not as soon and not as dramatically as it did under Graham's shadow.

Parachurch Movements

A *Newsweek* journalist once astutely remarked that "a complete list of all the evangelistic 'outreach' organizations and their missionary affiliates formed since the fifties does not exist. If it did, it would be thicker than most yellow pages."[43] Those enterprises were commonly called *parachurch* organizations because they stood outside or alongside mainstream evangelical denominations such as the Southern Baptist Convention and the (Southern) Presbyterian Church, US. The definition of a parachurch is not airtight. We might think of it as an association of like-minded persons coming from different denominational and different independent traditions for the purpose of achieving a particular evangelistic goal. Parachurches often looked and functioned like the religious counterpart to a single-purpose political action committee. Institutional fellow travelers, we might call them.

Parachurch organizations had their roots in independent institutions of various kinds that took hold before or during World War II. Representative examples of such early endeavors would include cooperative bodies such as the National Association of Evangelicals, college alliances such as InterVarsity Christian Fellowship, and missionary-sending agencies such as Wycliffe Bible Translators. More institutionalized expressions from that era would include magazines such as the *Sunday School Times*, radio programs such as the *Old Fashioned Revival Hour*, Bible institutes such as BIOLA (Bible Institute of Los Angeles), accredited colleges such as Wheaton, theological seminaries such as Asbury, and notable congregations such as Moody Tabernacle in Chicago.

Yet it was the post–World War II era that saw the main insurgence in the number, reach, and financial strength of parachurch organizations. Most of the important ones Graham had a hand in, either founding them or lending his considerable prestige and financial and organizational resources to their operations. Prominent examples included, in chronological order of their founding, Youth for Christ, World Vision International, Campus Crusade for Christ, *Christianity Today*, *Living Bible*, and Gordon-Conwell Theological Seminary.[44]

Graham's involvement in parachurch groups had a history. It grew from the independent impulse in his heritage. More precisely, it grew from the cooperative side of that independent impulse. It is important to remember that independence did not always foster cooperation. Sometimes it fostered (at least in the eyes of outsiders) a propensity to fight for purity regardless of the personal consequences. That propensity lay behind the founding of Bob Jones College and other independent schools and congregations throughout the United States. But Graham's instincts lay elsewhere. He believed with ever-growing conviction that combativeness, even in the interest of truth, served no one's interest, and least of all that of the gospel. More to the point, he was determined to step outside denominational structures in order to accomplish goals that could be better secured by joining hands and working together. The constructive bridge-building side of independence gave birth to cooperative evangelicalism. Cooperative evangelicalism in turn provided the rails for uncounted parachurch agencies.

In Graham's life the road to cooperative evangelicalism started way back in his adolescence and college days. Within a year of Billy's graduation from Wheaton, he threw his energies into Chicagoland YFC. That association, which embodied the organizational blueprint of most parachurch agencies, provided his first major public preaching outing (speaking before three thousand people at Orchestra Hall in May 1944 when he was just twenty-five years old), tens if not hundreds of speaking engagements through the late 1940s, two extended European tours, and, important for his later career, introduction to a network of like-minded and hugely talented young men like himself.[45] Through the 1940s Graham and YFC were so entwined one is left to wonder if one would have flourished without the other.

Several features of YFC played a role in Graham's career. Taken together they tell us important things about post–World War II culture. First, its meetings played out in Technicolor: they were fast moving, packed with arresting sights and sounds, featured engaging personalities, and focused on the lives and temperament of young adults. In all of these respects YFC fit the emerging media and cinematic attractions of the age. And then, YFC provided a platform for gregarious, talented, energetic, and visionary young men (or virtually all men). They were not seminary leaders bound by crusty traditions about the right way to climb the career ladder or the right way to present the gospel. Rather, they believed themselves free to innovate and follow whatever path was most effective. And third, YFC embodied the effervescence of an emergent religious movement. Just as there were no limits to what God could do, so also YFC zealots felt that there were no limits to what God's exuberant servants could do.[46]

Graham contributed to the growth of other parachurch organizations in varying degrees. We have seen that he effectively founded *Christianity Today*. J. Howard Pew's money and Carl Henry's brains were indispensable but Graham's imagination and resourcefulness made it happen. Within four or five years *Christianity Today* had become such a monument on the landscape of religious publishing that it seemed natural, as if it had always been there. But of course it had not. At the other end of the contribution continuum stood Graham's involvement in the early life of Fuller Theological Seminary. He lent his prestige but not much else. In 1959 Graham accepted an appointment to the Board but rarely attended any of its meetings. At one point, suffering a pang of conscience, he felt he really should resign. The chair persuaded him to stay on the roster, regardless. By then Graham's star had risen so high that one of the most valuable things he could do was simply lend his name.[47] In 2014 at age ninety-five Graham remained on the roster as a "senior trustee."[48]

Graham entered the cooperative/parachurch world when it was in a stage of rapid growth. He did not create that world, it had flourished in nineteenth-century reform and missionary societies, but his skill, resources, and imagination helped make it the sprawling and enormously powerful religious force it had become by the end of his public ministry.

Protestant Mainline

Graham may have grown up a "purebred fundamentalist," but he did not stay that way much beyond his first years of preaching on the Youth for Christ circuit.[49] In one of his earliest independent crusades, held in Augusta, Georgia, in 1948, he received the support of the local Council of Churches. Graham later recalled that some of the "ultra-fundamentalist" board members of Northwestern Schools—where he was president—did not like it.[50] He went anyway. That cooperation said as much about the council as it did about Graham. They saw in each other something worth nurturing. To be sure, things were not always so rosy. Graham's reception by the established churches in Britain and Scotland in the late 1940s and early 1950s proved a very mixed one. Though he received lavish praise he also received stinging criticism.[51] That being said, he attended most World Council of Churches meetings as an honored observer for the rest of his active life.

Those trips served as an eye-opener for a man who had spent nearly all of his adult life in the secure boundaries of American evangelical circles. In the United Kingdom he said he saw for the first time that Christians in the established churches loved Christ as much as he did. During the Scotland trip in 1955 in particular he started reconsidering some of his attitudes about historic Protestant churches.[52] Christian love seemed increasingly important to him. That did not mean, of course, that doctrine was unimportant, but it did mean that love counted too. "If a man accepts the deity of Christ and is living for Christ to the best of his knowledge," Graham wrote home to Ruth, "I intend to have fellowship with him in Christ."[53] If pressed, he surely would have added Christ's atonement and resurrection to the list, but deity served as shorthand for the larger point. Christian love was non-negotiable.[54]

One could argue that Graham's crusade in Madison Square Garden proved the most important public event of his career for multiple reasons. Conversations with potential organizers in New York had started as far back as 1951, less than two years after his "debut" crusade in Los Angeles. Those conversations culminated in a formal invitation from a cluster of evangelical churches in 1954. Graham declined, insisting that he would come only if a majority of congregations represented in the ecumenical Protestant Council of Churches, an affiliate of the National Council of Churches, participated. The broader invitation arrived the following year.[55] Graham's resistance to the initial invitation grew from a principled decision about ecumenical breadth. But he undoubtedly knew too that some of the leading mainline Protestant churches in the city, such as Marble Collegiate, First Calvary, and the Brick Church, enjoyed a long, rich history of mission and pastoral care in the city.[56] That history blurred the boundary between mainstream evangelical and mainline Protestant. As we have seen, one of his stated motives in launching *Christianity Today* in 1956 was to provide a literary voice for evangelicals *in* the mainline. Since this question was on his mind in 1956 it likely was buzzing around in his mind when he accepted the 1955 New York invitation, too.

When Graham opened the crusade in May 1957 some of the most prominent mainline Protestant clerics in the city, such as Henry Pitney Van Dusen, president of Union Theological Seminary, and John Sutherland Bonnell,

pastor of Fifth Avenue Presbyterian Church, supported him.[57] Though Bonnell, especially, fell in the moderate zone theologically, his career bore the
earmarks of impeccable mainline Protestant respectability. Bonnell served
the midtown Manhattan church from 1935 to 1962. His sermons saw regular reporting in New York newspapers, three million listeners heard his
weekly talks on the ABC network, and a clinic established in his church
blended psychological and spiritual guidance.

Over the years Graham accepted scores of invitations to speak in mainline Protestant seminaries and in secular colleges and universities. There was
little evidence that he changed anyone's mind theologically. There also
was little evidence that anyone changed his mind theologically. And there was
some evidence of audience hostility and some of condescension and some
that Graham may have mistaken a twitter for a chuckle. But on the whole the
encounters seemed remarkably amicable. Within minutes he brought audiences onto his own ground where he felt comfortable talking about human
sin, God's forgiveness, and new life in Christ. He did it with self-deprecating
wit, a relaxed style, a huge grin, and casual yet confident body language
that bespoke a desire to engage, not confront.[58]

Graham's encounters with mainline Protestant leaders call for analysis.
First it should be acknowledged that sometimes he remembered the stories
more favorably than his protagonists did. I know of no outright contradictions, but, for example, Graham recalled a warmer professional theological
relationship with Karl Barth than Barth did.[59] For another thing, it would
be cynical to think that Graham sought to make connections with mainline
Protestant leaders only because he knew they could open doors he wanted
opened, but it would be obtuse to assume that motive never entered his
mind. Graham was an ambitious man—ambitious for himself, his message,
and his movement. He wanted to know the people who had the power to
turn his ambitions into realities.

And then, it is clear that at a most basic level he wanted to know what
was going on in the culture and be part of it. He aimed to be a real participant and not an envious—let alone alienated—onlooker. Graham brought
a coherent theology of cooperation to his relations with mainline Protestant leaders. In contrast to Billy Sunday, for example, he sought an evangelical style as irenic and as broadly based as possible without giving up the
identifiable evangelical core. His ecumenism was not the vertical one of
the mainline Protestant: everyone has something valuable to contribute to
the tower of faith. Rather, his ecumenism was the horizontal one of the
bridge-builder: find the most basic common denominator—what can we all
agree on?—and then go from there.

Yet horizontal cooperation was not minimalist cooperation. It required fellowship, a genuine exchange of hearts, not just a polite shaking of hands. Graham said that he had studied what Scripture had to say about the relationship of orthodoxy to fellowship. He found passages both ways. But taken whole the Bible gave priority to fellowship.[60] On the eve of the 1957 New York crusade, Graham told the annual convention of the National Association of Evangelicals—the venue itself proved highly significant—that the "one badge of Christian discipleship is not orthodoxy, but love. There is far more emphasis on love and unity among God's people in the New Testament than there is on orthodoxy, as important as it is."[61] These may have been the most widely quoted words Graham ever uttered.

Three years after his New York crusade Graham would write in the impeccably mainline Protestant *Christian Century* that in his "ignorant piousness" he had once "'frowned upon'" men "so dedicated to Christ and so in love with the truth that I have felt unworthy to be in their presence." The *Century* was not his natural habitat, and neither was the venerable and venerated "How My Mind Has Changed" series in which the essay appeared. But he pressed on. "I have learned that although Christians do not always agree, they can disagree agreeably, and that what is most needed in the church today is for us to show an unbelieving world that we love one another."[62]

To be sure, Graham's quest for ecumenical fellowship with mainline Protestants had boundaries. He dismissed New York City's architecturally stunning Riverside Church as "impressive in a pagan sort of way" because it had no Christian symbols.[63] He suggested that cooperation with "extreme liberal and Unitarian clergy" was unlikely. They denied the deity of Christ, which he judged non-negotiable.[64] In the very same sermon/article in which he had said that the Bible gave priority to fellowship over separation, he also affirmed in bold letters: "Fellowship has its limits: We cannot commend or fellowship with those who live immoral lives or deny the deity of Christ."[65] Graham opposed *a priori* naturalism because it denied miracles and he deemed miracles (especially in the Bible and at the end of history) crucial to authentic Christianity. But he rarely publically attributed *a priori* naturalism to particular schools or to particular individuals. He worried, too, about nominalism, but he did not carefully define it and rarely publically attributed those shortcomings to particular schools or to particular individuals, either. The problem lay in the "ism."

One could argue that Graham could afford to be irenic toward mainline Protestant denominations and leaders for several reasons beyond his temperament and theology. It is plausible to think that his reflex instincts were less fundamentalist than an unself-conscious blending of fundamentalist and mainline Protestant attitudes. He came to emotional maturity in the South in the 1930s, but to ecclesiastical maturity in the Baptist South in the 1950s. In that immediate post–World War II period, said historian Elizabeth Flowers, "a stately group of silver-haired, golden-tongued, and grey-suited men" entered the ranks of the Southern Baptist Convention. They went by a variety of telling names: "genteel oligarchs, organization men, and new denominationalists." Established Baptists of that sort could afford to be graciously minded because liberals were too scarce to pose a serious or imminent threat.[66]

Beyond that, by the time Graham's star had risen high enough in the sky to attract the censorious attention of some mainline Protestant institutions and leaders Graham had already soared out of reach. That did not mean, of course, that the attacks did not hurt or that no one listened to them, but it did mean that he commanded the personal and institutional resources to ignore or respond to them as he saw fit. That independence—or even invulnerability—found re-enforcement in direct marketing, which the BGEA had pioneered in the early 1950s. Graham could navigate around the mainline whenever he wished. He simply did not need their financial or moral support, for he enjoyed direct access to the pocketbooks and heartstrings of millions already.

And finally, it is important to remember that the mainline was neither monolithic nor frozen in time. Different figures viewed Graham with different eyes. "Personally," said one cleric whose church had reluctantly lent its support to a crusade, "I don't care too much for Billy Graham or for what he preaches or for the way he preaches it. But I'm inclined to think the Almighty does."[67] Given the framing, one suspects these unidentified words, quoted by *Reader's Digest* editor Stanley High in 1956, came from a mainline Protestant pastor. One historian has shown that in New York in 1957 a window of mutual respect had opened surprisingly wide.[68] In 2007 John Buchanan, the editor of the *Christian Century*—which in times past had treated Graham with wariness—viewed his work with remarkable generosity.[69] Buchanan's attitude was not quite the same as chest-thumping support, Southern Baptist style. But it did betoken appreciation in a citadel of mainline Protestantism for diversities of gifts.

As noted, Graham would say, "I intend to go anywhere, sponsored by anybody, to preach the Gospel of Christ, if there are no strings attached to my message. I am sponsored by civic clubs, universities, ministerial associations, and councils of churches all over the world."[70] When his life and words are considered in their entirety, Graham clearly did not mean that correct belief was unimportant. But some items of belief were more important than others. The question was how to work with people of divergent views in the common cause of Christian evangelism. In his mature years Graham told one journalist that if it were possible to start his ministry all over again, without baggage, he would be an evangelical Anglican. He saw spiritual beauty in Anglican order.[71] Graham asked Richard Bewes, the rector of All Saints in London, to help officiate at his funeral.[72] Back in the 1950s, Bob Jones may have seen it coming.

Other Conservative Protestants

At one point or another Graham engaged virtually every definable Protestant group on the landscape. Many of them fell outside the evangelical mainstream either entirely or in one specific way or another. Graham explicitly or implicitly affirmed most of them as viable conversation partners even though he differed on particular beliefs or practices of particular groups, such as Mennonites' pacifism or Adventists' sabbatarianism or Methodists' episcopal polity. And with few exceptions the feeling proved mutual. The vast majority of Protestant periodicals from all parts of the religious landscape seemed not only to embrace Graham but also actively to seek his endorsement. A snapshot of his relationship with three of vastly different character illustrates the larger pattern: Eastern Orthodox, Latter-day Saints (Mormons), and Pentecostals. Regarding the first two, he said little, but what he did say was telling. Regarding the third, Pentecostals (or Charismatics), he said a lot, and that too was telling.

The Eastern Orthodox and the Mormons bore significant similarities in the evangelical universe. Evangelicals had little firsthand contact with the Orthodox. They occupied different social and linguistic locations, and generally different geographic ones, too. Even so, evangelicals regarded the Orthodox with a wary eye (though rarely as wary as their view of Catholics). The Orthodox seemed to substitute works for faith, and they got lost in a jungle of liturgy. Their Christianity was so dubious that evangelicals even projected a serious missionary effort to Orthodox lands.[73] The chasm between evangelicals and Mormons ran deeper. Though they spoke the same language, they occupied dramatically different geographic locations. Fired by a long history of bitter antagonism, the vast majority of evangelicals believed that Mormon doctrine and practices (especially their alleged secret

longing for reinstatement of polygamy) rendered them indubitably and forever out of bounds. Mormon Christianity was not only a sham but also—
and worse—positively dangerous because Mormons had the temerity to go
out and proselytize Gentiles.[74]

Graham did not directly challenge any of these prejudices but quietly
stepped around them. He did not comment on the Orthodox until he made
multiple extended trips to Eastern Europe and then to the Soviet Union in
the late 1970s and early 1980s. But in Eastern Europe he worked with the
Orthodox closely and without scruple about doctrinal or liturgical differences. On returning, he endorsed their Christian faith heartily.[75] He confessed that growing up in the South he knew next to nothing about the
Orthodox until he found himself face to face with them in Europe. There,
however, he discovered that they "believed everything I believed—only
more."[76] He was impressed that every Orthodox meetinghouse featured a
cross above the front portal.[77] Graham worried about the insensitivity of
evangelical missionaries in Orthodox lands.[78]

Mormons he handled more delicately. He knew perfectly well that virtually all of his fellow evangelicals regarded Mormons as non-Christian at
best and anti-Christian (anti-Christ) at worst. Yet he did not denounce
Mormon thought. More telling, he never held a crusade in Salt Lake City,
which would have meant drawing inquirers/converts away from their
local wards. That avoidance was significant. He held crusades in most major cities in the United States, and the financial cost—always an important
consideration—of doing business in Salt Lake would have been less than in
most sites. The preacher highlighted his close friendship with J. Willard
Marriott, a devout and well-known Mormon.[79] At a governor's prayer
breakfast in Massachusetts in 1982 he claimed Marriott as "one of the best
friends I have in the world."[80] Marriott gave Graham a pass to stay free in
any Marriott hotel in the world—which he gratefully used. There is evidence, too, of individual Mormons' warmly supporting Graham's crusades.[81] None of this should be taken to imply that Graham endorsed key
Mormon distinctives such as the supplemental revelation embodied in the
Book of Mormon. But it does reflect Graham's life-long attempt to build as
many bridges as possible.

Graham experienced multiple and extended relationships with Pentecostals and Charismatics. (Since the distinctions between those two traditions
were more important to them than to others, and since Graham seemed
uninterested in the distinctions, for economy I will describe both with the
historically older term *Pentecostal*.) He heartily affirmed Pentecostals'

contributions to the reinvigoration of the church.[82] Little wonder. Born at the turn of the century, their numbers had grown slowly until the early 1950s, when they seemed suddenly to explode with new adherents. In 1988 historian Peter W. Williams aptly said that Pentecostalism "may well be called *the* popular religious movement of the twentieth century."[83] By the end of the 1990s Pentecostal sects and Pentecostal-like spirituality and practices claimed the allegiance of (depending on how one measures things) twenty to thirty million Americans.[84] If the boundaries of Pentecostal, Charismatic, and neo-Charismatic are defined generously, and allowed to overlap with mainstream evangelicals, that figure might double or even triple.[85] By the 1970s many of the largest local congregations in the United States were no longer Baptist but Pentecostal, both white and black.

Graham, like most mainstream evangelicals, experienced few public interactions with Pentecostals until the 1960s. In the 1950s he had met the healing evangelist Oral Roberts—one of the three most famous Pentecostals of the century (the others being Aimee Semple McPherson and Kathryn Kuhlman)—twice in informal settings.[86] The two men bore similarities. Both were born in 1918 in the South. Both possessed only modest formal education but more than their share of moxie, determination, and ambition. They bore important dissimilarities too. Throughout his life, Graham gravitated toward partisan politics as a moth drawn to a flame, while Roberts remained for all practical purposes uninvolved in politics. More important, Graham represented mainstream evangelicals at their elite best (or worst, according to one's point of view), while Roberts represented an ecstatic, millenarian working-class movement that most evangelicals and mainline Protestants still viewed with suspicion.[87]

At the invitation of Carl F. H. Henry and Graham's "personal request," Roberts agreed to participate in the 1966 Berlin World Congress on Evangelism, sponsored and funded by the BGEA.[88] Roberts was too famous to be excluded from the conference but not famous enough to be included in the inner circle, at least not immediately. He was not accustomed to rubbing shoulders with evangelical heavyweights like Henry, Harold John Ockenga, and Anglican intellectual John Stott. One of Graham's close friends told him that Roberts was being treated like an "honorary leper."[89] So it was that Graham asked Roberts to dinner and to pray at the plenary session. "Our prayer," said Graham to the delegates, "is going to be led by a man that I have come to love and appreciate."[90] The following year Graham offered the dedication sermon at the recently opened Oral Roberts University. They remained fast friends until Roberts's death in 2009.

In the next three decades Graham interacted closely with Pentecostal leaders such as Assemblies of God General Superintendent Thomas F. Zimmerman, and he appeared repeatedly on Pat Robertson's *700 Club*.[91] He also made taped appearances on Jim and Tammy Faye Bakker's more controversial *PTL (Praise the Lord)* national television program.[92] To be sure, the interaction was limited. As far as I can tell, none of the Pentecostal stars mentioned—Roberts, Robertson, or the Bakkers—or the flamboyant divine healer Kathryn Kuhlman—ever joined the hundreds of guests that graced Graham's platform over the years. Yet one of Graham's proudest achievements was the massive BGEA-sponsored International Conference for Itinerant Evangelists in Amsterdam in 1986. Of the ten thousand participants from 174 countries, Pentecostals outnumbered non-Pentecostals.[93]

The preacher's willingness to associate with Pentecostals in highly visible venues merits close analysis. Without question he shared far more with them than not: mutual concurrence in the historic evangelical Protestant notions of Scripture alone, Christ alone, and faith alone. He also shared Pentecostals' profound sense of divine presence and embrace of the Holy Spirit. As with Pentecostals, Graham's worldview rested in divine providence: the personal God of Abraham, Isaac, and Jacob oversaw absolutely everything. Though Graham said relatively little about the devil and demons, he—like Pentecostals—always affirmed their literal palpable existence. Angels too, and he did say a great deal about them.[94]

Miracles, however, were a different matter. In principle Graham affirmed them but in practice largely ignored them. As noted, if readers looked long and hard enough they might find a rare reference to a change of weather coming to the rescue of a meeting or of the devil's opposition to a crusade strangely silenced. Here the contrast with Pentecostal literature, which teemed with references to miracles of all kinds taking place constantly and everywhere, was striking. The virtual absence of miraculous healing stories in Graham's preaching and publications was particularly striking.[95] When pushed, Graham affirmed miracles but allowed that they were rare and more likely at the end of the age—the timing of which he left blurry.[96]

The sum of it was this. On one hand, in practice, Graham treated miracles more as center/left mainline Protestants did than as Pentecostals did (excluding liberal mainline Protestants, who viewed miracles as purely mythical). He tended to treat miracles more as a salvific process in the believer's spiritual pilgrimage than as supernatural interruptions of nature. On the other hand, he left his audiences confident that God remained at the center of the story—or in the words of historian Roger G. Robins, that they inhabited "a world alive with divine promise."[97]

These considerations bring us to the doctrine and practice of speaking in tongues, commonly called, especially by outsiders, glossolalia. All Pentecostals esteemed tongues as one of the nine gifts of the Holy Spirit promised in I Corinthians 8–10. Virtually all white Pentecostals and many black and Latino Pentecostals went further and *also* designated tongues as the invariable sign of baptism of the Holy Spirit promised in Acts 2:4. The distinction between tongues as a *gift* given to some believers and tongues as a *sign* that all believers ought to receive proved fundamental to Pentecostals. In many Pentecostal groups persons could not be ordained unless they produced evidence that they had received tongues as a sign of Holy Spirit baptism. Needless to say the claim about tongues as an invariable sign of Holy Spirit baptism proved invidious. Whatever the intent, the effect proved very different: to draw boundaries and demarcate who was in and who was out.[98]

Graham affirmed the first claim—that the Holy Spirit gave tongues (and other gifts) to some believers to empower them for witness and service—but he denied the second claim—that the Holy Spirit also gave or wanted to give tongues to all believers as a sign of Holy Spirit baptism.[99] He mentioned his difference on this matter extremely rarely. Characteristically, he saw no reason to antagonize Pentecostals about a matter they considered non-negotiable.[100] Just as characteristically he recoiled from a teaching sure to repel the vast majority of mainstream evangelicals, not to mention the vast majority of mainline Protestants. The gift of tongues, Graham said, was exactly that: a gift. Believers should not pray for a specific gift, and it should not divide the church.[101] Building bridges was hard work. Graham saw no need to make it harder.

Pentecostals wanted more, however. A series of events that took place on December 9 and 10, 1982, spoke volumes about Graham's iconic status in Pentecostal culture. On December 9 he preached in the chapel of Evangel College, the flagship school of the Assemblies of God, the largest white Pentecostal denomination in the United States. Apparently time got away from him and he cut his sermon short in order to appear at a press conference. Just before the benediction one member of the audience stood and delivered a message in unknown tongues (glossolalia). Immediately afterward another person stood and interpreted the message in English. In Pentecostal culture, a public message in tongues ordinarily led to a public interpretation in the vernacular. The interpretation usually exhorted worshippers to a renewed life of faith. In the context of a Pentecostal worship service, the scenario that day was unexceptional: sermon, tongues, interpretation, and benediction.

The event had an afterlife, however. A startling narrative soon began making the rounds in Pentecostal circles. After the service, some said, a state patrolman and a denominational official declared that Graham had made an amazing claim in their presence: that the interpretation of the glossolalia message rehearsed *verbatim* what he had planned to say if he had not cut his remarks short. The story grew. Purportedly Graham repeated the claim in *Christianity Today* and on national television and vowed to reconsider his views about the Pentecostal teachings.[102]

About here, however, things grow murky. Graham's sermon notes for that day apparently have not been preserved (if they ever existed), and there is no transcript of the tongues interpretation, so the claim that the interpretation miraculously embodied the nonpreached part of the sermon cannot be verified. But other evidence casts doubt on the story. Graham spoke at Assemblies of God events in Springfield three times in the next thirty-six hours, and there was no evidence that he mentioned this manifestly supernatural miracle on any of those occasions.[103] And in any event, Graham's long track record of public remarks suggests that it would have been out of character for him to take such a clear stand on such a controversial doctrine and practice.[104] More likely he phrased his words to the patrolman carefully and inoffensively and Pentecostals heard what they wanted to hear.

The key point is that Pentecostals coveted—it seems not an exaggeration to say intensely coveted—his validation of their distinctive doctrine and practice. After all, the *Pentecostal Evangel*, the flagship periodical of the Assemblies of God, followed Graham's activities with meticulous care, year after year, as if he were one of their own.[105] At the same time, and equally important, Graham embraced Pentecostals without embracing all of their teachings. A classic balancing act that he had mastered many decades before.

Roman Catholics

Context is critical.[106] In 1950 evangelicals and Catholics eyed each other with deep suspicion. Most evangelicals felt that Catholicism was sub-Christian at best, and many believed that it was not Christian at all. Catholics substituted the fallible authority of the Church for the infallible authority of the Bible. They mistook works for faith and worshipped Mary and saints rather than the Father, Son, and Holy Spirit. They also paid political homage to a foreign pope instead of the duly elected leaders of the United

States. Those feelings ran deep. Graham remembered that when Herbert
Hoover beat Al Smith in the 1928 presidential election, Charlotte school-
children cheered. The children had no idea why—except that they were
supposed to cheer a Protestant Republican over a Catholic Democrat even
though the state had voted Democratic in every election since the Civil
War.[107] As late as 1957, when a fire killed students in a Chicago parochial
school, Moody Bible Institute, located in Chicago, refused to lower its flag
to half-mast.[108]

Catholics repaid evangelicals in kind. They felt historic Protestantism
was bad enough, for it placed salvation outside the sacraments of the
church. But evangelicals fell into even deeper error by placing priority on
individuals' interpretation of the Bible and individuals' quest for salvation
through private decision. And they disregarded the authority of the pope,
whom Christ himself had warranted through the word of the Apostle Peter.
Not a few Catholics believed that evangelicals were sub-Christian at best
or not Christian at all.[109]

Enter Graham. The year was 1950, and the place was the Catholic
stronghold of Boston. The Reverend Dr. Harold John Ockenga, the eminent scholar/pastor of Boston's historic Park Street Church, orchestrated
the crusade, which was Graham's first in New England. The meeting started
at Mechanics Hall on New Year's Eve 1949 with an overflow crowd. The
following day the crusade moved to Park Street Church at Ockenga's invitation. Owing to more overflow crowds, the campaign soon moved back to
Mechanics Hall, and then to the Opera House, and finally to the 13,000-
seat Boston Garden to accommodate the large numbers. Though originally
scheduled to run one week, the crusade ran through January 16. After a
respite in February and March (in which Graham took his crusade into
northern New England and then down to South Carolina), he returned to
Boston in April to finish the revival with a great outdoor meeting on the
Boston Common.

During his first visit to Boston, Graham had tossed aside four hundred
years of Protestant fear and hatred of Catholics, as well as Ockenga's strongly
anti-Catholic views, when he warmly accepted (perhaps sought) the endorsement of Archbishop (later Cardinal) Richard Cushing.[110] The archbishop in
turn tossed aside four hundred years of Catholic fear and hatred of Protestants when he ran a headline in the official newspaper of the Boston Archdi-
ocese: "BRAVO, BILLY!"[111] In the context of the times it would be hard to
exaggerate the boldness of each man's efforts to build a bridge between their
communities. Later that summer Graham sought an audience with President
Truman, using Boston's Catholic House Representative John McCormack

as an emissary. Graham asked McCormack to assure Truman that he—unlike most evangelicals—had not and would not criticize Truman's decision to send a diplomat to the Vatican. He wanted Truman to know that he was "anxious to bring all faiths together—rather than tear them apart."[112]

It was a promising start on both sides. In the next quarter century Graham enjoyed numerous friendships and productive interactions with Catholics. The list included (besides Cardinal Cushing) Peace Corps director Sargent Shriver, Francis Cardinal Spellman, and television pastor Bishop Fulton J. Sheen.[113] Graham made a point especially to herald his friendship with Sheen.[114] Some suggest that counselors sent inquirers with Catholic ties to Catholic churches if that was their preference.[115] Admittedly, other evidence suggests the opposite pattern: that counselors sometimes tried to steer inquirers away from Catholic churches or into neighborhood Bible studies led by evangelical Catholics. Clearly, patterns varied from site to site.[116] Nonetheless, Graham received glowing coverage in Catholic papers and from Catholic clergy.[117] Catholic and Protestant observers compared him favorably with Father Theodore Hesburgh, the iconic president of Notre Dame University.[118] When a journalist asked Graham what he would do if the pope invited him to preach in St. Peters, he said, "I would gladly and humbly accept it . . . [and] study for about a year in preparing." Graham admitted that he stumbled over the doctrine of papal infallibility, but there was not much else about which he and believing Catholics differed. Protestants paid too little attention to Mary, he mused.[119]

Yet boulders strewn on the path by centuries of hostility did not disappear easily. One of Graham's close associates, purportedly writing on his behalf, made clear that priests were not welcome in crusade meetings: people should know that "Roman Catholicism flourishes on ignorance."[120] Disdain ran both ways. One prominent Catholic theologian worried about Graham's "excessive emphasis on decision," "simplistic notion of salvation," "uncritical Biblicism," "[thin] theology," and, among many other dangers, "co-operation with liberal churches."[121] Catholic theologians and writers worried about Graham's insensitivity to the mystical power of the sacraments.[122] Many of the letters to Graham came from Catholics. Of those, many spoke of their priest's warnings about attending Graham's meetings. Even more spoke of their guilt or of their family's ostracism for doing so.[123] Graham was not naïve. He knew such resistance existed.[124] But he felt things were changing. Christians had more to worry about than struggling against each other.[125]

Until Graham met with Pope John Paul II in the late 1970s, a large share of the publicity about him and the Church centered on the 1960 presidential election. That contest pitted the Quaker Richard Nixon against the Catholic John Kennedy. The details of that controversial story are better left for the following chapter. Here the salient points are three. First, Graham made plain that, as a religion, Catholicism enjoyed a perfect right to its spot in the American sun. Second, Graham made equally plain that electing a Catholic president would be risky. If the president were a true Catholic he would place his loyalty to the pope above his loyalty to the Constitution. Third, Graham also made plain shortly before the election that if Kennedy won he would wholeheartedly support the new president. Graham kept that promise.

By far the most historically important relationship between Graham and the Church lay in his manifest admiration for Pope John Paul II. He visited with the pope three times. In 1990, he proudly told *Time* magazine that back in 1981—when Protestant-Catholic relations were just beginning to thaw—the pope had once grasped his thumb and said, "We are brothers."[126] Both men undoubtedly sensed, too, a different kind of bond—one that paralleled their shared faith. Both were always "on": 24/7/365. A single moral lapse would have triggered reverberations of incalculable scale among the faithful around the world. Graham did not deny that important doctrinal differences separated him and the pope. Yet he insisted that they agreed profoundly on essentials. He highlighted the pope's progressive stand on world poverty. When John Paul died in 2005, one journalist said that Graham judged the pontiff the "most influential force for morality and peace in the world in the past 100 years." The occasion for the journalist's attribution was as significant as the claim itself: the nightly television talk show *Larry King Live*, a microphone to the world.[127] Over the years Graham's fundamentalist former friends excoriated him for many things, including his stance on civil rights and working with mainline Protestants, but they especially deplored his rapprochement with Catholics.[128] His enemies knew his heart.

Jews

Untangling the relationship between evangelicals and Jews in post–World War II America is no small task. Fine scholars have devoted their entire academic careers trying to make sense of the twisting strands of anti- and philo-Semitism.

On one hand many evangelicals entertained both benign and malign stereotypes about Jews' so-called traits—their industriousness and intelligence as well as their avarice and sharp dealing. And they tried to persuade Jews to fulfill their religion by embracing Jesus as the Messiah. Most Jews regarded evangelicals' conversionary efforts with disdain. They thought evangelicals were asking them to eviscerate their faith by becoming Christians.[129] Many evangelicals seemed to think that Messianic Judaism, which encouraged converts to blend Christian theology with Jewish ritual, solved that problem. Few grasped that for the overwhelming majority of observant Jews, Messianic Judaism represented the worst of all worlds. Apostacy was bad enough but trying to have it both ways was even worse. Besides that, evangelicals could hardly escape the tarnish of two millennia of Christian persecution of Jews.[130]

On the other hand many evangelicals firmly believed that Jews represented God's truly chosen people. Jews had uniquely received the imprint of God's self-revelation in history. More important, long ago God had slipped into the human skin of a Palestinian Jew. That Jewish man—Jesus—bore the sins of the world and made possible God's reconciliation with humans everywhere. The whole of human history hinged on Jews. Jesus would not return until all of them had heard the gospel and received a chance to accept Jesus as Messiah. And people who persecuted Jews risked God's wrath.[131] Many evangelicals also embraced Zionism with gusto. They supported Israel's right to occupy its historic homeland and usually sided with Israelis in their perennial struggle against Palestinians and the Islamic world.[132]

Graham's own connection with Jews proved equally complex. On one hand he preached the good news of salvation through Christ to Jews as much as to every one else. He seemed only dimly to grasp that in the eyes of most Jews becoming a Christian meant ceasing to be a Jew. On the other hand he maintained close life-long friendships with prominent American Jews such as Rabbi Mark Tanenbaum and Rabbi Edgar Fogel Magnin, as well as powerful Israelis such as Prime Ministers Menachem Begin and Golda Meir.[133] He even invited Meir to speak at a crusade in St. Louis in 1973.[134] Television talk show host Larry King, culturally Jewish, invited Graham to be a guest on his late-night program, *Larry King Live*, at least twenty-four times. Graham might have held the record.[135] Though King claimed Graham as a friend, they talked frankly about religious differences.

Though Graham clearly was pleased when Jews professed faith in Jesus as the Messiah, and served as the "spiritual grandfather of the Lausanne Consultation on Jewish Evangelism," he refused to join evangelistic efforts that targeted Jews, and largely bypassed Messianic Judaism.[136] Once in

1991 he suggested that God's covenant with Jews was everlasting. "There are many passages in the Bible—Old Testament and New Testament," he noted, "that indicate that the Jewish people are in a special category of God's chosen people." He said he would not beg, coerce, or target them: "I have to leave it to the spirit of God and their own decision and choice."[137] He generally (though not always) supported Israel's cause in international affairs.[138] World Wide Pictures' 1970 film *His Land* presented Israel in—in the words of Judaism historian Yaakov Ariel—"favorable and glorious terms."[139] Graham denounced Christians who fell into the maw of stereotypes about Jews.[140]

Jews in turn liked Graham. "I may go to hear the great man when he preaches, maybe for the last time, to a bunch of really thirsty people, including me," wrote Rabbi Marc Gellman in *Newsweek* on the eve of Graham's final crusade in New York in 2005.[141] Graham received numerous awards from Jewish organizations for his pioneering work promoting respectful interfaith relations, such as the Silver Medallion Award from the National Conference of Christians and Jews and the Torch of Liberty Award from the Anti-Defamation League of B'nai B'rith.[142] Many Jews undoubtedly embraced him for his basic pro-God pro-decency pro-America stands. Graham told a Jewish friend that they worshipped the same God: "There is just this difference between us. You believe the Messiah is yet to come. I believe he has already come."[143]

And then the bomb dropped. On February 28, 2002, the National Archives released a tape of a conversation that took place between Graham and President Richard Nixon in the Oval Office thirty years earlier on February 1, 1972. On that fateful day Graham thought he was having a private conversation with Nixon and Nixon's chief of staff, H. R. Haldeman. The part of the conversation that involved Graham lasted off-and-on about one hundred minutes. Nearly one hour into the discussion, Graham, Nixon, and Haldeman fell to talking about how Jews "totally dominated" the media, as Nixon put it. A few minutes later Graham said: "And they're the ones putting out the pornographic stuff and putting out everything." After a short gap in the tape, Graham went on: "This stranglehold has got to be broken or the country's going down the drain." When Nixon concurred, Graham added: "If you get elected a second time, we might be able to do something about it." The conversation drifted on to the topic of (Nixon) "filthy" movies, as well as professors. "Ninety percent are atheists or worse," Nixon judged. Some fifteen minutes later, after Haldeman asserted Jews' control of television scripts, as well as *Time, New York Times, Washington*

Post, *Los Angeles Times*, NBC, CBS, and the White House press corps, Graham joined in: "I mean not all the Jews, but a lot of the Jews are great friends of mine. They swarm around me and are friendly to me because they know I am friendly to Israel (and so forth) but they don't know how I really feel about what they're doing to this country. And I have no power and no way to handle them." Graham soon started grumbling about postal rates going up. He said it would squeeze *Christianity Today* and its rival, the *Christian Century*, which Graham blasted as "the most left-wing of all the religious press in the country." The conversation—punctuated with four gaps in the tape—rambled on to John Connally, gifts for (Grady) Wilson and Graham, but nothing more about Jews. After Graham left the room, Nixon and Haldeman continued another twenty minutes. They talked about how they might strategically use Graham to handle the media. Nixon: "Well Billy's a, Billy's a . . . needs care." Just before the tape ended, Nixon said, "Well it's also the Jews. The Jews are irreligious, atheistic, immoral bunch of bastards. That goddamn girl the other night is Jewish."[144]

The release of the conversation ignited a firestorm. For understanding Graham's place in postwar American history it may be most helpful to break the reaction into how each of four groups dealt with it: Graham and his associates, the press, Jews, and most Americans.

Graham's own response moved from disbelief to unqualified apology. Initially he said nothing, apparently suspecting a hoax. After three days he issued a verbal and written apology without qualifications. "I cannot imagine what caused me to make those comments, which I totally repudiate. Whatever the reason, I was wrong for not disagreeing with the President, and I sincerely apologize to anyone I have offended." He said the views he expressed that day did not reflect his true feelings then, or now. He pointed to a lifetime of good relations with Jews and abhorred any kind of prejudice.[145] In 2006 he told *Newsweek*, "If it wasn't on tape, I would not have believed it . . . I guess I was trying to please. I felt so badly about myself."[146] When Larry King challenged him on the incident, his only explanation was to say that it was difficult to "take issue" with the president of the United States. "You said yes or you nodded your head or suchlike."[147] Yet Graham did not address the matter in the revised 2007 edition of his memoir, *Just As I Am*.

Graham's son Franklin and the BGEA reacted defensively. Franklin, president of the BGEA since 2001, asserted that his father's remarks were taken out of context. Franklin said his father was referring not to Jews per se but to the liberal biases of a "handful of elitists" who controlled "the major outlets at that time." Besides, Franklin added, the conversation was private and "many other people have had private conversations they wouldn't want to be made public."[148] The BGEA (apparently) made no official comment beyond publication of Graham's apology. In 2014 the incident received no mention on the official BGEA website biographical summary of Graham's life, or in the chronology of Graham's life produced by the Billy Graham Center Archives, or in the extensive museum renderings of his life at the Billy Graham Center at Wheaton College or in the Billy Graham Library in Charlotte.[149]

Others' reactions varied in nuance although not in substance. Most expressed shock because the remarks seemed so inexcusable and also so out of character. The *Chicago Tribune* had broken the story on February 28, 2002, and let Graham's incriminating words speak for themselves.[150] Graham's generally sympathetic biographer William Martin, the eminent historian Martin Marty, and the Jewish leader Michael Kotzin expressed incredulity, disappointment, and anger, respectively.[151] After Graham apologized, newspapers reported the apology with differing tones, ranging from condemnation of irreparably harmful remarks to willingness to accept an apology for a grievous mistake.

Jews' reactions are more difficult to measure. A scanning of a representative sample of periodicals suggests a range. They swept from angry denunciations to sadness that a good friend had betrayed them. According to journalist Allen Breed, "For some, the comments have all but erased the lifetime of good will Graham had built." "I fear, and it's with great sadness, that his legacy will be tarnished by this permanently," said James Rudin of the American Jewish Council.[152] Taken whole, the opinion among Jews about Graham seemed slowly to shift from anger to sadness to something close to forgiveness, albeit not overlooking it as if it had never happened.[153] Abraham H. Foxman, National Director of the Anti-Defamation League, accepted Graham's apology. Writing in March 2002, Foxman said that "even today" his words from 1972 were "chilling and frightening." Nonetheless, Foxman found the apology "full of sadness and repentance. This is the Billy Graham we thought we knew."[154] Michael Rapp, a Jewish leader in Cincinnati, said the incident proved that Graham was not a saint. "He is a human being like the rest of us."[155] "Jewish leaders," said *Newsweek* editor Jon Meacham in 2005, just after Graham's final crusade, "many of whom appreciated his support of Israel and his refusal to join other evangelicals in calls for the conversion of Jews, accepted his apology."[156] If Meacham was right, that turn may have said as much about Jews' generosity as about Graham's offense.

Absent systematic polling about the matter, the response of average Americans can only be inferred. For the vast majority of Americans who were alert to the controversy, probably the most damaging line was Graham's statement that Jews "do not know how I really feel about them and what they are doing to this country." Most seemed to think that Graham's life-long record of friendship with Jews and support for Israel outweighed his lapse, however shocking and regrettable. In a sea of millions of recorded words, what should one do with a half-dozen odious sentences?[157] The Kalamazoo, Michigan, *Gazette* represented scores: "Apology by Graham Should Be Accepted," ran one headline. Yet—tellingly—the subheadline judged Graham's charge of a Jewish stranglehold on the media "absurd."[158]

One of many problems in all of this was that Americans had come to expect better things from Graham. The slur loomed large precisely because it felt so jarring, so out of character. Perhaps the preacher disappointed Americans in a way other preachers could not because they had not been standing on a pedestal in the first place. Americans needed a figure like Graham. He let them down.[159]

Or perhaps the problem was at once more subtle and more devastating. Later we will see that in the eyes of many people, Graham's camaraderie with presidents had always been problematic. Now it spelled his undoing. Graham effectively admitted as much, at least if talk show host Larry King reported his words correctly. "I asked him," said King, about the anti-Semitic conversation with Nixon. We have already heard Graham's response: "So you either said yes or you nodded your head or suchlike." King minced no words: he found his friend's explanation disappointing.[160] Nixon pulled Graham down into the mud, and there was no evidence that he put up a fight.

In 2009 the Nixon Presidential Library released the transcript of another conversation between Nixon and Graham that involved Jews. This one took place on February 21, 1973, thirteen months after the first highly publicized one. Nixon phoned Graham in the early evening, the conversation lasted twenty minutes and ranged over several topics. Both Nixon and Graham expressed concern about the *rise* of anti-Semitism in America. They attributed it not to embedded prejudice against Jews but to provocative actions by the Israeli government and by activist American Jewish groups. They worried about the Israeli government's downing of a Libyan passenger plane the day before (taking the lives of 106 people), its threat to expel Christian missionaries (especially the Messianic Christian group Jews for Jesus), and the perceived overreaction of American Jews to Key 73 (an evangelical campaign to "Call the Continent to Christ"). Graham went on: "The Bible talks about two kinds of Jews. One is called 'the synagogue of Satan.' They're the ones putting out the pornographic literature. They're the ones putting out these obscene films" (apparently referring to *Last Tango in Paris*).[161]

This conversation received different interpretations. This time Foxman was less forgiving: "While never expressing these views in public, Rev. Graham unabashedly held forth with the president with age-old classical anti-Semitic canards."[162] A. Larry Ross, Graham spokesperson, on the other hand, said it proved Graham's concern for Jews. Their image should not be tarnished by counterfeit Jews, described in the New Testament book of Revelation as the "synagogue of Satan."[163] Graham historian Steven Miller said it showed that Graham really was part of Nixon's "kitchen cabinet."[164] However interpreted, the conversation received much less coverage in the secular and religious press than the 1972 exchange.[165]

In June 2002 Graham held a crusade in Cincinnati, his final one in that city. The eighty-three-year-old evangelist visited with Jewish leaders at Paul Brown Stadium. Facing a delegation of three rabbis, he looked them in the eye and said that the things he had said that day, thirty years before, were unforgivable. And then he said, "I'm sorry."[166] One observer remembered that when Graham entered the room the rabbis stood. He asked them to sit down, confessing, "I am the one who should be on my knees."[167] Sometimes even the best-built bridges needed major repair.

Other Religions

No aspect of American culture is more conspicuous—or daunting—to visitors to the United States than Americans' expansionist impulses. Americans share. They also market. Two stories about academic conferences reveal worlds within worlds. As one tale goes, at a meeting on the history of international missions held in India (sometime before 1987) one American participant grew defensive about the imperialist implications of the missionary enterprise. An international observer thereupon quipped, "Don't apologize. All Americans are missionaries."[168] And then at a conference on "Religion and the Marketplace in the United States" at the University of Heidelberg in 2011 another observer also astutely quipped, "Isn't the conjunction *and* in the conference title redundant?"[169] From beginning to end, sharing—evangelizing—missionizing—proselytizing—marketing—all verbs meaning roughly the same thing but with different connotations—proved intrinsic to the evangelical tradition. It was part of their DNA. That did not mean that all evangelicals did it, but it did mean that all or almost all evangelicals thought they ought to do it—and felt guilty if they did not.[170]

Graham inherited this expansionist universe. Evangelism—conceived in pretty much exclusively conversionary terms—prevailed at Bob Jones College and Florida Bible Institute. It likely never occurred to Graham that faith was a purely private matter. An unshared faith was no faith at all. Evangelism prevailed at Wheaton too. Wheaton bore a strong sense of mission to the entire world. Most evangelical colleges drew on a regional or ethnic constituency such as Florida Bible Institute or the (Dutch-immigrant–influenced) Calvin College. In contrast, Wheaton's student constituency was national and to some extent even international.[171]

In its own way Wheaton's culture proved acutely conscious of the wider world. Ruth Bell—later Ruth Bell Graham—had grown up a missionary kid in China and been educated at a missionary school in Korea.[172] Significantly, Graham majored in anthropology, not Bible or Christian education. Graham said he chose that major because he thought he too might become an overseas missionary.[173] Graham's main professor, Alexander Grigolia, who held a Ph.D. in anthropology from the University of Pennsylvania, was a learned and forceful man. He taught Wheaton students that despite apparent differences the human race suffered from a common disease, and that common disease was sin.[174] The gospel of Jesus Christ offered the only solution. Even so, in its own way, Wheaton's anthropology program proved expansive. It awakened students to the realities and sufferings of a world larger than most of them had known.[175]

Soon after Graham graduated from Wheaton in 1943 he started thinking and moving outward. In the spring of 1946 the evangelist and three associates took their gospel message to Great Britain. The following autumn Graham, along with his wife, Ruth, and Cliff and Billie Barrows, crossed the channel to hold meetings in Germany and France. The die was cast. By the end of his career Graham had preached the gospel in extended multiweek crusades in ninety-nine nations on six continents. He invested a staggering amount of his energy and financial resources in the organization of five global evangelization congresses: Berlin in 1966, Lausanne in 1974, and Amsterdam in 1983, 1986, and 2000. Each one reflected greater and greater degrees of diversity: from majority clergy to majority laity, from mostly male to a nearly equal number of females, from majority white to majority nonwhite with multiple ethnic identities, and from mostly

Western to mostly non-Western.[176] With good reason the historian Joel Carpenter would say in 2012 that the story of Graham abroad ultimately might well prove more important than the story of Graham at home.[177]

In his international travels Graham tried not to criticize other religions or cultures. "I consider myself a world citizen," he told the *San Jose Mercury News* in 1997. Regarding peoples of other countries he said, "I love them and respect them, and they have a right to their own beliefs and their own choices." Of course, he added, "I would be happy to see them get to know Christ and what Christ can do in their lives," but "I don't try to coerce people . . . They make up their own minds."[178] Evangelicals probably were no better or worse than other Protestants in how they viewed other cultures and religions. Graham followed the more progressive ones in his efforts not to depreciate, let alone demean, those who were different from himself.[179]

Definable reasons stood behind Graham's approach. For one thing, he saw no point closing doors to evangelism by gratuitously offending his audiences.[180] But more to the point, he consistently said that his sole task was to proclaim the gospel of Jesus Christ—and nothing more. This was of course partly a pragmatic decision. Graham understood that people grew defensive when their whole way of life fell under attack. He also understood that political leaders would close the door to return visits. But it was a principled decision too. It dated back to his Wheaton days: the world contained one race with one problem. God had called Graham to offer a solution, not a demolition.

Starting in the late 1960s, in response to direct questions from journalists about the fate of those who never heard the gospel, Graham offered the same response: that is God's call, not mine. In 1969 the *New York Times*'s Edward B. Fiske asked him about "those who never hear the Gospel preached? Do they automatically go to hell?" Graham gave Fiske the same answer he offered to other journalists who asked that question. "I don't like to speculate beyond what the Bible teaches," the evangelist replied. "You see, God hasn't intended to reveal everything to us. He doesn't try to satisfy curious minds. I think God is going to judge every man on the basis of the light that he has. And he'll make no mistakes. Nobody will deceive God. He knows our faults and our instincts. He knows the pressures."[181] A decade later Graham told an interviewer that he used to believe that people who had never heard the gospel were doomed for hell. "I no longer believe that," he stated. "I believe there are other ways of recognizing the existence of God—through nature, for instance—and plenty of other opportunities for saying 'yes' to God."[182]

Near the end of his ministry the BBC journalist David Frost raised the same question. Graham told him that people who live "according to the light that they have" are in a "separate category" from people, like Hitler, who have "shaken their fists at God." Frost pressed for details: "the person who never had a chance to know God, can, as it were, pass the test into heaven?" Graham responded, simply, "I would say that God, being a God of mercy, we have to rest it right there, and say that God is a God of mercy and love, and how it happens, we don't know. I'm not going to go beyond the teachings of the Scripture."[183]

Elsewhere, Graham said the same about Jews.[184] In 2006 *Newsweek* asked if heaven would be open to good Jews, Muslims, Buddhists, Hindus, or secular people. Graham responded without flinching: "Those are decisions only the Lord will make. It would be foolish for me to speculate on who will be there . . . I believe the love of God is absolute . . . I think he loves everybody regardless of what label they have."[185] The posture might be called a principled refusal to speculate about the ultimate fate of the nonbeliever.

Graham rarely addressed this question in his own writings but rather in response to journalists' hard questions. In his best-selling book *How to Be Born Again*, published in 1977, however, he did confront the problem. Though he spoke to it briefly, he gave the same answer: "God created all of us in His image; everyone is answerable to the light that He revealed to them. . . . When a man sincerely searches for God with all his heart, God will reveal Himself in some way." Significantly, he addressed these words not to the proverbial child in China who never heard the gospel but to the "pagans on Main Street, U.S.A." and the "pagans at Oxford [and] the Sorbonne."[186] The shade of Graham's one-time close friend Charles Templeton, who had reluctantly, painfully, moved from fundamentalism to agnosticism as he read more deeply in modern theology, may have been on his mind. He did not say.

It is important to be precise. Graham never embraced universalism (the idea that all people will be saved). He never denied the existence of hell—defined as separation from God. He always said that Jesus Christ offered the way to heaven, and usually he said the only way. He did not endorse other religions per se (although he came close to it when he spoke of God's enduring covenant with Jews). There is little evidence of Graham seriously studying other religions, let alone going out and asking partisans of other faiths what they thought about life's big questions. And following a provocative *McCall's* interview in 1978, he allowed *Christianity Today* to issue a "clarification" of his positions, denying universalism.[187] After an equally provocative *Newsweek* interview in 2006, he sent a brief appreciative letter to the editor—perhaps at the BGEA's instigation—reasserting that "only Christ can give us lasting hope—hope for this life, and hope for the life to come."[188] Yet the alleged clarifications clarified nothing. He never had asserted universalism and never had diminished Christ's exclusive role in the means of salvation. All that he ever had said, but said repeatedly and without qualifications, was that it was not his place to judge the destiny of souls. God and God alone made those determinations.

Through the first decade of the twenty-first century, the evangelical context was murky too. With rare exceptions, the movement's leaders held an absolutist position: rational adults who died outside Christian faith faced everlasting doom. Yet the evangelical missionary establishment was placing more and more—possibly a majority—of its financial and emotional resources into human-relief endeavors. Groups such as Compassion International, Samaritan's Purse, and World Vision International offered compelling examples of the broadening of evangelical outlooks. An outside observer could make a case that humanitarian aims increasingly competed with "purely" conversionary aims for a share of the grassroots dollar. The firmament was shifting.[189]

Probably Graham himself could not say precisely where he fell. Perhaps the real truth is that he remained "loyal to traditional formulations," as William Martin put it, but he also possessed the heart of a pastor.[190] His theological training told him one thing but his encounters with the real problems of real people in real situations pulled him in another direction. We might call it "emotional intelligence": the posture of a man who had talked to too many people of different life experiences to be willing to judge them.[191] Only God could do that.

In sum, Graham played a powerful role in two tectonic shifts that reconfigured the American cultural and religious landscape in the middle decades of the twentieth century. The first shift was the separation of a broadly amorphously evangelical river into two streams: mainstream evangelicalism (consisting of denominational and independent/cooperative evangelicalism) and independent/fundamentalism. Those two streams ran alongside a third one: the powerful mainline Protestant tradition. The three together did not own the whole of the religious landscape of course. Besides the vast Roman Catholic presence and the formidable Mormon influence, observers saw a large number of smaller currents surging vigorously—Mennonite, Adventist, Orthodox, and Jewish, among many others. But the Big Three seemed to capture the bulk of press attention. And one could make a case—not an airtight case but at least a credible one—that of the three, mainstream evangelicalism, flowing at the center, helped define the direction in which the other two would move.

The second tectonic shift is more difficult to describe but ultimately probably more important. Broadly stated, it dictated that bridges should span as many cultural and religious divisions as possible while still affirming the absolute truth of the Christian gospel. Graham seems never to have doubted that God had called him to do both at once. His trip to Romania in September 1985 held a great deal of symbolic significance. In that seven-city, eleven-day tour, he had preached in Orthodox and Reformed cathedrals; in Roman Catholic, Baptist, and Pentecostal churches; in a Jewish synagogue; and outdoors at an Orthodox monastery.[192] On some cultural and theological issues, such as the sinfulness of homosexual practice, he never budged. On some, such as the menace of communism, he did. But on almost all issues he not only insisted that it never hurt to talk but also that it was possible to talk charitably with people with whom he disagreed. He made a point to be spiritually confrontational: where do you stand with God? He made an equal point to be personally compassionate: where do you stand with your neighbor?

For a purebred fundamentalist it had been a long and remarkable process. "During most of my life I have been on a pilgrimage in many areas," he told an audience at the John F. Kennedy School of Government at Harvard in 1982. "I have come to see in deeper ways some of the implications of my faith and message."[193] If many people had seen Graham, it is equally true that he had seen many people. And they left their mark.

CHAPTER SIX

Pilgrim

The question of Graham and American political culture is vast. It has elicited books, theses, dissertations, scholarly chapters, popular articles, and uncounted website postings. Four sets of concerns defined his posture, and each spanned his entire career. The first was civil rights, the second presidents and politics, the third America's place in God's providence, and the fourth war, peace, and global justice. Graham's relation to the civil rights movement occupied part of an earlier chapter. In this one we turn to the latter three. Though some members of the journalistic and academic elite regarded Graham as regressive in some or all of these respects, I will argue otherwise.[1]

As Graham grew older, the nation's expanding vision for social justice at home and abroad powerfully influenced him. To be sure, he fell deep into the mire of political partisanship and never entirely extricated himself from it. And sometimes he evaded and backtracked. And he never doubted, even for a moment, that personal transformation formed the only firm foundation for enduring progress. Yet he gradually came to believe that the gospel transcended—or at least ought to transcend—partisan politics. He also came to believe that the movement from personal transformation to social justice was not automatic but required self-conscious attention.

Presidents and Politics

Graham's relation to presidents and politics proved both the best known and the most controversial part of his career. He prayed at four inaugurations of presidents of the United States and participated in one way or another in eight.[2] Graham spoke at most presidential prayer breakfasts, received the nation's two highest governmental awards for civilians, and maintained well-publicized friendships with innumerable mayors, governors, legislators, and judges.

Political figures of all ranks routinely attended his meetings. His 1952 meeting on the steps of the United States Capitol—the first religious service ever conducted there—drew forty thousand listeners, including Senators Richard Nixon and Lyndon Johnson, to hear the thirty-one-year-old evangelist.[3] One-third of the members of the U.S. Senate and one-fourth of the members of the House of Representatives asked for reserved seating.[4] Government dignitaries took him into their confidence, consulted with him, sought his advice, and asked him to serve as a quiet emissary on his international trips.[5] As indicated, Graham personally knew eleven successive presidents, forged friendships with ten of them, and became close friends with four (as well as their First Ladies).[6] *Time* journalist Nancy Gibbs would say that no other person in any field enjoyed such access to the pinnacle of American power: "He came with the office like the draperies."[7]

Graham's identification with politics ran deeper than just public associations, however. He admitted that he found the world of politics so fascinating that if he had not been an evangelist he probably would have tossed his proverbial hat in the ring.[8] From time to time admirers importuned him to run himself.[9] Associates said that politics absorbed the lion's share of his nontheological reading and television viewing time.

Graham's personal party membership remains elusive. Journalists and probably most Americans assumed that he was Republican.[10] That assumption bore a large measure of truth. On the whole he probably "had the soul of a mainstream, moderate Republican," as his political biographers Nancy Gibbs and Michael Duffy put it.[11] Yet the actual picture was more complex. Graham grew up a Democrat and retained that identification.[12] Many of his close friends were highly visible Democrats, including Hubert Humphrey, Sargent Shriver, John Connolly, both Clintons, and, above all, Lyndon Johnson. Graham joked that he could not spend much time with Johnson and still be a Republican.[13] He also was close to the liberal Republican senator Mark Hatfield, who often spoke at Graham's meetings.[14] In 1968, the newly nominated presidential candidate Nixon asked Graham's advice for choosing a vice president. Graham unsuccessfully urged Nixon to pick Hatfield.[15]

Graham took pride in saying that no one except his wife, Ruth, knew how he actually voted. Clearly intending to keep reporters off balance, he joked that once he voted twice because the machine was broken and so he used another one. Graham told the press that he usually voted a split ticket, choosing the man, not the party.[16] Graham wanted to maintain the image of a man who judged candidates and issues by their merits. Though he left no doubt that he supported Eisenhower, Nixon, Ford, Reagan, and both

Bushes, he did not *formally* endorse any of them. In order to minister effectively to Middle America, which in Graham's heyday was more politically mixed than it later became, it behooved him to keep some things at least partly to himself.

Graham's relation to the presidents offered a good window into the larger world of his relation to the political landscape. Of the eleven presidents Graham knew, his relationship with Truman was unique. Truman did not like him and made no effort to hide it. In the summer of 1950, as we saw earlier, they got off on the wrong foot when Graham and three associates landed a visit with the president in the Oval Office.[17] The Oval Office visit did not drop from the sky like a sacred meteor. Twice rebuffed in his desire to see the president, Graham finally secured an appointment by tapping the political influence of South Carolina Representative Joseph R. Bryson, North Carolina Representative Herbert Bonner, and Massachusetts Representative (later House Speaker) John McCormack.[18] The conversation was routine enough, but afterward Graham fell into the blunder of telling inquisitive reporters exactly what each of them had said. Truman never invited him back to the White House and refused to attend or endorse Graham's 1952 Washington, DC, crusade.[19] In 1967 Graham visited the aging Truman and apologized.[20] Even so, the former president made some unforgiving comments about the preacher in his autobiography published seven years later.[21]

Graham's growing dismay about Truman's handling of the Korean War probably played a role in the frostiness. In the beginning Graham supported Truman and what he initially considered Truman's aggressive prosecution of the war. Soon after the ill-fated Oval Office visit, Graham sent Truman a telegram assuring him: "I am praying for you during these critical hours that will decide the future of the world."[22] Before long, however, Graham started to attack Truman for dithering in Korea. Graham supported General Douglas MacArthur's bellicose policies in the war. And when Truman relieved MacArthur of command on April 11, 1951, Graham made clear that he, like most Americans, backed MacArthur.[23] On the eve of the 1952 election, the preacher wanted to know if the American people agreed with Truman's decision to go to war in the first place. He said he did not.[24] Though he did not say a great deal about the war—at least as compared with his many comments about the Vietnam conflict—he left little doubt that he thought America should fight to win or get out.[25] Truman seemed unwilling to do either one.

Eisenhower was another matter. The path that twisted from the mountains of western North Carolina to the office of the Supreme Allied Commander in Paris in the spring of 1952 led through the office of Texas oil tycoon Sid Richardson. Graham's tie with Richardson betokened his ease with big money in general and big oil money in particular. But the affinity between the preacher and the general was based less on a shared appreciation for capitalism than on Graham's conviction that Eisenhower—and Eisenhower alone—possessed the smarts to rid the world of communism. In the summer of 1952 Eisenhower announced he would run for president on the Republican ticket. Until then his party affiliation remained murky—perhaps a sign that Graham signed on more for the man than for the party.

Graham did not explicitly endorse Eisenhower in 1952 or in 1956, but his ringing encomia about Ike's wisdom and moral integrity left no doubt where he stood.[26] "I shall do all in my power during the coming campaign to gain friends and supporters for your cause. As always, you have my complete devotion and personal affection," Graham wrote Eisenhower on the eve of the 1956 election.[27] By Graham's account, however, they talked mostly about spiritual matters. The preacher prompted Eisenhower to reawaken and reaffirm his lapsed childhood faith. On Graham's recommendation, Ike and Mamie joined National Presbyterian Church. As Eisenhower neared death, he sought Graham's pastoral counsel.[28]

Graham's relationship with Kennedy ran on two rails. One pertained to Kennedy's membership in the Roman Catholic Church, the other to Kennedy's qualifications for the presidency. Countless Protestants, evangelical, mainline, and otherwise, held grave doubts about whether an honest Catholic could be president. Would he not face divided loyalties between the Vatican and the United States? Few doubted that Catholics enjoyed a perfect right to exercise their faith in the religious realm. But when their faith bore political implications—such as a pacifist Quaker being secretary of defense or a Christian Scientist being surgeon general—citizens had a right to ask.[29]

One of the murkier and more contested episodes in Graham's career bore on this question. On August 18, 1960, he and about twenty-five other conservative Protestant leaders, including the evangelical theologian Carl F. H. Henry, the evangelical scholar-pastor Harold John Ockenga, and the (more or less) mainline Protestant pastor Norman Vincent Peale, gathered in Montreaux, Switzerland. In his 1997 memoir Graham remembered that the meeting focused on strategies for evangelization. Peale, who strongly supported Nixon, asked if he could come, hoping to persuade Graham to endorse Nixon. Graham recalled that Peale addressed the group "briefly." Graham's memory had grown fuzzy. A letter Graham sent to Nixon near the time, August 22, 1960, allowed that the Montreaux group had "discussed at great length the many implications, particularly as related to the religious issue." Afterward Graham and Peale privately discussed the presidential race but Graham decided not to make a public endorsement.[30]

On September 7, 1960, several members of this group—minus Graham, who was vacationing in Europe—gathered in Washington, DC. The meeting consisted of 150 mostly conservative Protestant clergymen representing thirty-seven denominations. They discussed the problems that a Catholic presidency would pose for American democracy in general and for church/state separation in particular.[31] Peale presided. At the end of the day Peale read a brief press release, which articulated a five-point indictment of the Catholic Church's relation to American politics. Peale concluded: the "religious issue" in the "present political campaign is created by the nature of the Roman Catholic Church which is, in a very real sense, both a church and a temporal state."[32] The release backfired and Peale received fierce criticism in the press. Graham never publically endorsed the declaration or came to Peale's defense. Peale was privately dismayed by Graham's silence, but he said nothing in public.[33]

Though Graham had hosted the Montreaux "war council," as one historian put it, no one should have been surprised by Graham's reticence now.[34] The week before the Washington meeting he had privately advised Nixon to "stay a million miles away from the religious issue."[35] Explicitly raising it could boomerang. To be sure, Graham later admitted that "subconsciously" he too "had some questions as to what influence the Vatican might have over a Catholic President."[36] Yet in a letter Graham sent to Nixon the following summer, he reflected that he had been "reluctant to become tarnished as a bigot." Besides, Graham added, Kennedy's talk of "sacrifice and dedication . . . appealed to me."[37] And he disliked confrontations.

That storm soon blew over, but another one rolled in to take its place. Graham did not explicitly endorse Nixon, but he left no doubt where he stood. One week before the Montreaux meeting Graham had privately told Kennedy that he would vote for Nixon, "for several reasons, including a long-standing personal friendship."[38] Nonetheless, Graham added, if Kennedy won, he would try to unify "the American people" behind him and Graham would give Kennedy his "wholehearted loyalty and support." But

Graham *also* promised Kennedy that he would not raise the "religious issue publically during the presidential campaign."[39]

Technically Graham kept his word. He did not raise the religious issue publically during the campaign. But the line blurred. Less than two weeks after writing to Kennedy, Graham sent a letter to the two million American families on his mailing list, "urging them to organize their Sunday school classes and churches to get out to vote." Graham knew how they would vote, and why. In the same letter, Graham also encouraged Nixon to visit him in North Carolina in October. "This would most certainly be a dramatic and publicized event that I believe might tip the scales in North Carolina and dramatize the religious issue throughout the Nation without mentioning it publically."[40] Lest there be any doubt, on September 1, 1960, he told the presidential candidate: "Privately I intend to do all in my power to help you get elected."[41]

In October Graham overrode his better judgment and wrote an article for *Life* magazine explicitly endorsing Nixon. He made clear that his endorsement stemmed from his judgment that Nixon simply was better qualified by virtue of his "strength, knowledge, wisdom, and integrity as well as faith in God. . . . I am not against Mr. Kennedy, I am simply for Mr. Nixon."[42] Hours before the article was to go to press, the editor, Henry Luce, pulled it. Luce's decision followed a strongly worded appeal from John Kennedy. Luce also likely sensed, better than Graham himself did, that Graham would irreparably harm himself by falling so obviously into partisan politics. Graham quickly produced a substitute article, a simple recommendation to the American people to vote. Throughout his life Graham claimed that he had never publically endorsed a political candidate (except once long ago when he had endorsed John Connolly for governor of Texas). Yet Graham's strenuous just-under-the-radar advocacy for Nixon in 1960 and in later contests made his claim problematic.

Graham and Kennedy remained friendly but not warm. Earlier we saw that in January 1961, after the election but before the inauguration, Kennedy's father, Joseph, arranged for Graham and the president-elect to play golf together in Florida. More important, someone arranged for the two men to be photographed riding and schmoozing in a Lincoln convertible.[43] To some extent they needed each other: Graham needed access to Washington power corridors and Kennedy needed access to Graham's constituency. Or at least Kennedy surely wished to avoid stirring up needless resistance from Graham's constituency. After the golf outing, in the locker room, the preacher and the president-elect had a brief conversation about Jesus's

Second Coming. Graham later said that Kennedy told him that he was the only Protestant clergyman he trusted.[44] A Kennedy staffer later said that Graham caused the president to grit his teeth.[45] Both stories probably were true.

The relationship between Graham and Johnson constitutes one of the great friendship stories of American history.[46] However told, at the end of the day there can be little question that the two men admired and loved each other. Their wives were close too. The two men golfed, boated, and swam together. Along with Grady Wilson, Graham's downhome associate evangelist, Graham and LBJ even went skinny-dipping in the White House pool.[47] On occasion Graham and LBJ got down on their knees and prayed together. In 1965 Johnson attended Graham's crusade in the Houston Astrodome, the first visit by a sitting president. Several days after the election that seated Nixon in Johnson's place, Graham wrote: "I hope you will always remember that there is one country Baptist preacher from North Carolina who loves you, appreciates you, and hopes to see you often."[48]

Johnson feared death acutely.[49] When his heart began to give way, he asked Graham to preach his funeral: "Tell them a little bit about what I tried to do." And the preacher did. Describing Johnson's hope "to harness the wealth and knowledge of a mighty nation to assist the plight of the poor and underprivileged," Graham summed up his friend: "Lyndon Johnson was a mountain of a man with a whirlwind for a heart. He will stand tall in history."[50] Though there is no way to quantify such things, the evidence suggests that of all the presidents, Graham felt closest to Johnson. For that matter, one senses that Graham may have considered Johnson one of his dearest friends.

In many ways the friendship was a strange one. Johnson was no saint and Graham knew it. Johnson's language was bawdy, his manners coarse, and his extramarital affairs legendary.[51] Yet Graham was not a man to judge his friends on the basis of politics, theology, or personal behavior. Though Johnson was ten years older, the two men shared a great deal too. Both hailed from the South, enjoyed middle- or upper-middle-class standing, moderate formal education, and enormous talent and ambition. Most important, both found themselves driven by a world-encompassing vision of what they hoped to accomplish.[52]

Politics formed another bond. The 1964 election, which pitted Johnson against the conservative Republican senator Barry Goldwater, also pitted Graham against a great part of his natural constituency. He reported that he received more than one million telegrams urging him to support

Goldwater.[53] Graham effectively sat that one out, but he left little doubt that he favored his friend from Texas. The most historically significant part of the Graham and Johnson story involved Graham's steady and vocal support for Johnson's Vietnam War. Graham also supported Johnson's Great Society Program, but less vocally.

And then there was Nixon. An entire book could be devoted to the topic. Complex on many levels, Graham's relationship with Nixon represented both the highest and the lowest points of his career. Their friendship was an old one, going back to golf games in the early 1950s when Nixon was still a congressman from California. As with Johnson, the camaraderie ran deep. Nixon had somewhat humbler roots than Graham but their backgrounds were close enough that they both saw the world through the lens of entrepreneurial middle-class capitalism. Nixon's mother, Hannah Nixon, was devoutly Quaker. By the middle twentieth century the majority of Quakers stood on the center/left or left/left side of the theological and political spectrum. Hannah Nixon represented the evangelical minority. Graham liked to think that Nixon did too, although he wondered why Nixon was not more forthright about it.

From the outset Graham judged Nixon a very smart man with a commanding grasp of domestic and international affairs. Graham never doubted that Nixon possessed exceptional qualifications for high office. Repeatedly he spoke of Nixon's sharp intelligence, high moral character, and exceptional command of world politics. He once compared Nixon to Churchill.[54] Privately he told Nixon that God had been giving him "supernatural wisdom in handling difficult situations."[55]

Beyond all that, the two men simply liked each other—or at least, Graham liked and admired Nixon. Part of Nixon's friendship with Graham grew from his desire to use the preacher politically. A friend later said that Graham never saw how badly Nixon had "snookered him."[56] Even John Ehrlichman, a Nixon confidant, would say: "I'm not so sure that Nixon took Billy to heart."[57] Yet Graham's affection for Nixon ran deep. His dogged defense of the floundering president in 1973 and 1974 symbolized the strength of that affection. And he never abandoned his friend. After Nixon resigned, Graham tried with mixed success to continue the friendship. Graham's funeral sermon for Nixon ranked among the finest he ever delivered.[58]

Public connections and mutual endorsements proliferated. In 1957 Vice President Nixon visited Graham's New York City crusade. The crusade had moved for one day in July from Madison Square Garden to Yankee

Stadium, where Graham attracted one hundred thousand people inside the stadium and another twenty thousand in the parking lot. It was the largest crowd in the stadium's history. Nixon brought greetings from President Eisenhower. The event marked the first time a sitting vice president had spoken at a Graham crusade. For that matter, it probably marked the first time any sitting vice president had spoken at any outdoor revival meeting. Graham's star was soaring.

Graham possessed boundless admiration for Nixon. In the 1968 contest between Nixon and Senator Hubert Humphrey, as in the 1960 race between Nixon and Kennedy, Graham did not issue a formal or explicit endorsement of Nixon, but he made no attempt to camouflage his views either. One week before the election the press reported that Nixon's name was on Graham's absentee ballot.[59] The preacher not only prayed at Nixon's inauguration but also ventured to thank God for his presidency.[60] Two years later, days after the Kent State shootings, Nixon spoke, at Graham's invitation, at the University of Tennessee Knoxville crusade. It marked the first time a sitting president of the United States spoke at a Graham crusade. Critics saw it as little more than another presidential address at another Graham crusade. Historian Garry Wills's evisceration of the event in *Esquire* spoke volumes: "How Nixon Used the Media, Billy Graham, and the Good Lord to Rap with Students at Tennessee University."[61]

The relationship continued to thicken. On July 4, on the occasion of the Honor America Day that Graham and others had orchestrated, Nixon addressed the crowd massed on the Washington Mall. Honor Billy Graham Day in Charlotte in October 15, 1971, won another visit from the president. Some felt that Nixon's remarks about Graham that day crossed the line from honor to adulation.[62] Less than a month before the 1972 presidential election, Graham declared on the *Merv Griffin Show*: "Nixon is the most able and the best trained man for the job probably in American history. In an election year that divides people . . . I [have] to be honest."[63]

These events form the context in which Graham's reaction to Nixon's role in the Watergate controversy should be framed. The details of the low-level crime and high-level mendacity that led to Nixon's impeachment and forced his resignation in August 1974 have been rehearsed many times and need not detain us. The crucial point is that Graham continued to defend Nixon long after most Americans smelled a rat. When the first hint of something amiss came to light in 1972, Graham dismissed it as pettifoggery.[64] He pointed out that illicit undercover behavior was no stranger to the White House. Through 1973 Graham allowed that the Watergate events themselves were troubling but insisted that Nixon had nothing to do with them. As late as December he privately assured Nixon of his personal affection and "complete confidence in your personal integrity."[65] Graham maintained that posture through January 1974.

Finally, on April 29, 1974, the House Judiciary Committee received 1,200 pages of transcripts of Oval Office conversations. They showed that Nixon had participated in the cover-up virtually from the outset. The transcripts also showed Nixon's capacity for vulgarity and profanity. Graham finally muscled up the courage to start reading *New York Times* excerpts in the middle of May. "The thing that surprised and shook me most was the vulgar language he used. . . . I felt physically sick."[66] Elsewhere Graham admitted to weeping and throwing up.[67] Graham biographer Marshall Frady said Graham attributed Nixon's fall to "sleeping pills and demons." Graham insisted he was misquoted. But he was prepared to say that "all of Watergate was demonic because . . . it caused the American people to lose confidence in its institutions . . . almost as though some supernatural power of evil was trying to destroy this country."[68]

Graham's reference to Nixon's language left many journalists and historians appalled. They felt Graham had proved incapable of distinguishing between the minor issue of cussing and the major one of undermining the government.[69] On the face of it they were right. Graham did underscore Nixon's language. He even said that was what upset him "most." Yet deeper issues were involved too. First, Graham prided himself on his ability to judge character. Nixon had not revealed that side of himself, at least not to that extent. The preacher had heard the same language from Johnson, but Johnson did not pretend otherwise. Nixon did. The second, deeper issue involved the role of language in the evangelical subculture. As in all subcultures, language formed boundaries that separated insiders from outsiders. Graham also prided himself on not drawing boundaries, but Nixon was different. He pretended to be an insider yet his language proved that he was not. "Inwardly," Graham wrote, "I felt torn apart."[70] Nixon's crudity ripped the fabric of their friendship.

Graham's entanglement with Nixon marked a turning point. Until 1974 Graham had tumbled more and more rapidly into the vortex of partisan politics. When Nixon crashed, his muddy reputation soiled Graham's. The Nixon years represented the bottom of Graham's slide. After 1974 he tried, with mixed success, to avoid overt partisanship.[71] Graham acknowledged that Nixon's magnetism had clouded his judgment. In 1993 he would say, simply, that his friendship with Nixon had "muffled those inner monitors that had warned me for years to stay out of partisan politics."[72] He urged young evangelists to avoid his mistake. In a very real sense Nixon saved Graham, even though the salvation remained a work in progress to the end.

The preacher's relations with President Ford were friendly but not extensive. Religion was not a problem. Ford was Episcopal with evangelical leanings. In the fall 1976 Pontiac Stadium crusade, Ford may have asked Graham if he might speak (a reply letter from Graham to Ford implies this). Graham declined, saying that would look like a partisan endorsement before the fall election.[73] Ford's presidency marked the tipping point in which it became clear that presidents needed Graham more than he needed presidents.

Graham's relationship with Jimmy Carter, like his relationship with most presidents, started long before Carter entered the Oval Office and lasted long after he left it. Back in 1966 Carter agreed to host the showing of Graham's feature-length film *The Restless Ones* in Americus, Georgia. To Carter's surprise, he discovered that the BGEA insisted that all of its movie audiences had to be open to blacks and whites alike. Carter courageously faced down local hostility and integrated the meeting.[74] That was one bookend of their relationship. The other took place more than a half-century later in Charlotte, North Carolina, where Carter participated in the dedication of the Billy Graham Library in May 2007. The former president spoke with manifest respect and affection.

Conventional wisdom has held that the relationship between Graham and Carter remained friendly but not deep. Even though Carter's religious world paralleled Graham's—both men being evangelical Southern Baptists—the personal chemistry somehow never worked. Nancy Gibbs and Michael Duffy, historians of Graham and the presidents, even said that Graham's relation with Carter represented the "most complex and contradictory" of any in their book.[75]

Perhaps. On one hand it is true that Graham visited the White House comparatively infrequently, and the correspondence between them was scant and brief. Moreover, except for shared support for the (never ratified) SALT II nuclear nonproliferation treaties, they seemed not to find many reasons to interact. On the other hand, warmth and mutual kindness marked the correspondence that they (and their wives) exchanged.[76] In September 1979, the year before Carter's election contest with Reagan, Robert Maddox, Carter's religious liaison, told the president of a "cordial and gracious" meeting in Graham's home several days earlier: "Dr. Graham assured me he has complete confidence in, admiration and love for the President. He supports the

President wholeheartedly. He prays daily for the President." Maddox then added, undoubtedly saying more than he realized, "Dr. Graham does not care to be a highly visible figure at the White House." Even so, "Dinner at the White House, most any time, would please him."[77]

Historian Randall Balmer has documented that during this period Graham was working hard behind the scenes for Carter's defeat and Ronald Reagan's success in the 1980 presidential election. In early October 1979 Graham and Bill Bright of Campus Crusade convened several prominent conservative evangelical ministers in Dallas to pray together and settle on someone who could mount a successful campaign against Carter. About one year later, September 12, 1980, Graham pledged to Nevada senator Paul Laxalt, chair of Reagan's presidential campaign, that he would like to help Reagan's cause. But just eleven days after writing to Laxalt, Graham told Maddox, "As you know, with the Lord's help I'm staying out of it."[78]

Graham's political maneuvering with Carter and Reagan in 1979–1980 resembled his maneuvering with Nixon and Kennedy back in 1960. Then, it will be remembered, Graham promised Kennedy that he would not raise "the religious issue." But he worked hard to get out the vote among the two million families on his mailing list. He clearly assumed that most of them—who were overwhelmingly evangelical Protestant—would vote for Nixon, and he surely assumed too that they would do so partly for religious reasons. In the very same letter he invited Nixon to visit him in North Carolina. Doing so, he said, would "highlight the religious issue nationally."

Graham was never simple. Any reasonably objective observer would have to ask, what was going on in his head? Was it a question of duplicity, as Balmer has charged?[79] Or did rationales come into play that made sense to him even if not to others looking back twenty or thirty years later? Most likely Graham never saw any incompatibility between the things he said and did in one context and the things he said and did in another. The main reason was that when it came to politics he drew a fine line between the public and the private. He evidently saw no incompatibility between telling JFK he would not raise the religious issue and then giving Nixon advice on how to do precisely that. One was public, the other private. It pivoted on the perennial problem of what a prominent clergyman *should* say when he was wearing his collar, so to speak, and what he *could* say when he was not.

Two additional factors came into play. One was that Graham also drew a fine line between political support on one hand and pastoral counsel on the other. That principle evidently applied to his relationship with Reagan and Carter. He could work for Reagan politically even as he told Carter pastorally that Carter enjoyed his "love" and "wholehearted support." To be sure, this distinction gives Graham the benefit of the doubt. The other factor was one Graham seemed only dimly to understand about himself. Deep down he wanted to avoid confrontations, but he also desired to win as many people as possible to whatever cause he was championing. That was a tall order. The desire to get along *and* be persuasive all at the same time proved his undoing (especially with Nixon).

Reagan was a friend. Not a rollicking friend like Johnson, nor a politically intense friend like Nixon, but a friend with shared theological interests and common sympathy for free-enterprise capitalism. Both were masters of the camera as well as the microphone. Reagan liked to talk with Graham about eschatology—the theological study of how the world would end. Reagan had grown up in the mainline Protestant Disciples of Christ tradition, which had little interest in eschatological speculations. Though Graham wrote about dispensational premillennialism—most explicitly in *World Aflame* (1965)—he rarely preached about the details, evidently sensing that it was too arcane for mass audiences and divisive among conservative Protestants. The two men may have provided each other with a sounding board for those interests.[80]

But the deepest continuity between the preacher and the president lay in their approach to the world. Both articulated a large but simplified message of salvation, embraced a few exportable, stripped-down, time-tested principles, esteemed traditional verities, sought to make their words understandable by the masses, assumed there was no point speaking or preaching unless people understood them, knew how to assemble teams of able assistants and keep them, excelled in delegating, and proved loyal to friends. Above all, both knew how to inspire and lead.[81] When Reagan was shot, Graham was the first person Nancy Reagan phoned for advice and consolation.[82] Reagan had hoped that Graham would preach his funeral, but by then Graham was too weakened by age.

The friendships with the senior Bush and Clinton grew more from private affection than from public associations. In both cases the alliance reached far back into their prepresidential days. The networks of friendship with the political establishment were dense. Graham's associations with Senator Prescott Bush suggested deep connections with New England aristocracy. The Grahams and the Bushes routinely vacationed together.[83]

Yet Graham, burned by the Nixon years, declined publically to endorse Bush in 1988, though again he left no doubt where his sympathies lay. The key public event linking Graham and Bush was Graham's carefully framed support for the first Iraq War (narrated later).

At the dedication of the Billy Graham Library in 2007, former president Bill Clinton said that Graham had been "the most influential person" in his spiritual life. He said that Graham's own life had been marked by kindness, especially in private, when no one was looking. Graham paid a price with his more conservative supporters for his loyalty to Clinton as a friend.[84] He also paid a price with the secular media for a thoughtless remark on network television that seemed to minimize if not excuse the seriousness of Clinton's recent sexual misbehavior.[85] Though Graham said he did not agree with some of Clinton's policies, the main historical import of the relationship was that it existed at all.[86] Graham's quip in 2005 that Clinton would have made a fine evangelist himself aroused a firestorm from the right.[87] Once again Graham demonstrated that faith and friendship transcended differences about politics.

Graham's warm relation with the younger President Bush and his dutiful relation with later presidential contenders and President Obama bore few substantive implications for American history but significant ones for grasping the legitimating power of his presence. Bush's comments about how many years earlier Graham had helped turn a nominal faith into an active one bespoke the largely pastoral character of their relationship.[88] The 2008 and 2012 elections saw all three of the prime players—John Mc-Cain, Mitt Romney, and, after he became president, Barack Obama—making the expected pilgrimage to Montreat. Each of the players made certain, too, that photographers captured them on site. Those occasions served as a mark of political legitimation. These people are trustworthy, said the message. They have taken the time to visit the aging Billy Graham.

Graham and Presidential Culture

Graham's relationship with the presidents brimmed with implications for understanding the political significance of religion in modern America. The question journalists most often asked was, did his friendship—some said coziness—with presidents automatically preclude any kind of prophetic witness? Was it possible to play golf with a man year after year and realistically expect to challenge him about anything of consequence? Edward

Fiske's *New York Times Magazine* cover story, "Billy Graham: White House Chaplain," turned out to be one of the most widely circulated covers ever written about the preacher.[89] The essay offered a fair and actually quite sympathetic portrait. Yet the implication of the title—"White House Chaplain"— struck a nerve. Graham did not like it.[90]

Graham explained himself in several ways. First, speaking of presidents, he insisted that their relationships were primarily pastoral and secondarily collegial but rarely political.[91] He undoubtedly believed that claim to be true—he said it often—but it was not. The presidential correspondence and recorded conversations show that he gave substantive advice about how to win at the polls and in the polls.[92] And of course the "moral dimension" of policies remained fair game.[93]

That being said, the available evidence before, during, and after presidents' terms of office indicates that the relationships were *mainly* pastoral and collegial rather than political. For one thing, there is little or no evidence that any president actually changed his mind about a major decision as a result of Graham's intervention. But beyond that, the personal dimension really did show up everywhere. By one account Graham played golf with Nixon more than one hundred times.[94] After Johnson left the White House, he told Graham: "No one will ever fully know how you helped to lighten my load or how much warmth you brought into our house. . . . My mind went back to those lonely occasions at the White House: when your prayers and your friendship helped to sustain a President in an hour of trial."[95] Graham returned the sentiment: "Their personal lives, some of them, were difficult. But I loved them all, I admired them all. I knew that they had burdens beyond anything I could ever know or understand."[96]

Graham's second and third responses were pragmatic. He said—this was the second line—that if he publically criticized presidents about their policies he would never be invited back.[97] The one time he mildly but publically questioned a Johnson remark—a reference by Johnson to "declining morality"—Graham found immediately and the hard way that Johnson did not take criticism well.[98] Excluded from the Oval Office, he pointed out, he would have no access at all. And third, Graham felt that privately or publically advising presidents about how to do their job was not his calling.[99] He pilloried mainline Protestant clergy for expatiating about matters they actually knew very little about. He pointed to the fiascos of the Middle Ages when clerics tried to run states.[100]

How did Graham's relationships with presidents come about in the first place? A big part of the answer rested with the preacher himself. Until the middle years of his career, when presidents started to need him more than he needed them, he aggressively pursued the alliances. He let presidents know he could use a golf partner.[101] He praised them frequently and lavishly. In his eyes and in his words presidents had proved themselves men of exceptional skill, knowledge, and accomplishment. With each administration, he truly believed, providence had smiled on America. Graham also followed the rules. After he botched the visit with Truman, he maintained antiseptic confidentiality. Presidents knew they could talk and Graham would not. Presidents reciprocated. Johnson, for example, told Graham he should consider the White House his hotel whenever he was in town.[102]

Graham received direct rewards from the friendships. Presidents' support of his work in general and of him in particular gave him credibility. One aide, who worked closely with Graham in arranging his international crusades, felt that association proved especially influential in contacts with foreign leaders.[103] When photographers caught Graham out on the greens, rubbing shoulders with the most powerful man in the world, he believed that ordinary people would be more inclined to listen to him, to take his message to heart, and commit their lives to Christ.

Graham did not talk about another reward but common sense tells us it existed. The country boy from North Carolina surely felt a bolt of adventure as those relationships unfolded. Once, when playing golf with Kennedy, Graham double-bogeyed. The president joked, "I thought you played better than that." Graham quipped back, "Well, sir, when I'm not playing with the President-elect I usually do."[104] Though the exchange clearly unfolded in jest, it intimated Graham's awareness of Kennedy's power and what it might mean for his ministry and for him. Graham knew that at some level ordinary Americans were democrats in their heads but royalists in their hearts.

What did presidents gain? The short answer is, a lot. Legitimation topped the list. No one ever put it quite that baldly, but the photographic record told the story. Hundreds if not thousands of publically disseminated photographs showed presidents standing, sitting, talking, dining, or golfing with the preacher. Proximity served their purposes as much as his. Graham legitimated presidents by ratcheting up the stakes. More than once he suggested that the nation's prospects were hanging in the balance. In 1951 Graham hoped to persuade Dwight Eisenhower to run for president. At age thirty-two, he told Ike that he was praying that God would guide him "in the greatest decision of your life. Upon this decision could well rest the destiny of the Western World."[105]

Other presidents received similar velvet-mouthed compliments. As criticism of Lyndon Johnson started to mount, Graham reminded him that Lincoln, Wilson, and Roosevelt ranked among the "most criticized men in American history." For that matter, people "crucified Jesus within three years after He began His public ministry." Yet Johnson should take heart: "you could be the man who helped save Christian civilization."[106] In May 1968, looking at the upcoming presidential election, the preacher promised reporters in Portland, Oregon, that by September or October he might have to give up his (feigned) impartiality and make his choice of Nixon explicit: "I think that we are facing a crisis in the country of major proportions in which the very survival of the country is at stake."[107] In 1976 Graham assured Gerald Ford that he had been "one of America's great presidents."[108] With good reason, Arthur B. Krim, a noted financier and board member of the Lyndon Baines Johnson Foundation, would describe Graham as "sort of a president gatherer."[109]

The preacher provided more than legitimation, however. He also functioned as a barometer of Heartland opinion. One astute biographer intimated that when Graham spoke, America heard itself speaking to itself.[110] Graham's approval won votes for presidents. Nixon once told Graham that a barber in Oakland, California, a Democrat, had voted for Nixon because of his "confidence in your judgment."[111] The evangelist also functioned as a friend. Presidential aides told one set of reporters that almost everyone who saw the president wanted something. Graham did not. He did not need anything, either.[112] Camaraderie was energized by mutual recognition of the burden of responsibility. Graham said he understood the weight of their office. Presidents evidently sensed the weight of Graham's unofficial office too, the burden of being ultimately responsible for a vast evangelistic enterprise, with no lunch breaks.[113]

Graham undergirded presidents' credibility with the American people. After Truman, he virtually never challenged a president in public. There are good reasons to believe that people respected the preacher's judgment, not least because he knew presidents personally and they did not. More important, Graham assured Americans that presidents held their office by divine appointment. A rightly ordered society required a rightly selected leader. Absent moral failing or dereliction of duty, citizens should support them, at least until the next election. Besides, presidents just knew more about national and world affairs than most people did. Presidents were privy to classified information and behind-the-scenes negotiations with the power elite around the world.[114]

Finally, Graham really did, as he said, serve as a pastor. Eisenhower and Johnson asked searching spiritual questions. Kennedy and Reagan asked thoughtful theological questions. Both Bushes asked both. In later years Carter and Clinton spoke of Graham's ability to inspire their vision. Nixon may have come close to designating him the White House pastor (not quite the same as chaplain). "You will never know," wrote Johnson years after leaving office, "how much your love and support meant to me in the darkest days of my presidency." Not all of the relationships were of equal depth or longevity. But the deepest ones left a mark on both men's lives.

Counterfactual history has limited usefulness, but sometimes it throws actual history in a revealing light. So the question arises, how much influence would Graham have exerted if he had not known any president personally? By the same token, how much influence did he lose when he hitched his wagon to their stars? Historian/journalists Nancy Gibbs and Michael Duffy wrote a brilliantly perceptive biography titled *The Preacher and the Presidents*. Is it possible to imagine one titled *The Preacher without the Presidents*?

Religion and Political Culture

Graham's unique relationship with presidents formed part of the larger question of his view of American political life. How should religion and politics interact? On one hand, he felt individual Christians and individual preachers were obliged to participate thoughtfully and conscientiously in the political process. Graham nowhere considered, let alone endorsed, the Anabaptist argument against political participation. He also felt individual clergy members should feel free publically to advocate their political views, or not, as their conscience dictated.[115] On the other hand, churches themselves—especially entire denominations—should not.[116] Personally, he felt that he, too, should not, presumably because of the long shadow he cast as a prominent religious leader.[117]

Yet Graham drew a distinction between *partisan* politics—in which he did not (or claimed that he did not) engage—and *moral* politics, in which he did engage. Individual Christians, clergypersons, and organizations should take a position on questions of wide moral import. He did not articulate systematic criteria for identifying and separating the two, but he gave the example of the Panama Canal versus racial injustice.[118] The former clearly was partisan, the latter just as clearly moral. Treading lightly on partisan debates was a matter of common sense. They often required a kind of factual knowledge he did not possess. He refrained, for example, from commenting on the wisdom of local blue laws.[119] He said he just did not know enough about the ramifications. However, he grew testy when critics charged that he ducked the great moral issues of the day. He felt very strongly that he had commented on every issue of consequence. Perennially viewing himself as a social progressive, Graham seemed both confident and proud that he had addressed those issues in terms of wide moral principles, not Democratic or Republican agendas.[120]

Sticking with political questions with broad moral dimensions—ones that bore on the moral health of the commonwealth—required delicacy of touch. On multiple occasions Graham refused to sign declarations or formally testify before federal and state legislative committees about anything, including issues on which he agreed. He felt that if he signed one declaration or testified for one cause he would be pressured to support countless others. Where did one draw the line? And so it was that he publically supported Sargent Shriver's Anti-Poverty program, for example, or the SALT II agreement, but he would not testify before Congress.[121] He refused to sign petitions denouncing pornography, too, although he strongly supported the cause.[122]

In real life things were not so clear. More than once he fell off the wagon, even after the bitter experience of the Nixon years when he vowed to go and err no more. It seemed a case of—to change the metaphor—a proverbial moth drawn to the flame. By virtually all accounts, including otherwise sharply critical ones, Graham proved impervious to the temptations of greed and lust. But political power was another matter.[123]

Until the mid-1970s Graham insisted that he had avoided partisanship.[124] By that he meant that (with the Connolly exception) he had never *explicitly* or *formally* endorsed a particular candidate for office, as a newspaper might do the day before an election. In 1968 Graham tried to avoid the appearance of partisanship by praying at both the Republican and the Democratic national conventions. "I did not want people to think I was favoring one party over the other," he explained.[125] Americans, including Graham's ardent supporters, likely recognized that this was a distinction without much of a difference. Graham had made his views unmistakably—many felt painfully—clear time after time. Two months before the 1972 presidential election he told a press conference in California, without a trace of irony, that he did not know if he should use the word "'endorse'" but he *intended* to vote for Nixon.[126] And as we have seen, he waded, if not quite feet first, something pretty close to it, into the Carter/Reagan election, and would do so again with the Bush/Gore election in 2000.

A final point remains. From beginning to end, Graham found himself irresistibly drawn to the action, wherever it was, whatever it was. Action of the center/right variety usually proved most appealing, but not always. The key point is that for him the heart of the attraction was less the content of the politics than the fact that things were in motion and he wanted to be part of them. He appreciated the power of power. He possessed a shrewd instinct for discerning who counted. That did not mean that the powerless did not count. But it did mean that if revivals had to be worked up as well as prayed down, politics—secular politics, secular partisan politics—was part of the working-up enterprise. And in the process Billy Graham, every-day resident of Montreat, North Carolina—not Billy Graham International Christian Statesman—would contribute his energies and complications very much as any extraordinary ordinary citizen might do.

Providence and America

Both white and black Southerners of Graham's generation loved America. That is not to say that white Southerners always loved the U.S. govern-ment, the political and military machine that had invaded their land and left unspeakable suffering and poverty behind. But it is to say that they loved the noble ideals that animated the nation's founding. In their minds those ideals had inspired the building of a holy City on a Hill, operating under the watchful eye of a merciful God. The North had lost that vision to the greed of industrial capitalism and encroaching secularism. But the South believed they had kept it.[127]

The South also believed that it had established a providentially ordered society, marked by the rule of godly fathers, supportive families, and a con-tented class of "workers" and "servants." There, the Bible reigned. The Constitution of the Confederate States of America explicitly invoked God's blessing in its Preamble, in stark contrast to the virtual agnosticism of the federal Constitution. Sadly the South had lost its way, and God had pun-ished it by allowing Northern victory in the War between the States. But the ideals remained in the form of Lost Cause ideology. If Southerners re-turned to the godly, biblical faith they once knew, their glory might be restored.[128]

Graham's generation was not entirely blind to the substantial historical falsity of this Lost Cause ideology, but they were not entirely alert to it ei-ther. The part of the ideology that Graham inherited and maintained was the concept of the providential ordering of the society.[129] He rarely if ever spoke of the Lost Cause *per se*, but he did project the sense that God had a plan not only for his birth region but also for the entire American continent he loved. (God had a plan for other countries too, but that was another story.) Though God's aims for America would prevail—here was the rub— God had left many of the details up to individuals. Simply put, the end was predetermined but the means were contingent.

In America, providence and contingency took the form of a classic jeremiad. This term, drawn from the literary structure of the Old Testament book of Jeremiah, bore four tenets: 1. God had chosen and blessed this people for a particular task; 2. Americans had fallen away from that task; 3. if they persisted in their wicked ways they would run themselves into ruin partly because the wages of sin were death and partly because they had provoked God's just and holy wrath; 4. but if they returned to God, to holy living and a biblically ordered society (minus slavery, of course), God would restore them as citizens of a great land.[130] With good reason, President Dwight Eisenhower would quote Proverbs in his 1952 Inaugural Prayer: "Righteousness exalts a nation."

This jeremiad pattern had marked countless generations of Puritan and then mainstream evangelical preaching before Graham. He not only inherited and reproduced it but also articulated it in the most dramatic imagery possible. If Graham read the Almighty's designs rightly, America found itself simultaneously facing stark judgment and glorious hope. The nation lived in both the worst and the best of times. First came judgment. With his clock perpetually set at 11:57 PM, the darkness just before the dawn was the darkest darkness.[131] America deserved God's hostile verdict because of the evil deeds that America had inflicted on itself and on other nations. Like an Old Testament prophet he excoriated his land's moral bankruptcies. He saw a degree of evil unprecedented in American history, or at least since the Civil War.

Signs cropped up everywhere. They included racism, violence, corruption, greed, homelessness, immorality, nominalism, environmental degradation, child abuse, moral flabbiness, spiritual and physical hunger, and crime, both street and white-collar. America's very survival was at stake. The nation courted shame in the eyes of the world. America's racism in particular rendered his ministry abroad problematic. Though communist countries fell into their own sins, they at least avoided the moral slackness that marked American culture. And though communists posed a grave military and political threat, the evil that America inflicted on itself was even worse.[132]

In 1983 Graham released *Approaching Hoofbeats: The Four Horsemen of the Apocalypse.* The hardback jacket bore an ominous image of four galloping steeds. The imagery arose from the New Testament *Book of Revelation* or *The Apocalypse*. In it, four horsemen astride four horses—white, red, black, and pale—rode forth. They symbolized encroaching conquest, war, famine, and death, respectively. The mysterious equine quartet signaled the imminent end of the world and then the final judgment. Eleven years later Graham reissued the book with minor revisions under the grim title *Storm Warning*. The cover displayed a lightning bolt cracking across a blackened horizon, with text signaling doom: "With the Collapse of Communism the Nuclear Threat Has Diminished but Ominous Shadows of Deceptive Evil Loom on the Horizon."[133] Even so, the striking paucity of specifics of time and place amid the ample naming of general trends and biblical themes suggested that Graham's main aim was less apocalyptic than prophetic. He sought to arouse awareness of the urgency of the moment. People dithered at their peril.[134]

And yet the judgment part of the jeremiad formed only half the story. The other half invoked hope. As we have seen, if the alarm on Graham's clock was perennially set at 11:57 PM the backup was perpetually set at 12:03 AM. If Americans awoke and acted responsibly—*biblically*—as God's Word prescribed, the promise of hope would prevail. The formula for hope was both clear and achievable. Righteousness exalted a nation. The moral renovation of persons taken far enough would foster the moral renovation of the nation. Of course, radical moral renovation started with the new birth in Christ. But Graham was pragmatic enough to know that such a prescription would never win universal assent. So he often invoked the language of moral theism as, in effect, second best. Lives disciplined by the Ten Commandments would promote the moral renovation of the nation and, if universally applied, the world.[135]

Just as Graham saw evil everywhere he looked he also saw signs of a great and virtuous nation about to be born. In the evangelist's preaching America had positioned itself on the precipice of an unprecedented revival. Graham effectively took a cue card from the election campaign ad for his friend President Ronald Reagan: "It's morning again in America." Graham understood that the United States was not formally a Christian nation. Yet the nation's blueprints, the Declaration of Independence and the Constitution (and by implication the ideals of the Founding Fathers), were Christian in spirit, Christian values had shaped the nation's history, and most Americans were Christian.[136]

Granted, obstacles stood in the way. They had to be identified and removed. But they were just that: obstacles, not chasms. We will see that the later Graham distanced himself from the Christian right, partly because it elided economic justice. But as with the Christian right, progress required turning, both individually and corporately. Whether the turning hinged on repentance, which had a theological tonality, or regret, which had a more secular tonality, remained productively ambiguous for both Graham and the Christian right. Either way, his and the right's vision of an America morally reborn bore similarities.[137]

The exact relationship between the judgment and the hope visions also remained productively ambiguous. Sometimes they appeared to signal discrete, chronologically sequential dispensations (as dispensational premillennialists held). Sometimes they appeared to signal overlapping eras. And sometimes they appeared to signal interpenetrating planes of time. In his autobiography Graham recalled addressing Boston audiences in 1950: "Disillusioned and disconnected people seemed willing to try anything. It was a morally promising but exceedingly perilous time."[138] Graham absorbed a good deal of criticism because he projected signs of decline and renewal from a human's perspective and judgment and hope from a divine perspective.[139] Yet Graham's audiences, steeped in biblical metaphor, understood that history worked in fluid patterns. Partisans took the judgment rhetoric not with a grain of salt—that suggests flippancy—but as rhetoric of hope. Everything could be changed. The future lay squarely within their pragmatic can-do hands. After all, the nation had won the most terrible war in history. It now imagined making the entire world free of communism (and then terrorism) as well as hunger and poverty (and then environmental destruction).

Graham's view of America's place in the grand scheme of providence invites analysis. First of all, his prescription for America was not a call for a theocracy in which clerics would oversee the enforcement of the laws. Nor was it a call for a coercive moral establishment of the sort associated with the Christian right in the 1980s and 1990s. It was not even a call for a mass revival of stirring faith in the faithless. Rather, Graham called for America to return to its moral—even if not explicitly Christian—roots. Graham's command of early American history was shaky. But that was not the point. The task at hand was to recover—renew—the original vision, the vision that had made the land great.[140]

The remaining features of Graham's vision proceeded logically from the first one. The messenger urged fellow Americans to think about the momentousness of their providential obligations. *Momentousness* should be taken in the exact meaning of the term. Providence called them to focus on the moment at hand. They could not afford to wait a while, see what happened, and reserve action for a later day. Now was the day for action. And then he framed his discourses in public language. Though he often used stories drawn from private lives (anonymously), he did so in order to make a public point. Sometimes he wandered off script and the stories wandered with him. But the aim remained clear enough: to address fears that everyone—and not just a boutique corner of the population—was worrying about.

Providence applied first and last to the moral dimensions of public questions, not to the specifics of economic or political or military policies. When he endorsed capitalism, for example, or urged firmness in the fight against communism, he believed he was addressing the inner moral dimension of the times, like the marrow in a bone. So it was that he viewed providence's workings in national and eventually global terms. Except for a few icebreakers about the beauty of the site, he rarely preached about local or statewide or even regional matters. He spoke to all Americans about their entire land.

And finally, Graham left God in America's story. For many journalists and academics that move smelt of civil religion, which they knew had been used to justify the nation's actions, right or wrong. In 1970 theologian Reinhold Niebuhr dismissed "the Nixon-Graham doctrine of the relation of religion to public morality and policy" as "complacent conformity."[141] But Graham saw civil religion in a different light. Rightly framed, it gave the nation's story gravitas. It meant that the nation stood accountable not simply to its own interests but also to those of a higher tribunal.

These various traits, then—revival, momentousness, publicity, morality, expansiveness, and transcendence—marked Graham's rhetoric about America's place in the great rivers of divine providence. Throughout his career he sought to fix the events of his own ministry within this providential scaffold. When he helped launch *Christianity Today*, he said that each issue would take place within a national and international frame of reference. It would discuss "current subjects," "carry full news coverage," draw on the "wires of the Religious News Service . . . and at least one hundred reporters throughout the entire world," and serve as a "digest of what other magazines all over the world are saying."[142] In 2014 visitors to the Billy Graham Library viewed the photographic exhibits of his life in the context of the landmark events of national and international history.

Graham and the Almost-Chosen People

Like most Americans, Graham loved the land of his birth, but perhaps unlike most Americans, he loved it in quite different ways at different times of
his career. The events of July 4, 1970, offer a conspicuous, controversial,
and symptomatic place to start the story. Graham played the leading role,
at least symbolically, in the Honor America Day on the Washington Mall.
Though a wide range of political figures, including luminaries on the progressive left such as Senator George McGovern, and moderate left such as
Senator Hubert Humphrey, lent their support, the event acquired strongly
conservative Republican overtones. Little wonder, given the high visibility
of hard conservatives such as Bob Hope and Francis Cardinal Spellman.[143]
Nonetheless Graham felt that the underlying aim—independent of the bitter political controversies of the day over Vietnam—represented the great
majority of Americans. The flag, he said, belonged to everyone. Antiwar
protestors loved the flag as much as he did.[144] The disagreements lay in differences about how best to fulfill the American dream, not whether the
dream existed.

Over the course of his public ministry Graham displayed three distinguishable outlooks toward the American dream. They might be called
challenging America, embracing America, and transcending America. The
challenging outlook ran from the late 1940s through the early 1960s, the embracing outlook from the early 1960s through the early 1970s, and the transcending outlook from the early 1970s to the end of his active career. These
outlooks were not mutually exclusive. At all points all three of them played
a role. Yet viewed from afar each of them seemed to cast a definable profile
during the years noted.

In the first outlook, Graham projected a sharp critique of American life.
He excoriated it for the stubborn intractability of its sins and crimes. In his
thinking those two categories—sins and crimes—blurred because they both
rested on a distortion of the same underlying moral foundation. His critique took the form not of an anti-American tirade but of a prophetic call
to re-create a better America, the one envisaged in the Constitutional blueprint and in the Founding Fathers' vision. America enjoyed no special favor
in God's eyes. "While his views positioned him well within the cold warrior
mentality of the early 1950s," said Andrew Finstuen, a historian of Graham's
thought, "he was no simple apologist for American righteousness in the
face of Godless communism. . . . More than once he suggested that perhaps
the threat of communism was a judgment upon America's iniquities." In

1950, Graham asked a Burlington, Vermont, audience: "Why should God not destroy America tonight?"[145] Six years later he warned *Hour of Decision* listeners that the world rightly saw America as crime-ridden, with its economic prosperity rivaled by spiraling delinquency. "America has no special immunity from judgment from God," he declared. "God judges us by what we do, and iniquity is rising."[146] The future did not look good.

The second outlook saw Graham moving from a stance that challenged America toward an embrace of established powers. One sympathetic partisan astutely observed that Graham did not have much to embrace. He already *was* the establishment. Comfortable with the nation's power elite, he became a ready target for those who saw him as the high priest of civil religion—or what the conservative Jewish sociologist Will Herberg had tartly, and famously, called the religion of "the American Way of Life."[147]

The charge was not entirely fair. In 1960 Graham wrote in *Life*, which enjoyed a vast readership, that the nation's "quest for personal comfort, with a dearth of public services and surfeit of privately sold gadgetry," left it incapable of competing with the Soviet Union.[148] That same year another issue of *Life* splashed a photo of Graham, with two young African men, across its cover. The accompanying story said that in the previous six weeks Graham had preached the gospel to a "third of a million Africans, an overwhelming majority of them black."[149] The point was clear. Graham's message reached beyond comfortable white middle-class American audiences. Weeks after the shootings of Martin Luther King, Jr., and of Senator Robert Kennedy, Graham trembled in the face of the epidemic of violence. People abroad "read about it everyday. It's on the front pages every day. They wonder if we have gone mad in this country."[150] That period also hosted some of Graham's most determined efforts to empower evangelists of both sexes and multiple nationalities in the extraordinarily influential 1974 Lausanne Congress on World Evangelization.[151]

Yet the booster symbolism of serving as the Grand Marshal of the Tournament of Roses Parade in 1971 spoke worlds. And so did the Honor Billy Graham Day nine months later in his hometown of Charlotte (following the Billy Graham Appreciation Day three years earlier). The city's decision to dismiss public schools could be construed as a justifiable gesture of municipal pride, along with naming a lovely stretch of one of the city's highways the Billy Graham Parkway. The numerous businesses that closed that day acted within their rights too. But his remarks about growing up in hard times, killing rats, and surviving without government help rang false, at least to those who knew the family's history. The comment might have been technically true—his parents did go through a rough patch during the Depression—but it hardly represented the comparative economic comfort of his hometown years.[152]

Academic, business, civic, ethnic, geographic, media, political, religious, and even sartorial awards and honors—at least thirty-five—showered down on Graham in the decade following 1965.[153] Those encomia, along with honorary degrees, overnights in the White House, prayers at two presidential inaugurations, featured remarks at three presidential prayer breakfasts, well-photographed golf outings with high-ranking politicians, repeated appearances on network television talk shows, and fraternizing with some of the richest and most powerful men in America, betokened deep comfort with the culture. To be sure, there was no evidence that Graham compromised his core message in any of those settings, or that he strayed morally or financially. Yet the image of a man thoroughly at home with American life prevailed. His invitingly relaxed deportment on television talk shows appeared symptomatic of something deeper. Sometimes it was hard to tell where self-confidence ended and self-satisfaction began.[154]

The third outlook, transcending America, revealed a man markedly less comfortable with his role as the putative high priest of American civil religion. The debacle of the Nixon presidency, which Graham had strongly supported, signaled a turning point, if not consistently in practice, at least in aspiration. The sordid revelations released with the Nixon tapes saved Graham from himself. They forced him back to the drawing boards to reassess his real and perceived complicity in the smugness of that administration and by implication the smugness of his associations with other parts of the American establishment.

The years following the mid-1970s saw a man self-consciously trying to nudge the nation to transcend its vested interests. In 1980, looking back on the 1950s, he admitted that he "used to make the mistake of almost identifying the Kingdom of God with the American Way of Life." No longer. "I've come to see that other cultures have their own way of life that may be of just as great a value to them as our way of life to us."[155] That way of thinking persisted to the end of his career. In 1998 he suggested that Canada, "a peace-loving country," might be a model for Americans. It is "looked upon as a country that doesn't get involved in other people's affairs around the world. . . .We seem to have our people everywhere telling other people what to do."[156] Increasingly he turned his gaze to the fate of all nations on the planet: "We can go [into other nations] with a lot more humility and say that we're going to take our place among the nations of the world to make as fine a contribution as we can to world peace."[157] He increasingly disassociated himself from his America-only voice and endeavored to become a voice for the trials of dispossessed peoples everywhere.

In 2000 the respected CBS news anchor Dan Rather said that Graham defined America.[158] Many people judged that he represented simple decency, a basic American value.[159] Just as the Protestant mainline was shedding its custodial ownership of the American dream, Graham, like the Christian right, moved to claim it. But in a key different from the preponderantly judgmental ones he seemed to trumpet three and four decades earlier, and different, too, from the often triumphalist ones he seemed often to trumpet only one or two decades earlier. The notes of the final years—the late 1970s through the early 2000s—seemed more chastened than judgmental, more confident than self-satisfied. His mature message at its best called for the personal and social transformation of an entire world of almost-chosen people.

War, Peace, and Global Justice

One of the most durable conventions about Graham is that he was a hawk of the fiercest kind. The convention bears a large measure of truth for the Graham of the late 1940s, 1950s, and most of the 1960s. To a great extent the early Graham defined himself not only politically but also culturally and even theologically as a warrior against communism. As with millions of Americans, Graham's hatred and fear of communism was palpable, profound, and pervasive.

The story is long and complex.[160] Before plunging into it, however, four generalizations are helpful. First, Graham's attitudes toward communism not only changed but also zigzagged. The changes unfolded in different ways in different times and places. Second, Graham did not do it alone. The culture changed—and zigzagged—right along with him. Third, Graham and the West did not do it alone, either. The Soviet Union changed at the same time, and so did the Eastern Bloc nations, and, to a lesser extent, so did China and North Korea. Finally, Graham's star remained high long after the Cold War died. The Cold War helped propel him into public visibility but it did not keep him aloft. Other factors, including the culture's needs and his personal skills, did.

In the early years of his career Graham hammered the communist threat constantly. Next to the gospel message, by his own recollection, he preached about it more than anything else.[161] In 1953 the *Chicago Daily News* dubbed

Graham "Communism's Public Enemy Number One," a view echoed by Soviet newspapers.[162] Graham famously ridiculed "the pinks, the lavenders and the reds who have sought refuge beneath the wings of the American eagle."[163] The alarmist words on the front page of a "News Letter" of the BGEA, mailed to listeners of the *Hour of Decision* in July 1953, represented hundreds if not thousands of paragraphs in Graham's preaching and writing of that era. "This is no time to be lulled by the constant talk of 'peace' by the Communist spokesmen," he cautioned. *"Their program of world conquest is moving ahead at a steady pace."* British Guiana and Guatemala effectively have fallen, Graham warned. Communists intend "to bring Japan to her knees economically," then all of the Far East. "Other countries are to follow. *We are being gradually encircled.*"[164] Many of the most memorable lines Graham ever preached targeted the communist enemy: "Stalin's fixed purpose is to holster the whole world for communism"; "They have knifed their way across Laos"; "Communism is a fanatical religion that has declared war upon the Christian God."[165] Communism framed his image of the world, aroused his listeners' anxieties, and prompted them to take action.

Graham's attacks on communism started slowly but quickly gained momentum. The first comments turned up here and there in his preaching in the late 1940s. They appeared forcefully in his opening sermon in his first major urban crusade in Los Angeles in 1949. They reappeared with equal force in his first major outdoor meeting in the East: the revival sited on the Boston Common in the cold wet spring of 1950. The continually swelling audiences on both coasts and pretty much everywhere else suggested that the people eagerly embraced them.

Graham's fears stemmed from several sources. Perhaps the most proximate lay in his close association with the tycoon philanthropist J. Howard Pew. As noted, Pew founded and owned the Sun Oil Company. For many years he served as a major contributor to *Christianity Today*, to the staunchly evangelical Gordon Conwell Theological Seminary near Boston, and other evangelical enterprises. Pew probably was more interested in protecting free-market capitalism than in fighting communism. But since communism posed a threat to free-market capitalism it fell in the center of his crosshairs. Graham spent a great deal of time with other high-rolling conservative philanthropists like Pew. Association was not causation, but common sense suggests that these figures all influenced Graham's outlook.[166]

A second source grew from the widespread anxieties promoted by Wisconsin senator Joseph P. McCarthy. The senator's attacks focused on domestic threats, traitors at home, especially within the United States government. McCarthy has been sharply criticized. But in the very beginning— in the early 1950s—he seemed to many thoughtful Americans a brave patriot sounding the alarm. At one point Joseph Kennedy, John F. Kennedy's father, had contributed money to McCarthy's anticommunist campaign, and Robert Kennedy, John's brother, had worked for him.[167] Graham never met or corresponded with McCarthy but initially supported his aims of exposing traitors at home.[168] By 1954, however, Graham had followed Eisenhower and other establishment Republicans in moving away from McCarthy's extremism. He called the hearings "ridiculous."[169] And Graham's focus gradually shifted from the threats posed by domestic communism to those posed by its international counterparts.

If Pew and McCarthy formed immediate influences, the mood of the nation and palpable communist success abroad constituted mediate yet more menacing influences. The 1950s often have emerged in Americans' collective memory as a pleasant age of suburban expansion and household tranquility. Yet Hitler and Stalin's atrocities were recent enough to be a terrifying reminder of the cruelty humans could inflict. More concretely, communism seemed in many ways to be winning. Commies—as Americans commonly dubbed them—had acquired the Bomb (both A and H), overrun China, driven United Nations (UN) forces into a humiliating truce in Korea, hurled Sputnik into space before Americans had launched their own satellite, crushed Hungarian freedom fighters, and even beat American athletes in the 1956 Olympics. If Americans feared worldwide communism, they had reasons.

Graham shared other Americans' fears about the danger communism posed, but as a Christian he also brought concerns born of religion to the table. Communism threatened the American way of life at its roots. It represented a total system, encompassing and threatening every aspect of the culture, just as any authentic religion did. It drew its force from a sense of revelation, just as Christianity and Judaism did. Communism paraded as actively anti-Christian. More precisely, communism was not simply an alternative religion like Zen but an aggressive destroyer of souls. It manifested missionary zeal, with a track record of winning converts' hearts and souls. It employed deception and fostered treachery.

Communists added military might to missionary zeal. They possessed the power to destroy or at least inflict vast damage on the United States and other Western nations. When they acted, they acted with cruelty and inhumanity. And many Americans refused to see it. Still worse, America was unprepared. The nation had proved hapless after the Korean truce, shackled by its commitments to the United Nations. Individuals within the nation proved more interested in materialism and recreation than in moral rigor and hard work. Like a demonic religion—or even *as* a demonic religion—the communist threat was real, lethal, imminent, and violent.[170] Subtle, too. The communists quietly infiltrated churches and other institutions, working behind the scenes, invisibly. Communism represented the most grievous combination of threats imaginable, for it portended the annihilation of all that Americans held most dear.

Graham held all of these views, and many other men and women who commanded respect held some or all of them too, including such worthies as Dean Acheson and John Foster Dulles.[171] Far from being a voice crying in the wilderness, Graham found himself in good and strong company. Possibly he made communism more fearsome than any politician could do. He possessed the tools to leverage a political and military threat into a godless attack on an essentially Christian or at least Christian-influenced American way of life.

Yet Graham changed with the times. His assaults on communism continued with unabated ferocity through the 1950s and 1960s but began to taper off in the early 1970s, at least if the number of times he mentioned the threat is taken as a yardstick. In the late 1970s, they grew increasingly infrequent until they effectively disappeared in the early 1980s. In 1972 he said on national television that Christianity and communism might be reconcilable, at least to some extent, if communism were not atheistic.[172] In 1977 Graham told a church audience in Hungary: "I come from a different social system . . . we are bound together as brothers and sisters in Christ."[173] It is easy to imagine Graham speaking a quarter-century earlier about American and Hungarian Christians as brothers and sisters in Christ. It is difficult to imagine him speaking about the two social systems as "social systems." By the late 1970s Graham's worries centered more on the volatility of the Soviet Union as an unstable autocracy than on the worldwide conspiratorial ideology of communism. Yet even in reference to the Soviet Union, he would say in 1984, "We (the United States and Soviet Union) must learn to coexist and even be friends."[174]

These considerations about communism lead to Graham's views of America's wars. The preacher's outlook on the Korean War unfolded in two ways. First, as noted, it entwined itself with his view of Truman. Chest-thumping support in the beginning yielded to dismay about Truman's alleged dithering and then his firing of MacArthur. Though he did not say a lot about the Korean War, at least compared with his many comments about the Vietnam War, there can be little doubt that he thought the United States should fight the communist menace full force. Or leave. Distrust of the fledgling United Nations and, by implication, America's UN allies in Korea, shadowed his views too.[175]

Still—and this would be the second way—the war occasioned the publication of Graham's second book, *I Saw Your Sons at War: The Korean War Diary of Billy Graham* (1953). This slight volume of just sixty-four pages recounted his 1952 Christmas-season visit to troops at the front lines, casualties in hospitals, prayer meetings in local churches, and contacts with generals and Korean high officials. It carried photographs of Graham visiting severely wounded soldiers in a military hospital. The volume portended a ministry of global scope framed against the major events of the age.[176]

Though Graham's view of the Vietnam War was tangled, several overall comments seem warranted.[177] First, he moved from jut-jawed support for the administration's policies in the mid-1960s to professed neutrality, born of deep uncertainty, by the time the U.S. involvement ended in 1973. In the beginning his main fear centered on the domino effect: we must stop communist expansion now, over there, before it materializes here, on our doorstep. Graham pointed out that President Kennedy made the initial commitment of sixteen thousand soldiers and Johnson had inherited the burden.[178] In these respects Graham mirrored the views of many high-ranking figures in the United States government and millions of Americans too.[179] Despite some congressional misgivings, the 1964 Gulf of Tonkin Resolution, which authorized the use of conventional military force, won resounding support in the U.S. Congress.[180]

By the very end of the 1960s, however, Graham's support for how the administration was prosecuting the war started to waver, at least in his private communications. On April 15, 1969, he dispatched a thirteen-page letter to President Nixon. Declassified in 1989, the letter became one of the most important and controversial documents he ever wrote, at least in retrospect.[181] It purportedly reflected the views of a group of American missionaries in Vietnam, but it almost certainly expressed his own views too.[182] Graham acknowledged that the missionaries spoke from "hawkish" sympathies, but they also expressed deep dissatisfaction with how the administration had executed the war. Shades of the Korean War: fight or get out.[183]

The missionaries—presumably Graham too—outlined several possible scenarios. The majority of the options assumed that the Paris peace talks,

which had started the previous year, would not end productively and honorably. Under those circumstances, the thrust of the recommendations
involved five steps. First, turn the war over to the South Vietnamese government and military. It was, after all, their war. Second, withdraw "rapidly!"
The American presence corrupted the economy and poisoned the culture.
Third, empower South Vietnamese Special Forces for guerilla warfare. Their
methods might seem "brutal and cruel in sophisticated Western eyes," but
the Viet Cong used those methods every day to "spread terror and fear to the
people." Fourth, emphasize propaganda, especially psychological. And fifth,
"Use North Vietnamese defectors to bomb and invade the north. Especially
let them bomb the dikes which could over night destroy the economy of
North Vietnam."[184] The import was clear: attack and demoralize the civilian
population.

One sharply critical biographer of Graham wrote that the fifth part of
the plan would have taken a million lives.[185] Correct or not, there could be
little doubt that many civilians would have suffered and died. In the light of
the group's hawkish views, and its lament, stated earlier in the letter, that the
bombing of North Vietnam had stopped prematurely, waging war on the civilian population made sense as a strategic assumption. But the plan made
little sense morally, for it surely violated Christian principles of just war as
well as the Geneva Conventions.

There is no way to know if the document influenced anyone with power,
but it could not have instilled restraint. One interpretation of the event is
that Graham knew the consequences of the recommendation and pressed it
anyway. Another interpretation is that he did not know the consequences
and pressed it anyway. Either way, there was scant evidence that he possessed the training or experience to advise the president of the United States
about military strategy. Replicating a life-long weakness for speaking beyond his knowledge (a fault he admitted), he was simply out of his depth.[186]
Moreover, the letter undermined his repeated claim that he did not offer
Nixon—or any other president—specific policy recommendations.[187] And
it arrived at a time when Graham was entering the height of his political
influence.

A second overall observation is that in the late 1960s and early 1970s
Graham oscillated between noninvolvement and involvement. On one
hand, in public he spoke very little about the geopolitical details of the conflict. On the other hand, in public, with rare exceptions, he stood shoulder
to shoulder with Presidents Johnson and Nixon. Graham felt that God had
authorized civil authorities to do their job. Citizens should support them

unless they saw clear evidence of incompetence, moral turpitude, or violation of religious liberty. Besides that principled point, Graham projected a pragmatic one. Presidents usually knew things that ordinary people did not. Graham apparently did not suspect that his close friendship with Johnson and Nixon might have clouded his judgment about their judgment.[188]

As the 1970s wore on, Graham, like millions of Americans, grew increasingly ambivalent about the reasons for the war. He admitted that he was profoundly perplexed yet saw no way out. Repeatedly he said that he would keep his thoughts to himself and not take sides. Many Americans doubted that his neutrality was genuine or that his uncertainty ran very deep. They took his professed neutrality as tacit or even covert support for the war, especially in light of his refusal publicly to challenge the invasion of Cambodia in 1970 or the Christmas bombing of Hanoi in 1972. Dr. Ernest Campbell famously used the pulpit of New York's Riverside Church to accuse Graham of a "moral 'cop-out' " on the Cambodian bombing.[189]

Into the 1970s, Graham made statements that appeared to minimize if not trivialize the human cost of the fighting by universalizing the problem. In November 1969 the story of the My Lai massacre hit the headlines. According to the story, U.S. forces had gunned down some five hundred men, women, and children in cold blood. A military court convicted Lieutenant William Calley of killing twenty-two Vietnamese civilians. Graham claimed that the lieutenant represented the evil in everyone: "We have all had our Mylais in one way or another, perhaps not with guns, but we have hurt others with a thoughtless word, an arrogant act or a selfish deed."[190] From a Christian theological or human rights perspective the statement may have been factually true, but the way he framed it—in the highly visible venue of the *New York Times*, no less—appeared to thin out the atrocity by spreading it.

The early 1970s saw a man in turmoil. The lesson of the war, Graham told the British correspondent David Frost in 1970, was that "we should do more talking and less fighting."[191] In the spring of 1973, Graham supported Nixon's plan for an orderly withdrawal, yet he worried that the Paris peace talks would leave the South Vietnamese in peril and betray a nation that had trusted the United States. America, after all, had made promises. Fidelity remained an enduring American value. There, Graham undoubtedly touched a chord of approval. In June he told reporters that the Vietnam War had taught Americans that "we are not all-powerful and that America is not the Kingdom of God. We can go into it with a lot more humility. We have a lot to be proud of in the past; we have a lot to be ashamed of in the past."[192] Later, he said that America never should have gotten into a no-win land war in Asia in the first place.[193] In 1997 Graham told Larry King that he regretted that he had not spoken against it.[194]

Graham's position on the Vietnam War merits reflection. Considered whole, it placed a stain on his record. The problem was not that he took the wrong stand on the war by the light available to him (and many others) at the time, or that his views changed, at least to the point of finding the rationale for American involvement unconvincing. So did those of the journalism icon Walter Cronkite. The problem was different. First, he waffled. If he had taken a clear prowar stand, or a clear antiwar stand, or offered a clear explanation for changing his mind, then, all right, people differed on weighty matters of public policy. And sometimes they changed their minds. But his waffling looked like he was just putting his finger to the wind. Second, he dissimulated. Or at least he appeared to do so. On one hand, after 1970 or so he repeatedly said he was neutral about the war. On the other hand, his fervent public support for Nixon, continually paraded in front of the press without any hint of distancing, let alone criticism, left all but the most ardent partisans scratching their heads.

The first Iraq War presented a more seasoned Graham. One of the most reported incidents in Graham's life took place the evening of January 16, 1991. The preacher dined with President and Barbara Bush in the White House private quarters. The president told Graham that after dinner he would go on television and announce to the nation that he had ordered American jets to start bombing Iraq. Graham prayed with the president. Some observers took that moment as Graham's endorsement of the war, especially since he also had said, just seven days earlier, that the strong bore an obligation to protect the weak.[195]

Events at Fort Myer the following morning captured less attention but suggested that Graham saw this war less as a conflict to be won than as a burden to be borne. Standing before the assembled military brass, Graham prayed that the war would be brief, the casualties minimal, and the peace following it enduring.[196] And perhaps most important, he prayed that the United States would find itself on God's side, not the reverse.[197] There is no evidence that Graham had read Lincoln's searching ruminations on his own war, or Reinhold Niebuhr's *The Irony of American History*, but their concerns ran parallel paths. I am not suggesting Lincolnian or Niebuhrian wisdom. That was not Graham's gift or aim. But the times called forth from Graham a measured reserve not seen in the Korean and Vietnam eras.

That shift did not develop overnight, however. From the late 1940s through the late 1960s, Graham had consistently lined up with the hard-liners. This outlook found re-enforcement in an underlying assumption about the virtue of military discipline. Though Graham's only active-duty service had been a cadet-training program in college, he applauded the character-building benefits of service.[198] In a television broadcast aired in 1967 Graham compared the average Vietnam War soldier favorably with the average Korean War soldier. He cited the observation of officers in both wars that 70 percent of the Vietnam soldiers were willing to pull the trigger while only 35 percent of the Korean War soldiers proved willing to do so.[199] Not accidentally, the featured guests in the crusade meetings very often included generals, admirals, police captains, and male sports figures.[200] To be sure, from the outset, Graham had denounced militarism as one of the great sins of the age. Yet the young and the middle-aged Graham seemed to be altogether willing to unleash military power against international threats, as well as police and even National Guard forces against domestic disturbances.[201]

But he changed. In the late 1970s and especially in the 1980s Graham started to direct his attention to the threat of global nuclear annihilation. In 1979 he denounced the arms race as "insanity, madness."[202] Graham told reporters in a Honolulu press conference in 1986: "And now to try to pick up all these pieces when the rhetoric has been so strong on both sides, may be difficult. But it's got to be done if we're to survive."[203] The message was theologically complicated. Graham argued that history remained within God's hands and God would bring the human story to its ordained end. God would not allow humans to destroy the world. Yet Graham also felt that humans held a responsibility to do their part in executing God's plan. So it was that Graham gained a vision of the world as a whole: first one to be evangelized for Christ, and then one to be freed from the nimbus of nuclear war.

One of the most dramatic series of events in his career, filled with ironic twists, was his determined engagement with Eastern European nations in the late 1970s, his highly conspicuous trips to the Soviet Union in 1982, 1984, and 1992, and his less conspicuous yet telling forays into China in 1988 and North Korea in 1992 and 1994.[204] In all of those journeys, the key one, which triggered intense criticism at the time but praise later on, involved his decision to attend a peace conference in Moscow in May 1982. Graham knew, of course, that the meeting was little more than a charade, a propaganda ploy for the Communist party. But he also sensed that the threat of a nuclear holocaust had grown so grave that he had to take a stand for disarmament. The Moscow conference offered a platform with a global audience.[205]

The story of the opposition to Graham's trip before and after it took place was important in itself. It said a great deal about two things: Americans' view of the Soviet Union in the early 1980s and their evaluation of Graham's relationship with the wider world.[206] Before embarking on the trip, Graham received mixed support from the BGEA, resistance from his wife, and opposition from the State Department and the American ambassador to the Soviet Union, Arthur Hartman. Graham later said that Vice President Bush expressed others' concerns but remained neutral himself, while President Reagan privately supported him.[207] Just before Graham left, Reagan told him that he would be praying for him.[208] Solid confirmation came from former president Richard Nixon and former secretary of state Henry Kissinger.[209] Until the very night before the trip, Graham remained torn.[210] One close associate believed that he finally decided to go because of the advice of non-American counselors.[211]

The old anticommunist's motivations for opening a window in his mind and letting the "clean sea breeze" of a unique opportunity blow through call for reflection. Though he did not quite put it this way, undoubtedly the decision arose partly from a sense of adventure, doing what no other evangelist had done. Part of it came from his sense of calling, to carry the gospel to the corners of the world.[212] But he also said it was to highlight the necessity of mutual arms reduction or even disarmament in the face of possible global nuclear holocaust. Graham said the press would not listen to him if he did not go. He needed a platform, and the Moscow conference provided it.[213]

Though Graham's changing outlook undoubtedly had been brewing for years, three roughly contemporary events seem especially pivotal. In the spring of 1978 Secretary of State Henry Kissinger visited Graham at his home in Montreat. Kissinger described the consequences of a global nuclear exchange. Shortly afterward Graham toured the Auschwitz concentration camp in Poland. He found the visit traumatic. He admitted that the sight of the ovens caused him nearly to lose his composure. (I know of only one other instance in Graham's career when he did lose composure in public: when visiting survivors of a tidal wave in Andhra, Pradesh, India.)[214] "Visits to places like Auschwitz . . . made me reflect long and hard on the hawkish sentiments of my youthful years. I felt that I needed to speak out."[215] Seeing "the frightening capacity of nuclear and biochemical weapons to produce global genocide," and becoming "more sensitive to the numerous biblical injunctions for us to work for peace," prompted Graham clearly to see that "peace was a moral issue and not just a political issue."[216]

In Moscow Graham found his visit complicated in ways he did not expect. The actual conference proved, as he anticipated, a charade, largely a forum for extolling Soviet policies and lacerating America's. When Graham's turn came he offered a stirring call for new bilateral measures for peace: "Let us call the nations and the leaders of the world to repentance. . . . No nation, large or small, is exempt from blame for the present state of international affairs."[217] He removed his headphones when others attacked America. Graham spoke in Moscow churches, made his first visit to an Orthodox cathedral, talked with uncooperative Pentecostals holed up in the U.S. Embassy, and worked behind the scenes to secure the release of Jews who wished to immigrate to Israel.

The evangelist also made comments about life in the Soviet Union that he lived to regret. Some of the remarks, such as that more Christians worshipped on a Saturday night in Moscow than in Charlotte, or that he enjoyed caviar in Moscow, which he could not do at home, came with a twinkle in the eye, which the press did not or did not want to see. Graham deflected some of the attacks with his customary wit. When one reporter alleged that in a Moscow Baptist church one-third of the audience consisted of KGB agents, the preacher quipped, "I am glad to hear it. I always wanted to preach to KGB agents. They also need Jesus Christ."[218] But he also said, in earnest, that he saw a measure of religious freedom in the Soviet Union because Christians generally found themselves free to worship inside their churches or on their church grounds, but faced severe restrictions elsewhere. Graham later defended himself by pointing out that the comment was factually accurate: a *measure* of religious freedom existed. He implied that the Western press saw what it wanted to see in order to market a prescribed storyline.[219]

That last comment and other compliments about life in the Soviet Union ignited a storm of criticism at home. And it came from all quarters. Whereas before 1982 both the left and the right attacked him for different reasons, this time they attacked him for the same reason: gullibility. The conservative commenter George Will spoke for many. It was hard to say, said Will, which was more astonishing: Graham's "naiveté or his vanity."[220] The assaults on Graham were not quite universal. The *Christian Century*, perennially critical of him, offered qualified support.[221] His long-time friendly challenger Will Campbell was unabashedly generous: "I once accused him of being the court prophet to Richard Nixon," Campbell said. "But I have to say, he's God's prophet now."[222] Nonetheless, most Americans seemed puzzled at best. "Billy, won't you please come home?" pleaded William F. Buckley, Jr.[223] Even his friends acknowledged that he said some dumb things in his altogether typical desire to be liked.[224] And invited back. Which happened. A mass crusade attracting thirty thousand visitors in Moscow in 1984 marked the first evangelistic meeting of that magnitude in the nation's history.

The toxic fall-out from the 1982 visit eventually blew over. That did not mean Graham was impervious to the criticism. Clearly it hurt him, for it was fierce and it was personal. Eventually observers of all stripes came to see that several tactical missteps did not overshadow the strategic courage he had demonstrated. A decade later the distinguished newscaster Dan Rather, one of Graham's detractors after the 1982 visit, later publically judged that subsequent events had proved Graham right and his critics wrong.[225]

To the end of his public career, Graham maintained his call for mutual disarmament and negotiated efforts to achieve world peace. To be sure, he did not inch close to pacifism. He affirmed not only the right of self-defense but also, as noted, the obligation of the strong to protect the weak. And he said little about the warrants or absence of them for conventional warfare, per se. Yet given his earlier stridency about communism, the spread-eagle outlook of his constituency, and Reagan's famous "evil empire" speech delivered only ten months after the Moscow visit, Graham's commitment to new measures to achieve world peace was quite remarkable. In Moscow in 1982 he called for a "SALT X—the complete destruction by all nations of all atomic bombs, hydrogen bombs, biochemical weapons, laser weapons and all other weapons of mass destruction."[226] In the final twenty-five years of his ministry he preached about the threat of nuclear destruction repeatedly and in multiple places.

Graham's remarks in Duke University Chapel in 1985 proved typical of those decades. Speaking of the Geneva Summit, he told the worshipers, "Reagan and Gorbachev were pushed together by a terrible nuclear threat." He compared the potential nuclear catastrophe to the mythical sword of Damocles: "And that sword could fall at any moment and destroy the human race."[227] In his twilight years he said that he regretted that he had not openly opposed the Vietnam War, and that the United States never should have dropped nuclear bombs on Japan. It would be hard to find any prominent public figure, let alone prominent evangelist, who manifested a more dramatic change of view. How should we evaluate it?

The trip represented one of Graham's most courageous moments. It signaled his growing commitment to disarmament in the service of world peace. The deep sources of the change must be inferred from elusive data. They point to the cumulative impact of maturity and travel and willingness to open his eyes to the world's suffering. In another context he said, simply, "I've picked up a thing or two as I've been around and you can't help but change."[228] For some, he represented Teddy Roosevelt's classic "man in the ring." He stepped into the ring, got hit hard by the press and others, staggered a bit, then came back swinging.

Graham's growing concern about nuclear war formed part of a larger pattern of growing concern about humanity's travails. At all points in his career, he had targeted poverty and racism and injustice. To be sure, critics—and there were many—felt that he had not targeted those evils forcefully enough. They said that the means of redress that Graham emphasized—a renewed heart that led to structural reforms, rather than the reverse—were misconceived. Nonetheless, Graham *saw himself* as a "social liberal" and he took pride in it. Repeatedly he asserted that he had addressed every compelling social need. But in the final two decades of his public ministry, this one—peace and especially the elimination of nuclear weapons from the face of the earth—seemed to take precedence. "The Christian especially has the responsibility to work for peace in our world. Christians may well find themselves working and agreeing with nonbelievers on an issue like peace," Graham told the editor of the left-leaning evangelical magazine *JustLife*. "The Kingdom of God is not the same as the United States of America, and our nation is subject to the judgment of God just as much as any other nation. . . . We must seek the good of the whole human race."[229]

The year 1973 saw the now-famous evangelical social justice conference in Chicago, which resulted in the *Chicago Declaration of Evangelical Social Concern*. A stellar cast of well-known evangelical progressives signed it, including older ones such as David Moberg, Rufus Jones, Carl F. H. Henry, and Frank Gaebelein, and younger ones such as Leighton Ford, Paul Henry, Jim Wallis, John Perkins, Sharon Gallagher, Rich Mouw, and Ron Sider. It called for economic justice, peacemaking, racial reconciliation, and gender equality. Graham did not attend the conference, and he declined to sign the declaration, purportedly because he disagreed with a plank about feminism.[230] Probably he also declined because he saw no obvious place where the demands on him to sign declarations or testify would end. Still, Graham announced that he agreed with almost everything the document called for. "We have a social responsibility and I could identify with most of the recent Chicago Declaration of Evangelical Concern," he stated. "I think we have to identify with the changing of structures in society and try to do our part."[231]

Progressive sentiments of that sort were not new. He was not always consistent, but the general direction remained clear. In the 1960s he had publically supported Lyndon Johnson's War on Poverty. In 1967 he toured Appalachia with his friend Sargent Shriver and made a television movie, *Beyond These Hills*, on the region's distress. At the end of the decade he lent broad support to the progressive firebrand Jim Wallis and Wallis's magazine, *Post-American* (later *Sojourners*), as well as the Sojourners community itself. He called them "very radical and Marxian." Yet, as noted, Graham told one journalist: "I can agree with 90 per cent of what they have said and published. We should all read the book of Acts again."[232] Graham gave a widely quoted interview to *Sojourners* about his developing concerns about nuclear war.[233]

Graham's awakening to the social implications of the gospel manifested itself in the Lausanne Covenant too. The International Congress on World Evangelization met in Lausanne, Switzerland, in the summer of 1974. Though many hands contributed, Graham served as the principal convening and funding source. The organizers conceived Lausanne—as it came simply to be called—not as a rival but rather as an evangelical counterpart to the venerable World Council of Churches. Graham hoped to restore the priority of evangelization, but with social justice as its natural and necessary outgrowth. Lausanne sought representation from delegates from all parts of the world. In July 1974, 2,500 evangelicals from 150 countries and 135 denominations attended.[234]

At its conclusion, Lausanne organizers issued the Lausanne Covenant, which included a paragraph calling for the application of the gospel to world poverty, hunger, and suffering. The paragraph formed only one of fifteen. The others articulated traditional evangelical concerns, such as the "uniqueness and universality of Christ." Yet the fulsome paragraph on social justice was striking for its forthrightness: "We affirm . . . justice and reconciliation throughout human society for the liberation of men and women from every kind of oppression. Although reconciliation with other people is not reconciliation with God . . . nevertheless we affirm that evangelism and sociopolitical involvement are both part of our Christian duty."[235] Graham signed. The document was translated into twenty languages.[236]

Another important move centered on Graham's strong public support for World Vision International. Founded in 1950 by the visionary and flamboyant American evangelist Bob Pierce (another Youth for Christ product), World Vision endeavored to raise funds for missionaries and orphans in war-torn Korea. Pierce soon attained celebrity status among evangelicals by publicizing global suffering. He pioneered child-sponsorship programs and produced Christian films to bring images of a hurting world to American Christians. Graham joined the Board of Reference (later Trustees) in 1954, became chair in 1956, and served until 1960. He traveled with Pierce in Asia. In time World Vision would rank just behind the Red Cross as the second largest humanitarian organization in the world, and the largest Christian one. It would maintain offices in nearly 100 countries with 40,000 employees and an annual budget of more than 2.6 billion dollars.[237]

Pierce resigned from World Vision in 1967 as the organization grew beyond him. Two years later he took over a struggling evangelical mission organization, Food for the World, and in 1970 renamed it Samaritan's Purse. Pierce tried to replicate what he had started with World Vision. Pierce died in 1978, and the following year Graham's son Franklin Graham took control. With the elder Graham's support, Samaritan's Purse and the BGEA maintained close fraternal ties. Propelled by Pierce's signature words, "Let my heart be broken . . . with the things that break the heart of God," Samaritan's Purse pursued compassion ministries such as digging fresh water wells and providing food and medicine in victimized regions.[238] Though its ultimate goal of evangelism never fell in doubt, in 2013 the organization distributed more than $350 million in aid worldwide without regard to the prevailing religion or the ideology of the receiving culture.[239]

With the passing of the years the evangelist's vision seemed to grow larger and more inclusive. In an open letter apologizing for his anti-Jewish comments back in 1972, he said that "much of my life has been a pilgrimage—constantly learning, changing, growing, and maturing. I have come to see in deeper ways some of the implications of my faith and message, not the least of which is in the area of human rights and racial and ethnic understanding."[240] He distanced himself from the Christian right. In those years many evangelical leaders grew increasingly partisan and staked out their territory on one side or the other of the culture wars. In contrast, the mature Graham sought to soften boundaries, not harden them.

More to the point, Graham tried to stay out of the culture wars entirely. He refused to endorse the Moral Majority. Though he insisted that leaders of the Christian right such as Jerry Falwell and Pat Robertson remained friends, he found their mixing of religion and politics perilous. He worried that they evidenced too little concern for poverty and injustice. Graham targeted the unjust application of the death penalty (here differing from Ruth, who supported it). He called for humane treatment of Vietnam War refugees, saying it was unfair to fight a war for their future but not let that future unfold with our boundaries. He remained a teetotaler himself but allowed for moderate alcohol use by others. Nonetheless, he supported voluntary abstinence from alcohol because of the traffic fatalities and the miseries alcohol abuse caused. Though allowing for exceptional measures to protect the life of a mother, in general he saw abortion on demand as the taking of the life of the most innocent and helpless members of society. He repeatedly targeted the problems of global poverty and hunger and Christians' obligation to address them.[241]

Graham increasingly viewed himself speaking for the humanitarian interests of the entire world, not the United States alone. His vision steadily widened to see the world's suffering as one. The line between insiders and outsiders blurred. That perspective was not wholly new. As far back as 1971, even in his most establishmentarian years, the Chicago press heard him say that God was not on one side or the other. "We'd like to think that God is an American but God is not an American," he explained. "God is God of the whole human race and He loves that person in the middle of the tribe in Latin America as much as He loves an American."[242] That judgment grew more insistent as he aged. "I think of myself as a world citizen," he ruminated in 2002. "I've traveled over this world a great deal, and I feel that I am part of a great mosaic of the human race that God has created."[243]

The mature Graham's sermons revealed deepening convictions about the need for global justice: "How can we be indifferent to the millions and millions who live on the brink of starvation each year, while the nations of the world spend $550 billion each year on weapons?"[244] He spoke of the unequal distribution of earth's resources, the unequal availability of health care, the economic waste of global militarism, the need for population control to help combat worldwide hunger and poverty. Though the BGEA was an evangelistic, not philanthropic, organization, it made unheralded but large donations to international aid projects. Graham made a point to acquaint himself, firsthand, with suffering in the less-developed world. He backed up his words with his feet. William Martin's description of Graham's travels into the developing world prompted one Los Angeles *Times* review to reflect: "Most moving is an account of Graham's visit to an African leper colony where the oft-squeamish and somewhat hypochondriacal preacher clasped the stumps that one woman had for hands and joined her in prayer."[245] Captured by the press, private acts became public narratives.

One late-life interview revealed worlds within worlds about the evangelist's evolving thinking. In June 2005, the *New York Times*'s Laurie Goodstein asked Graham whether he anticipated a "clash of civilizations" between Christianity and Islam. His response was telling: "I think the big conflict is with hunger and starvation and poverty."[246] That same month, Graham preached his final crusade—fittingly, in Flushing Meadows, one of the most ethnically mixed sections of New York City. The crusade's counselors represented more than twenty language groups, including Arabic, Armenian, Korean, Portuguese, Punjabi, Russian, Tamil, and Mandarin.[247] That buzzing diversity symbolized just how much Graham's ministry had changed. In December of that year, television journalist Larry King asked Graham what he thought about his son, Franklin Graham, calling Islam "evil and wicked." Graham responded, "Well, he has [his] views and I have mine. And they are different sometimes."[248] No one should have been surprised.

Graham seemed to be hearing the voice of a new Jesus. In many ways he came to embrace the progressive evangelicalism of his friend Jimmy Carter. If the fiery youthful Graham had worried about lawlessness at home and communism abroad, the reflective older Graham worried more about loneliness at home and AIDS abroad. His increasingly progressive record on civil rights and nuclear proliferation, two of the most momentous challenges of the late twentieth century, moved him closer to the forefront of American Christians' social conscience. Not that he ever doubted his obligation to proclaim the gospel to everyone. But an enriched store of experiences—much of it purchased the hard way in a punishing schedule of evangelistic meetings abroad—brought with it a deepened and more far-reaching awareness of life's injustices and complexities. The pilgrim had come a long way.

CHAPTER SEVEN

Pastor

In 1968 John Corry, a contributing editor of *Harper's Magazine*, sat next to Billy Graham on a plane. The two men fell into a long and clearly very pleasant conversation. Before long Corry ordered a Bloody Mary. He hoped Graham would think it was just tomato juice. Then he thought, "What the hell," and plunged a swizzle stick into the drink. But then he reconsidered and slowly inched the drink over to the corner of his dinner tray, hoping Graham would not notice it. "His friends say that Billy Graham has found his natural home in a pulpit, but it is possible that he is even better when he confronts just one other person," Corry reflected. "Artlessness envelops him, sincerity is palpable, and good humor is nearly a weapon."[1]

This charming vignette said nothing about Graham's view of drink, but it did offer a glimpse into how Americans perceived and created him as a pastor. They saw him as a man of principles, but the principles came packaged in sugar. That combination embraced all three roles that clergy traditionally had held in American Christian history: office, profession, and vocation.[2] The pastoral office played the least important part of his story. Except for brief stints during college as an interim pastor, Graham served as pastor of an actual church for only eighteen months. By his own account he was not terribly successful, not least because he was away so much preaching at Youth for Christ and other kinds of meetings. He knew himself well.

The role of the clergyman as a trained professional—the second of the three traditional roles—fit him somewhat better. Though he read biographies avidly, there was little evidence that he routinely read the kinds of books seminary-trained pastors normally studied—homiletics, biblical criticism, systematic theology, church history, pastoral care—but he knew his Bible backwards and forwards, controlled the basics of evangelical Protestant theology, and mastered current events for placing it all in context. He also had a well-attested habit of asking questions of experts.[3] Graham's professional training, in short, took a form not taught in seminaries but well suited for his line of work.

Graham's greatest gift lay elsewhere. It was the role of the man called of God for the specific vocation of evangelism. Yet here things grew complicated.

The pastor as evangelist needed an audience—which is to say, he needed an audience in order to be who he was. The pastor and the audience created each other. To this point in the book we have focused on the first side of the equation: the evangelist himself. This chapter takes up the second side. We will look at the people in the audience who helped fashion him as pastor, who they were, how they responded to him, what they wanted from him, and what he gave back to them.

The Faithful: An External Profile

Historians have a better sense of the number of Americans who encountered Graham in person or via radio, television, books, or movies than they do of their class, demographic, cultural, and religious earmarks. But with allowance for the imprecision of the instruments and some generosity for educated estimates, we can construct at least a rough profile.

Class standing provides a baseline. As noted, Graham himself came from a middle- or upper-middle-class rural setting in a burgeoning region of the upper South. But it is also important to remember that he was shaped for ministry at Wheaton College, in a west Chicago suburb, and in churches in the immediate west Chicago area. In the 1940s, people who might be loosely called old-stock white middle-class Protestants of moderately conservative Republican orientation dominated the Wheaton vicinity.[4] Other parts of the Chicago area bore other ethnic earmarks—Irish, Czech, Polish, African American; other religious earmarks—Catholic, Orthodox, and Jewish; and other economic earmarks—upper and laboring classes. Graham's outlook on the world, the ethnic/religious/economic earmarks he took to be normative, or unexceptional, inevitably gained shape in those powerfully formative years. Many of Graham's followers likely gravitated toward a leader who at some deep level experienced and viewed the world as they did.

Graham said that his audiences represented a wide range of occupations and economic strata.[5] A bit paradoxically he also often said that they consisted of mostly ordinary people.[6] Apparently he meant that his audiences comprised all types, but with ordinary folks in the middle forming the largest part of them. There are good reasons to take Graham's perceptions seriously, as he was there, on site, and had a vested interest in rightly pegging the social profile of the people who supported him.

That being said, external evidence indicates that the cross-section bulged at the midpoint, more than he allowed. Sociologists and journalists who visited his meetings largely agreed that the faithful embodied the very middle of the middle class, in some studies slightly lower, in others slightly higher.[7]

That judgment corresponded with the long history of Protestant revivalism in the United States. Traditionally revivals appealed to middling folk in the eighteenth century and what came to be known as the middle class in the nineteenth century. Already prone to participate in public voluntary activities, the middle classes distinguished themselves by strong goal orientation, the financial means to travel to meetings, and a work schedule that permitted them to take time off.[8]

Though hardly a scientific survey, movies and newspaper photographs of the crowds in Graham's meetings recurrently showed people who fit that middle-class image.[9] In the early years, they appeared primly dressed in Sunday clothes, often coat and tie for men and hats for women. In the later years, something like up-town casual prevailed.[10] The occupational self-descriptions in the letters people sent also suggest that his audiences consisted mostly of middle-class people. One fine-grained sociological study found that the largest occupational groups were clerical and sales workers (27 percent), operatives (skilled labor; 17 percent), and professional and technical workers (12 percent).[11] And then there was body language. Setting aside the histrionics of Graham's earliest years, for most of his career the comportment of his body when he was preaching—active but tightly controlled—suggested nothing so much as middle-class sobriety.[12] Graham rarely if ever lost his composure behind the pulpit or in public.

Day laborers and organized labor remained underrepresented.[13] Graham and Walter Reuther, the long-term president of the United Automobile Workers union, were friends.[14] Nonetheless, observers rarely spoke of laborers in the audiences, and the testimonials and letters mirrored that absence. Graham hardly ever mentioned organized labor in his sermons. At least once he even lamented the paucity of laboring men in the churches that supported him.[15] The letters that people sent rarely spoke of strikes or other hints of labor-class consciousness.

Gender and age are clearer. Both sociologists' studies and journalists' observations affirmed the preponderance of women, about 60 percent.[16] That pattern corresponded with the long history of evangelicalism in general and revivalism in particular.[17] Some historians have argued that after World War II, women felt suburban malaise especially acutely.[18] Such women may have found themselves especially receptive to Graham's message of a larger meaning for their lives. The language of stable family values (before the term acquired partisan political connotations) may have spoken more persuasively to homemakers than to breadwinners. And a Hollywood face and physique did not hurt.

Outside observers, along with Graham himself, also commented on the comparative youthfulness of the visitors, a plurality of them probably being men and women in their twenties.[19] Moreover, the median age seemed to decrease over time.[20] With that demographic in mind, Graham's World Wide Pictures turned increasingly to a youthful audience with movies such as *The Restless Ones* (1963) and the documentary *The Lost Generation* (1971). The crusade meetings, for their part, featured youth-oriented artists ranging from Larry Norman to Kris Kristofferson, Johnny Cash, and Michael W. Smith.[21]

The racial composition of the faithful is more difficult to capture. Before 1953 Graham's audiences in the South were segregated. Though he occasionally preached to gatherings of blacks only, without doubt he preached mainly to whites.[22] As noted, at the 1957 Madison Square Garden crusade Graham recognized the comparative absence of minority attendees in a city marked by a large minority population. Among other responses, Graham held meetings in Harlem and Brooklyn, engaged an African American platform evangelist, and featured minority guest artists. Anecdotally, minority attendance grew, though the evidence is too sketchy to say much more than that.

The story of African American representation in Graham's meetings resembled ocean swells, rising, falling back, rising again, marking slow but steady progress overall. Graham claimed and clearly liked to think that the presence of minorities in his audiences paralleled their presence in the vicinity, and some external evidence supports that view.[23] With reference to the intensely watched crusade in Birmingham, Alabama, on Easter Sunday, 1964, for example, Graham said with pride that his audiences reflected the same proportion of whites and blacks as the area. So did the choir.[24] And other evidence confirmed the accuracy of Graham's report.[25]

Yet elsewhere the record proved variable. An insider historical study of the 1966 crusade in Greenville, South Carolina, for example, contained numerous photographs of audience members and platform speakers and guests. With the important exception of a full-page photograph of Ethel Waters singing, African Americans still proved to be minimally—certainly far from proportionally—represented.[26] African American attendance fell short of area representation in Washington, DC, in 1972, rose in Washington, DC, in 1986, fell short in Atlanta in 1973, but rose again in 1994.[27] One key difference between the unsuccessful and successful crusades hinged on the organization's effort to win African American support in the planning phases and in making black support visible throughout. In the second Atlanta crusade, for example, Cameron Alexander, pastor of the 6,000-member Antioch Baptist Church North, co-chaired the event, stage guests included Atlanta mayor Andrew Young, Coretta Scott King, and a youth night featured the African American Grammy Award–winning group Take 7 and the integrated DC Talk.

Two additional streams of evidence intimate—and *intimate* is all we can say—that black and white ethnic presence among Graham's followers remained small, possibly extremely small, through the mid-1980s (but probably rose after that). The first stream pertains to the identity clues of the men and women who sent letters to Graham. I examined a randomized sample of 164 of the thousands of letters that poured into his Minneapolis headquarters in 1950, 1961–1962, and 1982–1989.[28] Few if any of the writers of the letters made any sort of comment that revealed their racial or ethnic self-identification. More precisely, they did not do it in a casual or a positive or a negative manner. By casual I mean they did not convey that kind of information simply as a matter of information, which was a striking omission because—as we shall see—they often did say a lot about their lives in what might be called a literary form of small talk (especially children and the elderly). By positively I mean they did not speak of belonging to or worshipping in a historically African American Church (such as African Methodist Episcopal) or in a historically ethnic church such as the (German-speaking) Evangelical United Brethren. And by negatively I mean that they did not mention discrimination or exclusion for that reason. Very often they spoke of loneliness or feeling left out of things, but they did not attribute it to race or ethnicity.

The second stream of evidence about letter writers comes from the return addresses. Senders posted nearly two-thirds of the letters from small and large towns, and only one-third from small and large cities.[29] Though they came from all parts of the country (except the Mormon Intermountain West), the South and the wide band of states in the lower and upper Midwest claimed the absolute majority. Cities and towns with a strong black or white ethnic presence such as Chicago, Brooklyn, or El Paso made few appearances. It would be risky to make too much of such data, yet they seem consistent with other indicators of the predominantly northern European white composition of Graham's audiences and constituency.[30] Again, the aspiration for racial/ethnic diversity outpaced the achievement.

Yet aspirations counted. Though it is hard to generalize with great confidence, there is evidence that by the mid-1980s and certainly mid-1990s the proportion of minorities among Graham's supporters began to grow. The quarter-million people stretched across New York's Central Park on a Sunday afternoon in the fall in 1991 bore two distinctions. First it ranked as the largest crowd Graham had addressed in the United States, and the second largest in the park's history.[31] Second, it may have been, in the words of Mayor David Dinkins, the "most multicultural revival" in the city's history.[32] A veteran journalist judged that half of the crowd was composed of minorities.[33] Graham's final crusade, preached across the river in Flushing Meadows fourteen years later, probably ranked as the most ethnically mixed of his long career.[34]

Several reasons for the generally stronger record of minority participation in the later years emerge. For one thing, Graham talked about the racial challenge with increasing frequency and urgency as the decades slipped by. But probably a more important though less recognized factor played a role. At least from the mid-1980s forward the Graham organization made a concerted effort to involve African Americans in the planning of the meetings from the outset.[35] The number of black counselors grew too. Though the evidence is scanty, crusade captains apparently assigned counselors to potential inquirers without reference to race at least since the early 1980s.[36] Finally, Graham increasingly featured black guest artists and preached with manifest conviction about the moral fracture of a segregated society.

When we move from demographic earmarks of class, gender, age, and race/ethnicity to cultural earmarks of religious affiliation and cultural outlook, the picture becomes clearer. The great majority came from the mainstream evangelical denominations (or mainstream evangelical congregations tucked within mainline Protestant bodies). They were, in order, Baptist, and then, far down the list, Presbyterian, Methodist, Pentecostal, independent Bible Churches, and, surprisingly, Catholic. In the later years, Assemblies of God figured more prominently, possibly ranking third or even second. Peace bodies such as Mennonites, Amish, and Quakers, and confessional ones such as Lutherans and Episcopalians, appeared only rarely. Classic American-created sects such as Adventists and Mormons also appeared, but extremely rarely. (Groups pejoratively known in evangelical circles as cults, such as Jehovah's Witnesses, Christian Scientists, and non-Western religions, appeared virtually never.) This assessment draws on the amount of coverage given to Graham in denominational periodicals, the sponsoring churches in towns and cities, sociological observations, and theological (though rarely denominational) self-identification in the letters adherents sent.[37]

It would be easy to say that Graham's supporters were just Red Staters at prayer and leave it there. Undoubtedly the typical Graham supporter did feel more at home in Kansas than in Massachusetts. Yet a closer look suggests that the Graham supporter/Red State equation is too easy. Graham support overlapped Red States like transparencies in a geography book. Similar but by no means the same. For the outlook and lifestyle of Graham's constituents, the best indicators lie in the narrative observations of careful academics and journalists who year after year came up with a similar profile: solid, decent, frugal, patriotic, and hard-working.

Two brief descriptions, one from sociologist-historian William Martin, and the other from *Time* correspondents Nancy Gibbs and Michael Duffy, spoke for hundreds. Reprising reporters' accounts of the believers at a 1964 Boston crusade, Martin said they did not resemble champagne sippers at a Boston Pops concert nor bellowers at a Bruins slugfest. Rather, they came across as "sober," "earnest," "almost homespun." One journalist put it this way: "You would think you were in Kansas or Indiana or someplace else."[38] Turning to the men on Graham's staff at the 1986 Washington, DC, crusade, whom Martin himself observed, he said they reminded one of "the Lions Club in Dothan, Alabama." The women, mostly wives and secretaries, came across as "neat but unflashy, competent but ever friendly."[39] Gibbs and Duffy saw very much the same people: "His was still a congregation of Scout leaders pledging allegiance and homemakers wrestling with the grocery bill, who flew the flag without irony and spanked their kids when they cussed."[40]

Graham himself seemed to see that his followers exhibited a recognizable profile of lifestyles and cultural outlooks rather similar to the ones Martin and Gibbs/Duffy discerned. He golfed with presidents, dined with royals, vacationed with moguls, and schmoozed with anchormen. But he knew his core constituency lay elsewhere. In the spring of 1957 Graham told Vice President Nixon that four New York City newspapers had promised "full coverage and editorial support" for his upcoming crusade. But he was not receiving much coverage from the *Daily News*, "which has the largest circulation among the masses of people that we want to reach."[41] Once, when his friend Johnny Cash paid a visit to a Graham crusade, the audience erupted with thunderous applause. According to one journalist, "a grinning Graham whispered to Cash, 'Those are your fans, and they're the ones I want.' "[42] Graham spoke both for and to stable middle-class evangelicals, a social sphere bounded with white-picket fences.[43] They remind one of the lyric in a popular nineteenth-century evangelical hymn: "And let our ordered lives confess."[44] All of which is to say, Graham's audiences represented the kind of ordered world one might imagine on a Norman Rockwell cover.

The Faithful: An Internal Profile

It is daunting to move from the brightly lit landscapes of external behavior into the dimly lit hallways of internal motivation, for the move requires both caution and tolerance for a wide margin for error. But the faithful had their reasons, and they revealed them, or at least some of them, in letters, autobiographies, biographies, questionnaires, and interviews.

WHY DID THEY COME?

Seating at all crusades was free. Many of the larger ones required an admission ticket, but that too was free. Yet there was a cost. For many partisans, as we have seen, attending a Graham crusade meeting likely meant investing their time in the second or third worship service of the week.[45] It entailed the cost and trouble of getting there. Once there, they had to contend with surging crowds and the challenge of finding an empty chair or bench, often in rain or cold or heat or glaring sun. Given the gender and age of the typical visitor, it probably meant arranging for childcare, too.

Many said they came for the obvious reason: the experience of the worship service itself—entering into the music, seeing Graham in person, hearing him preach, and feeling the force of his invitation to come to Christ. Some said, too, that going was a way to witness for Christ at their workplace. Sometimes it helped assuage the guilt of not being able to muster the courage to share the gospel with others. Telling a co-worker what they did last night signaled enough.

Frequently another person lurked in the decision to attend. The BGEA's own studies revealed that the majority came in response to a personal invitation.[46] Knowing that, early on the BGEA developed a program called Operation Andrew, which called for inviting a friend. Often local churches arranged for buses to take believers along with a companion—ideally not a practicing Christian—to a meeting where organizers set aside sections for busloads. Besides boosting the number of visitors and potential inquirers, Operation Andrew drew the churches more deeply into the outcome. One careful sociological study concluded that "a crucial factor" in attendance at a crusade stemmed from "the extent of the local churches' efforts to mobilize for it."[47] Then too attendees often said they traveled to a meeting in order to please someone else, most commonly a spouse. One man with a drinking problem went to Graham's 1958 Charlotte crusade to "get out of the dog house with his wife."[48] Many came because they saw a change in the life of someone else. Seeing a person they respected or loved kick an addiction, especially alcohol, loomed large.

For some, the reasons for attending were not definably religious. They saw a Graham crusade as something of a spectacle—a media event not to be missed. Some made clear that they had no special affinity for Graham's message but knew he was a very famous person and did not want to miss seeing him. Some spoke of hoping to tell their grandchildren about it. Someday. And then we see a category of reasons that might be called liminal, explanations that involved factors not concrete yet utterly real. They did not know why they went. They just found themselves powerfully drawn to do so. Others spoke of expecting to convert or rededicate their lives to Christ after they got there. That frame of mind might be called time-out-of-time, a zone strangely different from the mundane. And some said they went at the Holy Spirit's direction. The Spirit left them no choice.

Graham captured the picture in a single wide-angle snapshot: They came for "all sorts of reasons."[49]

CHOREOGRAPHY OF CONVERSION

For many, the conversion experience started long before they got to the stadium.[50] Unlike the routine nuisances involved in going to work or to the mall, the effort of getting to the meeting registered in the memory bank not as time lost but as time invested. Often visitors arrived hours early, just to get a seat. That too was time invested. Recreational events such as a major league ball game or a rock concert bore some similarities, since anticipation was part of the experience. But this was different. Converts, as everyone else, lived their lives looking forward but made sense of them looking back. And looking back helped them frame the conversion experience in the language of ultimate things, a language not readily applied to ball games or rock concerts. It acquired a meaning different from the meanings of everyday affairs.

At the end of the service, Graham invariably issued an invitation for listeners to make a commitment to Christ. The great majority of times he called them to stand up and walk to the front. In massive structures such as Yankee Stadium or Soldier Field or the Rose Bowl the hike from the back bleachers to the podium took time—likely a good ten minutes—and the presence of mind to descend steep and crowded steps safely. Inquirers usually moved in pairs, as section captains assigned counselors of the same gender and similar age to fall in step with them. Converts remembered the aural universe of the ritual too, the silence of hushed crowds or the cadence of footsteps, especially in arenas with wood floors.

As we have seen, when inquirers got to the front, counselors led them to a waiting room around back to discuss the meaning of what they were doing, gave them a Gospel of John and other materials, and then asked them to fill out a decision card. When the number of inquirers was too large for them to go to adjoining rooms, Graham talked with them *en masse* in the pulpit/podium area. With his customary pragmatism Graham adjusted the pattern to the situation.[51] In university audiences, for example, where walking forward might create embarrassment, he asked students simply to raise their hands or slip a decision card to a counselor.[52] But in one way or another Graham called for a concrete gesture. Quiet decisions were too easy to forget.

The choreography of the conversion experience invites analysis from several angles. If in the eyes of skeptics the whole thing looked like a mindless response to mass suggestion, in the eyes of supporters it felt like an act of courage. The physicality of the experience cemented its reality. By providing a reference point in space and time it discouraged inquirers from reconsidering and turning back. For many, the ritual unfolded as memorable precisely because it played out through multisensory media.

Second, the ritual was both expressive and formative. As expressive it externalized a decision already made before Graham issued the invitation. As formative it externalized a decision under construction. Singing hymns, listening to Graham, and watching crowds move forward fostered repentance. Walking to the front under the eyes of family and friends constituted a form of penitence. Filling out the decision card—which inquirers knew would be forwarded to local churches—galvanized the conversion. For some, the decision to stand up and make the long trek to the front formed a door into the future.

Finally the ambience should be noted. Both insiders and outsiders consistently described the services in general and the invitation in particular as remarkably quiet, or riveted by ritualistic sounds such as those of "footsteps on creaking boards."[53] They saw tears here and there but on the whole few visible signs of emotion.[54] Nothing remotely approached the ecstatic fervor of Methodist revivals in the nineteenth century or Pentecostal revivals in the twentieth.[55] Graham's approach narrated the dramatic world of mainstream evangelical Protestants.

Everything pivoted on a self-conscious decision: choose Christ or do not choose Christ. But *choose*. If there was an unpardonable sin on Graham's roster, it was the sin of drifting. In every service, every sermon, every invitation, Graham aimed for "a verdict."[56] In principle he taught that Christ chose sinners but in practice he intimated that sinners chose Christ. To be sure, nostalgic music and earnest preaching flowed together to awaken desire.[57] And desire involved the heart. But they led to a concrete, self-conscious decision.

And why not? In an age when consumers were accustomed to choosing every other feature of their lives—spouses, occupations, churches, when to have children, whether to shop at a mom-and-pop store or at Sears—the experience of making a decision came naturally. That pattern proved especially cogent for the great majority of attendees who came from—as one wag put it—roll-your-own traditions of mainstream evangelical Baptists, Presbyterians, Methodists, and Pentecostals. In those circles choice already reigned.

The volitional essence of the conversion experience found re-enforcement in Graham's own conversion story, which he narrated virtually verbatim on countless occasions. He portrayed it as a tearless, seemingly unemotional decision to stand up, walk to the front, and commit his life to Christ. "I could not depend on my parents' faith," he explained. "Christian influence in the home could have a lasting impact on a child's life, but faith could not be passed on as an inheritance, like the family silver. It had to be exercised by each individual."[58] Four years later he received a life-defining mandate from above to commit his life to Christian service: "No sign in the heavens. No voice from above."[59]

Ruth Graham's experience re-enforced that script. Shortly after matriculating at Wheaton College, she went through something of a crisis of faith. She consulted Dr. Gordon Clark, a philosophy professor "known for his logic, his unemotional brilliance." Clark "factually and logically" outlined the reasons for believing that the Bible embodied "God's message to man." But at the end, Clark insisted, one must make a "leap of faith."

And so Ruth did, a self-conscious—evidently tearless—decision to embrace Christ and the Christian life. The feature to notice here is that in these autobiographical accounts neither Billy nor Ruth inherited a spiritual standing— "like the family silver." And neither was smitten from on high. Rather, both *chose* Christ through a self-conscious act of volition.[60]

The choreography of conversion revealed additional dimensions. For one thing, evangelical culture in general and Graham in particular typically described the experience as a definable event bounded in time and space. I say typically described because in his more thoughtful moments he knew things often were more complicated than that. "We are different temperaments," he told reporters in Cleveland in 1972. "We worship God in different ways."[61] The reporters' question was about the mingling of faiths, but the larger point held: "We are different temperaments." Yet the plain fact that numberless autobiographical accounts spoke of a very long process of spiritual awakening did not alter the standard narrative.

So what was going on? Why did he reshape the narrative to fit a precut scheme rather than real-life experience? Biblical and historical precedent formed one reason: Paul on the Damascus Road, Augustine in the Garden, and Luther in the Tower, for starters. Then too the American revival tradition had showcased the anxious bench where sinners marched to the front and mourned their sins once and for all. Moreover, a Reformation sense of grace as a work always in progress—simultaneously sinner and saint—remained comparatively foreign to mainstream evangelicals. But the most likely explanation is that evangelicals resisted the idea that dark nights of the soul, seasons of God's silence, after conversion, would be a normal part of the Christian journey. To be sure, novels such as Elisabeth Elliot's missionary classic *No Graven Image* (1966) provided a glimpse into the dark, the elegiac strains in some of the hymns offered a bit of that vocabulary, and the generalization fit Baptist and later Pentecostal supporters better than Presbyterian ones. Nonetheless, salvation narrated as an event, regardless of how it was experienced on the ground, provided a clean linear trajectory.[62]

Second, the internal choreography of conversion traced a delicate path between the personal and the communal. On one hand, inquirers walked alone, even when counselors accompanied them. They heard next to nothing about being a tiny part of the great river of Christian history, or of how salvation might be mediated through the sacraments of the church. One Catholic critic quipped that evangelicals effectively recited the Apostles' Creed backwards, starting with the life everlasting and ending up with the communion of saints almost as an afterthought.[63] On the other hand, the entire evangelical community involved itself in profound ways at every point. Counselors carefully directed inquirers to churches and Bible study groups. They followed up with local pastors and knocked on inquirers' doors to see how they were doing. Salvation started as a personal transaction between the inquirer and God but required ratification and re-enforcement from the extended family.

And if the conversion unfolded according to plan it manifested itself in a clarified vision of personal and social-ethical obligations. Admittedly, communal endorsement had its invidious side. By drawing lines between the saved and the unsaved it defined the boundaries of the social unit. The process enabled the community to know who it was and how it could strengthen itself in the face of a secularizing world. But communal endorsement also had its healing side. It gave individuals identity and helped fortify their lives in a battering culture. Graham's critics relentlessly carped that he preached a personal gospel. They missed the subtlety of the choreography. Graham's gospel started with heartfelt desire, expressed itself in personal choice, and culminated in the community.

Finally, the trek to the front and then to a counseling room backstage or counseling area in front turned the site into an altar in the truest sense. Granted, sometimes the event looked less than monumental. Inquirers' demeanor did not always inspire confidence that they grasped the meaning of what they were doing. "When one watches . . . two prepubescent boys poke one another and toss their hats in the air as they skip across the stadium infield toward the counseling area," said biographer William Martin, "or listen to a teenage girl tell her friend . . . 'There's nothing to it,' one comes to understand that not every decision flows from the deepest wellsprings of heart or mind."[64] But if we take countless inquirers at their word, especially in the aggregate, there can be little doubt that the site marked a place where decisive transformations either started or came to life with renewed clarity and vitality. Altars became doors.

Why Did They Commit?

First, the numbers. How many decision cards were turned in all told, and what percentage of the total attendance did they represent? In 2014 the BGEA's tally was remarkably exact: 3,229,121. Given 215 million total recorded attendees, that would be about 1.5 percent.[65] Other studies sponsored by the BGEA of "thousands of statistics" based on "hundreds of worldwide crusades" reported that approximately 4 percent of attendees walked forward.[66] Approaching the question with a different data set, the BGEA broke down the number of attendees and the number of inquirers in most of Graham's U.S. and some of his international crusades, meeting by meeting, starting with "evening church service" at Bostwick, Florida, on Easter Sunday, March 28, 1937.[67] By that selective reckoning, cumulative attendance totaled 82,774,083 and the cumulative inquirers 4,563,436—or slightly more than 5 percent.

Multiple caveats are needed, of course, since data on many overseas crusades were missing, many crusades especially in the later years featured associate evangelists, repeat attendees were not factored out, and other variables. Still, a ballpark of 3 percent seems defensible.

Converts in Graham meetings gave many reasons for going forward. Some were disarmingly mundane, mixing nostalgia with pilgrimage. In 1996 one Charlotte *Observer* journalist told the altogether typical story of Jane Long of Chester, South Carolina. Jane was an eighth-grader when Graham came to Charlotte in 1958. She went "just to sing in the choir." Jane had grown up Presbyterian, and a public demonstration of faith was not part of her heritage. But she "answered Graham's invitation." In college Jane found that being a Christian was not cool, fell into the party scene, divorced, and "spent years in the fast lane." But in the previous five years her faith had rekindled. And now Graham had come home for a final crusade. "'I'm gonna be there,' said Jane, now fifty-one. "'Wild horses couldn't keep me away.'"[68]

Some inquirers said they could not put their finger on a specific reason, they just felt an impulse to go forward. Others remembered that they felt uncertain about whether to go or not. For still others the decision was wrenching, leaving them frightened and shaking. A few—but surprisingly few—attributed their action to the nudging of the Holy Spirit (a difference from Pentecostal revivals, where the Holy Spirit routinely received credit for everything of significance). Yet not all of the recollections were so weighty. Graham quipped that he knew one crusader who walked forward just to catch a better view of him.[69]

Standing beside such reasons for committing—mundane, fuzzy, agonized, strategic—were the far more common testimonies that reflected a clear or at least fairly clear set of underlying motivations. These fell into two broad categories. The first involved different forms of obedience, the second different forms of a spiritual quest.

We might expect those motivated by obedience to recall that they were doing what God wanted them to do, but not many actually did. They seemed more comfortable talking about obeying Graham or other people or even themselves. Some said they followed the preacher's directives because of his determined attitude. He knew what he was talking about. His language was straightforward, free of theological mumbo-jumbo and qualifications. He took a stand without apology. Converts spoke too of his clarity, sincerity, and persuasiveness. Each term here was significant. Clarity: they understood what he was saying. Sincerity: they believed that *he* believed every word he said. Persuasiveness: his words overwhelmed doubts. And the reason was easy to see: Graham's narrative fit the narrative of their own lives. He made sense not only intellectually but also in the deeper sense that he found coherence where they found only incoherence. Graham became, in the words of historian Heather Vacek, "a public figure holding private pain."[70]

Obedience to others assumed both direct and indirect forms. Direct obedience seemed easier to describe. As noted, relatives figured large. Children, adolescents, and young adults walked forward because a parent urged them to go. More often spouses responded to their partner's wishes. Siblings and even grandparents played a role, though less often than parents and spouses. Friends encouraged friends and Sunday school teachers did their part.

President Bill Clinton remembered that in 1959, when he was thirteen, his Sunday school teacher had taken his class to a Graham crusade in Little Rock, Arkansas. He did not respond to the altar call—he had already done that four years before at Park Place Baptist Church in Hot Springs—but Graham modeled a presence that functioned as a conversion moment for the future president: At "that age where kids question everything . . . all of a sudden I said, 'This guy has got to be real, because he did this when he didn't have to.' . . . I never forgot it, and I've loved him ever since."[71] Individuals often acted reluctantly but stepped forward anyway in order to keep a promise to someone they loved or admired. The process worked in surprising ways too. Some acquiesced because others were going forward and they did not want to be left behind. There must have been people who wanted to go forward but did not because they feared ridicule. They did not leave a record.

Indirect obedience, though more elusive, remained powerful too. For some, going forward simply felt like a prudent thing to do. Graham's rise did, after all, parallel the rise of the age of the therapeutic. In many homes Norman Vincent Peale's *The Power of Positive Thinking* outpointed every book but the Bible.[72] Millions hoping to become happier people sought personal wellbeing through techniques that made them feel better about themselves. So, too, some converts spoke of how Graham's message challenged them to be nicer, or enhanced their self-esteem by giving them a new status in which they could take real pride. At a deeper level some spoke of the need to chisel out an identity for themselves. Becoming a newborn Christian helped.

Commitment as a response to some form of inner darkness formed another large category. Escaping hell motivated some. Sorrow for the harm they had done to other people and even to pets motivated others. For still others coming to Christ addressed the emptiness of a meaningless life, drifting without purpose. They variously sought freedom, or peace with themselves, or getting their priorities straightened out. Individuals wrote especially often about conversion as the final stretch of a very long search. Some sought a God who loved them, others a God who forgave them.

These reflections about why inquirers got up and walked to the front merit analysis. The first question that naturally arises is, how many of those decision cards represented—allowing for the imprecision of language—something like authentic commitment or recommitment to Christ? More simply put, how many took hold?

The short answer is that a great deal hinged on who was doing the counting. Debunking studies abounded. A survey of inquirers in a six-week stand in Seattle in 1951, for example, showed that of 6,354 decisions reported by the organization, the churches in that city received only 3,349 referral cards.[73] One-third of those came from children under fourteen, and prior church members accounted for about half. Or again: a 1971 Oakland, California, study claimed that one-third of 21,670 registered decisions gave false names and addresses.[74] In 1960 Graham's early biographer William G. McLoughlin summed up a variety of studies from around the United States and Great Britain. He concluded that "his crusades seemed capable of influencing only those already committed to his religious outlook. . . . Their impact on the community at large was superficial and ephemeral." McLoughlin then judged: "Now, as his decline begins, the burden of keeping the machine running is putting undue emphasis on publicity and fund raising."[75]

Yet other studies trumpeted different results. Two surveys by Robert O. Ferm, one of Graham's long-time associates, offered a case in point. One, of 2,400 deciders at Graham's 1957 New York crusade, found that 80 percent "had continued on in their Christian life" ten years later.[76] In the other, a study of "steadfastness" based on 400 randomly distributed questionnaires, Ferm tabulated that 97 percent had "persevered." The questionnaire was distributed on average four years after the reported decision. Ferm added that "a substantial percentage" had remained faithful for ten years or longer.[77] Another Graham aide looked at the results of the 1977 Cincinnati crusade soon afterward. He found that 87 percent of the people who accepted Christ had at least started attending church.[78]

The Graham organization sought to measure steadfastness in a different way by asking about effectiveness. An extensive study by the BGEA and Glenn Firebaugh, a Vanderbilt sociologist and statistician, analyzed ministers, lay leaders, and inquirers involved in the 1976 Seattle crusade. Firebaugh concluded that seven of eight lay leaders and two of three local pastors believed the crusade had "a positive effect," and that included pastors who had not participated in the crusade. That being said, only about one-tenth of the pastors and one-fifth of the lay leaders attested to numerical growth in church membership or affiliation. Deepening rather

than expanding seemed to be the key result. That conclusion found rein-
forcement in inquirers' evaluations of their own experience. Eighty-three
percent rated it positive or very positive, and 86 percent would do it
again.[79]

But debunking and trumpeting were not the only options. Some suggested more mundane ways to measure results. One writer observed, without a trace of irony, that after a Shreveport crusade, liquor sales went down
40 percent and Bible sales rose 300 percent.[80] Then, too, after a North
Carolina crusade the state department of revenue received a surge of un-
paid back taxes.[81] The scabrous English critic J. B. Priestley called it a draw.
Writing in the *New Statesman* in 1955, he judged "no great harm, no great
good, mostly a show."[82] An American theologian, fundamentally sympathetic to Graham's work, nonetheless felt that the preacher paid too little
attention to the spiritual balance sheet. If some found their lives transformed by the breadth of his vision, others went away disillusioned by the
narrowness of his solutions.[83] A *Reader's Digest* editor, also fundamentally
sympathetic, sought to reframe the question. The aim, he argued, was not
more Christians but deeper Christians—men and women more willing to
take up the cross.[84]

And then some looked to distant horizons, past and future. A distinguished religion editor touched on the power of memories. In 1996 Graham
came to Charlotte to preach one more time in his hometown. Billie Forbes
was waiting. Forty-seven years earlier she had been "introduced to Jesus"
at his 1949 crusade in Miami. Forbes still remembered "the moment and
the man who gave it to her."[85] A *Time* correspondent also turned to the
power of memory to measure success. In 1955 Graham had held his largest
crusade to date in London's great Wembley Stadium. When Queen Elizabeth visited San Francisco nearly thirty years later, she invited him to dine
with her aboard the royal yacht. As he boarded, "a high-ranking British
naval officer saluted and whispered to Graham . . . 'Wembley, '55.' "[86]

Graham himself proved both disarmingly realistic and surprisingly reflective. Near the end of his career he estimated that about one-fourth of
the inquirers would persist.[87] Seven years later, near the very end of his
ministry, he grew pensive: "A lot of people go by numbers. I don't. In some
crusades there are immediate results. In others, it might take 25 years to see
the results."[88] Elsewhere he reflected that if one person said yes to Christ,
he had succeeded.[89]

A final striking feature of the conversion literature is that it showed that
the majority—one-half to three-fourths—of conversions were actually not

first-time commitments but dedications or rededications by people who were already faithful church attenders.[90] And in one study, nearly all (96 percent) of those who came forward already possessed some kind of link with a congregation or denomination. In William Martin's apt words, the good news may have been " 'Good,' " but it hardly counted as " 'News.' "[91] Students of Graham's career often repeated these data, sometimes breathlessly, as if they constituted devastating information.[92] And to some extent they had a reason for doing so, since the BGEA and other revival supporters commonly projected the myth of the ubiquity of sky-blue conversions.[93] Life changes of that sort not only served as indisputable evidence of God's miraculous power but also validated the worth of the entire evangelistic enterprise.

Yet Graham never tried to hide the plain fact that most conversions were actually dedications or rededications. He told reporters in Los Angeles in 1968 that about 60 percent of the people "that come forward and make a commitment in this part of the country are already identified with the church."[94] Elsewhere he estimated that number at 75 to 80 percent.[95] But that pattern did not change the equation. Nominalism sapped Christianity's vitality. Pastors despaired of the lukewarm half-member.

Waking a faith grown drowsy proved just as hard and just as important as stirring first-time conversions. In 1955 Frank Tumpane, a columnist for the Toronto *Telegram*, visited one of Graham's meetings. Watching the inquirers stream forward, he found them "sober-faced," standing quietly in front of the platform. "How many of them will be backsliders?" Tumpane asked. "I don't know. But I think it's better to be a backslider time and time again than never to make an effort to move forward at all."[96] Graham's ability to prompt men and women to pause, take stock, and then shoulder the serious responsibilities of the Christian life, day in day out, may have said more about his impact on modern America than the sudden light of the textbook conversion.

And finally, many who started or more often restarted the Christian journey with Graham went on to something deeper. Henry Pitney Van Dusen, the president of Union Theological Seminary, strode to Graham's defense when Union Seminary's Reinhold Niebuhr dismissed his preaching as simplistic and Graham himself as a captive of Madison Avenue. "There are many, of whom I am one," said Van Dusen, "who . . . would probably never have come within the sound of Dr. Niebuhr's voice . . . if they had not been first touched by the message of an earlier Billy."[97] Both Billys—Sunday and Graham—had shown the path. Though Van Dusen did not cite Mr. Great-Heart in *The Pilgrim's Progress*, he might have: "But he had in his pocket a map of all ways leading to or from the Celestial City, wherefore he struck a light, (for he never goes also without his tinder-box)."[98]

The Letters

In the remaining sections of this chapter, I rely mainly on the manuscript letters, partly because they offer unparalleled immediacy and partly because they represent a rich (and still underutilized) resource for thinking about Graham's role in American life.[99]

The letters that the faithful posted to Graham for more than fifty-five years—from the founding of the BGEA in 1950 to his effective retirement in 2005 and beyond—merit a book by themselves. They flowed as an unending river from all parts of the world. The organization did not release data on the number of letters it received, but clues suggest that they totaled in the millions. In 1957, several weeks into his Madison Square Garden crusade, Graham said that he was receiving more than ten thousand letters a day.[100] In 1976 one student of the BGEA put the number at forty to fifty thousand letters per week and twice that number after a national telecast.[101] The following year the BGEA's business manager estimated 2.5 million a year.[102] In 1982, on the eve of Graham's Moscow conference, he reported ten to fifteen thousand a day.[103]

The letters arrived in a rainbow of colors and a jumble of shapes and sizes. About half were handwritten and half typed. The handwritten ones exhibited every imaginable style, ranging from exquisite calligraphy to childlike scrawling. Surprisingly, nearly all were legible. The authors clearly wanted Graham or his staff to be able to read them, and so they took time to make the lettering clear. Though most ran a few paragraphs, they varied in length from a few lines to many single-spaced typed pages. All age groups sent letters, including small children and nonagenarians. Yet insofar as it is possible to tell, a majority came from adults, ages twenty to forty who were beginning to face the responsibilities, rewards, and sorrows of adult life. As noted, about 60 percent of the letters bore conventionally female names.

The letters represented all educational levels, schooled and unschooled; they were grammatical and ungrammatical, eloquent and halting. A startling number of writers—likely the majority—laced their texts with supporting passages from the Bible, along with photos, requests for BGEA books and artifacts like calendars, and indications of the amount of money enclosed (rarely more than five or ten dollars). They proffered simple questions, contentious challenges, sage observations, and ruminations on the mysteries of life. Taken together, the postings told an epic story of despair and hope. And not a few were painfully funny, sometimes by accident but often by design.

The letters occupy both published and unpublished (or manuscript) forms. The published letters reside mainly in two venues, the monthly *Decision* magazine and in Graham's daily "My Answer" syndicated newspaper column. *Decision*, founded in 1960, usually ran eight to ten letters in each issue. "My Answer," launched in 1952, usually ran one question in each issue. The BGEA published a representative sample of one hundred letters in a volume titled *My Answer*, released in 1960, followed by a revised edition in 1972, and another revised edition in 2008. None of the answers carried dates. Since they were based on God's word, Graham believed, the answers were timeless and universal.[104] The *Decision* letters took the form of testimonials, while the "My Answer" letters always appeared as questions. Graham approved the responses, or at least the boilerplate for them, but editorial assistants wrote them. In both publications the letters were edited for style, content, and length. The BGEA destroyed virtually all of the letters, presumably owing to space and confidentiality.

For unexplained reasons several thousand letters received in the early 1960s and through the 1980s escaped the shredder.[105] In the following pages I draw occasionally on the published/edited letters but mostly on the manuscript/unedited ones. They offer a direct reading of how partisans perceived and constructed Graham as pastor. Unlike other media—which largely revealed Graham speaking *to* others, the letters reveal the emotional exchange *between* Graham and his audience. They enabled him to keep his finger on the pulse of broadly evangelical Americans and at the same time enabled them to know what he thought about their fears and aspirations.

WHY DID THEY WRITE?

Though every letter bore a unique literary thumbprint, they fell into several broad categories. The first one might be called "I am writing just to say hello." Those authors seemed to tell their life story for no special reason except that they just wanted to and thought Graham might enjoy reading it. Or an anecdote—a cute thing a grandkid said in Sunday school. This cluster also included a very large number that rendered Graham as the paradigmatic All American Male. Though rarely as graphic as journalists' sketches, they made clear that they found Graham, well, handsome. And many more hoped he would visit their town, maybe even stop in for a meal or just drop by for coffee.

But if some letters were bright and breezy, the great majority proved earnest. Of those, the bulk might be called something like "my life is a mess and I pretty much did it to myself." In order of frequency, they identified addictions, sexual sins, dishonesty, despair, and backsliding. Among addictions, writers most frequently named alcohol, but tobacco, gambling, and swearing were not far behind. In the later letters drugs appeared too. The addictive habit itself proved deadly enough. More frightening was the threat of losing a job or the affection of the people they loved (usually a wife). Not a few betrayed disgust with themselves for their weakness. Writers spoke of desperate efforts to break the habits that chained them. They had experienced no success at all or recurrent relapses. They requested Graham's advice about treatment programs. Very often they asked him simply to pray for them.

Sexual misconduct, especially adultery, ran a close second. A few spoke of affairs going on but more often they pointed to lapses long ago that lingered to haunt them. Would confessing make me feel good but hurt my spouse? Would it wreck my marriage? And what would happen to the kids? The very suspicion of adultery darkened many hearts too. So did the fear that the senders themselves might stray: "Is it okay, Dr. Graham, to go out for dinner with an attractive woman I work with if all we talk about is business?" Fornication appeared in the letters almost as insistently as adultery. Lust and masturbation too. The social protocols of the sexual revolution troubled many. They asked Graham how to manage when an adult child and their live-in partner came to visit. Evangelicals cut themselves no slack. They never chalked off sexual lapses as a predictable part of human nature or shifting morals of the age. Rather, they agonized and asked Graham to help.

Varieties of dishonesty and its consequences showed up more often than one might expect. Some letters were posted from jails, while others came from parents with incarcerated children. A striking number of writers confessed to theft, usually a long time back. A few spoke of an entire life of crime. Other forms of dishonesty, especially lying and cheating, ran like a red line through the documents. As with addictions, writers seemed to fear the future more than the past. If I did it once, many said in one way or another, what is to keep me from doing it again?

Not a few authors told Graham about dark clouds within. They spoke of paralyzing self-doubt, or of the inability to forgive themselves for the harm they had done, or feelings of utter worthlessness. Some used the language of depression, saying that morning after morning they struggled just to get out of bed and face a new day. A surprising number referred to the ever-present temptation of suicide. The actual or threatened suicide of family members, especially spouses, weighed heavily. Others reported that they had been mistreated or sexually abused as children and were still trying to get over it. And then there were dark clouds more spiritual than mundane. Once upon a time, the narrative often ran, things were right between God and me. But I drifted, wandered into party life, cheated on my spouse, divorced, and fell into one or another addiction. There is nothing I can do about the past now, I can't edit the film, but I need forgiveness. Dr. Graham, can you help me?

These reports bring us to a third large category. We might call it "my life is a mess, it's not my own fault, or only partly my own fault, but it still hurts." The list ran long. Health and money problems never went away, and writers just wanted Graham to know. As for health, the letter writers were probably split more or less evenly between those who worried about their own health and those who worried about the health of a loved one, most often a child. The bitter hurt that came with the illness, sickness, or disability of children clouded many pages. Money problems often centered on the moral dilemmas money created. Their primary concerns pertained to such things as the ethics of declaring bankruptcy or the humiliation of owing money and not knowing how to repay it. A few, but only a few, letters fretted about basic necessities. More often, Graham's grassroots followers worried not about the basics but about stretching modest salaries to get ahead. And when they could not, or feared they could not, they told him.

Affairs of the heart occupied many pages. I do not mean romances gone sour. Evangelicals undoubtedly experienced their fair share, but they rarely told Graham about them. What they did write about with great frequency and in revealing detail were the disappointments that friends, children, and especially spouses inflicted. Friends, including church friends, gossiped and backstabbed. Wayward children, including adult children, appeared often, adrift, wandering from job to job or even from spouse to spouse. Some adult children clearly remained unsaved, and worse, did not care. A mother of four told Graham that three of her children were walking with the Lord, but the fourth was not. Her heart broke for the one. Troubles with spouses figured exceptionally large. Writers talked about marriages on the rocks, spouses walking out, and of course the threat or reality of divorce. Again and again writers asked Graham if they should try to win the spouse back. Was it worth it? And even if they came back, could the marriage ever be patched up?

Many stories spoke of the pain that coming to Christ in a Graham revival had brought with it. Co-workers shunned converts, friends rued the real or expected loss of a convivial companion, and nonevangelical relatives saw the conversion as a tear in the family's fabric. One partisan, stepping away from the Catholic tradition into which she had been born, said it was the most difficult thing she had ever done.

Loneliness occupied a startling number of pages. In 1976 Graham said that next to marital problems, loneliness dominated the letters. "We're a lonely people on a lonely planet in a lonely world," he told a Chattanooga reporter in 1995.[106] The malaise took different forms. The most obvious was grief. Graham preached about Queen Victoria. On the death of her husband, Prince Albert, she would say, "There is no one left to call me Victoria."[107] Loneliness came in other guises, too. A silent grief fell when children left home and did not write or call. Others found themselves isolated in nursing homes. Many pages spoke of the hurt of spouses being alone together, when the other person paid no attention or did not care. For many the worst kind of loneliness gnawed when one partner became a Christian and the other one did not.

Problems dominated the letters, but not all of them. A plurality expressed gratitude. Some thanked Cliff Barrows and George Beverly Shea for the "blessing" that the crusade music brought to their hearts. They especially wanted to thank Shea for sticking to old favorites such as "How Great Thou Art" and "The Wonder of It All." Writers admired Ruth, especially her fortitude raising five kids mostly on her own. Not surprisingly, however, the great bulk of the gratitude letters focused on Graham himself. Some combined thanks with nostalgia. Long ago, many narratives ran, you turned my life around. I cannot imagine where I would be today if you had not led me to Christ. Prominent, too, were letters that thanked him for rousing them from the slumbers of a nominal Christian life. Most started by stating in so many words, I was born into a Christian home, but my parents did not take their faith very seriously, and neither did I. Then I saw you on TV and I knew something was missing. You stirred my dormant faith to life.

Many of the archived letters—presumably representing thousands more—expressed gratitude to Graham for leading them away from a life of sin and to Christ. Often challenging the smooth narrative of the prescribed conversion (as noted above), they painted a variety of conversion experiences. Some stretched over time, some became apparent only in retrospect, and some happened on the spot, in front of a television set. One mainline Protestant theologian targeted the blandness of the message: "For it promises a new life, not through painful religious experience but merely by signing a decision card. Thus, a miracle of regeneration is promised at a painless price by an obviously sincere evangelist. It is a bargain."[108] The critic undoubtedly got it right for some souls. But the ones who wrote repeatedly identified New Testament graces such as joy, hope, and peace as the result of their conversions. Perhaps the most frequent single sentiment ran, in one form or another, "you brought new meaning to my life." Some thanked him too for prompting them to join a church.

Not everyone found Graham so pleasing, however. This qualification opens a category that might be called "challenge" communications. Authors regularly vilified Graham for his ignorance of the Bible or for overlooking the key parts of it that did not suit his theology or purposes. Not knowing the Good Book was bad enough but willfully misinterpreting it even worse. Graham's teaching about the details of Last Things in general and the Second Coming of Christ in particular provoked the most hostile commentary. While secular critics felt he said too much, some writers felt he said too little. To them, the Bible offered a pristine blueprint for how history would come to an end. But Graham fell into vague generalities. Substituting platitudes for doctrine, he obscured important distinctions about exactly when and where and who would be saved. The preacher veered off track in other ways too. He ignored the Bible's "plain" or "clear"—two of the challengers' favorite words—teaching about divorce or abortion or capital punishment or much else. They disliked him for pretentiousness too. What qualified him to stand up there and act like he knew everything? Some thought his hair was too long.

Letters posed honest questions. A good many repeated the query he had spent sixty years trying to answer: What do I have to do to become a Christian? They asked factual questions: When was the Bible written? Conundrum questions: Why do the resurrection stories differ? Credibility questions: Do you really believe Methuselah lived 969 years? Some cut to the quick: Why is the Bible so hard to understand? Authors trusted Graham to give them the right answers about what the Bible *really* taught. They peppered him with queries about correct doctrine: Did babies who died automatically go to heaven? Which was correct: immersion or sprinkling? Did Jesus drink wine? Some letters started with a qualification such as, we know you are not a scholar, but then added, we trust you to tell us the correct answer anyway. Some struck chords that transcended time and place. Should I pray to be pregnant—or not to be pregnant? And some brought a smile, asking about marriage arrangements in heaven. Same woman? Forever?

Uncertainties abounded, and writers thought Graham could help. How to engage members of other denominations and religions bothered many. Was it okay to talk with outsiders at all? How could I lead them to Christ?

Were Catholics saved? Mormons? Figuring out the Christian ethics of daily life troubled many minds. Did buying life insurance imply lack of faith? What do you think about Christians who spend a lot of money on luxuries instead of giving it to the Lord's work? Not surprisingly, a large percentage of the queries in this genre pertained to sex, courtship, and marriage. Was it permissible to pet? Were sexual thoughts about the woman you plan to marry acceptable? Above all loomed the gnawing dilemma of marrying someone outside the faith. Marrying Jews or non-Christians such as Muslims virtually never arose, which said something about the boundaries of the social networks. The problem of marrying a person who practiced no religion at all came up frequently. But marrying a Catholic or a Mormon posed the most agonizing of dilemmas.

A few writers plunged deep. They asked Graham to explain or justify God's behavior. The loss of a child or a suicide cried for an answer. Some queried Graham about deep mysteries. Why was there so much suffering in the world? Would I see my husband in heaven? Why did God ignore my prayers? Why was God so silent?

Absences: Who Did Not Write? What Kinds of Letters Did Not Appear?

Who did not write? The letters did not necessarily represent a randomized sample of evangelicals, let alone Graham supporters. Common experience dictates that many, perhaps most, people would never share their thoughts with a celebrity preacher, even if they admired him. And others who in principle might be willing to share their thoughts would not in practice go to the trouble of addressing an envelope, buying a stamp, and hiking to a postal drop. Some details remain unknown. Were the people who wrote to Graham habitual scribblers? Did they write to other evangelists as well? Did they send letters to editors? Did the same writers send multiple letters?

It is important, too, to think about the kinds of letters that rarely landed in Graham's mailbox. The records contain very few communications that describe visionary or mystical or ecstatic experiences. Few if any identified the Pentecostal hallmark of speaking in tongues except to ask what he thought about it. Many spoke of healing, but most talked about the invisible mending of the spirit rather than the visible repairing of broken bones. Letters asking about etiquette—the stock-in-trade for Ann Landers–type columns—rarely showed up. Though the lines blurred, on the whole people seemed somehow to sense that Ann Landers and Billy Graham had different jobs. They asked about the morality of declaring bankruptcy but not about whom to invite to the wedding.

Also largely missing were letters about secular political affairs or about spiritual loss. Virtually no one asked Graham which political party to join or how to vote on a local school referendum. Given that mainline Protestant clergy regularly scored Graham for not getting into (the right kind of) politics enough, and given that many black Protestants, evangelical and otherwise, had blurred those lines for generations, this absence was striking. Failure letters also eluded Graham's eyes. A large number spoke of lapses and relapses but very few intimated deep doubts about their faith. There was no vocabulary for that. And no one said the journey was hopeless.

There is no way to know what percentage of the authors believed that Graham himself would read and respond, or believed their letters would be handled by a staff member, or gave the question any thought. A good-faith estimate is that about 20 percent fell into the first group, another 20 percent the second, and 60 percent into the third. Those who thought that Graham himself would respond revealed their assumptions in several ways. Some asked him not to show the letter to anyone else, including Cliff Barrows or his wife, Ruth. Some made a pre-emptive strike and requested a personal response. And some asked Graham to write back promptly since the problem was urgent. The second group—those who expected Graham not to write, usually started the letter with a sentence such as, "Dr. Graham, I know you will not read this letter yourself but . . ." The majority of writers seemed, however, not to think about the question at all. Or if they did, they seemed not to care one way or another.

The reasons for writing varied. Many were practical. They wanted a free book or a recommendation for a good church or to ask if the BGEA had a retirement community. Many indicated that they were enclosing a small contribution. There was indirect evidence, too, that some who could not or would not physically attend a church viewed writing to Graham as an acceptable substitute. Yet other reasons, likely too elusive for writers themselves clearly to discern, rippled just beneath the surface. Just writing about a concern or a joy gave it a name. A name made it more treatable if it was bad or more shareable if it was good. For some, writing to Graham functioned as a Protestant version of confessing to a Catholic priest. Telling him about their misdeeds evidently served as a form of absolution, even though he did not pretend to offer such a thing. And the postal wall that stood between the writer and the preacher provided a shield of anonymity, perhaps like the confidentiality of a Catholic confessional booth. Authors admitted with surprising frequency that they told him things they would not have shared with their own pastor.

A third reason is that many believed that Graham enjoyed a special relationship with God. Here we must be careful. Though Graham's followers often treated him reverentially, as if he were suprahuman, few if any intimated that they believed he actually was. At least not when they stopped to think about it. Still, they wrote, and they asked Graham to pray for them. Finally, one gains a sense that many writers felt they had no one else to turn to, nowhere else to unburden their problems and share their joys. Billy would care.

Graham's Responses

All letters received a personal response from BGEA staff. Since the kinds of issues people wrote about fell into a predictable range of categories, the return letters reflected categorical responses too. When the topics did not fit a predefined category, they received a more tailored reply. The BGEA did not keep carbons of the return letters, so we do not know exactly what they said. But the association did store thousands of the replies that Robert Ferm, Graham's long-term researcher and close associate, crafted for the "My Answer" column. Read cumulatively, they provide a sense of how Graham—or the Graham Voice—spoke to the times.

The first thing one notices is the absence of answers that might be construed as prosperity-gospel, let alone self-actualization or self-realization rhetoric.[109] Contemporaneous prosperity preachers, such as Graham's friend Oral Roberts and other paladins of the trade such as Kenneth Hagin and Kenneth Copeland, urged Holy Spirit–filled Christians to name any legitimate desire and then claim it through the power of the Holy Spirit. Yet prosperity notions and practices barely touched Graham's thinking or answer columns, at least if partisans read them in the commonsense way he intended. Faith in Christ solved the problem of sin, but it did not "pay the bills or cure every sickness. You will still have those problems."[110] And if Graham's constituents read and heard him rightly, the gospels of self-actualization and self-realization found no voice at all. The vessel was broken. It required replacement, not fixing up.

The crisis rhetoric that pervaded the *Hour of Decision* radio and television broadcasts and the crusade sermons (especially the earlier ones) found less space in the "My Answer" columns than they did in those other media.

In those sermons, as noted, the preacher usually started with a bill of particulars about the terrible predicaments of the day, and that backdrop spelled doom for individuals and the world if folks did not mend their ways. Urgency reigned. Tomorrow might be too late. "My Answer" columns and one-on-one exchanges presented a more pastoral tone. In a 1997 commencement address to a small college in Florida, the nearly octogenarian Graham had sage and gentle words for the young people just starting their careers: "I urge each of you to invest your lives, not just spend them. Each of us is given the exact same amount of seconds, minutes, and hours per day as anyone else. The difference is how we redeem our allotted time. . . . You cannot count your days, but you can make your days count."[111] Graham evidently sensed that the kind of social crises he had thundered about in days long past needed to be dialed down to a more human scale. He also evidently sensed that up close he needed to lower his voice.

But if the "My Answer" columns (both published and manuscript) avoided prosperity gospel and self-actualization uplift, and downplayed crisis rhetoric, they offered their own recognizable approach. Many—perhaps half—projected evangelical boilerplate. They repeatedly affirmed that nothing but the new birth in Christ afforded lasting peace—peace with self, with neighbors, and with God.

Yet Graham's repertoire was broader. He knew he was writing for non-Christians and nominal ones too. So for them, many "My Answer" columns and manuscript letters moved outside Christian revelation and projected principles of moral theism. They called for virtues that all men and women of good faith should seek: self-discipline, sobriety, and purity in one's personal life, forgiveness, fairness, and honesty in one's social life, and a commitment to work for justice for all people in one's public life. Moral theism blended evangelical theology with old-fashioned common sense. Many columns in this vein sounded like a page torn from Ben Franklin. Work hard, save for a rainy day, overlook slights, avoid tempting situations to begin with, and learn to deal with situations as they really are.[112] A grammar for everyday life, it might be called.

Three spheres of everyday life captured Graham's attention in especially memorable ways. One touched the trials of family life. Children need to see that their parents love each other.[113] And children need both discipline and love.[114] Parents can ruin their adult children's lives by refusing to turn them loose.[115] Marriages always require adjustment. Disagreements will come; accept each other's faults.[116] He offered practical tips: remember to talk with your spouse, remember the physical parts of marriage, remember the spiritual parts of marriage too, and remember that marriage like most of life rarely works out as expected.[117] A lot of the time you have to make do with Plan B. Eggs cannot be unscrambled.[118] Pray together.

The second subject touched addictions. The tyranny of unwanted habits chained lives in uncounted ways. Graham possessed an uncanny ability to discern the desperation of personal struggles to break free. He was careful not to pretend to be a fixer or a deliverer. He tried to steer people away from pop psychology and new-age gurus, urging them to seek the help of trained psychologists, psychiatrists, and other professionals. Yet he reminded them that their problems had a spiritual dimension too, one that lay beyond secular therapies. Name the evil, he said, confront yourself and what you have been doing to yourself and to others, especially the ones you love. Confess your addiction to God and ask God's help. Then move on.[119]

The third sphere of perennial troubles touched the gnawing sense of the meaninglessness of daily life. Graham repeatedly listed boredom on the register of modern trials. He spoke of how young persons, in particular, found no challenge or purpose to fill their lives. But not young persons only, for many seemingly successful adults found that they had "everything to live with but nothing to live for." A life committed to something they believed in—Graham clearly hoped they would choose the gospel, but any goal larger than personal self-fulfillment would help—seemed an apt response for that peculiarly modern malaise.[120]

The Faithful in Retrospect

Graham's critics repeatedly objected that his gospel had no bite. He called them to Christ but did not expect them to change in any fundamental way. At best, they said, his gospel came easy and at worst it equaled cheap grace. Reflecting on the corpus of documents that illuminate the lives of Graham's partisans, it is clear that many did find cheap grace in his ministry. He urged stewardship but did not ask followers to sell off a given percentage of their assets and give it to the poor. He urged witness for Christ but did not say that followers had to go on a two-year mission as Mormon young men did. He pressed for racial justice but did not call white inquirers to join sit-ins, let alone give up their unearned privileges. And so in one sense Graham's critics were absolutely right. Short of conspicuous misbehavior it was altogether possible to go through the motions and live as before.

But not if they internalized Graham's words as he meant them. Careful listeners heard a call for radical change, from the roots up, from the inside out. In one of the earliest sermons aired across the nation on the *Hour of Decision* Graham heralded exactly the same point he would press nearly six decades later in the final sermon of his long career. Re-creation had nothing to do with civilization, culture, refinement, or education: "God makes no attempt to repair the old man." Rather, the "supreme objective"—in a very real sense the sole objective—was the creation of a new person.[121] For some, such *re*-creation might require deep financial sacrifice or forsaking parents for a foreign mission field or taking a costly stand on a social issue. Graham rarely spelled out the consequences. His concern lay elsewhere. He aimed to address the wellspring of everything else, the volition. Rightly turned, fists became palms, selfishness became generosity, and cowardice became courage.

There is danger in overthinking the data, breaking it down into too many parts and losing sight of the big picture. Hundreds of thousands— perhaps millions—of Americans attested that Graham had played a pivotal role in their journeys. Other pastors had their jobs. He had his. It was to nurture the private life of a public faith.

Postscript A: Children's Letters

Children wrote to Graham with a range of concerns as broad and as deep as their parents'.[122] Most likely the great bulk of the children's letters, like the adults', fell into a shredder. But for unknown reasons several hundred posted in the early 1970s somehow survived. The letters show that children saw Graham as a combination of friend, confidant, advisor, and pastor in matters great and small. Graham had proved himself both credible and trustworthy. So it was that one young man would assure Graham, "I listen to you and believe every word you say."

Children were both generous and precise. Many posted photos of themselves and asked Graham to return the favor. They wrote poems, sketched and colored sunsets and pretty landscapes, enclosed lucky pennies, and sent handcrafted crosses. And of course they sent money, mostly coins, not rarely with the exact amount denoted lest there be any mistake.

Precision in other matters counted too. Frequently they gave their weight, height, age (down to the month), full name (including middle name), age of conversion and baptism, names of parents and siblings, and the age of everyone in the family. Pets' names often made the list too. Surprisingly often, children tabulated who was a Christian, or not. (The indefinite article "a" proved invariable. Cultural Christians did not figure in their mental worlds.)

Reading the letters with a straight face is not always easy. Eight-year-old Russ informed Graham—children usually addressed him by his full name, Billy Graham—that his own family was "going organic." Todd, fourteen, insisted that he "still loved God" yet admitted, "the most reason I'm writing you is to get stickers." Rob, six, confessed that he "was broke before today," but he now had $1.00 from his tooth, which he would send. To be clear, Rob wanted two big stickers and twenty small ones.

Pets, of course, played a large role in the correspondence. Ten-year-old Craig admitted that after leaving two parakeets in the car on a hot day, they ended up "three quarters dead," but prayer brought them back. Others had even better news. Scott happily reported that his dog had "just turned Christian." Kate wanted Graham to know that "her cat had kittens and she was allowed to keep one so I named the kitten Billy."

For children, as for adults, money loomed large. Many sent their savings—sums received for a lost tooth, a good report card, or washing dishes or raking leaves. Often they wished they could give more. Darlene wanted to do better than a quarter, but she urged Billy Graham to remember: "after all I'm only ten." Young Margaret lamented that she did not have her own checking account, then assured him, "God will help you . . . He is just testing your faith!" Some showed early signs of an entrepreneurial spirit. Kathy asked Graham to help sell a bunny for $1.50.

If Graham thought, at least in his bolder moments, that theology was too important to leave entirely to theologians, so did the children. No one used the word *theodicy,* but the problem of justifying God's ways to humans loomed large. Karen wondered: What do you do when you pray and your fish does not get well? The question was urgent: "Write me back." Another young questioner wondered, "What do you do if your dog is not all the way healed?" The sphere of theological problems included, not surprisingly, grades. Math and spelling figured especially prominently. Graham's prayers could help.

Children also sensed that Graham wanted Christians to work together. Chris observed that Graham talked as all three of his uncles talked, and they were priests. Yet ecumenism did not override denominational consciousness. Of those who raised the questions, most assured Graham that they were Baptists. Not all, however. Leigh Ann proudly informed Graham that *her* church is "Fairview Christian Reformed Church." Cooperation worked in deeper ways, too. For many children, the basic truths of the gospel seemed obvious. "God loves white and red and black and brown," young Sandra quietly insisted.

Questions of cosmology and creation also found their way into the letters. Linda, ten, cut right to the core: "I Love God because if he didn't make the world we wouldn't be here." Nine-year-old Mark knew that some things were worth fighting for. "My school teacher and I got in to a little scrap," he admitted. "Because he said the scientists thought that man was first one-celled and then gradually turned into man."

Graham's young writers had a heart for evangelism, just as Graham did. Entire cities needed the gospel. Young David invited Graham to hold a crusade at Veterans Stadium in Philadelphia—located at Broad Street and Pattison Avenue, he took care to note—because "who needs it better than Philadelphia?" And there were individuals. Ten-year-old Randy explained that witnessing at school was hard work. "I plot and plan to try to win people to Christ," he added with unflinching determination. Twelve-year-old Doug ran into resistance. He had witnessed to two people, yet "one boy I am working on . . . is a real sinner."

Evangelism required personal testimony too, and the children shouldered the obligation. Jane wrote that she had an "impaired leg." She went on to say that people asked her if she would like a normal leg, and her answer was always "No." This surprised people until she explained that her leg made her a better Christian: "I will have a normal leg in heaven."

Many pinpointed the year of their conversion. Kelley, eight, remembered that she had come to Jesus when she was just three. Carol, saved when she was "about 5," liked Graham best "because you do not say a lot of big words." Donald, eleven, discovered God's love back when he was five and learned the plan of salvation when he was six. Nonetheless, in the next three years, he drifted. "I started to cuss and be very nasty," he allowed. Yet Donald now understood that it was not enough just to ask Jesus to come into your life. You "must live like him" too. Others found that saying they were Christians was easier than being one. It required vigilance, which was an important part of a person's witness. At school, nine-year-old Linda heard the devil telling her "to plug up the toilet," but she didn't. Something told her that she could not be a real Christian if she did something like that.

Children heard Graham's messages in searching ways. They wanted to follow his advice, which they assumed would please God. They also understood that there was a price to pay. They strove to be good Christians, asked forgiveness for the things they had done wrong, wanted strength to witness to others, and realized that sending money (most often tooth money) was important.

The young authors somehow sensed the inevitable passing of time. "I pray that God will keep you alive for a hundred years," wrote Danielle. "Don't die until there is someone to take your place," pleaded Tim. Scott, nine, assured Graham: "Jesus is lucky to have a man like you." "God is going to give you a reward," said another. Mike, eight, judged: "I think you should go to heaven and be God's assistant."

Little wonder. If Graham had helped transform children's lives, he also had helped transform their parents' lives. After your services, wrote Maurice, exactly twelve and three-fourth's years old, "my dad has changed. He asked my sister and my brother and me all these things and at the end he said I love you all. So thank you Billy Graham."

Postscript B: Envelopes

The envelopes that spirited letters to Graham told their own story.[123] Perhaps the most striking story was the irregularity of the addresses. From 1950 to 2002 (when the BGEA moved to Charlotte, North Carolina) the ideal was: Billy Graham Evangelistic Association, 1300 Harmon Place, Minneapolis, MN 55403 (or later a box number). But uncounted envelopes fell wide of the mark. Since the letters nonetheless ended up where they were supposed to go, that success said something important about the sheer ubiquity of Graham's name recognition in the years of his ascendency.

Many envelopes bore no postal address at all, just *Billy Graham* scratched on the outside would do.

Mr. Billy Graham
The World

To Dr. Billy Graham
Evangelist
America

Send to Billy Graham
Don't Know Add Dress
Make Shore it is sent out at ones

Rev. Billy Graham
"Evangelist"
Who lives some where in
America
U.S.A.

The Rev. Billy Graham
Dear Mr. Postman I don't
Know the address of Rev. Graham,
to him. It really is important.
Thank you
Love
Linda

Billy Graham
Planet Earth

For some authors, U.S. geography remained murky. Or possibly Cliff Barrows's announcement about where to send "support" letters was not as crisply pronounced as the producers believed.

Billy Graham
Many Afflicts
Many Sodo

Reverend Billy Graham
Many Applause Many Sorrow
Los Angeles
Minneapolis, Minnesota

Vili Grim
Miniapoles Minesota

One sender correctly divined the city but saw no need to bother with the name. A photo of Graham pasted in its place seemed sufficient.

[Photo pasted]
779 Minneapolis MN

Clearly the effort was tongue-in-cheek, perhaps an affectionate acknowledgment that the sender understood Graham's own sense of humor.

Other envelopes indicated that the writers had done their homework
about Graham's life. The envelope bespoke awareness not only of Graham's
rural roots but also of his denominational identification—an identification
he did not hide but also did not emphasize.

> *Mr. and Mrs. Billy Graham Evangelist Charlotte North Carolina the
> farm near charlotte NC up in the mountains there or to his family
> home there or if don't know send to Baptist Church there anyone
> church Please or if can't find him send letter to international Place,
> Atlanta, GA 30320*

And some made plain on the envelope where they thought America's
pastor fit in the grand scheme of things.

> *Billy Graham*
> *Minneapolis MN*
> *In case of Rapture (never mind this letter)*

> *Heaven*
> *P.O. Box 779*
> *Minneapolis, MN 55540*

> *GOD'S MAN*
> *Minnesota*
> *USA*

CHAPTER EIGHT

Patriarch

If the morning of September 11, 2001, ranked as postwar America's defining moment, the morning of September 14, 2001, may have been Billy Graham's defining moment in the final decade of his public ministry. On that National Day of Prayer and Remembrance, the eighty-two-year-old evangelist joined a Catholic cardinal, a Jewish rabbi, a Muslim imam, a mainline Protestant pastor, and the president of the United States on the platform of Washington, DC's National Cathedral. Surrounded by the nation's elite and viewed by millions around the world, the four clergymen hoped to bring comfort to a grieving nation. They struggled to find meaning in the most deadly one-day attack Americans had suffered since the bombing of Pearl Harbor.

The names of the other speakers that day have largely drifted into the mists of memory, but not Graham's. Though he said that his comments applied chiefly to fellow Christians—he did not pretend to be all things to all people—they felt nonsectarian and broadly American. By that point in his career, Graham seemed to stand above divisions, somehow transcending the nation's multiple political and religious boundaries.

The scene was more complex than it first appeared, however. President George W. Bush selected the speakers. Given the nation's religious demographics, the president's decision to include two Protestants in the list of dignitaries seemed fitting enough. And his judgment that one of the Protestants should be an evangelical seemed equally fitting. Yet close consideration raised a question. Realistically, did Bush have any choice about whom that person would be? Could the speaker have been anyone except Billy Graham?

Americans needed a polestar that day. They needed a person to facilitate the transition from a familiar past to an uncertain future by providing a point of stability amid unsettling change. George H. W. Bush—the first President Bush—had called him the "nation's pastor."[1] So he was, not officially, of course, but effectively. For more than four decades Graham had helped mark many of the country's milestones. His presence served as a ritual balm, anchoring Americans in the past as they turned a corner into a new and uncertain future. Graham stayed with Lyndon and Lady Bird Johnson their final night in the White House and offered the inaugural prayer for President Richard Nixon the next day.[2] His official unofficial job, it seemed, was to preside over national occasions of turning and remembrance.[3]

Graham's homily at the National Cathedral constituted the preacher's final symbolic gesture for the nation as a whole. His remarks merit analysis for two reasons. First, they showed in concise form how he thought about theodicy, the justification of God's actions when they seemed horribly wrong. Graham did not try to rationalize the tragedy by saying, as commentators on both the left and the right had done that week, that it signaled God's punishment for Americans' misbehavior. Rather, some of God's actions remained stubbornly outside human reckoning. They somehow served God's unfathomable purposes, but beyond that, humans dared not speculate.

Second, Graham separated his remarks for two audiences. Some words were for everyone, and some were for Christians alone. The former drew on the nation's common moral foundation, while the latter drew on ideals based on the Old and New Testaments. For everyone, he argued, experience showed that suffering built character. For Christians, he argued, the Bible taught that life in heaven in God's presence would be glorious. No one would return even if they could. Graham understood his position. He spoke for the nation as a whole as well as for the specific Christian subset within the nation. In that sense he served more as the nation's patriarch than as its pastor.

The patriarch role did not materialize all at once but had been developing over many decades. When great old age finally stole on him the mantle fit easily.

Senior Decades

The years were good to Graham. He aged well both physically and spiritually. To be sure, he experienced his share of aches, pains, and trips to the Mayo Clinic.[4] Yet many believed that he grew even more handsome as he matured into his sixties and seventies. On the occasion of his seventy-fifth birthday a *Time* cover featured him with the same azure eyes, square jaw, and flowing mane, now silver-white. A slight grin and black turtleneck yielded an image of a mature yet vigorous—even virile—man, still safely unavailable. "A Christian in Winter," the cover read.[5] For nearly six decades he had remained on center stage—and not rarely the evening news, too.

But age took its inevitable toll. The man who once seemed invincible in vitality and stamina began to show the wear inflicted by the passing of the years. In 1992 Graham admitted that he suffered from Parkinson's disease.[6] The condition was serious, his wife remarked: "His Parkinson's disease is no joke. He's suddenly grown into an old man."[7] Still, the public saw something else, and that was resilience. One journalist observed that the "fire and energy" of Graham's youth had been replaced by a "gentleness brought on by the poignant reality that time is slipping."[8]

Graham had been thinking about the relationship between age and outlook on life for many years. As a middle-aged man, Graham—or an editorial assistant writing on his behalf—had responded to one letter writer who noted that he was seventy-two and had no living relatives. Feeling depressed, the writer asked Graham if there was anything left for a man his age. The preacher characteristically responded with a story about another elderly man. As the gentleman lay dying, he said, "I have found that all the sugar is at the bottom of the cup." So it was. "Life can grow sweeter and more rewarding as we grow old," Graham assured the writer.

Into his mid-to-late eighties, Graham soldiered on, crusade after crusade. In 2005, his final meeting, he had to be helped to a platform to speak.[9] Seven years later Senior Living magazine featured a white-haired yet smiling and still square-jawed Graham on its cover.[10] One admirer wrote that the preacher's ability to "accept illness and aging with peace" offered solace to others.[11] In Graham's next-to-final book, appropriately titled Nearing Home: Life, Faith, and Finishing Well, published in 2011, Graham acknowledged that he suffered infirmities. "Old age is not for sissies," he noted.[12] But quietly disappearing into the twilight was not in the cards. Nearing Home offered many nuggets of good common sense. It contained generous advice about prudent preparation for death. Get your things in order, see an attorney, write your will, and mend broken relationships with friends and family.

In some ways there was nothing new about such advice. From the early 1950s Graham had preached often and unflinchingly about the inevitability of death. He never evaded or whitewashed its centrality for understanding the rest of life. Unlike many fundamentalists and Pentecostals, who hoped for a miraculous "Rapture" before the Second Coming, Graham rarely if ever hinted that there would be an escape hatch. Death's jaws yawned wide for everyone. The frightfulness of the end occasioned some of Graham's most memorable phrasings. People, he said, tried to avoid the plain fact that death was the absolute enemy. It snatched them away in the prime of life, leaving behind loss, sorrow, and aimlessness.

People played word games, calling a cemetery a memorial park. Sin came, death reigned.

Graham admitted that when he offered the funeral homily for Richard Nixon he found the occasion difficult, as he looked on five living former presidents, their wives, and numerous dignitaries. Straying from his prepared text, he observed that there was a "democracy about death." Drawing here on John Donne, he reminded the mourners of death's grim universality: "'It comes equally to us all, and makes us all equal when it comes.' I think today everyone of us ought to be thinking about our own time to die, because we too are going to die and we are going to have to face Almighty God with the life that we lived here."[13] So it was when he received the Congressional Gold Medal in the Capitol Rotunda in 1996. He admitted to his distinguished guests that he had "wandered through Statuary Hall and looked at all those statues of some of the greatest men and women in our nation's history." Graham then added, perhaps with a pensive pause, "But one thing is true of everyone of them: They are all dead."[14]

Elsewhere Graham acknowledged mixed feelings about his own demise. He admitted that he did not look forward to the process of dying. He had seen many undergo its torments. But the end of it, the other side, was another matter. "I'm looking forward to it—I really am," he said. "I'll be happy the day the Lord says, 'Come on. I've got something better planned.'"[15]

Such equanimity in the face of death perhaps stemmed from a long maturing transformation in the man's personality and temperament. His largeness of spirit had grown increasingly evident as the years passed. Though he had made few if any concessions to theological liberalism, he had come to believe that his task was not to denounce but simply to proclaim a redeeming message. His breadth of outlook may have grown from his increasingly frequent contacts with impoverished and embattled Christians in the developing world and behind the Iron Curtain. And it may have been the kind of wisdom one expects from a man who had been blessed with sufficient years to see his numerous grandchildren grow to adulthood. Whatever the source, it is difficult to think of any modern world leader who manifested more earmarks of personal and spiritual maturation.

The Mantle

The question was perennial. At least since the mid-1980s the press had repeatedly speculated about Graham's mantle. Who would inherit it? Who would be the next Billy Graham? Though their curiosity was no doubt genuine, it also formed part of a story line. As the narrative ran, the evangelical movement sprawled everywhere. Graham's career provided a center and boundaries. If journalists gained a clear fix on his position they might also be able to gain a clear fix on the larger flow of American religious history, both in times past and in times to come.

At first, when reporters asked the preacher about successors, he steadfastly refused to answer. He felt that responding to that question would be arrogant.[16] It might imply that he felt that he had a mantle—a legacy—to pass on. "There might not be anybody to follow me," he told the *Charlotte Observer* in 1992. "It may be totally different. They don't need me. The gospel will still be the same."[17] In the mid-to-late 1990s, however, as Graham's elder son Franklin Graham ascended in the power structure of the BGEA—becoming CEO in 2000 and president in 2001—the senior Graham changed his mind. He expressed pride in Franklin's accomplishments.

Other groups had their own reasons for wondering about the legacy. For some mainline Protestants, Graham's theology and methods provided a foil against which they could define themselves. One historian astutely suggested that the mainline owed part of its resilience—its body tone—to its felt need to offset Graham's influence and provide something better.[18] And of course evangelicals, too, asked the question repeatedly, often to the point of obsession. Some seemed to fear that if the era of big-stadium mass evangelism passed, the entire tradition would stagger. A deeper fear lurked: they might lose the symbolic center. Just naming the denominations, agencies, leaders, theologies, ideologies, and political orientations that huddled under the evangelical umbrella would be no small task. Graham served as the umbrella. Without him, what would happen? How would they keep everyone working more or less together and moving more or less in the same direction? They needed a successor.[19]

Naming a successor posed problems, however. Where did Graham fit on the landscape? No one doubted that he remained an evangelical. But what kind of evangelical? Conservative? Moderate? Progressive? Some of all? And what was the yardstick of measurement? Theological? Social? Cultural? Throughout this book I have argued that Graham's core theological message remained consistent from beginning to end. His diagnosis of the human condition did not change. And neither did the prescription. The core gospel message—the authority of the Bible, the stranglehold of sin, the power of redemption through Christ, the necessity of a disciplined personal and social ethic, the command to share the gospel, and the promise of the life to come—all stayed the same. Still, his priorities, modes of delivery, awareness of the social implications of the gospel, attitudes toward the rest of the world, and, above all, openness toward those who differed from him did change, sometimes dramatically.

Beside the plasticity of Graham's personal legacy stood the plasticity of his institutional legacy. Unlike many big-name evangelists, he did not found a college, a denomination, or a mother church to carry his legacy beyond the final curtain. Graham did establish the BGEA, an independent evangelistic organization, which became one of the largest in the nation.[20] Whether it would survive the senior Graham's demise with the same robustness invited considerable debate. So the field remained open.

Yet here things grew murky. In the final decade or so of Graham's career he seemed to make a striking move back to the harder, more partisan positions of his earlier years. The problem was that virtually all statements during those final years were mediated through Franklin Graham and the BGEA. Franklin Graham's decision to feature Sarah Palin on the BGEA home page at one point implied the BGEA's endorsement of her strongly partisan views. Many assumed it implied the senior Graham's endorsement too.

In the summer of 2012, full-page advertisements, sponsored by the BGEA and featuring a bust-sized image of a clearly younger Billy Graham, appeared in North Carolina newspapers. The ads advocated passage of North Carolina Amendment One. That (ultimately successful) constitutional amendment prohibited the state from recognizing same-sex marriages or civil unions. Five months later, on the eve of the 2012 presidential election, full-page advertisements, also sponsored by the BGEA, appeared in major newspapers around the nation. Again, they carried a bust-sized image of Graham, younger than his ninety-four years, and they all but endorsed the Republican candidate, Mitt Romney.[21] About the same time, the BGEA's designation of the Church of Jesus Christ of Latter-day Saints (Mormons) as a "cult" disappeared from the website. As it happened, the Republican nominee for president, Mitt Romney, ranked as the best-known Mormon in the United States.[22]

Franklin insisted the ads represented the elder Graham's views too. Others questioned that claim.[23] They noted the senior Graham's advanced age. They also noted that the extremely conservative tone of the theological and political pronouncements of the past few years seemed inconsistent with Graham's thirty years of steady migration in a more progressive direction. They also seemed to undermine his principled (albeit imperfect) efforts to stay out of partisan conflicts in his later years. At least since the mid-1970s he had insisted that the gospel was neither liberal nor conservative, neither Republican nor Democratic, but transcended all mundane divides.

Another factor rendered the debate even murkier: the international charitable work of Samaritan's Purse, the BGEA's cousin nonprofit relief agency. Samaritan's Purse dramatically expanded the scope of the BGEA's World Emergency Relief Fund, which, by 1999, had contributed more than $10 million to aid projects.[24] In 2012 Samaritan's Purse distributed more than 350 million dollars to humanitarian relief projects around the world—including clinics, clean water, earthquake relief in Haiti, and tsunami relief in Japan—with few questions asked.[25]

But perhaps the debate about how seriously to take Graham's plunge into the culture wars at the end of a very long life, or his role in the rapidly expanding humanitarian reach of Samaritan's Purse, was irresolvable and in the end not very important anyway. His image and legacy had been firmly fixed in the public mind long before 2005. Many undoubtedly continued to see an anticommunist fundamentalist warhorse. Many others saw a man who had been growing more progressive culturally and more inclusive theologically, especially if inclusiveness was measured by his willingness to talk with people with whom he differed.

However Graham's legacy was defined, several leaders competed for the title. No one of consequence came right out and claimed to be the next Billy Graham, but not a few seemed to be standing in line. The most obvious inheritors were individuals who might be considered, for lack of a better term, conservative (or traditional) evangelicals on one side and liberal (or progressive) evangelicals on the other. The differences were less theological, strictly considered, than their attitudes toward the larger culture—to contest it or engage it—and toward secular politics. The principal contender for the conservative side was Graham's son Franklin. *Time* magazine called him "the anointed successor."[26] The principal contender for the more progressive side was less clear, but in the eyes of many Rick Warren, pastor of Saddleback Church in Lake Forest (Orange County), California, one of the first and largest of the megachurches, earned that role.[27] T. D. Jakes, pastor of Dallas's Potter's House, fit somewhere in the mix too.[28]

Yet the mantle was an expansive one. The options reached beyond individuals, conservative or liberal. The emergence of megachurches in the 1970s and afterward offered one possibility. Graham did not lend much explicit support to the movement, but aspects of his ministry did. Like Graham's work, megachurches projected anonymity coupled with internal

cell groups, an emphasis on the professional excellence of the musical programs, a folksy message more focused on redemption and hope than on
judgment and retribution, openness to a wider range of demographic groups,
and an enthusiastic engagement with newer forms of communication.[29]

Institutions lined up too. Perhaps the most conspicuous potential institutional successor was *Christianity Today*. Though the periodical was never
monolithic, through the mid-1980s or so, its theological and cultural center
of gravity fell to the center/right of the evangelical movement. After the
mid-1980s, it steadily inched toward the center in theological and center/
left in cultural positions. As the largest-circulation instrument of evangelical
thinking in the world, *Christianity Today* represented a formidable part of
Graham's legacy.

Yet what were the chances of any one person or any one institution actually replacing Graham? On the face of it, not very good. For one thing, the
long record of American religious history offered few reasons to believe
that a person of Graham's bundle of extraordinary "gifts and graces" would
come along again anytime soon. George Whitefield in the early eighteenth
century constituted a historical rival, but after him, the roster ran short.
Graham's perceptive biographer Marshall Frady captured the point: "Billy
is *sui generis*, a species unto himself. We are not going to look on his likes
again."[30] Besides, the job did not come with specs. There was no office—in
both meanings of the word—for someone to walk into. Graham fashioned
his own position. Then too, the evangelical movement had grown more
internally diverse, fractured along numerous lines. In principle that should
have meant that it needed a transcendent leader more than ever. In practice,
however, it seemed to work the other way around. The multiple factions,
each sporting its own brand of identity politics, appeared less inclined than
ever to accept a single leader.

That said, undoubtedly the most important reason that no replacement
emerged was that the criteria for an iconic figure of Graham's magnitude
were time and place specific. A particular set of social and cultural conditions produced his role. He rose in tandem with civil religion, the adoption
of "In God We Trust" as the official motto of the United States in 1956, and
the development of American Studies departments in colleges and universities, among many indicators of the desire for national consensus.[31] When
those conditions changed, so did the role. By the time the culture started seriously to fragment in the 1960s, Graham was already ascendant. But successors were not. The Internet, social media, three-day weekends, expanding

authority of the expert, and the diminishing authority of clergy rendered the Great Crusade era obsolete. Increasingly C. S. Lewis's words, uttered a half-century earlier, seemed exactly right: "The one single prayer God would probably never answer is represented by the word 'encore.'"[32]

But perhaps the pundits were asking the wrong question. The puzzle was not who would be the next Billy Graham, but rather how would Graham's legacy be perpetuated? What form would it take? By that reckoning the next Billy Graham would not be any one person or group or institution but a multitude of witnesses: preachers, journalists, authors, and ordinary and not-so-ordinary lay people who carried forward Graham's endeavors. They would do it without fanfare, barely knowing his name, or perhaps not knowing his name at all, but embracing his style of irenic, inclusive, and pragmatic evangelicalism, an evangelicalism that held firm convictions at the center but proved reluctant to make them a test of fellowship.[33]

Constructions of Leadership: Cracks in the Marble

Graham's legacy as a leader took multiple forms. For analytic purposes it may be clearest to break them into two broad categories: first cracks in the marble, and second contours in the marble. Or to put it more prosaically, some areas Americans found regrettable, while others they found admirable.

Gaining a clear view of the cracks in the marble takes both work and imagination, not because the cracks were so insignificant but because it is hard to cut through the benign grandfatherly images that came to prevail by the end of his ministry. In the glow of nostalgia, it is easy to forget that Graham, like all great leaders, made serious mistakes. And he was the first to say so. Some of the fractures looked minor but proved real and persistent. To begin with, Graham often seemed a notorious apple-polisher. His letters to a succession of U.S. presidents brimmed with superlatives about their qualifications for the job. In one of countless examples, he likened Eisenhower's first foreign policy speech to the Sermon on the Mount.[34] Where loyalty to leaders left off and flattery began was not always clear.

Another fracture was Graham's egregious namedropping. His autobiography overflowed with monikers of famous people of dubious relevance to his ministry. Reporters spoke of that habit in personal conversations.[35] He rehearsed names of celebrities and authorities in sermons, too, with little evidence that they served much substantive purpose. He invoked his international travels in much the same way: references with little substantive purpose. The trait grew more pronounced as the years slipped by and he came to know, dine, or golf with some of the wealthiest and most powerful men (mostly men) in the United States and elsewhere. Just as mainline Protestants sometimes measured their lives in terms of transformative books they had read, Graham seemed sometimes to measure his life in terms of famous people he had known.[36] Given his lack of advanced degrees and formal office, such associations served as a form of credentialing.

Graham's defenders were quick to point out that in many ways he was still just a star-struck country boy suddenly thrust into the limelight. And besides, those celebrities really were his "friends"—the people he really did schmooze with. How deep those friendships ran was another matter. One of the earliest widely shown photographs of Graham portrayed a spiffily dressed young preacher chatting with Jimmy Stewart, Spencer Tracy, and Katharine Hepburn in what appeared to be an elegant Hollywood home.[37] The invitation list to one state dinner that Graham attended in 1976 included Cary Grant, Henry J. Heinz II, J. William Fulbright, Alice Roosevelt Longworth, John D. MacArthur, and Queen Elizabeth and Prince Philip.[38] Some people found Graham's celebrity status thrilling while others found it unseemly for a man of the cloth.

The preacher's penchant for apple-polishing and namedropping marched with fondness for hyperbole. Some of the exaggerations involved the inflation of factual data but most of them involved inflation of qualitative categories. *Biggest, greatest, largest, worst, best, most glorious,* and *unprecedented* studded his preaching. Friendly observers could attribute hyperbole to youthful exuberance. After all, Graham rose very rapidly very early, while many of his chronological peers were still trying to figure what to do with their lives. Even so, the tendency toward hyperbole persisted into middle age and compromised his work.[39]

Four major problems proved more damaging to the effectiveness of his ministry than any of these minor ones. The first lay in his inability to stay out of partisan politics. As noted, in his mind voting and political participation seemed the moral responsibility of any thoughtful citizen, while overt partisanship seemed a misuse of the power of the pulpit and clerical standing. Nonetheless, in press conferences, correspondence with presidents, and the framing of sermons and articles, Graham repeatedly made clear exactly where he stood on partisan issues. If Graham had forthrightly acknowledged overt partisanship, as African American and mainline Protestant clergy routinely did, he probably would have escaped censure. Yet he did not. In his later years, after finding himself burned by Nixon's perfidy, he did try harder to go another way, and he urged young evangelists to do the same.[40] But he often failed. The lure of secular politics was just too strong to resist.

A second liability lodged in the widespread perception, especially in his middle-career years, and especially among more liberal Americans, that he was too close to the power Establishment. More precisely, he failed to use those relationships to effect change, at least in the direction his critics wanted. Charges of serving as "high priest of America's civil religion" dogged him.[41] Graham responded in several ways. He ran his own show. He did not imagine himself an emissary for any interest group, left, right, or otherwise. And he did not hide his relationships with wealthy or powerful or famous figures. They needed pastors and friends as much as anyone else. And evidence of personal material gain remained nonexistent. All of those responses were persuasive for die-hard partisans. But many others, including basically supportive ones, were left shaking their heads.

A closely related charge proved more difficult to rebut. Graham sometimes showed himself simply incapable of understanding the motivations of social and cultural dissidents. The press conferences of the 1960s and 1970s revealed a man tone deaf to the hurt and dismay that animated the counterculture.[42] At the same time, he showed genuine willingness to embrace dissidents as persons. They were created in God's image and therefore merited the same respect that Christians should give anyone else.[43] His tolerance of his son Franklin's rebellious youth offered a compelling image of a father allowing the unrepentant prodigal son not only to return home but also to live at home with smoke on his breath.[44]

A third widely perceived shortcoming was that he seemed distressingly prone to go along to get along. By that reckoning he adjusted his sails to every gust of the wind. The charge was recurrent and more than a little ironic. From the late 1940s he had insisted that within broad limits he would work with anyone who did *not* ask him to adjust his message. Here, precision is crucial. Few claimed that he knowingly contradicted himself, which is to say, that he intentionally lied. Rather, the problem lay in the perception that Graham artfully selected words in order to win favor with an audience.[45] Preaching was a hard dollar. Yet when did adeptness slide into adroitness? When did subtlety slide into sophistry?

A fourth charge targeted Graham's greatest gift: his ability to speak in diverse forums. For many Americans, especially those holding more liberal or secular outlooks, he exercised the gift too often and too glibly. For sure, garrulousness went with the territory. Graham was, after all, an evangelist, and talking was what evangelists did for a living. But he pushed the limits. He talked beyond his knowledge, both in sermons and in response to reporters' questions. Sometimes he recognized the fault and later retracted his words and apologized.[46] But very often journalists treated him as if he were an authority on sundry topics, and he obliged them. A closely related problem was Graham's inclination to speak in the declarative mode: to tell people how things were rather than to ask them. At the personal level, he enjoyed a reputation for asking lots of questions, especially of academics he trusted. Even so, when speaking about other faiths and cultures, he seemed rarely to ask their partisans how and why *they* saw the world as they did.[47]

Graham also appeared to possess little awareness of the legitimating power of his own presence, and that constituted a fifth problem. Without question, sometimes he *intended* to signal legitimation, as when he rode in an open convertible with President-elect Kennedy for the benefit of anxious evangelicals and Catholics alike. Yet many times he appeared not to intend legitimation and expressed astonishment when others inferred it. Why should dining with presidential candidate George W. Bush thirty-seven days before the 2000 election raise eyebrows?[48] How clearly did he grasp his power? How clearly did he grasp the difference between Billy Graham ordinary citizen and Billy Graham Protestant pope? When did simple naiveté become studied naiveté?

Academics in particular registered one more complaint. In different ways they claimed that Graham displayed little awareness of ambiguity, irony, and paradox in Christian theology or in U.S. history or anywhere else for that matter.[49] It was inconceivable that Graham could have written a searching, ruminative book like Reinhold Niebuhr's *The Irony of American History* or Thomas Merton's *Seven Story Mountain*. Did Graham's tone-deafness to ambiguity, irony, and paradox simply reflect his style of speaking directly, without qualifiers? Or did it grow from a deeper black-or-white reading of the world? With the Apostle Paul, Graham knew that people persistently did what they willed not to do and failed to do what they willed to do. His responses in the "My Answer" columns in particular showed acute awareness of the countless ways humans failed themselves. But for Graham, it often seemed, failures of that sort were remedied too easily. They signaled fixable breakdowns in the operating system rather than flaws inherent in the design.

Constructions of Leadership: Contours in the Marble

In the eyes of Graham's followers, his strengths greatly outweighed his weaknesses. For that matter, if the tone and extent of press coverage, religious and otherwise, can be taken as an index, probably a majority of all Americans, including those who would not count themselves supporters, acknowledged significant strengths.

The reasons for the power and longevity of his appeal were not incontestable. Evangelicals had proved that they were altogether capable of shifting loyalties as their interests dictated. In 1980, for example, more than half had abandoned Sunday school teacher Jimmy Carter for Hollywood actor Ronald Reagan. Politics trumped religion.[50] Graham himself gave them plenty of reasons to jump ship if they had wanted to—absentee father, friend of movie stars and liberal Democrats, refusal to endorse one or another sectarian distinctive, among others. But they did not. Decade after decade millions stuck with him, come what may. The reasons are not hard to find. They lodged in their appreciation for his character, mind, and charisma.

CHARACTER

For many, Graham's personal gifts grew from strength of character. That mosaic contained multiple pieces. One reflected a default preference for looking outward rather than inward. Differently stated, Graham proved invincibly extrospective, and many people liked that, as their fondness for the sunny-side-up personalities of Ronald Reagan and Bill Clinton demonstrated. Graham's memoir, *Just As I Am*, bore the perfect title. He told his own story in muscular, uncomplicated, straightforward language. That rhetoric mirrored the personality he presented to the public for six decades.

Graham betrayed few hints that he spent much time looking inward. And when he did, he saw mostly blue skies. "I don't have many sad days," he told *USA Today* in 2005.[51] He also saw few ambiguities. Except for an extremely brief period in the early days of his ministry when he said he experienced fleeting doubts about the Bible's authority, there is little evidence that big questions such as God's existence or his own vocation ever gave him serious trouble. If an extrospective orientation eclipsed irony it also eclipsed contemplativeness. The long lists of authorities he routinely cited in his sermons rarely if ever included the great mystics of the church. With the Holy Spirit's help, firm resolve, and common sense, he determined to take hold and march forward.

The same extrospective cheerfulness marked Graham's views of others. Biographers Nancy Gibbs and Michael Duffy sagely observed that he did not analyze motives. He just saw opportunities.[52] The "My Answer" columns offered ample evidence that he was acutely aware of the breakdowns in other folks' lives. But predictably, they received the same diagnoses and prescriptive resolutions he applied to himself: with the Holy Spirit's help, firm resolve, and common sense, they could take hold and march forward. As we have seen, psychologists, psychiatrists, and other mental health professionals had their rightful role, just as physicians did. But the spiritual realm required spiritual solutions. The Bible never hinted that spiritual solutions required health care professionals.[53]

Graham's irenic disposition constituted another striking feature of how Americans perceived and constructed his character. On the occasion of his seventy-fifth birthday, for example, the historian and Lutheran clergyman Martin Marty famously quipped that historically evangelists fell into two categories: "the mean and the non-mean." Marty placed Graham with the non-mean, for he consistently displayed the "fruit of the Spirit."[54] "Hot heads and cold hearts never solved anything," Graham would say.[55]

An irenic disposition blended with an irrepressible sense of humor. Both sympathetic and unsympathetic observers often overlooked this trait, though probably for different reasons. Graham's humor took multiple forms, sometimes corny, sometimes witty, and very often self-deprecating. He seemed to enjoy his own humor as much as anyone.[56] Not surprisingly, he received uncounted offers—many of which he accepted—to speak at banquets, weddings, and civic events. People appreciated a polished after-dinner speaker who knew how to tell a good joke, turn it to serious purpose, and then sit down.

Taken together, these character traits of an extrospective and irenic approach to life, coupled with humor, meant that millions ended up simply liking the man, whether or not they agreed with his theology or approach or anything else. The like-factor influenced religious outsiders, too. Martin's comprehensive biography sparkles with stories of journalists and others who met Graham with initial skepticism, even hostility, but came away impressed.[57]

Courage formed another feature of Graham's self-presentation, and that, too, said a lot about character. A peaceful disposition did not mean a timid one. So it was that he acquitted himself not only as amiable but also as an amiable protagonist. Grasping the proverbial sword of truth and armor of faith, he proved willing to step into the ring anytime, anyplace. Graham seemed never to back away from sharp questioning in secular universities, mainline seminaries, student unions, or no-holds-barred talk shows. He knew he was not equipped to tangle with academic questioners on their own territory. Yet remarkably quickly he shifted the discussion onto his own ground.[58]

Graham's remarks to public intellectuals at a TED (Technology, Entertainment, and Design) meeting in Monterey, California, in 1998 offered a case in point. After opening with the usual self-deprecating banter, he alluded to little-known technology data in the Old Testament. Then the punch: the human problems of lust, greed, hate, and prejudice loomed just as large back then as they did now. Technology had advanced but the human condition had not. Graham shifted the discussion from the delicate relation between religion and science (where he had little competence) to the delicate relation between sin and grace (where he did).[59]

The preacher's courage showed itself in other ways, too. From the mid-1940s, he regularly took his crusades into far-off sites around the world, when it would have been so much easier to tend familiar pastures back home in the South—and avoid uncounted harrowing flights along the way. Graham entered into physically dangerous situations in war-torn Northern Ireland, hoping to facilitate peace talks, as well as multiple trips to war zones in Korea and Vietnam, hoping to serve a chaplain role. Above all, time after time he challenged his friends, not his enemies, especially on civil rights. Confronting enemies took one kind of courage. Confronting friends took another kind. One of the most frequent charges, usually coming from the Protestant mainline, was that Graham did not "speak truth to power." By their lights perhaps not. But the answer depended on what one meant by truth.[60] In the eyes of many, he spoke the truth with the totality of his life.

Graham's character shone most brightly in the integrity of his personal life: financial probity, marital fidelity, devotional regularity, and recreational prudence. The record of financial probity suffered a small chink in the 1980s when the BGEA used money given for one purpose for something else. But the public soon forgot it, since no one, including Graham, profited personally. The misstep, in any event, prompted Graham and the BGEA publically to apologize and then to help form the Evangelical Council for Financial Accountability.[61]

Other lifestyle patterns counted too. His record of marital fidelity remained spot free. In an age when the sexual adventures of celebrities and sometimes even celebrity clergy seemed regular fare, Graham won approval for his chaste life. The same pattern of integrity marked his private devotional life.

At a time when polls showed that Americans prayed and read their Bibles remarkably often,[62] insiders' accounts of Graham's schedule attested to the rock-ribbed punctuality of his prayer and Bible reading. Here again a private practice became a public narrative. Recreation reflected the same consistency. Some evangelical stalwarts found travel to other cultures, especially Europe, where wine was routine at the dinner table, a moment of liberation. Graham did not denounce imbibing in moderation, but he did not do so himself. And he systematically avoided other behaviors such as smoking, gambling, and shady movies that evangelicals shunned in public but not always in private.

Graham keenly appreciated the public's taste for scandal, especially when they spotted misbehavior among holy men. Knowing human frailty, he took precautions to avoid temptation in the first place. While many Americans never could grasp what the private had to do with the public, Graham saw things differently. A broken covenant in the one realm implied fragility in the other realm. Integrity, he said, "means a person is . . . the same person alone in a hotel room a thousand miles from home as he is . . . with his family." Graham embodied, said William Martin, Americans' "best selves," the people they imagined themselves to be whether they lived up to those standards themselves or not. Appearances counted precisely because they were not just appearances.[63]

A final feature of Graham's public presentation of character received little explicit attention yet merits note for the implicit role it played in the eyes of everyday followers. Graham was a self-made man.[64] Though he rarely put it that way, his personal work ethic had to win respect from anyone who stopped to think about it. The vast and complex empire he created and maintained for six decades was unique in American religious history. It demanded long days, full weeks, wearisome trips, unfamiliar hotel rooms, and continual interactions with strangers, reporters, admirers, and skeptics alike. It also demanded a leather skin. Graham did not make a big deal of his work ethic. He freely admitted that he vacationed on sunny beaches and took a nap before preaching and clearly enjoyed sports. Yet insiders knew and the public sensed a man consistently at the tiller.

Mind

Gaining a fix on the kind of mind Graham possessed, as well as the kind of mind others believed he possessed, is no easier than gaining a fix on any other part of his public presentation. Yet the endeavor repays the effort, for it, too, tells us a great deal about the preacher's appeal.

First of all, Graham was blessed with extraordinary savviness. He knew how to get things done. He also knew the pitfalls and the landmines. Graham's business manager, George M. Wilson—a man widely respected for his shrewdness—once commented, not very subtly, that Graham possessed "innate common sense. That's something you don't get with a Ph.D."[65] Beyond savviness and common sense Graham proved master of the art of spotting talented associates—and keeping them. The core platform Team of Graham, Shea, and Barrows stayed together for six decades. He also relied on the real-world acumen of the leaders on his board, most of whom were businessmen. In addition, he knew what he did not know. He was adept at delegating and empowering talented subordinates to do their job without his micromanagement. Perhaps most important, he knew how to focus on doing what only he could do.

Graham never intimated that he felt the least bit hampered by not being a theologian or an intellectual (neither of which he ever pretended to be). He clearly felt he was plenty smart enough to do the job the Lord had called him to do. By all indications he seemed entirely at ease in both learned and socially elite circles. Press conferences showed that he could think quickly on his feet, possessed a prodigious memory, and proved capable of synthesizing large bodies of data. Graham actually—ironically—drew strength from the limitations of his formal education. Not pretending to have advanced training in theological disciplines, he paid no attention to technical arguments or intramural debates among theologians and church bureaucrats. The boundaries of his formal education freed him to keep his eye on the big picture.

What Graham did know, however, he knew well, and he knew how to deploy it. His impressive command of current events was enriched by a vast array of personal contacts with people of all stations and locations worldwide, won the hard way through relentless cycles of national and international travel. To be sure, the gift of ears did not show up as often as the gift of tongues. Still, the flow of information that he uncorked in press conferences left little doubt that he simply knew a lot about the world around him. If *expert* is defined as mastery of what one needs to know in order to do the job one has set out to do, then Graham proved himself an expert.

Controlling the external contours of current events was one thing, but discerning their internal moral meaning was another. Though Graham never jettisoned the premillennialism of his Bible school days (and probably not the dispensationalism either), premillennialism provided only a springboard to what he really wanted to talk about. If fundamentalist prophecy watchers

tumbled into soothsaying, Graham looked *through* the details for something else, for tokens of the human condition and of God's rescue plans. The
moral dimensions that Graham discerned in world events were not always
the ones mainline Protestants saw, and rarely the ones secular pundits saw,
but they resonated with many Americans' instinctive sense of priorities.

Finally, Graham thought seriously about things that mattered. His book
knowledge, including of course the Bible, proved entirely sufficient for his
purposes: to call people to faith. Here Graham, like his close friend Bishop
Fulton Sheen, who also commanded a vast television audience, showed that
not being an intellectual did not mean that he was anti-intellectual. Rather,
he just believed that there were simple yet profound answers to life's most
important questions. He also understood that some Christian theological
concepts, like sin, could be fruitfully translated to non-Christian and even
nonreligious categories. Such discernment helped him to speak the language of both Christian particularism and moral theism with conviction
and purpose.

The historian Andrew Finstuen concluded that Graham possessed the
gift of "intellectual virtue."[66] That virtue traded on curiosity, engagement,
agility, common sense, and deep insight. Billy Graham was no Karl Barth.
But then, Karl Barth was no Billy Graham.

CHARISMA

The concept of charisma has enjoyed multiple meanings. Most of them
suggest a trait somehow more elusive or even mysterious than a knack or a
talent. New Testament scholars, drawing on the Greek root of the word,
have thought of it as a divine endowment, while sociologists have conceived it as a rare ability to persuade people to follow. I use the term simply
to denote Graham's skill in communicating his gifts of character and mind
to an audience. It influenced them to esteem his words as not only intellectually true but also wholeheartedly or deep-down true.

Graham's charisma took a paradoxical form. Simply put, he was simultaneously inaccessible and accessible. On one hand he emerged in public
life as above the fray, uncompromised by partisan interests and sectarian
bickering. Besides that, the plain truth was that ordinary people had little
hope of actually meeting let alone getting to know him in person. Scarcity
amplified his appeal. On the other hand he emerged as proximate, intimately present in believers' lives by showing up in their mailboxes and on
their car radios and living room television sets, week after week, year after

year. The letters often read as if Graham were a personal friend, or easily could be. He also showed up in secular venues—network newscasts, celebrity magazines, and talk shows. In 1961 the Luce Clipping Service ranked Graham as their best client—above the Duke of Windsor, Mary Pickford, and the late FDR—with an average of five thousand clippings per month.[67]

Winsomeness came with a commoner's touch. The shimmering suits seemed strangely compatible with his downhome, "awww shucks" style. Visitors, we have seen, soon learned that he preferred to be called Billy or Mr. and not Dr. or Reverend.[68] Very few actually used the less formal address, but the gesture counted. Stories in the press brimmed with narratives of Graham striking up a conversation with strangers, stopping to chat with gardeners and skycaps, and remembering people's names years later.[69] More than a few critics thought it was a big show, contrived for the sake of flashbulbs. Yet many Americans apparently judged the style too consistent to fake. The private story gained public dimensions.

Within that context, Graham connected with Americans in a variety of ways. If good looks and smart attire provided the base, Graham's manifest easiness in his own skin materialized on televisions and even behind distant stadium pulpits as old-fashioned Southern charm. On talk shows in particular he came across as dashingly photogenic. He proved a lively guest, blessed with a quick smile, ready quip, and easy-going banter. He was not defensive, either. He once appeared on the *Merv Griffin Show* right after the *Playboy* model Joan Collins. When Griffin asked if he was "offended by open discussions of nudity," Graham said, "Of course not. . . . I just don't do it myself." Graham added that he had turned down twenty-five thousand dollars to write a story for *Playboy*. Griffin asked, "With your shirt on or off?" Graham shot back, "Well, I don't know. That wasn't in the contract."[70] Yet Graham rarely left character, either. He often said that in all settings he sought in one way or another to present the gospel. It was a remarkable (and instinctive) balancing act: a serious message lightly delivered.

Then, too, Graham proved skillful in the art of clear-channel communication. The high-powered European theologian Helmut Thielicke visited Graham's crusade in Los Angeles in 1963. After the crusade Thielicke wrote Graham: "When I have been asked . . . about your preaching, I have certainly not been too modest to make one or two theological observations." One can almost see the grin. But Thielicke went on: "My evening with you made clear to me . . . that the question should be asked in the reverse form:

What is lacking in me and in my colleagues in the pulpit . . . that makes Billy Graham so necessary?" He concluded: "We learn to see ourselves as various dabs of paint upon the incredibly colorful palette of God."[71]

Graham spoke the language of everyday folks, without seeming to talk down *or*—equally important—talk up for the sake of posterity. He used an old vocabulary to express old experiences, but in a context of global awareness and instant communication in which old experiences bore new meanings.

Theological specifics aside, Graham appealed powerfully to Americans' esteem for individualism. They were, after all, a people who embraced the American dream as, in William Faulkner's words, a "sanctuary on the earth for the individual man."[72] Things were of course more complicated than that. In Graham's meetings decisions for Christ were, as we have seen, prompted, confirmed, and exercised within the communal circle of the saints. Yet Graham demanded that his listeners make a choice, an individual choice, up or down. Secular pundits and mainline Protestant preachers might have valued a life of intellectual exploration—Living the Question, as the saying ran—but not Graham or his constituency. Life safely within the ark of God's love was best, life clearly outside the ark was at least understandable, but life wandering around the ark's perimeter, pondering the options, looked like the worst of all worlds.

Vision constituted a final appealing feature of Graham's charisma. Partisans saw a man of expansive instincts, embracing one opportunity after another, reaching wider and wider audiences geographically, culturally, demographically, and even musically. He made no small plans. Virtually from the outset of his career the North Carolina boy took his message to Great Britain, and then to the European Continent, and then to India, and eventually to six continents and nearly one hundred countries.[73] Though many American evangelists from the early nineteenth century forward—Charles Finney, Phoebe Palmer, Amanda Berry Smith, Dwight L. Moody, Aimee McPherson, and Billy Sunday, among others—had spirited their message overseas, none did it with the relentless global determination that Graham did. Long before most evangelicals sensed it, he intuited the "Next Christendom" emerging. The Berlin (1966), Lausanne (1974), and three Amsterdam (1983, 1986, 2000) evangelism congresses helped raise Americans' awareness of one of the most momentous developments of Christian history.[74]

Graham's expansionist vision moved outward culturally and demographically too. Seeking to be a voice among minorities formed a first step, among young adults a second one. Toward that end, the crusades featured an eye-popping and ear-tingling array of musical artists and styles, with special emphasis on groups like DC Talk aimed to appeal to youth. Then, too, as early as 1951 Graham's crusade counselors were trained to work with signers for the deaf.[75] *Decision* magazine was issued in a braille edition from the outset.[76]

Graham proved invincibly future-oriented. He admitted that the past just did not interest him very much. Jeremiads aside, he remained confident of his mission, of America, and of Christianity. He symbolized Americans' successes, not their failures. With an instinct for the strategic over the tactical, he saw himself and his life's work in a timeless framework. For sure, dangers lurked. Doom was inevitable if Americans did not mend their ways. But the conditional *if* was always there. That contingency gave history gravitas and urgency and meaning. Graham revealed no sense that he or America or the Christian gospel faced peril in any truly final way. Hope triumphed over judgment.

IDENTITY
These considerations bring us finally to the question of Graham's identity— how he viewed himself—and how that self-understanding functioned in the eyes of his supporters.

In some ways he appeared to all but the most devoted partisans as intensely self-promotional. Though hardly anyone called Graham vain, flashes of vanity abounded. The organization, after all, bore his name, and banners and countless other forms of advertising heralded it, often along with an Olympic-sized photograph, too. Just before the 1986 Paris crusade, for example, he told an organizer: "Get some more pictures up. I don't see my picture up enough."[77] Graham protested that he did not like all that attention but acceded because he knew his name and visage sold. Still, the sheer ubiquity of those markers raised the question of where necessary advertising ended and self-promotion began.

Other self-promotional traits intruded too. At one time or another ostentation, opportunism, swaggering, and moral elitism marred Graham's image. One unsympathetic journalist described a Graham entourage processing through the Atlanta International Airport, the celebrity preacher at the front, with silver hair, golden tan, blue eyes, a "walking mannequin who had sold his soul to the devils of modern image-making." The spectacle smacked of a Hollywood superstar sweeping into town.[78] And then there was the opportunism. Graham's correspondence with presidents brimmed with requests for meetings or for them to visit one of his crusades and offer a word of greeting.[79] When Graham received an invitation from President Gerald Ford to attend a state dinner in honor of Queen Elizabeth, Graham's photographer asked if they could obtain a photo of the preacher with Ford and the queen, or with the queen, or with the president.[80] From time to time Graham swaggered about his power with the people. In 1952, he boasted that he could deliver sixteen million evangelical votes with his word.[81] And sometimes, especially in the early years, Graham displayed more than a touch of the purple. In the run-up to the 1952 presidential election, he said he hoped to see all of the candidates. "I want to give them the moral side of the thing," the thirty-three-year-old evangelist ponderously observed.[82]

The core of the problem here was not the flashes of vanity, ostentation, opportunism, or moral elitism. Famous and powerful people regularly suffered from those vices and a lot worse. Rather, for the student of Graham's place in American history the problem is to figure out how we should separate ambition for himself from ambition for his cause. Where did one end and the other begin? And why did observers think that such a distinction was needed for a clergyman in the first place? Most people surely saw nothing wrong with a politician or entrepreneur or entertainer promoting self along with the party or business or profession. But if classic novels about clergy in America can be taken as an index, Americans revered religious leaders who kept their heads down.[83] Modest efforts to enjoy a spot in the sun were fine, but aggressive ones were not.

On the other hand, Graham's personal humility seemed to atone for the excesses of self-promotion. People who encountered him, personally or through film archives, including critics, almost always spoke of his humility, or at least likability.[84] Graham's photographer, Russ Busby, who likely spent as much time with him as all but the closest Team members, once observed that "the biggest asset Billy has is his honest humility. He has an ego, like the rest of us. Sometimes it takes off, but he brings it back under control. It takes a big ego to be a big preacher, but the difference between Billy and the others is that when God wants to speak to him, at least he can get his attention."[85] That comment and ones like it appeared so often in so many contexts over so many years, that it stretches credibility to suppose that Graham's unassuming view of himself was contrived for promotional benefit.

A potpourri of anecdotes drawn from a great range of possibilities suffices to make the point. In 1998, near the end of his storied career, Graham appeared on NBC's *Today Show* with Katie Couric and Matt Lauer. Ruminating with Couric about heaven, Graham surmised that seeing Jesus would be "the greatest thing." Then he added, without hesitation: "I'm sure he's going to look at me and say, 'You should have done a better job, and you failed here and you failed there.' But I think that overall, we're all going to get a reward of some sort." Later Lauer asked Couric, "If [Graham] says he's failed, what's the Lord going to say to the rest of us?"[86] Exchanges of that sort, manifestly unscripted, formed part of the public narrative.

Graham proved more critical of himself than many of his critics did. Dinah Shore once asked, "When people come to your rallies and say they have found Christ, how do you know?" Graham answered, simply, "We don't."[87] The preacher's view of his own life proved equally unremarkable. Time after time journalists queried how he thought he would be viewed by history. His response to news anchor Harry Smith paralleled others: "I don't want people to say good things about me because I don't deserve them; I want only the Lord to say something nice about me, to say well done thou good and faithful servant, but I am not sure I am going to hear it."[88]

In *Just As I Am*, an autobiography running 760 pages, Graham devoted one sentence to his 1973 crusade in Seoul, which attracted more than three million hearers in three days, and "more than one million in Yoida Plaza on the last day."[89] With eleven words, he dispatched that historic event.

Graham was not introspective, but he could be sharply self-critical, especially when caught out, as when the press exposed his odious remarks about Jews and the media. His memoirs, press conferences, and other writings brimmed with regrets, ranging from reading too little, accepting too many speaking invitations, spending too few hours with his children, foolishly offending President Truman, failing to criticize the Vietnam War, thoughtless comments to the press, his slander of Jews, and perhaps above all, falling into the muck of political partisanship (a failing he never entirely transcended).[90]

He apologized, too, for speaking beyond his knowledge too many times. When David Frost suggested that in his early days he "probably would have had an answer for everything," Graham agreed. "Yes"—we can almost see the dropped head—"probably out of ignorance or lack of study or lack of world travel and meeting with leaders all over the world. I've learned that there are some things I do not understand, certain things in the Bible I don't understand. And I leave that to God."[91]

Parochialism posed a special danger: "I used to think that if a person hadn't experienced what I had experienced, he wasn't a believer. It was my own ignorance." But things changed as he found "the opportunity to fellowship with people in other communities."[92] If Graham's efforts to avoid passing judgments grew as he did, so did his awareness of the cultural boundaries of his natal religious world.

Then, too, Graham lacerated himself for the sin of pride. That one was hard to figure. Flashes of vanity, yes, but pride seemed hardly apt. Graham insisted more often than anyone could count that his success baffled no one more than himself. Why did the Lord choose him? Graham had no clue. All he could do was accept the assignment.[93] Graham spoke often of his fear of somehow stumbling and failing to live up to the assignment. The anxiety seemed constant.[94]

Yet something else played a role, and that was Graham's refusal to diminish the magnitude of his accomplishments. They were real. And they produced awe, precisely because they represented God's work through him. To say otherwise would have insulted the work that the Lord had given him. Graham mastered the art of separating the task from the person charged with the task. From time to time, the ceaseless river of accolades caused him to lose his balance. But not for long. The historian David Aikman spoke for multitudes when he judged that the preacher's achievement lay not in how he handled adversity but in how he handled success.[95]

Graham and American Evangelicalism

Perspective is crucial. Graham did not build the edifice of modern evangelicalism. The key structures had been put in place, brick by brick, for three centuries. And countless hands had contributed every step of the way. Yet Graham's influence on the architecture of the structure proved so profound that many Americans effectively identified him with it. George Marsden once said that an evangelical could be defined as "anyone who likes Billy Graham."[96] The line was tongue in cheek, of course, but it bore an element of truth, especially if measured by public perceptions.

The story started at home, with the multiple ways Graham helped shape the movement's internal culture. For one thing, he prompted evangelicals to shift their focus from the venial sins of cussing, smoking, drinking, dancing, and premarital sex to the mortal sins of greed, lust, racism, and, above all, faithlessness. Which is to say, he prompted evangelicals to shift their focus from moral misdemeanors to moral felonies.[97] That did not mean that he started out that way. Nor did it mean that he ever winked at the misdemeanors, or got entirely beyond preaching about them himself. But it did mean that he helped evangelicals establish a sense of scale. In a closely related move, Graham also alerted evangelicals to the difference between core and peripheral doctrines. Not every doctrinal difference was worth going to the mat for. He brought many of them to appreciate, in other words, the philosopher William James's dictum: "The art of wisdom is the art of knowing what to overlook." Or at least, gaining a mature sense of which doctrines should—and should not—qualify as a test of fellowship.

Then, too, Graham helped evangelicals see that justice for everyone, regardless of social location, was not peripheral but central to evangelicals' affirmations and obligations. He did not always lead the way as boldly as he might have done, even by his own lights, but he was rarely very far behind the movement's shock troops, and far ahead of the great majority of his constituents. To be sure, Graham never retreated one inch from his conviction that enduring social change started with changed hearts. But if changed hands did not follow, hearts needed to go back into the shop for more work.

The preacher helped his co-workers both deploy and regulate their entrepreneurial impulses. He understood clearly what evangelists before him had understood more or less clearly: that communication tools were a wondrously adaptable medium. Media of every sort—radio, television, print, movies, Internet, landlines, contemporary music, among others—could be put to use for the Lord's work. Along those lines, Graham helped pry evangelicals loose from their venerable commitment to the *King James Version* of the Bible and try other ones, including, most notably, Kenneth Taylor's vernacular translation *The Living Bible*. Evangelicals had always been good at knowing what to do next. They had not always been good at knowing what *not* to do next, however. Sometimes they frittered away their energies on the temporary and the spectacular. Graham helped them calculate the long-term cost/benefit ratios.

Graham offered evangelicals more than vicarious status in the larger world. He taught them how to gain it themselves by learning to speak in wider and wider circles. If he first preached to Southern fundamentalists like himself, over time his voice echoed farther and farther. By the late 1940s he seemed to be addressing all evangelical Protestants, by the mid-1950s all Protestants, by the 1960s all Christians, by the 1970s and 1980s all faiths, and no faiths, seeking to bring about a safe, more humane world. To be sure, to the end of his career, he spoke as an exclusivist Christian, but at the same time he spoke to everyone, everywhere. In the process, he raised evangelicals from being both a marginal and a marginalized subculture to something closer to a parallel culture, with their eyes fixed on the distant horizon. If a surprising number of second- and third-generation post–World War II evangelicals left their religious ghettos and entered the "halls of power" in the outside world, Graham bore a measure of the credit.[98]

And then Graham, more than any one person, reshaped the waterways of American Protestantism.[99] First, he guided the separation of the broad evangelical river of the nineteenth century into two distinct substreams: new evangelical and fundamentalist. Second, he helped transform the new evangelical substream (in both its denominational and its cooperative forms) into a coherent and powerful stream in itself, running alongside the third stream of mainline Protestantism.

Graham and American Culture

When Graham gazed out on the Great Smoky Mountains from his hilltop home in North Carolina, he did not see distinct groups of potential listeners. He sought, rather, to address all Americans. Though his reach exceeded his grasp, the hope to embrace everyone, without exception, remained intact to the end of his active career. He drew on a sacred text he judged timeless and universal in order to proclaim a message he also judged timeless and universal.

In one sense that was exactly what he had been doing ever since he started preaching as an adolescent in the jails and mobile-home parks around Tampa, Florida. With the *Hour of Decision*, launched in November 1950, and reaching most parts of the country by the end of the year, Graham spoke as if every person in the nation might actually be listening. He framed his words in terms of national—actually international—crises that loomed large over every city, hamlet, and farmhouse. His goal of speaking to everyone never changed. The real or perceived consensus politics of the 1950s crumbled into identity politics in the 1960s and beyond. But when it came to the gospel message, Graham would have no part of it. He intended to preach for everyone.

The result confounded critics and admirers alike, for the "wrong" sort of people kept coming to Graham's meetings and tossing their support behind his work. Or at least they lined up alongside him as a friend of the larger good he was trying to achieve. The list included figures as (dramatically) different as Muhammad Ali, A. R. Bernard, Tony Blair, Bono, George H. W. Bush, Jimmy Carter, Eldridge Cleaver, Bill Clinton, Charlie Daniels, Bill Gaither, Kathie Lee Gifford, Al Gore, Nathan Hatch, Mark Hatfield, Jesse Helms, Jerome Hines, Larry King, Henry Kissinger, Cheryl Ladd, John

Lewis, Barack Obama, Luis Palau, Sally Quinn, Dan Rather, Ricky Skaggs, Donald Trump, Jim Wallis, Rick Warren, Louis Zamperini, and Efrem Zimbalist, Jr. The list could go on for pages.[100]

Graham offered a definably evangelical Protestant Christian message at the core, of course, but he also offered, in a nonjudgmental way, a set of consensual standards millions of Americans could embrace. His values constituted a polestar, a moral compass. Graham made traditional values—and not just evangelical ones—respectable, not laughable, as Archie Bunker fans might have it. Not a few Jews, too, admired his ability to combine evangelism with inclusivism and just leave the rest to God.[101] He reminded Americans everywhere that a good time was different from a good life.[102]

In the process, Graham enlarged the horizons of the possible.[103] Ordinary folks everywhere lived his breadth of vision, even if they did not enjoy his breadth of social connections. We really can be better people, he said, in so many ways. We really do possess the ability to choose the right. All we need is the will to do so. "A leader is a dealer in hope," Napoleon Bonaparte had observed generations before Graham's birth.[104] His words prefigured the preacher's vision. As much as anyone, and more than most other religious leaders of his time, he helped millions of everyday folks to be American, Christian, and modern all at once.

But above all, Graham's achievement for all Americans, his supporters and otherwise, lay in the offer of a second chance. Things had not always been that way. For many evangelicals, the new birth—being born again—bore an invidious edge: either you are in or you are out, either on the bus or off the bus. And for the early Graham, too. When the thirty-one-year-old evangelist asked President Truman about his "religious background and leanings," Truman responded: "I try to live by the Sermon on the Mount and the Golden Rule." Not good enough. "It takes more than that, Mr. President. It's faith in Christ and His death on the Cross that you need."[105] But for the mature Graham and, evidence suggests, for millions of his listeners, the new birth served less a way of telling some people that they were off the bus than a persuasive way of inviting "all aboard." Everyone.

So it was that the penultimate paragraph of his signature coffee-table photo book would ask, "How many times have you wished you could start over again with a clean slate—with a new life?" An ancient question for which there was a modern answer: "Allow . . . Christ to give you a brand-new start."[106] In the warm summer of 2005, in his last American crusade, in Flushing Meadows, New York—not many miles away from Madison Square Garden, the site of what may have been, way back in 1957, the most important outing of his life—"the years fell away and his voice hit the old familiar notes." A *Newsweek* editor heard the aging preacher say it one more time: "You must be born again. . . . Jesus said it's possible to start life all over again."[107]

Here Graham fit into a great tradition of reform. Regardless of differing political judgments about the most effective way to achieve it, the goal of a second chance remained as persistent as it was common. The aspiration stretched back to the beginnings of the Republic itself. "We have it in our power," declared Thomas Paine in 1776, "to begin the world over again." So it was that "New Deal," "Fair Deal," "New Frontier," "Great Society," "Morning in America," "Compassionate Conservatism," "Kinder, Gentler Nation," and "Change We Can Believe In" became the language of all Americans, not just Graham supporters. The mature preacher's growing social vision grew from a conviction that all people deserved another opportunity. That ideal differed from conservative notions of can-do entrepreneurialism as well as with liberal notions of social engineering. Rather, it simply said that Americans should receive a chance to make more of themselves than their genes and circumstances alone might dictate.

Louis Zamperini may have been the most famous inquirer or, as far as anyone could tell, convert of Graham's crusades. A record-setting high school, college, and Olympic track star, he joined the Army Air Corps in 1941 and became a B-24 bombardier. In May 1943 Zamperini's plane crashed into the Pacific, leaving him to endure forty-seven days on a life raft, fighting hunger, thirst, and sharks. The Japanese navy finally picked him up (rescued was hardly the word). Zamperini endured "unspeakable horrors" for two years in Japanese prisoner-of-war camps.[108]

When he returned to his home in Southern California at the end of the war, Zamperini's life unraveled, as he fell into a life of drinking and partying. His marriage was coming apart too. In October 1949 Zamperini's wife, Cynthia, persuaded him to go with her to the Graham revival, which was beginning to pick up speed, in the mammoth circus tent in downtown Los Angeles. Zamperini resisted. His memories of revivalists in his youth evoked images of holy-roller charlatans. Besides, he already was a Christian. He had believed in Christ since he was a kid. But to appease Cynthia, he went. Graham came across as a "clean-cut, all-American athletic type," in control of himself and his message. Zamperini found that just believing in Christ was not enough. The preacher called for a fundamental transformation from the ground up, from the inside out. "You must be born again." The second night, Zamperini walked the sawdust.[109]

The first sign of the change, Zamperini remembered, was going home and tossing out the booze, the cigarettes, and "a secret stash of girlie magazines." The second sign was a decision to tell others what had happened to him. And not just tell, but act. Zamperini returned to Japan as a Christian missionary, speaking of forgiveness. He went into real estate development, founded Victory Boys Camps for wayward boys, and maintained a six-decade ministry as a highly sought Christian inspirational speaker. When Zamperini died in 2014, his Pulitzer Prize–winning biographer, Laura Hillenbrand, captured his life with simple elegance: he was "the grandest, most buoyant, most generous soul I ever knew."[110]

Billy Graham, too, charted the path of his own life by the light of a second chance. "I've come to see in deeper ways some of the implications of my faith and of the message I've been proclaiming," he wrote in 1983, as he reflected on his call in Moscow the previous year for a "disarmament race." In Moscow he had said: "We as nations and as individuals need to repent over our past failures, the failure to accept each other, the failure to be concerned about the needs of the poor and starving of the world, the failure to place top priority on peace instead of war." But that perspective had taken time to mature. "I am a man who is still in process," the preacher quietly reflected.[111] Graham's pilgrimage toward a profounder understanding of the Christian faith testified to what it meant to receive the gift of another opportunity, another occasion to take a look and rethink one's deepest commitments. Maybe even a chance to redo the rest of one's life. Graham's legacy included the conviction that things old and broken really could become new and whole.

EPILOGUE

The road wound up and up the mountain, through laurel and rhododendron groves, past a great iron gate, finally spilling onto a graveled ridge with a spectacular view of the southern Appalachians. A German shepherd, snoozing on the driveway, lifted a wary eye. I felt unexpected anxiety. It was difficult to spend three summers and a sabbatical researching a man's life and then meet him in person. For a moment, before getting out of the car, I thought this was a bad idea—a *really* bad idea. I should go back to the quiet safety of my office in the university library. My wife, Katherine, safely buckled into the passenger seat beside me, felt the same way. Several months earlier she had given up idyllic days of retirement to pore through musty boxes of letters to the preacher. Our aim now was not to interview Mr. Graham in any formal way. He was nearly ninety, and the days of formal interviews were long past. Rather, we hoped only to meet the legend whose life and personality fill the pages of this book.[1]

The countless photographs we had seen of the spacious log home atop a mountain near the historic Presbyterian village of Montreat, North Carolina, came to life. Entering through the back door, as all visitors do, we were escorted by two nurses into a country kitchen, graced with a great stone fireplace and antique ironware, then down a long hallway festooned with family photos and mementos of world travel, and finally into a surprisingly small and cozy study. Mr. Graham was sitting in an easy chair. The flowing white hair and sky blue eyes immediately captured our attention. He stood with difficulty, first to shake Katherine's hand—a Southern gentleman to the end—and then mine. We expressed condolences about Ruth Bell Graham, his wife of sixty-three years, who had died several weeks earlier. Katherine, always better at those things than I was, chatted with him about his health and our beloved state of North Carolina. Mr. Graham said our town of Chapel Hill was one of his favorites. Though the once-commanding baritone had softened to a little more than a whisper, the Carolina drawl was still unmistakably that of Billy Graham.

After a few minutes, Mr. Graham's special assistant, standing nearby, said, "Billy, Grant is writing a book about you." Obviously puzzled, Mr. Graham responded, "Why? Why would you want to do that?" Taken aback, I finally mumbled, "Well, you have done some important things." Without hesitation, he said, "No. The Lord has done some important things through me." It was hard to know where to go from there. Though I had determined not to get into substantive matters, I could not help myself. I asked about Chattanooga. I said there is some disagreement among historians about whether you pulled down the ropes in Jackson, Mississippi, in 1952, or in Chattanooga, Tennessee, in 1953. Again without hesitation, he said, firmly, "Chattanooga. I remember it well. I walked out in the auditorium and pulled the ropes down. Some people did not like that."

Now rolling, I asked Mr. Graham if he remembered his trip to the peace conference in Moscow in 1982. The question triggered memories of his friendship with Mikhail Gorbachev, and then of his private talk with Winston Churchill back in the summer of 1954. Abruptly he directed the conversation back to Katherine, followed by a good deal of unexpected bantering. "What do you do, Katherine?" When she said she was a retired middle school guidance counselor, he asked how she liked retirement. He asked about our children and grandchildren and talked about his children and grandchildren and great-grandchildren, allowing that he had "about thirty" great-grandchildren.

Throughout the visit, Mr. Graham's wit sparkled. He wondered how we managed to live in Chapel Hill—the home of the University of North Carolina—with me teaching at Duke. With a wink he demanded, what happens in basketball season? He mentioned his Parkinson's disease.[2] "You know what happens when you get Parkinson's? Your handwriting gets illegible and your sermons longer." The conversation drifted to a book his nephew Kevin Ford was writing about how to avoid church conflict. "Kevin has a lot to write about," he grinned. Striking up a conversation with a watchful young nurse in the corner, I asked about her nursing background. She said she had gone to Duke School of Nursing. When I asked why not Carolina, Mr. Graham intervened: "Because Duke is easier to pronounce." And so it went.

A second visit followed in 2009. (A third one followed in 2011 and a fourth and final one a few weeks before his ninety-fifth birthday.) We found Mr. Graham frailer. He remembered us and invited us to have a seat. He noted that his vision had deteriorated, he could no longer read, and clearly he did not hear very well, either. But the flowing white hair and unmistakable rolling baritone remained the same. "What brings you to Montreat?" At first I thought he was spoofing, but I quickly realized that the question was genuine. It reflected the utter unpretentiousness so many other visitors had experienced and written about. He asked how the book was coming along. He demanded, with mock sternness, "How many chapters do you have?"

We told Mr. Graham that in the course of researching a work on his place in American history, we had discovered a cache of answered but long-forgotten letters that young children had posted to him in the early 1970s. We said that the letters brimmed with unintentional humor, comments about money, requests for stickers, observations on pets, theological questions about things great and small, and, above all, expressions of love and gratitude. We mentioned how most adults addressed him as Dr. Graham but children often called him Billy. He liked that. He wished everyone would call him Billy. "I don't have a doctorate, you know." He laughed heartily when we told him of the child who wrote that his Cocker Spaniel had become a Christian. And when we told him about another child who sent a dime, then added, "That's all I have. Get used to it." Mr. Graham said the children's letters touched his heart.

The time passed quickly as we rummaged over many topics. He chatted about good friends, now gone—Hank [Henry] Luce, David Frost, and Walter Cronkite, among others. We praised the handsomeness of the dog outside, and told him about our bulldog, and that opened a floodgate. A good deal of the conversation revolved around dogs, including his beloved Rottweiler mix, China, who did not get along all that well with the German shepherd. A sampler hung on the wall next to his chair. It said only, "Gal. 6:14." ["But God forbid that I should glory, save in the cross of our Lord Jesus Christ, by whom the world is crucified unto me, and I unto the world.] When I asked about the sampler and the Scripture passage, he said he wanted to preach one more time, on that passage. "It was [Charles] Spurgeon's favorite," he added, evidently for the benefit of a church historian.

An hour slipped by, he was tiring, and we stood to leave. Mr. Graham asked us not to go so soon. "You just got here." Remembering that I did, after all, teach in a divinity school, I offered to pray with him. He said, "I would like that very much," and extended his hand. Taking that glass-frail hand, which had gestured before more than two hundred million people in person, and hundreds of millions more on television, did not inspire much eloquence in me. But it did inspire an indelible memory. Leaving, Mr. Graham made us promise to "drop by" any time we were "in the neighborhood." The long drive back down the mountain was a quiet one. I knew it would take a while to process.

By the end of the four-hour drive home, five impressions stood out with clarity. The first pertained to something physical: the voice. Though Graham actually spoke very softly, his voice resonated. Historians have rightly invested considerable effort analyzing Graham's theology as well as his preaching style. Yet close up, it seemed evident that a lot of Graham's appeal rested in something as simple yet mysterious as the human voice. The second impression pertained to the wit—much of it self-deprecating—and his delight in bantering. In Mr. Graham's public performances, canned jokes at the outset of the sermons abounded, and the audiences clearly loved them. But wit was another matter. It did not come through very well on radio or television, and certainly not in the prose. But in person it bespoke a lightness of touch. In ineluctable ways it facilitated the expression of the charisma. The third impression centered on Mr. Graham's down-home, "awww shucks" style of self-presentation. I knew he had an uptown side too, but conversing one-on-one left little doubt that the default mode ran closer to the dairy farm than to the White House.

A fourth impression was the humility that virtually all visitors observed year after year. At times in Graham's long career, especially in his comfortable Establishment days, the humility got tied up with self-promotion. Exactly how they wound together defied easy untangling. Yet being with the man in person confirmed that humility—deep, authentic, the real thing—constituted the core of his identity. We were not the first to experience it.

And finally there was the preacher's faith. It commandeered my memory bank. It presented itself as at once the least and the most palpable of things, elusive yet everywhere. He did not wear it on his sleeve, as if he wanted to make sure we saw it. Rather, it seemed simply to bubble up. When he spoke quietly of how the Lord had chosen to use him, and he had no idea why, we knew it was not an act. He really believed it.

Retrospect and Prospect

Billy Graham enjoyed rare influence, but he was not alone. The ability to appropriate and deploy the trends of the age marked the careers and ministries of Martin Luther King, Jr., and of Pope John Paul II too. Each was very different from the other, yet each saw the world clearly and tried to change it dramatically. All three looked outside their own lives to see how they could help, and all three looked ahead of their lives to see how they could lead. They set in motion forces that came to fruition long after their careers had ended. All three sowed winter wheat. In the purportedly secular second half of the twentieth century, it is significant that three clergymen provided three of the most resonant voices Americans still heard. King, John Paul, and Graham spoke, respectively, of justice, solidarity, and transformation. Other voices gained an audience too, but those three ranked among the handful that scores—possibly hundreds—of millions of Americans took to heart, decade after decade. They constituted a touchstone for the nation's ideals.

This book started with three closely related yet distinct questions. The first was about Graham himself. How did he become "the least colorful and most powerful preacher in America"?[3] The second and more important one was about Graham and American religion. How did he help expand traditional evangelical rhetoric into the moral vocabulary that millions of Americans used to make sense of both their private and their public experiences? The third and most important one was about Graham and the great gulf streams of the nation's recent history. How did he help shape the consciousness of the culture that both created him and that he helped create?

I proposed one answer for all three questions. From first to last, Graham displayed an uncanny ability to adopt trends in the wider culture and then use them for his evangelistic and moral-reform purposes. If this thesis is right, or at least partly right, it helps explain Graham's rise in the evangelical world, evangelicalism's rise as a powerful force in American religion, and religion's rise as a powerful force in recent American history.

To say that Graham possessed an uncanny ability to adopt trends in the wider culture and then use them for his evangelistic and moral-reform purposes is another way of saying that he possessed an uncanny ability to speak both *for* and *to* the times. Speaking for required him to communicate in a register his listeners could hear. He legitimated their social location by guaranteeing that their values would count. He represented their points of view in mass media and in public forums. In all of this Graham was much like America itself: outgoing, pragmatic, visionary, and not terribly worried about subtleties. He embodied, as a *Newsweek* journalist said of Ronald Reagan, "America as it imagined itself to be—the bearer of the traditional Main Street values of family and neighborhood, of thrift, industry and charity."[4] He represented Plymouth Rock, *Life* magazine, and Little League baseball. Graham's ideals were those of average Americans.[5]

Yet the plain fact that Graham spoke for Heartland Americans should not obscure the more important fact that he spoke to them as well. He helped shape their consciousness. He influenced how they perceived their world, how they made sense of it, and then how they carried out those perceptions and interpretations in the long second half of the century. Speaking to Americans meant that he challenged them to live up to their self-professed values of biblical equality, moral integrity, and social compassion. It also meant hearts freed from dehumanizing lust, greed, hatred, and racism. The preacher from North Carolina touched their memories and called them to be the kind of people they knew they ought to be. Often they failed, and sometimes he did too, but perfection was never the point.

NOTE ON THE SOURCES

The literature by and about Billy Graham is vast. Though a comprehensive bibliography does not exist, the Billy Graham Center Archives (BGCA), Billy Graham Center, Wheaton College, Wheaton, Illinois, house thousands of primary and secondary documents, along with thousands of sermon notes. See the online catalog at http://www.wheaton.edu/bgc/archives/archhp1 .html, especially the tabs for "Billy Graham," "Searchable Online Data Base," and "Collections." The website also contains links to valuable summaries of aspects of Graham's career. The BGCA excludes Graham's personal papers, which are not available to researchers until twenty-five years after his death. Graham's autobiography, *Just As I Am: The Autobiography of Billy Graham* (San Francisco: HarperSanFrancisco; Grand Rapids, MI: Zondervan, 1997), revised and updated in 2007, certainly is ample enough, yet it remains curiously nonrevealing. More helpful are an early autobiographical essay, "I Was Born Again," *American Weekly*, January 16, 1955; and a three-part autobiographical essay, "Billy Graham's Own Story: 'God Is My Witness,'" *McCall's*, April, May, and June 1964. Graham's thirty-two books, published between 1947 and 2013, are mostly theological, sermonic, and devotional, but many of them contain autobiographical asides. For a nearly complete list with publication dates, see the Billy Graham Evangelistic Association's (BGEA) website, http://billygraham.org/about/biographies/billy -graham. The most autobiographical of the theological works is Billy Graham, *Nearing Home: Life, Faith, and Finishing Well* (Nashville: Thomas Nelson, 2011). Russ Busby, *Billy Graham, God's Ambassador: A Lifelong Mission of Giving Hope to the World* (Alexandria, VA: Time-Life Books, 1999), offers an authorized/official recounting of Graham's life, including scores of photographs. Ken Garfield, *Billy Graham: A Life in Pictures* (Chicago: Triumph Books, 2013), parallels and updates Busby's work, with arresting photographs and a useful and detailed narrative of Graham's life.

Graham has captured the attention of more than a score of biographers, ranging from hagiographic to sharply critical. George Burnham and Lee Fisher, *Billy Graham: Man of God*, 3rd ed. (Westchester, IL: Good News Publishers, no date), and Cecil Bothwell, *The Prince of War: Billy Graham's*

Crusade for a Wholly Christian Empire (Asheville, NC: Brave Ulysses Books, 2007), represent the extremes of the genre. By far the finest and most comprehensive biography is William Martin, *A Prophet with Honor: The Billy Graham Story* (New York: W. Morrow, 1991). An updated edition is scheduled for imminent release from Zondervan. Martin also has written a children's version: William Martin, *Prophet with Honor* (Grand Rapids, MI: Zonderkidz, 2013). Marshall Frady, *Billy Graham, a Parable of American Righteousness* (Boston: Little, Brown, 1979), is overwritten and tendentious yet contains perceptive insights into Graham's relation to American culture. David Aikman, *Billy Graham: His Life and Influence* (Nashville: Thomas Nelson, 2007), constitutes the best short biography, enhanced by its fluid prose and even-handedness. Stanley High, *Billy Graham: The Personal Story of the Man, His Message, and His Mission* (New York: McGraw-Hill, 1956), though consistently admiring, shrewdly captures ingredients of the early Graham's charisma. John Pollock's authorized book *The Billy Graham Story,* rev. ed. ([1985] Grand Rapids, MI: Zondervan, 2003), offers information, based on long association with the Graham family and organization, not available elsewhere. Roger A. Bruns, *Billy Graham: A Biography* (Westport, CT: Greenwood Press, 2004), presents a concise, readable overview. William McLoughlin, *Billy Graham, Revivalist in a Secular Age* (Ronald Press, 1960), was the first scholarly biography. It projects a negative profile but contains a detailed analysis of the inner workings of the BGEA. Though dated, the best short article-length biographical overview still is William Martin, "Fifty Years with Billy," *Christianity Today*, November 13, 1995.

The monographic literature about Graham (including more than a score of M.A. theses and Ph.D. dissertations) is extensive. Four masterful treatments of aspects of his career are Andrew S. Finstuen, *Original Sin and Everyday Protestants: The Theology of Reinhold Niebuhr, Billy Graham, and Paul Tillich in an Age of Anxiety* (Chapel Hill: University of North Carolina Press, 2009); Nancy Gibbs and Michael Duffy, *The Preacher and the Presidents: Billy Graham in the White House* (New York: Center Street, 2007); Steven P. Miller, *Billy Graham and the Rise of the Republican South* (Philadelphia: University of Pennsylvania Press, 2009); and Garth Rosell, *The Surprising Work of God: Harold John Ockenga, Billy Graham, and the Rebirth of Evangelicalism* (Grand Rapids, MI: Baker Academic, 2008). Harold Myra and Marshall Shelley, *The Leadership Secrets of Billy Graham* (Grand Rapids, MI: Zondervan, 2005), provides a perceptive analysis of Graham's administrative style, an important yet rarely addressed subject.

Journal articles and book chapters about Graham are too numerous to list, but two articles and two book chapters merit special notice: David Aikman, "Billy Graham—Salvation," in David Aikman, *Great Souls: Six Who Changed the Century* (Lanham, MD: Lexington Books, 2003), ch. 1; Peter J. Boyer, "The Big Tent: Billy Graham, Franklin Graham, and the Transformation of American Evangelicalism," *New Yorker*, August 22, 2005, available at http://www.newyorker.com/archive/2005/08/22/050822fa_fact_boyer?cur rentPage=all; Larry Eskridge, "'One Way': Billy Graham, the Jesus Generation, and the Idea of an Evangelical Youth Culture," *Church History* 67, no. 1 (1998): 83–106, doi:10.2307/3170772; and Mark A. Noll, *American Evangelical Christianity: An Introduction* (Malden, MA: Blackwell, 2001), ch. 3, "The Significance of Billy Graham." I tried out some of the ideas in this book in Grant Wacker, "Billy Graham's America," *Church History* 78, no. 3 (2009): 489–511. Essays on unexplored or underexplored dimensions of Graham's career will appear in *The Worlds of Billy Graham*, ed. Andrew S. Finstuen, Anne Blue Wills, and Grant Wacker, forthcoming.

Anthologies of personal reminiscences about Graham are useful if used with discrimination. Amy Newmark, Steve Posner, and A. Larry Ross, eds., *Chicken Soup for the Soul: Billy Graham & Me: 101 Inspiring Personal Stories from Presidents, Pastors, Performers, and Other People Who Know Him Well* (Cos Cob, CT: Chicken Soup for the Soul Publishing, 2013), is revealing because of the wide range of personalities who contributed, including some whose initial view of Graham was unfavorable. Collections of Graham's observations about a variety of topics are helpful too. One of the best for the range of subjects addressed and the carefulness of the documentation is Bill Adler, compiler, *The Wit and Wisdom of Billy Graham* (New York: Random House, 2007).

ABBREVIATIONS

BGCA Billy Graham Center Archives, 500 College Ave., Wheaton, IL

BGCA, Collection 1: Papers of Willis Graham Haymaker

BGCA, Collection 12: Records of BGEA Team Office: Executive Assistant for Team Activities

BGCA, Collection 15: Papers of William Franklin Jr. "Billy" Graham

BGCA, Collection 16: Records of BGEA Team Office: Crusade Procedure Books

BGCA, Collection 17: BGEA Crusade Activities

BGCA, Collection 19: Papers of Robert O. Ferm

BGCA, Collection 24: Records of Press Conferences

BGCA, Collection 26: Audio Tapes

BGCA, Collection 74: William Franklin Graham, Jr. "Billy," Ephemera

BGCA, Collection 141: Oral History Project

BGCA, Collection 191: Records of the *Hour of Decision* Radio Program

BGCA, Collection 345: Records of the Media Office

BGCA, Collection 360: Clippings File

NOTES

PROLOGUE

1 Michael Kazin, *A Godly Hero: The Life of William Jennings Bryan* (New York: Knopf, 2006), xx, and quoting Moses Hadas, "Introduction," *Greek Drama,* ed. Hadas (New York, 1965), 4.

INTRODUCTION

1 Billy Graham, *Just As I Am: The Autobiography of Billy Graham* (San Francisco: HarperSan-Francisco; Grand Rapids, MI: Zondervan, 1997).

2 I have based the following biographical overview on the well-known autobiographical and biographical texts listed in the Note on the Sources, especially Graham (1997, 2007), Aikman (2007), Frady (1979), Martin (1991), and Gibbs and Duffy (2007), as well as on my reading in readily available sources such as those posted on the website of the Billy Graham Center Archives (BGCA). I have not tried to document items of common knowledge about Graham. I have, however, provided citations for information that is not common knowledge or that represents my point of view in a particular way.

3 Reports about the date of Graham's pilgrimage down the aisle vary. Most, including his own, place it somewhere in the year after he turned sixteen. See, for example, Billy Graham, *Just As I Am: The Autobiography of Billy Graham*, rev. and updated 10th anniv. ed. (New York: HarperOne; Grand Rapids, MI: Zondervan, 2007), 25; and Billy Graham, "Billy Graham's Own Story: 'God Is My Witness,'" *McCall's,* April 1964, 196. Graham's close friend Grady Wilson said Graham was nearly seventeen. Grady Wilson, *Billy Graham as a Teen-Ager* (Wheaton, IL: Miracle Books, 1957), 11. I base the date of November 1, 1934, on a photocopy of a decision card he filled out that night, in my possession.

4 Graham, "Billy Graham's Own Story," April, 198.

5 Billy Graham, "I Was Born Again," *American Weekly,* January 16, 1955, 7.

6 Though commonly regarded as a CMA congregation, the Tab did not appear on the official list of CMA churches. I owe this information to Bob Shuster.

7 Edith Blumhofer, "Singing to Save: The Signature Sound of the Graham Crusades," in *The Worlds of Billy Graham,* ed. Andrew S. Finstuen, Anne Blue Wills, and Grant Wacker, forthcoming.

8 Russ Busby, *Billy Graham, God's Ambassador: A Lifelong Mission of Giving Hope to the World* (Alexandria, VA: Time-Life Books, 1999), 40.

9 Bob Shuster, "'I Learned to Look Straight at Them': The Apprenticeship of Billy Graham, 1937–1949," revised September 2013, available at http://www2.wheaton.edu/bgc/archives/Papers/BG3749/BG3749.html.

10 Blumhofer, "Singing to Save." Within the Billy Graham Evangelistic Association (BGEA), George M. Wilson, former business manager of Northwestern Schools and business manager of the newly formed BGEA, commonly ranked as a member of the Team. Sometimes Tedd Smith, the crusade pianist, also was included. However, for the broader public the platform Team of Graham, Shea, and Barrows remained most visible.

11 Charles Templeton, *Farewell to God: My Reasons for Rejecting the Christian Faith* (Toronto: McClelland and Stewart, 1996), 17–18; Charles Templeton, "Inside Evangelism: Touring with Youth for Christ and Billy Graham," in *Charles Templeton: An Anecdotal Memoir* (Toronto: McClelland and Stewart, 1983), available at www.templetons.com/charles/memoir/evang-graham.html.

12 Templeton, *Charles Templeton: An Anecdotal Memoir.*

13 By mainline Protestant—or mainline—I mean members of the theological center/left, and socially acculturated denominations, typically including Congregationalists, Disciples, Episcopalians, Lutherans, Methodists, (Northern) Baptists, and (Northern) Presbyterians. Needless to say this is an extremely rough definition of a complex social-cultural-religious tradition. The literature is extensive, but three books offer superb entry into it: Elesha J. Coffman, *The Christian Century and the Rise of the Protestant Mainline* (New York: Oxford University Press, 2013); David A. Hollinger, *After Cloven Tongues of Fire: Protestant Liberalism in Modern American History* (Princeton, NJ: Princeton University Press, 2013); and William R. Hutchison, ed., *Between the Times: The Travail of the Protestant Establishment in America, 1900–1960* (New York: Cambridge University Press, 1989).

14 In Chapter 7, I describe the demographic, social, and cultural characteristics of Graham's supporters, who might be called, very loosely, Heartland or Middle or average Americans. I take the concept of Heartland from William Martin, *A Prophet with Honor: The Billy Graham Story* (New York: W. Morrow, 1991), 309; Elizabeth Kaye, "Billy Graham Rises," *George,* December 1996, 140; Nancy Gibbs and Michael Duffy, *The Preacher and the Presidents: Billy Graham in the White House* (New York: Center Street, 2007), 161; Robert Wuthnow, *Red State Religion: Faith and Politics in America's Heartland* (Princeton, NJ: Princeton University Press, 2012), esp. Preface and 354–371; Lowell D. Streiker and Gerald S. Strober, *Religion and the New Majority: Billy Graham, Middle America, and the Politics of the 70s* (New York: Association Press, 1972), 23, 39, 78–81.

15 With the exception of New York in 1957 (attendance: 2.4 million), all of Graham's largest crusades were held overseas: London, 1954, 2 million; Scotland, 1955, 2.6 million; Australia and New Zealand, 1959, 3.4 million; and Seoul, South Korea, 1973, 3.2 million—including 1.1 million in attendance at the final service alone. Attendance at Graham's 1962 Greater Chicago crusade is listed at 704,900, and the 1963 Los Angeles crusade is given as 910,445. I owe this information to Elesha Coffman, who calculated it from http://www2.wheaton.edu/bgc/archives/bgeachro/bgeachron02.htm.

16 Busby, *Billy Graham: God's Ambassador,* 49.

17 William A. Doyle, "Bringing in the Sheaves: The Big (and Closely Guarded) Business of Billy Graham . . . ," *Corporate Report,* June 1977, 64.

18 According to one auditing firm, in the mid-1970s the BGEA ran on an overhead of 6.5 percent, compared with 8 percent for the Red Cross. Gerald S. Strober, *Graham: A Day in Billy's Life* (Garden City, NY: Doubleday, 1976), 100.

19 Graham and most historians place the event in Chattanooga in March 1953. There is some evidence, however, that it might have taken place in Jackson, Mississippi, the previous year. I discuss this question in Chapter 6. Graham, *Just As I Am,* 1997, 426.

20 Billy Graham to Richard Nixon, December 26, 1973, box 3, folder 7, Collection 74, BGCA.

21 Kempton, *New York Post,* September 9, 1960, quoted in Gibbs and Duffy, *The Preacher and the Presidents,* 92.

22 Regarding Franklin Graham, see the data quoted and cited in Grant Wacker, "Billy Graham's America," *Church History* 78, no. 3 (2009): 25, and note 38.

23 "Select Chronology Listing of Events," BGCA, http://www2.wheaton.edu/bgc/archives/bgeachro/bgeachron02.htm. This tabulation includes two crusades in Canada.

24 See, for example, Sally Quinn, "Sins of the Son: Sad Treatment for Billy Graham," *Washington Post,* July 1, 2013; William Martin, A. Larry Ross, and Michael Hamilton, "Has Billy Graham Suddenly Turned Political?" *Christianity Today,* October 19, 2012, available at http://www.christianitytoday.com/ct/2012/october-web-only/billy-graham-political-statements-history.html; "Franklin Graham's New Ally against Gays," Editorial, *Charlotte Observer,* March 20, 2014; Peter St. Onge "A Conservative Party for Rev. Billy Graham," *Charlotte Observer,* November 9, 2013; Steve Knight, "Billy Graham Is Not an Anti-Gay Bigot," *Huffington Post,* July 31, 2012, available at http://www.huffingtonpost.com/steve-knight/billy-graham-is-not-an-anti-gay-bigot_b_1716448.html. In contrast, Franklin Graham argues that his controversial views represent those his father would take if he were younger. See, for example, Tim Funk, "Franklin Graham: I'm Speaking Out Like My Father Did," *Charlotte Observer* online, March 26, 2014, available at http://www.charlotteobserver.com/2014/03/25/4793883/graham-im-speaking-out-like-my.html.

25 James T. Fisher, "American Religion since 1945," in *A Companion to Post–1945 America,* ed. Jean-Christophe Agnew and Roy Rosenzweig (Malden, MA: Blackwell, 2006), 44–63;

Patrick Allitt, *Religion in America since 1945: A History* (New York: Columbia University Press, 2003); James David Hudnut-Beumler, *Looking for God in the Suburbs: The Religion of the American Dream and Its Critics, 1945–1965* (New Brunswick, NJ: Rutgers University Press, 1994); George M. Marsden, *The Twilight of the American Enlightenment: The 1950s and the Crisis of Liberal Belief* (New York: Basic Books, 2014).

26 D. W. Bebbington, *Evangelicalism in Modern Britain: A History of the 1730s to the 1980s* (Boston: Allen and Unwin, 1989); Mark A. Noll, *The Rise of Evangelicalism: The Age of Edwards, Whitefield and the Wesleys* (Nottingham: Inter-Varsity Press, 2004).

27 The historical literature about the evangelical movement in America is vast. Works (with helpful bibliographies) that offer concise entries into the field include: Darren Dochuk, "Evangelicalism," in *The Blackwell Companion to Religion in America,* ed. Philip Goff (Malden, MA: Wiley-Blackwell, 2010); Randall Herbert Balmer, *Mine Eyes Have Seen the Glory: A Journey into the Evangelical Subculture in America,* 4th ed. (New York: Oxford University Press, 2006); and Douglas A. Sweeney, *The American Evangelical Story: A History of the Movement* (Grand Rapids, MI: Baker Academic, 2005).

"Classic" in-depth studies of the origin and development of the tradition in America in the eighteenth, nineteenth, and twentieth centuries (especially after World War II) include, respectively, Harry S. Stout, *The Divine Dramatist: George Whitefield and the Rise of Modern Evangelicalism* (Grand Rapids, MI: W. B. Eerdmans, 1991); George M. Marsden, *Fundamentalism and American Culture,* 2nd ed. (New York: Oxford University Press, 2006); and Joel A. Carpenter, *Revive Us Again: The Reawakening of American Fundamentalism* (New York: Oxford University Press, 1999).

Recent superior studies of aspects of the evangelical tradition in America since World War II include Kate Bowler, *Blessed: A History of the American Prosperity Gospel* (New York: Oxford University Press, 2013); Dochuk, *From Bible Belt to Sunbelt;* Larry Eskridge, *God's Forever Family: The Jesus People Movement in America* (New York: Oxford University Press, 2013); Elizabeth Flowers, *Into the Pulpit: Southern Baptist Women and Power since World War II* (Chapel Hill: University of North Carolina Press, 2012); Steven P. Miller, *The Age of Evangelicalism: America's Born-Again Years* (New York: Oxford University Press, 2014); Matthew Avery Sutton, *American Apocalypse: A History of Modern Evangelicalism* (Cambridge, MA: The Belknap Press of Harvard University Press, 2014); David R. Swartz, *Moral Minority: The Evangelical Left in an Age of Conservatism* (Philadelphia: University of Pennsylvania Press, 2012); Daniel K. Williams, *God's Own Party: The Making of the Christian Right* (New York: Oxford University Press, 2010); Molly Worthen, *Apostles of Reason: The Crisis of Authority in American Evangelicalism* (New York: Oxford University Press, 2014).

Enumerating evangelicals in contemporary America is a daunting task, partly because of the difficulty of deciding who should be counted. For example, should the 18.9 percent of American Catholics who identified themselves as evangelical in a 2008 survey be included? That being said, a figure in the range of 75 to 80 million people seems reasonable. Some of the key studies are summarized in Mark Chaves, *American Religion: Contemporary Trends* (Princeton, NJ: Princeton University Press, 2011), esp. ch. 7; and William Vance Trollinger, Jr., "Evangelicalism and Religious Pluralism in Contemporary America: Diversity Without, Diversity Within, and Maintaining the Borders," in *Gods in America: Religious Pluralism in the United States,* ed. Charles L. Cohen and Ronald L. Numbers (Oxford University Press, 2013), 105–118, esp. 105.

28 William R. Hutchison, *The Modernist Impulse in American Protestantism* (Cambridge, MA: Harvard University Press, 1976).

29 Countless sources, likely based on the Billy Graham Evangelistic Association biographical profile (http://billygraham.org/about/biographies/billy-graham/), claim 185 countries. Russ Busby's authorized/official pictorial biography lists 56 countries in what appears to be a complete register of the sites of Graham's crusades, or at least the major ones, through 1998. Busby, *Billy Graham, God's Ambassador,* 116–132. While there is some ambiguity about what counts as a distinct country (for example, Guam), the BGCA's chronology of Graham's life indicates that he spoke in 99 countries (preaching engagements are distinct from crusades). See http://www2.wheaton.edu/bgc/archives/bgeachro/bgeachron02.htm.

30 Martin, *A Prophet with Honor,* 418–419, details the historic Seoul meeting. All of the "standard" biographies of Graham listed above contain a variety of data about crusade attendance. One of the most comprehensive summaries is in Busby, *Billy Graham, God's Ambassador,* ch. 3. The attendance figures for many of the individual crusades, especially in the United

States, are listed in the BGCA's official chronology of his life, at http://www2.wheaton.edu /bgc/archives/bgeachro/bgeachron02.htm.

31 I discuss the development of Graham's media empire in Chapter 4.

32 I discuss Graham's relationship with U.S. presidents in Chapter 6.

33 Jeffrey M. Jones, "Obama, Clinton Continue Reign as Most Admired," *Gallup Politics,* December 30, 2013, table "Most Top 10 Finishes for Most Admired Man, 1946–2013," available at http://www.gallup.com/poll/166646/obama-clinton-continue-reign-admired-man -woman.aspx?ref=more. The article states that Graham "has never finished first, a spot typically taken by the sitting president, but has finished second on numerous occasions."

34 *Ladies' Home Journal,* July 1978, cited in Martin, *A Prophet with Honor,* 600, 716.

35 For a long though still partial list of the awards see the BGEA official biography at http:// billygraham.org/about/biographies/billy-graham/.

36 John Shelton Reed, "The Twenty Most Influential Southerners of the Twentieth Century," *Southern Cultures* 7, no. 1 (2001): 96–100, doi:10.1353/scu.2001.0012.

37 Kenneth L. Woodward, "The Preaching and the Power," *Newsweek,* July 20, 1970, 50.

38 Larry Woods, *CNN Take Two,* CNN, January 2, 1987. The context suggests Woods was speaking for himself, too.

39 *Billy Graham: A Prophet with Honor,* with Billy Graham and David Frost (Tullstar Productions, 1989), DVD.

40 Harold Bloom, "Billy Graham: The Preacher," *Time,* June 14, 1999, available at http://content .time.com/time/magazine/article/0,9171,991259,00.html.

41 Terry Mattingly, Scripps Howard News Service, "America's Pope: Billy Graham," *Daily News,* November 30, 2003, 22.

42 George H. W. Bush, quoted in Leslie Boyd and John Boyle, *Asheville Citizen-Times,* in "Graham's Spiritual Journey Finds Home," *USA Today,* May 31, 2007, available at http:// www.usatoday.com/news/religion/2007-05-31-billy-graham-library_N.htm.

43 Kempton, *New York Post,* September 9, 1960, quoted in Gibbs and Duffy, *The Preacher and the Presidents,* 91–92.

44 Marshall Frady, *Billy Graham, a Parable of American Righteousness* (Boston: Little, Brown, 1979), 14. Frady is quoting an unnamed and uncited "Baptist cleric," but the context makes clear that he agreed with the description.

45 Garry Wills, *Under God: Religion and American Politics* (New York: Simon and Schuster, 1990), 169.

46 I. F. Stone, quoted in Woodward, "The Preaching and the Power," 50.

47 I discuss the envelopes in Chapter 7.

48 Writer's name withheld, letter in BGEA Headquarters archives, Charlotte, NC.

49 Gibbs and Duffy, *The Preacher and the Presidents,* viii–ix.

50 Mrs. L. Diess to Vice President Richard Nixon, July 25, 1957, box 3, folder 7, Collection 74, BGCA. A Nixon office response memo said, "See if you can think of anything to say to this poor woman—obviously the Graham people do not think she is deserving of an appointment with Billy."

51 *Charlotte Observer,* August 18, 1968, quoted in Frady, *Billy Graham, a Parable of American Righteousness,* 447.

52 Bloom, "Billy Graham: The Preacher."

53 Martin E. Marty, "Reflections on Graham by a Former Grump," *Christianity Today,* November 18, 1988.

54 "The Top 100 Influential Figures in American History," *Atlantic,* December 2006, available at http://www.theatlantic.com/magazine/archive/2006/12/the-top-100-influential-figures-in -american-history/305384/.

55 Gallup poll, June 1, 1957, cited in Martin, *A Prophet with Honor,* 232.

56 A potpourri of headlines from newspapers in Boston in March and April 1950 alone, when Graham's career had barely cleared the ground, offers a taste of his influence in the press. "Billy Graham Leads His Evangelist Team in Stirring Tour of the Northeast," *Boston Daily Globe,* April 4, 1950, 17; "Billy Graham Draws Huge Portland Crowd," *Boston Daily Globe,* March 29, 1950, 1; "Throngs Again Pack Portland Hall as Billy Graham Inspires Converts," *Boston Daily Globe,* March 30, 1950, 1; "Evangelist's Sincerity Is Success Key," *Boston Sunday Herald,* April 2, 1950, 1; "Dr. Graham Sees Quisling Danger," *Boston Post,* April 5, 1950, 1; "Billy to Invade MIT April 21," *Boston Traveler,* April 6, 1950, 1. In addition, the *Boston Post* Souvenir Edition (c. April 1950) includes: "Thousands Repent for Billy Graham: Fiery Evangelist Leaves Indelible Trail in New England Tour," "Evangelist Could

Make Hollywood: Saving Souls Is His Ambition Not Pictures," and "Grueling Life Led by Preacher: Eats 4 Meals a Day, Keeps in Trim Like Prize Fighter." I owe all of these documents to Garth Rosell.

57 "Billy Graham: The Man at Home," *Saturday Evening Post,* March 1972, 43.

58 *Billy Graham: Ambassador of Salvation,* in series *Great Souls: Six Who Changed a Century,* hosted by David Aikman, with Billy Graham, Dan Rather, and David Frost, directed by Tom Ivy (Vision Video, 2002, dist. PBS).

59 Leonard I. Sweet, "The Epic of the Billy Graham," *Theology Today* 37, no. 1 (1980): 85–92, 85, doi:10.1177/004057368003700110.

60 Edith Blumhofer, *Aimee Semple McPherson: Everybody's Sister* (Grand Rapids, MI: W. B. Eerdmans, 1993), 3, 383–384. Blumhofer judiciously places McPherson's influence in the "millions" and notes that she made the front page of America's biggest newspapers "three times a week throughout the 1920s." McPherson also founded a small but sturdy Pentecostal sect, the International Church of the Foursquare Gospel. In 1993 the Foursquare, as it was commonly called, posted an international membership of 1.5 million. For Sunday, see Robert Martin, *Hero of the Heartland: Billy Sunday and the Transformation of American Society, 1862–1935* (Bloomington: Indiana University Press, 2002). Drawing on Sunday's contemporaneous authorized biographer, William Ellis, Martin states: "associates and admirers" argued that Sunday preached to 80 to 100 million people and was responsible for 100 million converts. Martin goes on: "Although such claims are probably extravagant, they accurately suggest the scope of the evangelist's enormous appeal" (xiii). Ellis puts attendees at 80 million and converts at 100 million but acknowledges that those figures are "estimate[s]." William T. Ellis, *Billy Sunday, the Man and His Message* (Philadelphia: John C. Winston, 1936), v. It is not necessary to minimize McPherson's or Sunday's importance in order to appreciate the uniqueness of Graham's power: his relationship with eleven successive U.S. presidents, ubiquity in American newspapers for nearly six decades, recurring stadium attendance records, and vast international media audience.

61 I discuss their role in Chapter 3.

62 Graham worried about being compared with the Gantry caricature. Frady, *Billy Graham, a Parable of American Righteousness,* 492–493. Producers created an opera version of *Elmer Gantry* in 2007. As it turned out, "Bible Belt" anxiety about the movie's influence may have been overwrought. William D. Romanowski, *Reforming Hollywood: How American Protestants Fought for Freedom at the Movies* (New York: Oxford University Press, 2012), 132, 148–149.

63 Willard L. Sperry, *Religion in America* (Cambridge: University Press; New York: Macmillan, 1946), 161–162, quoted in William G. McLoughlin, Jr., *Billy Graham, Revivalist in a Secular Age* (New York: Ronald Press, 1960), 3–4.

64 W. G. McLoughlin, Jr., "Billy Graham: In Business with the Lord," *The Nation,* May 11, 1957, 410.

65 Martin, *A Prophet with Honor,* 96. For one of countless journalistic descriptions of the early Graham's preaching style, see Harold H. Martin, "A Vivid Portrait of the Famous Revivalist Billy Graham," *Saturday Evening Post,* April 13, 1963, 18.

66 For a vivid and apparently eyewitness account of the early Graham's melodramatic preaching style and language—one of many—see Lewis W. Gillenson, *Billy Graham: The Man and His Message* (New York: Fawcett, 1954), 6.

67 Graham, *Just As I Am,* 1997, 668; Billy Graham, interviewed by Hugh Downs, *20/20,* ABC, December 20, 1979, videotape V8, Collection 74, BGCA; Woodward, "The Preaching and the Power," 54; Gerald S. Strober, *Graham: A Day in Billy's Life* (Garden City, NY: Doubleday, 1976), 46.

68 Merle Miller, *Plain Speaking; an Oral Biography of Harry S Truman* (New York: Berkley; distrib. by Putnam, 1974), 363.

69 Susan Hixon, quoted in Letter to the Editor from June M. Adamson, "Actions of Past Editors Remembered," *The* (University of Tennessee) *Daily Beacon,* August 25, 1995, quoted in Roger A. Bruns, *Billy Graham: A Biography* (Westport, CT: Greenwood Press, 2004), 120, and available at http://utdailybeacon.com/opinion/letters/1995/aug/25/actions-of-past-editors-remembered/.

70 Bob Jones, Sr., *Charlotte News,* March 4, 1966, quoted in Frady, *Billy Graham, a Parable of American Righteousness,* 248.

71 George Will, "Let Us Pray for a Little Skepticism," *Washington Post,* May 13, 1982, A31. Will's actual words were, "handcuffs are not America's most embarrassing export," but the context made clear that Graham filled that role. Will included other clergy members "on the left and on the right" in his indictment of Graham's "pious intentions."

72 Christopher Hitchens, "The God Squad," *The Nation*, April 15, 2002, 9.
73 Kaye, "Billy Graham Rises," 112, quoting Marshall Frady without citation.
74 Steven P. Miller, "Those Welkin Eyes: The Billy Graham Image," in *The Worlds of Billy Graham*, ed. Andrew S. Finstuen, Anne Blue Wills, and Grant Wacker, forthcoming.
75 James Morris, *The Preachers* (New York: St. Martin's Press, 1973), 387.
76 David Bruce, executive assistant to Mr. Graham, conversation with the author, January 17, 2014.
77 Louis Hofferbert, "Crossroads in the Life of Billy Graham," *Houston Chronicle*, October 10, 1965, part 3. Though there is no comprehensive biography focused on the "ordinary" or nonpublic Billy Graham, at least three volumes offer many details of that sort: Wilson, *Billy Graham as a Teen-Ager*; Strober, *Graham: A Day in Billy's Life*; and Hanspeter Nüesch, *Ruth and Billy Graham: The Legacy of a Couple* (Grand Rapids, MI: Baker Books, 2014). Mass-circulation popular magazines such as *Look, Sunday Parade,* and *Saturday Evening Post* featured countless biographical stories based on first-person interviews with Graham and his family. Though usually highly romanticized, they make clear that there was a real person behind the towering public myth. Hundreds of such articles are in Collection 360, BGCA.
78 Anne Blue Wills, "'An Odd Kind of Cross to Bear': Being Mrs. Billy Graham," in *The Worlds of Billy Graham*, ed. Andrew S. Finstuen, Anne Blue Wills, and Grant Wacker, forthcoming. I discuss Ruth's role in Chapter 2.
79 The exact figure was 29 percent. "Public Expresses Mixed Views of Islam, Mormonism," *Pew Forum on Religion and Public Life,* September 25, 2007, available at http://pewforum .org/surveys/religionviews07/. Stephen Prothero, *Religious Literacy: What Every American Needs to Know—and Doesn't* (San Francisco: HarperSanFrancisco, 2007), includes an entry for Graham. In a review, the American religious historian Mark Oppenheimer judged that he would have omitted the entry for Graham because he was "irrelevant today." Oppenheimer, "Knowing Not," *New York Times,* June 10, 2007.

1. PREACHER

1 Quentin J. Schultze, ed., *American Evangelicals and the Mass Media: Perspectives on the Relationship between American Evangelicals and the Mass Media* (Grand Rapids, MI: Academie Books/Zondervan, 1990), esp. Schultze's Introduction. The volume brims with references to Graham's role in the media revolution.
2 I adapt this sentence from one in William Martin, *A Prophet with Honor: The Billy Graham Story* (New York: W. Morrow, 1991), 155.
3 Billy Graham, *Peace with God* (Garden City, NY: Doubleday, 1953). I discuss the theological claims projected in this volume, as well as the book's extraordinary popular influence, in Chapter 4.
4 Martin, *A Prophet with Honor,* 220.
5 Billy Graham, "Christianity vs. Communism" sermon, *Hour of Decision* radio program, February 4, 1951, Minneapolis, audio tape T56j, Collection 191, BGCA, audio "Christianism vs. Communism" available at http://billygraham.org/audio/christianism-vs-communism/.
6 "Billy Graham Reflects on His Ministry," *Charlotte Observer,* March 23, 1986, 1.
7 Graham, in Russ Busby, *Billy Graham, God's Ambassador: A Lifelong Mission of Giving Hope to the World* (Alexandria, VA: Time-Life Books, 1999), 27.
8 David C. Steinmetz, "Billy Graham: Simple Message, Powerful Voice," *Orlando Sentinel,* June 28, 2005, available at http://articles.orlandosentinel.com/2005-06-28/news/STEINMETZ28 _1_evangelist-graham-christians.
9 Richard Brodhead, president of Duke University, quoted on Channel 14 News, Raleigh NC, September 29, 2007, 11 PM; quotation used with permission.
10 For the broader evangelical background, see Brendan Pietsch, "Dispensational Modernism" (Ph.D. diss., Duke University, 2011), 270–273; George M. Marsden, "Evangelicals, History, and Modernity," in *Evangelicalism and Modern America,* ed. George M. Marsden (Grand Rapids, MI: William B. Eerdmans, 1984); Grant Wacker, "Uneasy in Zion: Evangelicals in Postmodern Society," in *Evangelicalism and Modern America,* ed. Marsden.
11 Billy Graham, *Just As I Am: The Autobiography of Billy Graham* (San Francisco: HarperSan-Francisco; Grand Rapids, MI: Zondervan, 1997), 351.

12 Christian Smith with Melinda Lundquist Denton, *Soul Searching: The Religious and Spiritual Lives of American Teenagers* (New York: Oxford University Press, 2005), 162–170, 257–258, 262. Smith's phrase is "moralistic therapeutic deism."

13 Ami Eden, "'Focus' on Bloomberg's Jewishness," *Jewish Telegraphic Agency*, August 31, 2010, available at http://www.jta.org/2010/08/31/news-opinion/the-telegraph/focus-on -bloombergs-jewishness. Billy Graham, *Living in God's Love: The New York Crusade* (New York: G. P. Putnam's Sons, 2005), 68.

14 George M. Marsden, *Understanding Fundamentalism and Evangelicalism* (Grand Rapids, MI: W. B. Eerdmans, 1991), Introduction and Part 1; Ernest R. Sandeen, *The Roots of Fundamentalism: British and American Millenarianism, 1800–1930* (Chicago: University of Chicago Press, 1970), 285–289.

15 The primary and secondary literature on these conversations about the Bible in the middle-century years is extensive. I provide a brief introduction to some of the historical background in Grant Wacker, *Augustus H. Strong and the Dilemma of Historical Consciousness* (Macon, GA: Mercer University Press, 1985), chs. 5–7. See also George M. Marsden, *Reforming Fundamentalism: Fuller Seminary and the New Evangelicalism* (Grand Rapids, MI: W. B. Eerdmans, 1987), 224–230; Mark A. Noll, *Between Faith and Criticism: Evangelicals, Scholarship, and the Bible in America* (San Francisco: Harper and Row, 1986), esp. chs. 2, 3, and 7; Gary J. Dorrien, *The Remaking of Evangelical Theology* (Louisville, KY: Westminster John Knox Press, 1998), ch. 3; Sandeen, *Roots of Fundamentalism*, chs. 5 and 8. For a superior recent examination of the story—and the historical literature attending it—see Molly Worthen, *Apostles of Reason: The Crisis of Authority in American Evangelicalism* (New York: Oxford University Press, 2014), esp. chs. 2 and 3.

16 Graham became the first Vice President at Large of Youth for Christ in 1946. The first article of YFC's "Statement of Faith" affirmed: "We believe the Bible to be the inspired, the infallible, authoritative Word of God." See, for example, *Youth for Christ Magazine*, March 1946, 12, BGCA, Reading Room. The linking of the adjectives evinced the unselfconscious blending of meaning about the Bible's truthfulness in popular fundamentalist circles in 1946. About then, and certainly within a few years, fundamentalists began to bear down and parse exactly what each term denoted. See William Vance Trollinger, Jr., *God's Empire: William Bell Riley and Midwestern Fundamentalism* (Madison, WI: University of Wisconsin Press, 1990), 26, 29–30, 38, 152–153, 201n6. Trollinger does not explicitly state that Graham signed an inerrancy statement when he became president of Riley's Northwestern Schools in 1947, but given Riley's militant and venerable defense of the principle, he hardly would have importuned Graham to succeed him unless Graham wholeheartedly embraced it too. For the concept of inerrancy in the early Graham see George M. Marsden, *Reforming Fundamentalism: Fuller Seminary and the New Evangelicalism* (Grand Rapids, MI: W.B. Eerdmans, 1987), 113–115, 171, 207, 246. The "Statement of Faith of Fuller," which Graham embraced in the 1940s (171) and necessarily signed when he became a trustee in 1959, stated that the original Scriptures (that is, original autographs) "are plenarily inspired and free from error in the whole and in part" (113).

17 Leighton Ford, Graham's brother-in-law and long-term associate, presentation in a class at Duke Divinity School, April 1, 2008.

18 Graham, in Busby, *Billy Graham, God's Ambassador*, 27.

19 Editorial, *Christianity Today*, October 15, 1956, no page shown, in *Christianity Today* "Core Documents" Notebook, *Christianity Today* offices, Carol Stream, IL. The editorial reflected the views of both Graham and the first editor, Carl F. H. Henry.

20 Graham, *Just As I Am*, 1997, 291.

21 See, for example, Harold Lindsell, *The Battle for the Bible* (Grand Rapids, MI: Zondervan, 1976), esp. chs. 6 and 8.

22 Carl F. H. Henry, *Confessions of a Theologian: An Autobiography* (Waco, TX: Word Books, 1986), 123.

23 David Allan Hubbard, "What We Believe and Teach," *Theology, News and Notes* (Fuller Theological Seminary), Special Issue 3–4 (1976), quotation on 4. Fuller's doctrinal position contained the word *infallible* but applied it to "faith and practice," not to chronological, scientific, or historical details.

24 Billy Graham to "Dr. Fuller," May 16, 1964; Billy Graham to David Alan Hubbard, February 15, 1968, both in Fuller Theological Seminary Archives, Pasadena, CA. In 1984 seminary students and faculty members at Vancouver School of Theology and Regent College questioned Graham about his view of the fight about inerrancy that was splitting his own

denomination, the Southern Baptist Convention. Graham answered simply: "Both sides are going too far." The answer reflected his characteristic diplomacy—or evasiveness—but it also reflected his deep-seated view that faithful Christians might amicably agree to disagree, even on important questions like this, in order to pursue their larger agenda. He lamented the potential for schism. So too when Lindsell died on January 15, 1998, Graham said, with characteristic diplomacy (or evasiveness): "His stand on the authority of Scripture is one of his lasting legacies. . . . His writings will be used of God for many years to come to help hold the church to the Scriptures." See, respectively, Graham's comments in the question-and-answer period following an address at Regent College and Vancouver School of Theology, October 1984, audio available at http://www.regentaudio.com/products/billy-graham-at-vst -and-regent-college; Obituary, "Harold Lindsell, Evangelical Scholar, Author, Editor," *Los Angeles Times*, January 22, 1998. For the larger controversy over inerrancy at Fuller and in the evangelical subculture see, respectively, George M. Marsden, *Reforming Fundamentalism: Fuller Seminary and the New Evangelicalism*, pb. ed. (Grand Rapids, MI: W. B. Eerdmans, 1995), esp. Preface to the Paperback Edition and 179; and Worthen, *Apostles of Reason*.

25 Graham, "Let the Earth Hear His Voice," First International Congress on World Evangelization, July 16–25, 1974, Lausanne, Switzerland, in J. D. Douglas, *Let the Earth Hear His Voice: Official Reference Volume, Papers and Responses* (Minneapolis: World Wide Publications, 1975), 28.

26 Lewis William Gillenson, *Billy Graham: The Man and His Message* (New York: Fawcett, 1954), 6.

27 Graham's words come from Billy Graham, interview with David Frost, "Doubts and Certainties," on BBC-2, 1964, in David Frost and Fred Bauer, *Billy Graham: Personal Thoughts of a Public Man; 30 Years of Conversations with David Frost* (Colorado Springs: Chariot Victor, 1997), 72–74.

28 Jon Meacham, "Pilgrim's Progress," *Newsweek*, August 14, 2006, available at http://www .newsweek.com/pilgrims-progress-109171. A follow-up letter from Graham to the editor of *Newsweek* merits quotation for what it said about Graham's irenic spirit, acknowledgment of growth and change, and reaffirmation of Scriptural authority: "Like every other Christian, I see myself as a pilgrim journeying through life, looking expectantly to what God has promised in the future and yet yearning to be faithful in the present. Jon Meacham worked diligently to understand how my thinking on certain issues has grown over the years, and I commend him for seeking to capture my commitment to the Gospel I have always preached. The world is constantly changing, and I am only one in a long line of men and women who have sought to relate God's unchanging truth to the challenges of their time. As I grow older, my confidence in the inspiration and authority of the Bible has grown even stronger." Billy Graham, Letters to the Magazine [U.S. Edition], *Newsweek*, September 4, 2006, 22.

29 Mark Chaves, *American Religion: Contemporary Trends* (Princeton, NJ: Princeton University Press, 2011), 34–37, esp. Fig. 3.1. According to both the General Social Survey (GSS) and Gallup polls, since the 1970s, belief in an inerrant Bible declined from 40 percent to just over 30 percent of the population. That trend bottomed out between 1990 and the present. For evangelicals, the GSS data has about 60 percent saying the "Bible is the actual word of God and is to be taken literally, word for word" in the early 1980s, and that number is about 50–52 percent today. Mark Chaves, e-mail message to author, April 3, 2014. The survey data did not distinguish between inerrancy and literalism, a distinction that probably would have been irrelevant to everyday readers. See also Marsden, *Reforming Fundamentalism*, 302–303, for declining belief in inerrancy among Fuller Theological Seminary graduates.

30 Graham, "Let the Earth Hear His Voice," First International Congress on World Evangelization; and Douglas, *Let the Earth Hear His Voice*, 28.

31 Stanley High, *Billy Graham: The Personal Story of the Man, His Message, and His Mission* (New York: McGraw-Hill, 1956), 39.

32 My rendering of Graham from Billy Graham, interview by David Frost, *Doubts and Certainties*, BBC-2, 1964.

33 My rendering of Graham from Billy Graham, interview by David Frost, *Talking with David Frost*, January 29, 1993.

34 Billy Graham, *My Answer* (Garden City, NY: Doubleday, 1960), 10, available online at http://www.ccel.us/myanswer.toc.html.

35 Billy Graham, *Answers to Life's Problems* (Nashville: Thomas Nelson, 1988), ix–x.

36 Worthen, *Apostles of Reason*, chs. 2 and 3.

37 Graham, quoted in *San Diego Union-Tribune,* May 11, 2003, cited in Bill Adler, *Ask Billy Graham* (Nashville: Thomas Nelson, 2007), 56.

38 Graham, interview in Frost and Bauer, *Billy Graham: Personal Thoughts of a Public Man,* 116. The interview took place in 1981.

39 Graham, in Busby, *Billy Graham, God's Ambassador,* 27.

40 See, for example, Ross Douthat, *Bad Religion: How We Became a Nation of Heretics* (New York: Free Press, 2012), 49; Jon Meacham, "Pilgrim's Progress."

41 Andrew S. Finstuen, *Original Sin and Everyday Protestants: The Theology of Reinhold Niebuhr, Billy Graham, and Paul Tillich in an Age of Anxiety* (Chapel Hill: University of North Carolina Press, 2009), 192.

42 Billy Graham, interviewed by Jim Finnerty, *Jim Finnerty and Company,* KCRA (Sacramento, CA), September 9, 1982.

43 Billy Graham's decision card, November 1, 1934, photocopy in author's possession.

44 Frye Gaillard, "The Conversion of Billy Graham," *The Progressive,* August 1982, 26, available at http://search.opinionarchives.com/TP_Web/DigitalArchive.aspx?panes=1&aid=0460 8026_1.

45 Ibid.

46 Billy Graham, press conferences, Columbus, OH, January 28, 1963, audio tape no. T1 (side 1), transcript in box 4, folder 9, p. 5; Detroit, March 8, 1976, audio tape no. T88, transcript in box 4, folder 1, p. 17; both in Collection 24, BGCA; Lowell D. Streiker and Gerald S. Strober, *Religion and the New Majority: Billy Graham, Middle America, and the Politics of the 70s* (New York: Association Press, 1972), 53–56.

47 Billy Graham, press conference, Columbus, OH, July 9, 1964, audio tape no. T7, transcript in box 4, folder 14, p. 5, Collection 24, BGCA.

48 Harold Myra and Marshall Shelley, *The Leadership Secrets of Billy Graham* (Grand Rapids, MI: Zondervan, 2005), 141. I discuss these and related developments in greater detail in Chapter 6.

49 David Poling, "Billy Graham: God's Crusader," *Dayton Daily News,* September 29, 1974, 6.

50 But see Graham, *Just As I Am,* 2007, 154, for a relatively rare story of direct supernatural intervention in nature.

51 Joe E. Barnhart, *The Billy Graham Religion* (Philadelphia: United Church Press, 1972), 65.

52 Billy Graham, *The Collected Works of Billy Graham* (New York: Inspirational Press, 1993), 480; Billy Graham, *The Holy Spirit: Activating God's Power in Your Life* (Waco, TX: Word Books, 1978).

53 My rendering of Graham from Billy Graham, interview by David Frost, *Talking with David Frost,* January 29, 1993.

54 My rendering of Graham from *Dinah Shore Show,* "Dinah's Place," October 3, 1972, audio tape no. T45, Collection 345, BGCA.

55 The primary and secondary literature on dispensational premillennialism is large. The most perceptive study, with an extensive bibliography, is Pietsch, "Dispensational Modernism."

56 Classic dispensationalism involved more than speculations about how the world would end. The irredeemable apostasy of the established churches ranked high on the list. I see little evidence that Graham absorbed the broader claims of dispensational writers. Timothy P. Weber, *Living in the Shadow of the Second Coming,* enl. ed. (Grand Rapids, MI: Academie Books, 1983).

57 Graham citing himself, as quoted in the *Boston Globe,* 1950, in Graham, *Just As I Am,* 2007, 160.

58 Billy Graham, "Billy Graham: 25 Years an Evangelist, 55 Years a Man," *Eternity, Reprinted from Wittenberg Door,* November 1974, 28.

59 "Original Billy Graham Address, 1955," *Christianity Today* Editorial Offices, Carol Stream, IL, 3.

60 Billy Graham, *Approaching Hoofbeats: The Four Horsemen of the Apocalypse* (Waco, TX: Word Books, 1983).

61 Ibid., 257–269. For what might be called his earliest systematic statement, see Graham, *Peace with God,* 1953, ch. 17. Graham repeatedly pointed out that the New Testament referred to Christ's return more than 300 times. Graham, *Peace with God: The Secret of Happiness* (Nashville: W Publishing Group, 1984), 255.

62 Billy Graham, "Three Minutes to Twelve" sermon, *Hour of Decision* radio program, February 1953, pamphlet sermon no. 22, 1, 3, audio available at http://billygraham.org/audio/three-minutes-to-twelve/.

63 "Billy Graham Recalls Life in Charlotte at Rally," *Charlotte Observer*, October 27, 1985, C6.

64 Perry Miller, *The New England Mind; the Seventeenth Century* (New York: Macmillan 1939), ch. 16.

65 Billy Graham, *World Aflame* (Garden City, NY: Doubleday, 1965).

66 Billy Graham, *Storm Warning* (Dallas: Word Books, 1992), 26.

67 Ibid., 163–171, quotation on 168.

68 Graham, *World Aflame*, chs. 1 and 2.

69 See, for example, Graham's Oklahoma Bombing Memorial Prayer Service Address, April 23, 1995, available at http://www.americanrhetoric.com/speeches/billygrahamoklahomabombingspeech.htm; and "Remembrance" (regarding the September 11, 2001, tragedy) at the Washington National Cathedral, September 14, 2001, available at http://www.nationalcathedral.org/worship/sermonTexts/bg010914.shtml.

70 "Billy Graham Recalls Life in Charlotte at Rally," *Charlotte Observer*, October 27, 1985, C6.

71 Billy Graham, "Heaven" sermon, 1955, *Hour of Decision* radio program, pamphlet sermon no. 49, audio tape T265f, Collection 191, BGCA, audio available at http://billygraham.org/audio/heaven-2/.

72 Graham, in *Philadelphia Inquirer*, February 7, 1999, cited in Adler, *Ask Billy Graham*, 216; *Billy Graham: A Personal Crusade*, A&E *Biography*, hosted by Harry Smith (New York: A&E, 1999).

73 Billy Graham, interview by David Frost, *Talking with David Frost*, January 29, 1993, cited in Frost and Bauer, *Billy Graham: Personal Thoughts of a Public Man*, 166–167.

74 Nancy Gibbs and Richard N. Ostling, "God's Billy Pulpit," *Time*, November 15, 1993, 70. Graham added: "When the Scripture uses fire concerning hell, that is possibly an illustration of how terrible it's going to be—not fire but something worse, a thirst for God that cannot be quenched."

75 Harold H. Martin, "A Vivid Portrait of the Famous Revivalist Billy Graham," *Saturday Evening Post*, April 13, 1966, 21.

76 C. S. Lewis, *The Great Divorce* (New York: Macmillan, 1946).

77 Leighton Ford, e-mail message to the author, March 23, 2014.

78 Graham, *Living in God's Love: The New York Crusade*, 116.

79 Billy Graham, "Suffering: Why Does God Allow It?" *Decision*, August–September 1981, pamphlet sermon no. 263.

80 Billy Graham, "Death the Enemy," *Decision*, September 1975, pamphlet sermon no. 265, Graham is quoting an unnamed and uncited "columnist," but clearly he is speaking in his own voice too.

81 My thinking about the difference between content and function, and the community-defining function of media (print or spoken), is informed by Elesha Coffman, "The Measure of a Magazine: Assessing the Influence of the *Christian Century*," *Religion and American Culture: A Journal of Interpretation* 22, no. 1 (2012): 53–82, doi:10.1525/rac.2012.22.1.53.

82 Ibid.

83 An early *Hour of Decision* sermon, tellingly titled "Facts, Faith, and Feeling," asserted that Christianity was built on the plain fact of an empty tomb, then came faith, then came feeling. "They come in this order and the order is essential." Yet four years later, in the opening sermon of his landmark New York City crusade, Graham would say: "I want you to listen tonight not only with your ears, but the Bible teaches that the heart also has ears. Listen with your soul tonight." The difference between the sermons certainly was not irresolvable, but it was not insignificant either. "Facts, Faith and Feeling," pamphlet sermon no. 27, preached on the *Hour of Decision*, June 1953. Second sermon quoted in John Charles Pollock, *The Billy Graham Story: The Authorized Biography*, rev. and updated ed. (Grand Rapids, MI: Zondervan, 2003), 89.

84 For example, when in 1969 a reporter asked Graham if universities should be overhauled, he did not hesitate to comment on modern universities, which had become "too impersonal, too big." He cited the need for small classes, the desirability of reducing the student-teacher ratio, and reproducing the kind of small college system found at Oxford and Cambridge. Graham had never attended a university. He hardly could have known from first-hand experience the costs and benefits of different pedagogical arrangements. Billy Graham, press conference, New York, June 10, 1969 (recorded by W. Craig Hulsebos Family Radio News

WFME Newark, NJ), audio tape no. T37, June 10, 1969, transcript in box 1, folder 19, Collection 24, BGCA.

85 Kenneth L. Woodward, the former *Newsweek* Religion editor, would say that for all of Graham's openness to ecumenism with Catholics, he never grasped the power of Catholic—or for that matter any high church—sense of sacramentalism. Woodward, "Billy Graham Retrospective," *Daily Beast*, forthcoming.

86 Ken Garfield, "Graham's New Journey: Reflecting on His Past, Globe-Trotting Evangelist Works on Memoirs," *Charlotte Observer*, August 16, 1992, A1; Graham in *Ethnic News-Watch*, September 26, 1997, excerpted in Adler, *Ask Billy Graham*, 168.

87 Graham, in *San Francisco Chronicle*, September 25, 1997, excerpted in Adler, *Ask Billy Graham*, 168.

88 Graham, in *Arkansas Democrat Gazette*, September 16, 1989, excerpted in Adler, *Ask Billy Graham*, 168; Graham, in *Ethnic NewsWatch*, September 26, 1997, excerpted in Adler, *Ask Billy Graham*, 168.

89 Manny Fernandez, Glen Martin, and Don Lattin, "Ailing Billy Graham Inspires S.F. Crowd; He Welcomes Gays, All Believers," SFGate (*San Francisco Chronicle*), October 10, 1997.

90 Billy Graham, interviewed by Hugh Downs, *20/20*, ABC, December 20, 1979, videotape V8, Collection 74, BGCA; and quoted without citation in Myra and Shelley, *The Leadership Secrets of Billy Graham*, 317.

91 Graham, in *St. Louis Post-Dispatch*, October 11, 1993, excerpted in Adler, *Ask Billy Graham*, 71; see also Graham, in PR Newswire, September 28, 1992, excerpted in Adler, *Ask Billy Graham*, 72.

92 For example, Graham, on *Live at Five*, Jack Cafferty reporting, WNBC (New York), March 10, 1982. See also Peter J. Boyer, "The Big Tent: Billy Graham, Franklin Graham, and the Transformation of American Evangelicalism," *New Yorker*, August 22, 2005, available at http://www.newyorker.com/archive/2005/08/22/050822fa_fact_boyer?currentPage=all; Billy Graham, press conference, Detroit, October 11, 1976, audio tape no. T92, transcript in box 4, folder 6, p. 21, Collection 24, BGCA. Billy Graham, "Candid Conversation with the Evangelist," *Christianity Today*, July 17, 1981, 24; Billy Graham, press conference, Detroit, October 11, 1976, p. 16. Kenneth Bagnell, "Billy Graham Answers 26 Provocative Questions," *United Church Observer*, July 1, 1966, 12; Nancy Gibbs and Michael Duffy, "The Preacher and the Presidents: Billy Graham in the White House," interview by George H. Gilliam, American Forum, Miller Center for Public Affairs, University of Virginia, November 9, 2007, audio available at http://millercenter.org/events/2007/the-preacher-and-the -presidents-billy-graham-in-the-white-house. Martin, *A Prophet with Honor*, 293–294, states that Graham "acquiesced" in making Methodist Bishop Gerald Kennedy chair of his 1963 Los Angeles crusade. Kennedy acknowledged that he "doubted" the Virgin Birth.

93 Graham, quoted in Myra and Shelley, *The Leadership Secrets of Billy Graham*, 239.

94 Graham preached this 8.5-minute sermon September 25, 1949. The Los Angeles Meetings on Film, Into the Big Tent: Billy Graham and the 1949 Greater Los Angeles Campaign, BGCA Exhibit. The sermon can be viewed and heard at http://www2.wheaton.edu/bgc/archives /exhibits/LA49/07film.html.

95 Graham, *Living in God's Love: The New York Crusade*, 44, 75, 108, 124–125.

96 Kenneth L. Woodward, "The Preaching and the Power," *Newsweek*, July 20, 1970, 52.

97 Billy Graham, *Till Armageddon: A Perspective on Suffering* (Waco, TX: Word Books, 1981). For my awareness of the intimate relation between eschatology and everyday piety in the evangelical tradition I am deeply indebted to Pietsch, "Dispensational Modernism."

98 Andrew S. Finstuen, *Original Sin and Everyday Protestants*, 191–192.

99 I adapt this often-quoted line from G. K. Chesterton's 1908 classic *Orthodoxy*: Christianity, he wrote, "has not merely told this truth or that truth, but has revealed itself as a truth-telling thing." G. K. Chesterton, *Orthodoxy* (New York: John Lane, 1908), 289.

100 Numerous points in this section and in the following one I owe to the brilliant work of Harry Stout and Michael Kazin on the speaking styles of George Whitefield and of William Jennings Bryan, respectively. Neither Stout nor Kazin refers to Graham, and there is little evidence that Graham knew much about either Whitefield or Bryan as public speakers. Still, the parallels prove remarkable. Henry S. Stout, *The Divine Dramatist: George Whitefield and the Rise of Modern Evangelism* (Grand Rapids, MI: W. B. Eerdmans, 1991); Michael Kazin, *A Godly Hero: The Life of William Jennings Bryan* (New York: Knopf, 2006), esp. chap. 3. Not surprisingly, many theses, dissertations, and journal and magazine articles have focused on Graham's preaching. He also usually rates a chapter in anthologies of preaching,

such as Hughes Oliphant Old, *The Reading and Preaching of the Scriptures in the Worship of the Christian Church,* 7 vols. (Grand Rapids, MI: W. B. Eerdmans, 1998–2010), vol. 7, ch. 2, "Billy Graham," 61–85; William Martin, "Graham, William Franklin," in *Concise Encyclopedia of Preaching,* ed. William H. Willimon and Richard Lischer (Louisville, KY: Westminster John Knox Press, 1995), 167–169. That being said, professional homileticians—students of the *theory* of preaching—have paid relatively little attention to his work. Preaching scholars Clyde Fant and William Pinson conclude: "The complete bibliography on Billy Graham includes several thousand entries. One surprising fact emerges from a thorough study of this vast body of material: less than a dozen of these entries concern themselves with the preaching of Billy Graham. These articles examine either his crusade techniques, his theology, his decision services, his personality, or his approach to revivalism. Occasionally a line or two is devoted to a casual remark about a particular sermon or his preaching in general. But references to his preaching are usually confined to vague value judgments that are either uncritically approving or mildly patronizing." Clyde E. Fant and William M. Pinson, *20 Centuries of Great Preaching: An Encyclopedia of Preaching,* 13 vols. (Waco, TX: Word Books, 1971), vol. 12: *Marshall to King,* 290.

101 Graham, *Just As I Am,* 2007, 259; High, *Billy Graham: The Personal Story,* 90.
102 John Akers, special assistant to Mr. Graham, conversation with the author, January 17, 2014, Asheville, NC.
103 Graham, quoted in Pollock, *The Billy Graham Story,* 291.
104 Graham, in "Why God Allows Suffering and War," *Houston Crusade, 1965,* quoted in Graham and Bill Adler, *The Wit and Wisdom of Billy Graham,*158; Martin, *A Prophet with Honor,* 581.
105 Jean Graham Ford, Billy Graham's sister, e-mail message to the author, January 29, 2009.
106 Billy Graham, press conference, Asheville, NC, March 23, 1977, audio tape no. T93, transcript in box 4, folder 8, p. 15, Collection 24, BGCA.
107 Elizabeth Kaye, "Billy Graham Rises," *George,* December 1996, 142.
108 Graham, in *Monterey County Herald,* November 6, 2003, cited in Adler, *Ask Billy Graham,* 98.
109 Graham, quoted in Pollock, *The Billy Graham Story,* 94.
110 Billy Graham, interview with David Frost, *Doubts and Certainties,* BBC-2, 1964, in Frost and Bauer, *Billy Graham: Personal Thoughts of a Public Man.*
111 Name withheld by request.
112 Martin, *A Prophet with Honor,* 582.
113 This is a running list I compiled reading through the 322 sermon pamphlets published by the BGEA between 1951 and 1999.
114 Lois Ferm, "Billy Graham in Florida," *Florida Historical Quarterly* 60, no. 2 (1981), 177. David Malone, associate professor of Library Science and College Archivist, Wheaton College, e-mail message to author, June 10, 2014.
115 Busby, *Billy Graham, God's Ambassador,* 34; Martin, *A Prophet with Honor,* 69.
116 William Martin, "The Power and the Glory of Billy Graham," *Texas Monthly,* March 1978, available at http://www.texasmonthly.com/story/power-and-glory-billy-graham.
117 Robert C. Cooley, conversation with the author, July 1, 2007, Charlotte, NC. Cooley was president of Conwell Theological Seminary from 1981 to 1997. Graham served as chairman of the board of trustees from 1989 to 1994, which brought them into frequent contact.
118 Gerald Beaven, excerpted in Deborah H. Strober and Gerald S. Strober, *Billy Graham: An Oral and Narrative Biography* (San Francisco: Jossey-Bass, 2006), 135.
119 Billy Graham, "Hate vs. Love" sermon, *Hour of Decision* radio program, April 15, 1951, Shreveport, LA, pamphlet sermon no. 1, audio tape T66j, Collection 191, BGCA, audio available at http://billygraham.org/audio/hate-vs-love/. In 2012 the BGEA released audio recordings of 1,600 Graham sermons, going back to 1949, available at http://billygraham .org/tv-and-radio/radio/audio-archives/. In 2013 the BGCA made available 66,000 pages of notes of his sermons and more than 3,000 pages of actual transcripts, available at https:// public.share.wheaton.edu/sites/BGCArchives/BGSermons/Forms/AllItems.aspx.
  For three anthologies, see Billy Graham, *Revival in Our Time: The Story of Billy Graham: Including Six of His Sermons* (Wheaton, IL: Van Kampen Press, 1950); Graham, *The Challenge: Sermons from Madison Square Garden* (Garden City, NY: Doubleday, 1969); and Graham, *Blow Wind of God: Spirited Messages from the Writings of Billy Graham* (Grand Rapids, MI: Baker Book House, 1975).

120 Aimee Semple McPherson, quoted by her daughter, Roberta Semple Salter, interview with Matthew A. Sutton, New York, March 16, 2004, cited in Sutton, *Aimee Semple McPherson and the Resurrection of Christian America* (Cambridge, MA: Harvard University Press, 2007), 77.

121 Marshall Frady, *Billy Graham, a Parable of American Righteousness* (Boston: Little, Brown, 1979), 162.

122 Dean Minder, quoted in Busby, *Billy Graham, God's Ambassador,* 34.

123 John Akers, conversation with the author, January 17, 2014. See also Gerald S. Strober, *Graham: A Day in Billy's Life* (Garden City, NY: Doubleday, 1976), 62.

124 William Ferris and Charles Reagan Wilson, *Encyclopedia of Southern Culture,* vol. 1: *Religion,* ed. Samuel S. Hill (Chapel Hill: University of North Carolina Press, 1989), esp. entries for "Bible Belt," "Frontier Religion," "Fundamentalism," "Billy Graham," "Great Revival," "Pentecostalism, Preacher (white)," "Revivalism," and "Oral Roberts."

125 Graham's (usually) triple-spaced sermon notes, invariably with numerous apparently last-minute hand amendments—additions and cross-outs—are displayed in the Billy Graham Center Museum, Wheaton College, Wheaton, IL, and thousands of pages of them online at https://public.share.wheaton.edu/sites/BGCArchives/BGSermons/Forms/AllItems.aspx.

126 For example, see Graham's comments in Pollock, *The Billy Graham Story,* 94.

127 Gibbs and Duffy, "The Preacher and the Presidents," interview at the Miller Center for Public Affairs, University of Virginia, 2007, 18.

128 Boyer, "The Big Tent," 43.

129 Kenneth L. Woodward, "The Preaching and the Power," *Newsweek,* July 20, 1970, 53.

130 Cathy Lynn Grossman, "The Gospel of Billy Graham: Inclusion," *USA Today,* May 15, 2005.

131 John Akers, conversation with the author, January 17, 2014.

132 Carey Williams, editor at Baylor University Press, conversation with the author, November 12, 2010, Pittsburgh, PA.

133 For one of many references to this phrase see "Will Graham," in *Chicken Soup for the Soul: Billy Graham and Me: 101 Inspiring Personal Stories from Presidents, Pastors, Performers, and Other People Who Know Him Well,* ed. Steve Posner, Amy Newmark, and A. Larry Ross (Cos Cob, CT: Chicken Soup for the Soul Publishing, 2013), 174.

134 Graham, *Just As I Am,* 2007, 180.

135 Ken Garfield, "A Look Inside the World of Evangelist Billy Graham," *Charlotte Observer,* September 22, 1996, A2.

136 Graham, in *Dallas Morning News,* November 7, 1994, cited in Adler, *Ask Billy Graham,* 163.

137 *Time,* November 14, 1949, quoted in Graham, *Just As I Am,* 2007, 150.

138 Garfield, "A Look Inside the World of Evangelist Billy Graham."

139 David Poling, "Billy Graham: God's Crusader," *Dayton Daily News,* September 29, 1974, 4.

140 Pollock, *The Billy Graham Story,* 141.

141 David Frost, *Billy Graham Talks with David Frost* (Philadelphia: A. J. Holman, 1971), 73.

142 Billy Graham, "The Urgency of Revival" sermon, *Hour of Decision* radio program, January 3, 1954, pamphlet sermon no. 36, audio tape T208f,g, Collection 191, BGCA; Graham, "It Is Time to Seek the Lord," *Hour of Decision,* pamphlet sermon no. 158, 1966; Graham, "When Silence Is Yellow" sermon, *Hour of Decision* radio program, August 22, 1965, pamphlet sermon no. 156, audio tape T815c, Collection 191, BGCA.

143 Billy Graham, "Challenge to America," pamphlet sermon no. 145, *Hour of Decision,* 1963.

144 Billy Graham, "Revival or the Spirit of the Age," *Hour of Decision* radio program, April 27, 1952, Austin, pamphlet sermon no. 13, audio tape T120g, Collection 191, BGCA, audio available at http://billygraham.org/audio/revival-or-the-spirit-of-the-age/.

145 Quoted without citation in Aikman, *Billy Graham,* 42; Kaye, "Billy Graham Rises," 140.

146 Tom Allan, chair of the 1955 Glasgow crusade, quoted in Pollock, *The Billy Graham Story,* 79.

147 Martin, *A Prophet with Honor,* 90.

148 Approximate rendering of the concluding words of crusade sermon displayed on movie screen, Billy Graham Library, July 3, 2009.

149 Preaching professor Thomas G. Long has argued that the "efficacy" of Graham's sermons should be understood as "iconic and ritual events." Thomas G. Long, "Preaching the Good News," in *The Legacy of Billy Graham: Critical Reflections on America's Greatest Evangelist,* ed. Michael G. Long (Louisville, KY: Westminster John Knox Press, 2008), 13.

150 Graham, quoted in High, *Billy Graham: The Personal Story,* 89.

151 Jon Meacham, "Peace at the Last," *Newsweek,* July 3, 2005, available at http://www.news week.com/peace-last-121413.

152 Graham, in Busby, *Billy Graham, God's Ambassador,* 112.

153 These four autobiographical statements, written over a span of more than fifty years, describe Graham's tearless conversion with remarkable consistency. Graham, "I Was Born Again," *American Weekly,* January 16, 1955, 6; Graham, "Billy Graham's Own Story: 'God Is My Witness,'" *McCall's,* April 1964, 198; Graham, *Just As I Am,* 2007, 30–31.

154 My thinking about the role of desire in Graham's preaching grows from Michael Hamilton, "From Desire to Decision: The Evangelistic Preaching of Billy Graham," in *The Worlds of Billy Graham,* ed. Andrew S. Finstuen, Anne Blue Wills, and Grant Wacker, forthcoming.

155 Graham, quoted in Pollock, *The Billy Graham Story,* 89. These words do not appear in the text of the actual sermon. From the framing in Pollock, they seem to be introductory comments before Graham launched into the sermon.

156 Graham, *The Collected Works of Billy Graham,* 250.

157 Graham sermon, reported in *Columbus Dispatch,* September 23, 1993, cited in Adler, *Ask Billy Graham,* 164.

158 Lane Adams, excerpted in Strober and Strober, *Billy Graham: An Oral and Narrative Biography,* 9.

159 David Bruce, executive assistant to Mr. Graham, conversation with the author, January 17, 2014.

160 Graham, in Busby, *Billy Graham, God's Ambassador,* 101.

161 Graham, quoted in High, *Billy Graham: The Personal Story,* 52.

162 Kenneth L. Woodward, "The Preaching and the Power," *Newsweek,* July 20, 1970, 53. The organization's records indicate 3,229,121 Christian commitments in live crusades. David Bruce, e-mail message to the author, October 7, 2013.

163 W. E. Sangster, quoted without citation in High, *Billy Graham: The Personal Story,* 49.

164 Ruth Bell Graham reflection, posted in a glass cabinet in Billy Graham Library, Charlotte, NC, July 3, 2009.

165 For two of many examples: "I think the media and the papers have put me on a pedestal I don't deserve to be on. I'm not a great preacher. I'm just an ordinary proclaimer of the Gospel," *Post and Courier* (Charleston, SC), September 25, 1996, cited in Adler, *Ask Billy Graham,* 1; "I am not a great preacher and no one has ever accused me of being a great preacher. . . . My gift is communicating the Gospel in simplicity," Billy Graham, interviewed by Jim Finnerty, *Jim Finnerty and Company,* KCRA (Sacramento, CA), September 9, 1982.

166 Michael Duduit, "The 25 Most Influential Pastors of the Past 25 Years," *Preaching,* April 2010, available at http://www.preaching.com/resources/articles/11629162/.

167 "Pastors Poll: Graham Is 'Most Influential,'" *Christian Century* 122, no. 3 (2005): 13.

2. ICON

1 Graham, in Russ Busby, *Billy Graham, God's Ambassador: A Lifelong Mission of Giving Hope to the World* (Alexandria, VA: Time-Life Books, 1999), 22.

2 Billy Graham, *Just As I Am: The Autobiography of Billy Graham* (San Francisco: HarperSanFrancisco; Grand Rapids, MI: Zondervan, 1997), xiv–xv.

3 Ibid., 24, 52.

4 Stanley High, *Billy Graham: The Personal Story of the Man, His Message, and His Mission* (New York: McGraw-Hill, 1956), 77.

5 Graham, *Just As I Am,* 1997, 115–116. In this case the Northwestern board seemed more certain of providence's role than Graham himself was.

6 Ibid., 178, 181.

7 Ibid., 305, 299.

8 Graham, in Busby, *Billy Graham, God's Ambassador,* 22.

9 Lou Cannon, *President Reagan: The Role of a Lifetime* (New York: Simon and Schuster, 1991), 15.

10 Graham, *Just As I Am,* 1997, 413.

11 David Aikman, *Billy Graham: His Life and Influence* (Nashville: Thomas Nelson, 2007), 259–260.

12 Aikman, *Billy Graham: His Life and Influence,* 290. When I asked one associate how he hoped to spend the remaining years of his professional career, he answered simply: "To help Billy finish well." John Akers, special assistant to Mr. Graham, conversation with the author, February 1, 2009, Duke Divinity School Conference on Billy Graham and American Culture, Durham, NC.

13 The Billy Graham Center Museum was owned by Wheaton College but worked closely with the BGEA.

14 Busby, *Billy Graham, God's Ambassador,* exists in at least five editions, running from 1999 to 2007, and is housed in more than 750 libraries.

15 Of the more than 1,600 sermons, 1,256 were preached in the United States; audio recordings available at http://billygraham.org/tv-and-radio/radio/audio-archives/.

16 Digitized sermons database, available at http://www.wheaton.edu/BGC/Ministries/Archives/Sermons-of-Billy-Graham.

17 See, for example, [Billy Graham], "Text of Billy Graham's Sermon Opening His Crusade in Madison Square Garden," *New York Times,* May 16, 1957, 22.

18 For example, television first appeared at the World's Fair in New York in 1939. By 1949, 2.3 percent of households in the United States owned a set; by 1962 that number had risen to 90 percent; and by 1975 to 97 percent. Susan J. Douglas, "Mass Media: From 1945 to the Present," in *A Companion to Post–1945 America,* ed. Jean-Christophe Agnew and Roy Rosenzweig (Malden, MA: Blackwell, 2002), 81; and Edward D. Berkowitz, *Mass Appeal: The Formative Age of the Movies, Radio, and TV* (New York: Cambridge University Press, 2010), 164. For religious programming see Quentin J. Schultze, ed., *American Evangelicals and the Mass Media: Perspectives on the Relationship between American Evangelicals and the Mass Media* (Grand Rapids, MI: Academie Books/Zondervan, 1990), esp. Schultze's Introduction; Quentin J. Schultze, "Evangelical Radio and the Rise of the Electronic Church, 1921–1948," *Journal of Broadcasting and Electronic Media* 32, no. 3 (1988): 289–306, doi:10.1080/08838158809386703.

19 Catherine L. Albanese, *America: Religions, and Religion,* 5th ed. (Belmont, CA: Thomson/Wadsworth, 2013), 252; William Martin, "Mass Communications," in *Encyclopedia of the American Religious Experience: Studies of Traditions and Movements,* ed. Charles H. Lippy and Peter W. Williams (New York: Scribner, 1988), esp. 3:1716.

20 Albanese, *America, Religions, and Religion,* 252; Martin, "Mass Communications," esp. 3:1717.

21 Christopher Owen Lynch, *Selling Catholicism: Bishop Sheen and the Power of Television* (Lexington: University of Kentucky Press, 1998), esp. 7–8.

22 Graham, *Just As I Am,* 1997, 149.

23 William Martin, *A Prophet with Honor: The Billy Graham Story* (New York: W. Morrow, 1991), 117 and 636n117.

24 In early 1946 Hearst directed his Chicago editor to "Puff YFC [Youth for Christ]." Hearst's son, William Randolph Hearst, Jr., denied that his father sent a note with the same directive to the editors covering the 1949 Los Angeles revival. A Los Angeles *Examiner* editor said that Hearst urged them to "give attention to Billy Graham's meetings." Martin, *A Prophet with Honor,* 117–118, 636n117; Patricia Daniels Cornwell, *Ruth, a Portrait: The Story of Ruth Bell Graham* (New York: Doubleday, 1997), 106.

25 Billy Graham, *Revival in Our Time: The Story of Billy Graham: Evangelistic Campaigns; Including Six of His Sermons* (Wheaton, IL: Van Kampen Press, 1950), 15–16.

26 Graham, *Just As I Am,* 1997, 162; Alan Brinkley, *The Publisher: Henry Luce and His American Century* (New York: Alfred A. Knopf, 2010), 438.

27 Ken Garfield, *Billy Graham: A Life in Pictures* (Chicago: Triumph Books, 2013), 38.

28 See, for example, Billy Graham, press conference, Cleveland, July 10, 1972, audio tape no. T51, transcript in box 2, folder 4, Collection 24, BGCA.

29 Billy Graham, interview by Edward B. (Ted) Fiske of the *New York Times,* June 22, 1970, transcript in box 1, folder 24, p. 8, Collection 24, BGCA.

30 See, for example, Billy Graham, press conference, Albuquerque, March 12, 1975, audio tape no. T82, transcript in box 3, folder 33, Collection 24, BGCA.

31 Busby, *Billy Graham, God's Ambassador,* 152.

32 See, for example, Billy Graham, press conferences, Raleigh, NC, April 26, 1973 (audio tape no. T60, transcript in box 3, folder 3); Albuquerque, March 12, 1975 (audio tape no. T82, transcript in box 3, folder 33); and Detroit, March 8, 1976 (audio tape no. T88, transcript in box 4, folder 1); all in Collection 24, BGCA.

33 See, for example, Graham's (at least) two appearances on the *Dinah Shore Show*, "*Dinah's Place*," October 3 and 4, 1972, audio tape no. T45, Collection 345, BGCA.

34 Woody Allen interview with Billy Graham, 1969, posted multiple times on YouTube (e.g., http://www.youtube.com/watch?v=194zJ55LcVk, http://www.youtube.com/watch?v=K_poGs bBgpE), has been viewed more than 100,000 times.

35 See, for example, Billy Graham, press conference, Charlotte, NC, April 4, 1972, audio tape no. T46, transcript in box 1, folder 26, Collection 24, BGCA. Graham did feel, however, that the press misquoted or took out of context some of the statements he made in his famous/infamous trip to Moscow in 1982. Graham, *Just As I Am*, 1997, 509–510. Yet even there he defended the press, saying that there were "probably some misunderstandings due to the fact that I was flying around so fast and they were trying to keep up with me . . . and I don't blame them at all." Graham, on *Good Day*, John Willis reporting, WCVB (Boston), May 28, 1982.

36 See, for example, Billy Graham, press conference, Raleigh, NC, April 26, 1973, audio tape no. T60, transcript in box 3, folder 3, Collection 24, BGCA.

37 "Billy Graham: The Man at Home," *Saturday Evening Post*, March 1972, 45.

38 Andrew Walsh, personal conversation with the author, March 1, 2010, Hartford, CT.

39 Kenneth L. Woodward, "The Preaching and the Power," *Newsweek*, July 20, 1970, 51.

40 Lewis William Gillenson, *Billy Graham: The Man and His Message* (New York: Fawcett, 1954), 30.

41 See, for example, Billy Graham press conference, Houston, June 14, 1973, transcript in box 3, folder 6, Collection 24, BGCA.

42 Without quite saying so, Henry Luce's *Life* magazine left no doubt about Graham's prominence—if not pre-eminence—in the field. "Billy in Dixie: South Carolina Gives Revivalist Biggest Crowd He Has Ever Pulled," *Life*, March 27, 1950, 4.

43 See, for example, "Billy Graham's Finale," *Newsweek*, July 22, 1957, 57; "God in the Garden," *Time*, May 27, 1957; "Does a Religious Crusade Do Any Good?" interview with Billy Graham, *U.S. News and World Report*, September 27, 1957, 72–81.

44 See the examples in Martin, *A Prophet with Honor*, 321. For simple misrepresentation, see 300–301.

45 Published photographs of Graham, his family, associates, friends, and people he met in the course of his work range in the thousands, if not tens of thousands. The Busby (1999) and Garfield (2013) pictorial history volumes are the most polished. For another, see BGEA, *Meet Billy Graham: A Pictorial Record of the Evangelist, His Family and His Team* (London: Billy Graham Evangelistic Association, 1966), available at the BGCA, accession 021381. Thousands more appear in the magazine and newspaper clippings gathered in Collection 360: Clippings File, BGCA. One of the more important yet largely unstudied features of these materials is the countless published cartoons: "Cartoons, 1945–1982," box 3, folder 4, Collection 74, BGCA.

46 See, for example, the cover of *The Nation*, May 11, 1957. This issue carried an acidic article by W. G. McLoughlin, Jr., "Billy Graham: In Business with the Lord." Other caricatures, however, sometimes proved strikingly handsome. See, for example, David Hawley, "Billy Graham: 'God's Machine Gun,'" Hamilton *Spectator*, October 15, 1994.

47 William Martin, "The Power and the Glory: How a Towheaded Kid from North Carolina Became God's Best Salesman," *Texas Monthly*, March 1978, 99; available at http://www.texasmonthly.com/story/power-and-glory-billy-graham.

48 See, for example, Garfield, *Billy Graham: A Life in Pictures*, 113–114.

49 Busby, *Billy Graham, God's Ambassador*, 102–103.

50 Elizabeth Kaye, "Billy Graham Rises," *George*, December 1996, 145.

51 Cover, *Newsweek*, August 14, 2006.

52 Russell Chandler, "Hispanic Billy Graham," *Los Angeles Times*, July 2, 1980, B3.

53 Don A. Schanche, "Should the 'Pilgrim Pope' Stay Home?" *Los Angeles Times*, February 27, 1983, D2.

54 Jim Hoagland, "Qaddafi Takes on the World," *Washington Post*, May 20, 1973, A1.

55 Alice Murray, "Glamour and Theatrics Fight 'Spiritual Genocide,'" *New York Times*, April 1, 1973, GN134.

56 Sally Quinn, "Druid Priestess," *Washington Post*, May 1, 1970, C1.

57 "Zulu Evangelist Here for Crusade Support," *New York Times*, November 9, 1958, 64; "Zulu 'Black Billy Graham' in Philly," *Atlanta Daily World*, December 10, 1958, 2.

58 Junius Griffin, "Malcolm X Plans Muslim Crusade," *New York Times*, April 3, 1964, 23.

59 Cover, *Time*, September 17, 2001, available at http://content.time.com/time/covers/0,16641, 20010917,00.html.

60 Brooke W. Kroeger, "Jesse Shifting to Religion," *Chicago Defender* (Daily Edition), July 7, 1975, 4.

61 *American Experience: Walt Whitman*, directed by Mark Zwonitzer and Jamila Wignot, executive producer Mark Samels (PBS, 2008).

62 Joseph Alsop, "Matter of Fact . . . ," *Washington Post*, March 1, 1965, A17.

63 Judith Martin, "The Shape of Government: A Critical Evaluation," *Washington Post*, October 30, 1973, E3.

64 Nicholas Tomalin, "Provos in Holland Mix Trix with Their Politix," *Washington Post*, September 26, 1966, A1–2.

65 "Billy Graham: The Man at Home," *Saturday Evening Post*, March 1972, 46; Billy Graham, interview by David Frost, *Doubts and Certainties*, BBC-2, 1964.

66 Kenneth L. Woodward, "The Preaching and the Power," *Newsweek*, July 20, 1970, 51; Anne Graham Lotz, in the foreword to Billy Graham, *Living in God's Love: The New York Crusade* (New York: G. P. Putnam's Sons, 2005).

67 Worker, quoted without citation in Roger A. Bruns, *Billy Graham: A Biography* (Westport, CT: Greenwood Press, 2004), 4.

68 "Billy Graham: The Man at Home," *Saturday Evening Post*, March 1972.

69 Graham, quoted in Bruns, *Billy Graham: A Biography*, 3.

70 "Graham Says 'No' to Movies," Hollywood *Citizen-News*, November 11, 1949, 1, reproduced in Busby, *Billy Graham, God's Ambassador*, 49.

71 London *Evening News*, February 23, 1954, quoted in Martin, *A Prophet with Honor*, 175; also available on microfilm reel 6, Collection 360, BGCA.

72 Kenneth L. Woodward, "Billy Graham Retrospective," *Daily Beast*, forthcoming.

73 Cover, *Look*, July 31, 1951.

74 Thomas F. Downey, "Grueling Life Led by Preacher," Boston *Sunday Post Extra*, January 8, 1950 ("Gruelling" [sic] in original); cover, story by Curtis Mitchell, *Popular Science*, May 1965, 61–64, 202–205.

75 Marshall Frady, *ABC News*, December 20, 1979.

76 Rich Oppel, editorial, *Charlotte Observer*, August 23, 1992.

77 David Morgan, "The Face That's Everywhere," *Christian History and Biography* 91 (Summer 2006), 11.

78 Graham, *Just As I Am*, 1997, 85; Billy Graham, "Billy Graham's Own Story: 'God Is My Witness,'" *McCall's*, June 1964, 64.

79 Unnamed aide, quoted in Marshall Frady, *Billy Graham, a Parable of American Righteousness* (Boston: Little, Brown, 1979), 222.

80 John Corry, "God, Country, and Billy Graham," *Harper's Monthly*, February 1969, 37.

81 Ibid., 39.

82 Gerald S. Strober, *Graham: A Day in Billy's Life* (Garden City, NY: Doubleday, 1976), 59–60.

83 Pauline Presson, quoted in Frady, *Billy Graham, a Parable of American Righteousness*, 76, see also 72.

84 Martin, *A Prophet with Honor*, 79–80.

85 Photographs posted in Billy Graham Museum, Wheaton, IL (viewed August 2010).

86 Billy Graham, press conference, Philadelphia, June 7, 1972, audio tape no. T49, transcript in box 2, folder 1, Collection 24, BGCA; Graham, *Just As I Am*, 1997, xxi, and *Just As I Am: The Autobiography of Billy Graham*, rev. and updated 10th anniv. ed. (New York: HarperOne; Grand Rapids, MI: Zondervan, 2007) xxi; Frady, *Billy Graham, a Parable of American Righteousness*, 191.

87 "Billy Graham: Young Thunderer of the Revival," *Newsweek*, February 1, 1954, 44.

88 Busby, *Billy Graham, God's Ambassador*, 55, plus photographs throughout.

89 Francis Russell, "Billy and Aimee," *National Review*, June 29, 1971, 716, quoted in James Morris, *The Preachers* (New York: St. Martin's Press, 1973), 384. Russell was referring to how Graham looked when Russell first saw him in Boston in 1950.

90 Graham, *Just As I Am*, 2007, xxi.

91 Ibid., xix. Graham said that *Time* reported that the suits were pistachio green, but he remembered them as cream-colored. The light hue of a black-and-white photograph of the scene suggests that Graham was right—which may say something about the press's propensity to

make a good story even better. The photo also shows that the four men were similarly, though not identically, attired. Graham, *Just As I Am*, 1997, xix, and photo insert, 104.

92 Martin, *A Prophet with Honor*, 383.

93 Joel A. Carpenter, *Revive Us Again: The Reawakening of American Fundamentalism* (New York: Oxford University Press, 1997), ch. 9; Bruce L. Shelley, "The Rise of Evangelical Youth Movements," *Fides et Historia* 18, no. 1 (1986): 45–63, esp. 48–52.

94 Photograph of poster, displayed in Billy Graham Center Museum, Wheaton College, Wheaton, IL (viewed August 15, 2010).

95 Tommy Tomlinson, "First Crusade as Headliner: '47 in Michigan," *Charlotte Observer*, September 22, 1996, 12.

96 Photograph of poster, displayed in Levine Museum of the South, Charlotte, NC (viewed April 15, 2010).

97 Shelley, "The Rise of Evangelical Youth Movements."

98 Billy Graham, *Just As I Am: The Autobiography of Billy Graham*, 2007, 158. "Authorized News Release from the Billy Graham Headquarters New York Crusade, Inc.," September 3, 1957, 1, BGCA, provided courtesy of Bob Shuster, archivist.

99 Graham, *Just As I Am*, 1997, ch. 17, esp. 321.

100 See, for example, Dr. Ernest T. Campbell, "An Open Letter to Billy Graham," December 31, 1972, Sermons from the Riverside Church, available at https://archive.org/stream/sermono penletter00camp/sermonopenletter00camp_djvu.txt. Campbell, pastor of the Riverside Church in New York City, sharply criticized Graham for not taking a stand against the resumption of the bombing of North Vietnam, December 18–29, 1972, following the breakdown of the Paris Peace negotiations. See also Frye Gaillard, "Billy Graham: An Honest Look," *Charlotte Observer*, October 13, 1991, B5, for discussion of Will Campbell's change of heart about Graham following Graham's 1982 visit to Moscow.

101 Andrew Finstuen, "Professor Graham: Billy Graham's Missions to Colleges and Universities," in *The Worlds of Billy Graham*, ed. Andrew S. Finstuen, Anne Blue Wills, and Grant Wacker, forthcoming. For recent accounts that exhibit strikingly different memories of Graham's visit to Union in 1954 see Douglas John Hall, *Waiting for Gospel*, quoted in "Critical Perspective," *Christian Century*, June 26, 2013, 8, versus Margaret E. Towner, "Graham at Union," *Christian Century*, July 24, 2013, 6.

102 Graham, *Just As I Am*, 1997, 301; George Champion, interviewed by Lois Ferm, June 29, 1979, interview no. 359, tape T57, oral history interviews, final copies (stored separately), transcript in box 23, folder 14, Collection 141, BGCA. Martin, *A Prophet with Honor*, 182.

103 I discuss this episode in greater detail in Chapter 7.

104 Billy Graham, "The Home God Honors," sermon preached at the Los Angeles revival, 1949, in Graham, *Revival in Our Time*, 89–104.

105 Photo reproduced in Busby, *Billy Graham, God's Ambassador*, 95.

106 Graham, *Just As I Am*, 1997, 137–138.

107 David Frost, *Billy Graham Talks with David Frost* (Philadelphia: A. J. Holman, 1971), 40.

108 Billy Graham, press conferences, Atlanta, December 14, 1972 (audio tape no. T56, transcript in box 2, folder 12); St. Louis, October 15, 1973 (audio tape no. T67, transcript in box 3, folder 23); Detroit, October 11, 1976 (audio tape no. T92, transcript in box 4, folder 6), all in Collection 24, BGCA.

109 [William Martin], "Billy Graham: Evangelist to Millions," *Christian History*, August 8, 2008, available at http://www.christianitytoday.com/ch/131christians/evangelistsandapologists/ graham.html?start=1.

110 Billy Graham, press conference, San Diego, March 31, 1976, audio tape no. T89, transcript in box 4, folder 3, Collection 24, BGCA. See also Aikman, *Billy Graham: His Life and Influence*, 275; Strober, *Graham: A Day in Billy's Life*, 108; Joe E. Barnhart, *The Billy Graham Religion* (Philadelphia: United Church Press, 1972), 77, 80.

111 Christine Leigh Heyrman, *Southern Cross: The Beginnings of the Bible Belt* (New York: Knopf, 1997), chs. 3, 4, and epilogue; William Bradford Wilcox, *Soft Patriarchs, New Men: How Christianity Shapes Fathers and Husbands* (Chicago: University of Chicago Press, 2004), esp. 191; but see also Margaret Lamberts Bendroth, *Fundamentalism and Gender, 1875 to the Present* (New Haven: Yale University Press, 1993), epilogue.

112 James B. Gilbert, *Men in the Middle: Searching for Masculinity in the 1950s* (Chicago: University of Chicago Press, 2005), chs. 6–8; Craig Thompson Friend, "From Southern Manhood to Southern Masculinities: An Introduction," in *Southern Masculinity: Perspectives on*

Manhood in the South since Reconstruction, ed. Friend (Athens: University of Georgia Press, 2009), xi, xviii.

113 Billy Graham, "Father" sermon, Oklahoma City, June 17, 1956, *Hour of Decision* radio program, pamphlet sermon no. 68, audio available at http://billygraham.org/audio/father/.

114 Gail Collins, *When Everything Changed: The Amazing Journey of American Women, from 1960 to the Present* (New York: Little, Brown, 2009), esp. ch. 4.

115 For the ERA see Billy Graham, press conferences, Albuquerque, March 12, 1975 (audio tape no. T82, transcript in box 3, folder 33); Detroit, March 8, 1976 (audio tape no. T88, transcript in box 4, folder 1); both in Collection 24, BGCA. For women's ordination, see Billy Graham, press conferences, St. Louis, October 15, 1973 (audio tape no. T67, transcript in box 3, folder 23); Detroit, October 11, 1976 (audio tape no. T92, transcript in box 4, folder 6); both in Collection 24, BGCA.

116 Frost, *Billy Graham Talks with David Frost,* 39–41, quotation on 40.

117 Billy Graham, "Jesus and the Liberated Woman," *Ladies Home Journal,* December 1970, 40–44, 114–115. Graham said that this article elicited more letters than "they knew what to do with." Billy Graham, press conference, Lexington, KY, April 24, 1971, audio tape no. T40 (side 2), transcript in box 1, folder 30, Collection 24, BGCA.

118 Billy Graham, "Trust God with Your Marriage and Your Home," BGEA, sermon no. 264, taken from *Decision* magazine, May 1981.

119 Cornwell, *Ruth, a Portrait*; Wills, "'An Odd Kind of Cross to Bear': Being Mrs. Billy Graham," in *The Worlds of Billy Graham,* ed. Finstuen, Wills, and Wacker, forthcoming; Aikman, *Billy Graham: His Life and Influence,* 114, 280, 283. I have not tried to document well-known details about Ruth Bell Graham that are already amply covered in most biographies about Billy or Ruth Bell Graham and their sixty-three-year marriage. Ruth died in 2007.

120 Graham, *Just As I Am,* 1997, 72.

121 High, *Billy Graham,* 87; Busby, *Billy Graham, God's Ambassador,* 234; Ronald C. Paul, *Billy Graham, Prophet of Hope* (New York: Ballantine Books, 1978), 148.

122 See, for example, "A Day with Billy Graham," *Minneapolis Sunday Tribune,* Picture Roto Magazine, September 17, 1950, 4; Stanley Pieza, "Billy Graham: Has Bible—Does Travel," *Chicago's Sunday American Leisure Magazine,* May 27, 1962; "Billy Graham: The Man at Home," *Saturday Evening Post,* March 1972, 44; "Attractive Mrs. Graham Advises Listening to Teen-Agers," *Minneapolis Star,* September 11, 1969, Sec. B. Actress Andie MacDowell described her as: "beautiful. . . . I hope I look like that when I'm eighty. She has this unbelievable skin, elegance, and presence." Ruth Graham and Stephen Griffith, *Ruth Bell Graham: Celebrating an Extraordinary Life* (Nashville: W Publishing Group, 2003), 3. I owe these references to Anne Blue Wills.

123 Aikman, *Billy Graham: His Life and Influence,* 283; Billy Graham, *Dinah Shore Show,* "Dinah's Place,"* October 3, 1972, audio tape no. T45, Collection 345, BGCA. In the 1950s, in keeping with the ethos of the times, the press often denoted Ruth Graham by her husband's name: "Inside Our Home, by Mrs. Billy Graham," *Guideposts,* December 1955, cover.

124 Ruth Bell Graham, *It's My Turn* (Old Tappan, NJ: F. H. Revell, 1982), 65, 106; Billy Graham, press conference, Detroit, March 8, 1976, audio tape no. T88, transcript in box 4, folder 1, Collection 24, BGCA.

125 Busby, *Billy Graham, God's Ambassador,* 231.

126 Among hundreds of possibilities see the following. The titles of the articles are as revealing of journalistic sensibilities as the photos themselves: Vivane Peter, "Mrs. Billy Graham: Crusader's Wife," *Parade,* March 8, 1970, 1, 7; *Minneapolis Tribune Sunday Picture Magazine,* December 12, 1965, 1, 6; *Minneapolis Tribune This Week Magazine,* "Billy Graham Condemns Vacations from Decency," 9; "Resting Up to Save Souls," *Life,* December 26, 1955, 101; Lee Fisher, "How the Grahams Spend Sunday," *Crusader,* September, 1964, 10; "Illustrious Guests: Billy Graham," *Holiday Inn Magazine,* October, 1960, 15.

127 *Person to Person with Edward R. Murrow,* April 6, 1956, film F14 (copied to videotape V27), Collection 74, BGCA.

128 Busby, *Billy Graham, God's Ambassador,* 230–231.

129 Graham, *Just As I Am,* 1997, 713–715; Graham, "Billy Graham's Own Story: 'God Is My Witness,'" *McCall's,* April 1964, 206.

130 Graham, *Just As I Am,* 2007, 722.

131 Billy Graham, "Moral Degeneration and Its Cure" sermon, Honolulu, 1959, *Hour of Decision* radio program, pamphlet sermon no. 105, audio tape T471j, Collection 191, BGCA, audio available at http://billygraham.org/audio/moral-degeneration-and-its-cure/.

132 Billy Graham, *Freedom from the Seven Deadly Sins* (Grand Rapids, MI: Zondervan 1966), 63.

133 Billy Graham, "The Bible and Dr. Kinsey" sermon, September 13, 1953, *Hour of Decision* radio program, Pub. S31, audio tape T192f, Collection 191, BGCA, audio available at http://billygraham.org/audio/the-bible-and-dr-kinsey/.

134 Frost, *Billy Graham Talks with David Frost,* 114.

135 See, for example, Billy Graham, *My Answer* (Garden City, NY: Doubleday, 1960), 36, 62, 63, 66, available online at http://www.ccel.us/myanswer.toc.html. See also numerous sermons, running from the 1960s through the 1980s, that addressed the topic directly (http://billygraham.org/audio-cat/sermons/?s=sex) and indirectly (http://billygraham.org/audio-cat/sermons/?s=marriage). The topic came up in other contexts such as a symptom of declining morals or education in the schools.

136 See, for example, Graham, *My Answer,* 36, 79, 147–152, 166–167.

137 Robert Darden and Doug Duncan, "An Exclusive Interview with Billy Graham," *National Lampoon: The Door,* no. 155, September/October 1997, 5.

138 Frost, *Billy Graham Talks with David Frost,* 114–115.

139 Charles Hirschberg, "The Eternal Crusader," *Life,* November 1994, 107.

140 Graham, in *Time,* July 11, 1969, 65, quoted in Hanspeter Nüesch, *Ruth and Billy Graham: The Legacy of a Couple* (Grand Rapids, MI: Baker Books, 2014), 67.

141 See, for example, Cliff and Joyce Penner, "Designed by God: Sex—What Did God Intend?" *Decision,* February 1996, 32–35; Amy DeRogatis, "What Would Jesus Do? Sexuality and Salvation in Protestant Evangelical Sex Manuals, 1950s to the Present," *Church History* 74, no. 1 (2005): 97–137.

142 See, for example, Graham, *Just As I Am,* 1997, 668; Billy Graham, press conferences, Boston, December 19, 1970 (audio tape no. T39, transcript in box 1, folder 29); San Francisco, September 7, 1972 (audio tape no. T54, transcript in box 2, folder 7); Houston, June 14, 1973 (transcript in box 3, folder 6); all in Collection 24, BGCA. John Akers, conversation with the author, January 17, 2014, Asheville, NC.

143 Graham, in Chattanooga *Times Free Press,* September 28, 1996, cited in Bill Adler, *Ask Billy Graham* (Nashville: Thomas Nelson, 2007), 6; David Bruce, executive assistant to Mr. Graham, conversation with the author, July 12, 2010, Black Mountain, NC.

144 George M. Marsden, *Fundamentalism and American Culture,* 2nd ed. (New York: Oxford University Press, 2006), 4.

145 Graham, in "Candid Conversation with the Evangelist," *Christianity Today,* July 17, 1981, 26; Graham, in "Billy Graham Answers His Critics," *Look,* February 7, 1956; Graham, in J. H. Hunter, "He Came—He Saw—He Conquered," *Evangelical Christian,* May 1955, 215.

146 I borrow the term and the concept of theological borderlands from John G. Turner, *Bill Bright and Campus Crusade for Christ: The Renewal of Evangelicalism in Postwar America* (Chapel Hill: University of North Carolina Press, 2008), 20.

147 Billy Graham, "The Lost Chord of Evangelism," address prepared for April 3, 1957, previewed in *Christianity Today,* April 1, 1957, 26.

148 The story of Graham's decision to hold an extended crusade in New York in 1957 and to work with Catholics and mainline Protestants as well as evangelicals has been told—and retold—in all of the standard biographies. The most useful account is perhaps Aikman, *Billy Graham: His Life and Influence,* 132–136, because of Aikman's apparently unique access to acrimonious correspondence between Graham's father-in-law, L. Nelson Bell, and Bob Jones, president of the university of that name.

149 Sydney Ahlstrom quoted this apt phrase in Sydney E. Ahlstrom, *A Religious History of the American People,* 2nd ed. (New Haven: Yale University Press, 2004), 23.

150 Peter J. Boyer, "The Big Tent: Billy Graham, Franklin Graham, and the Transformation of American Evangelicalism," *New Yorker,* August 22, 2005, 44, available at http://www.new yorker.com/archive/2005/08/22/050822fa_fact_boyer?currentPage=all. I elaborate my use of the label "mainstream evangelical" in Chapter 4. Here it is sufficient to think of it roughly as the historically Reformed/Wesleyan Protestant tradition flowing in the middle, between fundamentalists on the right and mainline Protestants on the left.

151 James L. Snyder, *The Life of A. W. Tozer: In Pursuit of God* (Ventura, CA: Regal Books, 1991), 197. I am quoting Snyder quoting Tozer. The site and date of the event are not specified.

152 Martin, *A Prophet with Honor,* 240.

153 For one of countless examples see Ernest Pickering, "The Tragedy of Compromise," 1994, International Testimony to an Infallible Bible, available at http://www.itib.org/articles/tragedy _of_compromise/tragedy_of_compromise_3-4.html.

154 Woodward, "Billy Graham Retrospective"; Aikman, *Billy Graham: His Life and Influence,* 122, 129; Graham, *Just As I Am,* 1997, 273; by implication: Billy Graham, press conference, Washington, DC, December 22, 1964, audio tape no. T23, transcript in box 4, folder 16, Collection 24, BGCA; Ken Garfield, "In NYC, Graham Won't Be Preaching to the Choir," *Charlotte Observer,* September 22, 1991, A1. Referring to Graham's 1991 crusade in New York City, Garfield says, "It's a far cry from 1957, when Catholic leaders spurned Graham's 16-week New York crusade."

155 Martin, *A Prophet with Honor,* 173.

156 Unnamed newspaper, quoted in Graham, *Just As I Am,* 1997, 221.

157 Evans, quoted without citation in "Graham, Billy," *Current Biography Yearbook,* ed. Charles Moritz (New York: H. W. Wilson, 1973), 151.

158 *Yale Daily News,* February 12, 13, and 15, 1957, quoted in Martin, *A Prophet with Honor,* 227.

159 Busby, *Billy Graham, God's Ambassador.*

160 *Christian Century,* February 29, 1956, 261–263, quoted in Martin, *A Prophet with Honor,* 653n198.

161 Editorial, *Christian Century,* quoted in Martin, *A Prophet with Honor,* 227.

162 Walter Donald Kring, quoted in "Clergy Debates Graham Crusade," *New York Times,* May 13, 1957, 24.

163 Andrew S. Finstuen, *Original Sin and Everyday Protestants: The Theology of Reinhold Niebuhr, Billy Graham, and Paul Tillich in an Age of Anxiety* (Chapel Hill: University of North Carolina Press, 2009), esp. ch. 4.

164 Richard Wightman Fox, *Reinhold Niebuhr: A Biography* (New York: Pantheon Books, 1985), 266, 288–289; Reinhold Niebuhr, quoted in Mark Silk, "The Rise of the 'New Evangelicalism,' " in *Between the Times: The Travail of the Protestant Establishment in America,* ed. William R. Hutchison (New York: Cambridge University Press, 1989), 286; and Reinhold Niebuhr, "Differing Views on Billy Graham," *Life,* July 1, 1957, 92.

165 Niebuhr, re-quoted in *New York Post,* June 2, 1957, cited in Martin, *A Prophet with Honor,* 659n228.

166 William G. McLoughlin, Jr., *Modern Revivalism: Charles Grandison Finney to Billy Graham* (New York: Ronald Press, 1959), 520, 522.

167 Paul H. Lehman, quoted in Harold H. Martin, "A Vivid Portrait of the Famous Revivalist Billy Graham," *Saturday Evening Post,* April 13, 1966, 18.

168 Graham, quoted without source in John Charles Pollock, *Billy Graham, Evangelist to the World: An Authorized Biography of the Decisive Years* (San Francisco: Harper and Row, 1979), 56. Pollock curiously said the criticism came "in no fractious spirit" but does not explain.

169 Leon Wieseltier, "Washington Diarist Clippings," *New Republic,* October 8, 2001, available at http://www.newrepublic.com/article/washington-diarist-clippings.

170 Garry Wills, *Under God: Religion and American Politics* (New York: Simon and Schuster, 1990), 61.

171 Robert Sherrill, "Preachers to Power," *The Nation,* July 13, 1998, 14.

172 Clark Morphew, "With Nixon, Did Dr. Billy Graham Step Over Political Line?" *Evening Times Globe* (St. John, New Brunswick), June 30, 1994. (The short answer is yes, he did: "And the picture is not very pretty.") William Edelen, "Jesus Would Have Been Ashamed of This Book," review of Graham, *Just As I Am, Desert Sun* (Palm Springs, CA), May 17, 1997: "I believe he would be embarrassed for you and humiliated that you are using Jesus' name in your earthly con game."

173 Karl Barth, excerpted in Raymond Kemp Anderson, *An American Scholar Recalls Karl Barth's Golden Years as a Teacher (1958–1964)* (Lewiston, NY: Edwin Mellen Press, 2013), 168–169, 259–260, 350. See also Cornwell, *Ruth, a Portrait,* 204–205.

174 Daniel Aleshire, e-mail message to author, April 7, 2009.

175 Donald G. Bloesch, "Billy Graham: A Theological Appraisal," *Theology and Life* 3, no. 2 (1960), esp. 39–40. Bloesch, who identified with the United Church of Christ, taught more than three decades at University of Dubuque Theological Seminary.

176 Joel Carpenter, Institute for the Study of American Evangelicals consultation, Michilinda, MI, July 1, 2008.

177 King, in *Chicken Soup for the Soul: Billy Graham & Me: 101 Inspiring Personal Stories from Presidents, Pastors, Performers, and Other People Who Know Him Well,* ed. Amy Newmark, Steve Posner, and A. Larry Ross (Cos Cob, CT: Chicken Soup for the Soul Publishing, 2013), 200–204.

178 Martin E. Marty, *The New Shape of American Religion* (New York: Harper, 1959), 21.
179 Martin E. Marty, "Reflections on Graham by a Former Grump," *Christianity Today*, November 18, 1988, available at http://www.christianitytoday.com/ct/2008/octoberweb-only /142-23.0.html; this article is now a classic in Graham studies.
180 Marty, featured speaker, Worlds of Billy Graham Conference, Wheaton College, Wheaton, IL, September 28, 2013. See also Martin Marty, "Billy Graham Taught Christians New Ways of Being in the World," September 30, 2013, Martin Marty Center, University of Chicago Divinity School, available at http://divinity.uchicago.edu/sightings/billy-graham-taught -christians-new-ways-being-world-martin-e-marty. For additional comments by Marty about Graham, the *Christian Century*, and the mainline, see http://www.christiancentury.org /blogs/archive/2013-07/rough-treatment.
181 Harry S. Stout, *The Divine Dramatist: George Whitefield and the Rise of Modern Evangelicalism* (Grand Rapids, MI: W. B. Eerdmans, 1991), 46–47.
182 Graham, in Busby, *Billy Graham, God's Ambassador*, 244.
183 Graham, *Just As I Am*, 1997, 251.
184 See, for example, Billy Graham to Kenneth Woodward, Editor, *Newsweek*, June 21, 1969, July 27, 1970, and February 23, 1983; personal letters provided by Kenneth Woodward, in author's possession.
185 Graham, *My Answer*, 134.
186 "Billy Graham: The Man at Home," *Saturday Evening Post*, March 1972, 45.
187 Mandrell, in *Star Phoenix* (Saskatoon, Saskatchewan), September 13, 2003, cited in Adler, *Ask Billy Graham*, 236.
188 Nancy Gibbs and Michael Duffy, *The Preacher and the Presidents: Billy Graham in the White House* (New York: Center Street, 2007), xi.
189 Strober, *Graham: A Day in Billy's Life*, 106–107, 167.
190 Though President Barack Obama met with Graham in his home—the only sitting president to do so—in April 2010, I have not included President Obama in this list, given the brevity of their exchange. At the time, Graham encouraged "Christians everywhere to pray for our President . . . and for all those in positions of authority, and especially for the men and women serving in our military." BGEA, "President Obama Meets with Billy Graham," available at http://billygraham.org/story/president-obama-meets-with-billy-graham-2/.
191 That is an exaggeration, of course. Before Cronkite there was Edward R. Murrow. But the larger point holds: At a given time, Americans were prepared to elevate one person.
192 *Look*, quoted in Charles T. Cook, *The Billy Graham Story, "One Thing I Do"* (Wheaton, IL: Van Kampen Press, 1954), 42.
193 As noted, Graham perennially scored a niche on the Most Admired roster but, significantly, never at the top.
194 I discuss Graham's involvement in the 1960 election in Chapter 7.
195 "Dr. Graham Hails Kennedy Victory," *New York Times*, January 17, 1961, 24. The article added: "Dr. Graham, the evangelist, said Mr. Kennedy's victory . . . probably had reduced forever the importance of the religious issue in American elections."
196 Graham, *Just As I Am*, 1997, 393–396, photo insert 424+.
197 David R. Swartz, *Moral Minority: The Evangelical Left in an Age of Conservatism* (Philadelphia: University of Pennsylvania Press, 2012), ch. 4.
198 Jon Meacham, "Peace at the Last," *Newsweek*, July 4, 2005, 30.

3. SOUTHERNER

1 The literature on the Southernizing of America (and the reverse) is extensive. Darren Dochuk ably summarizes it in "Evangelicalism Becomes Southern, Politics Becomes Evangelical: From FDR to Ronald Reagan," in *Religion and American Politics: From the Colonial Period to the Present*, ed. Mark A. Noll and Luke E. Harlow, 2nd ed. (New York: Oxford University Press, 2007), esp. 300–303. Other key works include Darren Dochuk, *From Bible Belt to Sunbelt: Plain-Folk Religion, Grassroots Politics, and the Rise of Evangelical Conservatism* (New York: W. W. Norton, 2011); Peter Applebome, *Dixie Rising: How the South Is Shaping American Values, Politics, and Culture* (New York: Random House, 1966); John Egerton, *The Americanization of Dixie* (New York: Harper's Magazine Press, 1974); James N. Gregory, *The Southern Diaspora: How the Great Migrations of Black and White Southerners Transformed*

America (Chapel Hill: University of North Carolina Press, 2005), esp. chs. 1 and 6; Jack Temple Kirby, *Media-Made Dixie: The South in the American Imagination,* rev. ed. (Athens: University of Georgia Press, 1986); John Shelton Reed, *My Tears Spoiled My Aim, and Other Reflections on Southern Culture* (Columbia: University of Missouri Press, 1993), esp. ch. 10.

2 If we include George H. W. Bush, who was born and reared in New England but earned his fortune in Texas and represented a Texas district in the House of Representatives for two terms (1966–1970), all elected presidents hailed from the South or Sunbelt: Johnson, Nixon, Carter, Reagan, Clinton, George H. W. Bush, and George W. Bush.

3 Humphrey, McGovern, Mondale, Ford, and Dukakis.

4 Philip Goff, "'We Have Heard the Joyful Sound': Charles E. Fuller's Radio Broadcast and the Rise of Modern Evangelicalism," *Religion and American Culture: A Journal of Interpretation* 9, no. 1 (1999), 67, 86, 94–95, doi:10.2307/1123927.

5 *Park Ridge Gospel Herald,* January 16, 1941, 5, box 1, folder 7, Collection 15, BGCA.

6 "Billy Graham," in "The 100 Most Important Americans of the 20th Century: Special Issue," *Life,* Fall 1990, 12.

7 George M. Marsden, *Fundamentalism and American Culture,* 2nd ed. (New York: Oxford University Press, 2006), 240.

8 John Shelton Reed, "The Twenty Most Influential Southerners of the Twentieth Century," *Southern Cultures* 7, no. 1 (2001), 96.

9 Cover, *Our State: Down Home in North Carolina,* February 26, 1955.

10 Hubert F. Lee, "Billy Graham Presented 'Man of the South' Award by Wm. H. Barnhardt in Charlotte as 105,000 Watch," *Dixie Business,* Summer 1975, 8, quoted in Steven P. Miller, *Billy Graham and the Rise of the Republican South* (Philadelphia: University of Pennsylvania Press, 2009), 162; and Hubert Lee to the Honorable President Gerald Ford, December 12, 1974, Gerald R. Ford Presidential Library and Museum, Ann Arbor and Grand Rapids, MI. The letter states that the award was for the year 1974.

11 Gayle White, "Son of the South," *Atlanta Journal Constitution,* October 9, 1994, M1.

12 Jimmy Tomlin, "Man with a Mission," *Our State: Down Home in North Carolina,* July 2012, available at https://www.ourstate.com/billy-graham/.

13 Liston Pope, quoted in Kenneth L. Woodward, "The Preaching and the Power," *Newsweek,* July 20, 1970, 53.

14 See, for example, Billy Graham, *Just As I Am: The Autobiography of Billy Graham* (San Francisco: HarperSanFrancisco; Grand Rapids, MI: Zondervan, 1997), 448.

15 Billy Graham, press conferences, Raleigh, NC, April 26, 1973 (audio tape no. T60, transcript in box 3, folder 3), p. 14; Raleigh, NC, September 21, 1973 (audio tape no. T66, transcript in box 3, folder 22), p. 2; both in Collection 24, BGCA; Billy Graham, "Something Is Happening in America!" sermon, *Hour of Decision* radio program, March 14, 1971, Raleigh, NC, pamphlet sermon no. 199, audio tape T1105a,b, Collection 191, BGCA, audio available at http://billygraham.org/audio/something-is-happening-in-america/.

16 Billy Graham to Mervin E. Rosell, February 21, 1947, letter in possession of Garth Rosell.

17 Graham, *Just As I Am,* 1997, 3–4, 203; Billy Graham, "Billy Graham's Own Story: 'God Is My Witness,'" *McCall's,* April 1964, 124; David Aikman, *Billy Graham: His Life and Influence* (Nashville: Thomas Nelson, 2007), 21. For Southern male stereotypes see Ted Ownby, *Subduing Satan: Religion, Recreation, and Manhood in the Rural South, 1865–1920* (Chapel Hill: University of North Carolina Press, 1990), part 1, esp. ch. 5.

18 Michael Kazin, *A Godly Hero: The Life of William Jennings Bryan* (New York: Knopf, 2006), xiii.

19 Russ Busby, *Billy Graham, God's Ambassador: A Lifelong Mission of Giving Hope to the World* (Alexandria, VA: Time-Life Books, 1999), 32; Morrow Coffey Graham, *They Call Me Mother Graham* (Old Tappan, NJ: Fleming H. Revell, 1977), chs. 1 and 2.

20 Jean Graham Ford, Billy Graham's sister, conversation with the author, July 2, 2009, Charlotte, NC.

21 Graham, *Just As I Am,* 1997, 9.

22 Jean Graham Ford, e-mail message to the author, June 17, 2014.

23 Graham, *Just As I Am,* 1997, 4–6; Graham, "Billy Graham's Own Story: 'God Is My Witness,'" April, 124; William Martin, *A Prophet with Honor: The Billy Graham Story* (New York: W. Morrow, 1991), 61; Morrow Graham, *They Call Me Mother Graham,* 10–12.

24 Busby, *Billy Graham, God's Ambassador,* 30; Morrow Graham, *They Call Me Mother Graham,* 25.

25 Graham, *Just As I Am,* 1997, 17.

26 Ibid., 52.
27 Graham's mother, Morrow Graham, reported that she had wanted him to go to Wheaton instead of Bob Jones College in the first place but he did not because it was "so far away and much more expensive." Morrow Graham, *They Call Me Mother Graham,* 38.
28 Graham, *Just As I Am,* 1997, 60.
29 Pauline Presson and Roy Gustafson, quoted in Marshall Frady, *Billy Graham, a Parable of American Righteousness* (Boston: Little, Brown, 1979), 76 and 107, respectively. Graham, *Just As I Am,* 1997, 64. For recollections by fellow students at Wheaton about his clothes and shoes see W. Lloyd Fesmire to Mel Larson, March 10, 1953; Mrs. Helen Fesmire to Bob Shuster, May 10, 2010; Jane Levering to Bob Shuster, 2000, all in box 11, folder 4, Collection 74, BGCA. See also "In Search of Style," *Wheaton,* Spring 2011, 6, available at http://www2.wheaton.edu/alumni/magazine/spring2011.pdf, for the earliest known photograph of Graham at Wheaton, just after arriving in 1940, and headed into downtown Chicago to buy appropriate clothes for the campus where students dressed up.
30 Graham, *Just As I Am,* 1997, 64.
31 Jean Graham Ford, conversation with the author, July 2, 2009, Charlotte, NC.
32 Graham, *Just As I Am,* 1997, xviii; Billy Graham, press conference, December 29, 1967, Atlanta, audio tape no. T12, transcript in box 1, folder 7, Collection 24, BGCA; Nancy Gibbs and Michael Duffy, *The Preacher and the Presidents: Billy Graham in the White House* (New York: Center Street, 2007), 344.
33 See, for example, Billy Graham, press conference, Columbus, OH, July 9, 1964, audio tape no. T7, transcript in box 4, folder 14, Collection 24, BGCA.
34 Raymond D. Gastil, *Cultural Regions of the United States* (Seattle: University of Washington Press, 1975), 183, 197–198.
35 Hear, for example, his first sermon at his first major urban crusade: "Why a Revival," September 25, 1949, Christ for Greater Los Angeles Campaign, T5702, Collection 26, BGCA, audio available at http://www2.wheaton.edu/bgc/archives/exhibits/LA49/05sermons01.html#newaudio.
36 Laura Hillenbrand, *Unbroken: A World War II Story of Survival, Resilience, and Redemption* (New York: Random House, 2010), 370. Hillenbrand listened to audio recordings of Graham's preaching in the 1940 Los Angeles crusade.
37 Ronald C. Paul, *Billy Graham, Prophet of Hope* (New York: Ballantine, 1977), 2. I discuss the importance of Graham's voice and accent in the Epilogue.
38 Hanspeter Nüesch, *Ruth and Billy Graham: The Legacy of a Couple* (Grand Rapids, MI: Baker Books, 2014), 66.
39 Nathan Hatch, president of Wake Forest University, in *Chicken Soup for the Soul: Billy Graham & Me: 101 Inspiring Personal Stories from Presidents, Pastors, Performers, and Other People Who Know Him Well,* ed. Amy Newmark, Steve Posner, and A. Larry Ross (Cos Cob, CT: Chicken Soup for the Soul Publishing, 2013), 180.
40 Graham, *Just As I Am,* 1997, 45.
41 Andrew Walsh, conversation with the author, March 15, 2010, Hartford, CT.
42 Graham, quoted in Harold Myra and Marshall Shelley, *The Leadership Secrets of Billy Graham* (Grand Rapids, MI: Zondervan, 2005), 59, 63. I assume that the first quotation, which serves as a section heading with partial quotation marks, represented Graham's own words—and certainly his thoughts.
43 Ford, quoted in ibid., 252.
44 Gastil, *Cultural Regions of the United States,* 185; Samuel S. Hill, *Southern Churches in Crisis* (New York: Holt, Rinehart and Winston, 1967), 111, 114; Reed, *My Tears Spoiled My Aim,* 65–74; Samuel S. Hill, Jr., "The Shape and Shapes of Popular Southern Piety," in *Varieties of Southern Evangelicalism,* ed. David Edwin Harrell, Jr. (Macon, GA: Mercer University Press, 1981), esp. 98.
45 For the strong sense of localism and particularity that accompanied the emphasis on the personal, see John Shelton Reed, *One South: An Ethnic Approach to Regional Culture* (Baton Rouge: Louisiana State University Press, 1982), ch. 3.
46 Graham, quoted in Myra and Shelley, *The Leadership Secrets of Billy Graham,* 182.
47 Robert Drake, "The Lady Frum Somewhere: Flannery O'Connor Then and Now," *Modern Age* 29, no. 3 (1985): 217–218, 223.
48 For literary projections of multiple Souths see, for example, G. Lee Ramsey, *Preachers and Misfits, Prophets and Thieves: The Minister in Southern Fiction* (Louisville, KY: Westminster John Knox Press, 2008).

49 For media projections of the "Good South" see, for example, Kirby, *Media-Made Dixie,*142, 151, 170–174, 182–183; Charles Reagan Wilson, *Judgment and Grace in Dixie: Southern Faiths from Faulkner to Elvis* (Athens: University of Georgia Press, 1995), 32–36.

50 By mainstream evangelical I mean members of the theologically conservative, culturally accommodated denominations or quasi-denominations that sprawled across the states of the Old South and the Sunbelt. They typically included Southern Baptists, southern branches of mainline Protestant bodies—especially Lutheran, Methodist, and Presbyterian—as well as, more problematically, Pentecostals and Churches of Christ.

51 Richard Cooper. *Billy Graham: Preacher to the World* (Raleigh, NC: Creative Productions, 1985), 42.

52 James Peacock, "The South in a Global World," *Virginia Quarterly Review* 78, no. 4 (2002): 581–594.

53 David Bruce, executive assistant to Mr. Graham, conversation with the author, January 17, 2014, Asheville, NC.

54 I count 46 YFC events through 1960 (excluding events that took place in England or Europe), and of those, 7 took place in the "Old South"—Texas, Georgia, Mississippi—and the rest outside, mostly in Indiana, Illinois, Michigan, and Wisconsin. I count 30 regular crusades through 1960 (again, excluding foreign events). Of those, 14 took place in the Old South, and the rest outside. Not enough to constitute a clear majority, but certainly enough to dismiss the idea that Graham's work was limited to the Old South. "Select Chronology," http://www2.wheaton.edu/bgc/archives/bgeachro/bgeachron02.htm.

55 Miller, *Billy Graham and the Rise of the Republican South, 5–6*; Mary Norton Kratt, *Charlotte, North Carolina: A Brief History* (Charleston, SC: History Press, 2009), chs. 9 and 10; Thomas W. Hanchett, *Sorting Out the New South City: Race, Class, and Urban Development in Charlotte, 1875–1975* (Chapel Hill: University of North Carolina Press, 1998), ch. 7 and 225–228.

56 For the rise of the "new" middle and upper-middle nationally oriented middle class in the South, see Reed, *One South,* ch. 9, tellingly titled: "Grits and Gravy: The South's New Middle Class."

57 Uta Andrea Balbier, "Billy Graham in West Germany: German Protestantism between Americanization and Rechristianization, 1954–70," *Zeithistorische Forschungen/Studies in Contemporary History* 3 (2010), available at http://www.zeithistorische-forschungen.de/16126041-Balbier-3-2010.

58 British newspaper headline quoted without definite citation in Gibbs and Duffy, *The Preacher and the Presidents,* 47.

59 Josh Ozersky, *Colonel Sanders and the American Dream* (Austin: University of Texas Press, 2012), Introduction (titled "How to Become an Icon") and 130–131. Sanders's colonel designation was removed in the 1930s but reinstated by another governor in 1949.

60 Michael Parker, "Being Mayberry," *Our State: Down Home in North Carolina,* July 2012, available at https://www.ourstate.com/being-mayberry/. Dennis Rogers, "North Carolina Legend Andy Griffith Dies at 86," *News and Observer* (Raleigh, NC), July 3, 2012, available at http://www.newsobserver.com/2012/07/03/2176821/north-carolina-legend-andy-griffith.html.

61 Trevor Freeze, "Billy Graham among 'Most Admired' 55th Time," Billy Graham Evangelistic Association, January 5, 2012, available at http://billygraham.org/story/billy-graham-among-most-admired-55th-time/.

62 Anne Blue Wills, "Billy Graham, Man of God, 1949–1954," paper presented at the American Society of Church History Winter Meeting, San Diego, CA, January 8, 2010. Frady, *Billy Graham, a Parable of American Righteousness,* 318.

63 The historical literature on evangelical religion and evangelical religious culture in the South (broadly defined) is extensive. For superb entry points see Miller, *Billy Graham and the Rise of the Republican South,* ch. 2; the essays by Martin E. Marty, Wayne Flynt, William Martin, and Samuel S. Hill, Jr., in *Varieties of Southern Evangelicalism,* ed. Harrell; and the essays in Mark Silk and Charles Reagan Wilson, eds., *Religion and Public Life in the South: In the Evangelical Mode* (Walnut Creek, CA: AltaMira Press, 2005).

64 See, for example, the chapters by D. Edwin Harrell and Joseph R. Washington in *Varieties of Southern Evangelicalism,* ed. Harrell; the chapters by William E. Montgomery and Samuel S. Hill in Silk and Wilson, *Religion and Public Life in the South.* Hill's chapter on religion in Florida and Appalachia offers a particularly important corrective to the convention that Southern religion in the twentieth century was uniformly evangelical. See also Samuel S. Hill, Jr., "The Strange Career of Religious Pluralism in the South," *Bulletin of the Center for the*

Study of Southern Culture and Religion 4, no. 2 (1980), 17–25, available at http://jsr.fsu.edu /issues/vol14/hill.pdf.

65 Graham, "Billy Graham's Own Story: 'God Is My Witness,' " April, 125.

66 David L. Chappell, *A Stone of Hope: Prophetic Religion and the Death of Jim Crow* (Chapel Hill: University of North Carolina Press, 2004), 117–121, 140–145, 247n6, 273–276nn37–50.

67 For class divisions within Southern evangelicalism see Wayne Flynt, "One in the Spirit, Many in the Flesh: Southern Evangelicals," in *Varieties of Southern Evangelicalism,* ed. Harrell, esp. 25–26, 34, 42–44; Ted Ownby, "Evangelical but Differentiated: Religion by the Numbers," in *Religion and Public Life in the South,* ed. Silk and Wilson, 34; John Hayes, "Hard, Hard Religion: The Invisible Institution of the New South," *Journal of Southern Religion* 10 (2007): 1–24, available at http://jsr.fsu.edu/Volume10/Hayes.pdf.

68 All of these data come from an undated sheet in the Gerald R. Ford Library and Museum. It follows a *Dixie Business* cover sheet, dated Spring 1973. The sheet is titled "Billy Graham Atlanta Crusade June 18–24," and carries a "Subscribe to DIXIE BUSINESS" byline. The text is cast in present or future tenses but I have framed it in the past tense as a description of events that actually took place as prescribed.

69 Billy Graham, press conference, Raleigh, NC, April 26, 1973, audio tape no. T60, transcript in box 3, folder 3, Collection 24, BGCA.

70 Harold H. Martin, "A Vivid Portrait of the Famous Revivalist Billy Graham," *Saturday Evening Post,* April 13, 1963, 21.

71 Graham, *Just As I Am,* 1997, 22.

72 Paul, *Billy Graham, Prophet of Hope,* 21.

73 Kenneth L. Woodward, *Faith, Culture, Politics from the Era of Eisenhower to the Age of Obama,* forthcoming.

74 Curtis Freeman, " 'Never Had I Been So Blind': W. A. Criswell's 'Change' on Racial Segregation," *Journal of Southern Religion* 10 (2007), available at http://jsr.fsu.edu/Volume10/Free man.pdf.

75 Billy Graham, *Just As I Am: The Autobiography of Billy Graham,* rev. and updated 10th anniv. ed. (New York: HarperOne; Grand Rapids, MI: Zondervan, 2007), 628.

76 Reed, *One South,* ch. 11, tellingly titled "Below the Smith and Wesson Line: Southern Violence."

77 Ibid., ch. 10, esp. 135; Grant Wacker, "Uneasy in Zion: Evangelicals in Postmodern Society," in George Marsden, *Evangelicalism and Modern America* (Grand Rapids, MI: W. B. Eerdmans, 1984), 22–28.

78 Charles Marsh, *God's Long Summer: Stories of Faith and Civil Rights* (Princeton, NJ: Princeton University Press, 1997), esp. ch. 3.

79 Leighton Ford, conversation with the author, April 1, 2007, Charlotte, NC.

80 Photographs in popular mass circulation magazines of Graham playing golf, often with presidents and other dignitaries, number in the scores if not hundreds. For examples see "Resting Up to Save Souls," *Life,* December 26, 1955, 100; Martin, "A Vivid Portrait of the Famous Revivalist Billy Graham," 20; and Jim Huffman, "Fame Hasn't Spoiled Billy Graham," *Minneapolis Tribune Picture Sunday Magazine,* December 12, 1965, 10.

81 Graham to Richard Nixon, May 31, 1961, box 3, folder 7, Collection 74, BGCA. Graham's correspondence with presidents Eisenhower, Johnson, Nixon, and Ford is sprinkled with references to golf outings. Much of Graham's correspondence with presidents is in box 1, folders 11–14, and box 3, folders 6–7, Collection 74, BGCA. See also Graham, *Just As I Am,* 1997, 424+ for an iconic photograph of Graham riding in a convertible with newly elected President Kennedy "for a game of golf," and 680+ for Graham playing golf with President Ford.

82 For Bingay, Woodward, "The Preaching and the Power," 53; Graham, *Just As I Am,* 1997: 298 for Champion; 288, 290, 316, 362 for Pew.

83 D. Michael Lindsay, *Faith in the Halls of Power: How Evangelicals Joined the American Elite* (New York: Oxford University Press, 2007), 218–223.

84 Wacker, "Uneasy in Zion," 26.

85 This argument is sustained in virtually all of the sources cited above on the role of evangelical religious culture in the modern South.

86 Martin, *A Prophet with Honor,* 143.

87 Graham, *Just As I Am,* 1997, 415–416. Graham did not say who paid for these trips. The context implies that military officials viewed him as a chaplain of sorts and therefore covered the costs. Graham mentioned two Vietnam Christmas visits, 1966 and 1968. From the context I infer the latter.

88 Martin, *A Prophet with Honor*, 384.
89 Ken Garfield, "'My Mind and Heart Are Still in It' but Graham Says 72-Year-Old Body Balks at Rigorous Pace," *Charlotte Observer*, September 22, 1991, A6.
90 See, for example, Graham, *Just As I Am*, 2007, 626, 375.
91 Carl F. H. Henry, *Confessions of a Theologian: An Autobiography* (Waco, TX: Word Books, 1986), 346. Henry here reporting a conversation with Supreme Court Justice Tom Clark, who cited media reports that Graham had made this comment without reading the actual decision. Graham assailed on multiple grounds the Court's similar decision on prayer, *Engel v. Vitale*, 1962, the previous year. Billy Graham, "The Supreme Court Ruling on Prayer," *Good News Broadcaster*, August 1962, 19–20, Magazine Scrapbook for 1962, Collection 360, BGCA.
92 "Billy Graham: The Man at Home," *Saturday Evening Post*, March 1972, 105.
93 Billy Graham, press conference, Birmingham, AL, May 11, 1972, audio tape no. T47, transcript in box 1, folder 37, pp. 24–25, Collection 24, BGCA.
94 Billy Graham, press conference, St. Louis, MO, October 15, 1973, audio tape no. T67, transcript in box 3, folder 23, p. 4, Collection 24, BGCA.
95 Billy Graham, press conference, Columbus, OH, July 9, 1964, audio tape no. T7, transcript in box 4, folder 14, pp. 6–7, Collection 24, BGCA.
96 Billy Graham, press conference, Houston, June 14, 1973, transcript in box 3, folder 6, p. 3, Collection 24, BGCA.
97 Graham, on *News at 4*, John Beard reporting, KNBC (Los Angeles), July 22, 1985.
98 Billy Graham, press conference, Birmingham, AL, May 11, 1972, audio tape no. T47, transcript in box 1, folder 37, pp. 24–25, Collection 24, BGCA. Elsewhere Graham would make the same point in different words: "Any discussion of God can revolve around the Commandments, rather than getting into the differences in faith." Graham in Holly Graham Miller, "Hope for the Coming Generation," excerpted from *Saturday Evening Post*, November/December 1999, Beliefnet, available at http://www.beliefnet.com/Faiths/2000/02/Hope-For-The-Coming-Generation.aspx.
99 Billy Graham, press conferences, Atlanta, December 12, 1967 (audio tape no. T12, transcript in box 1, folder 7); New York, June 10, 1969 (transcript in box 1, folder 19), p. 14; Billy Graham, interviewed by Merv Griffin, *Merv Griffin Show*, October 12, 1972, audio tape T44, Collection 345, transcript box 2, folder 10; all in Collection 24, BGCA.
100 Billy Graham, press conference, Detroit, October 11, 1976, audio tape no. T92, transcript in box 4, folder 6, p. 11, Collection 24, BGCA.
101 Ibid., p. 14.
102 Graham, *Just As I Am*, 1997, 450. Graham goes on to imply strongly that Nixon made the White House Sunday worship services ecumenical at Graham's instigation (see p. 451).
103 Editor, "Billy Graham Reflects on His Association with the [Salvation] Army . . . ," *The War Cry*, December 9, 1989, 6–7.
104 Graham, in Barry A. Kosmin and Seymour P. Lachman, *One Nation Under God: Religion in Contemporary American Society* (New York: Harmony Books, 1993), back cover.
105 Jon Meacham, "The Prayer Breakfast Presidency," *Washington Post*, April 16, 2006, B1, available at http://www.washingtonpost.com/wp-dyn/content/article/2006/04/14/AR200604 1401908.htm.
106 All of the "standard" biographies treat Graham's relation to the civil rights movement at length, ranging from very positive to very negative. Steven P. Miller, "Billy Graham, Civil Rights, and the Changing Postwar South," in *Politics and Religion in the White South*, ed. Glenn Feldman (Lexington: University Press of Kentucky, 2005), 157–186, and Miller, *Billy Graham and the Rise of the Republican South*, offer a meticulous examination of this controverted subject. For meticulous and even-handed examinations of the subject and of much of the relevant literature see Martin, *A Prophet with Honor*, esp. 202, 296, and index entries for "race relations"; Miller, *Billy Graham and the Rise of the Republican South*; and Steven P. Miller, "Billy Graham, Civil Rights, and the Changing Postwar South," in *Politics and Religion in the White South*, ed. Glenn Feldman (Lexington: University Press of Kentucky, 2005), 157–186. For a shorter but incisive snapshot of the subject and the literature see Chappell, *A Stone of Hope*, 140–145, 247n6, 273nn37–50.
107 For Jackson, see *Billy Graham: Ambassador of Salvation*, in series *Great Souls: Six Who Changed a Century*, hosted by David Aikman, with Billy Graham, Dan Rather, and David Frost, directed by Tom Ivy (Vision Video, 2002, dist. PBS), quoted in Aikman, *Billy Graham: His Life and Influence*, 145, 8. For Clinton, see Peter J. Boyer, "The Big Tent: Billy Graham,

Franklin Graham, and the Transformation of American Evangelicalism," *New Yorker*, August 22, 2005, 44, available at http://www.newyorker.com/archive/2005/08/22/050822fa_fact_boyer?currentPage=all.

108 Martin, quoted in conversation with Myra and Shelley, *The Leadership Secrets of Billy Graham*, 144.

109 Darren Dochuk, "'Mr. Texas': Billy Graham, Entrepreneurialism, and Race Reform in the Sunbelt's 'Golden Buckle,'" in *The Worlds of Billy Graham*, ed. Andrew S. Finstuen, Anne Blue Wills, and Grant Wacker, forthcoming.

110 Billy Graham, "Why Don't Our Churches Practice the Brotherhood They Preach?" *Reader's Digest*, August 1960. See also Graham, *Just As I Am*, 1997, 63, 159.

111 Graham, *Just As I Am*, 1997, 12.

112 Jean Graham Ford, conversation with the author, July 2, 2009, Charlotte, NC.

113 Aikman, *Billy Graham: His Life and Influence*, 137.

114 Graham, *Just As I Am*, 1997, 63.

115 Ibid., 426. See also BGEA (as author), "Billy Graham Reflects on Friendship with Martin Luther King, Jr.," *Christian Post*, January 16, 2012, available at http://www.christianpost.com/news/billy-graham-reflects-on-friendship-with-martin-luther-king-jr-67267/.

116 The college yearbooks for the time Graham was enrolled seem to show only white students. The research of one historian of race at Wheaton indicated that most likely no African Americans graduated from the college between the 1920s and 1947. The one African American who graduated in 1947, C. Herbert Oliver, matriculated after Graham had graduated in May 1943. On the face of it, in short, there were no African American students at Wheaton during Graham's tenure. Graham may have misremembered the details, or the yearbook may have offered an incomplete record, or the students may have been visitors, or perhaps they may have been students in segregated military schools that shared the campus. I examined both the individual and the group photographs of the classes for the years 1941, 1942, and 1943 in *The Tower*, the Wheaton College annual yearbook, housed in the Wheaton College Archives and Special Collections. Visual identification is of course subject to error. I have pieced together the rest of this account from two sources; first, a lecture given by David B. Malone, associate professor of Library Science, Wheaton College, "Out of the Same Mouth Come Praise and Cursing: Race Relations at Wheaton College, 1840s–Present," at Faculty Development Day, Wheaton College, February 5, 2013, not paginated but appended to footnote no. 9, manuscript at Wheaton's Buswell College Library and in my possession; and second, the sedulous research of Bob Shuster, archivist, BGCA, e-mails to the author, February 26, 2013, and April 18, 2014. I wish particularly to thank Bob Shuster for his generous help. BGCA staff interviewed people whose time as students at Wheaton College overlapped with Billy Graham's. Some of these interviews mention African Americans, including T60, T66, T67, T72, and T79, Collection 74, BGCA; audio and transcripts of the interviews are available online within the content list of Collection 74: http://www2.wheaton.edu/bgc/archives/GUIDES/074.htm#9.

117 Martin, *A Prophet with Honor*, 169.

118 Stephen Olford, interviewed by Lois Ferm, August 10, 1970, interview no. 152, oral history interviews, final copy (stored separately), transcript in box 5, folder 27, pp. 15–16, Collection 141, BGCA.

119 Billy Graham, press conference, Jackson, MS, May 7, 1975, audio tape no. T84, transcript in box 3, folder 34, p. 14, Collection 24, BGCA.

120 Jerry Beryl Hopkins, "Billy Graham and the Race Problem" (Ph.D. diss., University of Kentucky, 1986), 44, 174n20.

121 Miller, *Billy Graham and the Rise of the Republican South*, 25–28, quotation on 28. Miller covers the shadings of Graham's many—and sometimes inconsistent—comments about race, segregation, and desegregation in the early 1950s with meticulous detail. I make no attempt to retrace his steps but only to highlight the primary events and turning points.

122 Graham, *Just As I Am*, 2007, 426. This is the "official" story, which Graham affirmed on several occasions and readily told me too when I first visited him in July 2007. That being said, the "ropes incident," as it came to be called, may have taken place in Jackson, Mississippi, the previous year. As late as 2010, Cliff Barrows, who was present at both the Jackson and the Chattanooga crusades, strongly insisted that it happened in Jackson. Frady, Martin, Miller, and Pollock support the Chattanooga story. See Frady, *Billy Graham, a Parable of American Righteousness*, 408–409; Martin, *A Prophet with Honor*, 171; Miller, *Billy Graham and the Rise of the Republican South*, 28, 230–231nn66–69; John Charles Pollock,

The Billy Graham Story: The Authorized Biography, rev. and updated ed. (Grand Rapids, MI: Zondervan, 2003), 113. For Jackson, see Barrows, quoted in Busby, *Billy Graham, God's Ambassador,* 213; and John Akers, special assistant to Billy Graham, e-mail message to author, September 1, 2010. The weight of the evidence favors Chattanooga but the jury is still out. More important than whether the ropes incident took place in Chattanooga in 1953 or in Jackson in 1952 is that three biographies (two sympathetic, one unsympathetic) published shortly afterward said nothing about the event at all: Charles T. Cook, *The Billy Graham Story, "One Thing I Do"* (Wheaton, IL: Van Kampen Press, 1954); Stanley High, *Billy Graham: The Personal Story of the Man, His Message, and His Mission* (New York: McGraw-Hill, 1956); and William G. McLoughlin, Jr., *Billy Graham, Revivalist in a Secular Age* (New York: Ronald Press, 1960). That omission suggests that the incident did not begin to loom large in Graham's memory until two decades later (see Miller, *Billy Graham and the Rise of the Republican South,* 231n67). The first edition of Pollock's authorized biography—published in 1966—similarly said nothing about the ropes incident. In that early work Pollock simply said that Graham "overruled protests" from the organizing committee and insisted that blacks should be allowed to sit anywhere.

123 "Instructions for Ushers," undated, The Greater Dallas Evangelistic Crusade with Billy Graham, 1953, box 1, folder 16, Collection 1, BGCA.

124 Graham quoted and the situation described in Pollock, *The Billy Graham Story,* 98. See also Martin, *A Prophet with Honor,* 171; Miller, *Billy Graham and the Rise of the Republican South,* 29. In his autobiography Graham mentioned the Dallas crusade—which he elsewhere pegged as "the largest single evangelistic audience in church history"—but said nothing about segregation. Graham, *Just As I Am,* 1997, 243. For "largest audience" quotation, see Francis Raffetto, "Graham Fills Cotton Bowl," *Dallas Morning News,* June 29, 1953, 1. One person who was present at the Dallas crusade (name withheld by request) told me that ropes separated the sections. The meetings began at 7:30 PM but the ushers took the ropes down at 7:00 PM. He did not know why. Chappell noted that in a revival in Houston in 1952 Graham had accepted segregated seating but insisted that the black section be removed from "an inconvenient place in the sun." It is possible that a similar reason dictated the rope policy in Dallas in 1953. Chappell, *A Stone of Hope,* 273n37.

125 Hopkins, "Billy Graham and the Race Problem," 51–52.

126 Anthony Lake Newberry, "Without Urgency or Ardor: The South's Middle-of-the-Road Liberals and Civil Rights, 1945–1960" (Ph.D. diss., Ohio University, 1982). Though Newberry does not speak of Graham specifically, in this period Graham fit Newberry's category of "cautious reformers." Later we will see that after the 1970s Graham moved to a more progressive, though not radical, posture (quotation p. 16; see also Epilogue, esp. 496–497).

127 Billy Graham, "Billy Graham Makes Plea for an End to Intolerance," *Life,* October 1, 1956, 138, 140, 143–144, 146, 151. Billy Graham, "No Color Line in Heaven," *Ebony,* September 1957, 99, 100, 102, 104.

128 Billy Graham, "Billy Graham Makes Plea for an End to Intolerance," 144.

129 Graham, "No Color Line in Heaven," 99.

130 Daniel Bell, *The End of Ideology* (Glencoe, IL: Free Press, 1960), 34, cited in George M. Marsden, *The Twilight of the American Enlightenment: The 1950s and the Crisis of American Belief* (New York: Basic Books, 2014), xxxi.

131 Howard O. Jones, *Gospel Trailblazer: An African American Preacher's Historic Journey across Racial Lines* (Chicago: Moody, 2003), chs. 11–13, esp. 143.

132 Howard O. Jones and Ralph Bell to Billy Graham, May 1, 1968, box 6, folder 12, Collection 12, BGCA; Forrest Layman to Howard O. Jones, May 6, 1968, cited in Martin, *A Prophet with Honor,* 682, note for p. 351.

133 Martin, *A Prophet with Honor,* 351, and corresponding note on 682. See also Roger A. Bruns, *Billy Graham: A Biography* (Westport, CT: Greenwood Press, 2004), 96.

134 Jones, *Gospel Trailblazer,* 134, 143; Howard Jones to Billy Graham, May 14, 1965; Howard Jones to Walter Smyth, May 14, 1965; Walter Smyth to Howard Jones, May 21, 1965; Billy Graham to Howard Jones, May 28, 1965; Billy Graham to Walter Smyth, May 28, 1965; all in box 80, folder 34, Collection 17, BGCA.

135 Jones, *Gospel Trailblazer,* 144.

136 Dr. Ralph Bell served from June 1, 1965, to December 31, 2004 (39 years) and Howard Jones served from June 1, 1957, to April 1, 1993 (36 years). Jones died November 14, 2010, in Seattle.

137 "Invocation Delivered at Billy Graham Evangelistic Crusade," July 18, 1957, New York, available through the Martin Luther King, Jr., Papers Project, at http://mlk-kpp01.stanford .edu/primarydocuments/Vol4/18-July-1957_BillyGrahamInvocation.pdf.

138 "Graham Says Country Needs 'Anti-Segregation Legislation,'" *Baltimore Afro-American*, July 27, 1957, available at http://news.google.com/newspapers?nid=2205&dat=19570723 &id=UuclAAAAIBAJ&sjid=bPUFAAAAIBAJ&pg=2636,4391383. The story indicated that the event took place on July 21; the audience was estimated at 3,000 (photo caption) and 8,000 (text of article). Both caption and text list the same location; they may refer to different events, but more likely one figure is a typographical error. The 8,000 figure corresponds with the estimate Jones offered.

139 Martin Luther King, Jr., to Billy Graham, August 31, 1957, available through the Martin Luther King, Jr., Papers Project at http://mlk-kpp01.stanford.edu/primarydocuments/Vol4 /31-Aug-1957_ToGraham.pdf.

140 Edith Blumhofer, "Singing to Save: The Signature Sound of the Graham Crusades," in *The Worlds of Billy Graham*, ed. Andrew S. Finstuen, Anne Blue Wills, and Grant Wacker, forthcoming.

141 Graham, *Just As I Am*, 1997, photo gallery preceding page 167. Haqq's tenure on the Team ran from 1957 to 1973. By 1964 another Indian, Robert Cunville, was preaching in Graham crusades and eventually became an associate evangelist (276); "Select Chronology," http:// www2.wheaton.edu/bgc/archives/bgeachro/bgeachron02.htm.

142 Henry, *Confessions of a Theologian*, 227.

143 Rufus Burrow, Jr., "Graham, King, and the Beloved Community," in *The Legacy of Billy Graham*, ed. Michael G. Long (Louisville, KY: Westminster John Knox Press, 2008), 168.

144 Miller, *Billy Graham and the Rise of the Republican South*, 67.

145 Rev. Martin L. King, Jr., letter to Billy Graham, July 23, 1958, available through the Martin Luther King, Jr., Papers Project at http://mlk-kpp01.stanford.edu/primarydocuments/Vol4 /23-July-1958_ToGraham.pdf.

146 Grady Wilson, letter to Rev. Martin Luther King, Jr., July 28, 1958, available through the Martin Luther King, Jr. Papers Project at http://mlk-kpp01.stanford.edu/primarydocuments /Vol4/28-July-1958_FromWilson.pdf.

147 Miller, *Billy Graham and the Rise of the Republican South*, 67–68. I wish especially to thank Aaron Griffith for helping me research this event.

148 Graham, *Just As I Am*, 1997, 359–360 (quotation on 360).

149 Ibid., 426.

150 Billy Graham, "Why Don't Our Churches Practice the Brotherhood They Preach?" *Reader's Digest*, August 1960. The phrase is usually attributed to King, who said it often in the 1950s and 1960s; the substance of the comment had been circulating in the press in one form or another since at least 1953. Ralph Keyes, *The Quote Verifier: Who Said What, Where, and When* (New York: St. Martin's Press, 2006), 54–55.

151 Graham, quoted in *New York Times*, April 18, 1963, 21.

152 Kennedy (timing) and *Washington Post* (utility) cited without attribution in Gibbs and Duffy, *The Preacher and the Presidents*, 111.

153 Martin Luther King, Jr., "Letter from Birmingham City Jail," April 16, 1963, available at www. africa.upenn.edu/Articles_Gen/Letter_Birmingham.html.

154 John Herbers, "35,000 in Alabama at Biracial Rites: Graham's Easter Service in Birmingham is Viewed as Helping to Curb Hatred," *New York Times*, March 30, 1964, 1.

155 Ibid., 15.

156 Miller, *Billy Graham and the Rise of the Republican South*, 109–112, quotation on 111.

157 "Rally Hears Graham in Birmingham," *Washington Post*, March 30, 1964, 3.

158 Herbers, "35,000 in Alabama at Biracial Rites," 1, 15. The *New York Times* account said the audience numbered 35,000 and the choir 3,000.

159 Numerous quotations and remarks from Graham, taken from *New York Times* and *Religion News Service*, 1965–1967, cited in Lowell D. Streiker and Gerald S. Strober, *Religion and the New Majority: Billy Graham, Middle America, and the Politics of the 70s* (New York: Association Press, 1972), 53–56.

160 Streiker and Strober, *Religion and the New Majority*, 55–59; Gibbs and Duffy, *The Preacher and the Presidents*, 142–143; Martin, *A Prophet with Honor*, 315; Miller, *Billy Graham and the Rise of the Republican South*, 128.

161 Gibbs and Duffy, *The Preacher and the Presidents*, 143, drawing on Doris Kearns Goodwin, *Lyndon Johnson and the American Dream* (New York: Harper and Row, 1976), 304.

162 Dochuk, *From Bible Belt to Sunbelt*, esp. 285–291.

163 Dwight Eisenhower to Billy Graham, March 30, 1956; and Billy Graham to Dwight Eisenhower, June 4, 1956; both in box 1, folder 12, Collection 74, BGCA.

164 Billy Graham, interview by Edward B. (Ted) Fiske of the *New York Times*, June 22, 1970, transcript in box 1, folder 24, pp. 12, 14, Collection 24, BGCA.

165 H. R. Haldeman, memorandum to Len Garment, January 16, 1970, box 3, folder 5 (or 7), Collection 74, BGCA.

166 Graham speech in Philadelphia, quoted in *Christian Century*, May 17, 1967, 645. I was led to this text by Martin, *A Prophet with Honor*, 346.

167 Frady, *Billy Graham, a Parable of American Righteousness*, 416; Michael G. Long, *Billy Graham and the Beloved Community* (New York: Palgrave Macmillan, 2006), 2, 132.

168 Graham, *Just As I Am*, 1997, 696.

169 Graham quoted in Martin, *A Prophet with Honor*, 351, and additional comments in the note on p. 682.

170 Ibid., 351.

171 Billy Graham, press conference, Los Angeles, May 13, 1968, audio tape no. T8, transcript in box 1, folder 10, p. 5, Collection 24, BGCA.

172 Gibbs and Duffy, *The Preacher and the Presidents*, 136.

173 Graham, *Just As I Am*, 1997, 430–431. These events are detailed in most of the standard biographies, most amply in John Charles Pollock, *Billy Graham, Evangelist to the World: An Authorized Biography of the Decisive Years* (San Francisco: Harper and Row, 1979), ch. 3, quotation on 36.

174 Martin, *A Prophet with Honor*, 506; J. Martin Bailey, "Billy Graham in Moscow: The Media Missed the Story," *Christianity and Crisis*, June 7, 1982, 155, 173.

175 See, for example, Billy Graham, press conferences, Columbus, OH, January 28, 1963 (audio tape no. T1 (side 1), transcript in box 4, folder 9), p. 5; Detroit, March 8, 1976 (audio tape no. T88, transcript in box 4, folder 1), p. 17; both in Collection 24, BGCA; Billy Graham to Lyndon Johnson, September 25, 1965, box 3, folder 6, Collection 74, BGCA.

176 Graham, quoted in Charles Hirschberg, "The Eternal Crusader," *Life*, November 1994, 114, quoted and discussed in Ken Garfield, "Graham Backs Mixed-Race Unions—But Not for His Own Children," *Charlotte Observer*, November 1, 1994, 1C. See also Streiker and Strober, *Religion and the New Majority*, 53.

177 Billy Graham, press conference, Detroit, October 11, 1976, audio tape no. T92, transcript in box 4, folder 6, p. 21, Collection 24, BGCA.

178 Mark G. Toulouse, "Christianity Today and American Public Life: A Case Study," *Journal of Church and State* 35, no. 2 (1993), 241.

179 Aaron Griffith, "*Christianity Today*, Race, and the Neo-Evangelical Quest for Respectability" (seminar paper, Duke University, 2013, ms. in author's possession). See also Henry, *Confessions of a Theologian*, 227, 270.

180 Henry, *Confessions of a Theologian*, chs. 13–15; Douglas A. Sweeney, "Christianity Today," in *Popular Religious Magazines of the United States*, ed. Mark Fackler and Charles H. Lippy (Westport, CT: Greenwood Press, 1995), 145–146.

181 Chappell, *A Stone of Hope*, 117, 120; Griffith, "*Christianity Today*," 9n30; Billy Graham to Richard Nixon, January 16, 1970, box 3, folder 7, Collection 74, BGCA.

182 Billy Graham press conferences, Columbus, OH, July 9, 1964 (audio tape no. T7, transcript in box 4, folder 14); Washington, DC, December 22, 1964 (audio tape no. T23, transcript in box 4, folder 16); both in Collection 24, BGCA; Billy Graham, *World Aflame* (Garden City, NY: Doubleday, 1965), 6; Billy Graham, press conference, Oakland, CA, June 25, 1971, audio tape no. T42, transcript in box 1, folder 23, p. 25, Collection 24, BGCA.

183 Mark Silk, "Franklin Graham Claims to Be Following in Billy's Footsteps," April 2, 2014, Spiritual Politics blog, Religion News Service, available at http://marksilk.religionnews.com/2014/04/02/franklin-graham-youre-billy/.

184 Gerald Durley, in *Chicken Soup for the Soul: Billy Graham & Me*, ed. Newmark, Posner, and Ross, 124–125.

185 See, for example, Graham, quoted in Joseph Neff, "Graham Hopes to Ease Racial Tensions . . . ," *Burlington County Times* (Willingboro, NJ), August 29, 1991, copy in Scrapbook 879, Acc. No. 08-53, Collection 360, BGCA; Billy Graham to Dwight Eisenhower, June 4, 1956, box 1, folder 12, Collection 74, BGCA; Graham, *World Aflame*, 7; Billy Graham, press conference, Washington, DC, December 22, 1964, audio tape no. T23, transcript in box 4, folder 16, p. 4, Collection 24, BGCA; Billy Graham, "Something Is Happening in America!" sermon, *Hour*

of Decision radio program, March 14, 1971, Raleigh, NC, pamphlet sermon no. 199, audio tape T1105a,b, Collection 191, BGCA, audio available at http://billygraham.org/audio/some thing-is-happening-in-america/.

186 Woodward, "The Preaching and the Power," 55.

187 Curtis Freeman, "Carlyle Marney: On Pilgrim Priesthood," *Baptists Today*, June 2002, 28–29, available at https://divinity.duke.edu/sites/default/files/documents/faculty-freeman/carlyle-mar ney.pdf.

188 Graham, on *Good Day*, John Willis reporting, WCVB (Boston), May 28, 1982. See also David Neff, "Graham and the Jews," *Christian History*, forthcoming.

189 Billy Graham, press conference, Detroit, March 8, 1976, audio tape no. T88, transcript in box 4, folder 1, p. 17, Collection 24, BGCA.

190 Dochuk, *From Bible Belt to Sunbelt*, 11, 185–189; Daniel T. Rodgers, *Age of Fracture* (Cambridge, MA: Belknap Press of Harvard University Press, 2011), 129–143; Michael O. Emerson and Christian Smith, *Divided by Faith: Evangelical Religion and the Problem of Race in America* (New York: Oxford University Press, 2000), ch. 4. In important ways the concept of color blindness informed the (in Steven Miller's words) "evangelical universalism" and the "politics of decency" that animated much of Graham's career. Miller, *Billy Graham and the Rise of the Republican South*, 3, 218–220.

191 Graham, *Just As I Am*, 1997, 201–202; Gibbs and Duffy, *The Preacher and the Presidents*, 70–71; Martin, *A Prophet with Honor*, 245–247.

192 Miller, *Billy Graham and the Rise of the Republican South*, 57.

193 *Arkansas Gazette*, September 13, 1959, A2, and September 14, 1959, A2, quoted in McLoughlin, *Billy Graham, Revivalist in a Secular Age*, 241n50. Miller, *Billy Graham and the Rise of the Republican South*, 57–60; Graham, *Just As I Am*, 1997, 201–202; Gibbs and Duffy, *The Preacher and the Presidents*, 71–72; Martin, *A Prophet with Honor*, 249–250.

194 Graham quoted and weather described in Boyer, "The Big Tent," 42. I infer the crowd size by dividing the estimated total attendance of 242,000 by the three nights the crusade lasted. Billy Graham, *Living in God's Love: The New York Crusade* (New York: G. P. Putnam's Sons, 2005), 13.

195 Laurel Griffith, "Just as We Were: When Billy Graham Came to Dothan," *Wiregrass Christian Family*, April 2010, 6–10; and Laurel Griffith, Dothan resident, conversation with the author, December 10, 2011, Durham, NC.

196 Graham, in *Dothan Eagle*, April 23, 1965, 1.

197 L. Griffith, "Just as We Were," 9.

198 The Rev. Dr. Harper Shannon, quoted in L. Griffith, "Just as We Were," 10.

199 Billy Graham, press conference, Albuquerque, March 12, 1975, 8.

200 Graham, on *The MacNeil/Lehrer NewsHour*, April 17, 1992, cited in Bill Adler, *Ask Billy Graham* (Nashville: Thomas Nelson, 2007), 161.

4. ENTREPRENEUR

1 This apt phrase is a chestnut in American religious studies, probably going back to Charles Finney's *Lectures on Revivals* (1868): Lecture 1: "What a Revival of Religion Is": "*Religion is the work of man*. It is something for man to do." Charles G. Finney, *Lectures on Revivals of Religion*, ed. William G. McLoughlin (Cambridge, MA: Belknap Press of Harvard University Press, 1960), 9.

2 These different yet related developments probably have received more attention from historians than any other sustained tradition in American religious history. As noted in the Introduction, the primary and secondary historical literature on the movement is vast. I have summarized some of the key texts in Note on the Sources.

3 Of the many biographies of Moody, two of the strongest include Bruce J. Evensen, *God's Man for the Gilded Age: D. L. Moody and the Rise of Modern Mass Evangelism* (New York: Oxford University Press, 2003); James F. Findlay, *Dwight L. Moody, American Evangelist, 1837–1899* (Chicago: University of Chicago Press, 1969).

4 Of the many biographies of Sunday, two of the strongest are Lyle W. Dorsett, *Billy Sunday and the Redemption of Urban America* (Grand Rapids, MI: W. B. Eerdmans, 1991); and Robert F. Martin, *Hero of the Heartland: Billy Sunday and the Transformation of American Society, 1862–1935* (Bloomington: Indiana University Press, 2002).

5 Of the countless primary and secondary accounts of these revivals and revivalists (evangelicals were indefatigable self-promoters) the best overall is Joel A. Carpenter, *Revive Us Again: The Reawakening of American Fundamentalism* (New York: Oxford University Press, 1997).

6 Garth Rosell, *The Surprising Work of God: Harold John Ockenga, Billy Graham, and the Rebirth of Evangelicalism* (Grand Rapids, MI: Baker Academic, 2008), esp. chs. 4–6; J. Edwin Orr, *The Second Evangelical Awakening in America: An Account of the Second Worldwide Evangelical Revival Beginning in America in the Mid-19th Century, with Appendices Dealing with the Beginnings of the Mid-20th Century Movement* (London: Marshall, Morgan and Scott, 1952), 160–201.

7 Orr, *The Second Evangelical Awakening in America*, 196, 198–199.

8 Barbara Hudson Powers, *The Henrietta Mears Story* (Old Tappan, NJ: Fleming H. Revell, 1957), available at http://ccel.us/mears.toc.html; Rosell, *The Surprising Work of God*; Garth Rosell, *Boston's Historic Park Street Church: The Story of an Evangelical Landmark* (Grand Rapids, MI: Kregel, 2009).

9 Rosell, *The Surprising Work of God*, ch. 4. In the following generation Southern California evangelical pastors J. Vernon McGee and (African American) E. V. Hill also exercised influence far beyond their region. Hill worked especially closely with Graham and served on the Board of Directors of the BGEA. Darren Dochuk, *From Bible Belt to Sunbelt: Plain-Folk Religion, Grassroots Politics, and the Rise of Evangelical Conservatism* (New York: W. W. Norton, 2011), chs. 6–9.

10 Carpenter, *Revive Us Again*, chs. 5–10.

11 Philip Goff, "'We Have Heard the Joyful Sound': Charles E. Fuller's Radio Broadcast and the Rise of Modern Evangelicalism," *Religion and American Culture: A Journal of Interpretation* 9, no. 1 (1999): 67–95, 67, doi:10.2307/1123927; Quentin J. Schultze, "Evangelical Radio and the Rise of the Electronic Church, 1921–1948," *Journal of Broadcasting and Electronic Media* 32, no. 3 (1988): 289–306, esp. 301–302, doi:10.1080/08838158809386703.

12 Contrary to conventional wisdom, revivals—or at least tame ones—did flourish in some mainline Protestant circles in the early years of the century. See Grant Wacker, "The Holy Spirit and the Spirit of the Age in American Protestantism, 1880–1910," *Journal of American History* 72, no. 1 (1985): 45–62, doi:10.2307/1903736.

13 These quotations and additional data about Graham's entrepreneurial accomplishments are taken from Russ Busby, *Billy Graham, God's Ambassador: A Lifelong Mission of Giving Hope to the World* (Alexandria, VA: Time-Life Books, 1999), ch. 3.

14 Graham, in ibid., 103. Elsewhere Graham said: "If I talk to one person and get him to say yes to Jesus Christ, I consider that to be a successful meeting" (ibid., 101).

15 Billy Graham, *Just As I Am: The Autobiography of Billy Graham* (San Francisco: HarperSanFrancisco; Grand Rapids, MI: Zondervan, 1997), 134.

16 Graham, reported in St. Louis *Post Dispatch*, October 13, 1999, cited in Bill Adler, *Ask Billy Graham* (Nashville: Thomas Nelson, 2007), 36.

17 Billy Graham, press conference, Detroit, March 8, 1976, audio tape no. T88, transcript in box 4, folder 1, p. 26, Collection 24, BGCA.

18 For the problem of exaggeration in the Pentecostal movement, see David Edwin Harrell, *All Things Are Possible: The Healing and Charismatic Revivals in Modern America* (Bloomington: Indiana University Press, 1975), 68, 76, 99–116, 196; and Kate Bowler, *Blessed: A History of the American Prosperity Gospel* (New York: Oxford University Press, 2013), 263.

19 Billy Graham, press conference, Cleveland, July 10, 1972, audio tape no. T51, transcript in box 2, folder 4, p. 5, Collection 24, BGCA.

20 Kenneth L. Woodward, *Faith, Culture, Politics from the Era of Eisenhower to the Age of Obama*, forthcoming.

21 Brendan Pietsch, "Dispensational Modernism" (Ph.D. diss., Duke University, 2011), 50–69.

22 Mark Chaves, *American Religion: Contemporary Trends* (Princeton, NJ: Princeton University Press, 2011), ch. 9.

23 For a sampler of examples see Busby, *Billy Graham, God's Ambassador*, 46–47, 53; see also the headlines of the Boston newspapers for January through March, 1950, cited in Introduction, note 58.

24 For cold and wet see John Charles Pollock, *The Billy Graham Story: The Authorized Biography*, rev. and updated ed. (Grand Rapids, MI: Zondervan, 2003), 72; for heat see Busby, *Billy Graham, God's Ambassador*, 119; for driving rain and freezing wind see ibid., 128; for lack of toilet facilities see Graham, *Just As I Am*, 275; for a lightning storm in an outdoor

meeting see William Martin, "The Power and the Glory of Billy Graham," *Texas Monthly,* March 1978, 98, available at available at http://www.texasmonthly.com/story/power-and -glory-billy-graham.

25 For preaching stamina in the 1949 Los Angeles crusade see Graham, *Just As I Am,* 1997, 158; for the same in the 1957 Madison Square Garden crusade see Curtis Mitchell, *God in the Garden; the Story of the Billy Graham New York Crusade* (Garden City, NY: Double-day, 1957), 9; for peripatetic rushing from one event or crusade to another see, for example, Graham, *Just As I Am,* 1997, 165.

26 William Martin, *A Prophet with Honor: The Billy Graham Story* (New York: W. Morrow, 1991), 253, 576.

27 C. Eric Lincoln, "Cultism in the Local Church," plenary address, annual meeting of the Society for Pentecostal Studies, Cleveland, TN, November 5, 1983.

28 Billy Graham to President Harry Truman, December 26, 1951, box 1, folder 11, Collection 74, BGCA.

29 Busby, *Billy Graham, God's Ambassador,* 250; "Billy Graham: The Man at Home," *Saturday Evening Post,* March 1972, 106; Gerald S. Strober, *Graham: A Day in Billy's Life* (Garden City, NY: Doubleday, 1976), 57. Strober said that Graham received more than 8,000 invitations each year. The Billy Graham papers at Fuller Theological Seminary contain a hand-written note, dated February 27, 1967, apparently by Fuller Seminary president David A. Hubbard, about a conversation with Billy Graham. It indicated that Graham had received 17,008 invitations to speak the previous year. Billy Graham Papers, Fuller Theological Seminary Archives, Pasadena, California.

30 Martin, "The Power and the Glory," 153.

31 Most biographies and numerous articles examine the meticulous planning that went into the crusades. For a concise, exceptionally helpful overview see Martin, "The Power and the Glory," 153–156.

32 Willis G. Haymaker, interviewed by Lois Ferm, January 29, 1971, interview no. 97, tape T3, oral history interviews, final copies (stored separately), transcript in box 4, folder 22, pp. 31–32, Collection 141, BGCA.

33 "Committee Sees Chance to Fulfill Budget in Advance," *Charlotte Observer,* July 27, 1996, G2. See also the "Carolinas Crusade," September 26–29, 1996, Procedure Book, Collection 16, BGCA.

34 David Bruce, executive assistant to Mr. Graham, conversation with the author, January 17, 2014, Asheville, NC. For detailed accounts of the orchestration of individual crusades, see "Records Relating to Specific Campaigns, Rallies and Tours; Jan 1950–Sep 1970," boxes 1–5, 7, and 9, Collection 1, BGCA.

35 Strober, *Graham: A Day in Billy's Life,* 26–27; "Carolinas Crusade," September 26–29, 1996, Procedure Book, Collection 16, BGCA.

36 Graham, *Just As I Am,* 1997, 213.

37 For a detailed account of the BGEA's strategies for promoting a major Graham crusade, and of Graham's self-promotional strategies, see Martin's narrative of the 1986 Greater Washington, DC, crusade, in Martin, *A Prophet with Honor,* ch. 1. Later, Martin aptly states, Graham always showed a "keen appreciation for the role self-promotion could play in an evangelist's career" (78). In his memoir Graham said, without a hint of irony: "Golf gave me not only a way to relax but also, when played with well-known people, a chance to exercise my ministry in a relaxed, informal way." Graham, *Just As I Am,* 1997, 200.

38 Busby, *Billy Graham, God's Ambassador,* 57 (identification line too small to decipher on the reproduced page).

39 For examples see Busby, *Billy Graham, God's Ambassador,* 127, 128, 130.

40 Ibid., 130.

41 Gerry Beaven, quoted in Marshall Frady, *Billy Graham, a Parable of American Righteousness* (Boston: Little, Brown, 1979), 296.

42 Advertisement clip, Elaine Corral, co-anchor, Fox, KTVU (Oakland, CA), September 24, 1997.

43 Poster shown in Busby, *Billy Graham, God's Ambassador,* 46.

44 Roger G. Robins, "Worship and Structure in Early Pentecostalism" (M.Div. thesis, Harvard Divinity School, 1984), 11.

45 See, for example, *Billy Graham, God's Ambassador,* with Billy Graham and David Frost, directed by Michael Merriman (Gaither Film Productions, 2006), DVD. For musical and preaching clips from the 1957 New York Madison Square Garden Crusade, which represent

the tenor of most of the larger crusades, see http://www.wheaton.edu/bgc/archives/exhibits /NYC57/11sample59.htm.

46 I owe this line of thinking to Andrew S. Finstuen, *Original Sin and Everyday Protestants: The Theology of Reinhold Niebuhr, Billy Graham, and Paul Tillich in an Age of Anxiety* (Chapel Hill: University of North Carolina Press, 2009), 138.

47 Edith Blumhofer's various works on American evangelical hymns in general, and on the Billy Graham crusades in particular, have alerted me to the importance of this understudied area. See Edith Blumhofer, "Singing to Save: The Signature Sound of the Graham Crusades," in *The Worlds of Billy Graham*, ed. Andrew S. Finstuen, Anne Blue Wills, and Grant Wacker, forthcoming; Edith L. Blumhofer, *Her Heart Can See: The Life and Hymns of Fanny J. Crosby* (Grand Rapids, MI: W. B. Eerdmans, 2005). See also Stephen Marini, "From Classical to Modern: Hymnody and the Development of American Evangelicalism, 1737–1970," and Daniel Fuller, Philip Goff, and Katherine McGinn, "'Sing Thy Power to Save': Music on the 'Old Fashioned Revival Hour' Radio Broadcast," both chapters in *Singing the Lord's Song in a Strange Land: Hymnody in the History of North American Protestantism*, ed. Edith L. Blumhofer and Mark A. Noll (Tuscaloosa: University of Alabama Press, 2004); and Thomas E. Bergler, "'I Found My Thrill': The Youth for Christ Movement and American Congregational Singing, 1940–1970," in *Wonderful Words of Life: Hymns in American Protestant History and Theology*, ed. Richard J. Mouw and Mark A. Noll (Grand Rapids, MI: W. B. Eerdmans, 2004).

48 "8 Great Days of Revival Meetings" poster, shown in Busby, *Billy Graham, God's Ambassador*, 35.

49 Harold H. Martin, "A Vivid Portrait of the Famous Revivalist Billy Graham," *Saturday Evening Post*, April 13, 1963, 22. Graham's sermons lasted a mere 3.5 to four minutes. Vincent Hogren, "Billy Graham's Own Hours of Decision," in Billy Graham, *America's Hour of Decision: Featuring a Life Story of Billy Graham, and Stories of His Evangelistic Campaigns in Portland, Ore., Minneapolis, Atlanta, Fort Worth, Shreveport, La., Memphis, and the Rose Bowl, Pasadena, California* (Wheaton, IL: Van Kampen, 1951), 12.

50 For most of the years of Graham's public ministry, the platform Team consisted of Barrows, Graham, and Shea, while the full Team consisted of pianist Tedd Smith, business manager George M. Wilson, and associate evangelists Grady Wilson and T. W. Wilson. Other associate evangelists included Ralph Bell, Joe Blinco, Ralph Cunville, Leighton Ford, Roy Gustafson, Akbar Abdul-Haqq, Howard Jones, and John Wesley White.

51 Unidentified woman, quoted in Joe DePriest, "Return Engagement," *Charlotte Observer*, September 14, 1996, G1.

52 Cliff Barrows, quoted in Willa J. Conrad, "8,000 Sign Up to Make a Joyful Noise," *Charlotte Observer*, September 13, 1996, C1.

53 Billy Graham, *Billy Graham Talks to Teen-Agers*, 14th ed. (Wheaton, IL: Miracles Unlimited, 1958), 16. I owe this reference to Owen W. Reagan, "Sing a New Song: The Rise and Transformation of Contemporary Christian Music, 1970–2000" (ms. in author's possession).

54 Billy Graham, press conference, Cleveland, July 10, 1972, audio tape no. T51, transcript in box 2, folder 4, p. 2, Collection 24, BGCA.

55 Graham, quoted without citation in Harold Myra and Marshall Shelley, *The Leadership Secrets of Billy Graham* (Grand Rapids, MI: Zondervan, 2005), 307.

56 Blumhofer, "Singing to Save."

57 Leighton Ford, quoting George Beverly Shea, conversation with the author, January 20, 2014, Charlotte, NC.

58 Photograph, "Barrows, Graham, and Shea," on the BGCA website for the exhibit "Into the Big Tent: Billy Graham and the 1949 Christ for Greater Los Angeles Campaign," available at http://www2.wheaton.edu/bgc/archives/exhibits/LA49/02pictures.html: under "Exhibit Index" choose "Photographs," photo is on top left.

59 Pictured in Busby, *Billy Graham, God's Ambassador*, 46.

60 I owe this point to Blumhofer, "Singing to Save."

61 I have pieced together the basic biographical data about Barrows and Shea in this and the following paragraph from the standard biographies of Graham and his crusade ministries.

62 Cliff Barrows, in *Chicken Soup for the Soul: Billy Graham & Me: 101 Inspiring Personal Stories from Presidents, Pastors, Performers, and Other People Who Know Him Well*, ed. Amy Newmark, Steve Posner, and A. Larry Ross (Cos Cob, CT: Chicken Soup for the Soul Publishing, 2013), 27.

63 "Pamphlet about the Meetings," on the BGCA website for the exhibit "Into the Big Tent: Billy Graham and the 1949 Christ for Greater Los Angeles Campaign," available at http://www2.wheaton.edu/bgc/archives/exhibits/LA49/02pictures.html: under "Exhibit Index" choose "Preparation," pamphlet is fourth row down, center column.

64 Blumhofer, "Singing to Save."

65 Graham, *Just As I Am*, 1997, 85.

66 Blumhofer, "Singing to Save." Historian Edith Blumhofer merits special credit for her original research and insights about the significance of Barrows, Shea, and music in the crusades.

67 Ibid.

68 I attended this event at the Grove Park Inn, Asheville, NC, November 7, 2013. I witnessed the scene and heard the remark. It is also recorded on a DVD of the event, "Billy Graham's 95th Birthday," recorded December 16, 2013, in my possession, courtesy of David Bruce, executive assistant to Billy Graham.

69 Blumhofer, "Singing to Save."

70 Ibid.

71 My comments about testimonies in crusade meetings grow from informally listening to them on *Hour of Decision* telecasts during my research as well as the following transcripts of testimonies, housed at BGEA, Charlotte: Andre Thornton, Columbus, 1993, BGC-2040; Cindy Todd, Orlando, 1983, BGC-2006; Dan Reeves, Denver, 1987, BGC-2003; Gary Cuozzo, Meadowlands, 1991, BGC-2031; Jack Kemp, Anaheim, 1985, BGC-2020; Joe Gibbs, Portland, 1992, BGC-2033; Ray Perkins and Mike Kolen, Birmingham, 1972, BGC-2045; Tom Landry, Irving, TX, 1971, BGC-2049.

72 See, for example, Will Vaus, *My Father Was a Gangster: The Jim Vaus Story* (Washington, DC: Believe Books, 2007); Charles W. Colson, in Vernon K. McLellan, ed., *Billy Graham: A Tribute from Friends* (New York: Warner Books, 2002), 43–46.

73 Hamblen, quoted in AP release, likely *Los Angeles Times*, November 5, 1949, pictured in Busby, *Billy Graham, God's Ambassador*, 50.

74 See, for example, the remembrances by John Carter Cash and Roseanne Cash in *Chicken Soup for the Soul*, ed. Newmark, Posner, and Ross, chs. 17 and 18, respectively. See also Michael Streissguth, *Johnny Cash: The Biography* (Cambridge, MA: Da Capo Press, 2006), chs. 9 and 14, and pp. 177–179.

75 For reflections on the functions of personal testimony in the evangelical revival tradition, see Grant Wacker, *Heaven Below: Early Pentecostals and American Culture* (Cambridge, MA: Harvard University Press, 2001), ch. 3.

76 Billy Graham, interviewed by Peter Wilson, KRON (San Francisco), September 24, 1997.

77 "Carolinas Crusade," September 26–29, 1996, Procedure Book, Collection 16, BGCA; Billy Graham and Charles G. Ward, *The Billy Graham Christian Worker's Handbook: A Layman's Guide for Soul Winning and Personal Counseling* (Minneapolis: World Wide Publications, 1984). For a concise yet remarkably comprehensive description of the organizational blueprint for the planning of crusades, recruiting, training, and work of counselors, and follow-up procedures, see BGEA (as author), "How Does a Crusade Work?" available at http://www.beliefnet.com/Faiths/Christianity/Protestant/2004/01/How-Does-A-Crusade-Work.aspx. For another concise and exceptionally helpful overview of the crucial role of counselors see William Oscar Thompson, Jr., "The Public Invitation as a Method of Evangelism: Its Origin and Development" (Ph.D. diss., Southwestern Baptist Theological Seminary, 1979), 180–184. Though historians usually give credit to Sunday, Mordecai Ham implemented many of the counseling and follow-up procedures that Graham adopted. Graham may have witnessed and experienced them firsthand in the Ham revival in Charlotte in 1934 when Graham himself professed conversion. Ham's determination to avoid "merely 'professing' people and 'swapping' proselytes" may have prompted Graham to be sensitive to the distinction between inquirers and converts. Edward E. Ham, *Fifty Years in the Battlefront with Christ* (Louisville: Old Kentucky Home Revivalists, 1950), 256, quoted and described in Thompson, "Public Invitation," 164.

78 "New York Crusade," May 15–September 1, 1957, "Crusade Counseling and Follow Up" (Book 1), Procedure Books, Collection 16, BGCA; Martin, "The Power and the Glory," 153–154.

79 Exactly how the option of selecting a church "of their choice" worked out in practice is not clear, since the evidence is inconsistent. I discuss it in Chapter 5.

80 Graham, *Just As I Am*, 1997, 178–179.

81 Wacker, *Heaven Below*, 130–132.

82 Myra and Shelley, *The Leadership Secrets of Billy Graham*, 111–112; William C. Christian, "Electronic Evangelism," *Business Automation*, June 1962, 28–33.

83 McLoughlin, *Billy Graham, Revivalist in a Secular Age*, chs. 7–8.

84 Myra and Shelley, *The Leadership Secrets of Billy Graham*, 47, 51; Harold Myra, e-mail message to the author, May 9, 2014.

85 Maynard Good Stoddard, "Billy Graham: The World Is His Pulpit," *Saturday Evening Post*, March 1986.

86 Graham, *Just As I Am*, 1997, 185.

87 Martin, *A Prophet with Honor*, 25, 104, 107, 125, 138–139, 205, 227, 564, 637.

88 Ibid., 152. Frady, *Billy Graham, a Parable of American Righteousness*, 270.

89 Graham, quoted in Frady, *Billy Graham, a Parable of American Righteousness*, 271.

90 Graham, *Just As I Am*, 1997, 175.

91 Ruth Graham, quoted in Frady, *Billy Graham, a Parable of American Righteousness*, 283.

92 Billy Graham, press conference, Detroit, October 11, 1976, audio tape no. T92, transcript in box 4, folder 6, p. 10, Collection 24, BGCA.

93 William A. Doyle, "Bringing in the Sheaves: The Big (and Closely Guarded) Business of Billy Graham . . . ," *Corporate Report*, June 1977, 66.

94 Graham, *Just As I Am*, 1997, 180.

95 Frady, *Billy Graham, a Parable of American Righteousness*, 258, 279.

96 David Bruce, conversation with the author, January 17, 2014.

97 I owe both insights—about trust and about independence—to Robert Cooley (conversation with the author, July 1, 2007, Charlotte, NC). Cooley was president of Gordon Conwell Theological Seminary from 1981 to 1997. Graham served as chair of the board of trustees from 1989 to 1994, which brought them into frequent contact.

98 John Akers, special assistant to Mr. Graham, conversation with the author, January 17, 2014, Asheville, NC; Steven P. Miller, *Billy Graham and the Rise of the Republican South* (Philadelphia: University of Pennsylvania Press, 2009), ch. 6; Charles E. Hambrick-Stowe, "'Sanctified Business': Historical Perspectives on Financing Revivals of Religion," in *More Money, More Ministry: Money and Evangelicals in Recent North American History*, ed. Larry Eskridge and Mark A. Noll (Grand Rapids, MI: W. B. Eerdmans, 2000), 100–102; Darren Dochuk, "'Mr. Texas': Billy Graham, Entrepreneurialism, and Race Reform in the Sunbelt's 'Golden Buckle,'" in *The Worlds of Billy Graham*, ed. Andrew S. Finstuen, Anne Blue Wills, and Grant Wacker, forthcoming; Darren E. Grem, "The Blessings of Business: Corporate America and Conservative Evangelicalism in the Sunbelt Age, 1945–2000" (Ph.D. diss., University of Georgia, 2010), 52–68; Darren E. Grem, "*Christianity Today*, J. Howard Pew, and the Business of Conservative Evangelicalism," *Enterprise and Society* 15, no. 2 (2014): 337–379, doi:10.1093/es/khu012; Sarah R. Hammond, "'God Is My Partner': An Evangelical Business Man Confronts Depression and War," *Church History: Studies in Christianity and Culture* 80, no. 3 (2011): 498–519, doi:10.1017/S000964071100062X.

99 Busby, *Billy Graham, God's Ambassador*, 38.

100 *Oiltown, U.S.A.*, with Billy Graham, Colleen Townsend, Peter Power, directed by Dick Ross (World Wide Pictures, 1953); Dochuk, "Mr. Texas."

101 Graham, *Just As I Am*, 1997, 108.

102 Hambrick-Stowe, "Sanctified Business," 101.

103 Martin, *A Prophet with Honor*, 341–342.

104 Billy Graham, press conference, Raleigh, NC, September 21, 1973, audio tape no. T66, transcript in box 3, folder 22, p. 5, Collection 24, BGCA.

105 John Akers, conversation with the author, January 17, 2014.

106 Woodward, *Faith, Culture, Politics*; "Billy Graham: The Man at Home," *Saturday Evening Post*, March 1972, 42.

107 Willmar Thorkelson, "The Billy Grahams at Home," *Christian Herald*, November 1973, 33.

108 See, for example, Jane Wolfe, *The Murchisons: The Rise and Fall of a Texas Dynasty* (New York: St. Martin's Press, 1989), 233–234.

109 Reverend John Huffman, long-term friend of Graham, conversation with the author, January 20, 2012, Pasadena, CA.

110 David Bruce, conversation with the author, January 17, 2014.

111 The four other women board members were Mary C. Crowley (1974–1986), Betty Jane Scheihing (1987–2004), Ruth Shanahan (1992–2010), and Marjorie Geiser (1992–2011). "BGEA Board from 1950 to Current" [2014].

112 Goff, "We Have Heard the Joyful Sound"; Schultze, "Evangelical Radio and the Rise of the Electronic Church"; Larry K. Eskridge, "Evangelical Broadcasting: Its Meaning for Evangelicals," in *Transforming Faith: The Sacred and Secular in Modern American History*, ed. M. L. Bradbury and James Burkhart Gilbert (New York: Greenwood Press, 1989).

113 "KTIS from the Ground Up," xi, in special section after p. 11, *Pilot: The Magazine of Northwestern College* (Orange City, IA), Spring/Summer 2009, available at http://www.unwsp .edu/c/document_library/get_file?uuid=8e8de1e2-04ab-435d-8c94-90e4dcd85bce&groupId =1979620.

114 Exact data are hard to pin down. By one authority, more than 150 ABC-affiliated stations carried the first broadcast; within weeks, the program had won 20 million listeners. In 1997, 664 stations in the U.S. and 366 around the world carried it. "Billy Graham Evangelistic Association," in *Prime-Time Religion: An Encyclopedia of Religious Broadcasting*, ed. J. Gordon Melton, Phillip Charles Lucas, and Jon R. Stone (Phoenix: Oryx, 1997), 28–29. A web-based compilation of old-time radio ratings shows that, for the 1951–1952 to 1955–1956 seasons (the only ones tabulated), the *Hour of Decision* topped all religious programs. Among the top 25 programs of all types, for each of those seasons, it ranked 14, 15, 7, 6, and 4. See "Radio Ratings: Radio's Most Popular Programs of the Golden Age," compiled by Danny Goodwin, available at http://www.old-time.com/ratings/index.html. In 1990 the *Hour of Decision* was still being beamed from 690 stations, but by then it had become less an evangelistic tool than a medium of keeping contact with followers. Martin, *A Prophet with Honor*, 553. In 1950 Graham also launched Billy Graham Evangelistic Films, later renamed World Wide Pictures. The latter has produced at least thirty-five feature length films, shown around the globe since 1953. Records show 1.5 million viewers and two million decisions for Christ. Martin, *A Prophet with Honor*, 136, 553. Information on 33 of the films is available at http://billygraham.org/tv-and-radio/worldwide-pictures/.

115 Billy Graham, "Revival" sermon, Atlanta, November 5, 1950, *Hour of Decision* radio program, audio tape T43j, Collection 191, BGCA, audio available at http://billygraham.org/audio /revival.

116 Some programs involved filmed segments of crusades, but most were set in a television studio designed to look like a study or living room.

117 Martin, *A Prophet with Honor*, 232.

118 Graham, *Just As I Am*, 1997, 433. For World Wide Pictures, see ibid., 433–437, and http:// billygraham.org/tv-and-radio/worldwide-pictures/ for information about thirty-three of Graham's feature-length movies.

119 Busby, *Billy Graham, God's Ambassador*, 161.

120 Billy Graham, press conference, Oakland, CA, June 25, 1971, audio tape no. T42, transcript in box 1, folder 23, p. 24, Collection 24, BGCA.

121 Graham, *Just As I Am*, 1997, 283, 232.

122 Ibid., 283, 232. The two assistants were Robert O. Ferm and Lee Fisher. For Ferm, see telegram from Billy Graham to Lois Ferm, undated [probably early 1954], box 13, folder 3, Collection 19, BGCA; and personal letters from Robert O. Ferm to family in box 13, folder 3, Collection 19, BGCA, especially those dated March 18, 23, 25, 28, 29, April 12, 14, 17, and 18, 1954. Since Ferm intended the letters for immediate family members (some of whom may be living), I do not quote them. The letters are available for public inspection by any researcher. Ferm worked for Graham off and on from 1954 to 1978. For Fisher, see Lee Fisher, interview with Robert O. Ferm, Oral History no. 70, January 1976, box 3, folder 39, Collection 141, 4, and tape T15a (incomplete), Collection 141. Fisher worked for Graham from 1951 to 1974. He did not explicitly detail his role as a "researcher and writer" but implied that in his twenty-three years sitting behind a typewriter "in a little study" he provided materials for Graham's sermons (11). I was alerted to the Ferm and Fisher materials by Michael G. Long, *Billy Graham and the Beloved Community* (New York: Palgrave Macmillan, 2006), 227–232, 256–257.

123 Busby, *Billy Graham, God's Ambassador*, 161.

124 Graham, *Just As I Am*, 1997, xiv, 731–735.

125 Reproductions of sermon notes are available at https://public.share.wheaton.edu/sites/BGCArchives/BGSermons/Forms/AllItems.aspx.

126 George Burnham, "Graham Book, *Peace With God*, Puzzles Author Janet Baird," Chattanooga *News-Free Press*, March 28, 1953, copy in Scrapbook 169, Acc. No. 88-41, Collection 360, BGCA. The clipping did not state whether Baird's draft was the final one or the one Graham

tossed out. In 1978–1979 Robert O. ("Bob") Ferm, Graham's regular writer for the daily "My Answer" newspaper column, said that he "assisted in the preparation" of *Peace with God*, but he did not elaborate. Robert O. Ferm, interviewed by Lois Ferm, June 21, 1978, and January 10, 1979, interview no. 331, tape T1 (part 1) and T21 (part 2), oral history interviews, final copies (stored separately), transcript in box 3, folder 37, Collection 141, BGCA.

127 John Akers, conversation with the author, January 17, 2014. The sermon notes on the BGCA website show considerable variation of form, ranging from fairly sketchy outlines to complete scripts. Most of the outlines contain numerous cross-outs, red underlines, and amendments in Graham's handwriting, presumably made by Graham just before preaching them. The scripts may have been the written base of crusade sermons, or secretarial transcriptions of crusade sermons, or texts for sermons prepared for time-sensitive radio broadcasts. The outlines grow more prominent and eventually predominant in the later years. BGCA, Collection 265, available at https://public.share.wheaton.edu/sites/BGCArchives/BGSermons /Forms/AllItems.aspx.

128 Finstuen, *Original Sin and Everyday Protestants*, 5. Owing to multiple publishers, sales figures for *Peace with God* are difficult to pin down. The BGEA simply says more than two million. David Bruce, executive assistant to Billy Graham, e-mail message to author, July 21, 2014. However, BGEA photographer Russ Busby reported sales of more than three million and translation into fifty languages. Busby, *Billy Graham, God's Ambassador*, 161.

129 Ibid., 136.

130 Reinhold Niebuhr, "The King's Chapel and the King's Court," *Christianity and Crisis*, August 4, 1969, available at http://www.religion-online.org/showarticle.asp?title=454.

131 Compare, for example, Graham's own rendering of his controversial meeting with other evangelical leaders in Montreaux, Switzerland, in 1960, with Shaun Casey's account of the meeting. Graham, *Just As I Am*, 1997, 391–392; Shaun Casey, *The Making of a Catholic President: Kennedy vs. Nixon 1960* (New York: Oxford University Press, 2009), 123–124, 135.

132 Rupert Shortt, "Saver of Millions?" *Times Literary Supplement*, November 7, 1997, 35.

133 Colman McCarthy, review of *Just As I Am: The Autobiography of Billy Graham*, *The Nation*, September 22, 1997, 30–32.

134 Andrew Delbanco, "The Church of Appearances," review of *Just As I Am*, *New Republic*, October 6, 1997, 31–36.

135 Joanne C. Beckman, review of *Just As I Am*, *The Christian Century*, October 8, 1997, 888; David Crumm, "Billy Graham's Honesty and Greatness on Display," review of *Just As I Am*, *Chicago Tribune*, June 2, 1997, available at http://articles.chicagotribune.com/1997-06-02 /features/9706020007_1_billy-graham-world-politics-christianity; James A. Nuechterlein, review of *Just As I Am: The Autobiography of Billy Graham*, *Commentary*, August 1, 1997, available at http://www.commentarymagazine.com/article/just-as-i-am-the-autobiography -of-billy-graham; Mark Noll, "The Innocence of Billy Graham," review of *Just As I Am*, *First Things*, January 1998, available at http://www.firstthings.com/article/1998/01/001-the-inno cence-of-billy-graham; "Prince Billy," review of *Just As I Am*, *The Economist*, June 19, 1997, available at http://www.economist.com/node/597390; Andrew Sullivan, "Evangelist to the World," review of *Just As I Am*, *New York Times Book Review*, July 6, 1997, available at http://www.nytimes.com/books/97/07/06/reviews/970706.06sullivt.html; Larry Witham, "Billy Graham's Life and Times," review of *Just As I Am*, *Insight on the News*, July 28, 1997, 37. Significantly, the long list of the encomia published in the front matter of the second edition seemed mostly to refer to the man, not the book. Billy Graham, *Just As I Am: The Autobiography of Billy Graham*, rev. and updated 10th anniv. ed. (New York: HarperOne; Grand Rapids, MI: Zondervan, 2007). See, for example, the excerpts from *Just As I Am* from the *New York Times Book Review*, *Chicago Tribune*, and *USA Today*, and *Los Angeles Times*.

136 Graham, *Just As I Am*, 1997, 723–724.

137 Kenneth L. Woodward, "A Career in God-Talk," review of *Just As I Am*, *Commonweal*, August 15, 1997, 22.

138 Graham, *Just As I Am*, 2007, 711.

139 Circulation figures: Timothy T. Clydesdale, "Decision," in *Popular Religious Magazines of the United States*, ed. P. Mark Fackler and Charles H. Lippy (Westport, CT: Greenwood Press, 1995), 206; 1980: Pollock, *The Billy Graham Story* (2003), 110; BGEA: http://

billygraham.org/news/media-resources/electronic-press-kit/ministry-facts/. For other estimates see, for example, Martin, *Prophet with Honor,* 250.

140 *Christianity Today,* advertising information, as of May 14, 2014: print circulation at http://www.christianitytodayads.com/print-media/christianity-today; number of page views and unique visitors, and visitor demographics at http://www.christianitytodayads.com/christian ity-today/.

141 Graham, *Just As I Am,* 1997, 284–294.

142 Wilbur Smith to Billy Graham, February 22, 1951; Billy Graham to Charles E. Fuller, May 1, 1956; both in Seminary Archives, Fuller Theological Seminary, Pasadena, CA.

143 Billy Graham to Harold Lindsell, January 25, 1955, letter in my possession, courtesy of Harold Myra.

144 "Original Billy Graham Address 1955," *Christianity Today* Editorial Offices, Carol Stream, IL. I wish to thank David Neff for supplying this document. See also Graham, *Just As I Am,* 1997, 284–285.

145 Billy Graham, Interview, "In the Beginning . . . ," *Christianity Today,* July 17, 1981, 26.

146 "Original Billy Graham Address 1955," 4.

147 Graham, *Just As I Am,* 1997, 291. Both documents articulated additional aims but these seem the key ones.

148 Elesha J. Coffman, *The Christian Century and the Rise of the Protestant Mainline* (New York: Oxford University Press, 2013).

149 "Original Billy Graham Address 1955," 2.

150 Billy Graham to Carl F. H. Henry, October 23, 1956, 2, Graham here reporting the views of "several other competent people." The second quotation came from "one man," whom Graham did not identify. Letter in *Christianity Today* editorial offices, Carol Stream, IL. Graham felt that his own article contained "too much spinning dust and purple prose." Decades later Graham regretted sending that letter of critique to Henry, saying that if he had been more mature he might not have done so. Billy Graham to Gilbert Beers and Harold Myra, April 6, 1984, copy of letter in my possession, courtesy of Harold Myra.

151 Billy Graham to Harold Lindsell, January 25, 1955, copy of letter in my possession, courtesy of Harold Myra.

152 Carl F. H. Henry, *Confessions of a Theologian: An Autobiography* (Waco, TX: Word Books, 1986), 227; Mark G. Toulouse, "*Christianity Today* and American Public Life: A Case Study," *Journal of Church and State* 35, no. 2 (1993), 241; Aaron Griffith, "*Christianity Today,* Race, and the Neo-Evangelical Quest for Respectability" (ms. in author's possession).

153 Griffith, "*Christianity Today.*"

154 Henry, *Confessions of a Theologian,* 227. The reporter was Frank Gaebelein, later the Headmaster of the evangelical Stony Brook School on Long Island.

155 Billy Graham to President Richard Nixon, January 16, 1970, box 3, folder 7, Collection 74, BGCA.

156 Graham, *Just As I Am,* 1997, 288; Hambrick-Stowe, "Sanctified Business," 101; Grem, "*Christianity Today,* J. Howard Pew, and the Business of Conservative Evangelicalism."

157 In the first issue of *Christianity Today,* October 15, 1956, the masthead listed Graham as a "Contributing Editor" (about fifty other people also held this designation). In the 1960s and 1970s he held the same title. In the 1980s the masthead listed him as "Founder." In the 1990s he was called Chairman of Board of Directors and Founder. In 2014, the magazine's website named him Founder and Honorary Chairman.

158 Henry, *Confessions of a Theologian,* ch. 13–15, esp. 269, and 183. This is my inference based on Henry's description of the seemingly continual power struggles within the magazine's leadership (mostly L. Nelson Bell, Harold John Ockenga, and J. Howard Pew) about its editorial direction. Graham emerges as more of a vigilant observer than a direct participant. See also Darren E. Grem, "*Christianity Today,* J. Howard Pew, and the Business of Conservative Evangelicalism," esp. 356–359, 366. Graham asserted that Pew did not try to control the magazine's editorial policy (288), but Grem offers persuasive evidence that Pew did strive, occasionally directly but more often indirectly, to influence the magazine's direction (359, 364, 366–367).

159 Harold Myra, e-mail message to author, June 20, 2014; David Neff, e-mail message to author, June 21, 2014. My quotation is from Myra, who in turn quotes Graham's long-term friend, Harold John Ockenga. See also Billy Graham interview, "In the Beginning . . . ," 26–27. Myra later served the magazine as executive editor and Neff as editor-in-chief.

160 Grem, "*Christianity Today,* J. Howard Pew, and the Business of Conservative Evangelicalism," 369–374.

5. ARCHITECT

1 For the general history of post–World War II America I have drawn on William H. Chafe, *The Unfinished Journey: America since World War II,* 7th ed. (New York: Oxford University Press, 2011); David Edwin Harrell, Jr., Edwin S. Gaustad, John B. Boles, Sally Foreman Griffith, *Unto a Good Land: A History of the American People* (Grand Rapids, MI: Wm. B. Eerdmans, 2005), chs. 30–37.
2 For the tension between anxiety and possibility in the fifteen years following World War II, especially in religious culture, I have drawn on Patrick Allitt, *Religion in America since 1945: A History* (New York: Columbia University Press, 2003), ch. 1; Andrew S. Finstuen, *Original Sin and Everyday Protestants: The Theology of Reinhold Niebuhr, Billy Graham, and Paul Tillich in an Age of Anxiety* (Chapel Hill: University of North Carolina Press, 2009), ch. 1; James David Hudnut-Beumler, *Looking for God in the Suburbs: The Religion of the American Dream and Its Critics, 1945–1965* (New Brunswick, NJ: Rutgers University Press, 1994).
3 Ross Douthat, *Bad Religion: How We Became a Nation of Heretics* (New York: Free Press, 2012), chs. 1, 8.
4 George M. Marsden, *The Twilight of the American Enlightenment: The 1950s and the Crisis of Liberal Belief* (New York: Basic Books, 2014), xxxii.
5 Robert N. Bellah, "Civil Religion in America," in *American Civil Religion,* ed. Russell E. Richey and Donald G. Jones (New York: Harper and Row, 1974), esp. 33.
6 Joel Carpenter, "Revive Us Again: Alienation, Hope, and the Resurgence of Fundamentalism," in *Transforming Faith: The Sacred and Secular in Modern American History,* ed. M. L. Bradbury and James B. Gilbert (New York: Greenwood Press, 1989), esp. 113–116.
7 Douglas A. Sweeney, *The American Evangelical Story: A History of the Movement* (Grand Rapids, MI: Baker Academic, 2005), chs. 1, 7; George M. Marsden, *Fundamentalism and American Culture,* 2nd ed. (New York: Oxford University Press, 2006), part 5; D. G. Hart, *That Old-Time Religion in Modern America: Evangelical Protestantism in the Twentieth Century* (Chicago: Ivan R. Dee, 2002), chs. 4–6. D. G. Hart, *Deconstructing Evangelicalism: Conservative Protestantism in the Age of Billy Graham* (Grand Rapids, MI: Baker Academic, 2004), part 1. In Part 1 of this provocative volume Hart argues for the *appearance* of a more or less coherent evangelical movement, while in Part 2 he "deconstructs" it into its quite different component parts. My aim is not to enter this lively debate but simply to argue for the breadth and power of a coherent evangelical mainstream at the center, both real and perceived, while acknowledging that the centrist mainstream harbored internal divisions and shared the landscape with a variety of conservative Christian competitors.
8 Molly Worthen, *Apostles of Reason: The Crisis of Authority in American Evangelicalism* (New York: Oxford University Press, 2014), esp. chs. 6–9; Donald W. Dayton and Robert K. Johnston, eds., *The Variety of American Evangelicalism* (Knoxville: University of Tennessee Press, 1991); Hart, *Deconstructing Evangelicalism,* part 2.
9 *New Historical Atlas of Religion in America,* ed. Edwin Scott Gaustad and Philip L. Barlow (New York: Oxford University Press, 2001), 79–89, 363–367, 402.
10 Elizabeth Flowers, *Into the Pulpit: Southern Baptist Women and Power since World War II* (Chapel Hill: University of North Carolina Press, 2012), ch. 3.
11 The chronology of Graham's parents' church affiliations is difficult to pin down. I have built this account from Morrow Coffey Graham, *They Call Me Mother Graham* (Old Tappan, NJ: Fleming H. Revell, 1977), 16; Louis Hofferbert, "Crossroads in the Life of Billy Graham," *Houston Chronicle,* October 10, 1965; Billy Graham, *Just As I Am: The Autobiography of Billy Graham* (San Francisco: HarperSanFrancisco; Grand Rapids, MI: Zondervan, 1997), 4, 22, 25; William Martin, *A Prophet with Honor: The Billy Graham Story* (New York: W. Morrow, 1991), 56; William Oscar Thompson, Jr., "The Public Invitation as a Method of Evangelism" (Ph.D. diss., Southwestern Baptist Theological Seminary, 1979), 164.
12 Graham, quoted in Randall T. Ruble, *Bicentennial History of the Associate Reformed Presbyterian Church, 1950–2003* (Grand Rapids, MI: McNaughton and Gunn, 2003), 379.

13 Jean Graham Ford, Billy Graham's sister, conversation with the author, July 3, 2009, Charlotte, NC; Morrow Graham, *They Call Me Mother Graham*, 28–29.

14 Graham, *Just As I Am*, 1997, 23–24.

15 Kenneth W. Russell II, "Mordecai F. Ham: Southern Fundamentalist" (M.A. thesis, Western Kentucky University, 1980), 10, 23, 58.

16 Graham, *Just As I Am*, 1997, 22, 25.

17 Ibid., 25. Morrow Graham, *They Call Me Mother Graham*, 25–26; Martin, *A Prophet with Honor*, 32.

18 Ernest R. Sandeen, *The Roots of Fundamentalism: British and American Millenarianism, 1800–1930* (Chicago: University of Chicago Press, 1970), chs. 3–4; Brendan Pietsch, "Dispensational Modernism" (Ph.D. diss., Duke University, 2011), esp. 268–270.

19 Graham, *Just As I Am*, 1997, 41–42.

20 Sandeen, *Roots of Fundamentalism*, chs. 9–10.

21 Graham, *Just As I Am*, 1997, 32.

22 Ibid., 55.

23 Ibid., 56–57.

24 Gerald S. Strober, *Graham: A Day in Billy's Life* (Garden City, NY: Doubleday, 1976). Strober stated that the typical crusade won support from 80 percent of local churches (37).

25 See, for example, the *Dixie Business*, Spring 1973, data discussed in Chapter 3, note 68. For the 1982 Raleigh, NC, crusade: out of 14 counselor applications, 7 (50%) were Methodist and Baptist, 2 (14%) were Catholic or Anglican/Episcopal, and 5 (36%) were unaffiliated.

Out of 54 decision cards, 27 (50%) were Methodist and Baptist, 10 (19%) were Catholic or Anglican/Episcopal, 10 (19%) were other Protestant denominations or other (one each Baha'i, Church of Jesus Christ of Latter-day Saints, and Greek Orthodox), and 7 (13%) were unaffiliated.

Copies of the counselor applications and decision cards are in my possession, courtesy of Dr. Fred Brooks, chair of the 1973 Raleigh Crusade. Fred Brooks possesses the 1982 materials because his wife, Nancy Brooks, served as a counselor in the 1982 crusade. The counselor applications are dated 1982 and the decision cards are undated. Dr. Brooks affirms they all came from the 1982 crusade. Fred Brooks, e-mail message to the author, May 16, 2014.

26 Graham, *Just As I Am*, 1997, 34. On my third personal visit with Mr. Graham, July 23, 2010, I asked him why he chose Bob Jones College, which was unaccredited. He said Jones had spoken at his Sharon High School and the young Graham found his preaching style forceful, charismatic, and compelling.

27 "Gospel Tabernacle of Tampa," WPA Church Records, State Library and Archives of Florida, available at http://floridamemory.com/items/show/248832.

28 Lois Ferm, "Billy Graham in Florida," *Florida Historical Quarterly* 60 (October 1981), 177. Graham's transcript revealed courses in Bible introduction, history, analysis, doctrine (homiletics), and geography. He also "studied" hermeneutics, prophecy, church history, comparative religions, ethics, and personal evangelism.

29 Robert Shuster, BGCA archivist, e-mail message to author, May 15, 2014.

30 Graham, *Just As I Am*, 1997, 66–67; Advertisement for Gospel Tabernacle, *Wheaton Record*, April 2, 1943, 4, Wheaton College Archives, Wheaton, IL.

31 Robert L. Niklaus, John S. Sawin, and Samuel J. Stoesz, *All for Jesus: God at Work in The Christian and Missionary Alliance*, 125th anniv. ed. (Colorado Springs: The Christian and Missionary Alliance, 2013), chs. 9–11.

32 *Bulletin of Wheaton College*, Wheaton, IL, *1940–1941 Catalog* (April 1940), available at http://espace.wheaton.edu/lr/a-sc/archives/publications/catalogs/1940-1941catalog.pdf. I owe this reference to David Malone.

33 See the demographic breakdown discussed in Chapter 7.

34 D. Michael Lindsay, *Faith in the Halls of Power: How Evangelicals Joined the American Elite* (New York: Oxford University Press, 2007).

35 Nathan O. Hatch and Michael S. Hamilton, "Taking the Measure of the Evangelical Resurgence, 1942–1992," in *Reckoning with the Past: Historical Essays on American Evangelicalism from the Institute for the Study of American Evangelicals*, ed. D. G. Hart (Grand Rapids, MI: Baker Books, 1995), 400–401.

36 Christian Smith with Michael O. Emerson, *American Evangelicalism: Embattled and Thriving* (Chicago: University of Chicago Press, 1998); Tamney, *Resilience of Conservative Religion*, esp. ch. 7; Smidt, *American Evangelicals Today*, esp. chs. 6–8.

37 Samuel S. Hill, conversation with the author, October 1, 2006, Durham, NC. See also Matthew Bowman, *The Urban Pulpit: New York City and the Fate of Liberal Evangelicalism* (New York: Oxford University Press, 2014), 283–285.

38 George M. Marsden, *Reforming Fundamentalism: Fuller Seminary and the New Evangelicalism* (Grand Rapids, MI: W. B. Eerdmans, 1987); Rudolph Nelson, *The Making and Unmaking of an Evangelical Mind: The Case of Edward Carnell* (New York: Cambridge University Press, 1987), 80.

39 Worthen, *Apostles of Reason*, 83; Garth Rosell, *The Surprising Work of God: Harold John Ockenga, Billy Graham, and the Rebirth of Evangelicalism* (Grand Rapids, MI: Baker Academic, 2008), chs. 2, 8; Rudolph Nelson, *The Making and Unmaking of an Evangelical Mind*, chs. 5–9, esp. ch. 5. George M. Marsden, *Reforming Fundamentalism*, esp. ch. 3.

40 See, for example, [Billy Graham], "A Discussion at the Harvard Law Forum: Evangelism and the Intellectual," *Decision*, October 1962, 7–8; Andrew S. Finstuen, "Professor Graham: Billy Graham's Missions to Colleges and Universities," in *The Worlds of Billy Graham*, ed. Andrew S. Finstuen, Anne Blue Wills, and Grant Wacker, forthcoming.

41 Martin, *A Prophet with Honor*, 383.

42 Peter J. Boyer, "The Big Tent: Billy Graham, Franklin Graham, and the Transformation of American Evangelicalism," *New Yorker*, August 22, 2005, 44, available at http://www.new yorker.com/archive/2005/08/22/050822fa_fact_boyer?currentPage=all.

43 Kenneth L. Woodward, *Faith, Culture, Politics from the Era of Eisenhower to the Age of Obama*, forthcoming.

44 The academic literature on the history and sociology of the parachurch movement is large. One of the best entry points is Michael S. Hamilton, "American Evangelicalism: Character, Function, and Trajectories of Change," in *The Future of Evangelicalism in America*, ed. Candy Gunther Brown and Mark Silk (New York: Columbia University Press, forthcoming).

45 YFC played a crucial (and understudied) role in the rise of post–World War evangelicalism in general and Billy Graham in particular. Joel Carpenter, "Youth for Christ and the New Evangelicals' Place in the Life of the Nation," in *Religion and the Life of the Nation: American Recoveries*, ed. Rowland A. Sherrill (Urbana: University of Illinois Press, 1990), 128–151; Joel A. Carpenter, *The Youth for Christ Movement and Its Pioneers* (New York: Garland, 1988); Bruce L. Shelley, "The Rise of Evangelical Youth Movements," *Fides et Historia* 18, no. 1 (1986): 45–63.

46 Billy Graham, "God Did It!" pamphlet, Youth for Christ International, Wheaton, IL, c. 1950.

47 Marsden, *Reforming Fundamentalism*, 167, 290; Billy Graham to Charles E. Fuller, September 4, 1958; Billy Graham to Wilbur Smith, January 21, 1963; Billy Graham to David Allan Hubbard, February 15, 1968, all in Fuller Theological Seminary Archives.

48 Billy Graham's first year on the Board of Trustees was 1959 (invited 1958). In the fall 1991 catalog he was still listed as a trustee. In the fall 1992 catalog he was listed as an emeritus trustee. The seminary therefore regarded his service as: trustee: 1959–1991, senior trustee: 1992–present. Len Tang, Assistant to the President of Fuller Theological Seminary, e-mail message to author, May 15, 2014; Cliff Penner, chair, Board of Trustees, Fuller Theological Seminary, e-mail message to author, May 15, 2014.

49 Marsden, *Fundamentalism and American Culture*, 4.

50 Graham, *Just As I Am*, 1997, 119 ("ultrafundamentalist" in original).

51 Martin, *A Prophet with Honor*, 173–175, 321; Graham, *Just As I Am*, 1997, 213, 221.

52 Woodward, *Faith, Culture, Politics*.

53 Graham, *Just As I Am*, 1997, 251; see also 119 and 696.

54 Billy Graham, "Candid Conversation with the Evangelist," *Christianity Today*, July 17, 1981, 26; Graham, in "Billy Graham Answers His Critics," *Look*, February 7, 1956; Graham, in J. H. Hunter, "He Came—He Saw—He Conquered," *Evangelical Christian*, May 1955, 215.

55 Graham, *Just As I Am*, 1997, 299.

56 Bowman, *The Urban Pulpit*.

57 Peter Steinfels, "Dr. John S. Bonnell, 99, Is Dead; New York Presbyterian Preacher," *New York Times*, February 26, 1992.

58 See, for example, Billy Graham, "Evangelism and the Intellectual," Harvard Law School Forum, April 1, 1962, audio (scroll down page for audio link) available at http://www3.law .harvard.edu/orgs/hlsforum/multimedia/. More broadly, see Finstuen, "Professor Graham."

59 Graham, *Just As I Am*, 1997, 694; Karl Barth, excerpted in Raymond Kemp Anderson, *An American Scholar Recalls Karl Barth's Golden Years as a Teacher (1958–1964)* (Lewiston, NY: Edwin Mellen Press, 2013), 168–169, 259–260, 350; Uta Andrea Balbier, "Billy Graham in West Germany: German Protestantism between Americanization and Rechristianization, 1954–70," in *Zeithistorische Forschungen/Studies in Contemporary History* 7 (2010), H. 3, 9, available at http://www.zeithistorische-forschungen.de/site/40209072/default.aspx. Barth liked Graham personally. Graham's recollection of a warm reception and invigorating hour-long conversation with literary giant C. S. Lewis found confirmation in Lewis's own recollection of the one time they met, in 1954. Lewis later told interviewer Sherwood Wirt: "I had the pleasure of meeting Billy Graham once. We had dinner together during his visit to Cambridge University in 1955, while he was conducting a mission to students. I thought he was a very modest and a very sensible man, and I liked him very much indeed." Graham, *Just As I Am*, 1997, 258; Lewis quoted in Sherwood Eliot Wirt, "C. S. Lewis on Heaven, Earth and Outer Space," CBN Network, post date not stated, available at http://www.cbn.com/special /Narnia/articles/ans_LewisLastInterviewB.aspx. The interview, not dated, was taken from *Decision*, September 1963.
60 Billy Graham, "Fellowship and Separation," sermon pamphlet no. 140, *Hour of Decision*, 1961, 1, reprinted from *Decision*, August 1961. It is not clear if this sermon was actually preached on air as it is not available in the BGEA sermon audio files or in the BGCA sermon note files. I owe the information about the printed source to Bob Shuster.
61 Graham, "The Lost Chord of Evangelism," *Christianity Today*, April 1, 1957, 26, an advance printing of remarks Graham later delivered April 15, 1957, in Buffalo, NY.
62 Billy Graham, "What Ten Years Have Taught Me," *Christian Century*, February 17, 1960, 188. I was led to this article by Martin, *A Prophet with Honor*, 294.
63 Graham, *Just As I Am*, 1997, 96. Graham is here quoting with obvious approval the view of his wife, Ruth, on a trip they took to New York City, apparently in 1946.
64 Ibid., 160; Martin, *A Prophet with Honor*, 218. In his memoir Graham reported cryptically that Catholic and Unitarian clergy visited his 1950 Boston meetings but he did not elaborate (167).
65 Billy Graham, "Fellowship and Separation," sermon pamphlet no. 140, *Hour of Decision*, 1961, 8, reprinted from *Decision*, August 1961.
66 Flowers, *Into the Pulpit*, 30.
67 Stanley High, *Billy Graham: The Personal Story of the Man, His Message, and His Mission* (New York: McGraw-Hill, 1956), 100.
68 Mark Silk, "The Rise of the 'New Evangelicalism': Shock and Adjustment," in *Between the Times: The Travail of the Protestant Establishment in America, 1900–1960*, ed. William R. Hutchison (New York: Cambridge University Press, 1989). For a darker view of the relationship, however, see Bowman, *Urban Pulpit*, 283.
69 See, for example, John Buchanan, "Graham's Gift," *Christian Century*, October 2, 2007, 3.
70 Graham, quoted in *Ottawa Citizen*, June 15, 1998, cited in Bill Adler, *Ask Billy Graham* (Nashville: Thomas Nelson, 2007), 81.
71 Kenneth L. Woodward, "A Career in God-Talk," review of *Just As I Am*, *Commonweal*, August 15, 1997, 22; Woodward, *Faith, Culture, Politics*.
72 Leighton Ford, Graham's brother-in-law and long-term associate, e-mail message to author, January 21, 2009.
73 For example: a standard church history published by the firmly evangelical Zondervan Publishing House includes a foreword by Earle E. Cairns, long-term Wheaton College history professor, stating simply that the "theological development" of the Eastern Church "stagnated after the Council of Chalcedon" in 451 CE. Eastern Orthodoxy receives no further mention in this otherwise comprehensive synopsis of European and American church history. Robert C. Walton, *Chronological and Background Charts of Church History* (Grand Rapids, MI: Academie Books, 1986), chart 22. Another popular evangelical guide to modern church history does not mention Eastern Orthodoxy at all. John D. Hannah, *Charts of Reformation and Enlightenment Church History* (Grand Rapids, MI: Zondervan, 2004). See also Richard J. Mouw, "Educating for the Kingdom," *Fuller [Theological Seminary]: Theology, News and Notes*, Spring 2014, 30, reprint of presidential inaugural address, November 8, 1993. Mouw, former president of Fuller Theological Seminary, here publically laments evangelicals' failure to appreciate Orthodox efforts to bring spiritual renewal to mainline churches.
74 The primary and secondary historical literature on evangelical opposition to Mormonism is extensive (if not vast). For a valuable entering wedge see John-Charles Duffy, "Conservative

Pluralists: The Cultural Politics of Mormon-Evangelical Dialogue in the United States at the Turn of the Twenty-First Century" (Ph.D. diss., University of North Carolina at Chapel Hill, 2011), 46–68, available at https://cdr.lib.unc.edu/record/uuid:f4d52b55-a90b-432a-831c -5bfa189103ee.

75 Woodward, *Faith, Culture, Politics.*

76 My rendering of Graham's comments in the question-and-answer period following an address at Regent College and Vancouver School of Theology, Vancouver, British Columbia, October 1984, audio available at http://www.regentaudio.com/products/billy-graham-at-vst -and-regent-college.

77 *Billy Graham: A Personal Crusade,* A&E *Biography,* hosted by Harry Smith (New York: A&E, 1999).

78 Graham, in Pittsburgh *Post Gazette,* June 1, 1993, cited in Adler, *Ask Billy Graham,* 28.

79 Graham, *Just As I Am,* 1997, 456.

80 Massachusetts Governor's Prayer Breakfast, June 1, 1982, sermon no.1728; notes for sermon in box 26, folder 131, Collection 265, BGCA, available at https://public.share.wheaton.edu /sites/BGCArchives/_layouts/15/WopiFrame.aspx?sourcedoc=/sites/BGCArchives/BGSermons /1704_FileCabinet_611982_MassachusettsGovernorsPrayerBreakfast_Boston,MA_Massa-chusettsGovernorsPrayerBreakfast_-_1728.PDF&action=default. In 2012 the room keys for the Marriott Hotel in Charlotte, NC, bore a photo of Billy Graham and Lyndon Johnson chatting.

81 For example, Robert L. Millet, Professor Emeritus of Religion, Brigham Young University, to the author, May 19, 2014: "I read *Just As I Am* when it was first released in 1997. It was a life-changing experience for me. . . . My Dad, an active and very involved LDS Church leader in Louisiana, had always admired Billy—had appreciated his sermons, his sincerity, his devotion to a grand cause, and, as Dad would say, "because he always kept his nose clean." . . . Graham's influence for good among rich and poor, black and white, high and low—including serving as spiritual advisor to several presidents of the United States—was almost overwhelming to me . . . I remember being filled with emotion, sensing deep down the hand of God upon this simple North Carolina preacher. It was a lesson for a lifetime: Miracles are wrought in the lives of those who surrender themselves to the promptings and purposes of the Almighty." See also Richard N. Ostling and Joan K. Ostling, *Mormon America: The Power and the Promise* (San Francisco: HarperSanFrancisco, 1999), xvi, 204.

82 Billy Graham, press conference, Detroit, March 8, 1976, audio tape no. T88, transcript in box 4, folder 1, p. 28, Collection 24, BGCA.

83 Peter W. Williams, *Popular Religion in America: Symbolic Change and the Modernization Process in Historical Perspective* (Urbana: University of Illinois Press, 1989), 144; Grant Wacker, *Heaven Below: Early Pentecostals and American Culture* (Cambridge, MA: Harvard University Press, 2001), Introduction.

84 Wacker, *Heaven Below,* "Appendix: U.S. Pentecostal Statistics," 271–272.

85 R. G. Robins, *Pentecostalism in America* (Santa Barbara, CA: Praeger, 2010), 141.

86 David Edwin Harrell, *Oral Roberts: An American Life* (Bloomington: Indiana University Press, 1985), 179.

87 David Edwin Harrell, *All Things Are Possible: The Healing and Charismatic Revivals in Modern America* (Bloomington: Indiana University Press, 1975), chs. 5 and 9.

88 R. O. Corvin (?), quoted in Harrell, *Oral Roberts,* 200.

89 Harrell, *Oral Roberts,* 201. The quotation came from Calvin Thielman, pastor of the Presbyterian church in Montreat, NC, Ruth Graham's home congregation.

90 Graham, quoted by Roberts, in Harrell, *Oral Roberts,* 203.

91 David Edwin Harrell, *Pat Robertson: A Life and Legacy* (Grand Rapids, MI: William B. Eerdmans, 2010), 41, 330, 219–220.

92 Graham may have appeared on *PTL* November 8, 1978, based on videotapes of *PTL* broadcasts held in the Flower Pentecostal Heritage Center, Springfield, MO. Darrin Rodgers, director of the FPHC, e-mail message to the author, February 15, 2014. A log of *PTL* programs 1979–1989 lists Graham's name several times but these seem to be tapes of events (press conferences and a banquet), probably held elsewhere, at which he appeared. Log supplied by Darrin Rodgers.

93 [William Martin], "Billy Graham," *Christian History,* August 8, 2008, 3, available at http:// www.christianitytoday.com/ch/131christians/evangelistsandapologists/graham.html ?start=1.

94 Billy Graham, *Angels: God's Secret Agents*, rev. and expanded ed. (Waco, TX: Word Books, 1986), ch. 6.

95 Alan Bestic, 1971, quoted without citation in James Morris, *The Preachers* (New York: St. Martin's Press, 1973), 367. Bestic is referring to Graham's mass circulation periodical *Decision*, which features testimonials. One would expect to find miraculous healing stories there, if anywhere, in the Graham corpus.

96 I examined Graham's view of miracles in Chapter 1.

97 Robins, *Pentecostalism in America*, 147.

98 Wacker, *Heaven Below*, 44, 148–149.

99 Billy Graham, *The Collected Works of Billy Graham* (New York: Inspirational Press, 1993), 409, 417, 480–482.

100 Billy Graham, press conference, Birmingham, AL, May 11, 1972, audio tape no. T47, transcript in box 1, folder 37, p. 15, Collection 24, BGCA.

101 Billy Graham, press conference, Tulsa, OK, October 17, 1972, audio tape no. T55, transcript in box 2, folder 11, p. 14, Collection 24, BGCA. Billy Graham, press conference, Houston, June 14, 1973, transcript in box 3, folder 6, p. 6, Collection 24, BGCA.

102 "Billy Graham," in Vinson Synan, *Voices of Pentecost: Testimonies of Lives Touched by the Holy Spirit* (Ann Arbor, MI: Vine Books, 2003), 62–66. Two letters to Thomas F. Zimmerman, general superintendent of the Assemblies of God (author does not have permission to identify the senders), July 1, 1982, and October 12, 1983, and Zimmerman's responses, July 29 and October 12, 1982, affirm the claim in Synan. All letters are on file at the Flower Pentecostal Heritage Center, Springfield, MO.

103 The incident merits a full article, less to confirm or disconfirm its factual veracity than to analyze the oral dynamics of a popular religious tradition and what it said about Graham's status as a source of legitimation in American religious culture. Suffice it to say that Graham spoke at a banquet at the Assemblies of God Headquarters, Springfield, MO, the evening of December 9 and did not mention the incident. He also preached at the Assemblies of God Headquarters the following day—December 10, 1982—and his sermon notes do not show any indication of the event. The notes were drafted December 6, but heavily amended in his personal hand, and therefore could have shown awareness of any events that took place the previous day, December 9. A lengthy question and answer session with the college faculty followed the sermon on December 10. The transcript of the Q & A session ran twenty-three single-spaced pages. Graham did not mention the event there, either. To the best of my knowledge, he did not publically speak or write about it at any point in his public ministry. Moreover Zimmerman sent a thank you letter to Graham on December 13 that said nothing about the event. Zimmerman also wrote to Trooper S. M. Kaunley, the original source of the story, on December 13 and said nothing about it. Transcript of December 9 speech: "Evangel College Oral History / Dr. Billy Graham / Banquet, Assemblies of God Headquarters, December 9, 1982." December 10 sermon: Billy Graham, sermon no. 1807, "Christian Education," All-School Faculty Meeting, Evangel College, December 10, 1982; Graham's notes for the sermon are available at https://public.share.wheaton.edu/sites/BGCArchives/_layouts/15/Wopi Frame.aspx?sourcedoc=/sites/BGCArchives/BGSermons/933_FileCabinet_12101982_All -SchoolFacultyMeeting_Springfield,MO_ChristianEducation_-_1807.pdf&action=default. Transcript of the discussion with faculty following the sermon: "Evangel College Oral History / Billy Graham / Joint Faculty Meeting / A/G Headquarters Auditorium / December 10, 1982," transcribed by Betty Chase, January 1991. Transcripts of Graham's December 9 speech and the faculty discussion on December 10 are in the author's possession (courtesy of Darrin Rodgers, director of the FPHC, March 13, 2014) and are archived at the Flower Pentecostal Heritage Center, Springfield, MO. I wish to thank Darrin Rodgers, director of the Flower Center, for his assistance in narrating these events. My interpretation of this event is not necessarily his.

104 David Bruce, executive assistant to Mr. Graham, conversation with the author January 17, 2014; John Akers, special assistant to Mr. Graham, conversation with the author, January 17, 2014, Asheville, NC.

105 A word search for "Billy Graham" in the *Pentecostal Evangel*, the flagship periodical for the Assemblies of God, yielded the following data. Between 1913 and 2002, 774 different issues of the magazine spoke about Graham. He was first mentioned in 1946, when his public career had barely begun. Another search of the magazine, running from 1957 to 1996, yielded 184 mentions of Graham in the current news section, "Passing and Permanent" or "The Present World" (the name of the section changed several times), and 30 articles of varying

length about his ministry. See also for example a ten-page booklet, Jack Hayford, *Fifty Years of Integrity: Fifty Years of Billy Graham's Success* (Lake Mary, FL: Strang Communications, 1995), reprinted in Jack W. Hayford, *The Leading Edge* (Lake Mary, FL: Charisma House, 2001), ch. 1, "Let's Learn from Billy Graham"; Synan, *Voices of Pentecost*, ch. 20. I owe these references, as well as the data about the first word search, to Darrin Rodgers, Director of the Flower Pentecostal Heritage Center, Assemblies of God, Springfield, MO. Rodgers adds: "In my experience most Pentecostals have lionized BG, although some of the more conservative Pentecostals and old-time Pentecostals have accused Billy Graham of 'easy-believism.'" Rodgers, e-mail message to author, June 26, 2014.

106 Mark A. Noll, *American Evangelical Christianity: An Introduction* (Malden, MA: Black-well, 2001), ch. 7. Evangelicals were not alone. For Mainline Protestant wariness (at best) or hostility (at worst) to Catholics, see Benny Kraut, "A Wary Collaboration: Jews, Catholics, and the Protestant Goodwill Movement," in *Between the Times,* ed. William R. Hutchison, esp. 212–226.

107 Graham, *Just As I Am,* 1997, 390.

108 Deborah H. Strober and Gerald S. Strober, *Billy Graham: An Oral and Narrative Biography* (San Francisco: Jossey-Bass, 2006), 140.

109 Noll, *American Evangelical Christianity,* ch. 7, esp. 116.

110 See, for example, Harold John Ockenga, "The Challenge of the Christian Culture of the West," *Fuller [Theological Seminary] Theology, News and Notes,* Spring 2014, 13. Ockenga was the first president of Fuller Seminary. This talk, originally given October 1, 1947, was his "Opening Convocation" address.

111 Graham, *Just As I Am,* 1997, 161.

112 "acm," memorandum to Mr. Connelly, January 31, 1952, summarizing the content of a telephone call from Graham that morning, box 1, folder 11, Collection 74, BGHA.

113 Graham, *Just As I Am,* 1997, 397, 423; Martin, *A Prophet with Honor,* 345; Lowell D. Streiker and Gerald S. Strober, *Religion and the New Majority: Billy Graham, Middle America, and the Politics of the 70s* (New York: Association Press, 1972), 73; Roger A. Bruns, *Billy Graham: A Biography* (Westport, CT: Greenwood Press, 2004), 81.

114 Graham, *Just As I Am,* 1997, 693.

115 Ibid., 357; Martin, *A Prophet with Honor,* 223 and the extensive note on page 658, which substantiates the claim, but acknowledges possible conflicting evidence; Michael Kernan, "Billy Graham: Paradox, Power, and Glory," *Braniff Place* 3, no. 5 (1974), 13. My e-mail conversations with a counselor at the 1970 New York crusade and with the chair of the 1973 Raleigh, NC, crusade, yield a more qualified picture. In the former case, inquirers received encouragement simply to involve themselves in "a local church," without further specification. In the latter case, inquirer decision cards were sent to the church of the inquirer's choice, including Catholic churches. Douglas Jacobsen, e-mail to the author, June 20, 2014, and Frederick P. Brooks, e-mail to the author, June 19, 2014. More broadly, see James Beam [Kenneth Woodward], "I Can't Play God Anymore," *McCall's,* January 1978, 158.

116 Despite Graham's statements to the press before the 1957 New York crusade that Catholics (and Jews) would be sent back to their own congregations, a senior BGEA official said that in practice that did not happen. Local pastors and church leaders oversaw the assignment of inquirers' information cards. Usually committees sent the card to the church that inquirers identified (or that brought them to the meeting through Operation Andrew). They did not send cards to congregations they considered incompatible with Christian teachings. Also, usually they did not send cards to Catholic priests. Rather, the committees tried to set up neighborhood Bible studies for Catholic inquirers with evangelical Catholic leadership. The official professed no knowledge of Jewish inquirers (if any) being sent to a synagogue. David Bruce, conversation with the author, January 9, 2014, Asheville, NC. See also the *1957 Madison Square Garden Procedure Book,* which lumped Catholics, with Unitarians, as a "questionable group," and urged ministers to assign them to Episcopal churches. "New York Crusade," May 15–September 1, 1957, *Procedure Books* (Book 1), 30, Collection 16, BGCA.

117 For example, Charles W. Dullea, S.J., "What About Billy Graham?" *Catholic Digest,* July 1972, 51–58; Tim Funk, "Graham Crusade Inspires Idealism Wherever It Goes," *Charlotte Observer,* September 21, 1996, G1. "Graham to Try Message of Unity in Racially Divided NYC," *Charlotte Observer,* September 18, 1991, A1; Funk, "Graham Crusade Inspires Idealism Wherever It Goes"; Sherwood Eliot Wirt, *Billy: A Personal Look at the World's Best-Loved Evangelist* (Wheaton, IL: Crossway Books, 1997), 213.

118 Billy Graham, interviewed by Edward Wakin, "Rev. Billy Graham and Father Theodore Hesburgh: Revival Tents and Golden Domes," *U. S. Catholic*, March 1976, 6–14; Nathan Hatch, in *Chicken Soup for the Soul: Billy Graham & Me: 101 Inspiring Personal Stories from Presidents, Pastors, Performers, and Other People Who Know Him Well*, ed. Amy Newmark, Steve Posner, and A. Larry Ross (Cos Cob, CT: Chicken Soup for the Soul Publishing, 2013), 179–180.

119 Graham, "Rev. Billy Graham and Father Theodore Hesburgh," 7, 10.

120 Martin, *A Prophet with Honor*, 295.

121 Charles W. Dullea, *W. F. "Billy" Graham's "Decision for Christ": A Study in Conversion* (Rome: Pontifical Universitas Gregoriana, 1971), 6. Ironically Dullea was more positive in his popular writing (e.g., "What About Billy Graham," cited above).

122 Kenneth L. Woodward, "Billy Graham Retrospective," *Daily Beast*, forthcoming.

123 I discuss the letters in Chapter 7.

124 See examples from Gustave Weigel, S.J., and the Reverend John E. Kelley of the National Catholic Welfare Council, in Martin, *A Prophet with Honor*, 229.

125 Graham, *Just As I Am*, 1997, 273; Billy Graham, press conference, Washington, DC, December 22, 1964, audio tape no. T23, transcript in box 4, folder 16, p. 3, Collection 24, BGCA.

126 Graham, interview with David Aikman, "Preachers, Politics, and Temptation," *Time*, May 28, 1990, 14; Mandy McMichael, "Ties that Bind: Evangelicals and Catholics Together?" (ms. in my possession), carefully documents Graham's growing embrace of Catholics.

127 Michael Ireland, summary of Larry King interviews of Billy Graham (April 2, 2005) and Jim Caviezel (April 1, 2005) on *Larry King Live*, "Billy Graham: Pope John Paul II Was 'Most Influential Voice' in 100 Years," Christian Broadcasting Network, undated, available at http://www.cbn.com/spirituallife/BibleStudyAndTheology/Perspectives/ANS_PopeGrahamCaviezel.aspx. The quoted material is Ireland speaking for Graham. In 1970, Graham told David Frost that Pope John XXIII and Dwight L. Moody ranked as the most important religious leaders of the twentieth century: David Frost, *Billy Graham Talks with David Frost* (Philadelphia: A. J. Holman, 1971), 77–78.

128 Bruns, *Billy Graham: A Biography*, 81.

129 Yaakov S. Ariel, *An Unusual Relationship: Evangelical Christians and Jews* (New York: NYU Press, 2013).

130 Yaakov S. Ariel, *Evangelizing the Chosen People: Missions to the Jews in America, 1880–2000* (Chapel Hill: University of North Carolina Press, 2000).

131 Ariel, *An Unusual Relationship*.

132 Shalom Goldman, *Zeal for Zion: Christians, Jews, and the Idea of the Promised Land* (Chapel Hill: University of North Carolina Press, 2009).

133 Graham, *Just As I Am*, 1997, 301, 509, 511, 536, 353, 450, 497.

134 Strober, *Graham: A Day in Billy's Life*, 128.

135 Billy Graham, interviewed by Larry King, *Larry King Live*, CNN, June 16, 2005, transcript available at http://transcripts.cnn.com/TRANSCRIPTS/0506/16/lkl.01.html. King described himself as Jewish, adding, "while I may not think there is a God," and "although I was raised in a religious home, I don't believe in God." Larry King, in *Chicken Soup for the Soul*, ed. Newmark, Posner, and Ross, 201–203.

136 Graham, *Just As I Am*, 1997, 301; David Neff, "Graham and the Jews," *Christian History*, forthcoming; Graham, in *Virginian Pilot* (Norfolk), January 15, 2000, in Adler, *Ask Billy Graham*, 115; Ariel, *Evangelizing the Chosen People*, 215, 265–266. It is difficult to document that something does not exist, but Graham's massively comprehensive memoir does not mention Messianic Judaism, Jews for Jesus, or key leaders of those movements, such as Louis Goldberg and Martin Chernoff. In 1957 the American Association for Jewish Evangelism "prepared at the request of the [BGEA]" a brief "Principles of Approach to Jewish People." The document articulated biblical passages that supported Jesus as Messiah, but stressed the multiple steps counselors should take to avoid offending Jewish inquirers such as avoiding discussion of the Trinity, Virgin Birth, and hell. In Beam [Woodward], "I Can't Play God Anymore," Graham purportedly opposed evangelical groups such as Jews for Jesus that specifically targeted Jews, presumably by Christianized or Messianic Jews (158). In Editorial, "Graham's Beliefs: Still Intact," *Christianity Today* January 13, 1978, however, he purportedly qualified the *McCall's* statement (49–50). That being said, I have found no concrete acts of support of such groups.

137 Graham, quoted in *New York Times*, September 16, 1991, cited in Adler, *Ask Billy Graham*, 117. To be sure, dispensationalist fundamentalism harbored a line of thought that at the end of time most Jews would convert to (fundamentalist) Christianity. In that sense, God's covenant with them was everlasting. Yet, as noted above, Graham rarely showed interest in the details of dispensationalism, and the context of his remark does not hint that it should be understood in that framework.

138 Strober and Strober, *Billy Graham: An Oral and Narrative Biography*, 98; Neff, "Graham and the Jews."

139 Ariel, *Evangelizing the Chosen People*, 198. World Christian Videos advertises *His Land*: "Prophecy fulfilled in the Holy Land! Take a musical journey into the soul of a nation and see prophecy fulfilled," available at http://www.worldchristianvideos.org/Video~FL~631.

140 Lewis William Gillenson, *Billy Graham: The Man and His Message* (New York: Fawcett, 1954), 13.

141 Marc Gellman, "The Spiritual State: Words of Faith," *Newsweek*, June 8, 2005, available at http://www.newsweek.com/spiritual-state-words-faith-120307.

142 Neff, "Graham and the Jews."

143 Graham, quoted in Wirt, *Billy: A Personal Look*, 186.

144 To my knowledge, there is no "official" transcript of this conversation. My rendering draws on John Prados, *The White House Tapes: Eavesdropping on the President* (New York: New Press, 2003), 238–255, and my own and two research assistants' transcription of the relevant parts of tape 662, February 1, 1972, National Archives and Records Administration, Nixon Presidential Materials, available from the Miller Center, University of Virginia, http://millercenter.org/presidentialrecordings/rmn-e662a.

145 Billy Graham, "A Statement by Evangelist Billy Graham on Intolerance and Prejudice Following Release of Nixon White House Tapes," Billy Graham Evangelistic Association News Release, March 16, 2002, available at http://www.prnewswire.co.uk/news-releases/a-statement-by-evangelist-billy-graham-on-intolerance-and-prejudice-following-release-of-nixon-white-house-tapes-155747745.html.

146 Graham, in Jon Meacham, "Pilgrim's Progress," *Newsweek*, August 14, 2006, 42.

147 Graham, paraphrased by King, in *Chicken Soup for the Soul: Billy Graham & Me*, ed. Newmark, Posner, and Ross, 201.

148 Ken Garfield, "Evangelist Says Father Spoke against Media Elite . . . ," *Charlotte Observer*, April 3, 2002, 1B. The first two quotes are Garfield quoting Franklin Graham, the third is Garfield's rendering of Franklin Graham's words. Garfield again quotes Franklin Graham: "Any time you have a private conversation with anybody released, your confidence has been broken."

149 "Billy Graham and the Billy Graham Evangelistic Association—Historical Background," BGCA, available at http://www2.wheaton.edu/bgc/archives/bio.html; "Select Chronology . . . ," BGCA, available at http://www2.wheaton.edu/bgc/archives/bgeachro/bgeachron02.htm. It should be said, however, that the BGCA continued to collect and make available to any researcher the extensive coverage of the incident in the press in *Scrapbook 2002*, in Collection 360, open shelves, BGCA.

150 James Warren, "Nixon, Billy Graham Make Derogatory Comments about Jews on Tapes," *Chicago Tribune*, February 28, 2002.

151 "On Tape: Billy Graham Tells Nixon of Jewish 'Stranglehold' on U.S. Media," Religion News Service, March 1, 2002. Available at http://www.beliefnet.com/News/2002/03/On-Tape-Billy-Graham-Tells-Nixon-Of-Jewish-Stranglehold-On-U-S-Media.aspx.

152 James Rudin, quoted in Allen G. Breed (AP), "Image Tarnished at the Twilight of His Career: Billy Graham Weathers Storm over Past Remarks about Jews," *Peninsula Clarion* (Kenai, AK), March 22, 2002.

153 Rebecca Phillips, "Jews React to Billy Graham News," Beliefnet, undated, available at http://www.beliefnet.com/Faiths/Judaism/2002/03/Jews-React-To-Billy-Graham-News.aspx.

154 *ADL . . . Newsletter*, "ADL Accepts the Rev. Graham's Apology," March 19, 2002, available at http://archive.adl.org/presrele/chjew_31/4056_12.html#.U6wlOI1dXBw.

155 Rapp, quoted in Ken Garfield, "In Person, Graham Makes Apologies to Jewish Leaders, Evangelist Regrets Remarks during '72 Talk with Nixon," *Charlotte Observer*, June 27, 2002, A2.

156 Jon Meacham, "Peace at the Last," *Newsweek*, July 4, 2005, 31, available at http://www.newsweek.com/peace-last-121413.

157 See, for example, William Buckley, Jr., "Billy Graham, By His Deeds," *Washington Times,*
     March 23, 2002; Cal Thomas, interviewed by Deborah Caldwell, "A Little Glitch," Belief-
     net, undated, available at http://www.beliefnet.com/Faiths/Christianity/2002/03/A-Little
     -Glitch.aspx.

158 Editorial, Kalamazoo (Michigan) *Gazette,* March 6, 2002.

159 Newspaper headlines from different parts of the nation in the two weeks following the 2002
     revelation of the 1972 incident showed a great variety of responses, ranging from "Graham-
     Nixon anti-Semitic tapes leave Jewish leaders aghast" (Tucson *Arizona Jewish Post,* March
     8, 2002), to "Graham is entitled to forgiveness for remarks" (*Roanoke Virginia Times,*
     March 10, 2002). The typical ones, however, seemed to run between these extremes: "When
     words come back to haunt us even saints suffer" *(Mobile Alabama Register,* March 3,
     2002); "Graham missed chance to speak truth to power" (*Charlotte Observer,* March 11,
     2002); "Hidden prejudice tarnishes a public legacy" (*St. Petersburg Times,* March 9, 2002).
     These papers, and perhaps scores more, in *Scrapbook 2002,* in Collection 360, open shelves,
     BGCA.

160 Larry King, in *Chicken Soup for the Soul: Billy Graham & Me,* ed. Newmark, Posner, and
     Ross, 185.

161 "Richard Nixon/Billy Graham, February 21, 1973," Miller Center/University of Virginia
     Presidential Recordings Program," Tape no. 043-161, http://whitehousetapes.net/transcript
     /nixon/043-161http://whitehousetapes.net/transcript/nixon/043-161.

162 Foxman quoted in Cathy Lynn Grossman, "In Nixon Tapes, Billy Graham Refers to 'Syna-
     gogue of Satan,'" *USA Today,* June 24, 2009, available at http://usatoday30.usatoday.com
     /news/religion/2009-06-24-graham-tapes_n.htm.

163 Ross quoted in ibid.

164 See, for example, the range of responses described in Cathy Grossman, "Is 'Synagogue of
     Satan' Really Just an Attack on Jews?" *USA Today,* June 24, 2009, available at http://content
     .usatoday.com/communities/religion/post/2009/06/68465115/1; and Steven Miller, "Billy
     Graham, Nixon, and Jews as God's Time Piece," Religion in American History, usreligion.
     blogspot.com, June 2009, available at http://usreligion.blogspot.com/2009/06/billy-graham
     -nixon-and-jews-as-gods.html.

165 I base this inference on "Religion in the News: 2009," PewResearch Religion and Public Life
     Project, March 25, 1010, available at http://www.pewforum.org/2010/03/25/religion-in-the
     -news-2009/; and Tom Heneghan, "What Were the Top Religion News Stories of 2009?"
     FaithWorld, December 17, 2009, available at http://blogs.reuters.com/faithworld/2009/12
     /17/what-were-the-top-religion-news-stories-of-2009/.

166 Ken Garfield, "In Person, Graham Makes Apologies to Jewish Leaders, Evangelist Regrets
     Remarks during '72 Talk with Nixon," *Charlotte Observer,* June 27, 2002, A2.

167 David Bruce, conversation with the author, January 17, 2014, Asheville, NC. See also Boyer,
     "The Big Tent," 52.

168 Arnold Rose, quoted in William R. Hutchison, *Errand to the World: American Protestant
     Thought and Foreign Missions* (Chicago: University of Chicago Press, 1987), 1. Hutchison:
     "Arnold Rose gave the response quoted . . . when a fellow academic, at a conference in India,
     admitted to having been a missionary." Leroy S. Rouner, conversation with author. The event
     is not dated.

169 A bystander at the train station in Heidelberg, guessing I was an American, cordially asked
     what brought me to that city. When I stated the title of the conference, he responded as
     indicated.

170 Hutchison, *Errand to the World;* Grant Wacker, "Billy Graham, Christian Manliness, and
     the Marketing of the Evangelical Subculture," in *Religion and the Marketplace in the United
     States,* ed. Philip Goff, Jan Stievermann, and Detlef Junker (New York: Oxford University
     Press, forthcoming). For the broader expansionist impulse, which evangelicals exemplified in
     a particularly forceful way, see James H. Moorhead, "The American Israel: Protestant Trib-
     alism and Universal Mission," in *Many Are Chosen: Divine Election and Western National-
     ism,* ed. William R. Hutchison and Hartmut Lehmann (Minneapolis: Fortress Press, 1994).

171 I owe this idea to Paul Erickson.

172 Graham, *Just As I Am,* 1997, 73.

173 Ibid., 73.

174 Ibid., 65; Alexander Grigolia, *Custom and Justice in the Caucasus: The Georgian Highland-
     ers* (Philadelphia: n.p., 1939). Though I do not know of any direct connection, the

international orientation of Grigolia's work likely influenced Graham's outlook, especially since Grigolia had published it only the year before Graham matriculated. Wheaton tradition remembered Grigolia as young and able. Grigolia clearly influenced Graham, perhaps not least because Grigolia figured in Wheaton lore for using an alarm clock to remind himself when it was time to go to bed at night. Ability: John Charles Pollock, *The Billy Graham Story: The Authorized Biography*, rev. and updated ed. (Grand Rapids, MI: Zondervan, 2003), 30. Alarm clock: *Oshkosh Daily Northwestern*, April 24, 1939, 16, available at http://www.newspapers.com/newspage/43462275/.

175 Michael S. Hamilton, "The Fundamentalist Harvard: Wheaton College and the Continuing Vitality of American Evangelism, 1919–1965" (Ph.D. diss., University of Notre Dame, 1994), 81–83.

176 Graham rightly took pride in his and the BGEA's critical role in orchestrating and largely funding the landmark Berlin, Lausanne, and Amsterdam congresses. These events are recounted in Graham, *Just As I Am*, 1997, ch. 31, and in Martin, *A Prophet with Honor*, throughout (see index).

177 Joel Carpenter, conversation with the author, July 1, 2008, Michilinda, MI. A fully orbed examination of Graham's international ministry remains to be written. Besides the relevant events arranged chronologically in Martin, *A Prophet with Honor*, the most fulsome study remains John Charles Pollock, *Billy Graham, Evangelist to the World: An Authorized Biography of the Decisive Years* (San Francisco: Harper and Row, 1979), part 4; John Charles Pollock, *To All the Nations: The Billy Graham Story* (San Francisco: Harper and Row, 1985), part 3, esp. ch. 23.

178 Graham, quoted in San Jose *Mercury News*, September 5, 1997, in Adler, *Ask Billy Graham*, 24.

179 Sarah E. Ruble, *The Gospel of Freedom and Power: Protestant Missionaries in American Culture after World War II* (Chapel Hill: University of North Carolina Press, 2012), chs. 1 and 2; William Lawrence Svelmoe, *A New Vision for Missions: William Cameron Townsend, the Wycliffe Bible Translators, and the Culture of Early Evangelical Faith Missions, 1896–1945* (Tuscaloosa: University of Alabama Press, 2008), esp. ch. 8.

180 John Akers, conversation with the author, January 17, 2014, Asheville, NC.

181 Graham, quoted in Edward B. Fiske, "The Closest Thing to a White House Chaplain," *New York Times Magazine*, June 8, 1969, 4, available at http://www.nytimes.com/books/97/07/06/reviews/graham-magazine.html.

182 Beam [Woodward], "I Can't Play God Anymore." Graham made stronger statements in a televised interview with California pastor Robert Schuller. Billy Graham, interview by Robert H. Schuller, "Say 'Yes' to Possibility Thinking," *Hour of Power*, May 31, 1997; transcript cited in Robert E. Kofahl, "Billy Graham Believes Catholic Doctrine of Salvation without Bible, Gospel, or Name of Christ," excerpt available at http://www.biblebb.com/files/tonyqa/tc00-105.htm. That being said, the BGEA strenuously disputed the validity of this interview. Steven Porter carefully tracked the controversy in "Billy Graham and the Wideness of God's Mercy" (ms. in author's possession). For this whole section on Graham and other religions, I am deeply indebted to Steven Porter's careful and brilliant work.

183 David Frost, *Billy Graham: Personal Thoughts of a Public Man* (Colorado Springs: Chariot Victor, 1997), 166. The interview took place January 29, 1993 (174).

184 Graham, paraphrased by Larry King, in *Chicken Soup for the Soul: Billy Graham & Me*, ed. Newmark, Posner, and Ross, 201; see also Wirt, *Billy: A Personal Look*, 186.

185 Graham, in Jon Meacham, "Pilgrim's Progress," *Newsweek*, August 14, 2006, 43.

186 Graham, *The Collected Works of Billy Graham*, 185.

187 "Graham's Beliefs: Still Intact," *Christianity Today*, January 13, 1978, 49.

188 Billy Graham, Letters to the Magazine, *Newsweek*, September 4, 2006, 22.

189 David R. Swartz, "Global Reflex"; and Amy Reynolds and Stephen Offutt, "Global Poverty and Evangelical Action"; both in *The New Evangelical Social Engagement*, ed. Brian Steensland and Philip Goff (Oxford University Press, 2013).

190 Martin, "Graham, William Franklin," 169.

191 Unidentified Graham associate, quoted in Harold Myra and Marshall Shelley, *The Leadership Secrets of Billy Graham* (Grand Rapids, MI: Zondervan, 2005), 119.

192 Russ Busby, *Billy Graham, God's Ambassador: A Lifelong Mission of Giving Hope to the World* (Alexandria, VA: Time-Life Books, 1999), 146.

193 Billy Graham, "Religion, Morality, and Politics," address at the John F. Kennedy School of Government, Harvard University, April 20, 1982, quoted in "Billy Graham: Advocate for Human Rights in America," in *Billy Graham: Footprints of Conscience* (Minneapolis: World Wide Publications [BGEA], 1991), 9.

6. PILGRIM

1 For example, Cecil Bothwell, *The Prince of War: Billy Graham's Crusade for a Wholly Christian Empire* (Asheville, NC: Brave Ulysses Books, 2007).

2 Graham prayed at Richard Nixon's first inauguration, the George H. W. Bush inauguration, and both Clinton inaugurations. For a list of Graham's inaugural prayers and sermons, see http://www2.wheaton.edu/bgc/archives/inaugural01.htm.

3 *Billy Graham: A Personal Crusade,* A&E *Biography,* hosted by Harry Smith (New York: A&E, 1999).

4 Sam Wellman, *Billy Graham: Unto All the Nations* (Uhrichsville, OH: Barbour, 1996), 106.

5 See, for example, Billy Graham, *Just As I Am: The Autobiography of Billy Graham* (San Francisco: HarperSanFrancisco; Grand Rapids, MI: Zondervan, 1997), xxii, 626, 629.

6 I am not counting President Barack Obama, who visited briefly in Graham's home after he became president. I will say more about the significance of that meeting later in the chapter.

7 Nancy Gibbs and Michael Duffy, "The Preacher and the Presidents: Billy Graham in the White House," interview by George H. Gilliam, American Forum, Miller Center for Public Affairs, University of Virginia, November 9, 2007, audio available at http://millercenter.org /events/2007/the-preacher-and-the-presidents-billy-graham-in-the-white-house.

8 Billy Graham, press conference, Columbus, OH, January 28, 1963, audio tape no. T1 (side 1), transcript in box 4, folder 9, p. 8, Collection 24, BGCA.

9 Graham, *Just As I Am,* 1997, 410; John Corry, "God, Country, and Billy Graham," *Harper's Monthly,* February 1969; Lori Lyn Bogle, *The Pentagon's Battle for the American Mind: The Early Cold War* (College Station: Texas A&M University Press, 2004), 99.

10 Murray Kempton, *New York Post,* September 9, 1960, quoted in Nancy Gibbs and Michael Duffy, *The Preacher and the Presidents: Billy Graham in the White House* (New York: Center Street, 2007), 92.

11 Ibid., 344.

12 Graham, *Just As I Am,* 1997, xviii. In 2005 Graham told Katie Couric that he was a Democrat. Billy Graham, interviewed by Katie Couric, "I Hope They'll Say That He Was Faithful," *Today,* June 23, 2005, video and transcript available at http://www.today.com/id/8326362 /ns/today/t/i-hope-theyll-say-he-was-faithful/. He made a similar claim to Larry King: Billy Graham, interviewed by Larry King, *Larry King Live,* CNN, May 7, 1997.

13 Billy Graham, interviewed by Larry King, *Larry King Live,* CNN, January 21, 1997.

14 David R. Swartz, *Moral Minority: The Evangelical Left in an Age of Conservatism* (Philadelphia: University of Pennsylvania Press, 2012), 77.

15 Graham, *Just As I Am,* 1997, 446–447. Though in 1973 Graham and Hatfield had a falling out over the Vietnam War, they eventually reconciled. Conversation between Richard Nixon and Billy Graham, February 21, 1973, Presidential Recordings Program, Miller Center, University of Virginia, tape no. 043-161, transcript and audio available at http://whitehouse tapes.net/transcript/nixon/043-161; Mark Hatfield, in *Billy Graham: A Tribute from Friends,* ed. Vernon K. McLellan (New York: Warner Books, 2002), 91.

16 Billy Graham, press conference, Atlanta, November 5, 1964, transcript in box 4, folder 15, p. 2, Collection 24, BGCA.

17 Graham, *Just As I Am,* 1997, xvii–xxi.

18 Ibid., xvii.

19 David L. Holmes, *The Faiths of the Postwar Presidents: From Truman to Obama* (Athens: University of Georgia Press, 2012), 7.

20 Graham, *Just As I Am,* 1997, xxi.

21 Truman, in Merle Miller, *Plain Speaking: An Oral Biography of Harry S. Truman* (New York: Berkley, 1974), 363.

22 Billy Graham, telegram to Harry Truman, November 29, 1950, box 1, folder 11, Collection 74, BGCA.

23 Billy Graham, "Hate vs. Love" sermon, *Hour of Decision* radio program, April 15, 1951, Shreveport, LA, pamphlet sermon no. 1, audio tape T66j, Collection 191, BGCA, audio available at http://billygraham.org/audio/hate-vs-love/; Danny R. Day, Jr., "The Political Billy Graham: Graham and Politics from the Presidency of Harry S. Truman through the Presidency of Lyndon Baines Johnson" (M.A. thesis, Wheaton College Graduate School, 1996), 40.

24 Graham, address on eve of the 1952 election, cited in Marshall Frady, *Billy Graham, a Parable of American Righteousness* (Boston: Little, Brown, 1979), 254.

25 Graham, *Just As I Am*, 1997, 196–197, quoting Graham diary entry during his visit to the Korean War zone in December 1952; Billy Graham, *I Saw Your Sons at War: The Korean Diary of Billy Graham* (Minneapolis: Billy Graham Evangelistic Association, 1953), 63. The armistice was not signed until the following July 27, 1953, long after Truman's watch had ended.

26 Graham, *Just As I Am*, 1997, 189.

27 Dwight D. Eisenhower to Leonard W. Hall, quoting a letter from Graham to Eisenhower, September 3, 1956, box 1, folder 12, Collection 74, BGCA.

28 Gibbs and Duffy, *The Preacher and the Presidents*, 39, 43, 76.

29 Billy Graham to Richard Nixon, August 28, 1960, box 3, folder 7, Collection 74, BGCA; Shaun Casey, *The Making of a Catholic President: Kennedy vs. Nixon 1960* (New York: Oxford University Press, 2009), 179.

30 Billy Graham to Richard Nixon, August 22, 1960, box 3, folder 7, Collection 74, BGCA; Graham, *Just As I Am*, 1997, 391.

31 Casey, *The Making of a Catholic President*, 136–144.

32 "Protestant Groups' Statements," issued by the National Conference of Citizens for Religious Freedom (and another group), reprinted in *New York Times*, September 8, 1960, 25.

33 Graham, *Just As I Am*, 1997, 392; Gibbs and Duffy, *The Preacher and the Presidents*, 86–87; Casey, *The Making of a Catholic President*, 135, 143–144; Carol V. R. George, *God's Salesman: Norman Vincent Peale and the Power of Positive Thinking* (New York: Oxford University Press, 1993), 200–201, 209–210. Graham later apologized for "inadvertently" contributing to Peale's embarrassment by urging Peale to go to the meeting, which, by some accounts, Graham had helped organize. See also John A. Huffman, *A Most Amazing Call—One Pastor's Reflections on a Ministry Full of Surprises* (self-published, 2011, available on Amazon .com), 70–71.

34 Casey, *The Making of a Catholic President*, 125, 135.

35 Billy Graham to Richard Nixon, September 1, 1960, box 3, folder 7, Collection 74, BGCA.

36 Kenneth L. Woodward, "The Preaching and the Power," *Newsweek*, July 20, 1970, 54.

37 Billy Graham to Richard Nixon, ca. August 15, 1961 (date not shown), box 3, folder 7, Collection 74, BGCA.

38 Graham, *Just As I Am*, 1997, 192.

39 Billy Graham to John F. Kennedy, August 10, 1960, available at "God in America" (PBS), http://www.pbs.org/godinamerica/timeline/grahamletter.html.

40 Billy Graham to Richard Nixon, August 22, 1960, box 3, folder 7, Collection 74, BGCA.

41 Billy Graham to Richard Nixon, September 1, 1960, box 3, folder 7, Collection 74, BGCA.

42 Billy Graham, unpublished letter to *Time* magazine, undated, box 3, folder 7, Collection 74, BGCA. The letter is appended to another one from Graham to Nixon, dated May 31, 1961, in which Nixon asked for a copy of the unpublished letter to *Time*. The letter was scheduled to go to press October 20, 1960, but Henry Luce pulled it the night before October 20. Graham likely wrote the letter shortly before October 20, 1960.

43 Graham, *Just As I Am*, 1997, photo following 424.

44 Ibid., 397.

45 Staffer, quoted in Woodward, "The Preaching and the Power," 54.

46 Martin, *A Prophet with Honor*, 299; Russ Busby, *Billy Graham, God's Ambassador: A Lifelong Mission of Giving Hope to the World* (Alexandria, VA: Time-Life Books, 1999), 178.

47 The group included Congressman Homer Thornberry as well. Billy Graham, interviewed by Monroe Billington, October 12, 1983, transcript available at http://www.lbjlibrary.net/assets /documents/archives/oral_histories/graham_b/Graham-B.PDF.

48 Billy Graham to Lyndon Johnson, November 18, 1968, box 3, folder 6, Collection 74, BGCA.

49 Billy Graham, interviewed by Monroe Billington, October 12, 1983.

50 Graham, quoted in Busby, *Billy Graham, God's Ambassador*, 179. These words differ slightly from Graham's recounting in *Just As I Am*, 1997, 404.

51 Billy Graham, interviewed by Monroe Billington, October 12, 1983; William H. Chafe, *Private Lives/Public Consequences: Personality and Politics in Modern America* (Cambridge, MA: Harvard University Press, 2005), 223–224; Graham, on ABC News *Prime Time Live,* December 17, 1992, cited in Bill Adler, *Ask Billy Graham* (Nashville: Thomas Nelson, 2007), 148.

52 Gibbs and Duffy, *The Preacher and the Presidents,* 343.

53 Martin, *A Prophet with Honor,* 302. Graham himself put the figure at 1.2 million. Richard V. Pierard, "Billy Graham and the US Presidency," *Journal of Church and State* 22, no. 1 (1980), 123n83.

54 Billy Graham, "Billy Graham's Own Story: 'God Is My Witness,' " *McCall's,* June 1964, 64.

55 Billy Graham to Richard Nixon, August 22, 1960, box 3, folder 7, Collection 74, BGCA.

56 Unnamed friend, quoted in Martin, *A Prophet with Honor,* 435.

57 Ehrlichman, quoted in Roger A. Bruns, *Billy Graham: A Biography* (Westport, CT: Greenwood Press, 2004), 117.

58 "Remarks by Dr. Billy Graham at Richard Nixon's Funeral," transcript available at http://watergate.info/1994/04/27/billy-graham-remarks-at-nixon-funeral.html. Also CNN broadcast of Nixon's funeral, April 27, 1994, videotape V62, Collection 74, BGCA.

59 Woodward, "The Preaching and the Power," 54.

60 *Billy Graham: A Personal Crusade,* A&E *Biography,* hosted by Harry Smith (New York: A&E, 1999).

61 Garry Wills, "How Nixon Used the Media, Billy Graham, and the Good Lord to Rap with Students at Tennessee U," *Esquire,* September, 1970, 119–122.

62 Martin, *A Prophet with Honor,* 386–387.

63 Billy Graham, interviewed by Merv Griffin, *Merv Griffin Show,* October 12, 1972, audio tape T44, Collection 345; transcript box 2, folder 10, p. 16, Collection 24, both BGCA.

64 Billy Graham to Richard Nixon, October 21, 1972, box 3, folder 7, Collection 74, BGCA.

65 Billy Graham to Richard Nixon, December 26, 1973, box 3, folder 7, Collection 74, BGCA.

66 Graham, *Just As I Am,* 1997, 457.

67 Martin, *A Prophet with Honor,* 431.

68 Billy Graham, interviewed by Hugh Downs, *20/20,* ABC, December 20, 1979, videotape V8, Collection 74, BGCA.

69 Martin, *A Prophet with Honor,* 432, 695n431.

70 Graham, *Just As I Am,* 1997, 457.

71 Graham virtually endorsed George W. Bush publically. Gary Scott Smith, *Faith and the Presidency: From George Washington to George W. Bush* (New York: Oxford University Press, 2006), 374.

72 Graham, *Just As I Am,* 1997, 445.

73 Billy Graham to Gerald R. Ford, September 10, 1976, Gerald R. Ford Presidential Library and Museum, Ann Arbor and Grand Rapids, MI.

74 Graham, *Just As I Am,* 1997, 491.

75 Gibbs and Duffy, *The Preacher and the Presidents,* 247.

76 Carter signed (at least one) letter simply "Jimmy"—Jimmy Carter to Billy Graham, April 7, 1977; handwritten note from Ruth Graham to Mr. President and Rosalynn, November 6, 1979 and another from Ruth Graham to Rosalyn, December 11, 1980; Billy Graham to Rosalynn: "You and your family are daily in my prayers . . . We thank God for your Christian witness." "Graham, Billy" File, White House Central File, Jimmy Carter Presidential Library and Museum, Atlanta, GA.

77 Robert Maddox to Jimmy Carter, September 5, 1979, "Graham, Billy" file, White House Central file, Jimmy Carter Presidential Library and Museum, Atlanta, GA.

78 For the Graham and Bright meeting in Dallas, see Gibbs and Duffy, *The Preacher and the Presidents,* 260–262; Randall Balmer, *Redeemer: The Life of Jimmy Carter* (New York: Basic Books, 2014), 119–122; William C. Martin, *With God on Our Side: The Rise of the Religious Right in America* (New York: Broadway Books, 1996), 205–207. For more details and primary references regarding Graham's letters to Paul Laxalt and to Robert Maddox, see Balmer, *Redeemer,* 119–121, 242–243nn1–7. See also Carl F. H. Henry, *Confessions of a Theologian: An Autobiography* (Waco, TX: Word Books, 1986), 386.

79 Balmer, *Redeemer,* 122. Elsewhere Balmer slightly softens the charge: "evangelicals themselves might be chagrined to learn about some of the backroom machinations of preachers like Jerry Falwell and even Billy Graham . . . [whose] actions . . . probably crossed the line between honest mistakes and outright duplicity" (xxvi).

80 David Aikman, *Billy Graham: His Life and Influence* (Nashville: Thomas Nelson, 2007), 229.

81 I borrow this picture of commonalities from Martin, *A Prophet with Honor,* 434; Lou Cannon, *President Reagan: The Role of a Lifetime* (New York: Simon and Schuster, 1991).

82 Aikman, *Billy Graham: His Life and Influence,* 233.

83 "Billy Graham Visit at VST [Vancouver School of Theology] and Regent College," Vancouver, 1984, available at http://www.regentaudio.com/products/billy-graham-at-vst-and-regent-college.

84 Graham, *Just As I Am,* 1997, 652–653; "Billy Graham: Pastor to Power," *20/20,* hosted by Charles Gibson, August 10, 2007, excerpt available at http://abcnews.go.com/2020/video/billy-graham-pastor-power-3474754.

85 Graham regarding Clinton: "I—I forgive him. I don't know what the average person—but, I mean, certainly I forgive him. Because I know the frailty of human nature and I know how hard it is—and especially a strong, vigorous young man like he is. And he—he has such a tremendous personality that I think the ladies just go wild over him." Graham, interviewed by Katie Couric, *Today,* NBC, March 5, 1998. For one biting response, see Arianna Huffington, on *Hardball with Chris Matthews,* CNBC, March 6, 1998. Huffington: "What is this? A kind of hormone excuse? . . . To hear that from Jerry Springer is one thing, to hear it from Billy Graham was extremely disappointing."

86 Graham, *Just As I Am,* 1997, 653.

87 Nancy Gibbs and Michael Duffy, "Billy Graham: Hillary's Solace," *Time,* August 8, 2007, available at http://content.time.com/time/nation/article/0,8599,1650798,00.html.

88 George W. Bush, Amy Newmark, Steve Posner, and A. Larry Ross, eds., *Chicken Soup for the Soul: Billy Graham & Me: 101 Inspiring Personal Stories from Presidents, Pastors, Performers, and Other People Who Know Him Well* (Cos Cob, CT: Chicken Soup for the Soul Publishing, 2013), 60–61.

89 Edward B. Fiske, "The Closest Thing to a White House Chaplain," *New York Times Magazine,* June 8, 1969, available at http://www.nytimes.com/books/97/07/06/reviews/graham-magazine.html.

90 Willmar Thorkelson, "The Billy Grahams at Home," *Christian Herald,* November 1973, 31.

91 See, for example, Graham, *Just As I Am,* 1997, 415; Billy Graham, press conference, Columbus, OH, July 9, 1964, audio tape no. T7, transcript in box 4, folder 14, p. 8, Collection 24, BGCA.

92 See, for example, the exceptional number of times Graham appears in Daniel K. Williams, *God's Own Party: The Making of the Christian Right* (New York: Oxford University Press, 2010), under index entries for "Graham, Billy," especially "Republican Party, association with," and for Nixon.

93 Graham, *Just As I Am,* 1997, 505; Billy Graham, press conference, Baton Rouge, LA, October 19, 1970, transcript in box 1, folder 27, Collection 24, BGCA; Garry Clifford, "Billy Graham, First of the Big-Time TV Preachers . . . ," *People,* February 16, 1981, available at http://www.people.com/people/archive/article/0,,20078616,00.html, quoted in Gibbs and Duffy, *The Preacher and the Presidents,* 277.

94 Gustav Niebuhr, "Billy Graham: Loyal to Longtime Friend in Triumph and Defeat," *Washington Post,* April 28, 1994, A12.

95 Lyndon Johnson to Billy Graham, February 11, 1969, box 3, folder 6, Collection 74, BGCA.

96 Graham interview, January 17, 2006, cited in Gibbs and Duffy, *The Preacher and the Presidents,* xii.

97 "Billy Graham: Pastor to Power," *20/20,* hosted by Charles Gibson, August 10, 2007.

98 Graham, *Just As I Am,* 1997, 406; Billy Graham, telegram to Lyndon Johnson, September 15, 1967, box 3, folder 6, Collection 74, BGCA.

99 Graham, *Just As I Am,* 1997, 415.

100 Graham, in Corry, "God, Country, and Billy Graham," 39.

101 See, for example, Billy Graham to Dwight Eisenhower, November 18, 1959, inviting himself to play golf with the president at Augusta, box 1, folder 12, Collection 74, BGCA; White House memorandum from "b." to "Don": "Billy Graham called to let the Vice President know he is in Washington and available for golf. . . . He is at the Willard Room 702." June 14, 1960, microfilm, reel 1, box 299, Series 320, BGCA (in this case Nixon was of course still vice president).

102 Billy Graham to Lyndon Johnson, April 5, 1966, box 3, folder 6, Collection 74, BGCA.

103 John Akers, special assistant to Billy Graham, conversation with the author, January 9, 2014, Asheville, NC.

104 Graham, *Just As I Am,* 1997, 394–395.
105 Graham, *Just As I Am,* 1997, 189. Writing a half-century later, Graham poked fun at himself: "Nobody would accuse me of understatement."
106 Billy Graham to Lyndon Johnson, July 11, 1965, box 3, folder 6, Collection 75, BGCA.
107 Billy Graham, press conference, Portland, OR, May 15, 1968, transcript in box 1, folder 11, Collection 24, BGCA. Graham did not explicitly name Nixon but no one could doubt that he meant Nixon.
108 Graham added: "For some mysterious reason unknown to us, Mr. Carter won." Billy Graham to Gerald R. Ford, November 24, 1976, Gerald R. Ford Presidential Library and Museum.
109 Arthur Krim, interviewed by Michael L. Gillette, June 29, 1982, New York, p. 22, Oral History Collection, Lyndon Baines Johnson Presidential Library and Museum, Austin, TX.
110 Frady, *Billy Graham, a Parable of American Righteousness,* vii.
111 Billy Graham to Richard Nixon, (probably) March 27, 1962, box 3, folder 7, Collection 74, BGCA.
112 Gibbs and Duffy, "The Preacher and the Presidents," interview at the Miller Center for Public Affairs, University of Virginia, 2007.
113 Graham, *Just As I Am,* 1997, 593.
114 See, for example, Billy Graham, press conference, Atlanta, December 29, 1967, audio tape no. T12, transcript in box 1, folder 7, p. 3, Collection 24, BGCA.
115 Billy Graham, press conference, Columbus, OH, January 28, 1963, audio tape no. T1 (side 1), transcript in box 4, folder 9, p. 11, Collection 24, BGCA.
116 Ibid., 10–11.
117 Billy Graham, press conference, Los Angeles, May 13, 1968, audio tape no. T8, transcript in box 1, folder 10, p. 12, Collection 24, BGCA.
118 Billy Graham, press conference, Baton Rouge, LA, October 19, 1970, transcript in box 1, folder 27, p. 16, Collection 24, BGCA; Graham in Marguerite Michaels, "Billy Graham: America Is Not God's Only Kingdom," *Parade,* February 1, 1981, 6–7, quoted in Bruns, *Billy Graham: A Biography,* 139.
119 Billy Graham, press conference, Columbus, OH, July 9, 1964, audio tape no. T7, transcript in box 4, folder 14, p. 9, Collection 24, BGCA.
120 Billy Graham, press conferences: Houston, June 14, 1973, transcript in box 3, folder 6, p. 3; Raleigh, NC, April 26, 1973, audio tape no. T60, transcript in box 3, folder 3, pp. 10–11; both in Collection 24, BGCA.
121 Gibbs and Duffy, "The Preacher and the Presidents: Billy Graham in the White House," interview at the Miller Center for Public Affairs, University of Virginia, 2007.
122 "The Man Behind the Crusades," *Charlotte Observer,* September 14, 1996, 1C.
123 Michael S. Hamilton, "Something Big for God: Billy Graham," *Christianity Today,* forthcoming.
124 Billy Graham, "Billy Graham's Own Story: 'God Is My Witness,'" June, 64; Deborah H. Strober and Gerald S. Strober, *Billy Graham: An Oral and Narrative Biography* (San Francisco: Jossey-Bass, 2006), 11.
125 Graham, *Just As I Am,* 1997, 448.
126 Billy Graham, press conference, Santa Barbara, CA, September 6, 1972, audio tape no. T53, transcript in box 2, Collection 24, BGCA.
127 Drew Gilpin Faust, *The Creation of Confederate Nationalism: Ideology and Identity in the Civil War South* (Baton Rouge: Louisiana State University Press, 1988), esp. ch. 2.
128 Charles Reagan Wilson, *Baptized in Blood: The Religion of the Lost Cause, 1865–1920* (Athens: University of Georgia Press, 1980).
129 Charles Reagan Wilson, *Judgment and Grace in Dixie: Southern Faiths from Faulkner to Elvis* (Athens: University of Georgia Press, 1995), ch. 2 and Afterword.
130 Harry S. Stout, *Upon the Altar of the Nation: A Moral History of the American Civil War* (New York: Viking, 2006), esp. xvii–xxi.
131 Billy Graham, "Three Minutes to Twelve" sermon, February 1953, *Hour of Decision,* pamphlet sermon no. 22, audio available at http://billygraham.org/audio/three-minutes-to-twelve/.
132 Graham, *Just As I Am,* 1997, 160, 170; Billy Graham, press conference, New York, July 29, 1968, transcript in box 1, folder 13, p. 6, Collection 24, BGCA.
133 Billy Graham, *Approaching Hoofbeats: The Four Horsemen of the Apocalypse* (Waco, TX: Word Books, 1983); Billy Graham, *Storm Warning* (Dallas: Word Publishing, 1992). Other printings have different covers.

134 See, for example, Billy Graham, "What Is God Like?" sermon, *Hour of Decision* radio program, July 22, 1956, pamphlet sermon no. 4, audio tape T341j, Collection 191, BGCA, audio available at http://billygraham.org/audio/wha-is-god-like/.

135 Billy Graham, *My Answer* (Garden City, NY: Doubleday, 1960, 185, available online at http://www.ccel.us/myanswer.toc.html; Billy Graham, "The Unfinished Dream" sermon (from Honor America Day, July 4, 1970), *Hour of Decision* radio program, July 5, 1970, Washington, DC, pamphlet sermon no. 189, audio tape T1069a,b, Collection 191, BGCA, audio available at http://billygraham.org/audio/the-unfinished-dream/.

136 For Graham in the context of American traditions about Christian values and the state see Jon Meacham, "The Prayer Breakfast Presidency," *Washington Post*, Sunday April 16, 2006, B1, available at http://www.washingtonpost.com/wp-dyn/content/article/2006/04/14/AR200 6041401908.html.

137 Billy Graham, press conference, Atlanta, April 24, 1973, audio tape no. T59, transcript in box 3, folder 2, pp. 17–18, Collection 24, BGCA.

138 Graham, *Just As I Am*, 1997, 170–171. For the broader outlook in evangelical and, behind that, Puritan culture that informed Graham's words see Timothy P. Weber, *Living in the Shadow of the Second Coming*, enl. ed. (Grand Rapids, MI: Academie Books, 1983); and Harry S. Stout, *The New England Soul: Preaching and Religious Culture in Colonial New England* (New York: Oxford University Press, 1986), ch. 4.

139 William G. McLoughlin, Jr., *Billy Graham, Revivalist in a Secular Age* (New York: Ronald Press, 1960), 71, 144–145.

140 Billy Graham, "Men Must Be Changed before a Nation Can," in John K. Jessup and others, *The National Purpose* (New York: Holt, Rinehart and Winston, 1960), esp. 63–64; Billy Graham, "Four Great Crises" sermon, *Hour of Decision* radio program, July 7, 1977, New York, pamphlet sermon no. 88, audio tape T391f, Collection 191, BGCA, audio available at http://billygraham.org/audio/four-great-crises/.

141 Reinhold Niebuhr, Introductory Essay, in Stephen C. Rose, ed., *Sermons Not Preached in the White House* (New York: R. W. Baron, 1970), quoted in Woodward, "The Preaching and the Power," 55.

142 "Original Billy Graham Address 1955," *Christianity Today* Editorial Office, Carol Stream, IL.

143 Gibbs and Duffy, *The Preacher and the Presidents*, 187–190.

144 Billy Graham, interview by Edward B. (Ted) Fiske of the *New York Times*, June 22, 1970, transcript in box 1, folder 24, p. 8, Collection 24, BGCA.

145 Andrew S. Finstuen, *Original Sin and Everyday Protestants: The Theology of Reinhold Niebuhr, Billy Graham, and Paul Tillich in an Age of Anxiety* (Chapel Hill: University of North Carolina Press, 2009), 129.

146 Billy Graham, "God and Crime" sermon, *Hour of Decision* radio program, April 22, 1956, pamphlet sermon no. 63, audio tape T328f, Collection 191, BGCA, audio available at http://billygraham.org/audio/god-and-crime/.

147 Will Herberg, *Protestant, Catholic, Jew: An Essay in American Religious Sociology* (Chicago: University of Chicago Press, 1983), 30.

148 Graham, quoting diplomat George Kennan, cited in George M. Marsden, *The Twilight of the American Enlightenment: The 1950s and the Crisis of Liberal Belief* (New York: Basic Books, 2014), xxxvii.

149 "Billy's Bountiful African Harvest," *Life*, March 21, 1960, 29.

150 Billy Graham, press conference, New York, July 29, 1968, transcript in box 1, folder 13, p. 6, Collection 24, BGCA.

151 John Charles Pollock, *Billy Graham, Evangelist to the World: An Authorized Biography of the Decisive Years* (San Francisco: Harper and Row, 1979), chs. 15–19.

152 Martin, *A Prophet with Honor*, 384.

153 Graham's awards are listed in the BGCA's "Select Chronology Listing of Events in the Life of Billy Graham . . . ," available at http://www2.wheaton.edu/bgc/archives/bgeachro/bgea chron02.htm. The awards include the Speaker of the Year Award (for "effective, intelligent and responsible communication in a democracy") from Delta Sigma Rho-Tau Kappa Alpha (1965), the Torch of Liberty Award from the Anti-Defamation League of B'nai B'rith (1969), and Salesman of the Decade Award from the Direct Selling Association (1975).

154 See, for example, Graham's multiple appearances in the early 1970s on nationally syndicated talk shows, including interviews with Johnny Carson (T42), Merv Griffin (T44), Dinah Shore (T45), the *Today* show (T38, T47), all in Collection 345, BGCA; interview with Dick

Cavett (T18), Collection 74, BGCA; and interviewed by Woody Allen, *Kraft Music Hall,* September 21, 1969, available at http://www.youtube.com/watch?v=194zJ55LcVk.

155 Billy Graham, Associated Press, February 1, 1980, cited in Adler, *Ask Billy Graham,* 185.

156 Billy Graham, *Calgary Herald,* June 24, 1998, cited in Adler, *Ask Billy Graham,* 23.

157 Billy Graham, press conference, Houston, June 14, 1973, transcript in box 3, folder 6, p. 16, Collection 24, BGCA.

158 Dan Rather, interviewed by David Aikman, for *Billy Graham: Ambassador of Salvation,* in series *Great Souls: Six Who Changed a Century,* hosted by David Aikman (2002), cited in Aikman, *Billy Graham: His Life and Influence,* 4.

159 Though I use the term "decency" somewhat differently, I owe it to Steven P. Miller, "The Politics of Decency: Billy Graham, Evangelicalism, and the End of the Solid South" (Ph.D. diss., Vanderbilt University, 2007).

160 The historical literature on anti-communism in America is extensive. Graham's name possibly shows up as often as any person outside the government. See, for example, William Inboden, *Religion and American Foreign Policy, 1945–1960: The Soul of Containment* (New York: Cambridge University Press, 2008); Jason W. Stevens, *God-Fearing and Free: A Spiritual History of America's Cold War* (Cambridge, MA: Harvard University Press, 2010); Andrew Preston, *Sword of the Spirit, Shield of Faith: Religion in American War and Diplomacy* (New York: Alfred A. Knopf, 2012); Stephen J. Whitfield, *The Culture of the Cold War,* 2nd ed. (Baltimore: Johns Hopkins University Press, 1996).

161 Graham, *Just As I Am,* 1997, 381.

162 Chicago *Daily News,* June 11, 1955, 1, quoted in Martin, *A Prophet with Honor,* 167.

163 Graham, quoted in Harold Bloom, "Billy Graham: The Preacher," *Time,* June 14, 1999.

164 "Decision" News Letter of the Billy Graham Evangelistic Association, Minneapolis, July 1953, 1, from BGEA, Charlotte, NC.

165 Billy Graham, "Christianity vs. a Bloodless Religion" sermon, *Hour of Decision* radio program, September 16, 1951, Hollywood, CA, audio tape T88j, Collection 191, BGCA, audio available at http://billygraham.org/audio/christianity-vs-a-bloodless-religion/; Billy Graham, "The Urgency of Revival" sermon, *Hour of Decision* radio program, January 3, 1954, pamphlet sermon no. 36, audio tape T208f,g, Collection 191, BGCA; Billy Graham, "Christianity vs. Communism" sermon, *Hour of Decision* radio program, February 4, 1951, Minneapolis, audio tape T56j, Collection 191, BGCA, audio "Christianity vs. Communism" available at http://billygraham.org/audio/christianism-vs-communism/.

166 Darren E. Grem, "*Christianity Today,* J. Howard Pew, and the Business of Conservative Evangelicalism," *Enterprise and Society* 15, no. 2 (2014): 337–379, doi:10.1093/es/khu012.

167 Thomas C. Reeves, *The Life and Times of Joe McCarthy: A Biography* (New York: Stein and Day, 1982), 203, 442, 463, 498. For a revisionist view of McCarthy, which may make Graham's short-term appreciation for him more compelling, see Arthur Herman, *Joseph McCarthy: Reexamining the Life and Legacy of America's Most Hated Senator,* 1999, Introduction, available at http://www.nytimes.com/books/first/h/herman-mccarthy.html; Alonzo L. Hamby, "Reds Under the Bed," review of Herman, *Joseph McCarthy, New York Times,* December 12, 1999, available at http://www.nytimes.com/books/99/12/12/reviews/991212.12hambyt.html.

168 Frady, *Billy Graham, a Parable of American Righteousness,* 238–239.

169 Billy Graham to Dwight Eisenhower, May 10, 1954, box 1, folder 12, Collection 74, BGCA; Graham, *Just As I Am,* 1997, 381; Aikman, *Billy Graham: His Life and Influence,* 187–188.

170 The deeply, if not essentially, religious character of communism resonated in Graham's sermons of this era. Not surprisingly, the first sermon he preached in the Los Angeles revival in 1949 targeted the communist threat. (Sermon available at http://www2.wheaton.edu/bgc/archives/exhibits/LA49/05sermons01.html.)

171 Inboden, *Religion and American Foreign Policy.*

172 Graham, on the *Dinah Shore Show,* "*Dinah's Place,*" October 3 and 4, 1972, audio tape no. T45, Collection 345, BGCA.

173 Graham, quoted without citation in John Charles Pollock, *The Billy Graham Story: The Authorized Biography,* rev. and updated ed. (Grand Rapids, MI: Zondervan, 2003), 150.

174 Graham, quoted in Tim Funk and Ken Garfield, "Graham: Message Is Same, Man Has Changed," *Charlotte Observer,* September 24, 1996, 1A, cited in Adler, *Ask Billy Graham,* 25.

175 See, for example, Billy Graham, "America's Decision" sermon, *Hour of Decision* radio program, August 2, 1953, pamphlet sermon no. 28, audio tape T186f, Collection 191, BGCA.

176 Graham, *I Saw Your Sons at War.*
177 All of the standard biographies examine Graham's relation to the Vietnam War at length. For a particularly perceptive treatment, see Richard V. Pierard, "Billy Graham and Vietnam: From Cold Warrior to Peacemaker," *Christian Scholar's Review* 10, no. 1 (1980): 37–51.
178 Billy Graham, press conference, December 29, 1967, Atlanta, audio tape no. T12, transcript in box 1, folder 7, p. 4, Collection 24, BGCA.
179 William H. Chafe, *The Unfinished Journey: America since World War II,* 7th ed. (New York: Oxford University Press, 2011), 251.
180 Chafe, *The Unfinished Journey,* 270–272; James T. Patterson, *Grand Expectations: The United States, 1945–1974* (New York: Oxford University Press, 1996), 603–604.
181 Billy Graham, "Confidential Missionary Plan for Ending the Vietnam War," April 15, 1969, box 3, folder 7, Collection 74, BGCA. See Martin, *A Prophet with Honor,* 685n365, for government provenance.
182 Martin, *A Prophet with Honor,* 367.
183 Graham, "Confidential Missionary Plan," 1.
184 Ibid. The quotations are from pages 7, 9, 10, respectively.
185 Bothwell, *The Prince of War,* 110.
186 I discuss this trait in a wider context in Chapter 8.
187 Graham, *Just As I Am,* 1997, 415.
188 Pierard, "Billy Graham and the US Presidency," 126.
189 David Poling, "Billy Graham: God's Crusader," *Dayton Daily News,* September 29, 1974, 6.
190 Billy Graham, "Billy Graham: On Calley," *New York Times,* April 9, 1971, 31.
191 David Frost and Fred Bauer, *Billy Graham: Personal Thoughts of a Public Man* (Colorado Springs: Chariot Victor, 1997), 53.
192 Billy Graham, press conference, Houston, June 14, 1973, transcript in box 3, folder 6, p. 16, Collection 24, BGCA.
193 Billy Graham, press conference, Lubbock, TX, May 6, 1975, audio tape no. T83, transcript (dated May 7) in box 3, folder 35, p. 9, Collection 24, BGCA.
194 Billy Graham, interviewed by Larry King, *Larry King Live,* CNN, January 21, 1997.
195 Graham, quoted in "U.S. Religious Leaders . . ." (AP), January 10, 1991, cited in Gibbs and Duffy, *The Preacher and the Presidents,* 302.
196 Graham, *Just As I Am,* 1997, 586.
197 Gibbs and Duffy, "The Preacher and the Presidents," interview at the Miller Center for Public Affairs, University of Virginia, 2007. Except for Graham's September 14, 2001, Service of Remembrance homily in the National Cathedral (available at http://www.nationalcathedral.org/worship/sermonTexts/bg010914.shtml), he said little of consequence about the second Iraq war. He was eighty-one when it started and nearly ninety when American troops withdrew in 2009.
198 In 1944 Graham enrolled in the U.S. Army chaplain training program, but owing to a severe bout with mumps he never served. He was discharged owing to the imminent end of the war. Graham, *Just As I Am,* 1997, 67, 93.
199 Billy Graham, interviewed by Ben Haden, "Billy Graham on Vietnam," *The Bible Study Hour,* no date. Transcript in the LBJ Presidential Library, Austin. The transcript is not dated but the accompanying correspondence is dated March 2, 1967. See also Loyd Hackler to George Christian, White House Memorandum, April 28, 1967, summarizing Billy Graham comments on the *Bible Study* radio program: "He heard of one former Berkeley protestor who was drafted and is now a superb soldier; Graham credited the change to discipline and a challenge." Billy Graham, "Transcript of Television Broadcast: Billy Graham on Vietnam," moderated by the Reverend Ben Haden, *Bible Study Hour,* 9–10, transcript not dated but likely April 1967, as the broadcast was almost certainly the one described in White House Memorandum for George Christian from Loyd Hackler, April 28, 1967, both documents in LBJ Presidential Library, accession number for Hackler ND19/CO312//F05//PR12//FG1//RM.
200 Edith Blumhofer, "Singing to Save: The Signature Sound of the Graham Crusades," in *The Worlds of Billy Graham,* ed. Andrew S. Finstuen, Anne Blue Wills, and Grant Wacker, forthcoming.
201 Anne C. Loveland, *American Evangelicals and the U.S. Military, 1942–1993* (Baton Rouge: Louisiana State University Press, 1996).
202 Graham on *CBS Evening News,* March 29, 1979, quoted in Pierard, "Billy Graham and Vietnam," 37.
203 Billy Graham, press conference, Honolulu, August 8, 1984, audio tape no. T158, transcript in box 4, folder 25, p. 2, Collection 24, BGCA.

204 The story of Graham's journeys into Eastern Europe and, especially, the Soviet Union in the late 1970s and 1980s appears in most of the standard biographies, but most extensively and meticulously in Martin, *A Prophet with Honor,* chs. 29–31.

205 Graham, *Just As I Am,* 1997, 500–502; Graham, in Busby, *Billy Graham, God's Ambassador,* 138.

206 John Akers, "To Go or Not to Go: Billy Graham and Moscow, 1982," in *The Worlds of Billy Graham,* ed. Andrew S. Finstuen, Anne Blue Wills, and Grant Wacker, forthcoming.

207 Graham, *Just As I Am,* 1997, 500–501; Martin, *Prophet with Honor,* 499.

208 Ibid., 502; Graham, in Busby, *Billy Graham, God's Ambassador,* 142; Graham in Frost and Bauer, *Billy Graham: Personal Thoughts,* 192.

209 Busby, *Billy Graham, God's Ambassador,* 142.

210 John Akers, conversation with the author, January 17, 2014, Asheville, NC.

211 Leighton Ford, presentation in a class at Duke Divinity School, April 1, 2008, Durham, NC.

212 John Akers, conversation with the author, January 17, 2014.

213 Martin, *Prophet with Honor,* 499. Martin quotes Graham in this respect but the original source is not clear.

214 See photograph of Graham dabbing his eyes. Russ Busby, *God's Ambassador,* in unpaginated frontmatter.

215 Graham, *Just As I Am,* 1997, 485.

216 Ibid., 486.

217 Graham's remarks in Moscow, ibid., 505.

218 Graham, in Busby, *Billy Graham, God's Ambassador,* 144.

219 "Billy Graham Visit at VST and Regent College," Vancouver, 1984, audio available at http://www.regentaudio.com/products/billy-graham-at-vst-and-regent-college.

220 George Will, interviewed by Martin Agronsky, *Agronsky and Company,* May 17, 1982.

221 James M. Wall, "A Few Kind Words for Billy Graham," *Christian Century,* May 26, 1982, 619.

222 Campbell, quoted in Frye Gaillard, "Billy Graham: An Honest Look, Martin's Biography Written with Fairness, Thoroughness, Respect," *Charlotte Observer,* October 13, 1991, 5B Bookweek.

223 Buckley, quoted without citation in Sherwood Eliot Wirt, *Billy: A Personal Look at the World's Best-Loved Evangelist* (Wheaton, IL: Crossway Books, 1997).

224 See the comments of Ed Robb, director of the neoconservative Institute on Religion and Democracy, quoted in Wall, "A Few Kind Words," 619.

225 Dan Rather, on *The Bible and the Wall* (BG syndicated television program), 1990, quoted in Martin, *A Prophet with Honor,* 616.

226 Graham, *Approaching Hoofbeats,* 153–154.

227 "Graham Says He's Praying for Peace," *Charlotte Observer,* November 18, 1985, C2. Audio of sermon available at http://library.duke.edu/digitalcollections/dukechapel_ua17010003cs0294/.

228 Billy Graham, interviewed by Jim Finnerty, *Jim Finnerty and Company,* KCRA (Sacramento, CA), November 9, 1983.

229 "Global Citizens, Global Peacemakers: An Interview with Billy Graham," in *JustLife '88: Election Study Guide for Justice, Life and Peace,* ed. Kathleen Hayes and Ronald J. Sider (Grand Rapids, MI: William B. Eerdmans, 1988), 9.

230 Graham purportedly said this to Mark Hatfield, cited in Wesley Granberg-Michaelson, *Unexpected Destinations: An Evangelical Pilgrimage to World Christianity* (Grand Rapids, MI: W. B. Eerdmans, 2011), 77.

231 Billy Graham, "Watergate," *Christianity Today,* January 4, 1974, 9–19, quoted in Swartz, *Moral Minority,* 182.

232 David Poling, "Billy Graham: God's Crusader," *Dayton Daily News,* September 29, 1974, 6.

233 Billy Graham, in "A Change of Heart: Billy Graham on the Nuclear Arms Race," *Sojourners,* 8 (August 1979), 12–15, cited in Richard V. Pierard, "Billy Graham and Vietnam: From Cold Warrior to Peacemaker," *Christian Scholar's Review* 10, no. 1 (1980): 37–38. Pierard does not state the title of the original article in *Sojourners,* but it can be accessed at http://sojo.net/sites/default/files/images/A-Change-of-Heart.pdf. The cover of that issue bore a photo of Graham preaching, with the logo: "Billy Graham: Preaching against the Arms Race." Pierard cites similar remarks by Graham on CBS Evening News, March 29, 1979, text printed in *Christianity and Crisis,* 39 (April 30, 1979), 111, and commentary on the CBS News interview in Colman McCarthy, *Los Angeles Times,* June 24, 1979. On the occasion

of Graham's ninety-third birthday, Jim Wallis, CEO of *Sojourners,* described a breakfast meeting with Graham about 1975 (exact date not specified). Wallis quoted Graham: "'I think that you will be a leader for the next generation of young Christians. And I am a leader for the older establishment of evangelicals. There are people who would divide us, and pull us apart; but we can't let them do that. I want them to know that I agree with you on more things than they would imagine, and I thought we should start talking together.'" Wallis quoted Graham in a later conversation: "'My calling is to preach the gospel of personal salvation, and yours is to preach the social implications of that same gospel. So I think our ministries are complementary.'" Jim Wallis, "From Jim Wallis to Billy Graham, on His 93rd Birthday: 'Thank you!'" *Sojourners,* posted November 7, 2011, available at http://sojo .net/blogs/2011/11/07/jim-wallis-billy-graham-his-93rd-birthday-thank-you.

234 Brian Stanley, *The Global Diffusion of Evangelicalism: The Age of Billy Graham and John Stott* (Nottingham, UK: IVP, 2013), ch. 6; Richard V. Pierard, "Transformation after Lausanne: Radical Evangelical Mission in Global-Local Perspective," *Covenant Quarterly* 68, no. 3–4 (2010): 74–75; Richard V. Pierard, "Lausanne II: Reshaping World Evangelicalism," *Christian Century* 106, no. 24 (1989): 740–742. Graham's attention to the developing world was not new. One of the earliest books produced by the BGEA-related Grason Company chronicled his six-week mission tour across Africa in 1960. Nearly every page of the slim volume featured striking, unposed black-and-white photographs of Graham and nationals, or nationals alone or in groups without Graham. Western missionary faces, common fare in mission-related books, remained nearly absent. Tom McMahan, *Safari for Souls: With Billy Graham in Africa* (Columbia, SC: State-Record Co., 1960).

235 "The Lausanne Covenant," 1974, available at http://www.lausanne.org/en/documents/lausanne -covenant.html.

236 Alister Chapman, *Godly Ambition: John Stott and the Evangelical Movement* (New York: Oxford University Press, 2012), 137–138, 142–143, 148–149; Billy Graham, *Just As I Am: The Autobiography of Billy Graham,* rev. and updated 10th anniv. ed. (New York: HarperOne; Grand Rapids, MI: Zondervan, 2007), 573–574. To be sure, Graham held reservations about the direction that the Lausanne Continuation Committee (the permanent organization that emerged from the conference) took the following year, seeking to combine evangelization with social witness. But for him the question was not whether the *gospel* itself bore a mandate for social witness but what the mandate for this particular organization should be.

237 David P. King, "Seeking a Global Vision: The Evolution of World Vision and American Evangelicalism" (Ph.D. diss., Emory University, 2012), 1; David King, "The New Internationalists: World Vision and the Revival of American Evangelical Humanitarianism, 1950–2010," *Religions* 3, no. 4 (2012), 924; Steve Gray, Central Records-Global Knowledge Management, World Vision International, e-mail message to the author, April 3, 2014; and David P. King, e-mail message to the author, June 27, 2014. The exact dates of Graham's service on the Board of Reference are not certain. The dates that I have stated represent Gray's and King's best judgments.

238 Bob Pierce, quoted in King, "Seeking a Global Vision," 51.

239 Ibid., 211–215; David Bruce, executive assistant to Billy Graham, e-mail to author, July 2, 2014; "Samaritan's Purse Consolidated Statement of Activities for the Year Ended December 31, 2013," 4, available at http://static.samaritanspurse.org.s3.amazonaws.com/pdfs/2013Sa-maritansPurseAuditedFinancials-PublicDisclosure.pdf.

240 Graham, quoted without citation to original source in Pollock, *The Billy Graham Story,* 130.

241 See Graham in "Candid Conversation with the Evangelist," *Christianity Today,* July 17, 1981, 21–22; Graham in Colin Greer, "Change Will Come When Our Hearts Change," *Parade,* October 20, 1996, 6; Aikman, *Billy Graham: His Life and Influence,* 149, 155–156, 160; Martin, *Prophet with Honor,* 442–443, 522–524; Frye Gaillard, *Southern Voices: Profiles and Other Stories* (Asheboro, NC: Down Home Press, 1991), 121–122, 126.

242 Billy Graham, press conference, Chicago, May 24, 1971, audio tape no. T41, transcript in box 1, folder 31, p. 11, Collection 24, BGCA.

243 Billy Graham, in *Billy Graham: Ambassador of Salvation,* in series *Great Souls: Six Who Changed a Century,* hosted by David Aikman (2002), quoted in Aikman, *Billy Graham: His Life and Influence,* 7.

244 Billy Graham, in "Facts on File," *World News Digest,* February 13, 1981, cited in Adler, *Ask Billy Graham,* 192.

245 Michael D'Antonio, "Playing It Safe in the Pulpit," review of *A Prophet with Honor: The Billy Graham Story,* by William Martin, *Los Angeles Times,* November 10, 1991, available at http://articles.latimes.com/1991-11-10/books/bk-2227_1_billy-graham-s-success.

246 Laurie Goodstein, "Spirit Willing, One More Trip Down Mountain for Graham," *New York Times,* June 12, 2005, available at http://www.nytimes.com/2005/06/12/national/12graham .html. See also Ken Garfield, "Crusade Will Show a Softer Graham," *Charlotte Observer,* June 23, 2005, A1.

247 Gibbs and Duffy, *The Preacher and the Presidents,* 339–341.

248 Billy Graham, interviewed by Larry King, *Larry King Live,* CNN, December 25, 2005, rush transcript available at http://transcripts.cnn.com/TRANSCRIPTS/0512/25/lkl.11.html. The transcript has Graham saying, "he has my views," but, from the context, it is obvious that Graham meant that *Franklin* has "his views." In the interview, Graham added that Franklin "doesn't hold that position now."

7. Pastor

1 John Corry, "God, Country, and Billy Graham," *Harper's Monthly,* February 1969, 39.

2 E. Brooks Holifield, *God's Ambassadors: A History of the Christian Clergy in America* (Grand Rapids, MI: William B. Eerdmans, 2007), 2. I draw on Holifield's categories but I have renamed and adapted them to Graham's career.

3 John Akers, special assistant to Mr. Graham, conversation with the author, January 17, 2014, Asheville, NC.

4 Keith Call, *Wheaton* (Charleston, SC: Arcadia, 2006); Ann Durkin Keating, *Chicagoland: City and Suburbs in the Railroad Age* (Chicago: University of Chicago Press, 2005), 109, 132–133. Billy Graham, *Just As I Am: The Autobiography of Billy Graham* (San Francisco: HarperSanFrancisco; Grand Rapids, MI: Zondervan, 1997), 65.

5 Billy Graham, interview by Edward B. (Ted) Fiske of the *New York Times,* June 22, 1970, transcript in box 1, folder 24, p. 19, Collection 24, BGCA.

6 Graham, *Just As I Am,* 1997, xxv, 216, 228, 250, 295; Billy Graham, press conference, Albuquerque, NM, March 12, 1975, audio T82, transcript box 3, folder 33, p. 6, Collection 24, BGCA.

7 William G. McLoughlin, Jr., *Billy Graham, Revivalist in a Secular Age* (New York: Ronald Press, 1960), 184; Edward B. Fiske, "The Closest Thing to a White House Chaplain," *New York Times Magazine,* June 8, 1969, available at http://www.nytimes.com/books/97/07/06 /reviews/graham-magazine.html. William Martin, "The Power and the Glory of Billy Graham," *Texas Monthly,* March 1978, 152, available at http://www.texasmonthly.com/ story/power-and-glory-billy-graham. Donald A. Clelland, Thomas C. Hood, C. M. Lipsey, and Ronald Wimberley, "In the Company of the Converted: Characteristics of a Billy Graham Crusade Audience," *Sociology of Religion* 35, no. 1 (1974), 47–49, doi:10.2307/3710342; Kurt Lang and Gladys Engel Lang, "Decisions for Christ: Billy Graham in New York City," in *Identity and Anxiety: Survival of the Person in Mass Society,* ed. Maurice R. Stein, Arthur J. Vidich, and David Manning White (Glencoe, IL: Free Press, 1960), 418; Lowell D. Streiker and Gerald S. Strober, *Religion and the New Majority: Billy Graham, Middle America, and the Politics of the 70s* (New York: Association Press, 1972), 13. See also Frederick L. Whitam, "Revivalism as Institutionalized Behavior: An Analysis of the Social Base of a Billy Graham Crusade," *Social Science Quarterly* 49, no. 1 (1968), 117–118. Whitam's study reinforces the findings of these observers about the middle-class preponderance among Graham's followers, but it targeted crusade deciders rather than attendees, and focused on New York City, both of which may have been atypical. Though Whitam's study generally emphasized middle-class presence, one questionnaire emphasized upper-middle-class presence (118).

8 Paul E. Johnson, *A Shopkeeper's Millennium: Society and Revivals in Rochester, New York, 1815–1837* (New York: Hill and Wang, 1978); Michael J. McClymond, ed., *Embodying the Spirit: New Perspectives on North American Revivalism* (Baltimore: Johns Hopkins University Press, 2004), esp. ch. 1; Grant Wacker, *Heaven Below: Early Pentecostals and American Culture* (Cambridge, MA: Harvard University Press, 2001), ch. 11.

9 See the people filing into the large meeting tent in Graham's 1949 springboard revival in Los Angeles, in *Canvas Cathedral,* the first Billy Graham film, BGCA.

10 See, for example, Russ Busby, *Billy Graham, God's Ambassador: A Lifelong Mission of Giving Hope to the World* (Alexandria, VA: Time-Life Books, 1999), for 1949: photos following table of contents and p. 51; Ken Garfield, *Billy Graham: A Life in Pictures* (Chicago: Triumph Books, 2013): for 1961, p. 61, for 1960s(?), p. 82, for 1978, p. 87, for 1996, p. 23.

11 Whitam, "Revivalism as Institutionalized Behavior," 119.

12 Busby, *Billy Graham, God's Ambassador;* and Garfield, *Billy Graham: A Life in Pictures.*

13 Whitam, "Revivalism as Institutionalized Behavior," 119. In Ferm's study, based on a randomized sampling of 400 inquirers, only twenty (5%) identified as laborers, the others being (to take only the "A's" in a long alphabetical list) account representative, accountant, actor, advertising executive, armed services personnel, artist, attorney, auditor, auto dealer. Robert O. Ferm with Caroline M. Whiting, *Billy Graham: Do the Conversions Last?* (Minneapolis: World Wide Publications, 1988), 25–28.

14 Billy Graham, press conference, Baton Rouge, LA, October 19, 1970, transcript in box 1, folder 27, p. 8, Collection 24, BGCA.

15 Billy Graham, "Organized Labor and the Church" sermon, *Hour of Decision* radio program, August 31, 1952, Ocean Grove, NJ, pamphlet sermon no. 18, audio tape T138j, Collection 191, BGCA, audio available at http://billygraham.org/audio/organized-labor-and-the -church/.

16 I base the claim for female preponderance on outsiders' observations and on, for example, Fiske, "The Closest Thing to a White House Chaplain"; Clelland et al., "In the Company of the Converted," 49, 52, 54; Marshall Frady, *Billy Graham, a Parable of American Righteousness* (Boston: Little, Brown, 1979), 226; Ferm and Whiting, *Billy Graham: Do the Conversions Last?* 22.

   In addition, in a sample of letters 164 of the writers had names that could be identified as distinctively male or female; of those, males constituted 39% and females 61%. First names of the people who sent letters in my random sample: A. J., Aaron, Alan, Albert, Alberta, Allen, Ann, Arnette, Arlene, Arlette, Barb, Barbara (2), Bernice, Betty (3), Beverly, Bob, Bonnie, Brainerd, Butch, Cal, Carole, Carolyn, Charlena, Charles, Claude, Clay, Conrad, Cynthia (2), Daniel, David (4), Debbie, Debra, Dennis, Don, Donald, Donna (2), Dora, Dwayne (2), Ed, Edith, Edwin, Eleanor, Emmanuel, Ernest, Florence, Francois, Frank, Gail, George, Graham, Hal, Harrill, Helen, Henry (2), Herb, Howard, Ira, Irene, J.B., J. M., James (2), Jamie, Janet (2), Jean, Jeanette, Jeannie, Jeffrey, Jennifer, Jim, Joanne, Joel (2), John (4), Joyce, Judith, Judy, Julie, Karen, Katherine (2), Kathy (2), Ken, Kim, Lee, Leila, Lilla, Lisa, Loretta, Lorna, Loraine, M. B., Margaret, Marie (2), Marilyn, Marsh, Mary (3), Marylee, Maurice, Melinda, Michael (3), Minnie, Mrs. B, Myrtle, Nancy (2), Nora, Patti, Patty, Paula, Ralph, Raymond (2), Reg, Rob, Robert (3), Ron, Rose (2), Ruth, Samuel (2), Sarah (2), Sheree, Sharon, Sheree, Steve, Susan (2), Sylvia, Tammy, Theresa, Thomas, Tony, Trish, Virginia (2), Wanda, William (2), Winston, Zoe.

17 Catherine A. Brekus, ed., *The Religious History of American Women: Reimagining the Past* (Chapel Hill: University of North Carolina Press, 2007), Introduction.

18 Andrew S. Finstuen, *Original Sin and Everyday Protestants: The Theology of Reinhold Niebuhr, Billy Graham, and Paul Tillich in an Age of Anxiety* (Chapel Hill: University of North Carolina Press, 2009), 18; Robert A. Orsi, *Thank You, St. Jude: Women's Devotion to the Patron Saint of Hopeless Causes* (New Haven, CT: Yale University Press, 1996), ch. 3.

19 Clelland et al., "In the Company of the Converted," 165; Ronald C. Wimberley, Thomas C. Hood, Donald Clelland, C. M. Lipsey, and Marguerite Hay, "Conversion in a Billy Graham Crusade: Spontaneous Event or Ritual Performance?" *Sociological Quarterly* 16, no. 2 (1975), 165, doi:10.1111/j.1533-8525.1975.tb00935.x; Billy Graham, press conferences: Baton Rouge, LA, October 19, 1970, transcript in box 1, folder 27, p. 4; Chicago, May 24, 1971, audio tape no. T41, transcript in box 1, folder 31, p. 2; both in Collection 24, BGCA; Ferm and Whiting, *Billy Graham: Do the Conversions Last?* 23–24.

20 Billy Graham, on *Dinah Shore Show,* "Dinah's Place," October 3 and 4, 1972, audio tape no. T45, Collection 345, BGCA.

21 Larry Eskridge, "'One Way': Billy Graham, the Jesus Generation, and the Idea of an Evangelical Youth Culture," *Church History* 67, no. 1 (1998), 86, 102, doi:10.2307/3170772.

22 James L. McAllister, "Evangelical Faith and Billy Graham," *Social Action* 19, no. 5 (1953), 22–23.

23 See, for example, Billy Graham, press conferences: Chicago, May 24, 1971, audio tape no. T41, transcript in box 1, folder 31, p. 4; Cleveland, July 10, 1972, audio tape no. T51, transcript in box 2, folder 4, p. 4; both in Collection 24, BGCA; Whitam, "Revivalism as Institutionalized Behavior," 120.

24 See, for example, Graham in Busby, *Billy Graham, God's Ambassador*, 214; Billy Graham, press conference, Cleveland, July 10, 1972, audio tape no. T51, transcript in box 2, folder 4, p. 4, Collection 24, BGCA.

25 See Chapter 3.

26 Lewis F. Brabham, *A New Song in the South: The Story of the Billy Graham Greenville, S.C., Crusade* (Grand Rapids, MI: Zondervan, 1966).

27 White churches tried to mount a crusade in 1972, but black churches did not support it partly because black churches had not been consulted. The crusade did not occur at all for that reason. William Martin, *A Prophet with Honor: The Billy Graham Story* (New York: W. Morrow, 1991), 409. Several news outlets noted the change from the failed crusade attempt in Washington, DC, in 1972 to the crusade held there in 1986. For the 1986 crusade, the organization sought black church support, and the first seven nights of the crusade were held at the downtown convention center because of its access to local (presumably more African American) residents. An event was held at the suburban RFK stadium only on the final night. Patrice Gaines-Carter, "The Making of a Crusade: Yearlong Planning for Billy Graham in D.C.," *Washington Post*, April 24, 1986, C1; "Billy Graham's Washington Crusade Gains the Support of Black Church Leaders," *Christianity Today*, June 13, 1986.

In Atlanta in 1973, several black church leaders protested the event, and the crusade audience was primarily white. "Billy Graham Plans Crusade Aimed at Youths' Problems: Disillusionment Cited," Associated Press report in *The Toledo Blade*, June 17, 1973, 15; "Graham Opens Georgia Crusade," Associated Press report in the *Florence Times—Tri Cities Daily*, June 19, 1973, 8; Marjorie Hyer, "Billy Graham Out of Favor with Black Christians?" *Tuscaloosa News*, reprinting *Washington Post* piece, July 1, 1973, 6E. In 1994, however, Graham visited several black churches to promote his crusade, and "demanded racially integrated support" as a condition of his preaching in Atlanta. Some black clergy and leaders were still not impressed, and refused to participate. But others supported Graham's work. Gayle White and Tom Oder, "Before the Crusade—Graham Makes Rounds; Drops by 3 Churches," *Atlanta Journal-Constitution*, October 24, 1994; Gayle White, "A Commitment to Racial Unity," *Atlanta Journal-Constitution*, October 25, 1994; "Graham Hopeful of Uniting Races in Atlanta Crusade," Associated Press story in *Tuscaloosa News*, October 25, 1994, B4; Frederick Robinson, "Billy Graham-Style Evangelism—Can Crusade Bridge the Gap between Races?" *Atlanta Journal-Constitution*, October 28, 1994, A18; "Graham Crusade, 'Deeper Than a Handshake,' " *Christianity Today*, December 12, 1994, 62.

28 It is of course difficult to prove that something did not exist. But the letters proved remarkably forthright and self-revealing in numerous other respects—especially those from children and self-identified elders—as I try to show below.

29 Out of a randomized sample of 164 letters drawn from the folders described in Note 99, below, 155 had legible return addresses. Based on reports from the 1980 United States Census, a majority of the individuals who wrote to Graham lived in large or small towns and a plurality resided in the Southern United States. Of the 155 legible letter return addresses, 25 came from *large cities* (500,000+), 25 from *small cities* (100,000 to 499,999), 33 from *large towns* (25,000 to 99,999), 72 from *small towns* (24,999 or fewer), and none from rural box numbers. Only 16 percent of letters originated in large cities while small towns alone nearly triple that figure by boasting 46 percent of Graham's received correspondence. When combined, individuals from large and small towns represent more than two-thirds (68 percent) of the people who wrote to Graham. Source: 1980 populations, from City Population, 2014, http://www.citypopulation.de/USA.html. In terms of regional origin of the writers to Graham, 59 lived in the South, which exceeds the 32 writers from the West, 31 from the Midwest, and 25 from the Northeast. With 38 percent of the correspondence, Southern provenance constitute a clear plurality when compared to the West (21 percent), Midwest (20 percent), and Northeast (16 percent). The remaining 8 writers (5 percent) had international addresses. My research materials, available at the Duke Divinity School Library, include a full listing of the names of the places.

Serious analysis of the cultural significance of residence in towns rather than cities falls outside the scope of this book. Though towns were commonly regarded as repositories of traditional values (and sometimes as cultural backwaters), they might have been sites of rapid rural/urban interface. Daniel T. Lichter and David L. Brown, "Rural America in an Urban Society: Changing Spatial and Social Boundaries," *Annual Review of Sociology* 37, no. 1 (2011): 565–592, doi:10.1146/annurev-soc-081309-150208.

30 Whitam, "Revivalism as Institutionalized Behavior," 120; Clelland et al., "In the Company of the Converted," 53–54.

31 Billy Graham, *Just As I Am: The Autobiography of Billy Graham* (San Francisco: HarperSan-Francisco; Grand Rapids, MI: Zondervan, 1997), 324.

32 Dinkins, quoted in Ken Garfield, "250,000 Answer Graham's Call to Repentance: Diverse Audience Fills Central Park," *Charlotte Observer,* September 23, 1991, A1.

33 Ibid.

34 Nancy Gibbs and Michael Duffy, *The Preacher and the Presidents: Billy Graham in the White House* (New York: Center Street, 2007), 339–341.

35 It is difficult to determine when the BGEA began systematic efforts to insure that the planning committees were racially integrated from the *outset*. One account, framed in Jackson, Mississippi, in 1975, seems simply to presuppose it. A reminiscence by an African American university dean intimates that was not the case in the early 1960s but by 1994 Graham was personally making sedulous efforts to assure African American participation at all stages. See, respectively, Gerald S. Strober, *Graham: A Day in Billy's Life* (Garden City, NY: Doubleday, 1976), 36; and Gerald Durley, in *Chicken Soup for the Soul: Billy Graham & Me: 101 Inspiring Personal Stories from Presidents, Pastors, Performers, and Other People Who Know Him Well,* ed. Amy Newmark, Steve Posner, and A. Larry Ross (Cos Cob, CT: Chicken Soup for the Soul Publishing, 2013), ch. 30.

36 For the racial integration of counselors, and assignment of them to inquirers without reference to race, see Sherwood Wirt, *Billy: A Personal Look at the World's Best-Loved Evangelist* (Wheaton, IL: Crossway Books, 1997), 129. An executive assistant stated that when he joined the BGEA in 1972, assignments without reference to race were simply presupposed. David Bruce, executive assistant to Mr. Graham, conversation with the author, January 17, 2014.

37 Norris R. Johnson, David A. Choate, and William Bunis, "Attendance at a Billy Graham Crusade: A Resource Mobilization Approach," *Sociology of Religion* 45, no. 4 (1984), 390, doi:10.2307/3711301. Whitam, "Revivalism as Institutionalized Behavior," 125. Though Whitam's categories do not apply precisely, they generally support my reading of the letters. Most letter writers did not identify a denomination, per se. Most revealed a broadly evangelical (or blended Reformed/Wesleyan) theology, focused on conversion, life of faith in Christ, with little sense of ecclesiology, sacrament, confession, historic tradition, or sectarian distinctives such as vegetarianism, healing, speaking in tongues, or hard dispensationalism.

38 Martin, *A Prophet with Honor,* 309, journalist unnamed.

39 Ibid., 25.

40 Gibbs and Duffy, *The Preacher and the Presidents,* 161.

41 Billy Graham to Richard Nixon, March 28, 1957, box 3, folder 7, Collection 74, BGCA. Founded in 1919, the *Daily News* ranked as the nation's first successful tabloid paper. It reached a circulation of two million by the 1940s. "New York Daily News," *Encyclopedia Britannica,* available at http://www.britannica.com/EBchecked/topic/412434/New-York-Daily -News. "Favored by lower-end white-collar workers, subway riders commuting into the city, the *Daily News* featured short punchy stories and impressive photography." Matthew Bowman, New York City religion historian, e-mail message to the author, May 31, 2014.

42 Graham, quoted in Elizabeth Kaye, "Billy Graham Rises," *George,* December 1996, 140.

43 I adapt this sentence from Michael Kernan, "Billy Graham: Paradox, Power, and Glory," *Braniff Place,* 1974, 13, and from Frady, *Billy Graham, a Parable of American Righteousness,* 234.

44 The words came from the hymn *Dear Lord and Father of Mankind,* adapted by Garrett Horder in 1884 from John Greenleaf Whittier's poem, "The Brewing of Soma," published in 1872.

45 Finstuen, *Original Sin and Everyday Protestants,* 138.

46 Ferm and Whiting, *Billy Graham: Do the Conversions Last?*

47 Johnson, Choate, and Bunis, "Attendance at a Billy Graham Crusade," 300.

48 Joe DePriest, "Return Engagement," *Charlotte Observer,* September 14, 1996, 1G.

49 Graham, *Just As I Am,* 1997, 153.

50 The historical and theoretical literature on religious conversion is extensive. I note some of the texts that inform my thinking in Grant Wacker, "Pearl S. Buck and the Waning of the Missionary Impulse," *Church History* 72, no. 4 (2003), 868n34. See especially Lewis R. Rambo, *Understanding Religious Conversion* (New Haven, CT: Yale University Press, 1993). For a superior entry into the historical literature see John M. Mulder, ed., *Finding God: A Treasury*

of Conversion Stories (Grand Rapids, MI: Wm. B. Eerdmans, 2012), esp. Introduction. John Charles Pollock, *The Billy Graham Story: The Authorized Biography*, rev. and updated ed. (Grand Rapids, MI: Zondervan, 2003), 219, drawing on a study of David MacInnes of crusade attenders in Great Britain in 1984.

51 Graham, *Just As I Am,* 1997, 241, 259.

52 I attended one meeting of Graham's crusade at the University of North Carolina, Chapel Hill, in 1982, and saw that pattern.

53 For one of many descriptions supporting this point see Harold H. Martin, "A Vivid Portrait of the Famous Revivalist Billy Graham," *Saturday Evening Post,* April 13, 1963, 18. See also Stanley High, *Billy Graham: The Personal Story of the Man, His Message, and His Mission* (New York: McGraw-Hill, 1956), 50, 56, 91; Kaye, "Billy Graham Rises," 142. See also Frady, *Billy Graham, a Parable of American Righteousness, 5,* who speaks of Graham's insistence on quiet, even in a vast stadium audience. Billy Graham, "Billy Graham's Own Story: 'God Is My Witness,'" *McCall's,* May 1964, 184, borrowing words of a reporter at his 1954 Harringay, London, crusade.

54 Martin, *A Prophet with Honor,* 29; Ferm and Whiting, *Billy Graham: Do the Conversions Last? 58.*

55 Wacker, *Heaven Below,* ch. 6.

56 High, *Billy Graham: The Personal Story,* 66; Billy Graham, press conference, San Francisco, September 7, 1972, audio tape no. T54, transcript in box 2, folder 7, p. 11, Collection 24, BGCA.

57 My thinking about the role of desire in Graham's preaching grows from Michael Hamilton, "From Desire to Decision: The Evangelistic Preaching of Billy Graham," in *The Worlds of Billy Graham,* ed. Andrew S. Finstuen, Anne Blue Wills, and Grant Wacker, forthcoming.

58 Graham, *Just As I Am,* 1997, 28, emphasis added.

59 Graham, in Busby, *Billy Graham, God's Ambassador,* 30.

60 Ruth Bell Graham, *It's My Turn* (Old Tappan, NJ: Fleming H. Revell, 1982), 47. See also Martin, *A Prophet with Honor,* 449; and Patricia Daniels Cornwell, *Ruth, a Portrait: The Story of Ruth Bell Graham* (New York: Doubleday, 1997), 48.

61 Billy Graham, press conference, Cleveland, July 10, 1972, audio tape no. T51, transcript in box 2, folder 4, p. 9, Collection 24, BGCA.

62 Roger Lundin and Mark A. Noll, eds., *Voices from the Heart: Four Centuries of American Piety* (Grand Rapids, MI: W. B. Eerdmans, 1987). This fine work features seventeen American writers from a variety of vocations—Emily Dickinson to Woodrow Wilson—ruminating in depth on the life of God in the life of humans. Significantly, no evangelical (except Charles Finney in the middle nineteenth century) is included in the collection. Both Noll and Lundin write from within the tradition.

63 Kenneth L. Woodward, *Faith, Culture, Politics from the Era of Eisenhower to the Age of Obama,* forthcoming.

64 Martin, *A Prophet with Honor,* 550.

65 Brent Rinehart, Manager, Public and Media Relations, BGEA, e-mail message to David Bruce, executive assistant to Mr. Graham, October 7, 2013, forwarded to author by David Bruce, October 7, 2013. Mr. Rinehart adds that this number does not, of course, include commitments prompted by Graham's vast electronic and print media ministry.

66 Ferm and Whiting, *Billy Graham: Do the Conversions Last?* 17. See, however, page 21 which reports 3.4%.

67 BGCA "Select Chronology Listing of the Life of Billy Graham," available at http://www2 .wheaton.edu/bgc/archives/bgeachro/bgeachron02.htm.

68 Joe DePriest, "Return Engagement," *Charlotte Observer,* September 14, 1996, G1.

69 Billy Graham, press conference, Albuquerque, March 12, 1975, audio tape no. T82, transcript in box 3, folder 33, p. 13, Collection 24, BGCA.

70 Heather Vacek, conversation with author, November 18, 2008, Chapel Hill, NC.

71 Clinton, quoted in David L. Holmes, *The Faiths of the Postwar Presidents: From Truman to Obama* (Athens: University of Georgia Press, 2012), 220, see also 218.

72 Miller, "Popular Religion of the 1950's"; Carol V. R. George, *God's Salesman: Norman Vincent Peale and the Power of Positive Thinking* (New York: Oxford University Press, 1993), 129–131.

73 Frady, *Billy Graham, a Parable of American Righteousness,* 220.

74 *Christian Century,* September 13, 1972, 891, cited by "Mr. Butler," in Billy Graham, press conference, Albuquerque, New Mexico, March 12, 1975, 13.

75 William G. McLoughlin, Jr,, *Billy Graham: Revivalist in a Secular Age* (New York: Ronald Press Company, 1960), 193, 195.

76 Robert O. Ferm, interviewed by Lois Ferm, June 21, 1978, and January 10, 1979, interview no. 331, tape T1 (part 1) and T21 (part 2), oral history interviews, final copies (stored separately), transcript in box 3, folder 37, p. 11, allin Collection 141, BGCA.

77 Ferm and Whiting, *Billy Graham: Do the Conversions Last?* 138–139. Martin reports a different Ferm study of the New York crusade which showed that one in five deciders could not be reached afterward; one-third of the remaining 80% had not been involved in church before and, of those, 90% (that is, about a quarter of the deciders) had become members or were studying to do so. Martin, *A Prophet with Honor,* 237–238 and 662n237.

78 Sterling Huston, cited in Ken Garfield, "Groundwork Underway for Graham Charlotte Crusade," *Charlotte Observer,* January 31, 1996, C1.

79 Editors and Glenn Firebaugh, "How Effective Are City-wide Crusades?" *Christianity Today,* March 27, 1981, 24–29. Internal evidence in the article suggests the study was undertaken in 1980.

80 Charles T. Cook, *The Billy Graham Story: "One Thing I Do"* (London: Marshall, Morgan and Scott, 1954), 43.

81 Ibid., 86.

82 Priestley, quoted in High, *Billy Graham: The Personal Story,* 228.

83 Daniel Aleshire, e-mail message to author, April 7, 2009.

84 High, *Billy Graham: The Personal Story,* 252.

85 Ken Garfield, "Child of Charlotte, Child of God as Billy Graham's September Crusade Nears, Memories Help Mold a Museum Exhibit," *Charlotte Observer,* April 20, 1996, G1.

86 David Aikman, *Great Souls: Six Who Changed the Century* (Waco, TX: Word Books, 1998), 58.

87 David Frost and Fred Bauer, *Billy Graham: Personal Thoughts of a Public Man* (Colorado Springs: Chariot Victor, 1997), 72. In the 1993 interview, Graham said inquirers and converts "will be there five or ten years from now." The context suggests he meant not just five or ten years but something like "for keeps."

88 Graham, quoted in *The Tennessean,* May 26, 2000, cited in Bill Adler, *Ask Billy Graham* (Nashville: Thomas Nelson, 2007), 36.

89 Graham, in Busby, *Billy Graham, God's Ambassador,* 101.

90 Martin, *A Prophet with Honor,* 708n550. See also William Martin, "The Power and the Glory of Billy Graham," 156; Ferm and Whiting, *Billy Graham: Do the Conversions Last?* 29, 101.

91 Martin, *A Prophet with Honor,* 708n550.

92 Wimberley et al., "Conversion in a Billy Graham Crusade," 162; Whitam, "Revivalism as Institutionalized Behavior," 123; Johnson, Choate, and Bunis, "Attendance at a Billy Graham Crusade," 887; David Bennett, *The Altar Call: Its Origins and Present Usage* (Lanham, MD: University Press of America, 2000), 225.

93 Curtis Mitchell, *God in the Garden; the Story of the Billy Graham New York Crusade* (Garden City, NY: Doubleday, 1957), 12–19.

94 Billy Graham, press conference, Los Angeles, May 13, 1968, audio tape no. T8, transcript in box 1, folder 10, p. 19, Collection 24, BGCA.

95 Billy Graham, press conference, Columbus, OH, January 28, 1963, audio tape no. T1 (side 1), transcript in box 4, folder 9, p. 5, Collection 24, BGCA. See also Ferm and Whiting, *Billy Graham: Do the Conversions Last?* 84.

96 Frank Tumpane, quoted in High, *Billy Graham: The Personal Story,* 223.

97 Van Dusen, "Billy Graham," *Christian Century,* April 2, 1956, 40 (and interview with Fox), quoted in Richard Wightman Fox, *Reinhold Niebuhr: A Biography* (New York: Pantheon Books, 1985), 266.

98 John Bunyan, *Entire Works,* ed. Henry Stebbing (London: J. S. Virtue, 1860), 128.

99 The manuscript letters that constitute the bulk of the evidence for the remaining sections of this chapter are housed at the BGCA. The BGCA prohibits copying or any use of the letters that might reveal the identity of the writers. I also feel an ethical obligation not to identify or quote letters obviously intended for Graham or his staff, not for outside researchers. Except for a handful of published letters, I have limited my analysis to the larger themes that they raise, and avoid quoting them directly (though I have paraphrased particular sentences or parts of sentences).

The letters I examined are largely from "Counseling letters" (letters sent to Graham that were considered for "My Answer" column), in box 28, folders 1, 2, 6, 7; box 29, folders 1–3; box 30, folder 6; box 31, folder 6; box 33, folders 3–8, all in Group I.C, Collection 575,

BGCA. Other letters are from "Appreciation notes, 1948–1950," box 3, folder 1, Collection 74, BGCA; and "My Conversion Story" questionnaires, box 20, folders 4–6, Collection 19, BGCA. I estimate that these collections contain more—possibly far more—than five thousand letters. I read approximately five hundred, and took careful notes on 164. (It is a time-consuming process because of the difficulty of deciphering handwriting, even on carefully scribed letters.) I wish especially to thank Katherine Wacker and Aaron Griffith for helping me research these documents.

100 Graham, *Just As I Am,* 1997, 318.

101 Strober, *Graham: A Day in Billy's Life,* 94.

102 William A. Doyle, "Bringing in the Sheaves: The Big (and Closely Guarded) Business of Billy Graham . . . ," *Corporate Report,* June 1977, 66.

103 Graham, *Just As I Am,* 1997, 502.

104 By the late 1950s "My Answer" saw publication in 200 papers with a daily circulation of about 28 million. Stanley High, "Billy Graham: The Personal Story of the Man," *Reader's Digest,* May 1957, 222–223, cited in Douglas T. Miller, "Popular Religion of the 1950's: Norman Vincent Peale and Billy Graham," *Journal of Popular Culture* 9, no. 1 (1975), 72, doi:10.1111/j.0022-3840.1975.0901_66.x. According to historian Andrew Finstuen: "My Answer" appeared [six] days a week in newspapers across America. In the fifties alone, the column generated 15,000 letters a week . . . By the end of the decade, "My Answer" ran in more than 150 papers and reached more than 16 million readers." Staff writers, particularly Robert Ferm, produced all of the responses. "Graham made no secret of this collective authorship. . . . Every column, however, passed through Graham's hands for final approval and editing. In fact, the *New York News–Chicago Tribune* syndicate would accept only columns with Graham's handwriting visible on the draft." Finstuen, *Original Sin and Everyday Protestants,* 143.

105 The years for which I found and read letters include 1950, 1958, 1961–1962, 1981–1989 (except 1987).

106 Graham, quoted in Chattanooga *Times Free Press,* June 23, 1995, cited in Adler, *Ask Billy Graham,* 206.

107 Billy Graham, "Despair of Loneliness" sermon, *Hour of Decision* radio program, October 5, 1952, Pittsburgh, pamphlet sermon no. 19, audio tape T143g, Collection 191, BGCA, audio "Loneliness of Despair" available at http://billygraham.org/audio/the-loneliness-of-despair/.

108 Reinhold Niebuhr, "Differing Views on Billy Graham," *Life,* July 1, 1957, 92, excerpts available at http://www2.wheaton.edu/bgc/archives/exhibits/NYC57/05sample28.htm.

109 For the surge of prosperity teaching that accompanied but rarely penetrated Graham's ministry see Kate Bowler, *Blessed: A History of the American Prosperity Gospel* (New York: Oxford University Press, 2013). For cultural background, which many evangelicals increasingly embraced, but with no intentional encouragement from Graham, see Todd M. Brenneman, *Homespun Gospel: The Triumph of Sentimentality in Contemporary American Evangelicalism* (New York: Oxford University Press, 2014).

110 Billy Graham, *My Answer* (Garden City, NY: Doubleday, 1960), 115, available at http://www.ccel.us/myanswer.toc.html.

111 Graham, commencement address to Palm Beach Atlantic College, 1997, quoted in *Ledger* (Lakeland, FL), cited in Adler, *Ask Billy Graham,* 204–205.

112 Charles H. Lippy, "Billy Graham's 'My Answer': Agenda for the Faithful," *Studies in Popular Culture* 5 (1982), 28–29.

113 Graham, *My Answer,* 26–27.

114 Ibid., 49.

115 Ibid., 14.

116 Ibid., 25.

117 Ibid., 33–34, 21.

118 Ibid., 36, 38.

119 Ibid., 121, 132, 141.

120 Ibid., 186, 189–190.

121 Billy Graham, "Christianity vs. Communism" sermon, *Hour of Decision* radio program, February 4, 1951, Minneapolis, audio tape T56j, Collection 191, BGCA, audio "Christianism vs. Communism" available at http://billygraham.org/audio/christianism-vs-communism/.

122 Katherine Wacker helped research and provide ideas about the significance of these letters. All of the letters detailed in Postscript A of this chapter are archived at the BGEA headquarters in Charlotte, NC. I wish to thank retired corporation counsel Stephen Scholle for allowing

me to see them. I changed the children's identities and corrected some misspelled words, but otherwise the quotations are original.

123 Most of these envelopes are displayed in public glass cases at the Billy Graham Museum and Library in Charlotte, NC. See also Martin, *A Prophet with Honor*, 551; Busby, *Billy Graham, God's Ambassador*, 248; Rich Oppel, "The Autumn of Billy Graham," *Charlotte Observer*, August 23, 1992.

8. Patriarch

1 Bush, quoted without direct citation in David Aikman, *Billy Graham: His Life and Influence* (Nashville: Thomas Nelson, 2007), 234. This final chapter addresses features of Graham's career that I have discussed and documented in earlier chapters. Here, I document only claims that are specific to this chapter.

2 Billy Graham, *Just As I Am: The Autobiography of Billy Graham* (San Francisco: HarperSanFrancisco; Grand Rapids, MI: Zondervan, 1997), 416.

3 See, for example, Graham's Oklahoma Bombing Memorial Prayer Service Address, April 23, 1995, available at http://www.americanrhetoric.com/speeches/billygrahamoklahomabombingspeech.htm.

4 Graham, *Just As I Am*, 1997, 424–425, 495, 601–602, 663, 741.

5 Cover, "A Christian in Winter: Billy Graham at 75," *Time*, November 15, 1993.

6 In 2000 doctors at the Mayo Clinic rediagnosed the condition as hydrocephalus.

7 Ruth Graham, quoted in *Tampa Tribune*, October 23, 1998, cited in Bill Adler, *Ask Billy Graham* (Nashville: Thomas Nelson, 2007), 228. Ruth added: "But there's a silver lining. Along with it, there's sweetness and gentleness."

8 Ken Garfield, "On Opening Night, Graham Reflects on Historic Crusade," *Charlotte Observer*, March 18, 1993, 1A.

9 Billy Graham, *Living in God's Love: The New York Crusade* (G. P. Putnam's Sons, 2005), 13.

10 *Senior Living Resource Magazine*, Summer 2006, front cover.

11 Marsha Tennant, "What I Really Know about Billy Graham," *AARP Bulletin*, April 11, 2012, 38.

12 Billy Graham, *Nearing Home: Life, Faith, and Finishing Well* (Nashville: Thomas Nelson, 2011), 61.

13 Graham, *Just As I Am*, 1997, 464.

14 Billy Graham, "Hope for America," sermon no. 2671, Congressional Gold Medal Presentation, May 2, 1996, notes for the sermon available at https://public.share.wheaton.edu/sites/BGCArchives/_layouts/15/WopiFrame.aspx?sourcedoc=/sites/BGCArchives/BGSermons/635_Awards1973-1976_521996_CongressionalGoldMedalPresentation_CapitolRotunda,Washington,DC_TheHopeForAmerica_-_2671.pdf&action=default.

15 Karyn Spellman, "Graham Defies Doctors, Addresses Baptists," *Charlotte Observer*, June 23, 1995, A2.

16 Nancy Gibbs and Michael Duffy, "The Preacher and the Presidents: Billy Graham in the White House," interview by George H. Gilliam, American Forum, Miller Center for Public Affairs, University of Virginia, November 9, 2007, audio available at http://millercenter.org/events/2007/the-preacher-and-the-presidents-billy-graham-in-the-white-house.

17 Graham, quoted in Ken Garfield, "Graham's New Journey: Reflecting on His Past, Globe-Trotting Evangelist Works on Memoirs," *Charlotte Observer*, August 16, 1992, 1A.

18 Mark Silk, "The Rise of the 'New Evangelicalism': Shock and Adjustment," in *Between the Times: The Travail of the Protestant Establishment in America, 1900–1960*, ed. William R. Hutchison (New York: Cambridge University Press, 1989), 297.

19 *Christianity Today*—in many ways the unofficial official voice among mainstream evangelicals—proved remarkably cold-eyed about Graham's successor. In 1988, on the occasion of Graham's seventieth birthday, the magazine editorialized that there would be no successor, any more than Jonathan Edwards or Charles Fuller saw a successor. Still, the editor would add: "Billy Graham is an evangelist. In some ways he is 'the evangelist.' Certainly he is the evangelist of our time." That the magazine saw a need to raise the question at all in 1988 and again in 2008 was telling. Editorial, "The Evangelist of Our Time," *Christianity Today*, November 18, 1988, reissued online October 14, 2008, "The Evangelist of Our Time," available at http://www.christianitytoday.com/ct/2008/octoberweb-only/billy-graham-evangelist-of-our-time.html.

20 In 1995 the BGEA ranked as the fourth largest evangelical nonprofit in the nation, behind Campus Crusade for Christ, Christian Broadcasting Network, and Focus on the Family. John W. Kennedy, "The Son Also Rises," *Christianity Today*, December 11, 1995, 58, available at http://www.christianitytoday.com/ct/1995/december11/5te058.html.

21 See, for example, a full-page advertisement in the Raleigh *News and Observer*, May 6, 2012, A8. Significantly, this ad bore a banner at the top: "Paid Political Advertisement."

22 Ruth Moon, "Should the Billy Graham Evangelistic Association Have Removed Mormons from 'Cult' List? A Roundup of Views," *Christianity Today*, October 19, 2012, available at http://www.christianitytoday.com/ct/2012/october-web-only/should-billy-graham-have -removed-mormons-from-cult-list.html. In March 2014 the BGEA's mass circulation periodical, *Decision*, featured Russian President Vladimir Putin on the cover. The stated purpose was not to endorse all of Putin's policies but to signal approval of his opposition to same-sex unions. Franklin Graham, "Putin's Olympic Controversy," *Decision*, February 28, 2014, available at http://billygraham.org/decision-magazine/march-2014/putins-olym pic-controversy/.

23 See the discussion in the Introduction.

24 Russ Busby, *Billy Graham, God's Ambassador: A Lifelong Mission of Giving Hope to the World* (Alexandria, VA: Time-Life Books, 1999), 225.

25 Samaritan's Purse Consolidated Financial Statements, December 31, 2013, available at http://static.samaritanspurse.org.s3.amazonaws.com/pdfs/2013SamaritansPurseAuditedFi nancials-PublicDisclosure.pdf.

26 "Billy and Franklin Graham" (part of "The 25 Most Influential Evangelicals in America"), *Time*, February 7, 2005, available at http://content.time.com/time/specials/packages/article /0,28804,1993235_1993243_1993276,00.html.

27 Gibbs and Duffy, "The Preacher and the Presidents," interview at the Miller Center for Public Affairs, University of Virginia, 2007.

28 Cover (photo of T. D. Jakes), "Is This Man the Next Billy Graham?" *Time*, September 17, 2001, available at http://content.time.com/time/covers/0,16641,20010917,00.html.

29 Scott Thumma and Dave Travis, *Beyond Megachurch Myths: What We Can Learn from America's Largest Churches* (San Francisco: Jossey-Bass, 2007); David E. Eagle, "Historicizing the Megachurch" (ms. in author's possession).

30 Frady, in *Billy Graham: A Personal Crusade*, A&E *Biography*, hosted by Harry Smith (New York: A&E, 1999).

31 See, for example, John K. Jessup and others, *The National Purpose* (New York: Holt, Rinehart and Winston, 1960); George M. Marsden, *The Twilight of the American Enlightenment: The 1950s and the Crisis of Liberal Belief* (New York: Basic Books, 2014).

32 C. S. Lewis, quoted in Harold E. Helms, *God's Final Answer* (Maitland, FL: Xulon Press, 2004), 155.

33 I owe this idea to Kenneth L. Woodward, "Billy Graham Retrospective," *Daily Beast*, forthcoming.

34 Robert Sherrill, "Preachers to Power," *The Nation*, July 13, 1998, available at http://www .highbeam.com/doc/1G1-20913892.html.

35 Jon Meacham, "Pilgrim's Progress," *Newsweek*, August 13, 2006, available at http://www .newsweek.com/pilgrims-progress-109171.

36 Historian Elesha Coffman showed that mainline Protestants partly defined their personal trajectories—their "faith journeys"—in terms of life-changing books they had read. Coffman, "'I Had Not Yet Learned to Read Books': The Role of Texts in Liberal Protestant Conversion Narratives," paper presented at the American Society of Church History, Washington, DC, January 3, 2014.

37 Busby, *Billy Graham, God's Ambassador*, 48.

38 Invitation list for state dinner with Queen Elizabeth II and Prince Philip, July 7, 1976, box 1, folder 14, Collection 74, BGCA.

39 William Martin, *A Prophet with Honor: The Billy Graham Story* (New York: W. Morrow, 1991), 273, 583, 603; Nancy Gibbs and Michael Duffy, *The Preacher and the Presidents: Billy Graham in the White House* (New York: Center Street, 2007), 116.

40 Ken Garfield, "Just a Few Observations on My Way Out the Door," *Charlotte Observer*, April 30, 1994, C6; George M. Marsden, *Fundamentalism and American Culture*, 2nd ed. (New York: Oxford University Press, 2006), 38. Graham, *Just As I Am*, 1997, 724.

41 James Morris, *The Preachers* (New York: St. Martin's Press, 1973), 387.

42 See, for example, Billy Graham, press conference, Columbus, OH, July 9, 1964, audio tape no. T7, transcript in box 4, folder 14, p. 11, Collection 24, BGCA; Graham, *Just As I Am*, 1997, 421; Kenneth L. Woodward, *Faith, Culture, Politics from the Era of Eisenhower to the Age of Obama*, forthcoming. When I visited the Billy Graham Library and Museum in Charlotte, NC, in 2009, the sixth display room contained fourteen televisions running simultaneously, focused on events of the 1960s. One featured a video of 1960s "turmoil"—rather than "protest" or "civil disobedience."

43 Larry Eskridge, "'One Way': Billy Graham, the Jesus Generation, and the Idea of an Evangelical Youth Culture," *Church History* 67, no. 1 (1998), 86–89, doi:10.2307/3170772.

44 Ibid., 89–90; Franklin Graham, *Rebel with a Cause* (Nashville: Thomas Nelson, 1995), chap. 4, esp. 52.

45 See, for example, Steven P. Miller, *Billy Graham and the Rise of the Republican South* (Philadelphia: University of Pennsylvania Press, 2009), 22; Ronald C. Paul, *Billy Graham, Prophet of Hope* (New York: Ballantine, 1977), 156, for the *Christian Century*'s contention of "canny" tactics in the 1957 Madison Square Garden crusade; Charles R. Ashman, *The Gospel According to Billy* (Secaucus, NJ: Lyle Stuart, 1977), 237, for "Score Card" of "Souls Allegedly Saved."

46 Harold Myra and Marshall Shelley, *The Leadership Secrets of Billy Graham* (Grand Rapids, MI: Zondervan, 2005), 170; Graham, in *St. Louis Post-Dispatch*, October 11, 1993, cited in Adler, *Ask Billy Graham*, 71.

47 It is difficult to document that something did not take place, but I cannot identify any place in the Graham corpus that reveals serious *engagement* with partisans of other religions.

48 Gibbs and Duffy, *The Preacher and the Presidents*, 337–338.

49 Andrew S. Finstuen, "The Prophet and the Evangelist," *Books and Culture: A Christian Review*, July 1, 2006, http://www.booksandculture.com/articles/2006/julaug/3.8.html.

50 Randall Balmer, *Redeemer: The Life of Jimmy Carter* (New York: Basic Books, 2014).

51 Cathy Lynn Grossman, "The Gospel of Billy Graham: Inclusion," *USA Today*, May 15, 2005, available at http://www.usatoday.com/news/religion/2005-05-15-graham-cover_x.htm.

52 Gibbs and Duffy, *The Preacher and the Presidents*, 108.

53 Graham, *My Answer*, 141.

54 Martin E. Marty, "Reflections on Graham by a Former Grump," *Christianity Today*, November 18, 1988, http://www.christianitytoday.com/ct/2008/octoberweb-only/142-23.0.html ?paging-off.

55 Myra and Shelley, *The Leadership Secrets of Billy Graham*, quotation without source on 90.

56 Hear, for example, the rapid-fire wit and laughter in the question-and-answer period following an address at Regent College and Vancouver School of Theology, Vancouver, British Columbia, October 1984, audio available at http://www.regentaudio.com/products/billy -graham-at-vst-and-regent-college. The transcripts of Graham's press conferences brim with the parenthetical "(Laughter)." See, for example, Billy Graham, press conference, Atlanta, June 25, 1973, audio tape no. T63, transcript in box 3, folder 8, p. 9, Collection 24, BGCA. When a reporter asked him who would be the next Billy Graham, he quipped, "I hope there will never be another one. I think you've had enough of me. (Laughter)."

57 See, for example, Martin, *A Prophet with Honor*, 182.

58 Andrew S. Finstuen, "Professor Graham: Billy Graham's Missions to Colleges and Universities," in *The Worlds of Billy Graham*, ed. Andrew S. Finstuen, Anne Blue Wills, and Grant Wacker, forthcoming. For a classic—and delightful—case in point, listen to Graham's address, "Evangelism and the Intellectual," Harvard Law School Forum, April 1, 1962, audio (scroll down page for audio link) available at http://www3.law.harvard.edu/orgs/hlsforum/multimedia/.

59 Billy Graham, "On Technology and Faith," TED talk, February 1998, http://www.ted.com/ talks/billy_graham_on_technology_faith_and_suffering. This talk has over a million views.

60 Gibbs and Duffy, *The Preacher and the Presidents*, 342–343; Gibbs and Duffy, "The Preacher and the Presidents," interview at the Miller Center for Public Affairs, University of Virginia, 2007.

61 Martin, *A Prophet with Honor*, 472.

62 According to one 2012 study, "about half of Americans read the Bible on their own, and four in five people who read it as part of their personal lives open it at least once a month. And far and away the No. 1 reason they pick up Scripture is for personal prayer and devotion." David Briggs, "The Lord Is Their Shepherd: New Study Reveals Who Reads the Bible—and Why," The ARDA: Association of Religion Archives, March 7, 2014, available at

http://blogs.thearda.com/trend/featured/the-lord-is-their-shepherd-new-study-reveals-who
-reads-the-bible-%E2%80%93-and-why/. Prayer practices show similar patterns: "For
many Americans, every day is a day of prayer. More than half (55%) of Americans said they
pray every day, according to a 2013 Pew Research survey, while 23% said they pray weekly
or monthly and 21% seldom or never. Even among those who are religiously unaffiliated,
21% said they pray daily. Another survey we conducted in 2012 found that 76% of Americans agreed with the statement 'prayer is an important part of my daily life,' a percentage
that has remained relatively stable over the last 25 years." Michael Lipka, "5 Facts about
Prayer," Pew Research Center, May 1, 2014, available at http://www.pewresearch.org/fact
-tank/2014/05/01/5-facts-about-prayer/.

63 Busby, *Billy Graham, God's Ambassador*, 209; Martin, *Prophet with Honor*, 383.
64 Gibbs and Duffy, *The Preacher and the Presidents*, 12–13; Woodward, *Faith, Culture,
Politics*.
65 Wilson, quoted from 1987 interview with Martin, cited in Martin, *A Prophet with Honor*,
561.
66 Finstuen, "Professor Graham," my emphasis.
67 Document in box 10, folder 6, Collection 19, BGCA.
68 Martin, *A Prophet with Honor*, 601; see also Epilogue below.
69 William Martin, "Fifty Years with Billy, Part 2: The Impact of Billy Graham's Ministry to the
World," *Christianity Today*, November 13, 1995, 29.
70 Graham, interviewed by Merv Griffin, *Merv Griffin Show*, November 16, 1983.
71 Thielicke letter excerpted in Leighton Ford, "Is It Still Gospel Preaching?" *Leadership Journal*, Winter 2008, available at http://www.christianitytoday.com/le/2008/winter/17.26.html.
72 Faulkner, quoted in "On Privacy," *Harper's*, July 1955, cited in Lou Cannon, *President Reagan: The Role of a Lifetime* (New York: Simon and Schuster, 1991), 16.
73 John Charles Pollock, *Billy Graham, Evangelist to the World: An Authorized Biography of
the Decisive Years* (San Francisco: Harper and Row, 1979).
74 Philip Jenkins, *The Next Christendom: The Coming of Global Christianity* (New York: Oxford
University Press, 2002); Michael S. Hamilton, "American Evangelicalism: Character, Function,
and Trajectories of Change," in *The Future of Evangelicalism in America*, ed. Candy Gunther
Brown and Mark Silk (New York: Columbia University Press, forthcoming).
75 Billy Graham on KRON (San Francisco), NBC, September 24, 1997; Sherwood Eliot Wirt,
Billy: A Personal Look at the World's Best-Loved Evangelist (Wheaton, IL: Crossway Books,
1997), 114.
76 Wirt, *Billy: A Personal Look*, 120.
77 Bob Evans, conversation with William Martin, November 12, 1987, quoted in Martin, *A
Prophet with Honor*, 548.
78 Dale S. Russakoff, "Billy Graham: He Walks, He Talks, He Sells Salvation," *Harvard Crim-
son*, December 12, 1973, available at http://www.thecrimson.com/article/1973/12/12/billy
-graham-he-walks-he-talks/.
79 See, for example, Graham forthrightly importuning Truman to attend a crusade meeting and
"bring a few words of greeting." Billy Graham to Harry Truman, December 23, 1951, box
1, folder 11, Collection 74, BGCA.
80 Russ Busby, BGEA, to Larry Speaks, White House Press Office, July 2, 1976, Gerald R. Ford
Library and Museum, Ann Arbor and Grand Rapids, MI.
81 Gibbs and Duffy, *The Preacher and the Presidents*, x.
82 Graham, quoted in "Rockin' the Capitol," *Time*, March 3, 1952, cited in Gibbs and Duffy,
The Preacher and the Presidents, 29.
83 Consider, for example, virtuous protagonists such as Henry Maxwell in Charles Sheldon's *In
His Steps*, Harry Donner in Conrad Richter's *A Simple Honorable Man*, John Ames in Mari-
lynn Robinson's *Gilead*, or Margaret Sparhawk in Elisabeth Elliot's *No Graven Image*. For
the reverse imagery, consider Theron Ware in Harold Frederic's *The Damnation of Theron
Ware*, Elmer Gantry in Sinclair Lewis's *Elmer Gantry*, and Abner Hale in James Michener's
Hawaii. Ambiguous figures such as "Andrew" in Pearl Buck's *Fighting Angel* are ambiguous
precisely because promotion for self and cause cannot be distinguished.
84 See, for example, Marshall Frady, *Billy Graham, a Parable of American Righteousness* (Boston: Little, Brown, 1979), ix; Michael G. Long, *Billy Graham and the Beloved Community*
(New York: Palgrave Macmillan, 2006), ix; Saul Braun, "Nearer Silent Majority to Thee,"
Playboy, February 1971, 120.

85 Busby, quoted in William Martin, "Fifty Years with Billy, Part 2," 5.

86 Graham, interviewed by Katie Couric, *Today*, NBC, March 5, 1998.

87 My rendering of Graham on the *Dinah Shore Show*, "Dinah's Place," October 4, 1972, audio tape no. T45, Collection 345, BGCA.

88 My rendering of Graham on *Billy Graham: A Personal Crusade*, A&E *Biography*, hosted by Harry Smith (New York: A&E, 1999).

89 Graham, *Just As I Am*, 1997, 618. Graham said "1 million."

90 For one of many examples of Graham both retracting and earnestly apologizing for a thoughtless comment (in this case, about AIDS possibly being a judgment from God), see Graham in St. Louis *Post-Dispatch*, October 11, 1993, cited in Adler, *Ask Billy Graham*, 71. See also Billy Graham, *Just As I Am: The Autobiography of Billy Graham*, rev. and updated 10th anniv. ed. (San Francisco: HarperOne; Grand Rapids, MI: Zondervan, 2007), 721–722, 744–745.

91 Graham, quoted in David Frost, *Billy Graham: Personal Thoughts of a Public Man; 30 Years of Conversations with David Frost* (Colorado Springs: Chariot Victor, 1997), 143.

92 Graham, quoted in Calgary *Herald*, December 7, 1991, cited in Adler, *Ask Billy Graham*, 46.

93 Graham, *Just As I Am*, 2007, 743.

94 John Akers, special assistant to Mr. Graham, conversation with the author, January 17, 2014, Asheville, NC.

95 David Aikman, *Great Souls: Six Who Changed the Century* (Waco, TX: Word Books, 1998), 58.

96 George M. Marsden, *Understanding Fundamentalism and Evangelicalism* (Grand Rapids, MI: W. B. Eerdmans, 1991), 6.

97 Andrew S. Finstuen, *Original Sin and Everyday Protestants: The Theology of Reinhold Niebuhr, Billy Graham, and Paul Tillich in an Age of Anxiety* (Chapel Hill: University of North Carolina Press, 2009), 149, 151.

98 D. Michael Lindsay, *Faith in the Halls of Power: How Evangelicals Joined the American Elite* (New York: Oxford University Press, 2007).

99 Peter J. Boyer, "The Big Tent: Billy Graham, Franklin Graham, and the Transformation of American Evangelicalism," *New Yorker*, August 22, 2005, available at http://www.newyorker.com/archive/2005/08/22/050822fa_fact_boyer?currentPage=all.

100 I have drawn this list, with an eye to diversity of social location, mostly from first-person tributes to Graham in Amy Newmark, Steve Posner, and A. Larry Ross, eds., *Chicken Soup for the Soul: Billy Graham & Me: 101 Inspiring Personal Stories from Presidents, Pastors, Performers, and Other People Who Know Him Well* (Cos Cob, CT: Chicken Soup for the Soul Publishing, 2013); Vernon K. McLellan, ed., *Billy Graham: A Tribute from Friends* (New York: Warner Books, 2002). Not included in these volumes: Bono, quoted in Pat Boone, *Thank You, Billy Graham* (DVD, 2006), cited in Nüesch, *Ruth and Billy Graham*, 23; Donn Downing, "Ex-Panther Eldridge Cleaver: 'I Just Wish I Could Be Born Again Every Day,'" *People*, October 25, 1976, available at http://www.people.com/people/archive/article/0,,20067024,00.html; I infer Ali's support from Graham's comments, in Graham, *Just As I Am*, 2007, 695. In 2009 a glass display case at the Billy Graham Library contained a poem by rock star Bono for Graham. Bono signed it "with much love and respect."

101 See, for example, Yechiel Eckstein (133) and Steven Posner (14, 16), in *Chicken Soup for the Soul*, ed. Newmark, Posner, and Ross. Posner asked about the "fate of those that do not bear his faith," and received the same answer: "That's between the person and God" (14).

102 I have adapted this line from Leonard I. Sweet, "The Epic of Billy Graham," *Theology Today* 37, no. 1 (1980), 91, doi:10.1177/004057368003700110.

103 I draw this notion from Michael Kazin, *A Godly Hero: The Life of William Jennings Bryan* (New York: Knopf, 2006), xx, who in turn draws it from Moses Hadas, "Introduction," *Greek Drama*, ed. Hadas (New York: Bantam Books, 1965), 4.

104 Napoleon I, Emperor of the French, *Napoleon in His Own Words,* trans. Herbert E. Law and Charles Lincoln Rhodes (Chicago: A. C. McClurg, 1916), 52, available at http://archive.org/details/napoleoninhisown00napo.

105 Graham, *Just As I Am*, 1997, xx.

106 Graham, quoted in Busby, *Billy Graham, God's Ambassador*, 270.

107 Jon Meacham, "Peace at the Last," *Newsweek,* July 3, 2005, 29, available at http://www.newsweek.com/peace-last-121413.

108 Helene Elliott, "He Has Quite a Story to Tell," *Los Angeles Times*, January 26, 2007, available at http://articles.latimes.com/2007/jan/26/sports/sp-elliott26.

109 Louis Zamperini, Lois Ferm interview with Louis Zamperini, May 16, 1976, "Into the Big Tent: Memories 14," available at http://www2.wheaton.edu/bgc/archives/exhibits/LA49 /09memories14.html.
110 Laura Hillenbrand, *Unbroken: A World War II Story of Survival, Resilience, and Redemption* (New York: Random House, 2010), 376. Laura Hillenbrand, quoted in [Editor], "Olympian Louis Zamperini dies at 97," *ESPN Olympic Sports,* July 3, 2014, available at http://espn .go.com/olympics/story/_/id/11171984/war-hero-olympian-louis-zamperini-dies-97. See also Ira Berkow, "Louis Zamperini . . . Dies at 97," *New York Times,* July 3, 2014, available at http://www.nytimes.com/2014/07/04/arts/louis-zamperini-olympian-war-survivor-unbroken -dies.html?_r=0.
111 Billy Graham, *Approaching Hoofbeats: The Four Horsemen of the Apocalypse* (Waco, TX: Word Books, 1983), 155, 152, 155.

Epilogue

1 I have conflated details of our four visits with Mr. Graham at his home in Montreat, North Carolina, in 2007, 2009, 2011, and 2013. I wish to thank especially Dr. John Akers, special assistant to Mr. Graham, for arranging the first two visits, Jean Graham Ford and Leighton Ford (sister and brother-in-law) for arranging the third visit, and the Reverend David Bruce, executive assistant to Mr. Graham, for arranging the fourth.
2 As noted in an earlier chapter, in 2000 the Mayo Clinic rediagnosed the condition as hydrocephalus, but Mr. Graham still called it Parkinson's.
3 James Morris, *The Preachers* (New York: St. Martin's Press, 1973), 387.
4 Richard Darman, *Newsweek,* quoted in Lou Cannon, *President Reagan: The Role of a Lifetime* (New York: Simon and Schuster, 1991), 435.
5 This sentence adapted from Marshall Frady, *Billy Graham, a Parable of American Righteousness* (Boston: Little, Brown, 1979), 16; and Nancy Gibbs and Michael Duffy, *The Preacher and the Presidents: Billy Graham in the White House* (New York: Center Street, 2007), 161.

ACKNOWLEDGMENTS

The UNC basketball coaching legend Dean Smith is, without question, the most famous person in my hometown of Chapel Hill, North Carolina. Smith liked to say that when you make a basket be sure to thank the person who tossed you the ball. Whether this book makes any baskets readers will have to judge, but I do know that many people tossed me the ball. Properly thanking them is impossible since mere words hardly suffice, and risky too, for I probably have overlooked some of the most important ones. But I will give it a try.

Among the people who helped, deans come first, and then librarians and archivists close behind. My two deans at Duke Divinity School, first Greg Jones and then Richard Hays, gave me lightened committee assignments and spot cash from the dean's discretionary fund for travel and research assistants. More important, they provided unceasing encouragement. Librarians and archivists include Roger Loyd, former library director of Duke Divinity School, Paul Ericksen, director of the Billy Graham Center Archives, Wayne Weber, BGCA archivist, and especially Bob Shuster, BGCA archivist and Billy Graham polymath.

Generations of research assistants set aside their own work to retrieve books, compile statistics, track down fugitive page numbers, and make themselves available at all hours of the day and night (and weekends) to talk me down from the anxieties of the Brave New World of digitized research. They included Chris Blumhofer, Charles Cook, Seth Dowland, Rebekah Eckland, Andrew Klumpp, Sean Larson, Mandy McMichael, Scott Muir, Wen Reagan, Dan Rhodes, Heather Vacek, and Kevin Walters. Katie Benjamin and Aaron Griffith deserve special credit for guiding me through the final stages and working above and beyond the call of duty. Both of them researched and provided comments on several especially important paragraphs.

The roster of friends who offered ideas could fill the Chapel Hill yellow pages under the category "Encouragers." A partial list includes Dan Aleshire, Uta Balbier, Randy Balmer, Dan Bays, Peggy Bendroth, Shane Benjamin, Dave Bere, Susan Boehmer, Jim Bratt, Cathy Brekus, Fred Brooks, Nancy Brooks, Richard Bushman, Jon Butler, Julie Byrne, Joel Carpenter, Heath

Carter, Bob Cooley, Mike Cromartie, Heather Curtis, Darren Dochuk, Seth Dowland, Larry Eskridge, Curtis Evans, Tim Frakes, Tim Funk, Ken Garfield, Philip Goff, Franklin Golden, Jen Graber, Stephen Graham, David Hall, Ken Hall, Ed Harrell, David Heim, David Hempton, Judith Heyhoe, Sam Hill, Bruce Hindmarsh, Barbara Hofmaier, Brooks Holifield, David Hollinger, John Huffman, Jake Jacobsen, Nate Jones, Peter Kaufman, Michael Kazin, David King, Byron Klaus, Mark Labberton, Jim Lewis, Roger Lundin, Lucie Marsden, Martin Marty, Steven Miller, Shirley Mullen, Harold Myra, David Neff, Shenan Nieuwsma, Maggie Noll, Ron Numbers, Allen Poole, Dan Ramirez, Russ Richey, Darrin Rodgers, Sarah Johnson Ruble, Steve Scholle, Jan Shipps, Mark Silk, Larry Snyder, John Stackhouse, Randall Stephens, Skip Stout, Jonathan Strom, Matt Sutton, Angela Tarango, Bill Trollinger, Andrew Walsh, David Weaver-Zercher, John Wilson, and John Witvliet.

Current and former colleagues at Duke—Jeremy Begbie, Kate Bowler, Jack Carroll, Mark Chaves, Liz Clark, Ellen Davis, Stanley Hauerwas, Dick Heitzenrater, Hans Hillerbrand, Richard Jaffe, Xi Lian, Rick Lischer, Randy Maddox, David Morgan, Maurice Ritchie, Kavin Rowe, Warren Smith, David Steinmetz, Jim Travis, and Will Willimon—and at UNC—Yaakov Ariel, Brandon Bayne, Randall Styers, and Molly Worthen—offered insights sufficient to fill another book.

Many others tossed me the ball. This book would never have gotten off the ground without John Akers, David Bruce, Mike Crisp, and Jean Graham Ford and Leighton Ford, who opened doors in the Graham organization and became fast friends in the process. Friends from forever ago—Don Argue, Scott Kelley, Malcolm Reid, Russ Spittler, Wayne Warner, Everett Wilson, and Ray Woody—helped prevent a five-year project from turning into a ten-year marathon. They did it by recurrently asking the most innocent of questions, "So, how's the book coming along?" Rich Mouw wagered his presidential reputation on my behalf. Andrew Finstuen and Anne Blue Wills wagered their professional reputations in order to edit with me an anthology of essays on Graham's place in American life.

Friends who took the time to offer detailed, unflinching, and incredibly helpful critiques of the entire manuscript include John Akers, David Bruce, Aaron Griffith, George Marsden, and Mark Noll. Edith Blumhofer, Kate Bowler, Elesha Coffman, Nathan Hatch, Greg Jones, Brendan Pietsch, and Ken Woodward played their own very special roles. The kindness of Laurie Maffly-Kipp stands behind every paragraph, first for arranging a hide-away office at UNC, and second for swapping ideas and war stories over more mugs of strong black coffee at the Open Eye than anyone should consume in a lifetime. She gave the words friend and colleague new meaning. Dr. Fred Irons left a light on for me.

All students of Graham owe a special debt to William Martin. I have read his magisterial biography and brilliant articles about Graham so often it is hard to know where his ideas end and mine begin. I have tried to flag specific points of dependence in the endnotes, but I am sure I have missed some. It suffices to say that his work and generous advice fill these pages.

Fellowships and conversations with students and faculty colleagues in other schools made the book possible. Funding for leave time came from a Henry R. Luce III Fellows in Theology Fellowship, a Louisville Institute Grant for Independent Research, and a Louisville Institute Grant for Summer Research and Travel. I tried out ideas about this project at a variety of schools and conferences. They included the American Theological Society, Assemblies of God Theological Seminary, Campbell University, Columbia University, Davidson College, Eastern Nazarene College, Emory University, Ethics and Public Policy Center, Evangel University, Fuller Theological Seminary, Gordon Conwell Theological Seminary, Heidelberg University, Indiana University/Purdue University, Messiah College, North Park Theological Seminary, Northwestern College, Simpson College, Southern Baptist Theological Seminary, Trinity College (CT), University of Denver, University of North Carolina at Charlotte, University of Tennessee at Chattanooga, and Wheaton College (IL).

Some of the ideas in this book were worked out in an earlier or different form in the following: "'Charles Atlas with a Halo': America's Billy Graham," essay review of *Prophet with Honor: The Billy Graham Story*, by William Martin, in *Christian Century*, April 1, 1992, 336–341; "The Billy Pulpit: Graham's Career in the Mainline," in *Christian Century*, November 15, 2003, 20–23; "Billy Graham's America," *Church History: Studies in Christianity and Culture*, September 2009, 489–511; "Billy Graham, Christian Manliness, and the Marketing of the Evangelical Subculture," in *Religion and the Marketplace in the United States*, edited by Philip Goff, Jan Stievermann, and Detlef Junker (New York: Oxford University Press, forthcoming); and "Children's Letters to Billy Graham," with Katherine Bowman Wacker, *Christianity Today*, forthcoming.

Editors and a teacher played key roles. Kathleen McDermott, Executive Editor for History at Harvard University Press, offered astute advice on how to shape the argument, chapter by chapter. She mixed patience with pressure in just the right measure. Christine Thorsteinsson, Senior Manuscript Editor at Harvard University Press, turned barbaric sentences into civilized ones. And she knew when (to pirate a line from Billy Graham) "obscurity was reaching for profundity." Anne McGuire, Assistant Production Editor, turned gnarly footnotes into lucid prose and tracked elusive references back to their headwaters in the original sources. My graduate school mentor, William R. Hutchison, died nearly nine years ago. I still have not reached the place where I—like most of his former students—can draft a sentence without wondering, "WWBT" (what would Bill think)?

Family counts most. My omnicompetent stepfather, Dave Zeller, and entrepreneurial brother, Dan Wacker, helped me remember that the world is wider than the library. Our incorrigible but beloved English bulldog, Jedd Wacker, helped me remember another enduring truth: beauty lies in the heart, not the face. Last I checked, my five young grandchildren, to whom this book is dedicated, claimed parents. Which brings me to my daughters, Laura Stern and Julia Wacker, and their husbands, Andrew Stern and John Beck. Long ago each of them saw that the world was wounded, and each committed their lives to vocations that tried to do something about it. I am proud of them.

My wife, Katherine, has been part of the project from the beginning. She helped me research Chapter 7 by deciphering scores of letters to Graham in the Billy Graham Center Archives. More than once she had to stop because of her eyes. They were perfectly fine, but uninvited tears kept clouding her vision. That is when I figured out that the letters contained a major part of Graham's meaning for America. Four times she accompanied me up the mountain to see the man himself. And she heard me talk about the project more hours than any spouse should have to bear. Since her patience was unmerited, it equaled pure grace, and grace is always amazing. Katherine's support stands behind every page of the book in ways more profound than she will ever know. She has been the polestar of my life for nearly a half-century now. It must be love.

INDEX